T0354002

Imagining and the Transformation of Man

1964 Lectures

NEVILLE

Order this book online at www.trafford.com
or email orders@trafford.com

Most Trafford titles are also available at major online book retailers.

(1964 lectures unabridged, verbatim, and all transcribed from tapes recorded in live audiences in Los Angeles, CA. Reel-to-reel transcriptions and books compiled by Natalie.)

Printed in the United States of America.

ISBN: 978-1-4907-3111-7 (sc)
ISBN: 978-1-4907-3112-4 (hc)
ISBN: 978-1-4907-3113-1 (e)

Library of Congress Control Number: 2014905189

Trafford rev. 11/13/2014

www.trafford.com

North America & international
toll-free: 1 888 232 4444 (USA & Canada)
fax: 812 355 4082

OTHER WORKS BY NEVILLE

Your Faith Is Your Fortune
The Search
Awakened Imagination
He Breaks the Shell
The Neville Reader (reissue of *Neville or Resurrection* containing):

> *Out of This World*
> *Freedom for All*
> *Feeling is the Secret*
> *Prayer—the Art of Believing*
> *Seedtime and Harvest*
> *The Law and the Promise*
> *Resurrection*

The Awakening: 1963 Lectures

CONTENTS

NOTE FROM AUTHOR

(This is Neville's last piece of writing, given to me by Mrs. Goddard after his death in 1972. Neville felt "that the chapter Resurrection needed something to lead into it.") Natalie

Introduction to *Resurrection*

If I tell you what I know and how I came to know about it, I may give hope to those who would gladly believe the Bible but who do not understand it or who may have thought that the ancient scriptures are but a record of extravagant claims. Therefore, the reason for this report from me, rather than from another whose scholarly knowledge of the scriptures is more erudite, is that I am speaking from experience. I am not speculating about the Bible, trusting that my guesses about its meaning are not too wide of the mark. I will tell you what I have experienced that I should convey more of God's plan than the opinions of those who may know the Bible so intimately that they could recite it from end to end, although they have not experienced it.

He who knows something out of his own experience knows something that makes the finest and wisest opinion look shadowy. True knowledge is experience. I bear witness to what I have experienced. Looking back, I do not know of anything that I heard or read to call forth this knowledge. I did not receive it from man, nor was I taught it, but it came through a series of supernatural experiences in which God revealed himself in action for my salvation.

He unveiled me. And I am he. We mature only as we become our own Father.

I do not honestly expect the world to believe it, and I know all the varieties of explanation I myself should give for such a belief had I not experienced it. But I cannot unknow that which I have experienced. When it occurred it was the most amazing thing that every happened to me. I could not explain it with my intelligence. But God's plan of redemption unfolded within me with such undeniable insistence that finally it became both a mystery and a burden laid upon me. I literally did not know what to do with what I knew. I tried to explain it to friends, and I know that with all good will they could only think, "Poor Neville, he has evidently had a very bad time."

From the first experience, I felt commissioned. I could not unknow it, and I am burdened with that knowledge. The warnings of my friends could make no difference to the truth I had experienced. That truth remained. Whether I could be a living instrument of it or not, I could not say at all. But until I put it into words so that others could read it, I did not feel that I had accomplished the work I was sent to do.

Now that I have written it, I feel that I have finished what I came to do. And that is to reveal the true identity of Jesus Christ. Jesus is the I AM of everyone. He is the Lord, the one God and Father of us all, who is above all and through and in all. Therefore, if the words *Lord, God, Jesus* convey the sense of an existent someone outside of man, he has a false God. Christ is the Son of God. The Son of God is David, the sweet psalmist of Israel.

It's the Father's purpose to give himself to all of us, to each of us. And it is his Son, David, calling us Father, who reveals the Father's gift to us. The Father's gift of himself to us is not discovered until the very end. And all discovery implies suffering to be endured in the process of discovery.

The Father became as we are that we may be as he is. He is never so far off as even to be near, for nearness implies separation. He suffers as us, but we know it not. God as Father is made known only through his Son, David. The core and essence of David's work is his revelation of the Father. Can one come to an identity of oneself with the Father without the Son's revelation of him? Personally, I feel quite sure the answer is no, one cannot. "No one knows the Son except the Father, and no one knows the Father except the Son and anyone to whom the Son chooses to reveal him."

If two different witnesses agree in testimony, it is conclusive. I now present my two witnesses: the internal witness of the Spirit, my experience, and the external witness of scripture, the written Word of God.

Neville
September 1972

FOREWORD

(to 1964 book)

Welcome to the world of practical imagining, of visionary and mystical experiences, of a deeper appreciation of the meaning of life, the inward journey, and the eternal ancient wisdom revisited.

We are led to the truth when we are ready for it. I was led to Neville when answers had to be found, where changes in thinking had to take place in order to expand spiritual awareness. The first most compelling concept encountered was that a change in attitude begets a change in the outer world, stated by Neville as "imagining creates reality." It followed that one's world is a reflection of one's inner thinking plus the attendant emotions; and that to dwell on anything you desire, feeling the possession of it in the present moment, remaining faithful to that feeling of having it now, believing it wholeheartedly, produces that result.

I tried it and it worked. To my joy, a three-and-a-half-month trip to Europe, all expenses paid, came in within about a month after doing an imaginal act of feeling myself flying in a jet over the ocean and then seeing through the window well-know landmarks of Europe below. I did not lift a finger to make it so, told no one about it, and it came out of the blue. This is the pragmatic and provable law that everyone can test endlessly to their satisfaction. It's truly the way to everything in the world; and it's being done by every person every moment of time, either wittingly or unwittingly. It's a magical overcoming of limitation when done deliberately. And it is, you learn, God the I AM, your "I am," in action.

Neville taught from his own visions, mystical experiences, discernment (not speculation) and Bible study, not only that imagining creates reality but that every soul is destined to spiritually awaken eventually as God, yet retaining one's individual identity. He never claimed to be more than the messenger of this eternal story that all will one day experience...a gift which can't be conjured or earned. This book of 1964 talks (the second in a series) chronicles a continuing growth in understanding of his six major visions that began in 1959 with the last one occurring after three-and-a-half years. Through extensive study and insight, he found these visions paralleled those in the Bible, the story of Christ; and they proved to be the keys to explaining the hidden mysteries of the prophetic Old Testament and their fulfillment in the New Testament. Perhaps an appropriate analogy would be the Rosetta stone and what it did for the Egyptian hieroglyphics. Once understood and accepted, the larger picture emerges. The questions "Who am I? What am I doing here? Where did I come from? What is the purpose of life?" are all answered in this new at the same time ancient revelation. A sense of power is returned to the individual, plus a great sense of peace comes knowing life really does have a glorious meaning...in spite of the seeming chaos and horrors of the world.

As Browning said in his *Paracelsus,* "Truth is within ourselves; it takes no rise in outward things...There is an inmost center in us all where truth abides in fullness...and to know rather consists in opening out a way whence the imprisoned splendor may escape, than in effecting entry for a light supposed to be without." Neville's teaching gives us the way to that center and how to help open out the way so that the imprisoned splendor may escape. So the story needs time to be understood, to be heard repeatedly, and to be internalized by the seeker. And that is why the eleven years of his lectures are so precious and unique, gradually leading one through the process that culminates in an awakened individual.

Study of this higher level of being helps stir the sleeping giant in all who have been made by their Inner Being into the good soil, that is, made ready to awaken. To awaken is to personally experience those same six visions. These are the signs that the transformation has been completed, and that our divine heritage has been returned. (As encouragement to all, this writer can also bear witness to experiencing the last of the six visions.) Then we can go back to eternity expanded and triumphant having overcome death and the illusion of this world.

Natalie 7/2014

ACKNOWLEDGMENTS

Deepest thanks to Neville for being the source of these wonderful insights. The inspiration they will forever engender in readers of his work is undeniable and it is that which is the incentive to preserve his lectures for posterity.

In memory and thanks to William Machgan for his love of Neville's teachings which led him to lend support to this project.

To all who will find help in these volumes, grateful thanks for your interest and for helping spread the good news.

N.

THE SHAPING OF THE UNBEGOTTEN

1/7/64

Tonight's subject is "The Shaping of the Unbegotten." Naturally, we turn to the greatest book in the world to guide us in telling you what I feel about the shaping of the unbegotten, and that book is the Bible. The entire Bible is the word of God. No matter how far it may exceed the limits of our logic—there is much in it that doesn't make sense—but don't tamper with it. Leave it just as it is and time will prove that it is true.

Here, the first decision, the first creative act, we find in the very first chapter of Genesis: "And God said, 'Let us make man in our image, after our likeness'...so God created man in his own image, in the image of God he created him" (Gen.1:26,27). Now, when you read it carefully what are the words "let us"? Let us, well, they could stand simply for the plural of majesty or God first consults with divine beings other than himself. You can take it as you want. But if I search the scriptures I must come to certain conclusions. He asked, "What's the greatest commandment in the world?" and the answer to that question was this, "Hear, O Israel, the Lord our God is one Lord" (Deut.6:4). The word translated "the Lord" by definition means "I AM." It is Yod He Vau He. The word translated "our God" is the word Elohim; it's a plural word, "gods." Then it ends on the note "I AM", again. But there's a little word in there "one Achad," one Lord. This is a compound unity, one made up of others. So we can put it into this statement, "Hear, O Israel, the I AM, our I AMs, is one I AM." So here is by this decision that man is to be made into the image of God. Well, who made it and who started the entire process? We say God.

Now let me share with you a vision of mine of just a week ago, a week ago today. I came out of it about 5 A.M. Here, I was taken in Spirit to read one passage, or one of God's eternal pages, in his divine history. For history is simply the unfolding of God's purpose, a movement of events from his Promise towards its fulfillment. So I was taken in Spirit and here I came upon a scene, a man about 6'5", a tall, majestic creature. He personified courage, and this courage was based upon his faith in God, his absolute trust in God's ability to execute his Promise. Here was this giant of a man, I would say, 6'5" looking off into space at an enormous distance. It was not only space, as I looked at his eyes, he as looking into time. Looking far, far away in time to that *moment* in time when the Promise would be fulfilled, as could be said when it was fulfilled, "Your father Abraham rejoiced that he was to see my day; he saw it and was glad" (Jn.8:56). He was standing under an oak tree. The oak tree wasn't very tall, maybe the height of this room, and it almost was bare of leaves, just a few leaves, so you could actually see the entire structure of the tree, all of the branches. They were twisted and curled, like the human brain. If I could have drawn a line around this tree, it would have been the perfect expression of the human brain with all of its convolutions. And in the tree a serpent with a human face; and I knew that that serpent was articulate, but it didn't speak. But there it was, alive, the personification of wisdom and power. It seemed infinitely wise, and it seemed omnipotent in its power, as I stood there looking at the man who simply looked off into time, and this tree, knotted and twisted like the human brain, and then coiled in the tree, a serpent with a human face…then the vision began to fade. As it faded, a book came before my eyes. It's the Bible, opened at the 17th chapter of the Book of Genesis, and I began to read it, all in my vision. I read the first verse and then it faded.

So I got out of my bed, went into my living room, and got the Bible and completed the chapter. The chapter begins this way, "When Abram was ninety-nine years old the Lord appeared unto Abram and said to him, 'I am God Almighty; walk before me and be blameless'" (Gen.17:1). In this chapter he makes a covenant with Abram. He first changes his name, and the change of name must be consummated and sealed by the act of circumcision. Every male on that day, including his son Ishmael, at the age of thirteen must be circumcised. And Abraham, at ninety-nine, he had to be circumcised. Then he makes you a promise that this son Ishmael will not inherit your kingdom; but I will give you a son and you will call his name Isaac, and *he* shall be your heir. We are told he fell on the ground and laughed because it seemed to him ridiculous...or maybe he rejoiced at the good news. You can interpret as you will. I would say, he rejoiced at the good news. But it is said in the book, he prostrated himself and laughed, and said, "I, a hundred years old?" For the Promise was made, It would not be given you today; but next year I'll return in the spring, and your son will be born. It seemed summer to me when I saw the scene...it seemed summer. And so, it would be spring if you took it in the way that you and I measure time and pregnancy.

So I began to dwell upon this. I wondered, Why the serpent? So you search the scriptures again, and here, man begins his journey after being beguiled by a serpent. "The serpent beguiled me," said she, "and I ate of it." Then comes the banishment into a world that is a strange world. Well, who is the serpent? If I told you the serpent in the ancient world was called Jesus Christ, would you be shocked? The serpent is Jesus Christ. And yet, you are told, "He's our savior." Well, he who banished me also redeems me?--yes. Now listen to these words in the Book of Romans, the 11th chapter, the 32nd verse, "For God has consigned all men to disobedience that he may have mercy on all." It was God and only God who consigned men to disobedience. So the first fundamental sin recorded in scripture is the *disobedience* of man. And so, the disobedience was ordered by God that God could have mercy on all. If I were pure, never could I taste of the sweets of the forgiveness of sin. How could I? There would be no need for the forgiveness of sin. I would never know the sweetness of it, to forgive sin. If I were holy, could I ever behold the tears of him who loved me and still loves me, in the midst of his anger, as he puts me through the fire? For that is my destiny: to go through the fires of affliction that I may come out as his image, come out *as* God. So God actually becomes man that man may become God. That's not poetry, that's fact. And when Spirit possesses a man, he clothes himself with that man, puts him on as you would put on an outer garment. So God is wearing every garment in this room; every child born of woman is a garment, an outward garment that God is wearing. The day will come when he completes his work *in* man, and he unveils, takes it off and that man is God. That's the purpose. So God becomes as I am with all my limitations that I may become as he is without limitations.

Now, in the scriptures I read it there is not a slightest reference in the works of Paul speaking of the prenatal existence of Christ as a man. These are his words: "Jesus Christ, who, though in the form of God...emptied himself, taking the form of a slave, being born in the likeness of men. And being found in human form became obedient unto death, even death upon a cross" (Philip.2:6). His form was that of God, and he exchanged it for that of a slave; and so *he* is the slave, playing all these parts. When he completes it and we awake, we are he: "Christ *in* man is the hope of glory" (Col.1:27). Were he not *in* man he could not emerge from man. So Christ *in* man is putting us through all the paces, and he's doing all the suffering. For when he comes out, I am he. Therefore, "If any man should ever say to you, 'Look, here is the Christ!' or 'Look, there he is!' do not believe it" (Mark 13:21). Do not believe it for the very simple reason, although it may not now appear to you what you shall be, know this much when he appears you will be like him (l John3:2). Therefore, if he does not look like you now, don't look at any man and think of that man "There is Christ." For when you see Christ, he's going to be just like you. He *became* you, and transformed you into his likeness by taking upon himself your likeness.

He puts himself through the paces, and when he has completed the work, and he unveils it, you are he. "For he who began a good work *in you* will bring it to completion at the day of Jesus Christ" (Philip.1:6). That day is called "the day of the Lord." It was shown me so clearly, when man comes into what is known as the eighth, the day of the Lord, he has entered into the kingdom of God. It's called by a strange name, which I've never used before, but I came across it recently "the ogdoad." I wondered, what is the ogdoad? Looking it up, it's simply the eighth number. That's all that it is called, the 8th number. He comes into the 8th, which is a new first day. At the end of the 7th day, then he rose on the first day after the Sabbath, which is a new first day or the 8th day. That's not explained but it's implied. When one comes into the 8th number, in Hebrew it is a Cheth, and its symbolical value is "an enclosure, a protection, a completely protected area," called "the kingdom of God." An entirely new generation, an entirely new creation, and therefore a new body to function in a new world; and that's the body that he's working on and weaving in us, an immortal body.

Now, why the serpent? Why of all of the things of the world *that* should be the symbol of God, I do not know. I only tell you my vision; I saw it. Christ is defined in the scripture as "the wisdom and the power of God"; in the very first chapter of Paul's letters to the Corinthians, "Christ, the wisdom and the power of God" (1Cor.1:24). And looking at that face, all that you could think of was infinite wisdom and infinite power. At the moment you wonder, "Why a serpent, a human face?" And yet, not a thought crossed your mind but wisdom and power woven into that face. The eyes of the man, no. I did not catch his eye. I simply stood and looked...but his eye was away into the distance, both in time and in space. I knew then he was looking at the fulfillment of the Promise, and the words came back from the 8th chapter of the Book of John, "Abraham rejoiced that he was to see my day; he saw it and was glad" (verse 56). "You, not yet fifty and you know Abraham? Abraham saw you?" Yes, said he. "Before Abraham was, I AM." But how could he tell anyone in this world? That creature that symbolized him, who was the very cause of the so-called fall of man, it wasn't man's fall, God *deliberately* fell. You go back and you search it all over again, and the word translated God, Yod He Vau He, the verb is He Vau He, its original meaning was "to fall or to cause to fall; to blow or to cause the wind to blow." And the word "wind" and "spirit" are one in both Hebrew and in Greek. He caused it all; therefore in the very last he can forgive all.

So he actually clothes himself with every being born of woman. So don't look for him elsewhere, you aren't going to find him. He is closer than your breathing, closer than your hands and feet; he is your own wonderful human Imagination. That's God. Just as he clothed himself with you, you are called upon now to exercise that same power and clothe yourself with your noble concepts in this world. Everything that is lovely, everything that is of good report, clothe yourself with it and actually put it on like an outward garment. You can stand here now or sit here now and imagine that you are elsewhere; and clothe yourself with the reality of that elsewhere-ness. You can clothe yourself with the reality of success, of health, of anything in this world. You do the same thing that God did for you: He clothed himself with you. Put the human being upon himself like an outward garment and walks saying "I am." For that's his name. He has no other name: This is my name forever...the name by which all generations must know me. So as you are seated here you're saying "I am." But you don't stop there, you say "I am John, I am Mary" and so you come down and condition it when you know what John means to you in the world, and you let it remain there. You limit yourself by the evidence of your senses and what reason dictates, and there you remain.

But, the limitless is in you, and he asks you to exercise it. Exercise it by assuming that you are *now* the man that you want to be, remain faithful to that assumption, and live in it. It will come to pass; for the whole movement of events brings this promise, which is now God's promise to you, to fulfillment. You have a desire? That's God speaking to man. Clothe yourself with it, just as though it were true. And this is the shaping of the unbegotten. When the curtain goes up and you're exposed as he, you who *began* in time have no beginning, for God so completely became you. He has no parents, he has no origin; he's the origin of all. He has no ending of days; he's the beginning and end of all. And so, you will know how can this thing happen—I who *began* in time at the completion of God's work upon me, when he gives himself to me, that I did not begin in time. I am before and I am after. I am not something that began when he completes his work. And it's God's purpose to give himself to me as though there were no others in the world, just God and I, and the same to each person in the world.

So when he completes that purpose, we have no beginning...and that's called Melchizedek in scripture: without father, without mother, without beginning, without end of days. All enter into that same order of being: no beginning, no end. What a strange mystery! That here we are created in our image, and yet when the image is completed, image of the invisible God, that seal that was created and therefore began in time, doesn't. It is God—one with the gods who made the decision to transform man into their image…and so becomes more and more, like the sands of the sea, said he, like the stars of the heaven. You cannot number that which is being created, and yet, though created, it is one with the creator, therefore, not created. It's God begetting himself, his actual self, individualizing himself as you, individualizing himself as every being in the world. When you see him one day, you see yourself. But you will see yourself with such beauty of features and such majesty of features and such strength of character that you would never dream in eternity that you could ever be that. And yet, that is exactly what you are moving toward. When one day he awakes, this whole thing will be as a dream to him, the God awake. But it took this entire dream to produce his purpose which was to give himself to you.

So when we see Isaac in the 17th chapter (verse 18), hereafter, do not see Isaac or think of him as the result of generation. See Isaac as the begetting of the unbegotten, the shaping of the unbegotten...that's Isaac. He's just as you are told, they said, he laughs or he will laugh, and he does when you see him one day and he'll be the symbol of *your* awakening. He will laugh, just as you are told: He beheld my day; he saw it and he was glad. He rejoiced that he would see it, and he saw it, and he was glad. The laughter is confirmed; he *does* laugh. So every little sign in that story is true, and day after day, men and women all over the universe are coming as witnesses to the truth of God's word. So the call has gone out since the first born took place and the call is "Call the next witness." Go and call him. He will come, when prepared, with his witness, because he must come to witness to the truth of God's word. And he's called, and God's word is true. So we have two witnesses, one is the external witness of scripture, and the second is the internal witness of the Spirit. So, bring me the witnesses, for if two different witnesses agree in principle it's conclusive. So bring the witnesses... and everyone will one day be a witness to the truth of God's word. For these things are eternal. They did not die and leave the world forever. They did not die; they live forever in an internal imaginative world. For that creature that I saw, that majestic man, is part of the story of the 17th chapter of the Book of Genesis. It was *that* that was starting a journey. When you read it carefully, he goes on a long, long journey into a land where he'll be mistreated and abused, but when he comes out his possessions are great.

And so that's you. But that's the *symbol* of the journey. And you start with that courage, a courage based upon your faith in God, for there's no courage comparable to that which comes as a result of one's faith in God. So, if I heard this very moment the voice of God, and it said to me the most impossible thing in the world, I would not allow reason to tamper with the word of God. I would know that he who promised is capable of executing that which he promised. And so, that courage comes only from faith in God.

When you hear it one day, you never question it. You never question the voice, and though reason denies it, your senses deny it you are supported by what you heard. Memory hasn't faltered, you know what you heard, and having heard it you do nothing, just as in my case I was told, "Do nothing." I heard the voice speak in the very depths of my soul, "That which I have done I have done. Do nothing"…and then a wonderful picture before my eyes, where he had revised a decision of a superior of mine. God revised it and then told me to do nothing. So I did nothing, and nine days later that revision was an objective fact. My superior called me in, unasked by me, and then once more corrected his decision by completely revising it...just as I was told in the depth of my soul, "Do nothing." So that superior had no choice in the matter. He thought he had a change of heart, a change of attitude. He did have a change of attitude, but it was induced by God. God is playing all the parts in the world.

So when you know what you want this night, just assume that you have it, and put it on just as God put this garment on. Assume that you have it. Because all things by a law divine in one another's being mingle, all of us. Therefore, if I put it on I will influence every being in the world who can be of assistance in bringing to pass that which I have assumed. If you can be used, you'll be used, without your knowledge, without your consent. If it takes 10,000 to aid the birth of what I'm assuming, 10,000 will be used, for we are all one. And God has plotted it and planned it so that you will know, in the end, we *are* one. So, "Hear, O Israel, the Lord our God is one Lord" and that *one* Lord is simply a compound unity, the gods. Therefore, all will play their part in concert to produce what was the decision in the beginning: "Let us make man in our image."

And while man is being made in the image of God, man has been given the freedom to make mistakes; for he was invited in the beginning to disobey and yet forgiven for his disobedience. For he was actually invited to disobey, and made to disobey by God, who assumed the picture of a human face and that which could only be the human spine. So you look up the word tree in the biblical concordance and what do you see, "the spine, the back-bone, the carpenter, the gallows." Therefore, who is on the gallows?

You're told in the 3rd chapter of Galatians it is Christ Jesus. He is cursed for man's sake. We are told the serpent was cursed. Well, read the 3rd chapter of Galatians, "Cursed be every one who hangs upon a tree." And Christ became the cursed for man, hanging upon the tree. What tree?—this tree. So all of the wise men of the world, "All of the gods of the earth and the sea sought through nature to find this tree, but their search was all in vain, there grows one in the human brain." That's where the tree is. That's the tree of life.

And so, the very trunk of that tree, which would be the serpent that you saw, would be the human spine, that spinal cord. One day you'll know it. And yet human...when you see the face it's human. But what is the nature of that body? You can only hint at it. I'll tell you that it is love. Love is the human form divine. Human face...but how would you describe a body made only of love, complete love? The fullness of love is the body, the human body divine, but you can't describe it. How would I describe the beauty of it? How would I describe the color? You can't describe it. But I'll tell you, love *is* the human form divine. And that's what is being formed *in* man, so he'll be clothed in it and that will be his immortal body, his eternal body in an eternal world. That's when the work is completed and that which has no beginning shapes itself, and you are that which he shapes, and you are immortal. And you and I are one.

Doesn't seem to make sense, for I respond to one name and you respond to another, and without loss of identity we are still one. The gods are individualized and yet *one* God. There's only *one* Jehovah, *one* Savior, and yet *unnumbered* gods, and altogether form *one* Jehovah. The proof that they are one: they all have the same son. Not many little sons running around, *one* son, and *that* son is *God's* only begotten Son. Everyone will look right into the eyes of God's only begotten Son and know without any uncertainty he's *my* son. Therefore, then and only then do you really know who you are. It takes the Son to reveal the Father: "No one knows who the Son is except the Father, and no one knows who the Father is except the Son and any one to whom the Son chooses to reveal him" (Mat.11:27). So when that choice is made and the day of the Lord is upon you, the Son appears and calls you Father. Then you know who you are. You never knew it until then.

But you also know, at that very moment, everyone will be called Father by this same Son, this eternal youth. Then you know beyond all doubt there were never two of us, just a fragmented being, individualizing himself as unnumbered children, each like himself. For the Father and the Son are one. And so, if I emptied myself, the being who emptied himself to become me was in the form of God, then he'll reclaim it. He became me by emptying himself of the form of God and took upon himself the slave form, and was born in the likeness of man. Being born in the likeness of man, then he became obedient unto death, even death upon the cross of man (Phil.2:7). This is that tree spoken of in scripture...the only tree. This is the tree on which he's nailed.

When the drama is over there will be a rejoicing beyond the wildest dream of all of us here who go through the bath of pain. For, we are taken through these furnaces of affliction and you wonder "Why? What have I done?" There's no one to tell you what you did. People speculate and they try to bring in all kinds of extraneous things and tell you that you must have been horrible in a last incarnation or something, that you did this, that, you did the other. Then they read your stars for you, then they read the teacup leaves for you, then they do numbers, all of these, trying to convince you that you did something of which you are totally unaware…can't remember a thing that I have done. And yet, you haven't done a thing, God did it. Read the 9th chapter of John: "Master, who sinned, this man or his parents that he was born blind?" "Neither this man, nor his parents, but that the works of God be made manifest" (verse 2). No past incarnation is the result that resulted now in this act.

God is an infinite, merciful being. God is not a God of retribution; he forgives everything in the world. He's a God of love. Even though we form a garment that he wore and it was blind. Because the being wearing it will one day appear, and that being that seemingly now is going through hell with his blind state will be just like the wearer of that garment, and he won't be blind. I saw it. I saw it so clearly. For those who had no arms, no eyes, all members missing, and then as I walked by, out of some invisible storehouse every missing member came and fitted itself perfectly into what was empty sockets, or empty arm sockets, and they were made perfect. You could not improve upon them, everyone was perfect. So that in the end all are made perfect; for you are told, As your Father is perfect, be ye perfect. For he's actually begetting himself and he's perfect and he's holy. So everyone will be holy, everyone perfect.

But while it's taking place, it seems so difficult to believe in a God of love. I promise you that you will stand in his presence one day, and you can't think of anything but love. No other attribute in the world...you don't entertain the thought of might, of wisdom, of any other attribute, just love. You look right into his eyes and here is infinite love. You'll be embraced and be incorporated into his body, forever part of the *one* body that is God. And so, even though you are in the world and seemingly fragmented, you are still there in the body of God. For there's no place where one can go that he is not. After you are incorporated into the body of God, I can say truly, I am here in this room talking to you but I am still there. I have never left him since the incorporation. There's been no divorce, no separation, and so, you can be sent and still be one with the being who sent you.

That is a peculiar, strange statement to make but it's true. You are sent, and yet you haven't left the being who incorporated you into his body. So you are one with the one who sent you, so you can truly say, "He who sees me sees him who sent me." If you want to see the one who sent me, alright, look at me, *he's* the one who sent me. So when I saw him, he looked just like me. And so you'll say the same thing. I'll look at you, and if I'm curious who sent you, you can say, if you see me, you see the one who sent me. Only, when I see the one who *really* sent you, I will see you raised to the nth degree of perfection, the nth degree of all that is majestic in this world; that you could not improve upon it when I see the being who really sent you, but just like you. So there will be no loss of identity, and yet there will be a tremendous, how would you put it, increase. Because I inherit not only the kingdom, I inherit God. That is his purpose, that I inherit him. So without loss of identity I become something greater, one with the being who incorporated me, and I am he.

Now, if you are here for the first time tonight, I'm not apologizing, but this is more mystical than most people like to hear. Thursday night it's on a different level. It is on what we'll call the practical level. I'll show you a being who is far, far great than John. "John, the greatest born of woman, of all those born of woman, no one was greater than John; yet I say unto you, the least in the kingdom is greater than John" (Mat.11:11). And I'll show you that "least" in the kingdom. He's right where *you* are, but you don't know it…or maybe you do. But if you do know it and don't feed him, then I would say you don't know it. And so you must feed him by exercising him, and then you know it.

A friend of mine in San Francisco this past fall took the series of lectures; then he got married, and thought he would go off to Mexico City. He wrote me this past week. I got the letter I think it was on Saturday morning. He said, "I took your tapes with me, but then I didn't have a machine to play them. All over the City of Mexico I looked and couldn't find a machine. One who had one wanted an outrageous price for it, but was reluctant even then to sell it." Then he told me what he did, how he came into a border state to find one and looked all over for three or four days and couldn't find one. So he despaired and thought, "Well now, why did I make this 1,600 mile trip?" Then he said to himself, "Here, I'm not even applying the law. I haven't done a thing about finding a machine in my Imagination. I've gone looking through the eyes of man; I've done nothing about really getting it." He said, "I sat down and took that machine in my mental hand, at the border going into Mexico, where no one would question my right to have it. Everything in Mexico is actually taxed a hundred per cent. You paid a hundred dollars for it they'll tax you a hundred dollars for it, no matter what you bring in. If you receive a gift from this country, when you go to receive it at the post office, they value it at a hundred per cent tax on it. And so, here I had my machine in my Imagination, going through the Customs without any difficulty and no tax on it.

"I was just about to depart, and I went downstairs. I went into a little jewelry store, and I said, "I don't suppose you would know of anyone in this city who would have"—and he mentioned the machine he wanted—"to play my tapes?" He said, "Isn't it strange, I have one here. I don't sell them, but a customer of mine left one here in the event I knew of someone who would be of interest." "Let me see it." It was exactly what he wanted to play the same speed. So with that, he asked the man what he wanted. He said, I'll bring him over. The man wanted $200 for it. "Well, he said, it's worth the $200, but I only have fifty on me, and my money is in Mexico, and there's not one person in this city of Nogales who knows of me. They don't know me, so I can't prove that I am the person that I tell you that I am. Will you take my fifty dollars and give me the machine and I'll send you the money?" The man shook on it and said yes. He said, "I went through Customs as though I didn't have it. I didn't hide it from the man; the Customs official did not question my right to have it. I told him the truth, I have tapes to be played, and I must have this machine. Not one penny tax on it. So I went back with my machine.

"Now," he said, "having done that, this is what happened to me. I've proved the law, now that I've proved the law I'll try it again. I had a little boat and I went to this little island. My wife and I went ashore, and we left the boat I thought safely anchored. There was no wind when I went ashore and suddenly we looked up and the boat is a quarter mile out to sea, and an enormous wind. So I started after the boat. I didn't think I could make it and I was getting more and more tired and the boat was going faster away with the wind. The tide is against me. So suddenly, where the wave came from I don't know, the wave lifted me up, an enormous wave. At the crest of the wave I could see a boat with three men in it. It was a little motor boat. I screamed and waved my hands on top of this wave, and they looked because the wind was going in their direction and they could hear me. They came towards me, took me aboard, went and got my boat for me, and brought me back to the shore.

"But, he said, before I jumped into that ocean, Neville, in my Imagination I took the little boat and anchored it on that beach again. I did the whole thing in my Imagination before I plunged into that water. I could never have made it physically, because I was getting more and more tired, and the boat was going faster away. On the heels of these two experiences, this is what I had, a dream, I dreamt this. I dreamt that I was in San Francisco in the sheriff's office and he tells me that I am named sheriff of the City of San Francisco. I told him I didn't want to be a sheriff, but he said, 'You *are* the sheriff.' So, he said, I didn't want to be the sheriff, so I woke and wrote down the dream. I went back to bed and I re-dreamed it; but this time a little change, I *am* the sheriff. I am wearing the uniform, I have my badge, and I am the sheriff, and there's a gun. I don't use a gun—wouldn't have one in my house—but there is the gun, part of my equipment. I have on my uniform; it's the sheriff of San Francisco. So I woke and wrote that down. Well, you told us the story of Joseph, and Joseph said to Pharaoh, the doubling of a dream means that God has fixed the thing and it will shortly come to pass. A double dream means a thing is...that no one can alter it."

So he had the double dream. Well, it's a symbolical dream. He has already proven the law. For the first time in his life he had to prove this law before he *could* be an operator of the law, a protector of the law. So he dreams that he now represents the law. His confidence is built now on faith in God. Before, it was faith in his position as a businessman, faith in the pigment of his skin (he's an Irishman), all these things. That was his faith. Now, these are not his faith any more. His faith is in God. He has proven God's law. So he has a dream where God speaks to him through the medium of dream, and in the dream he is wearing the uniform of law. So now you live by law, from now on.

So I ask every one to try it. What is the nature of the dream to prove to you that you accepted God's law, I don't know. He doesn't have to repeat himself. He can give you a dream this night if you really live by law that would convince you beyond all doubt when you wake tomorrow morning that you've *accepted* God's law. What better dream than this to prove to this man he really now has accepted God's law? He's not going to try to get things the hard way; he's going to get things by God's way which is by God's law. So, all these things happen to us as we really pitch in and make *his* law *our* law.

Now we'll go into the Silence, and try to clothe ourselves in a noble concept of self, whatever it is. Don't limit it to what reason allows, just simply sit quietly and clothe yourself with it like an outward garment, and feel the reality of the thing that you are imagining. Now let us go.

THE ONE GREATER THAN JOHN

1/9/64

Tonight's subject is "One Greater Than John." I think you will find this a most practical approach to this teaching. When we open the Bible we think it is just a normal book. May I tell you, it is not; it is divine history and all the characters in scripture represent states of consciousness, from Adam to Jesus, every one. They're not individuals as you and I are; they're simply representatives of these states of awareness. And the very last before the page turns into an entirely new age is called John. And so we are told in the earliest of the gospels, which is Mark: "After John was arrested, Jesus came preaching the gospel of God" (John 1:14). *After* John was arrested then he appears preaching the gospel of God. What is this story trying to tell us?

So here, let me share with you my experience. I didn't know it either, but I'll tell you how this thing works. John, we are told, is the very last of the great of the prophets. As we're told, "Of those born of women, none is greater than John; yet the least in the kingdom is greater than he" (Mat.11:11). None greater than John in this world, yet the least in the kingdom is greater than he. And John came not eating or drinking. If you take that on this level, that's nonsense, because the body could not survive. Another gospel states it, "He came neither eating bread nor drinking wine." That tries in some way to, well, explain what he did not eat or drink. Well, there's no statement in the law of Moses against eating bread or drinking wine—unless you are one of the Nazarenes and it's true as to wine, but certainly not eating bread. The last supper was the eating of bread and the drinking of wine. But he came, neither eating bread (if you want to take it that way) nor drinking wine. But the Son of man came eating and drinking, and they called him a glutton and a drunkard, a friend of tax collectors and sinners. But we think, this night, of one *greater* than John, who was the *greatest* in this world, yet not equal to the least in the world called the kingdom of heaven. Now these are only states of consciousness through which every man passes. If you are not now in the state of John, may I tell you, you're *going* to be some time in the state of John; if not now in this present little environment, when the wheel turns and it returns, you will be *in* that state. Everyone passes through the state of John before he comes into the state of Jesus Christ.

Now, what is the state of John? We come into this world ...now let me share with you my own personal experience. I was born in a very limited environment, small little island in the West Indies called Barbados. My father ran a little grocery store, but it was a general store, not only groceries but meat, fish, fowl, liquor, wine. I mean, it supplied everything for the table. I was raised in that environment where it seemed the most normal, natural thing in this world to eat anything that was placed on the table, and so I did. I left Barbados at the age of seventeen and came to America, believing as I did everything placed before me that was edible was right. And then, I fell into a state, the state called John. John came not eating or drinking. And then I fell into the state where I gave up all the things that I did normally as a boy, right through until I was seventeen years old. I fell into the state at the age of twenty, a little after twenty, say, twenty-one, where I would not eat any meat, any fish, fowl, not even eggs. Naturally, in those days I didn't drink so that was not giving up wine, but that couldn't cross my lips. I did violence to my own appetites, because as a child, as a boy, I indulged in everything that my father placed before me. And suddenly I gave it all up and for seven years I was a strict vegetarian, teetotaler, celibate. John represents that state in man's ongoing when he does violence to his appetite. And yet life is nothing more than the appeasement of hunger. God gives to every man in this world a hunger that he can, if he knows God's law, satisfy. He can clothe himself with the fulfillment of his dream and satisfy it. But there's a state where man passes through, and it is called John the Baptist, where he does violence to his appetite.

I met a friend of mine in New York City, his name was Abdullah. He said to me in 1933 (I met him in '29)...and he did everything, he ate everything, he drank everything. He didn't smoke only because he just didn't enjoy it, but he did *everything*. An old, old man, he was then in his late eighties when I met him. And he said to me, "So you're going to Barbados? You want to go to Barbados?" I said yes. Now, this is where the good news of the kingdom comes in. Then, when I met him, I did not eat flesh in any form, I did not drink alcohol in any form, and no smoking and a celibate. He said, "Well then, you are *now* in Barbados." I said, "I'm in Barbados?" This is on 72nd Street in New York City, where the buildings can go thirty and forty stories high. Barbados, if you find a three-story building, you're lucky...the little one and two-story buildings, and no sidewalk, but *no* sidewalk. One little tiny street we call Broad Street, to this day we call it Broad Street, and that's the only place that has a sidewalk. All the other areas no sidewalks, you walk in the street or you walk in the gutter, but there is no such thing as a sidewalk.

And he said to me, "Now *clothe* yourself with Barbados. Put it on as you would another garment, just as you would another garment, so that you would smell the tropics and you would see what you would see were you in Barbados." Well, I did to the best of my ability, and I clothed myself with Barbados. And when I thought then that night—the first night that I clothed myself with Barbados---I thought of New York City, and I saw it 2,000 miles to the north of me. Then I had succeeded in clothing myself with Barbados. I fell asleep in the assumption I am in Barbados. Well, the days went on from this I would say, late October through November, and yet I am not physically in Barbados. So I tried to open up my discussion with Abdullah, and I said, "Ab, I did all that you told me. I clothed myself with Barbados, I am sleeping in Barbados, and yet here I am in New York City." He would not talk to me. He turned his back upon me the very first time I brought it up; he walked towards his studio and slammed the door in my face. And if you knew Abdullah as I knew him that was no invitation to come in.

So, if I am clothing myself in Barbados and with Barbados, then I must be faithful to this clothing. That's the good news spoken of *after* John is arrested, not before. John is doing violence, trying to gain the kingdom of heaven by being good. And he said to me, "You're so good you're good for nothing. And you're trying to get into the kingdom by being good. You don't eat meat, no kind of meat, you don't drink any alcoholic liquor, so you're so good. And you're celibate at the age that you are today, and so all the fires you've bottled up in you, trying to be good." So I kept on wearing my garment: I am in Barbados. On the morning of the 4th of December a letter came to my door, stuck under the door, from my brother giving reasons why he wanted me to come to Barbados, and enclosing in that letter a ticket for Barbados. I had not gone home to Barbados in eleven years. I made no request. I didn't write the family. My brother Victor writes me saying that you must come and no response other than yes would he accept, and enclosing a little draft to buy shirts, if I need them, or a pair of shoes, and stating in the letter that use the check to the fullest advantage. Charge everything and when I arrived in Barbados, well, he would board the ship and pay all expenses that I had signed. If I use the bar, use the bar. He didn't know I wasn't drinking. But, all expenses...the tipping of the steward, the tipping of everyone in that ship. He would board the ship, take care of all my expenses, but I must come! Then he gave me his reasons for it, he justified why. I went down to that ship on the morning of the 6th and got my passage and off I went.

Before I went, Abdullah said to me, "So you're going to Barbados. May I tell you, you're going to die but you will not *surely* die…but you will die." He didn't explain. Like Blake he never would tell me the interpretation of his statement "you will die." Well, I went off thinking, well, I'll die, die in Barbados. I didn't die in Barbados but I died: I died to everything that I was doing. I lived in Barbados for three months, which is the Christmas season and everyone is entertaining. I'm returning from America after eleven years, and party after party is given for my honor. It's Christmas, it's New Years, they're all drinking, all having fun, and I simply drank water. Mother prepared all kinds of meals, and I would have just a vegetable meal. She never heard of it. We were raised supplying the entire island with meat, with fish, with fowl, with everything...with all the wine...everything was home… and I just said, no, I would take vegetables. I was there for one solid three months.

I came back to that ship going north. And the night I entered that ship, we sat maybe six or eight people at table, and we all introduced ourselves. "My name is Neville Goddard," and so I would shake hands, and this one is so and so-—you all introduce yourself aboard ship. Then the man to my right said to the waiter, "Let us see what you have for wine." The waiter brought the wine list, he said, "We'll have that." I didn't say wine, so he ordered that wine. Then came the first course, soup. So I didn't ask if there's meat stock in this as I'd done for seven years; I drank the soup. Then he brought the second course, it was fish; I ate the fish. He brought the third course, it was meat; I ate the meat; all the time pouring down the wine. Every thing that I had *not* done in seven years I *did* that night, and then from then on for the ten or twelve days at sea 'til I got off the ship in New York City. Then I understood what he meant "you will die."

That *state* called John the Baptist, which does violence to itself, you *must* pass through it. If you are not now in it, you *will* be in it. It's part of the eternal drama of God. God has prepared a way to redeem himself. It's God and only God playing all these parts. So God has prepared the way to bring himself back individualized as you. There's no other way. So from Adam to Jesus Christ they are only states of awareness through which God and only God passes. And the last state of the old dispensation is John the Baptist. That is the last stage. And so, man *must* pass through that state. Don't try to invite it. It happens, and you don't understand why it happens. In my own case, raised normally, with all the food before me, because my father made a living feeding us by selling this, fish, fowl, meat, eggs, butter, everything that was normal, all the rum in the world. We make rum in Barbados. He drank heavily; my father was a very heavy drinker. All these things were exposed to us, so we took it and suffered it.

My Father, the depths of my own being, moving me through all these furnaces, put me into a state where I was married at the age of eighteen, father at nineteen, separated at twenty. And then *I* became so disillusioned with marriage, I vowed I would have not a thing to do with sex—my *own* disillusionment, my own, not hers, my own. That was part of the play where he put me through these furnaces and brought me out seven years later. I know friends of mine who have been in that state of John the Baptist for fifty years, and they have died in it. But the wheel turns; they will come out, the wheel turns. Although they cease to be here as a flesh and blood being, they were in it when they died. Others came out after forty years. Here was George Bernard Shaw...he died in it after seventy years. He was ninety years when he died. He was a strict vegetarian and a teetotaler. He was in it, but he died *in* it; he had not come out. He died not believing in Christ. He died an atheist. He didn't know the good news. My friend Abdullah who taught me this story, he was in it for forty years. He hadn't touched anything that was meat, especially pork. He was born and raised in the Jewish faith, and for forty years he touched nothing that was meat. But certainly he, not only forty years, but from the time of birth up until he was almost eighty years old, he hadn't touched pork. And then came the same thing to him that happened to me.

So man passes through this state called John the Baptist, and he comes into the state called Jesus Christ. Jesus Christ is the freedom of the world. So, it's said of John he came not eating or drinking. It is said of Christ, called the Son of man, he came eating and drinking; and they say of him, "Behold, a glutton and a drunkard, a friend of tax collectors and sinners." So you pass through it and then you know what he is talking about. He doesn't come to destroy the law. He said not one little dot will be rubbed out of the law, all will be fulfilled, but he interprets the law as John could not interpret it. John thought that by doing violence to his appetite he would get into the kingdom. He thought that he could scare a man into salvation. And the next state beyond John tells you you can't do it that way. He interprets the law and shows the law as something that is mental, not physical. And then he puts it this way: "You have heard it said, 'You shall not commit adultery.' But I say to you anyone who looks on a woman lustfully has already committed the act of adultery with her in his heart" (Mat.5:27). He takes it from a physical state to a mental state. If I look upon a woman lustfully and I think I can get away with it, and it seems pleasant, I may be inclined to do it. If I contemplate that act along with its consequences for myself and my family, I may restrain the impulse. But, he tells me that's not good enough—in the contemplation of the act I did it. So, causation is mental, it's not physical. John didn't know that. The state called John didn't know that. If I restricted myself and resisted the impulse, I thought, "Well, am I not wonderful! I have just abided by the law 'ye shall not do.'"

Then comes the next state called Jesus Christ, and that state tells me that wasn't good enough; the wheel is turning and you are going to do it tomorrow. The wheel will turn now and tomorrow when it turns all over again, you will be performing the act. And you'll wonder why has this happened to me to the disgrace of my family and myself? Because you thought by the restraint of the act you didn't do it. And now he interprets the law for us, and tells us the very contemplation of the act *was* the act. And so, when one gets to that point where they don't even contemplate it, well, then off the wheel of recurrence we are lifted, one by one. And that is the story of the one that is greater than John.

So everyone is moving through a series of states, and it starts from Adam through, well, we can stop the Adam and start it from Abraham, for that's where *real* civilization begins. So you start from Abraham and you come all the way through into Jesus Christ. And they're only states of consciousness where God passes through individualizing himself as you. And everyone goes through the state called John the Baptist. So of all those born of women, none is greater than John, yet the least in the kingdom of God is greater than John. So how great we are in this world, that doesn't really matter; because the least in the kingdom of God has a greatness beyond the wildest dream of this world. The least has a greatness...you can't conceive the greatness of the least in the kingdom. And he's brought there not by anything he's done. For, may I tell you, I did nothing to do it; I fell into it. But who made me fall into it?—God. And so, we can't take any credit for having fallen into the state called John.

It seemed to me, if I reflect upon it, prior to when I fell into it, that I was disillusioned in marriage. A young man of eighteen getting married, and then being a father at nineteen, and then at twenty separated, and becoming disillusioned. And then pledging myself *not* to have anything to do in the sexual world and then to give up completely all the food that I loved. I love food, love all the things that the world would offer. And then to go through it and a man would tell me on a certain day, "You're going to die, but not really die." And then you're bewildered—"I'm going to die, but I'm not going to die"—what is he talking about? Well, he was talking about the state. I will die to that state. And when after the things happened and I said to him, "What did you mean and who told you that I would die and yet not really die?" He said to me, "The Brothers." That's all that he would tell me: "The Brothers told me that you would die and not really die. The Brothers told me you were coming to me." And what did he mean by the Brothers?—the Elohim, the gods who made us all in their own image.

So tonight, may I tell you, let me share with you the good news. You are told, the very first words given into the world in the mouth of Jesus Christ in the earliest gospel is in Mark, the 14th and 15th verses. The words are: "After John was arrested, Jesus came into Galilee, preaching the gospel of God, and saying, 'The time is fulfilled, the kingdom of God is at hand; repent, and believe in the gospel.'" The first words put into his mouth. Someone asked the other night concerning changing the picture of this world—the word is "repent" in the first statement made in that gospel. "Repent" is "a radical change of attitude towards anything that happens to you in this world." I don't care what is happening, repent! Don't let it happen as it is happening. Change it in your mind's eye, solely, as I did standing in New York City, without one nickel in my pocket, not a nickel, and Barbados is 2,000 miles away, across water, so you can't walk; and he tells me, "You are *now* in Barbados!" I'm in Barbados and Barbados is 2,000 miles away across water. "Clothe yourself with Barbados. If you *are* in Barbados, how would you know you are? Look at the world." For motion is relative: I can only detect that I have moved relative to something that is stationery to my motion. So, New York remains where it is, and if I assume that I am in Barbados, and I think of New York, I should see it 2,000 miles to the north of me. So, I clothe myself with Barbados and think of some stopping place where if I *am* in Barbados that vision would tell me where I am. So I think of Barbados…and there it is 2,000 miles to the north of me. So I sleep in that state, to find that someone 2,000 miles away is *moved* to bring me…a ticket to go to Barbados, with a little small check to buy the necessary things to get aboard the ship.

So you clothe yourself in a state. That's the good news: "I bring you the good news of the kingdom of God," for man is rising into a kingdom where everything is subject to his imaginative power. But before you get there you start to test it here...and you test it. So I'm telling you of a kingdom. What kingdom? The kingdom of God, well, what is it? It's a place beyond the wildest dream of earth, the world of Caesar, where when you arrive there everything is subject to your imaginative power. But I'll tell you, start it right here. And how do you do it? You clothe yourself with this state just as though it were true, and as you clothe yourself with it, wait. As you're told, those who really believe do not make ___(??). If they really believe it, they don't *make* it so, it *is* so.

That's why when I discussed it with Abdullah he never discussed it with me. When I asked him how would I go there he wouldn't even answer me. Because what he was trying to show me was, "If you really are clothed with the feeling of *being in* Barbados, how could you and I sit down and discuss how you're *going* to get there? How could we possibly discuss this?" And so, he wouldn't discuss it with me. "If you really are doing what I told you to do...you say you are in Barbados...well, then you can't discuss how you're going to go." If I said to you, "You are now rich," and today you owe rent, can you and I discuss how you are going to become rich if I tell you that you *are*, and ask you to clothe yourself with wealth? If I ask you to clothe yourself with any state in this world; and then it doesn't hatch out tomorrow because tomorrow is not the moment of hatching out, but you're anxious; and then you say to me, "But where is it coming from, how will it come?" should I really discuss it with you? Would not...that is a lack of faith on your part if you say, well, I'm wearing it. If I'm wearing it, it should be just as real to you as the room is real.

That's the good news of the kingdom. If I really want anything in this world, I clothe myself with it, just as though it were true, and then let it hatch out. All things have moments between the moment of assumption and the fulfillment of that assumption. We either believe it or we don't believe it, and not a thing I can do to persuade you to believe it. I can just simply throw it out, and in this audience this night there are those who will accept it and those who will reject it...not a thing I can do about it. I can only tell you of the kingdom of God and tell you these are the *states* through which we pass.

So, I hope you've passed through the state of John the Baptist. But it makes no difference. If you haven't passed through, I'll tell you, you *will* pass through it. And so, when the wheel turns as it will turn; for all come to the inevitable end and so everyone will make their exit from this world; and if they haven't before they exit from this world passed through John the Baptist, they will when the wheel comes back again pass through it. For there is no death; nothing dies in God's world. It *seems* to die, but the world does not end where my senses seem to disappear from it...it doesn't. So if the wheel is turning and turning, and you and I are turning on the wheel until by...except after John the Baptist, before we are plucked from the wheel, we begin to live by the promise called the gospel or the good news of God.

So here, this night you take it and test it. If you test it, may I tell you, you'll prove it in performance; if you don't test it, you will never know. And so, it is Christ *in you* that you must test. Christ became man, God became man, that man may become God. So this John the Baptist spoken of in scripture is not a little man born of Elizabeth, who was a cousin of Jesus. Forget it! These are only related states—a cousin is a relative—and so these are related states that's all. It hasn't a thing to do with my cousin born of my sister. No, that's not the cousin. They were cousins separated in time: John came before and Jesus followed. Jesus is not *a* man. Jesus is the fulfillment of God's plan, God's promise, God's purpose, where he comes forward and he awakens *as* himself, and that self is Jesus Christ.

So, the last state man passes through is John the Baptist, where he does violence to himself. Now, he is clothed in camel's hair and a leather girdle. The most external parts of a man is hair and skin; so he's clothed in camel's hair and a leather girdle. So here, he's...the most *external* thing that man could ever have on a body would be the camel's hair and the leather girdle. And he said, "If you will accept it, he is Elijah come again." Go back and read the story of Elijah. He was clothed in camel's hair and a leather girdle. It means that the mind is clothed with something external. I think if I give to the poor, if I contribute to the church, if I go to church every Sunday, and I do all the external things then I am now getting into the kingdom of heaven. So I abide by all *external* things and that doesn't get me any place into the kingdom of heaven.

Then I begin to do violence to my appetite. I restrain the impulse to do this, that, or the other, not knowing that life itself is nothing more than the appeasement of hunger, and God and only God gives me the different hungers. And the final hunger he gives me is the hunger for the *word* of God. The very last hunger, as told us in the Book of Amos: "I will send a famine upon the world. It will *not* be for bread or a thirst for water, but for the hearing of the word of God" (8:11). And so, the last hunger to come upon man is to hear the word of God. To hear it is to experience it. I want to experience the reality of what is said in scripture. And so I will hear it, and I'm so hungry to hear it I will experience it; then comes man's *individual* experience. So man must experience scripture for himself to understand how wonderful it is. When he experiences scripture, the hunger that preceded the experience is now satisfied by the experience.

And so that is what comes out when he enters into the state called Jesus Christ. Jesus Christ is the flower, the fulfillment of God's purpose. So in the end there's nothing but Jesus Christ. So then we are told, in that day or, "On that day the Lord is one and his name one," and that name is Jesus. All come out as he. But they must pass through the state called John the Baptist, and John is but a state. And all must pass through that state doing violence to themselves in the hope that in some way it is seen by someone above him, and by that seeing he enters into the state called salvation. You cannot save yourself. No man can save himself. It's the gift of grace; it's the gift of God. You could this very moment become the most strict vegetarian in the world, teetotaler, non-smoker, celibate—go to the extreme state and make yourself so impotent that you couldn't possibly even entertain the thought—and yet you cannot by such violence to yourself enter the kingdom of God. The kingdom of God is entered by grace. But you pass through the violence to self, and then you come out.

May I tell you, when you do come out, there'll always be those who mock you...always those. So, when he comes into the world they call him a glutton, and they call him a drunkard and the friend of sinners. And may I tell you, when I came back after seven years of this *rigid* discipline, and those who saw me in this meeting one night, when I got up and suddenly confessed what I am now doing, that a few ladies in the audience cried. Because they thought they had in me some personal savior, and I became to them an image that cracked and broke; and they saw in me now an utter failure, one who normally drank and normally ate meat. To them I was a complete disillusioned being. And it happens to every being in this world. You'll pass through it. I am sharing with you my own experience. And no man can speak with any grater authority than when he speaks from experience; for a truth that man knows from experience he knows more thoroughly than he knows anything else in this world, or than he can know that same truth in any other way.

So if I tell you of this experience, you may believe me or you may disbelieve me. Even those who believe me will not know it to the extent they *will* know it after they themselves have had the experience. And so you pass through. But don't encourage it, don't this night say, "I will simply go on a vegetable diet, I will give up liquor, I'll give up smoking, I'll give up sex in the hope that I'm going to pass through this state." It doesn't come that way. It comes in a strange way...it came to me in the strangest way. I ordered the most wonderful roast beef, may I tell you—I was in Syracuse, New York—and I love my meat, and I ordered the most wonderful roast beef. And as I put my knife into it, I actually felt I was cutting the animal alive. I took the plate and pushed it away. I could not take one piece from that plate...and for seven years I couldn't. So it happened that way. I couldn't touch a piece of meat, a piece of fowl, an egg or fish for seven years. But it happened…I was ___(??) for seven years. And I ordered from the menu roast beef, as I always loved it, and as it was delivered I just thought it would be marvelous, and as I put my knife right into it, I was cutting into the animal and pushed the whole thing away. For seven years it was that way. And coming back to the States I did everything I had not done in seven years. That's how you pass through the state called John the Baptist and come into the state called Jesus Christ.

But before you are lifted off the wheel, you must prove that this is *good* news. And *good* news is that everything in this world that you want you can have if you clothe yourself with it. It doesn't mean you're lifted off the wheel, but clothe yourself with it. You want to be rich? How would you feel were you rich? You want to be healthy? How would you feel were you healthy? You want to be free of all embarrassment? How would you feel this night if you were not embarrassed, that not a thing in this world could embarrass you? How would you feel were it so? And you *clothe* yourself with these states, one after the other, and be faithful to the clothing that you wear, and let it unfold in your world. It will! It will completely unfold in your world and you will see it. Then as you practice with it and actually believe in the good news of the kingdom of God, suddenly, when you least expect it, one after the other, a series of events that God predetermined to awaken *himself* will awaken within *you*. Because, God has prepared a way for himself to return individualized as you, completely prepared, and no one can stop the way. He's prepared that way, and so, at very end, all of a sudden the series begins to unfold, and you are it unfolding; and you are he— the one who became you and took himself through the furnaces, all through John into Jesus Christ—and you awake *as* he.

There's not a thing I can tell you to persuade you to accept it. And I wouldn't raise a finger to make it so, because I am not convinced by speculation: I am convinced by knowing having experienced it. And so, if all the great teachers of the churches of the world stood before me in opposition, it would make no difference to me whatsoever. They, too, will pass through these states because they aren't elected to these states by men. So the heads of all the great churches of the world, if they stood before me now, I could say to them, if you have not experienced it, you will. And your greatness in this world is as naught, it is nothing, for the least in the kingdom is greater than you; for the least in the kingdom has a greatness that you cannot measure by anything on earth. And if you have not experienced this, no matter how great you are with all the medals pinned upon you by men who vanish in this world, it is as *nothing*. But the day will come you'll go through John the Baptist. He's not a man who lived 2,000 years ago. He represents a state of consciousness that's eternal, through which every *soul* must pass, and passing through they do violence to their appetites. They come out of it and enter the state called Jesus Christ; and they believe the story of the good news of God, and actually prove it in performance. They prove it and prove it until that moment in time when they're lifted off the wheel of recurrence, and they enter the kingdom of God.

But, here we are told concerning John, the law and the prophets *until* John. It starts the great law and all through the great prophets *until* John (Mat. 11:13)...there comes a stop...from *then* the good news of the kingdom is preached. And everyone enters the kingdom violently. I read here in the most recent scholarly works this passage, which is the 16th chapter, the 16th verse of the Book of Luke, and these great scholars, and there were hundreds of them in discussion, and they confessed it doesn't make sense. It only adds confusion to confusion, based upon an earlier passage that they can't understand what he means that all of a sudden everyone enters the kingdom *violently*, and this thing happens *after* John. Well, may I tell you, it's true; it happened to me, and I can't tell you how violent you are when you enter—not angry but sheer, sheer energy. You use a power that you have never heard of on earth. We speak of a power, of blowing up a whole city with one bomb, blowing up a country with a bomb. It doesn't compare to the power that you exert in that moment of entrance into the kingdom of God. When you are whipped up in the form of a spiral into your own skull, it is as though it takes that energy to ram you into the eternal structure that God has predetermined; as though the whole vast skull is being *filled*, and you fill one niche forever and forever. But you move into it with such power the whole thing radiates, the whole thing shakes like an earthquake; as though the whole vast world is an earthquake. And then suddenly when you are completely in it and then riveted in, then it subsides, and it's all quiet, and you return here to the world of Caesar. So the world is stating in that 16th verse of the 16th chapter of Luke: "Everyone enters it violently." May I tell you, it must, because it takes an *enormous* power to drive you into that part prepared for you. It's been waiting for you since the beginning of time, and you move into that one part prepared for you, and you move in so forcibly the whole structure vibrates. Then it subsides and you're back.

So, you go home this night and clothe yourself in the joy of being the man, the woman that you want to be. I tell you it will not fail you! Now let us go into the Silence.

* * *

Q: (inaudible)

A: Yes, my dear, certainly. The lady's question is "Do you think we could have gone through the state of John in a life before this?" Why certainly, I wouldn't doubt that for one moment, and come out of it knowing that these things are not necessary for the kingdom of God...with all the temptations of the world. For we have all kinds of cults in this world who are playing as a cult. They don't know it's the state called John the Baptist, inviting everyone into it. They give up wearing fur, they give up eating meat, give up drinking, give up smoking, give up sex, and they're all inviting us into that cult, and they call themselves houses of religion. But, people are persuaded to enter that, and then they give up all these things, and do violence to their appetites. You might have passed through that. I'm not saying that you did or did not. So I'm saying to you, to answer your question, certainly, many of us could have gone through that state and in this world tonight you could be called into the kingdom of heaven. Because you're told, when the question was asked, "Tell me, Lord, is it now that you will restore the kingdom to Israel?" And he corrected their question and then answered, "It's not for you to know the time or the season which is fixed by God by his own authority. But you'll receive power *after* the Holy Spirit has come upon you" (Acts 1:6). Therefore, wait for the promise, just wait for it. You could have gone through it, and this very night...it is my constant hope that everyone who hears me is this very night lifted up into the experience, because, I can't tell anyone the thrill of being *aware* of the fact that you are a part of the kingdom of God. And there should be no delay beyond that moment in time when God calls you. And I'm ___(??) quite sure there is no delay.

Q: (inaudible)

A: Well, my dear, when this thing happens from above and you are awakened from this deep, deep sleep...

Q: (inaudible)

A: Oh, I didn't even know I was asleep. I didn't know when I was awakened in my skull to find myself completely enclosed within my skull and my skull is a sepulcher. And it's not a little tiny place like this here, for I only wear a seven-size hat, and I couldn't get into a seven-size hat. So it's not this, but it is my skull. And so here, I awake. I find myself waking but unlike the usual waking which comes every morning when I awake. This is something different—I'm waking, and I awake in my skull. My skull is a tomb, it's a sepulcher. And here I am completely awake now for the first time in thousands of years, but I am entombed. That's the resurrection. The resurrection begins the whole drama. And then out I come, being born like a child. The birth is symbolized in that of a babe wrapped in swaddling clothes. So, this series of events differs completely from all other mystical experiences.

BINDING AND LOOSING

1/14/64

Tonight's subject is "Binding and Loosing." It may be an odd title, but you'll find it a very practical one. When we open the Bible, we are in the midst of mystery. But I promise you, every one of you, everyone in the world will one day experience scripture for himself; and then and only then will he know how truly wonderful it really is. It's all true. Don't change it. Don't attempt to change it. It's altogether true when you experience scripture for yourself.

This segment is taken from the gospels...that is, not the gospels, but in the Book of John we are told: "If you forgive the sins of any, they are forgiven; if you retain the sins of any, they are retained" (20:23). That is true, and one day you will experience that in depth. But tonight, on this level, we'll show you how altogether marvelous it really is here before you experience that in depth. But I mean every sin is forgiven in depth, everything. But, on this level, you and I can forgive it.

But now we must search the scriptures. We're told this is said to the disciples. And you might think you are not a disciple. May I tell you that you are *if* you are willing to accept the story of Jesus Christ as told you in the 9th chapter of the Book of Acts—that Saul went out to find all the disciples of The Way. The early Christians were not called Christians; they were called people of The Way; those who believed in a certain *way* of salvation. And he went out determined to find anyone that he could find of The Way, whether they be male or female, and bring them bound into Jerusalem to be condemned. Now here in the scriptures, if you read the story on the surface there was no woman made a disciple. But in the 9th chapter of the Book of Acts they are—anyone, regardless of sex, who accepts this way of life is a disciple. So I say to you, if you believe this story, the story of salvation, you are a disciple, and to *you* it is said, if you forgive a sin, it's forgiven; if you retain a sin, it's retained. What a responsibility!

But in the same book, the wonderful Bible, we are told, "Without the shedding of blood there is no forgiveness of sin." Without the shedding of blood there is no forgiveness of sin. You'll read that in the 9th chapter of the Book of Hebrews (verse 22). Now, these words are true. Then what does it mean? To this very day, in the year 1964, there are those who believe on a certain day called the Day of Atonement that some living being must be destroyed for the salvation of those who will adhere to the law; and they keep it literally. I'm not taking it on that level; that's the most external of all levels, where we do everything on the outside in the hope of appeasing some god. I take it on the next level, the psychological level, where you and I tonight can prove beyond all doubt the truth of this law. And it *is* true, without the shedding of blood there is no forgiveness of sin. If you take it literally, it would be the twenty-fourth chapter of the Book of Exodus, where something alive was slain, and then the blood was sprinkled on the altar and then sprinkled on those who were present. And then came the atonement, and you wonder what is this atonement? The English word "atone" originally meant "at one." It's an at-one. I must perform a certain act to become attuned or at-one with a state. But, how could I do it? I do it only by the shedding of blood.

Now we are told, when man really discovers it, it is the blood of Christ Jesus that must be shed. Well, how could I shed the blood of Christ Jesus? Yet I am told, without the shedding of blood there is *no* forgiveness of sin; therefore, what is sin now? Sin is "missing the mark." If I have a goal in life and I do not realize it, I am sinning. I don't care what the world will tell me, it's the one sin of scripture if I have a goal. .And I am told: "If I had not come unto them and spoken unto them, they would not have sin; but now that I have spoken unto them, they have no excuse for their sin" (John15:22). If someone did not come into my world and tell me that I am not adjusted to the environment into which I am born, I could transcend it. I am not the being that seemingly appeared in this world and that is it, I could transcend *it.* If I am *told* I could transcend my environment, and then I desire to transcend it and don't, I am sinning. If someone didn't come into my world and tell me I could transcend my environment, I wouldn't know sin. But someone comes into my world and tells me I can transcend the being that I am; and at that moment he stirs me, and disturbs me, and makes me ambitious to transcend that which I am, and if I don't realize the being that I would like to be, then he made me a sinner. So to whom did he come? He said, I did not come to the righteous, I came to the sinners. I came to *make* them sinners and then to redeem them. Those who are complacent, who are satisfied with what they are, I did not come to the righteous. "I came not to the righteous but to the sinners." So he comes into the world and tells man a story.

But now, what is the blood of Christ that I have to shed? I'll tell you: Christ is your own wonderful human Imagination. "Christ in you is the hope of glory" (Col.1:27). It is Christ in you that must be awakened from this death. So, if I would now shed his blood, how would I shed my own Imagination's blood? Well, now I am in a certain state. I am aware that I am a certain man, and I desire to transcend it; I want to be other than the man that I am. I have to *die* to that man; therefore, blood is shed. I detach myself mentally from the man that I am now keeping alive and I become at-one with that state of consciousness, the new man, that I want to make real in this world. So we are told in Ephesians, "Be imitators of God as dear children" (5:1). And we are told in the same book, Ephesians, "He creates in himself *one new* man in place of the *two*, so making peace" (2:15). He creates in himself one new man in place of the two and this way he makes peace. So if I am now disturbed because I'm not the man I want to be, there's conflict, there's war. The only way I can find peace is to create *in myself* the one *new* man. I must *become* the man that I want to be.

A very able, in fact, the greatest writer in the English language put it into the character called Hamlet, and tried through this story to instruct on it. We think because he's a playwright, well, that was simply written for entertainment, that was written simply to entertain the world, don't believe it! One of the greatest educators of all time you'll find in Shakespeare. So, here he takes Hamlet and Hamlet is now made to tell his mother how to transcend herself. He said to her: "Assume a virtue, if you have it not. Refrain tonight; and that shall lend a kind of easiness to the next abstinence: the next more easy; for use can almost change the stamp of nature" (Act 3, Sc 4). And you try it. You can take it tonight and restrain tonight. Restrain what?—the impulse to sleep in the consciousness of being thwarted, of being the man that you don't want to be. And, just this one night restrain the impulse to fall asleep in that state. But don't fall asleep in a vacuum; fall asleep now by assuming a virtue that you have not.

For she didn't have the virtue of mercy when she actually aided in the destruction and death of her husband, through a passion that she wanted to, I would say, appease. And so, she certainly was not merciful, she was not one of pity, she was not one of love, and so, he asked her to *assume* a virtue if she had it not. What virtue? Well, he didn't name it for her. He allowed her to select the virtue that she would like to assume, which currently she did not possess; and told her if tonight you would refrain the impulse to fall asleep in your last night's concept, and this night fall asleep in the assumed virtue, just once, tomorrow night you'll find it easier, and the next night still more easy. For I tell you that even if it doesn't happen the next day, the next day you can always change the stamp of nature. So, if you came into this world stamped with the venom that is yours, the horror that is yours, the unmerciful picture that is yours, it can still change that stamp of nature if you'll try it tonight. So he tried to persuade her to assume it.

So I will say to you tonight, if you want to be successful, if you want to be...I don't care what it is, but you name it. I hope it is something lovely, something marvelous. If the whole vast world tells you that you could not do it, I have been sent to tell you that you can transcend your environment. You can transcend anything in this world that you seem to have at birth, or you seem to have today. You can transcend it by assuming the feeling of the wish fulfilled. I will tell you that Imagination will do *nothing* for us, nothing that we wish, *until* we have assumed the wish fulfilled. It will do nothing until we have assumed the wish fulfilled; and Imagination is Christ. And so, if I now give up my present concept of myself and dare to assume that I am the man that I want to be, have I not died to my former state? And *that* was the shedding of blood; that is the shedding of blood on the psychological state. I don't go out and buy a turtle dove, or buy a bullock, or kill some little animal in this world in the hope of appeasing God. I shed the blood of Christ, and the blood of Christ is my own wonderful human Imagination; for God became man that man may become God. He actually became us!

So if I am told when I started the dream that whatever—anything in this world no matter what it is—if you forgive it, it is forgiven; if you retained it, it is retained. But am I not told I must not ask for your consent. I don't ask for your permission to do it, and I need not tell you I am doing it. Maybe you are totally unaware that I am doing it. Therefore, if you are unaware that I am doing it, and I'm doing it without your knowledge or your permission, then is it not true that "All that I behold, though it appears without, it is within, in my Imagination, of which this world of mortality is but a shadow"? If I don't need your permission to forgive you, and I need not tell you that I am actually forgiving you and I perform an inner act which results in an outer change in *your* world, are you not within me? *If* I do it. Well, is it done? May I tell you, I could tell you unnumbered stories to support that claim. It *is* true!

A lady called me yesterday morning to thank me for something she'd asked of me on the morning of the 29th of December when I spoke to Dr. Palmer. She asked me for a certain something, and it was, would I please release her from this problem. And so, in my Imagination I simply assumed that she had called and told me of the good fortune or the good news which she called yesterday morning. But then she shared with me a lovely piece of good news. She said, "You know, I can't come to you at night any more, I don't like to go out at night, but I do put into practice what I heard from you over the years. And a friend of mine called me up—she goes to Santa Barbara in the summer and goes to New Mexico in the winter. In New Mexico she lives in a trailer. She called me and told me that they told her that the trailer had changed hands, that is, the place where they're all parked, and that she wanted to sell. So I said, 'Alright, it's done. You have the check in your hand and it's all done.' Then she called me back and told me that she had just heard from the people who were living there that there are seventeen trailers for sale, and because of the change in management, all things are going to pot, and that no one can get anything for a trailer today. I said, 'I'm not asking you why you're going to sell it; you want to sell it; and you sold it for the sum of money that you want.' She went off to New Mexico and within one hour after she arrived—in spite of the seventeen trailers for sale—she sold *her* trailer at the price she had stated, not one penny less, not a penny more. Someone within one hour bought her trailer in that trailer camp.

And if that works once, and you can repeat it, and then repeat it, and repeat it, we have found the law of the forgiveness of sin. For sin is only missing the mark. And if no sin can be forgiven without the shedding of blood, I have found what the shedding of blood is. The shedding of blood is the Christ blood. Well, Christ is my Imagination. And I gave up that which I made alive. If I give up something I made alive, I shed its blood. I took myself out of one state and put it in another state. So I put it in one state called "the check is in your hand"; therefore, I took it from the state where you are *trying* to sell and put it into the state where you *have* sold. I take it from one state where you are *not* the man you want to be, and put it in the state where you *are* the man that you want to be. So, in making this transformation I die to one state; and in dying to this state I then fulfill the Book of Ephesians, "He creates in *himself* one *new* man in place of the two, so making peace." And so, he makes peace.

In the *depths* of yourself you'll see that's done. That's another depth. But on this level it's done here. One day you will know how he does that in depth, and that is when he becomes you. And, not you and another, not you *and* God, God actually becomes you. And you will know then what it means to be one with God and what it means for the whole vast world to *be* God. He has one wonderful symbol by which he reveals it, and that is his Son; that, "No one knows who the Father is except the Son; and no one knows who the Son is except the Father" (Mat.11:27). And so when the Son appears and reveals you as Father, and you know he's going to reveal everyone as Father, then you know we are all one; we aren't really two. For, if I am the father of your son, and you *know* that son and I know that son, and we are both the father of the same son, then we are one. Although seemingly we are fragmented into numberless parts, if all are the Father of the one Son, then we are one God, one Father. So that day will come when you will know that.

But before it comes to you individually, you can take this marvelous revelation and try it on this level. So you are commissioned to go into the world and forgive sin. If you retain it, it's retained; if you forgive it, it's forgiven. And whatever you forgive is forgiven. So try it. Start this very night trying to forgive sin, by starting with yourself first. Look at yourself this very night, and ask yourself if you really are the man, the woman, that you really want to be. If you're satisfied, perfectly alright, but I doubt that anyone is *really* satisfied. For when he comes into the world he comes and he brings disturbance. "If I had not come unto them and spoken unto them, they would have not had sin; but now they have no excuse for their sin" (John15:22). So when Christ comes into the world of man he disturbs them. Prior to the coming, they were quite satisfied to adjust to the environment in which they were born, and perform the external act of sacrifice, so that once a year they could perform some little sacrificial act. But then one who heard him clearly said, "I see as I pass by that you are observing days and weeks and seasons and years. I am afraid I have labored over you in vain" (Gal. 4:10).

So when one thinks that only one day of the year atonement comes, I have labored over you in vain. Atonement comes at every moment in time. *Every* moment is the at-one. One can attune or atone, and so create in himself *one* man in place of the two. And so the two are always the man that I am and the man that I want to be. If the man that I want to be is in conflict with the man that I am—and it must be if I *want* to be it—I'm confessing I'm not it. The minute I *want* to be something I'm confessing I'm not that, therefore, there's war, there's conflict. And so, I must now create in myself *one new* man in the place of the two. So when I go to bed this night I must dare to assume that I am the man that at the moment my reason denies, my senses deny. And how do I know that I'm in it? Just how would I know that I'm really *in* this state and I've brought about this one new man in myself? By looking at the world...if I don't see the world as I *would* see it were I the man that I want to be, then I'm not in that state. I haven't yet created in myself the one new man. But if tonight I assume—___(??) assume the virtue if you have it not. That virtue may be any kind of virtue. So, I assume that I'm...and I name it...and then I look at my world, my frame of reference, to reflect confirmation of the man that I want to be. I will see then on the faces of my friends' expressions implying that they see in me the man that I want the world to see. So I will hear them speak about me. I will see them and just see that face reflecting what I am. Then I am in it.

And so, I tried to tell this in a strange way, saying thinking *from* what you want instead of thinking *of* what you want. If I think *of* what I want, I'm in conflict because I am not there. If I think *of* and I really want it, then the being thinking *from* and thinking *of* what he wants, these two are in conflict. I must resolve it. So that when I think *of* and it's really something that I want to realize, I must resolve it and create in myself the one *new* man so it becomes a state *from* which I think. And then I think from it, instead of thinking of it. If you do it this way it works. But how it works no one knows. No one could devise the means employed by that state *from* which you think to bring it to pass. I could not, on reflection, have devised the means employed to bring about the state that I had realized in my world, I couldn't. I would not be wise enough as a normal person to actually devise the means. But man not knowing this, he goes out trying to work out the means instead of applying God's law. God's law is: You cannot do it unless you do it by the shedding of blood. So you give up what you are to become what you want to be; and that's dying. So you die to one state and you live to another state. So without the shedding of blood there is no remission of sin. And yet I'm invited to remit sin, to forgive it.

So I can take the words now, "atonement, forgiveness, remission," all these things, and put them and call them, really, synonyms, they're all one. If I forgive...what is the challenge to a man to forgive? It challenges a man's ability to enter into and partake of the nature of the opposite state of consciousness. I'll forgive you, forgive myself. So I take myself, I'll forgive myself for being today, and I'll name it. Then what would be the solution of my present problem? Alright, can I assume that I am now it? It challenges my ability to enter into *that* state to the point where when I view the former state it's a something away behind me. It's something that was. I can say today, I remember when—remember when what?—when I was not that.

I remember when someone told me, "You will never in eternity earn a dollar using your voice." That's a fact! That was in my school, I went to school and she said to me, "You know, you'll never...you're the one in the class of forty...and listen to Neville, he will never be able to earn a dollar using his voice. So use him as an example and see what you should avoid." And so, they all *are* really using their voices to order a meal, or to sell a shirt at Macy's. They are using their voices, but she was wrong there too. But they're not using their voices in the theatrical world where we all hoped one day to use it. It was a little theatrical school in New York City called the ___(??) School, and I was singled out as the horrible example of things that one should *not* do. Well, then I began to apply this law, to assume that *I am* the man that I want to be, and then let things happen. I could not have devised it. I took no more lessons I assure you. When I left there that was the end of my schooling. And so, I never once took a lesson in the use of the voice. It just happened that I had something to say and then I said it. That's all that matters. Whether I said it correctly, I mean in the proper use of words, it made no difference to me once I said it. But I said it with feeling because I had experienced it. So I wasn't trying to become a church in the use of words, I wasn't trying to become some great user of words, just to be normal and to tell it as clearly and with all the feeling I possibly could muster. For I knew that I had experienced it and if I could tell it with *feeling* I would persuade others to try it.

And so I tell you, you don't have to have anything more than you have now—just a dream, a dream of something other than what you are, some noble dream. Then this night believe the great Bard: "Assume a virtue if you have it not. Refrain tonight; and that shall lend a kind of easiness to the next abstinence and the next more easy; for use almost can change the stamp of nature." And in my own case, I completely changed the scene. It changed my stamp of nature, for I certainly was not stamped with this. But I desired to tell it and then went out to tell it. The first time I started, six people came, all through sympathy. I sent out fifty penny postal cards. In those days there was such a thing as a penny card, and I sent out the large amount of fifty cents worth. Out of the fifty, my friends, all of the theatrical world, six came, and six came just because they were sympathetic, and they came almost to pay their respects. Because there were only six in the place that could have taken care of fifty. They either were embarrassed, but whether embarrassed or not, these were embarrassed out of dollar bill. Because I didn't charge, didn't have the courage to charge, and so you pass the basket among the six. When they saw only six they each gave a dollar. And so, that paid the rent. And I started that way and never turned back, every night dreaming my dream of telling this story.

Then six months later, a man who was in the same building, speaking to an enormous crowd—all things being relative, I spoke to six, and when he invited me, oh, six months later, I had grown to twenty—and so, he had an enormous audience of about 600 people, and he thought that he would simply snuff me out by inviting me to take the platform. So I took the platform and he paid me the large amount of twenty-five dollars for that night to take his platform and talk to his 600. I learned afterwards he invited me for one purpose, that when I faced this audience I would be so nervous they would see that he's not the one to visit anymore, and so he'd rub me out completely. But may I tell you what happened? The very next night I spoke upstairs in my little place of fifty and I got 200 of his. They were all down the hallway. And then they kept on coming night after night—I spoke twice a week then—and so they came. I had no place for them, and the management in Steinway Hall said, "You can't continue this way. I'm getting all kinds of complaints because they're all in the hallway. I must rent you a bigger place." I said, alright, rent me a bigger place. He rented me a bigger and it still overflowed and overflowed and overflowed, until finally we had to move out of Steinway Hall.

So it all started by my dream. I simply went to bed assuming a virtue that I did not possess. I assumed it and assumed it and assumed it. So I tell you that Imagination will not do a thing for us until we have imagined the wish fulfilled. Just like a little child, it cannot be compelled; it must be persuaded. The child must be persuaded; you can't compel it; it resents it. Well, Imagination is just like that. And in all the stories of Christ he's always depicted as a little child: "And a little child shall lead them." And just like a child, it must be persuaded, not compelled. And so this night I can't compel myself to believe something, I must pretend it's true, and play the game of pretending, and assume it and assume it. If I dare to assume that I am what at the moment reason denies and my senses deny, and fall asleep in that assumption just as though it were true, may I tell you from experience, it becomes true.

On reflection, when you look back and see how it worked out, you could never have devised the means employed to bring it to pass. You never could have done it. I could never have thought of the means of being invited by this man to take his audience. It came suddenly. He sent his secretary downstairs to invite me to come upstairs on a Thursday night, which was my off night—I spoke on Wednesdays and Fridays—and he sent this lady downstairs and asked me to come upstairs the following night, because he had to go to Washington. It was true, he did, he had to go to Washington and he was the honored guest at one of the great ___(??) meetings. And so, this was the great night of the banquet and he was the honored guest. And so I took his platform and, naturally, I was very happy to do it. But I didn't realize the consequences. I had been sleeping in my dream and this is how it works. So it didn't work out as he had plotted it. He was used by my Imagination to bring it to pass, because all of us are interwoven: "All things by a law divine in one another's being mingle." So that if I'm assuming that I am what I want to be, I don't need your permission, your consent, to use you if you can be used to bring my assumption to pass. I'll use you and a billion like you if it takes a billion to bring it to pass. Therefore, when you look in the morning's press and you see these strange things, don't be disturbed. It happened because someone is dreaming.

Did you read last week's *Life Magazine* of MacArthur? I did. I'm very interested in the man and I read the story of Gen. MacArthur. But the very end, the very last paragraph, when he was leaving West Point, he quoted what the general who addressed this fine body of men said. He said: "Before you take off that uniform, you will be at war. It is always so, it's part of the tradition of our country. You will be at war; therefore, prepare your nation for that war." He quotes it just as the man said it to him. Well, if everybody that graduates from that great group of men are addressed in that manner—go out and prepare yourself first, and prepare your community, and then your state, and your country for the inevitable war—what do you expect? It's all Imagination. Imagination *creates* reality. The whole vast world is God made visible; and God *became* man that man may become God. He is sunk in us as our own wonderful human Imagination, so what are we doing with our Imaginations?

I tell you that the story of scripture is true. I stand before you as a witness to it. I have experienced the story of Christ Jesus. Everything said about him in scripture has happened in the soul of my being. Everything, from his resurrection, to his birth, the discovery of the fatherhood of God, and the ascent into heaven, and the descent of the dove, which is the symbol of the Holy Spirit. Everything recorded I have experienced. That comes in the depth of the soul. But these same experiences lifted to the psychological level can be *invaluable* here in the world of Caesar. You and I can take it in the world of Caesar and do the most fantastic things with it. On the highest level, the level of John who wears the outer garment of skin and hair you've outgrown. You need not do that...no stalking of a bird to redeem yourself, no killing of a bullock or a lamb or a ram and offering *it* to redeem yourself. That's on the very surface of it all.

But below it, on that psychological level, you can use it to the most marvelous state in this world. Take every person that you know and without their consent represent them to yourself as being what you would like them to be, and see them actually become it. See them become it! Like my friend who went to San Francisco, Freedom, a total stranger on the street was asking for money, and he doesn't give him money, but in his mind's eye he sees the man gainfully employed. He refuses the money but sees him gainfully employed, and then when he is satisfied that this imaginal act is true he goes upon his way. And then, four months later that same man is coming down the street, comes up to my friend Freedom, extends his hand, and says, "I don't suppose you remember me?" "Oh yes I do." And then, said the man to my friend Freedom, "I want to thank you for not giving me the money that I asked you for four months ago; for had you given me that money I would today be asking for money. Because you *didn't* give it to me, I went out that very day and got myself a job. I am still on that job, and I am now gainfully employed, and it has great possibilities of growth in this world." And he thanked him for it...a total stranger. But he knew the art of forgiveness: how to actually create in himself one *new* man instead of this conflict. A man begging for money? No. I'll create in myself one new man, a man who is gainfully employed.

So I say everyone can do it. You are a disciple. Don't think that the disciples from Peter down to Judas are the twelve disciples. Read the 9th chapter of the Book of Acts. Both women and men if they *really* accept this way of life they are disciples. Anyone who accepts the way of life, and this is the way of life, they're called "the people of The Way". We take the phrase "the people of The Way" and we now give it the name Christ. It's a lovely name; to me it's a beautiful name. The word Christ means Messiah. It is *the way* of salvation. But it is a *way* of salvation, not a being outside of yourself who saves. For listen to these words from the 43rd of Isaiah: "I am the Lord your God, the Holy One of Israel, your *Savior*...and besides me there is no savior...I know not any" (verses 3,11). There is no Savior besides the Holy One of Israel, and his name is I AM: "I am the Lord your God, the Holy One of Israel." So the I AM within you is the great being that sunk himself in you and became you. He's your own wonderful human Imagination.

And you try it. Try it sincerely. If tomorrow you don't get the fruit, so what? Let me quote that lovely passage from Habakkuk: "The vision has its own appointed hour; it ripens, it will flower. If it be long, then wait; for it is *sure* and it will not be late" (2:3). So the vision, your vision of yourself, you want to be and you name it. Alright, you drop a seed into the ground today. It could be a little acorn, it could be a corn, it could be some other kind of seed, and every seed has its own appointed hour. One will grow overnight, one will grow in a week, one will grow in a month, one will grow in a year, but it has its own appointed hour and it ripens and it will flower. If it seems to you long, wait, for it is sure and it will not be late. Not for itself. All things bring forth after their kind. That's part of the eternal plan—the identical harvest (Gen.1:11). You can't plant one thing and expect to grow something other than what you planted. And so, whatever you plant you plant it in your own wonderful Imagination by assuming that you are what you want to be.

So he comes into our world and disturbs it. Had he not come into my world and told me that I am not really anchored to the environment in which I was born, that I could transcend it, well then, I would have no ambition to be other than what I was at birth, and remain in that environment. For when Christ comes into the world, he comes not to bring peace but a sword. He disturbs the whole vast world when he comes; and then he shows man how in himself to bring peace, how to create in himself *one* new man in place of two, so making peace. But at first you can't make peace unless first there is war. So he makes war first and then shows you how he is going to make peace. He disturbs you that you may be other than what you seem to be; and then shows you how to make peace, how to bring about *one* new man instead of two.

Now let us go into the Silence.

* * *

___(??) that when you begin to practice this art of forgiveness and you master it, and you will if you practice it, don't think for one moment because you've mastered the art that then you could work in cooperation with God to bring a new order into being. That new order is coming whether you forgive or not. It is only given to us to cushion the blows on this level. But that new order is coming, in fact, it has come. The door is open and no one can shut it. And so the order has come. If you want to continue adjusting yourself to the environment in which you were born, it will not delay your entrance into the kingdom of heaven. It is only given to you to adjust yourself on this wheel of recurrence while you are on it, until that moment in time when God, in his own wonderful mercy, lifts you off into the kingdom of heaven.

Now are there any questions, please?

Q: Could you relate what you said tonight about forgiveness to your chapter called *The Pruning Shears of Revision*?

A: Yes, definitely. Revision is forgiveness. I tried to freshen it as it were, because the word today...after 2,000 years the ship has grown barnacles. And all these words, like atonement, like forgiveness, certain groups have claimed the right and the only right to forgive; that an individual can't forgive; only if you wear the frock you can forgive, and he has assumed the right and the only right to forgive. It isn't that in scripture at all; everyone in this world can practice the art. A little child five years old, whose grandmother comes here (she's here tonight) who actually brought about reconciliation between divorced parents by playing a little game that the grandmother had devised. So when you go to bed tonight...(tape omission).

Q: Is it necessary to do the revision, as Jesus said, prior to praying? If you have hurt your brother, go back and forgive him? Is the revision necessary for more effective work?

A: It's effective any moment in twenty-four hours. If I injured you, then we are in conflict in me, not in you. I must resolve it if I so desire. I *should* desire it because I am going to prove to myself, as I have already proven, that you are really not another. You do not know as yet that you are the being talking to you. You do not know it as yet and yet you are. Without loss of identity you will be the same wonderful being you are but more so and yet one with the Speaker. And the one being that's going to prove it to you is that you are really the father of my Son, my Son David. You are his father and your mother is his father, and your grandmother. Every being in this world that is seemingly of another sex they are the *father* of my Son. So the fatherhood of God is real.

So if in the process you do not realize this and someone offends us, and I don't know he's my very being only reflecting something I have done of which I have forgotten, that he only bears witness of my own disturbance—I think *he* is the cause. He isn't the cause; it's in me. Somewhere along the line.when I read this thing on Gen. MacArthur...I've always admired the general, I still admire him...so I, tonight, regret that he wrote it, really, because to me he's greater than what he's written in the first installment. In my mind's eye, I think he's a perfectly marvelous person. But when as a young man he was being sent off into the world, well trained, at the head of his class, a way ahead of any of them, and he is told: "Before you take that uniform off you will be at war, and this is inevitable" says the gentleman who addresses the class. It has always happened and it always will, he said, therefore prepare your country for it. Well, what can you expect when every class that's coming out this day, out of Russia, out of China, out of England, out of...they all have classes coming out trained to protect their land. If that is the charge given—undoubtedly it's a similar charge given to all of them—are we concerned, or should we be disturbed when we see these explosions all over the world? It's inevitable, said he.

Well, I say to you, Christ came into the world. He's sunk in you as your wonderful human Imagination, and he disturbs you by telling you you can be what you want to be. That's war. But he puts you into an environment that is limited and starts you in life as a slave. For we're all slaves: you come in and you have no money, no social background, no intellectual background, but nothing, and there you start. And he tells you that you can dream, and by daring to assume that you are the man you would like to be, you can become it. It's going to cause conflict in this world—"I didn't come to bring peace but a sword." Because, the minute you begin to dream, things are going to happen, and people are going to be disturbed. But their disturbance brings to birth the fulfillment of your dream. The whole thing is disturbed—you can't stop it—all of a sudden it comes to birth, and you *are* the man, and you dream from then on. And dreams are always disturbing the world.

One day, a friend of mine, flying up from San Diego to Los Angeles, he came home for dinner that night—he's a Navy man, not any more, but he was in the Navy during the last war. He said, "I had the strangest experience today. I didn't realize it but I was down on the water's edge, but flying above the water, I saw this little tiny small little ship moving off, and it was leaving a wake behind it. And do you know, Neville, that wake kept on going long after my eye could see it; and I know a bit of the structure of this world of ours, *that* thing unless interfered with is going to reach the Orient, that wake. That he disturbed the water and that thing is moving, and it will go on forever and forever. Until some shoreline stops it, it's going to go right on." Well, you know, mind disturbs something and it influences everyone that it hits.

Goodnight.

THE LARGER VENTURE

1/16/64

The subject tonight is "The Larger Venture." Sir Winston Churchill made the statement that "The destiny of mankind is not determined by material computation. But when great causes are on the move in the world, then we realize that we are spirits, not animals, and that something is going on in space and time and beyond space and time, which, whether you believe it or not, spells duty." Now you and I, today, we have a certain duty. If you are not satisfied with the being that you are, then you have a definite responsibility to be the being that you want to be. That's scripture. And so, causes are moving in the world...and you and I *can* be the being that we want to be.

Let me turn now to the 20th chapter of 1st Kings. It's a fantastic chapter. Read the entire thing when you go home tonight, I'll only just cover it lightly. But a prophet, an unknown prophet, said to a fellow, "Strike me, at the command of God" and he didn't. He said, "Because you did not obey the command of the Lord, as you depart from me you will be killed by a lion." And so, as he departed he was killed by a lion. Then he said to another fellow, "Strike me, at the command of the Lord," and he struck him and wounded him. Then he disguised himself with a napkin over his eyes and waited for the coming of the king of Israel. Then he said to the king as he came by, "I went into the midst of the battle; and a soldier turned and brought me a man and said to me, 'Keep him; if by any means he disappears, your life shall be for his life, or else you will give a talent of silver.' And as your servant was busy here and there, he was gone." And the king said to him, "So shall your judgment be; you *yourself* have decided it."

And so, here is a story of man too busy, so busy he substitutes physical action for sustained thought. I give you a man to keep, what man? You tell me what you want to be...that's the man. I would like to be and you name it—I would like to be this, that or the other man. By man I mean generic man. So the ladies now are in the same boat as it were...the lady that you would like to be, the man that you would like to be. And so, here is a man to keep, but you're so busy with the thousand and one things—I was here and there, and he was gone. And so, he escaped out of your consciousness. You don't remain faithful to the man that you want to be, and so the judgment is upon you, and you yourself pass judgment upon yourself. We're so busy we can't remain faithful to the assumption that I am that which I want to be, and remain faithful to it. You read it carefully, it's the 20th chapter of 1st Kings (verse 35). It's a fantastic story, because he succeeded and succeeded, and then in the very end he was unfaithful. He did not remain faithful to that which he really wanted to be in this world.

Now let me share with you a story. I've told it time and again, but after all, the same stories are told over and over again in scripture. They are only in the gospel of John six signs—not called miracles—six signs, six stories. And they're repeated after 2,000 years because they came from the Lord. Now let me share with you a story I've told you unnumbered times. But there are those this night who never heard it before and they should hear it, and you should hear it again. How one remains faithful to that which the Lord proclaims. I was in the army, I was thirty-eight, eligible for discharge; made my application; within four hours it came back "disapproved." That night I applied God's principle, his law, and this is his principle—read it in the 37th chapter of the Book of Psalms: "Take delight in the Lord, and he will give you the desires of your heart. Commit yourself, your way, to the Lord; trust in him, and he will act" (verse 4). Read it carefully, the 37th chapter of the Book of Psalms. Take delight in the Lord...just delight in the Lord. Well, the word Lord is Yod He Vau He which defined is I AM. Take delight in the Lord and he will give you the desires of your heart. Commit your way to the Lord—the Lord, I AM, Yod He Vau He—trust in him, trust in I AM, and he will act.

So I went to bed. That day I saw the piece of paper, and my captain said, "I'm awfully sorry for you, Neville, but I am very happy that I have a man just like you going through this war with me." Alright, so he wanted me to go through the war with him, but I didn't. I wanted to go back to New York City and live a lovely normal life with my wife and my child. So that night I said nothing to my captain, I applied the law; I delighted in the law of the Lord. "Take delight in the Lord and he will give you the desires of your heart." My desire was to be in New York City, honorably discharged. That was my desire. How would I now delight in the Lord and the Lord is I AM? So, I *assumed* that I am in New York City. To prove that I really *am* in New York City I viewed the world, and I saw it as I would see it *were* I in New York City, but just as I would see it. Not as vividly as I'm seeing this room now, but I gave it as much of the tones of reality, as much of the sensory vividness as I possibly could muster. I felt it natural as far as I'm concerned, and saw it so clearly in my mind's eye, and then I slept in my Imagination in New York City.

That very night as I was sound asleep—as you're told, "He will act." Listen to the words, "Delight in the Lord, and he will give you the desires of your heart. Commit your way to the Lord; trust in him, and he will act"—well, that night as I did this he acted. Suddenly before my eyes came a piece of paper, just like the paper I saw that day that I had signed and it came back "Disapproved" and signed by my colonel. Then a hand came out of the nowhere and a hand scratched out the word "Disapproved." It did not scratch out my colonel's name; it left the authority of my colonel just as it was. It simply revoked his decision, and a greater authority which was the hand of God wrote in "APPROVED" and wrote it in a bold, bold script above the statement "Disapproved." Then the voice said to me from the depths of my soul, "That which I have done I have done"—that was his statement. Now he addresses me, "Do nothing." "Do nothing" he said to me. May I tell you, there are times in this world of ours when the most difficult thing in the world is to do nothing; and yet there are times when the *only* thing to do is do nothing. And so I woke with the words ringing in my mind. I saw the revision... I saw the whole thing revised. Instead of "Disapproved" I saw it scratched out—"APPROVED." Then the voice said, "That which *I* have done *I* have done." Now, "Do nothing."

So I walked for the next nine days in the assumption that it was done. If there was any goldbricker in this world, I was it. Every morning early I would get up...my friends, I wrote their letters for them. I had a Chinese next to me who made my bed for me, and for that I wrote his letter. I had about four or five men in my company that they couldn't read or write, and they would say to me, "You tell her I love her. You tell her I'm very lonely." I said, "Alright. You ___(??)" and I would write these letters every week to girls back wherever they were. For that they would do all kinds of things for me. And so for the next nine days I didn't really appear when they called reveille. Or when they got out and they all called names, they would say Neville Goddard or Goddard, and someone would say, "Here." I wasn't there. I was so completely lost in this belief that I am out I didn't attend any one of these early morning calls, not one. I mean it; I tell you I didn't attend one. I was out, completely out, because I heard the voice of God, and God said to me, "That which I have done I have done. Do nothing." And I did nothing, literally. Nine days later, the very colonel who disapproved my request called me in, I didn't seek him, and here he called me in and then wrote the very word "Approved," and that day I was on a train for New York City. But I *lived* in New York City nine days before in this way.

Listen to the words, the 37th chapter of the Book of Psalms, the 3rd and 4th verses: "Take delight in the Lord, and he will give you the desires of your heart," all your desires. "Commit your way to the Lord; trust in *him*, and he will act." Well, didn't he act that night? Well, who is the Lord? The Lord is I AM; there is no other God in this world, but *none*. When you meet him it is yourself personified. There is only God in this world, and God is your own wonderful I-am-ness. One day you will meet him, the most majestic being in the world; it's yourself personified. He personifies himself as you here and puts him through the paces in hope that you'll remember who projected himself here, and that you will believe in him, and it will come to pass.

So here, this is the greater venture. They were so busy…this king of Israel, so busy he could not keep what was entrusted to him. And the prophet said to him at the very end, "You have passed judgment on yourself." He thought he was really judging the prophet. Then the prophet took the cloth from his eyes, and this king saw the prophet and realized it was his own judgment: That he had allowed the king of Syria to go free when he was condemned by the Lord. So he had removed this little cloth and said, Alright, so once you pass it on me, you pass it on yourself. Listen to it carefully. "I was in the field in the midst of the battle; and suddenly a soldier came to me and said, 'Keep this man; you keep him and if by any means he escapes, your life shall be for his life...if by any means.' And as I was busy here and there, he was gone." And that is the life of man. I tell you this night you can be the man, the woman, you want to be. Keep it; but if by any means he escapes you, then your life shall be for his life. So I tell you, you name it. You want to be this lady, this man, this person, you name it, but you must *keep* him. But if by any means he escapes, his life, your life shall be for his life: You remain just as you are. But if you keep him by assuming that you are—as God assumed that he is this being, your being. Every being in this world to become alive God had to assume that he is that being. And he wears me just like an outward garment; he wears you like an outward garment. And so, we are told to wear our assumption just like an outward garment as God wears us like an outward garment.

Here was a lady in New York City...and to show you how this thing works...this lady went into the hospital, many years before, and I met the nurse who took care of her. She was violent. I mean they considered her the incurable case...violent to the point where she could never be let out of this mental hospital. But she *was* let out. I was not then in her world. She came to my meetings. A lady of means—she had all the money that it took to travel all over the world—and she went off to Europe with her children, leaving behind her a lovely home and her maid. When she returned nine months later, having spent nine months in Paris, there was no furniture. She went to everything in this world that you could call the right thing to do—the police, private detectives, everything—and at the end of quite a long search, no furniture. *Then* she came to me.

Now she knew my teaching, she came to me before. It never occurred to her to come to me first; she went to the authorities first. And then, we sat in the Silence and she and I agreed that she had her furniture. I asked her to assume that she was sitting in her own place where she had paid the rent, and here, lovely pictures of her children on the piano, and all the things were there, as they ought to be there. She did it. And then she went down to her bank on Madison Avenue, and coming out of the bank she turned in the wrong direction. When she realized her mistake, only one block away, there were these familiar ankles, and it was her maid. She looked up and here's the maid. She held the maid, no scene. She took the maid into a taxicab and made the maid take her to the place where she had stored the furniture. The maid was waiting for this wealthy woman not to come back. At the end of a year she would dispose of it. She knew the woman's eccentricity, she'd been in a mental institution, and the maid knew all these things, and simply moved it out after the lady went off to Paris. And out of the *nowhere* she finds her, when the entire police department and her private detectives in New York City could not find where this furniture was. And she found it, because suddenly she found a man, and I said, "Hold onto this man; don't let him go."

Now you are told in the end of the Book of John: So they come into the garden and they're looking for a savior, one called The Lord Jesus of Nazareth. He said to them, "Whom do you seek?" and they answered, "Jesus of Nazareth." He answered, "I am he" (John18:4). When they heard it they all fell to the ground, as the world falls to the ground when they discover that the savior of *their* world is *their own* I-am-ness. They can't believe it. They've been taught to believe that some God in space, something outside of himself, is his God. And one day he discovers my own consciousness is God, the only savior in the world; and when he hears it, all that he believes in falls to the ground as it were. When he regains his composure, he can't believe it, so he asks the same question. So the one asked the question, "Whom do you seek?" Again they make the same answer, "We seek Jesus of Nazareth" and he replies, "I told you that *I am he*; now that you've found me, let these go, but do not let me go" (verse 8).

Don't let *me* go after you have found me, but let everything in this world go that you thought could be your protector. Don't let me go.

So man finds his own wonderful I-am-ness, called in scripture, "The Lord." So, "Take delight in the Lord"—take delight in the I AM—"and he will give you the desires of your heart. Commit your way to the Lord (to I AM); trust in the Lord (I AM), and he will act." And so, man comes and he finds the being that saves him, and it's his own wonderful human Imagination. So he loses himself in his own wonderful Imagination. But he acts: He creates the scene which would imply the fulfillment of his dream. Then God acts; your own wonderful I-am-ness goes into action after you prepare the scene for him to execute in this world. "By him all things were made; without him there was nothing made that is made." So I create the scene implying the fulfillment of my dream. And so I'm in New York City and honorably discharged. And that night the grand I AM acts.

So some psychiatrist would tell me, "That was your own imagination." And when I say no, I wouldn't say that. "And when you saw the paper come before your eyes and a hand out of the nowhere scratched out the word disapproved and then write in approved, that's your own imagination." I said yes it was. "And then the voice said, 'That which I have done I have done. Do nothing,' that's your own imagination." I said yes...but it worked! So if I have evidence for a thing, what the world thinks about it, it's no matter. So people tell me, "My own Imagination"...while he remains in the army for the next four years. I had that experience. A very close friend of mine (I haven't seen him in years) but he was in the army until the other seventeen million were discharged. And I wrote him what I did, but he was a Freudian, and he knew exactly how this thing should *not* work, so he never applied it. So he remained for the next four years in the army. And to this day he will *still* not believe it. But he told me himself, "When I come to your meetings, I like it, but I put my feet into the carpet and I stick my hands on the chair and I hold on firmly to keep my sense of the profoundness and the reality of things." So for the next four years he was still holding onto the chair in his barracks, and he wanted out as much as I did. I told him exactly how to do it, to believe in the Lord, actually *believe* in the Lord, and the Lord is my own wonderful I-am-ness.

So tonight if you could believe in the Lord, the Lord being your own wonderful Imagination. So when you go to bed, "I am" and you name it; and then to prove that you are in that state you see the world, and you see the world as it *would* be seen were you *now* the being that you want to be. You see it exactly as you would see it. And seeing it, you may not hear the words. When I told this story, I wrote it down in detail, and a friend of mine, being very, very practical, and he read my manuscript for me, he said,

"Neville, may I delete the mystical aspects of this story, because someone reading it not knowing of you would think unless they had the experience, the mystical experience, it wouldn't work." I was persuaded by him not to incorporate it when I really should have incorporated it. You don't have to hear the voice. If you believe in him, he acts anyway. In my case, my belief was so intense that I heard the voice and saw the paper and saw the hand and saw everything. It was God's hand. It was God's voice. And his voice is my voice. My own I-am-ness was speaking to myself. That's God. There is no other God. God became man that man may become God. So he sunk himself in me as my own wonderful human Imagination. But he is still I AM. Go to them and tell them I AM that I AM. I AM has sent you unto them. Go and tell them. But if you hear the words or see the pictures, it doesn't mean that he is more active in this case than he is if you do *not* hear his words or see the pictures. I tell you, you will bring about everything in this world if you believe in God. And God is your own wonderful human Imagination, and his name is I AM. That's his name.

So this is the greater venture. One turned the fields...I am in the field of the battle, I went into the midst of the battle (this is the battle); and someone said to me, "Keep this man; but if by any means he is gone, then *your* life shall be for his life." "And, O king, as I was busy here and there, he was gone." Then the king said, "So shall it be unto you. You, yourself, have pronounced the judgment, the decision." And so he was gone. I was so busy...maybe the morning's paper, maybe the news on the radio or the TV, maybe some little rumor persuaded me that things aren't as they ought to be—I'm going to lose my job when I get my Social Security—and I let the man go. I let him go…and then the judgment is upon myself. I tell you it is true—"Do not let me go." Who is speaking? "I AM he," said he. I want Jesus; I want the savior of the world. "I am he. Let these men go, but don't let me go." And the world thinks it's some little being that dramatized this picture 2,000 years ago. This is the ___(??) drama. God actually sunk himself in humanity, became every child born of woman. God is in man as man's own wonderful human Imagination. When he says, "I am," that's God. But he's been taught to believe that there's another God outside in space to whom he bows; and all orthodoxies the world over speak of another God, and worship the false God, and have built up fantastic things around some God that does not exist. The only God that exists dwells *in* man as man's own wonderful human Imagination, that's God.

And the day will come, may I tell you, every story told in scripture you will experience. Man must experience scripture for himself to know how wonderful it really is. In the depths of his soul he goes through this experience. On the next level it is this, the psychological level. On the level man simply goes through all the outer things that mean nothing, all the outer rituals and doctrines that mean absolutely nothing...not really to change his world. But below it, where we're talking this night, it changes every thing in this world. As I stand before you, that's exactly how I got out of the army. It was the year 1943 and the month was March. My friend was my age and he could have gotten out that very month, but he would not believe me. He did not believe in God. He *thought* he believed in God. And he wrote a book, and in this book he wrote a chapter on me, and he said, "Neville is an atheist." Well, an atheist is one who does *not* believe in God. An agnostic is one who is on the verge, he doesn't know whether he believes in God or not. He's not against God, but he's not yet convinced. But an atheist is a Khrushchev, one who does *not* believe in God.

I do not know of anyone who walks the face of this earth who believes more in God than I do. Because I stood in the presence of God and God is man: It is yourself personified. You meet yourself, and you can't conceive of the beauty and the majesty and the glory of the being that you meet when you are brought into the presence of the ___(??), and you meet yourself: It is God. You're embraced and incorporated into your very being. He went astray into a world for educative purposes. It's an ever-expanding illumination that is God. So he simply assumed a limitation and projected himself in this limitation. Emptied himself of his original form and took upon himself the form of man, this limitation, and became obedient unto death, even death upon this cross (Phil.2:6). Finding himself in this form, he became obedient to all the limitations of the flesh. And one day he calls you back. You have gone through all of the hell of the world, all the fires he could ever conceive, and he brings you back. He brings you into his presence, and you stand in the presence of yourself. There's nothing but God, only God. Every being in this world is God.

So I tell you, believe. Listen to the words, "Those who believe will not make haste." I didn't know it, I tell you. For those nine days in the army I walked as I walked on air, really I did. And when the world would say... well, as I told you earlier, one of the most difficult things in this world when one is anxious, has a wife, has a child he hasn't seen in three months, a little child two months old, and you're hungry to kiss and smell that little child, and the hunger for that embrace of a baby. For I do not know of any odor in this world comparable to the odor of a child, I do not know it. I can't conceive of any odor—perfumes, flowers, all these things are lovely—but the odor of a baby. I personally know of no odor in the world more desirable than the odor of a baby. And here was this baby and I'm denied it, a thousand miles away. So, I simply lost myself and I performed the act.

So, listen to the words, "Take delight in the Lord, and he will give you all the desires of your heart. Commit your way (that is, your action) to the Lord; trust in him, and he will act." So I did it. I assumed that I am in New York City. I am looking out on the world proving that I am in New York City, for were I in New York City I would see the world from New York City. So I saw it *from* New York City. I didn't think *of* New York, I thought *from* New York, and slept in it. And that very night he acted. My intensity was so great, suddenly the paper comes before my face, he scratches out "Disapproved," he writes in "APPROVED," and then he speaks to me directly. Having said to me, "That which I have done I have done," now believe it. "Do nothing." And if you have ever gone through this you'll know that it is the most difficult thing in this world when you are so anxious, to do nothing. And yet, there are moments as it was in my case when it was the only thing to do, to do nothing. And so I did nothing. And then, I didn't appeal, he calls me nine days later and here I am that very day on a train to New York City.

So I tell you it will not fail you if you believe in God. If you think God is hanging on the wall, or if you think he is in some other place, you don't know God. Listen to these words, the 3rd chapter of 1st Corinthians, the16th verse, it is that "the Spirit of God dwells *in* you…*you* are the temple of the living God." The *Spirit* of God dwells in you...you are the temple of the living God. So the Spirit of God dwells in me and his name is I AM then I know who he is. I'm not going to walk down the street and tell people when I meet them, "Look at God." No. He is not this garment; he *dwells* in this garment. He's Spirit. He is not this thing that you see, he *dwells* in this that you see, and he's my own wonderful human Imagination. When I meet him he's myself...as I *have* met him…as you will one day.

So begin this night to believe in God. Believe in him more than anything else in this world; and not a thing can fail you if you believe in God. Try it. I could tell you unnumbered stories, but *you* try it. It's far better if you had the story yourself. I could go on telling stories and you might say, well, he is more mystically inclined, maybe he is more so and so. Don't let anyone persuade you that Neville is more God than you are. You can't find a better God, a more God or less God than the God that is in you as I AM. Only one God: "So on that day the Lord will be one and his name one" (Zech.14:9). If he's one and his name one, not one is better than the other. No one is better than the other. But we do not believe the same ___(??) in God, and billions of us don't believe in *the* God; we believe in some little totem pole, something on the outside.

So you read carefully this night when you go home the passages that I have mentioned. Read the 28th of Isaiah, the 16th verse; the 37th Psalms, rather, the 4th and 5th verses; read the 20th chapter of the Book of 1st Kings; and something that I quoted earlier from the 18th chapter of John. "Whom do you seek?" "Whom do I seek? I seek Jesus." "I am he." And standing before you now the name is Neville. But the first one to discover the fatherhood of God was Jesus Christ. Its discovery came by the discovery of the Son. And so, the Son called him...called what...called Jesus Christ "Adonay." May I tell you that in the end there is only Jesus Christ; and everyone who finds the Son and the Son calls him, as he will, "my Father" is Jesus Christ. So in that day the Lord will be one and his name one. There will be *nothing* but Jesus Christ, for Jesus means "Jehovah saves." Nothing but Jehovah...and he saves himself. He sent himself fragmented into this world for a greater expansion of the being that he is. He brings it all back... and the name is Jesus Christ.

It's a mystery, but you dwell upon it. Jesus Christ is the father of David. "What think ye of the Christ? Whose son is he?" and they said, "The son of David." "Why then did David in the Spirit call him Lord? If David thus calls him Lord, how can he be David's son?" (Mat.22:42). So David calls him Father, and David is God's only begotten son (Psalm 2:7). You must spiritualize the mission of David. So we see David—and we spiritualize the mission—who calls everyone who is awake Father. The one he first calls is Jesus Christ, and everyone thereafter though he's called by other names is Jesus Christ.

Now let us go into the Silence.

* * *

Q: (inaudible)

A: The first beginning of tithing is when Abraham came back from the storeroom of the king that he tithed with Melchizadek. He gave Melchizadek a tenth portion of all that he had. And man today believes that if I give to charity ten per cent of what I earn, or I give to any organization that I love in this world that's tithing God. It isn't. Give to all the charitable organizations in this world that you love, that you admire, give it ___(??), but that's not tithing of scripture. We're told that if I tithe with God I get it back a hundred-fold. Whatever I assume that I am becomes magnified a hundred-fold, good, bad or indifferent. I give it to God. You're told when you go into a church and you give a dollar you're giving it to God, so the minister tells you. Then he puts it in his own bank and buys his own home, buys his clothes. No criticism of the minister, he was taught to believe that he could be the intermediary between you and God, and some ___(??) or other for himself, and he thinks that God has chalked it up to you. It isn't so.

God is your own wonderful human Imagination—the tithing must be to God. So everything you assume as true you have given to God, good, bad or indifferent. When it comes back, it always comes back shaken down and multiplied, whatever you give. If you want to give to churches, give to churches. We give to charity. My wife and I send our little checks every year to three or four. The Red Cross always gets a check, other charities get a check, and so we give as members of society. We're all members of this grand society, and so we contribute, based upon our income, a small amount. But that does not in any way qualify me for any return from God. I tithe with God when I assume that I am the man that I want to be. Or if I don't assume it, I'm still tithing; I'm giving that…the negative state…and he gives it back to me multiplied.

Q: (inaudible)

A: ___(??) is the story of sacrifice, where animals were sacrificed, and the high priest would go into the Holy of Holies once a year, where he had to repeat the sacrifice of this blood…where the sacrificial story of Christ is not repeated (Heb. 9:3). In depth, when Christ actually awakes in man he enters into a place already prepared for him. For Christ *in man* is awakened. In that moment when he actually awakes and moves up—as we're told in the 3rd chapter of John, "As Moses lifted up the serpent in the wilderness, so must the Son of man be lifted up"—when that is accomplished and you re-enter that place already prepared for you, you are fixed in it forever and forever. That is only once, you never return. But on this level, we can take the story, well, on a psychological level. I am crucifying Christ and shedding his blood every moment of time when anyone asks anything of me, because I will die to what he seems to be and I will live to what he wants to be. So I am shedding his blood all through the day. But the time will come when he actually tears that curtain and enters—as you'll read in that 9th chapter and the 10th chapter of Hebrews. The curtain is torn from top to bottom, and then he goes up into heaven for once and forever. That will happen to every individual being in this world. Until that happens, when he actually tears that curtain and goes up, he is still in this world of Caesar, shedding his blood, transforming individuals into their dream fulfilled. So the 9th and 10th deals with the shedding of blood but the blood of Christ. And when you see it, may I tell you, it's the most wonderful golden living liquid light. You see the blood...it isn't blood, it's gold, it's liquid golden light. As you look at it, you know it is yourself. You are the blood of Christ that he shed for you, and you *fuse* with it. Fusing with it you become one with the blood of Christ, and up you go into the place prepared for you.

Goodnight.

THIS IS MY NAME FOREVER

1/19/64

Tonight let us discuss the name. If you find this name or believe in it, really there is nothing impossible to you…if you really believe in it. Moses said to God: "If I come to the children of Israel and say to them, 'The God of your fathers has sent me unto you,' and they ask me, 'What is his name?' what shall I say?" The Lord said, "I AM who I AM"—sometimes it is translated "I AM what I AM" or "I AM that I AM"—but any form of the verb "to be." I AM who I AM. Then he said, "Say this to the children of Israel, 'I AM has sent me to you. The Lord God, the God of your father Abraham, and Isaac, and Jacob has sent me unto you: this is my name forever, and by this name I shall be known throughout all generations.'" No change in this name, my name forever. This comes in the Book of Exodus, the 3rd chapter (verses 13-17). If you read the Book of Exodus you will find that this is sheer power completely unmodified by any justice, any love, no mercy, no pity, no peace, sheer power. So Moses stands in the presence of power. That's the first revelation of God and it's I AM. May I tell you, when you believe it that's how you use it. Your first use of it is sheer power unmodified by any mercy in this world…just power.

So in this same Book of Exodus he is told to go to Pharaoh and tell Pharaoh to let his children go free; then he hardens the heart of Pharaoh. Therefore he's playing all the parts. He sends his servant Moses to tell Pharaoh to let the children of Israel go free; then he hardens the heart of Pharaoh. So who is playing all the parts? Since Jehovah, which is I AM, is the primary actor in every event, if you adopt this name of God this is what will happen to you. If you really believe it and adopt it, then the cult of heroic personalities will be unable to take any foothold in your faith. You can't turn to any being in this world as an important person in your life, but no one. You can't point to anyone. This night a great man is making his exit from the world, and we all admire him as a person, but when you adopt the name of God, the God of Israel, and actually believe in the God of Israel, which is I AM, and know he plays all parts, then you cannot really turn to any cult of heroic personalities. You'll find none in Israel, none whatsoever. There's only I AM.

So the first revelation is sheer power. You can do it and you're invited to do it. So Pharaoh, who was condemned by the world, was hardened by the very one who asked him to set the children of Israel free. So when you see it, you can say at the very end of the drama, "Father, forgive them; they know not what they do" (Luke 23:34). For God the Father played all the parts. But you don't know he is God the *Father* in the early stages of the revelation of the name; the name is revealed as sheer power, nothing but power. And then it unfolds itself and finally comes to the end, and the end is God the Father. And the Father is infinite love...but we don't know that until the very end. So we are told, "In various and many ways God spoke to our fathers through his servants the prophets; but in these last days he has spoken to us through a Son" (Heb.1:1). *Now* we know he speaks through a son then he must be a father. You can't speak through your son unless you are a father, and the Son reveals the Father (Mat.11:27).

But until you reach the point where you see the Son and know who God the Father is, you are moved to use sheer power. And so, you are invited to use power. So, may I tell you how to use it? The name is simply I AM. It's not Neville, it's not John Brown, it's not Mary Smith, it's not any name outside of I AM. That's God and it is infinite might. You could this night seated here close your eyes to the obvious and dare to assume that you are now the one that you desire to be, and assume that you are it. Don't ask how...this is a power, sheer power, and in a way that no one knows this assumption would rearrange the entire structure of your world and mirror the fulfillment of that assumption. You could this very moment assume that you are elsewhere, though you are here, and you have no means of getting there. And suddenly, if you dare to assume it, believing in the name, the only name the God of Israel possesses, I AM, if you dare to assume it, then a bridge of incidents would form itself across which you would be compelled to move. You would move across this bridge of events leading up to the fulfillment of your assumption...if you believe in the *name* of the God of Israel.

You never leave Egypt until you accept the God of Israel, no one leaves it. Everyone is in Egypt. Every one is buried in a coffin, as told us so beautifully in the seed plot of the Bible, which is Genesis: "In the beginning God..." it begins, and the Bible ends, that is, the Book of Genesis "...in a coffin in Egypt" (Gen. 1:1; 50:26). And who is put into a coffin in Egypt?—Joseph the dreamer. Well, who is the dreamer? Aren't you a dreamer? "Behold this dreamer cometh," Joseph, the prototype of the fulfillment of God's purpose (Gen. 37:19). He said, "You meant it for evil"—you meant it to be evil to me—"but God meant it for good" (Gen. 50:20). So God played both parts. He made you sell me into Egypt, and yet he did it for a purpose: That I would show the whole vast world who God is. He's the dreamer; the dreamer in man is God. When you say "I am" that's God. The Bible recognizes only one source of dreams: All dreams, all visions proceed from God (Num. 12:6; Job 33:15). So as I stand here I can dream a day dream or I can close my eyes and fall into a little nap and have an uncontrolled night dream. Or I can open my eyes upon the world and ignore the entire world and have a controlled day dream...still the same dream. This is the power that is God which is I AM.

So if you accept the God of Israel, you begin to move out of Egypt. That is the beginning of the exodus. But man has great trouble in keeping the tense; he's always turning here, turning there, turning elsewhere. He can't seem to be faithful to the tense: the tense is "I am." If I say, "Thou art," I'm away. If I say, "He is," I'm away. If I use the word Lord and think of something else than "I am," I'm away. If I use any name used in scripture for God and do not allow it to register in me as "I am," I'm completely away. So the Yod He Vau He—which is "the Lord" in scripture which means "I AM"—it is the verb "to be." But it has no sound, there are four consonants, and no one can really sound it. My old friend Ab tried to explain to me how to sound it, but he couldn't sound it. You can't sound Yod He Vau He in Hebrew, there's no way to sound it. But we have added something to it and tried to give it a sound; we call it Jehovah, some call it Yahweh. But you can't sound the name; it's the unpronounceable name this power that is I AM. If you always remember that when they use the word Adonay they use the word Adonay for the saying Yod He Vau He; because they can't sound Yod He Vau He they say Adonay. Sometimes they use another word ___(??), Aleph Lamed, and they will use many words. But no matter what word you hear for God, you can always remember it is I AM and no one else. Then you can't go wrong.

All things are possible to God. If a man can stand before a board and simply see on that board what he wants to see, which if he saw it would imply that he owned the building, well, who's looking at it?—I am. Well, what are you seeing? I am seeing and I tell him exactly what I am seeing. Well, if I am seeing it, it would imply I own the entire block...and that's all that I do... so I am doing it, and two years later without a nickel in the pocket I owned the block. And this is true, I'm not manufacturing this, I'm telling you a true story. That building was bought in 1924 for $50,000 and he didn't have a penny in his pocket. He sold it this past year for $840,000, and there is no tax on capital gain. That is the man who is my second brother, who is simply looking and simply using God's only name which is I AM

This is sheer power when it first reveals itself to man. So we go forward condemning Pharaoh. Why condemn Pharaoh when the being who plays Pharaoh plays the part of Moses? He's playing all of the parts in the world, but every part. After you *use* it—and quite often unwisely, unlovingly, unmercifully—still in the end there is no condemnation. You're moving towards a predetermined end to find that God is Father and infinite love is God. But tonight I share with you my own knowledge and use of this name in power. I can also share with you (and I will) this name in its final state in love. For when you come to the very end of the unfolding of the name, you are God. So you start in the beginning…and so you are told: "I have tried you in the furnaces of affliction. For my own sake, for my own sake, I do it, for how should my name be profaned? My *glory* I will not give to another" (Is. 48:10).

God alone is praise unto God; Spirit alone is praise unto Spirit; life alone is praise unto life. So If I would receive the praise, the glory of God, I must become God first. And so here are the words in the 17th of John, "Father, glorify thy Son that the Son may glorify thee" (verse 1). The Son can't glorify the Father until the Father first glorifies the Son. Now he makes the statement: "I have accomplished all the works thou gavest me to do; now, Father, glorify thou me with thine *own self* with the glory I had with thee before that the world was" (verse 4). Well, who is asking this question?—you and I when we have finished the work. When we've accomplished all of the work given us to do, we only ask for the return of the glory that we gave up to assume the limitation of flesh. For the one that is asking is the creative power and wisdom of God personified as man.

So to come here we came with a purpose. And to come here we were the creative power and the wisdom of God. For that's who Christ is, as told us in the Book of Corinthians, 1st chapter of 1st Corinthians: "Jesus Christ, the power of God and the wisdom of God" (verse24), and so here personified as man. But when he's completed the work—which is the unfolding of the name of God—when it comes to the very end and he ___(??) as God the Father, now "I've accomplished the work thou gavest me to do; now, Father, glorify thou me with thine own self with the glory that I had with thee before that the world was." And so God glorifies the Son that the Son may glorify the Father, because the Father alone is glory unto the Father. So you can't really glorify the Father until the Father first glorifies you. And he doesn't glorify you until you come to the very end. When you return, that creative power has returned from its mission. Having accomplished all that it was sent to do it comes back…and then it returns. And the Father glorifies it first that it, in turn, will glorify the Father.

So this is the great mystery of this name. So in the Book of Exodus when Moses begins to sing the song called The Song of Moses, he said, "God is a man of war; the Lord is his name" (15:3)…only power, sheer power, "God is a man of war." For he saw it, every child died that was the first child, from he who sat on the throne to the one who was in the dungeon. Go and ask him to let my people go, but I will harden his heart; and then you tell him that every firstborn this night will die, from Pharaoh's firstborn to the lowest in the land of Egypt. And that night they all died, and the firstborn of the cattle died. They said, "We are dead men, let these people go." Well, who did it? Was it not the same God? Only *one* God plays all the parts in the world. There's nothing but God; God is playing every part.

But now, if you want to really start the exit from the world of death, you must accept the name of the God of Israel. This is monotheism in the extreme. You can't have two gods and be a true Israelite and only the Israelite comes out of Egypt. As told us, "Truly thou hast been good…the pure in heart," the 73rd chapter of the Book of Psalms (verse 1). Then he looks and he sees Nathan, who was called Nathaniel "the gift of God"; and he said, "Behold, the Israelite indeed, in whom there is no guile" (John 1:47). No two gods; just one God. So he calls Israel. He *only* calls Israel a man after his own heart, an Israelite indeed in whom there is no guile, and he calls him. Well, if there is no guile, then you are only worshipping one God. But, to worship means "worthy of one's attention"…so you pay attention to the headlines tomorrow morning, you pay attention to something else tomorrow, are you paying any attention to I AM? Would you spend five minutes tonight before you go to bed, or five minutes tomorrow, just to contemplate being, just being—not John, not Mary, not anyone in this world, simply being—for that is to worship God. So you worship only I AM. So you dwell upon just being. You'd be amazed what you will see and what will happen as you dwell upon being. You've never seen such glorious light as you dwell just upon being. This golden, golden light begins to appear all around you, liquid light. As we are told in the Book of Wisdom, like gold in the furnace he has tried us and received us unto himself as pure gold (Prov. 17:3). That's right, molten gold. You are tried in the furnace and all of a sudden you turn into molten gold, and he receives you unto himself as pure molten gold

Then you leave this world, called the world of Egypt, which is the coffin. So then he was placed in the coffin in Egypt—the very last verse in the book, the 50th chapter of the Book of Genesis—"And he was put into a coffin in Egypt" (verse 26). But he exacted a pledge from his brothers that he would not be left in Egypt; they would take him out of Egypt and bring him into the land that was promised. So the whole vast world could be almost within that little statement, "In the beginning God…in a coffin in Egypt." And then the dreamer is dreaming this fantastic dream of life. All must dream the dream of life, but he will come out of it when he discovers the name of God.

The first discovery of the name is sheer might, sheer power. I saw it so clearly when I was a lad in my twenties, taken into the divine society, and the first one I encountered was infinite might, sheer might, not a shred of mercy in his presence, no peace, no love. But in the same society was infinite love who embraced me; and at that moment of the embrace I became one with him, fused with infinite love that is the ultimate God. Then I was sent back before the first one, sheer might. I had to start there. It was might who commanded me to go into the world and tell the story, it wasn't love. Love embraced me, and while mingled with love I was brought before might for the second time, and might sent me into the world with this ringing command in my ears "Time to act!" That was the word, with emphasis on "act." "God only acts and is in all existing beings or men. So let us to him who only *is* give decision" (Blake, *Mar. Heaven and Hell*, Plt.15). He only acts.

I started in that manner, trying to test it, and it worked like a charm. Then from then on the name itself began to unfold into higher levels. Always might, but from the higher and higher levels, until you finally reach the ultimate, and the ultimate is love. God is infinite love and God is Father. But you will never know the Father save through the Son, so the Son reveals you to yourself. When God's only begotten Son stands before you and you know that he is your Son, then you know who you are—you are the Father. So can't you see in this affirmation, I AM, this strange, wonderful unity of God and man? "That is my name forever." When I say "I am" and you say "I am," well, isn't this a strange, wonderful revelation of the unity of man and the oneness with God? Then we understand that greatest of all statements when asked what is the greatest of all commandments and he answered, "Hear, O Israel: The Lord our God the Lord is one" (Deut. 6:4). "Hear, O Israel: The Lord"—the word translated "the Lord" is I AM. The word Elohim would be "the I AMs"; it's gods, it's plural. Then comes again "The Lord, I AM, is one." So here is a compound unity, one made up of others. So, all of us together form the one Lord that is the God of Israel.

So no one departs from this fabulous world of death until he first accepts the God of Israel, which is I AM. Then he starts. He may make numberless mistakes. As you're told, in the journey they turned back, they made every effort to go back into Egypt…because they forgot the tense. They couldn't quite remain faithful to the tense, which is I *am*. So they brought in ___(??), they built a golden calf, and they built something else, they made something else…all in conflict with the Second Commandment, "Make no graven image unto me" (Deut. 6:8). Well, the graven image need not be something physical, it could be an idea. I met a wonderful person they will tell you, come and hear him, come and hear her. Oh, he is so altogether near God. So you forget "I am" and you go to "he is." That's not God; it's not out there at all. God does not wear the name called Neville or John Brown; these are masks, forget them—it's simply I AM. So wherever you are in this world, whatever you're doing, if you could only remember the name of God and call upon it, *instantly* you would be—redeemed from whatever you are if you call upon it—in another state.

He said, "I am the Lord." Rightly translated it would be "I am the I am." "I am the Lord your God, the Holy One of Israel, your Savior…and besides me there is no Savior, I know not any. I know no other Savior, I am the first and I am the last; and there is none beside me." Read it in the Book of Isaiah, the 43rd chapter, the 41st, the 44th (Is.43:3,11; 44:6; 41:4). Tie them together and see this wonderful revelation of the name of God who is the Savior of the world. So tonight, instead of praying to someone, may I tell you, if the name of the God I worship is I AM, then it follows only *what* I am. Can I pray aright? I can't pray aright in any other way other than by *what* I am. He doesn't hear my words. There's a little story told that Michael turned to the Lord and said, "Allow me, Sire, but I think you've made a great mistake in permitting man to learn how to talk." All of the prayers were coming up and it sounded just like Babel, everyone was asking something entirely different, all were asking. So he said, "If you did not allow them to talk, we could then understand what they were praying for." God said to him, "I never listen to what they say; I listen only to their lives." That's all…I listen only to their lives…so only what *I am* is answered. No prayer of mine goes beyond the roof but the prayer of what I am. That's all that I can answer.

So this night if I would be healthy, I must assume that I am. If I would be wealthy, I must assume that I am. Don't ask anyone in this world for permission. If I would be anything, I must assume that I am; for that is asking in the only name that really responds. I only listen to their lives. And my assumption need not be based upon the evidence of my senses, it need not be based upon reason. My assumption at that very moment that I assume it will actually build a wonderful series of events; and then I, standing here, will be compelled to walk across this series of events, across that bridge of incidents, and move exactly where the assumption leads me. I have done it time and time again. When things seemed so black, I couldn't turn for light, I didn't know where to turn. Had no money, had none of this, none of that, and I dared to assume that I was the man that I wanted to be, and I was where I wanted to be—which would have taken quite a fortune. And strangely enough it all came out of the nowhere. I didn't have to put my hand in the pocket of another to get it. I did nothing of which I was ashamed to get it. It just happened. But on reflection one is inclined through past training to believe it would have happened anyway, and that's when you go back to another god, and forget the God of Israel. One must ever remember the God of Israel, and the God of Israel is your own wonderful human Imagination. That's the God of Israel…that's the God that created the whole vast world and brought it into being and sustains it. Not a thing comes into this world unsupported by your own wonderful imaginal act. It does not remain in the world without such support, and when it ceases to receive that support, it vanishes as though it were never present. That is the God of whom I speak. This is the God of Israel, your own wonderful human Imagination which I speak of as I AM, that's God. Start this night, because you are encouraged to do it. Go back to the Book of Exodus…it's sheer power. If you are in business, try it.

The day will come you'll move through the entire series and come right up to the fulfillment of it all, and find him to be the God of love, not only the God of love but Father. So God has to give you in the end himself to receive glory, because he cannot receive glory from anyone but himself. So to receive glory from you, he has to give you himself; and he's a father, so he gives you himself as father, and in so doing he gives you his son. Then you see his son and his son calls you Father. And you know it, there's no doubt in your mind as to who he is, he is *your* son. You look into this heavenly face, which is God's only begotten son (Ps.2:7), and you know that you are his father and he is your son. Then the drama is over.

But the inheritance which is God himself cannot be actualized, or is, at least, not fully realized by you who has had the experience so long as you still wear the garment of flesh. This is a veil of forgetfulness, this is amnesia, this little garment, complete amnesia when you step into this world and assume the limitations of the garment of flesh. So you play the part, and then you hear from those whom he has sent into the world the real meaning of his name and the power of his name. You take it and you use it. If it proves itself in performance, does it really matter what others think? What do we know in this world better and more thoroughly than that which we have experienced? Do we know anything in this world more thoroughly than what we've experienced? So if I've experienced it, does it really matter what anyone in this world would tell me? I will say to you, you haven't experienced it or you would not tell me that it is wrong. Had you experienced it you would have agreed with me, and so you haven't experienced it. Wait…you will experience it.

After a man has *experienced* God, it doesn't really matter what the world would say about there is no God. Many of them say there is no God, doesn't really matter. They go blindly on not knowing first they're going to find him as power…that's when they first find him. When they find him as power they're going to use him and misuse him, and as they misuse him, who's misusing him? God's misusing him. He's misusing his own name. He hardens Pharaoh's heart and then kills all the firstborn…in one night they all die. The locusts come and devour all the land. Every plague, one after the other, is the use of power; but in this way a strange, peculiar *misuse* of it. Well, that's alright, you're invited to use it and misuse it. Then comes the pain…he puts you through the furnaces. "I'll try you in the furnaces of affliction. For my own sake, for my own sake, I do it, for how shall my name be profaned? My glory I will not give to another" (Is. 48:10). So he has to bring me into that state that is just like himself before he can give me his glory, that I may reflect his glory. He can't possibly give it to me until I become one with him. He takes me through all these furnaces, and finally I become molten gold and can be quickly molded into his image. In the twinkle of an eye that molten gold takes on his image, and then you ascend right up into heaven with God the Father forever and forever.

I can share it with you; I can't convince you by words. I can only tell you it starts with the first revelation of the name and the first revelation is power, sheer, unmerciful power, that's power. He's called a God of war, and this is his name. But after you've gone through it and you see it and you've used it unmercifully, you will come out of it. And you'll use it on a higher level and a still higher level and finally you reach the highest level, and it's the level of love where God is *infinite* love. And may I tell you, there is no power in the world comparable to God. We speak of this power on this level, but *love* is greater than all. That's the greatest of all, for it's the ultimate of God that is love.

So tonight, you take this wonderful name and you try it. It won't fail you! I promise you, it won't fail you…just "I am." Forget what you've done in this world, forget what people think that you are; forget all the little tags people put upon you. Do take off everything and simply dwell on "I am." Repeat it to yourself quietly without any audible sound, just "I am." You'll be amazed what happens…just "I am." Then in that I-am-ness clothe it with your wish fulfilled. Just try it. I'm telling you what I have experienced. This is not any theory, this is not speculation, this is pure experience. It comes that way in an ultimate bliss. I can't tell anyone in words what it is to reach a state where there is no one but "I am." You are *infinite* being… pulsing, liquid light. There's no world, no people, nothing, just "I am." It's a state beyond any way that man could describe in words. And so, you and I, separate as we are seemingly, in that state we are one.

So if you bear his name—as we're told, Go and call my daughters from the ends of the earth, and call my sons from afar, all those who are called by my name (Is. 43:6)—aren't you called by his name? Before you say anything in this world you say "I am," don't you? Well, that's the name. Call my daughters from the ends of the earth and call my sons from afar, *all* who are called by my name. Well, we're called by the name because "I am"…you can say "I am." If you first are not aware of being, then you can't be aware of being anything. You must first be aware of being by saying "I am." Call all my daughters, call all my sons, who are called by my name, and let them know that I am the only Savior. Besides me there is no Savior. He calls them all and gives himself to the called.

But tonight, if you are now looking for a better job, or *a* job, or a change in your social world, or your physical world, or whatever it is, start with the sheer power of God which is I AM. And then, God can conjure anything in this world. *All* things are possible to God. Then dare to assume that I am…and you name it. As you named it…it is *that*…then "I am." So what should I say? Just say, "I am that I am." When you go to them, just simply say, "I AM has sent me unto you." That's all that you say. Some will believe you and some will not. That's all that you say, just say, "I AM has sent me unto you…for that's my name forever…throughout all generations" (Ex. 3:14). So tonight, you just simply assume that I am…and then you name it. The minute that you name it you put *"that"* on it, and then affirm it, "I am." You say "I am healthy"—the word healthy would become "that" in the sentence—I am. "I am wealthy, I am." "I am employed, gainfully employed, I am." So that sentence—in the middle "gainfully employed" becomes "that" in the sentence. I am and you affirm it. Then fall asleep in that statement just as though it were true, and test God and see. As you're told, "Come test me and see. Do you not realize that Jesus Christ is in thee?—unless of course you fail to meet the test" (2 Cor. 13:5). "Jesus Christ is the power and the wisdom of God" (1 Cor.1:24). It's this power. So you try it this night and see if you do not externalize in your world that which you are affirming as true of yourself.

Now let us go into the Silence.

Q: (inaudible)

A: To me, the four rivers are the four senses in man. The ancients never spoke of five senses; they spoke of four—sight, sound, scent, and then they joined taste and touch together. And so these are the chief outlets of man in this age. So sight, sound and scent were the three and then taste and touch they joined as four because both depended on contact. To taste you must contact that which you taste, and touch you must contact it.

Q: How would you interpret that when you read it? I was reading it again and I thought, well now, how can this mean me…and I couldn't quite figure it out.

A: Well, my dear, I've answered it as clearly as I can. The four senses that go out of Eden…Eden is all within you. The whole vast book is all about you. The whole drama unfolds within your own wonderful human Imagination. So as Blake said: "Man has no body distinct from his soul. That called body is a portion of the soul discerned by the senses, the chief inlets of the soul in this age." Although he used the word "five senses" in his own wonderful poem, he confines it to four. Every mystic confines it to four senses, because the sense of touch and the sense of taste depend upon contact. And he said that's the closed Western gate in man. Man hasn't quite opened up that gate as yet. If he could only open the Western gate, he would look into the immortal worlds which, he said, is his task: "I rest not from my great task, to open the eternal worlds, to open the immortal eyes of man inward into the worlds of thought, into Eternity, ever expanding in the bosom of God, the human Imagination" (*Jer.*,Plt.5, Ln.17). But that Western gate in man is closed, so these immortal eyes are closed, the immortal senses are closed. But he takes the Western gate, which is the sense of touch…that's closed.

Q: Neville, where's that question of "Call my daughters from the ends of the earth"?

A: That's from Isaiah, that's from the 41st chapter, and take the 43rd and tie it with it. "Call my daughters from the ends of the earth and my sons from afar off, all those who are called by my name." See, there are two Isaiah's. So the second Isaiah begins with the 40th chapter and does not go beyond the 44th chapter from what I quoted this night. Start from the 41st—they're all very short chapters—41st or 43rd, and both of them put them together.

Q: Neville, would you recap a little bit of what you said on Jan. 5th about the first to be sealed?

A: That was Judah. That's the 7th chapter of the Book of Revelation, and the 144,000 who are sealed, which spells the name of Adam. Aleph, Daleth, Mem is one plus four plus forty. But in Hebrew when you get the zero after the figure you could multiply it indefinitely. So Adam really is 144,000...that's the *whole* will be sealed. Nor one can be lost because everyone is God. There's only God playing all the parts. But Judah is the first one in the twelve. Because there were twelve, and each twelve had twelve, well, twelve times twelve is 144. So the first one called to be sealed is Judah, so that he was the fourth of the fourth generation from Abraham, and he was the one who held the scepter and from him it could never depart. So that was the fourth one and the fourth name of the fourth son. We come through this doorway called the fourth, because the fourth letter is Daleth, and that is the door.

But strangely enough, when you start to seal them, Judah comes first in the 7th chapter of Revelation (verse 5). We're all one; there aren't two of us in this world. But man doesn't know it as yet; and there's no condemnation if you don't know it and you think the other fellow is doing something that is wrong, as people do it all day long. Every morning's paper, someone goes to the bank and takes what isn't his. And so all day long he doesn't know the power of God as yet. Perfectly alright, for the being playing that thief is God. The one who is going to arrest him is God. The one who will guard him in jail, that's God. God plays all the parts in the world; there's nothing but God. There's no room for anyone—there's only Achad, only one.

Q: What is the significance of Joseph exacting the promise from his brothers not to leave him in Egypt?

A: Again, in keeping with the promises of the scripture, all the promises must be fulfilled. Joseph is the dreamer. Do not leave me in the coffin, awaken me. As told us in the 44th chapter of the Book of Psalms, "Rouse thyself! Why sleepest thou, O Lord?" (verse 23). Not another, it is the Lord who is sleeping. He's only a prototype of the dreamer that is God. It is God who imposed upon himself all these limitations. In fact, tyranny is nothing more than the division of this spiritual substance against itself. God became fragmented...this is the rock that became broken...now he's gathering every little piece to put it back together. So when it's all brought back together, it's a far greater rock than it was before. So here, we scatter this creative power and then we bring it back. And each brings back the work allotted it, and it comes back and all become one once more, and it's a far greater power than it was before.

So everyone is playing...that's why when the Bible speaks of incest, well, anyone you know has to be incest if it's all God and you are God. And "Reuben went up unto his mother's bed" and we just judge harshly for his going to his mother's bed. And we speak of all these strange things of scripture that we don't understand that the whole vast world would have to be. There isn't one so-called crime known to man that isn't openly discussed in scripture. We have nothing new in the world concerning crime. We speak of genocide, we speak of destroying a whole city, read scripture. Complete wiping out entirely of a whole being and all its offspring…that's the sheer destructive power. And finally it moves towards that which we call Christ Jesus when he finds the Father. And here's a revelation of the Father, and when you stand in the presence of the Father, well, I can't describe it. You've never known such love; you can't describe such ecstasy. People talk of love here, why it's like living in separate rooms. Suppose you wanted someone passionately in this world and you were barred by steel bars, and you couldn't even touch the other, well, that's more remote. This thing called love of God, you can't conceive of the intimacy of this love. You become one with infinite love, and it is an ecstasy beyond the wildest dream of man…and that's love. The ultimate is love.

So the whole vast scattered world is being drawn one by one by one. "I will gather you one by one, O people of Israel" (Is. 27:12). You aren't gathered in twos or in groups, one by one. And when you are called into the presence of infinite love, you stand in the presence of man, and here is love, and love embraces you. Then you know for the first time in eternity what love really means. And you're there forever… until tomorrow after the whole drama is over, a new play is written, and a new fragmentation for a still greater expansion of God.

Goodnight.

THE SUPREME IDEAL

1/21/64

Tonight's subject is "The Supreme Ideal." But really this is a misnomer, because it would have to be relative to the level on which man is placed. For what is to me today a *supreme* ideal would not be my ideal tomorrow after I've obtained it. But you can, if you have an ideal, you can realize it, and one *should* have an ideal. Here is a formula by which it can be realized: You sow a thought and you reap an act; you sow an act and you reap a habit; you sow a habit and you reap a character; you sow a character and you reap a destiny. So it all goes back to the thought that you sow.

Here, two stories come to mind. I think, in fact I know, you are familiar with both of them. Here is a North American Indian who had an idea, and he sowed it. I'll show you later how to sow the idea. He wanted to be a hero, he wanted to die a hero, and he wanted to be given a hero's funeral. To make it...to summarize it briefly...he joined the forces, went off to Korea, was killed in action, and the body was shipped back to this country. At the moment of internment a question was asked, "Is he a Caucasian?" and when it was discovered that he was not a Caucasian the minister had to execute the law by which he operated this little church, and he said, "I'm sorry, but I'm not permitted to allow it here." Of course the whole country went up in arms. Then President Truman who was then in office, offered the widow a plot of ground in Arlington. The entire country was made conscious of it. TV had it, radio had it, newspapers had it, all the magazines spoke about it, and it was the *biggest* thing of the time. So here, his destiny was to be a hero, to die a hero, and to be buried as a hero. It all started with an idea when he either wittingly or unwittingly sowed that thought. Then it simply fulfilled itself, because he lived in it, it became a habit, it became his character. He *had* to be killed in action.

And, of course, the most recent one of a similar nature, here is now our president, the late president. I haven't read it in a paper, I haven't heard anyone say it, but this is the law and the law operates regardless of individuals in this world. But we know he was a very great student of history. In fact, he won the Pulitzer Prize for his book *Profiles in Courage* based upon historical characters where these were to him after investigating and doing great research, they were to him the great giants in our land when it came to courage, political courage. So he must have been aware of that strange tradition in our land that goes back 120 years, beginning in 1840, when our president died in office. And then the cycle of twenty years—twenty years later when the next one also died in office, but this time he was assassinated. Then came 1880, then came 1900, 1920, 1940, and 1960, and every president elected in the cycle of twenty years died in office. Well, no one can tell me a man as great as he was, the great student of history, wasn't aware of it, and might have again, unknowingly, toyed with the idea of going down in history; for he certainly had a sense of destiny. So we go back to the idea that is planted, and then it becomes a habit of thinking, then it becomes one's character, and finally it fulfills itself as one's destiny.

So here, we can take any idea...and maybe take a noble idea…but, how can I plant a thought? First of all, a thought unless it moves man into action is not creative. A thought by itself does nothing, doesn't affect anything. So how do I take a thought and sow it that I can really make it become effective and it moves through this series from a thought, to an act, to a habit, to a character, to a destiny? Well, the Bible teaches it, and you listen to it carefully, this is from the 4th chapter of the Book of Hebrews: "Good news came to us just as it came to them; but the message they heard did not benefit them, because it did not meet with faith in the hearers" (verse 2). It did not meet with faith in the hearers. For are we not told in the same book, the 11th chapter, that "By faith we understand that the world was created by the by the word of God" —by faith—"so that what is seen was made out of things which do not appear" (verse 3). For the word created it, but without being mixed with faith it would be impossible to create anything. It had to be mixed with faith. So if I take an idea this night, say this noble concept as far as I can conceive it, I must mix it with faith. Can I persuade myself that it is so? Well, I have discovered from my own personal experience that I do it when I *feel* it. I must in some way persuade myself through feeling, so I captured this phrase, "Assume the feeling of the wish fulfilled." I always start in the end; the end is where I start from. So I take an idea but the idea that I see it in my mind's eye *fulfilled.* I occupy the end, the fulfilled state; there I then view the world and see that world mentally as I *would* see it were it true.

So I start in the end; the end is where I start from. In my end is my beginning. And then it takes me through...it becomes almost a habit of thinking. The next day it seems easier, and the next day it almost becomes my character; and finally I find myself fulfilling it in a way I could not have devised. I didn't know how it happened. I couldn't have worked it out. I could not have placed myself in some state where I could just simply devise the means by which it came to pass. It seemed on reflection that it would have happened anyway. But it wouldn't have happened anyway. It just simply happened that way. So I know exactly what I want, occupy the end, viewing the world *from* the end, and seeing it in bloom as it were, seeing it fulfilled. Then it becomes a habit, and finally that's my destiny. So on this level anyone can be free, anyone.

There is another level, it is God's level, and that's God's concern. He gives us this technique on *this* level—for you and I, while he's working out our destiny, we can modify the pain, modify the blows, modify all these pressures in this world by the same technique by which he does it. For this is how he does it...and so the same five terms...but they are changed in the way *he* does it. In the 8th chapter of the Book of Romans, and the terms used there: "Those whom he foreknew he also predestined to be conformed to the image of his Son. And those whom he predestined he also called; and those whom he called he also justified; and those whom he justified he also glorified" (Rom. 8:29). So there still are five stages, beginning with foreknowledge and ending with glorification.

Well, what is the glorification? It's himself, as revealed in the Book of John, "O Father, I have finished the work which thou gavest me to do...now glorify thou me with thine own self" (John 17:5). He's asking God to give him himself. That's the story. So the end is the gift of God to man, which will be given to every being in this world, because you and I can't modify it, you and I can't change it. We're allowed within the framework of his plan to do all kinds of things, like dying as a martyr, dying as a great hero, going down in human history. But we are told everything that happens here will vanish, everything. "It will all simply vanish like smoke and wear out like a garment...but my salvation is forever and my deliverance will never end" (Is. 51:6). So his plan is the overall plan. But within his purpose as he said, "As I have planned it, so shall it be. As I have purposed it, so shall stand" (Is. 14:24). And no one will change it, so be assured of salvation. Be *assured* of it! No one in this world could scare you out of it, because they haven't a thing to do with it. It's all God's plan. God actually became man that man may become God.

Well now, it brings me to this picture of the night—that is, the plan by which it unfolds. It is a very interesting plan. I'm here to speak from experience about this plan. But it's so difficult to change the meaning of an event once certain interpretations of that event become fixed in the public mind. So we read the plan; the plan is in scripture, it's told in the gospels... that's the plan. God actually played the part; it's an acted parable. Only as the parable was acted out could man see the key to unlock scripture. Scripture was a closed book until it was acted out, the acted parable. Then we could go back into scripture and understand it. We didn't understand it before. And having seen the key given to us by the acted parable, we then could apply it. We can't unlock it, we just simply wait, and the thing unfolds in us.

Now we are told, the call has gone out to the world, the whole vast world, and the call is this, "Bring the next witness"; for God has taken his place in the divine circle, in the divine council, and there he stands in judgment. He doesn't judge anyone harshly and he's not judging anyone with retribution. He's only asking for a witness to the truth of his word, so "Bring the next witness." And "God has taken his place in the divine council; in the midst of the gods he holds judgment" (Psalm 82:1,6). And so, as you have the experience, you're brought into the divine council. And it starts in this manner. Believe it, I have experienced it. I have witnessed so far to almost all the things told in the gospels. I wouldn't say everything but *almost* all. And it starts with the call. First of all, I am preordained as you are. Those whom he foreknew...we're all locked within him, like brain cells in the mind of the great thinker. Then he brings one out, one by one; for we're not brought in pairs, we aren't brought in groups, we're too precious. As we are told, "I will gather you one by one, O people of Israel." You are too unique to be called in pairs, only one by one. But *everyone* will be called, and called for what purpose? Called to witness to what?—to the truth of scripture.

So, when you are called, you don't have to say anything outside of the first confession of faith; for you are in the presence of God, and you confess that presence. What is the greatest thing in the world? It would have to be God. But you don't use the word "God"; that's a human name. And so, what is the greatest thing in the world? And you answer automatically from scripture, "Faith, hope and love, these three; but the greatest of these is love" (1 Cor. 13:13). At that, you are incorporated into the body of God, and there, forever; it is your body from then on. You're one with God because he embraces you and you fuse and become one being. At that moment then you are sent—to be called is to be sent—and yet you're not separated from the being in whom you are incorporated. So I stand here talking to you and yet I am one with God. I can't show him to you. I'll try in words; but I can't *show* him to you; for God is spirit, God is Father. So as you are sent into the world, you're sent to bear witness to the truth. He said, "Thy word is truth" and then starts the series of events, all based upon scripture.

Now, let me go back to a passage I've never touched before from this platform. It's taken from the Book of Luke, and when you read it you think it's an old, old man. His name is Simeon. Simeon was told, "You shall not see death until you see the Lord's Christ, the Lord's anointed" (Luke.2:26). Then, moved by the Holy Spirit, he was moved in *Spirit* into the temple. Now let me stop there for you must search scripture: "*You* are the temple of the living God and the Spirit of God dwells in you" (1Cor. 3:16). So you are not taken into any temple where men made it with their hands; you're taken to the temple of your own being. So, moved by the Spirit he's taken to a temple. Now the word Simeon means "to hear intelligently; to hear with understanding." What do you hear with understanding? Well, we go back to Nehemiah, the 8th chapter, the 8th verse: "So they came into the temple and then they read from the book of God the law of God, and they read it clearly so that those who heard *understood* what was read." They read it with understanding. So the word Simeon is "one who hears with understanding." And he heard the word of God and God's promise that he would not see death *until* he had seen the Lord's Christ. So coming into the temple, he comes up and here is the child, the babe. He takes the babe in his hands and lifts him up and then he makes this pronouncement, "The child shall be a sign." He states it: "It shall be a *sign* that is spoken against. It shall be for the fall and the rising of many in Israel. Now, O Lord, let your servant depart in peace...for my eyes have seen the Lord's salvation" (Luke 2:27,33). So when you read it you think it's another. It never occurred to you that it could be you. It never occurs to anyone that he's reading about himself.

Somewhere a long time ago you heard God's promise to you. You heard it in some way; you either read it in scripture or you heard it. For all this is done to you. And you believed it; it was mixed with faith in you. But you didn't see it, you only heard it. "I have heard of thee with the hearing of the ear" and then you go on blind, you haven't yet seen him. And so Simeon did not see until the final moment before his death. You think it means the death of this body? No, he's now going to die to the wheel of recurrence. He's reached the end, and he wants to depart quickly, like Paul: "The time of my departure has come. I have finished the race, I have fought the good fight, I have kept the faith. And now is laid up for me a crown of righteousness" (2 Tim. 4:6). Righteousness is faith. For this one, Simeon, was called a man who was devout and righteous. It was said of Abraham that Abraham was a righteous man, and his righteousness was accounted for faith.

So, to plant the idea you must mix it with faith. So I can tell you of the pattern that you will unfold. You may this night deny it, for this child shall be a sign that is going to be disputed. Some will reject it and some will accept it. But even those who reject it tonight will ultimately accept it. Because you will be prepared as time moves on to accept it, because everyone must accept it to fulfill it. You can't fulfill God's purpose which is to give himself to you until you first accept his promise. For his promise is to man, but man has to mix the promise with faith for it to become a saving word. And so, it'll be done—how and when I do not know. Maybe everyone here has already accepted it, I do not know. There's no way that I can look at you, mortally, with my mortal eyes and see. I only know that in God's own good time it happens in the twinkle of an eye. It could be this very night that everyone here, or one here, will go through the series of events leading up to complete freedom and death to the wheel of recurrence. Why should I die to the wheel of recurrence? Well, listen to these words: "The creature was made subject unto vanity, unto futility, not willingly but by reason of the will of him who subjected him in hope that the creature would be set free from this bondage to decay, and obtain the glorious liberty of the sons of God" (Rom.8:20). That no one is free, really free, until he is set free as a son of God.

Then what is the difference between that and this? Well, I'll show you the difference...or tell you the difference. I have had moments when I was taken in Spirit, when Spirit possessed me, and suddenly I looked upon *this* world, the world that I'm seeing now, and I tasted at that moment of a power this world knows nothing about. The power that belongs to *that* world...when you and I, being resurrected into *that* world, everything is subject to our imaginative power. I looked upon this world...and I stopped it. Everything froze, as though they were all made of clay; then I started it, and it moved on. I stopped it, and it stopped. I discovered then, not a thing in this world was independent of my perception of it. It all simply was dead...the world was dead. But I didn't know it and I didn't believe it until I tasted of the power of *that* world, the world to come, where man by resurrection enters that world. Then you understand scripture, "As the Father has life in himself, so he has granted the Son also to have life in himself" (John 5:26). That's life. And then I discovered the origin of life was my own Imagination, that life is nothing more than an activity of Imagination. For when I stopped the activity people couldn't move, and when I released that activity and allowed it to function people could walk. A bird flying, when I stopped it, the bird couldn't fly, and it didn't fall; and when I released it, it continued in its flight. Then, I'm not a scientist, but when I came back from that experience I knew in spite of all the wise men in this world that what we call gravity is only relative. It only is on *this* sphere, and it's a grand illusion.

And now we come to that passage which to me is so difficult to explain. It's taken from Paul's letter to the Corinthians. Bear in mind this letter was written before the gospels. The first letter in the New Testament, the first book, is Paul's letter to the Galatians, and in this he makes the statement, "My little children, with whom I am again in travail until Christ be formed in you" (Gal. 4:19). My little children, with whom I am again in travail until Christ be formed in you. "In Christ" is "to be *formed* in Christ." To be "in Christ" is formed as Christ. Is he doing it? He said, "Little children, with whom *I am* again in travail until Christ be formed in you." Now listen to this passage from the 4th chapter of 1st Corinthians, he said, "You have many tutors"—some translators say thousands of tutors, some translations say countless tutors—"You have countless tutors in Christ...but only one father. *I became* your father in Christ Jesus through the gospel: I urge you, then, be imitators of me" (verse 15).

Now isn't that the most arrogant, arrogant statement in the world—"Be imitators of me"! A man is speaking to you, his name is Paul, and he's telling you that you have numberless teachers in Christ, people who are leading you concerning *their* concepts of Christ, but you only have one father, and he is your father. Well, that's the height of arrogance for a man to make that bold claim...and yet, it's a true claim, what he's telling you. But there must be some missing book of Paul because he doesn't spell it out in anything I've read of Paul. I've read the Bible backwards. I haven't seen anything where Paul spells it out, so there must be some missing letter of Paul. For he tells you...or makes this bold statement...what he's telling you is this, the time of his departure has come; he's leaving this wheel of recurrence, and *he* will be turning it from above. It will be the being that is now one with Christ Jesus. For there aren't many little Christ Jesuses; there's only one Christ Jesus. So everyone who is incorporated into his body *is* Christ Jesus, and *he* is the creator of the universe, and therefore he's bringing out himself from this turning wheel.

Paul is telling you, you have many instructors, numberless instructors, but only one father; and I became your father *in* Christ Jesus through the gospel. He discovered the way of salvation. He went through the experiences; for these are his words, "When it pleased God to reveal his Son *in me*...then I conferred not with flesh and blood" (Gal. 1:16). To whom would I turn to explain what I have experienced? What man in this world could tell me what I experienced when I tell them I stopped men in their tracks, without their consent, without their knowledge, and they couldn't move and they were dead? And then I released in me, not in them, I released an activity in me, and they continued to move. I stopped a bird in flight, and it couldn't move and it didn't fall. And then I released an activity in my own Imagination and it continued in its purpose, and went to the limb where it intended when I stopped it. I could have held it there forever. What scientist in this world could explain that power to me? Well, that's the power that is *your* power, tomorrow, when God pulls you out of the wheel of recurrence and incorporates you into his body, which is Christ Jesus. And you, *as* Christ Jesus, will be turning this wheel; and therefore, you are told, I became your father. I am bringing you out, being born, and when I bring you out, you and I are one. I'll bring you out, said Paul. And yet, when the Son comes out, that he's bringing that glorious liberty, the Son is one with the Father. For, "As the Father has life in himself, so he has granted the Son also to have life in himself."

It's a peculiar passage, and when you read scholars' interpretations of it, you just have to smile. The best they can get is this, that if a teacher instructs and converts someone to his way of thinking, then he became their father. That's the best they can do with that passage. That if a man can convert someone to his way of thinking and you accept his way of thinking, then he fathered your thinking. That's the best they can do with it. Hasn't a thing to do with that. You become one with an entirely different world, free, free forever, because everything there is subject to your imaginative power. And you will turn the wheel. When I say the wheel, it's the wheel of recurrence. You will allow all the freedom within your plan to bring sons out. You're begetting sons, because you are father. He said, "I *became* your father in Christ Jesus through the gospel." Then he makes this bold claim, "I urge you, be imitators of me." For that statement is in his next letter to the Ephesians, only he calls it God. He's telling you who he is. He said, "Be ye imitators of *God* as dear children." Now he tells you in this letter, "I became your father in Christ Jesus through the gospel" and then he tells you, "Be imitators of me." He's telling you who he is: There is only God. So when you are raised up out of this wheel of recurrence, you are not some little thing flying through space, you *are* God. God is begetting himself, drawing himself out of this predetermined play. When you come out and you are incorporated into the body of God, you *are* God. There won't be many little gods running around. Without loss of identity you are still God.

It doesn't make sense...and on this level it certainly doesn't make sense. You read the morning paper, you turn on the TV...this past Sunday, just in an idle moment I turned it on. Here is this brilliant philosopher speaking and he is telling us that today the majority of the people of the world do not believe in God. They have no feeling about immortality. As far as he personally goes, he said, "I don't believe in God. Death is the end." A brilliant mind…alright, with *that* mind, how could I ever explain to him that scripture is the only reality in the world? And according to this rabbinical principle that goes back for unnumbered centuries, what is not written in scripture is nonexistent. How would I tell *that* statement to *that* mind when he knows that he is living in an age that never occurred before? How could I explain to him it has always happened? That the present is not receding into the past, it's advancing into the future? That the bygone is not bygone, it's oncoming? And the wheel is turning and this whole vast wheel is turning, and it always has been turning. But man has so short a memory he can't remember beyond a little, small section of time. He has no knowledge of the past.

So when I tell him, and quote from Ecclesiastes, "There is nothing new under the sun. Is there a thing of which it is said, 'See, this is new'? I tell you it has been already in ages past...but there is no remembrance of former things, nor will there be any remembrance of things to come after, among those who will come after," well, who will believe that? We think we are living in an age no one has ever known or dreamed of before, the atomic age. And to tell men it always *has* happened, that everything is eternally *present* to God. But you and I, on the wheel of recurrence, when we were made subject to it—listen to it again, "The creature was made subject unto futility, *not* willingly but by reason of the will of him who subjected him in hope...that he will be set free from this bondage of decay, and obtain the glorious liberty of the children of God." So we didn't ask for it.

I'll tell you, I was in a world where I saw they wouldn't believe one word I told them concerning *this* world. They had not yet arrived here, and they spoke of this world not as Earth, they spoke of it as Woodland, and they did not believe that anyone ever returned from Woodland. To them it was the limit, it was death. And it *is* death, but we don't believe that here. So in scripture we are told, in the 5th chapter of Ephesians, "Awake, O sleeper, and arise from the dead, and Christ will give you light" (verse 14). The call is to us, "Awake, O *sleeper*." Now, he associates this profound sleep with death, for he said, "Awake, O sleeper, and arise from the dead." That's exactly what happens. When you first awake, that comes first, you find where you are, and you are where only the dead are placed, in a sepulcher. Only the dead are placed in a sepulcher and you are in a sepulcher, but it's your skull. But you first *awake*; you awake in your skull to find you are completely sealed in a sepulcher, and the sepulcher is your skull.

So in that 5th chapter of Ephesians, "Awake, O sleeper, and arise from the dead, and Christ will give you light." Well, what is the light? Listen to the words, "In him was life, and the life was the light of men" (John 1:4). So life in him, and he gives you light, he gives you life. And he's the Father, so "as the Father has life in himself, so he has granted the Son also to have life in himself" if you awake. But may I tell you, you will awake, for that is his most mighty action in the world. He *awakens* you, and you've never in your life felt such power when he awakens you. You awake to find yourself in a grave where only the dead were placed, and then you come out. And then comes the story of Simeon; for you do pick him up in your hands and he's a sign. He's a sign that this day this great event took place in eternity. Then you pass through these signs, one after the other; leading up to complete deliverance from this wheel of recurrence.

So the Bible, I tell you, is true from beginning to end. Not as people try to rationalize it...leave it just as it is. You will experience it. For every man must experience *in himself* scripture to understand how perfectly marvelous it really is. He does, he experiences scripture. Then when it comes to the end of this little time, you are Simeon, the one who heard. You went through hell, may I tell you, and you come to that point in time where now you see; and so you say with Job, "I have heard of thee with the hearing of the ear, but now my *eye* sees thee." That's your departure from the wheel of recurrence. But while you are on it, bear in mind God's five terms. And you cannot take these five terms and come to any other conclusion other than predestination; therefore, you are predestined to be conformed to the image of his Son. You're going to be, regardless of what you've done in this world. If you've been a murderer, if you are a murderer, if your future state is to be one; if you've been a thief, if you are a thief, I don't care what you have ever done you are *predestined* to be conformed to the image of God.

But in the meanwhile, take this formula: Sow a thought and reap an act, sow the act and reap a habit, sow a habit and reap a character, sow a character and reap a destiny. It is my hope that you do not wish to die a hero's death or some martyr's death, but that you really want to live fully and graciously in this world of ours, live lovingly. If you want money, let no one tell you you shouldn't have money. If you want to extend yourself and be a great artist in this world, let no one tell you that you shouldn't be a great artist. You can be anything in this world that you want if you know how to sow the first thing—to sow the thought. You can't sow a thought in itself, you have to embed it, embed the thought with faith. It must be mixed with faith, and I call that feeling. I assume the feeling of my wish fulfilled and the thought is planted. I don't do anything beyond that. If I did it, on reflection it seems a habit now; then after a little while it seems just my character. As my old friend Abdullah used to say, and this was·his statement, "I willed it so to be, I still will it so to be, and I will *will* it so to be until that which I have willed is perfectly expressed." I haven't forgotten what I willed, said he, I willed it so to be. I *still* will it so to be. I will continue to will it so to be until what I have willed is perfectly expressed. So I will assume that I am that which I want to be. I'm still assuming that I am it. I will continue to assume that I am it until what I have and still am assuming is externalized and is expressed.

All that is in the framework of God's purpose for us, and his purpose is to give himself to us, not as another but as himself. He has one and only one way to reveal it. He gives us the only thing in this world that could ever prove to man that he's God: he gives us his Son. His Son comes right into our world and he calls us "Father." That's the only symbol in the world that could convince a man he's one with God. Because God, remember, as you're told in the 18th verse of the 1st chapter of John: "No one has ever seen God; but the only Son, in the bosom of the Father, he has made him known." For God is Spirit; so suddenly the Son appears and calls *you* Father. You don't see your face reflected in the mirror, you're Spirit…but you're real. You're more real than the whole vast world and yet you're Spirit. And the Son reveals you to yourself. So he who is in the bosom of the Father makes him known. But no one has ever seen God…but the Son, who is in the *bosom* of the Father, he makes him known. So he comes out.

Well, where is that bosom? May I tell you, it's your own wonderful human Imagination. It explodes one moment, completely explodes, and as it explodes, here stands David and he calls you "Father." So Blake, in speaking of this wonderful thing that is man, he said, "The human Imagination"…"ever expanding in the *bosom* of God, the human Imagination." So we are in the bosom; and then it explodes one day and out comes God's Son, and he calls me Father, as he has called or he will call you Father. And therefore we are one. All of us are one, one being, all incorporated into one body and that body is Christ Jesus. So until it happens to you, take the formula: from the thought, through the habit, through the character, up to destiny. Just take it right through and apply it.

Here in this audience tonight—and I didn't know it until just before I took the platform—is a lady who was here about five weeks ago. No one knows her, so she need not be embarrassed. She's been married for a long, long time, longer than most people, especially in California, in other words, forty-odd years. She has a grown family. And then, like so many men in this world, I don't know what gets into them, I don't know, but at a certain peculiar moment in time they seem to fly the coop, and they get going. So she came to me here in this very hall five weeks ago and told me her tale of woe. I told her, "I can't do it now, but in my Silence I will take you. So when I go into the Silence tonight, I will hear the good news you want me to hear. First of all, do you want him back?" And she said, "Certainly, after forty-odd years of marriage? I want no one else. He might have gone off with someone else, I've been told he has, but I don't care, I want him back." So, in my Silence...I only spent a minute in the Silence...that night when she went home he was at home, took her hand, so she tells me, kissed her hand and kissed her hand, and said, "Please come with me to Palm Springs." That's where he was. He went on...she didn't ask any questions (I hope she didn't)…leave him alone. But he came back, that very night he was home waiting. While we were in the Silence here, he just had to steer his ship right straight to that place and go there. I tell you, imagining creates reality! But an imaginal act must meet with faith to become effective in this world. And so, when I sat in the Silence and believed it, I *really* believed it. I heard the lady's voice...and so five weeks later she tells me. And, may I tell you, we are neighbors, she's next door, but she didn't call me up and tell me. But I didn't care, I *knew* it had worked. If she never told me, I still felt it had worked, and that's all that matters.

So now let us go into the Silence and take what is to us the supreme ideal, whatever it is, relative to our present state, so that we can transcend what we are by becoming what we want to be. We do it by a simple technique of sowing an idea. But the idea must have acceptance on your part, which is you must mix it with faith. For it did not help those who heard the same thing that we heard—why?—said Paul, because the message did not meet with faith in the hearers. So, "Without faith, you cannot please him." Now let us go.

* * *

Q: (inaudible)

A: ___(??) Biblical Concordance, the Biblical Concordance of James Strong. And it says...like the word Simon, Simon Peter, Simon is another form of Simeon, but they both mean "to hear, to listen, but listen with intelligence, listen with understanding." So in that 8th chapter, the 8th verse of Nehemiah, when they came into the temple, the book of God was read to them *clearly* so that it was given understanding. So when they went out they *understood* that which was read. You must first of all hear and you must hear with understanding. A word spoken in some tongue other than your own tongue may have meaning but not for you. Therefore, it would mean nothing to you if someone spoke to you in a tongue that is not your tongue, and yet to themselves it has meaning. So they must speak so that you can understand, and then you either respond or you don't respond. So, "This child shall be a sign that shall be disputed." So you tell the story of the child. And as I said earlier, it's one of the most difficult things in the world to change the meaning of an event once certain interpretations of that event become fixed in the public mind. And so, if this is a story that happened 2,000 years ago, it's difficult then to persuade man that it is *taking place* now, because, no, he can't believe it's related to himself. Yet the whole Bible is your story and you *must* experience scripture.

Q: What's "God's boring of the ear"?

A: The boring of the ear and the opening of the eye. Man doesn't really hear the heavenly sphere…it is all here...the ears are not yet bored. We are really...this is a real veil that is over the being that you really are. It's *that* being that is being brought out, and this is completely a seal; you're sealed in this. Man doesn't hear. The vision I've heard has always been in the depth of the soul, not with these ears, because no one around me heard it. When I'm told, "That which I have done I have done. Do nothing"—no soldier in the barracks heard it. I'm the only one who heard it; therefore, I could not have heard it with these ears. Well, when you hear it, it is so commanding it's amazing that others didn't hear it. It seemed that the whole world should have heard it, because a voice of real authority speaks. So the ears are not bored, here, but in the depths they are.

Q: Who are those you referred to as being in Woodland?

A: Woodland? Those not yet made subject to this vanity. This is taking place all the time, and they will be made subject to it but not willingly. When I talked with them, they did not believe me that I returned from this place, because to them this is death, and no one returns from the grave. This really is death. When you come here, you are sealed in your skull. And although you die, *seemingly* die, and you are buried, and I can see the thing decay and the skull decay, you still don't die. You find yourself clothed in a skull. You don't die. So in the 3rd chapter of Genesis and the wisest creature which is God himself clothed in that of a serpent, and he said to the woman, "Did God say to you that if you ate of the fruit of the tree of the garden that you would die? And she said, 'If I ate of the fruit of *this* tree, I would die.' He said, "You will not surely die." He's contradicted himself. He said, "You'll die." But we do die but we don't *really* die. The wheel is turning, and so, the earth does not terminate at that point where my senses cease to register it. A ship starts off to sea and it has a mast, and as it recedes in the distance, it vanishes, gets lower and lower and finally it's out of sight. But it hasn't fallen off the earth. Space is curved, but so is time. And so, you vanish, but you don't cease to be. And you're coming out of this.

So the people from Woodland...that is, this is called Woodland, but those who are not yet in Woodland they've got to come here. God must reach the limit of contraction, the limit of opacity, which is called death, and it's this world. When he awakes you...and the words come in the same order they do happen, "Awake, you sleeper, and arise from the dead." And it comes that way. You are first awakened to find that you must have been dead because you are in a tomb. These are the words of the 5th chapter of Ephesians, "Awake, you sleeper." Now, to whom is he speaking? He is speaking to himself, because God became man that man may become God. Now listen to the 44th Psalm, "Rouse thyself! Why sleepest *thou*, O Lord?" Arouse thyself. Why sleepest *thou*, O Lord? It's deep calling unto deep. And finally at that moment in time, the most intense vibration will awaken you. You awake to find that you must have been dead because you are in a tomb. You know the tomb, and it's called Golgotha. Golgotha is your skull...and you *know* you're in your skull. You push and you come out of your skull. How long you've been entombed, well, that's speculation...I don't really know. Blake said 6,000 years. He might have been trying to do it with the biblical day, a thousand years was a day, and on the 6th day he succeeded in making man, and man was the image of himself. So he might have been using that biblical measuring rod. But he makes the statement that I walk up and down in 6,000 years. "I behold the visions of my deadly sleep of 6,000 years, circling around thy skirts like a serpent of precious stones and gold. I know it is myself." He said of the gold, "I know it is myself"; and then, myself is my own creator, "O my Divine Creator and Redeemer." And then, *as* this you go up into a new heaven already prepared to receive you. So everyone is going to go up.

And so you're told, listen to these words (they're so altogether true) in the 3rd chapter of John: "As the wind blows where it wills and you hear the sound of it, but you cannot tell where it comes from and where it goes; so it is with every one who is born of the Spirit" (verse 8). Now when you read that you'll say, what is he talking about? But every word then is true; you can't displace it. As the wind blows where it wills...well, when it happens to you, you only are concerned about the unearthly wind. The wind is the most unearthly sound in the world, the wind. The word wind and Spirit are the same in both Hebrew and in Greek. But he uses the word wind, and you think in terms of wind. I can't tell you why, but you do. You hear it, and all you can think of is wind and wondering why and where is it coming from? So you are told, "As the wind blows where it wills and you hear the sound of it, but you cannot tell where it comes from and where it's going; so it is with every one who is born of the Spirit." Happens in the same strange manner, you are born of the Spirit, of the wind. And so, you can't change that verse in the 3rd chapter of John. Scholars labor with it, what is this all about? Don't touch the Bible, leave it. You're going to live it; you're going to experience it.

Q: Neville, could this unfold without the experience of the skull?

A: I can't see how one who is buried in his skull can awaken and not find himself *in* the skull. No one can bring you out while you are dead from the skull. You are placed in the tomb and then you escape from the tomb in which they've placed you. And it's a skull, it's a tomb. You're told it's called Golgotha, called Calgary, and you're told it's one in which a man has never yet lain. You're unique. You're in one prepared for you. No one was ever yet placed in that skull.

Q: What I was trying to say, I'm sure I have had the experiences, but I haven't fulfilled the skull. The skull I haven't discovered…

A: Well, to me, that experience of the skull is the greatest of all, for that is the birth from above. That's the spiritual birth. As you are told in John, again, "That which is born of flesh is flesh; that which is born to the Spirit is Spirit." One must be born of Spirit. God is begetting himself, and God is Spirit. And so I tell you I've shared with you what I have experienced.

Now goodnight.

NO OTHER FOUNDATION

1/23/64

Tonight's subject is "No Other Foundation," and this we take from the 3rd chapter of 1st Corinthians: "No other foundation can anyone lay than that which is laid." Then it names the foundation and calls that foundation Jesus Christ (verse 11). So when you hear the word you might think of a man, something outside of yourself. The whole vast world does. I know the Christian world does, and the Jewish world does. The Christian world accepts this outside leadership, called Jesus Christ; and the Jewish world cannot accept Jesus Christ as the savior of the world. So here we have one billion people in the world who will, when they hear the word Jesus Christ, think in terms of an external leader. And yet this is the *foundation* of the world. Now, what is this foundation? "No other foundation can anyone lay than that which *is* laid, which is Jesus Christ." May I tell you that this foundation, Jesus Christ, is your own wonderful human Imagination, that *that* is Jesus Christ.

Let me now turn to a chapter that is not read, not very often, really. It's from the 1st Book of Samuel, the 8th chapter. The people of Israel demand a king to rule over them, and so the prophet turned to the Lord and made Israel's request. The Lord said, Give them what they want. They want a king to rule over them? Give it to them; for they have rejected not you, they have rejected me. Give them what they want; they have rejected me, they have not rejected you. But warn them solemnly what is going to happen to them by their choice of a king to rule over them. And then this is what the prophet was told by God to tell them. First of all, he will take your sons for the army, your daughters to become the cooks and the servants of the king, he'll take your property, he'll take your money, he'll take *everything* that you possess, and when he's taken everything, then he'll take you. And in *that* day you will cry out to be saved from a king of your own choosing, but then I will have no ears to hear you. After he's taken everything, you will cry to be saved from what you yourself decided on and I will have no ears to hear you (verses 4-18). Look into the world today and men want some *external* leadership, someone to lead them into paradise on earth. Then dictators rise, and here is the ___(??) save the world. The first thing he does gets them all into the army. They had no desire to be in an army. Then he appropriates and confiscates all property. Then he takes their money. He takes everything and reduces them to slavery. And then they cry...and there's no one to hear their cry. This is eternally true as long as man thinks in terms of some external leader that is God.

The *only* God is I AM; there is no other God. "When I go to the people of Israel and they ask me, 'Who sent you?' what should I say?" The voice came back, "Say unto them I AM sent you." Just I AM...I sent you. "When I say to them I am the one sent by the God of your fathers, the God of Abraham, the God of Jacob, the God of Isaac, what then must I say?" "Just say I AM has sent you" (Ex.3:14). There is no other foundation in this world for anything I don't care what it is. If you think some leader outside of yourself can save you, then you think in vain. You're simply building up a picture in your mind's eye which will lead you into a certain group that will one day want some dictator or something outside of self to lead you into some comfortable world. There is no being outside of self that could ever lead you into what you want. The only God in this world is your own wonderful human Imagination. When you say "I am," that's God.

Well now, how will I go about proving this "there's nothing but God"? Well, you can prove it. Dare to assume that you are now the man, the woman that you want to be. Having assumed it, look at the world mentally and see that world reflect your assumption. For if I am now the man that I want to be, I have a frame of reference, you, and others that I know across this country and in other parts of the world. And if I *am* the man that I want to be, and dare to assume that I am it, they would know it. They would know it by the grapevine, things would get around, and they will become aware that Neville became the man that no one would ever dream that he ever could become. All right, so they would gradually become aware of the man that I am. So now, not waiting for them to become aware of it, I let them see it now. I dare to assume that I am *now* that man that I want to be and if in time I become it and they become aware of it, haven't I found the foundation stone? Are we not told, "All things were made by him and without him was not anything made that was made (John 1:3)?" Well, I think now of something not here. I think of it. The very act of thinking of it, isn't that an action that is creative? Well, the Bible recognizes only one source of a dream, whether that dream be a day dream or the dream of the night, all dreams and all visions proceed only from God. They have no other source of a dream. Well, I now think of something that is not here, and I enact in my mind's eye a lovely drama implying the fulfillment of a dream. Well, that's a dream, and the Bible recognizes only one source of any dream, be it a daydream or a night dream, well, haven't I found God? If God is the *only* foundation stone out of which all things come, and I have just discovered the source out of which my dream came, haven't I found him?

Well, God is your own wonderful human Imagination. If you're not willing to accept it, and like the children of Israel in that 8th chapter of 1st Samuel you insist on an external leadership, alright, that's your privilege (verse 10). But I must warn you, so he said to the prophet Samuel, warn them solemnly of the consequences of their choice, but grant them exactly what they want. They want a leader outside of themselves? Give it to them. You can't take it from them, but warn them of the consequences of their choice. They will become slaves. Everything in this world will be taken from them. And then when everything is taken, they'll cry out to be saved from the king of their own choosing, but I will have no ears to hear them. They'll go through the furnace of furnaces after they've made their choice to be led by something external to God.

And so he said to the prophet, "They did not reject *you*, they rejected *me* to be king over them." Like a man rejecting his own consciousness as king over himself. I want to be and I name it, and I think if I could only meet the right people... something outside of myself. I am rejecting the king over my own being which is the true God. And then, haven't you heard it said, someone will come home and say, "Who do you think I met today?" and they mention some person, to them a very important person. He will know so and so, who will introduce me to so and so, and then I will definitely get the job that I want. They're rejecting God. They're rejecting the only God in the world which is their own wonderful human Imagination. There is no other God. And so I think I'm going to become rich because I know rich people, or that some rich person met me at a party and he's going to introduce me to someone else, who in turn will introduce me to someone else, and through this contact I will really get what I want. I have rejected God, the only God. There is no other foundation in this world but God, and God is your own wonderful human Imagination. And by him—it's personified, it's called "him" not "it"—by him all things are made and without him there is not anything made that is made. In him is life, and that *life* is the light of men.

Well, I know from my own personal experience that I have assumed, when reason denied it, when my senses denied it, that I was the man that I wanted to be. I assumed it. I had no reason in this world to believe I could ever become it; I simply assumed it. I believed it. Then I rested in my assumption just as though it were true. Then things happened. And I can't tell you *how* they happened. On reflection you will say to yourself, "Well, it would have happened anyway." It always happens so naturally that you would think if you didn't do what you did, it would have happened anyway. And so you're misled to believe, well, maybe that isn't causation after all. Maybe this thing really would have happened and the whole thing would have moved like a river flowing. But it isn't. Had you not assumed that you were the man, the woman that you wanted to be, not a thing would have happened in the direction that it did happen. I find it time and time and time again, and it always works that way; not only for myself the being speaking to you but for myself in the form of the *seeming* other; for there is no other.

And so, I take anyone's request, and it seems to be another, but he, really, and she, is not another. There isn't "another" in this world; there's only I AM and you can't divide it. So when you say "I am," you're including every being in this world. There is not a being but God, and God is I AM. So when you say "I am," you're calling upon God's name, the only name, the only foundation stone, the only rock, and there is no other rock. So tonight you could assume that you *are* the being that you want to be, and assume it to the point where it's reflected in your mind, where you can see reflected on the screen of the mind confirmation of your assumption. You see people seeing you as they *would* see you were it true, and then fall asleep. That's all that you do. You desire, and God gave me the hunger to be other than what I seemingly am at the moment, and he who gives me that hunger can satisfy the hunger. So the whole thing begins with knowing God.

So the whole vast world teaches man that God is something outside of himself, and he isn't. God became man that man may become God. And because there's only God, "All that I behold, though it appears without, it is within, in my Imagination" and *my* Imagination is God. Divine Imagination is sunk in man as human Imagination. Because the only source of all phenomena is God, and God is *Divine* Imagination sunk in me as *my* Imagination, then it still is only Divine Imagination. The only difference between the two is when I am keyed low on this level it seems to take a little bit longer between my assumption and the fulfillment of that assumption. If I were now functioning on high levels, my assumption would be externalized immediately. Man is rising gradually into that world where everything is subject to his imaginative power and instantaneously. On this level, it's a limit of time, a little interval of time between the assumption and its fulfillment.

So I don't care what has happened to you this day and how dark the day looks, *believe* in God. And the only God, and I mean this, the *only* God is your own wonderful human Imagination. There is no other God. But may I tell you, when you meet your Imagination, you're going to see it personified as yourself, the most glorious being you've ever seen. You're going to meet yourself one day. When you meet him, you've never seen such beauty, such joy, such radiated strength in your life as yourself made visible. Because God is a person, and you'll meet him, and it's just like you, raised to the nth degree of beauty, majesty, strength, courage, character, all the pronouns in the world you can think of that are great. Like mercy, pity, peace, love, all embodied in one being, and it's just like you. You'll meet him...but it's all your own wonderful I-am-ness.

So you can start this night, start tonight and test it. It will not fail you, but you've got to test it. If when you leave here this night you think, well now, that was alright, but I still am not going to take any chances, because I do believe there must be something other than myself, some other God, and so, I'll try it, *but* I don't want to blaspheme against God. I was taught to believe in some God other than my own consciousness, and that man tells me that God is my Imagination. That is difficult to grasp. It's so much easier to believe that God is something outside as the priests and the rabbis and the ministers of the world talk about. It's so much easier to believe in *that* kind of a God, and hope that he will look upon me and see me in a good light; and then have compassion upon my weakness, and then grant me what I want. It's much easier to believe in *that* kind of a God.

But I tell you there were those who believed in that God…and you read it when you go home, it's a very short chapter, the 8th chapter of 1st Samuel. Oh, do read it, not more than a few verses: Go and tell them, Samuel, the consequences of their request but grant it. They have not rejected you; they have rejected *me* to rule over them as king. They will not accept the God which was revealed to them in the very second book of the Bible, for Samuel comes afterwards. In the second book of the Bible he said: "When I go to the people of Israel and I say to them, 'The God of your fathers, the God of Abraham, the God of Isaac, and the God of Jacob, sent me unto you' and they say to me, 'What is his name?' what should I say?" "Just say unto them, 'I AM has sent you'," that's all. When they ask for the name of the God who sent you and you claim that that God is the God of Abraham, the God of Isaac, and the God of Jacob, just say "I AM has sent you."

Man finds it difficult to keep the tense. He always speaks of thou art or he is, but never I am. So one comes into the world bringing I-am-ness, and they said of him, he speaks not like the scribes, he speaks as one having authority. No one can speak with authority unless he speaks from experience. And so, he comes saying, *I* say unto you...for I testify to the things that I have seen and things that I have heard. If you would not believe the things that I have seen and heard on this level, how would you believe the things that I have seen and heard from heaven? How can I tell you of heavenly things if you will not believe me when I speak of earthly things? And so, the being speaking is your own wonderful I-am-ness.

And may I tell you as I stand before you, every character in scripture, from the beginning to the end, is *buried* in you. That is where the fathers are buried and every one you are going to resurrect. When you resurrect them, one after the other, you'll know them more intimately than you know any being in this world. Every one will rise. And who resurrects any being in this world?—only God. Jehovah is the resurrecting power of the world. So when he resurrects, and Jehovah's name is I AM, *you* will know who you really are. For you'll lift up one after the other. And may I tell you when you lift them up and you see them, and you know them forever, you've *always* known them, but they've died. All these are the fathers who died and were buried in Egypt, and Egypt is your own wonderful, wonderful being. That's where they're all buried.

One day the tree begins to bloom and out comes this one. Out comes Joseph, and Joseph is the last of the seed plot, the Book of Genesis. The book begins, "In the beginning God..." and it ends "...in a coffin in Egypt." That's how the book begins and ends. In the beginning is God, I AM, and then the last one, in a coffin in Egypt. Who was the coffin? Joseph. Well, he is the prototype of Imagination. That's the first symbol that appears in the world of Imagination; for he was the dreamer. He interpreted all the dreams; he knew exactly what the meaning of a dream was. He saved, by his dreams, his brothers who sold him into Egypt. He saved his father. He saved the world from starvation by his dream. Then he died and was buried in Egypt, but he made all those who came with him pledge they would not leave him in Egypt. They would raise him out, take his body out and take it into the land that was promised.

May I tell you the day will come...and I know, tonight, one. I have been waiting for someone to meet him, for confirmation of those that I have seen. And one could tell me this past week, "I saw Joseph." When you see him, you don't have to ask one word, "Who are you?" you know who he is. There are millions of Josephs in the world, but there is only one Joseph. There are millions of Davids; there's only one David. There are millions of Abrahams but only one Abraham. These are distinct characters that live forever, not in some past but in some imaginative eternity, all buried in man. When you look into his eyes and you see Joseph, he is not as the world thinks him to be at all. This radiant being of youth and strength; not what the world thinks he ought to be, an old man. Yet, there is no doubt in your mind who you're looking at. You don't have to ask one question concerning, "Who are you?" So the entire Old Testament is *buried* in man, and it lifts itself up in man as man begins to awake. So the New Testament is only the fulfillment of the Old. The New interprets the Old, not vice versa. Not until it begins to awake in man can the Old be understood. All of a sudden the whole thing begins to appear, and every character of the Old Testament unfolds in the mind of man. Then you meet them one after one after one, and you stand thrilled beyond the wildest dream as they begin to appear within you. They *all* appear...and it's *God* awakening in you. So I tell you, believe it, they will appear.

But until they begin to break forward and appear in you, believe what I tell you concerning this foundation stone. The foundation stone is your own wonderful human Imagination, and that is God. Tonight you can assume that you are now the lady, now the gentleman that you want to be. And name...if it's money, you want money...alright, name it. Everything can be dreamed into this world. It's all a dream anyway. If you want fame, name it. I don't care what you want in this world, dare to *assume* it, and wear *it* as God wears you. You say, "How can God wear me?" well, his name is I AM. If I ask you, "Who are you?" before you put the little tag on it you are going to precede it by saying "I am" and then you're going to name it. You'll say "I am John, I am Mary" so before you say John, before you say Mary, you said "I am." That's God's name. So God is wearing you. You said you are Mary, but before you said Mary you said "I am." So God is wearing Mary. Get back and feel yourself "I am." That is God. There's nothing but God in this world and God wears all in this world. And because all things are possible to God you can by assuming that you are what you want to be bring it into being.

Believe me when I tell you, you can search the scripture from beginning to end and you cannot find any reference in scripture where a dream was associated in any way other than with God. Listen to these words in the Book of Numbers, "I will speak to you in a dream (the Lord is speaking) and I will make myself known unto you in a vision" (Num. 12:6). You can go through the entire scripture...go through the Book of Job..."In a dream, in a vision of the night, when deep sleep falls upon man, then I open the ears of man and speak to him in a dream" (Job 32:14). He opens the ear and speaks to man in a dream, unstops him, but he speaks to man in a dream. So if the only source of dream in scripture is God, the *only* source, well, you and I know how we can dream. Many a time I've asked myself,

"What do you want?" and then dared to assume it, and then fell asleep in the assumption that I had it, and then in the day, or the week, or the month, or the year, it happened. That assumption on my part built a dream into a fact. It built some little bridge of incident across which I moved, not knowing why, and I moved across this little bridge of incident, and when I got to the end of the bridge there was the fulfillment of my dream. I realized it.

So tonight, you take a dream and you wear it as God wears this dream. You say this is not his dream. Now listen to this carefully...it is said in the beginning that he brought forth from a man a woman, and then he told man to cleave to her and do not leave her until you become one. He brought forth woman out of man and then said to *cleave* to her. Leave everything, but don't leave her, cleave to her, and then you'll become one. Do you know what it means? Well, you think of the man, of the woman you would like to be, just think of it. I don't care what it is, the most noble concept of the world, think of it. Did it come out of you? Didn't you think of it? Isn't it your emanation? Well now, *you* out of whom it came must cleave to it, wear *it* as though you *were* it until you adhere and you become *it*. Then you'll crystallize it in this world. You are God's dream; you are God's desire. God so desired you, you came out from God, and then God wore you. To fulfill his own command, he cleaves to you; he doesn't let you go, for no matter where you go you are always saying "I am." No matter where you go in this world you say "I am." You never point to something other than yourself and speak of *it* as "I am." Wherever you are, whatever you're feeling, you say, "I am poor, I am rich, I am known, I am unknown, I am wanted, I am unwanted, I am weak, I am strong." No matter what you are saying you're saying, "I am." And that is God, and he's wearing it.

Well now, you think of someone or think of some thing that you want to be in this world and wear *it* as God wears you. Cleave to *it* as God cleaves to you. Just as God has made himself one with you and the whole story unfolds within you, then the story in the outside world will unfold in the outer world. Whether it be health or wealth or being known or being unknown, it all unfolds in the same way that you will unfold based upon God's eternal plan. You can't fail if you try it...but you've got to operate it. We are the operant power; it doesn't operate itself. We and we alone operate it. And so, there is no other foundation but God, and that foundation is your own wonderful human Imagination, when you say "I am."

The day will come—and I've experienced it so I'm not theorizing, I'm telling you what I've experienced—all the characters of the Old Testament, they all appeared before me, and I know the relationship between us, every one. The great one that comes at the very end is David. When David comes, God's only begotten Son reveals me as God. It takes the Son to reveal you as God the creator. So God's purpose is to give himself to you, but so *give* himself to you that you have no doubt of that gift. God so loved you he gave his only begotten Son to you as *your* Son, and so the Son appears and calls you Father. When you see him you have no doubt as to who he is. But all the others come; every one will be resurrected. For you must resurrect every being; and the only power in the world that resurrects is God.

Listen to these words carefully, "Man is reborn by the resurrection of Jesus Christ from the dead." He is reborn by the resurrection of Jesus Christ from the dead (1 Pet. 1:3). Well, who is Jesus Christ? It's God, and Jesus Christ is your own wonderful I-am-ness, that's Jesus Christ. "Christ *in you* is the hope of glory." So when you are told in the Book of Jeremiah, the very first chapter, he said unto Jeremiah and Jeremiah replied, how can this be, seeing that I *know* nothing and I'm only a child? The word Jeremiah means "Jehovah will rise." If Jehovah will rise, Jehovah must have fallen. So who fell? The word Yod He Vau He, the verb He Vau He, meant in its original form "to fall"—that's what it really meant—or "to cause to fall; to blow, or to cause the wind to blow." That's what the word Yod He Vau meant; that's the original form of it, which we translate today as I AM.

So who fell? Speak to Jeremiah. Jeremiah simply means, "Jehovah will rise." If he will rise, he must have fallen. And he did: God became man that man may become God. He *sunk* himself in us, and divine imagining is one with human imagining. But he will rise, and when he rises, everything that he foretold will rise in us. And you will see why these characters are as they are in scripture. They are eternally true; they didn't live in some long past, they are now alive in the most marvelous imaginative eternity buried in man, and they rise in man, and then you meet one after the other. They all know you, because *you* resurrect them. When you meet Abraham, he knows who you are. You are the God who told of the story to Abraham. When you meet Joseph, you know who he is and he knows who you are. You're the God of them all, God of all the fathers. Then you meet David, and David knows you and calls you "Father." And that's the end of it. But every one of them you meet. They are eternally true. And this play goes on and on, because in every child born of woman God's eternal play is buried, and then it takes root and it grows. Then comes that moment in time when the fullness of time has come and it begins to take flower, and the beings appear and the flowers appear. These are these eternal characters that appear, and you meet them one after the other. When the last has come, you depart from this wheel of recurrence.

I would not deceive you. I would not for one moment mislead you. I am speaking from experience. I'm telling you what I, personally, have experienced. I did not hear it from a man; I didn't read it in a book. I am telling you what I know, and I tell you what I experienced and share it with you. Buried in everyone is the Old Testament, and the New Testament only explains it. Because every one will awaken in you, in the Old Testament; then you'll understand the key given to us in the New. And it's not some being, one unique being of unnumbered centuries ago, no, it's you: you are Christ Jesus. And you *unlock* the scriptures. Scripture must be experienced in me. He said, scripture...I've come only to fulfill it: "Scripture must be fulfilled in me," and they didn't understand it. There was only an Old Testament, and he said, The Old Testament must be fulfilled in me.

How could the Old Testament be fulfilled in you when you came *after* the Old Testament? For we are told there were 400 years between the last book of the Old Testament and the first book of the New. That's a perfect number, 400 years, and 400 is the cross, it's the tau, the 22nd letter of the Hebrew alphabet. And there must be between the last book of the Old and the first book of the New 400 years. So I've come...I've borne the cross...I have come then to *interpret* the Old. The Old interprets itself: it awakens in me. And you tell it to everyone who has ears to hear. Some will hear it and believe it, and some will hear it and reject it; but, nevertheless, you tell it. So between the two books there's the interval of 400 years, which is symbolized by the cross, the tau.

As the whole thing unfolds you know you are on the end. But you also know don't judge anyone who rejects it. Everyone will eventually accept it, so don't judge them. Leave them alone, because you were just where they are at one time in your life. Every person who would now cut your head off for saying what you say, you were in that same state once upon a time. Only I plead with you this night to read that 8th chapter of the 1st Book of Samuel, and do not...if the whole vast country wants an external leader and centralized government where they're going to give you everything and you do nothing, they will finally take you. That's life.

Take a simple little thing like here in Cuba...they all say to the world... don't you recall Ed Sullivan's picture? He brought him on the stage on a Sunday night. Ed Sullivan still goes on because people have very short memories. But I saw it vividly and recall it, he brought him on and put his arms around him and embraced him as "the George Washington of Cuba." He *embraced* him, and there he hugged him before the whole vast country because Sullivan has a huge rating...and here is the George Washington of the country. He went off to Washington and he rode with Mr. Eisenhower, and he met all of the powers of our country, and here was this grand George

Washington. It was Christ embodied, and all Cuba hailed him as their savior; they wanted some external savior. First thing he did, took them all in and made them soldiers, without their consent. Then appropriated all the money...American property, $2 billion, all the money...and then he took everything and took more and more and completely enslaved them. Now they can't...they're crying out to another god to save them from a god of their own choosing, and there's no God to hear them.

So I ask you not to let yourself be led into that blind alley. The *only* God in this world is your own wonderful human Imagination. And when you turn it over to another to lead you into what you consider security, what you consider some wonderful state in this world, you are simply giving yourself over into anti-Christ, for Christ is your own I-am-ness. To turn from your own wonderful Imagination and give it to something else is to serve anti-Christ.

Now let us go into the Silence.

* * *

Now are there any questions? None? Well, when you go home...

Q: (inaudible)

A: The Bible says, Take no thought what you should wear and what you should eat, and then draws the analogy of the birds of the air, that they're fed without effort, and the lilies of the field grow without effort. If you will simply do what most of the Bible tells you, "When you pray, *believe*"—is that taking thought?—"When you pray, believe that you *have* received, and you *will* receive." That's the 11th chapter, the 24th verse of the Book of Mark, which is the earliest of the gospels. So when you pray, that is, when you desire—because to pray means to desire; you pray for something, you desire something—then believe you have received, and you will. But then don't take thought as to *how* this thing is going to come to pass, for "your Father has ways and means that ye know not of, his ways are past finding out." So it may come in unnumbered ways that you could never devise. On reflection, everything that has happened to me after I have assumed that I am what I want to be, I virtually as a man could not have devised it. I would have thought of a thousand other ways that it should have come, and it didn't come that way at all. But everything that I have ever done by applying this law, on reflection it seemed natural and yet I could not have devised the means. So take no thought as to *how* it's going to happen. But when you do pray, believe that you have received, and you will receive.

So may I invite you all this night, when you go home, that you may be encouraged to believe *only* in God, read that 8th chapter of the 1st Book of Samuel. Don't turn to any God outside of yourself. I don't care what he looks like. He may come as a tall, majestic being. And so, when even the prophet Samuel was over taken by the height of the first one, "Surely *he* is the Lord's anointed," and the voice said to Samuel, "I have rejected him. God sees not what man sees. Man sees the outward appearance of things and God sees only the heart" (1 Sam. 16:7). So don't judge by any outward appearance. Who knew the motive behind this takeover in Cuba…the takeover in so many parts of Africa today? In one week a Democracy is taken over. Who knows the motive behind this façade? So I tell you don't trust anything outside of God, and God is your own wonderful human Imagination. If you are faithful to God, God will use every being in this world to fulfill your assumption...because there's *only* God. But the minute you turn from God to another, then you're going to pay the price and he warned you solemnly the price you're going to pay. He's going to make you a slave the minute you turn on him. So he said to the prophet Samuel, "They did not reject *you*, they have rejected *me* as king over them." And the only one that should be king should be God, and God's name is I AM. See, the day is coming when the Lord will be king over all the earth. On that day his *name* will be one...only one, on that day. When you say "I am," are they two? On that day the Lord will be one and his name one...when he is king over all the earth. So you make God king over all the earth and the God that you would make is I AM.

Goodnight.

PURIFIED BY THE DEATH OF YOUR DELUSIONS

1/28/64

Tonight's subject is about one's delusions: "Purified by the Death of Your Delusions." You may find it, well, I don't say you will find it profound, no, but I've always felt that whatever is most profoundly spiritual is in reality most directly practical, and you'll find this very practical. But, it does take us into other areas.

Possibly the most...if I could choose among the Beatitudes, I would choose the sixth, if I could choose. But it seems arrogant on anyone's part to choose among the great Beatitudes. The sixth Beatitude is "Blessed are the pure in heart, for *they* shall see God" (Mat.5:8). This is a profound statement because man becomes what he beholds, and no man becomes God until he can see God. It's God and God alone who unveils himself that man can see him. But it's an everlasting expansion of the unveiling, as we are told so clearly in Paul's letter to the Corinthians, the 3rd chapter of 2nd Corinthians: "And we all, with unveiled face, beholding the glory of the Lord, are being changed into his likeness from one degree of glory to another; for this is by the Lord who is the Spirit" (verse 18). So he unveils himself in our presence and we at that moment are transformed into the image of what we behold. We invariably become what we behold. The veil that we wear is this garment, and so he simply lifts it and exposes himself, and we behold him as we become him.

But, we are told there's a condition imposed upon it. And you might think, can I meet the condition? Let me repeat it, the condition is: "Blessed are the pure in heart, for they shall see God." You might wonder which is the more difficult, the condition or the promise, purity of heart, or seeing

God? Well, let me tell you from my own experience, God is infinitely merciful. He initiates the process by which you and I are purified. You could sit from now to the end of time and you couldn't purify yourself. God initiates the entire plan of purification, and then devises the means by which we are purified. It happens so suddenly; you'll never dream in eternity how it happens.

So let me share with you a story told to me this past year in the city of San Francisco, this past fall. He's one perfectly marvelous chap. He was born in Boston, Massachusetts, the only child of parents who came here from Ireland, raised in a very rugged environment where he thought if he fought daily he was a man. Come home with bloody noses, black eyes, and he thought *that* was the way to live. He went through life that way. Then came the 2nd World War, and so he went off to war. He was a sergeant in this company and he found himself in New Guinea. The Japanese had pinned them down, the entire company was flat on their faces, dug in, and they couldn't move. He said, "Neville, let me now make a confession. Raised in my limited environment, in an Irish environment in Boston, Massachusetts, I had two extreme hates in my life, not dislikes, hates: I *hated* Jews and I *hated* Negroes." You can't justify a prejudice, because you can't. There's no reason in God's world why one should hate anything. But he hated; that was his confession.

He said, "I as a sergeant gave this Jew, who was a private, every dirty thing in the world to do when I was his superior. And here we are now pinned down in New Guinea by Japanese machine gun fire. We couldn't move. If I barely raised my head I would feel on my steel helmet the bullets ricocheting off my helmet. You couldn't budge; they had us completely pinned down. And this Jew to my left said to me, 'Sarge, do you have any hand grenades?' and I said yes, and I detached three from my belt, and could get them to him without being detected. And this Jew jumped up suddenly and completely wiped out the entire nest of Japanese snipers with their machine guns. He was severely wounded, but it wasn't mortal. At that very moment, I overcame all of my prejudices for the Jew. All the walls of Jericho came tumbling down, all of these ancient evils *in me* collapsed. And then I understood that statement which I had read but I didn't understand it before: You see these buildings and you're so proud of them—as I was proud of my prejudices—I was an Irishman and I was Catholic, better than any other religion in the world, better than any person in the world, and all these were things that I hated. And then suddenly I remembered this statement: You see these buildings? Not one stone will be left standing upon another that will not be thrown down (Mat. 24:2). And the ancient prejudice, the ancient evil, crumbled within me, and I not only did not *hate* the Jew, I *loved* them. So when I came back to this country and worked myself into a position where I had my own business in masonry—bricks, mortar, everything that went into the building of a building using masonry I supplied in San Francisco—and the Jew got the first chance at any job available."

"Then came something that happened by accident seemingly and some explosion took place in the factory and I am burning. My body is aflame, my overalls are burning, and all of the Caucasians in the place they didn't rush to save me. A Negro rushed forward, threw me on the floor, rolled me over, and put it out, burning himself in the process. I was lit, burning, but he was burned. At that very moment, my hate turned to love. So today in my business in San Francisco, you want a job, you either must first be a Jew or a Negro. My hate turned into love. For I could not have plotted that, I couldn't have planned it. It just happened that it happened this way."

Well, I'll tell you, it happened that way because God planned it that way. God *became* man that man may become God. There is nothing but God in this world. And so, when you sit there this night and you say "I am" that's his name. That's his great name, his only name. So, I am what? I am prejudiced? Alright, that's the wall he is going to tear down. I am prejudiced against this, that or the other? He will bring it down. As he brings it down, he unveils himself at a certain level, and lifts your veil, and you behold him, and you become what you behold. So, as we are told: And we all, with unveiled face, beholding the glory of the Lord, are changed into *his* likeness from one degree of glory to another; for this is by the Spirit of the Lord who is the Spirit.

And so, don't plot it, it's going to happen. If tonight you're prejudiced, may I tell you, you are not outside of salvation. God has plotted *the way* of salvation for you, and will place you into a situation just like this chap. His name is Bill Donovan...you can't get a more Irish name...well, here is Bill, and today you couldn't meet a nicer person. But to show you how he was really searching for God, when he came West he went alcoholic, with all of his prejudices, he went alcoholic, completely blind. He was searching for the Spirit and he saw the false spirit in the form of alcohol. He didn't know it. And then he joined AA, and for the last dozen years Bill hasn't touched a drop. Took me out to dinner, he knows I take a drink, he said, "Neville, you have all you want, but Becky and I (his wife) we never touch a drop. We both were AA and met in AA because of our problem." I didn't tell him then that he was searching. He knew it in the depth of his soul he was searching for God and saw God in some spurious form of alcohol. That's really what it is; it's simply *another* form. It's spirit, the same word spirit, spirit is alcohol. And so, he was searching for it and saw it in a form that was false. And then, joined it, and now today you couldn't in any way tempt him to take one little drop, he just doesn't want it. But he overcame the prejudice and then all these things crumbled within him.

So I say, if today you are prejudiced, don't be concerned. Everyone in this world is prejudiced, and these things are built around them that God may awaken. So you are placed into an environment where you don't know it. He was brought into this little environment in Boston, surrounded with a certain prejudice, a hatred, and he grew into it. And then God placed him in a certain environment where the two he hated most were his saviors in this world. The Jew saved his entire company and the Negro saved his personal life, and today the two are the most employed in his very successful business. So I say it works this way. So don't be, if you have it this night, don't be concerned. God will plot it; God will plan it. The initiative for man's salvation is with God, and, may I tell you, it isn't prompted by any good deed that man has done. Man's salvation is by grace and grace alone. No one can earn it. No one in this world is good enough to *earn* salvation. Salvation is becoming God: God became man that man may become God. And it's a series of unveiling, unveiling, unveiling, where suddenly man *awakens* to find himself transformed: this finite, fallible being transformed overnight into an entirely different being. And yet, the veil has not been completely lifted...another veil, and still another veil, for Truth is an ever-increasing illumination. But, it is all man.

So here, man is purified by the *death* of his delusions. But listen to this carefully, for this is from the greatest, in my mind, the greatest mystic that ever walked the face of this Earth, William Blake. He claimed that the entire poem *Jerusalem* was dictated by God, so he claimed. I wouldn't question Blake's right to make that claim. He makes it not only in the poem itself but in his letters to his friends, and they're all on record. Well, here is his statement, he claims it was dictated: "Then those in eternity who contemplate on death said thus." Who are they in this great eternity who contemplate on death and what is the death on which they contemplate? May I tell you, the beings contemplating are those who said, "Let us make man in our image," the Elohim, the gods. Let us make man in our image by the same process of unveiling ourselves; and because man becomes what he beholds, they'll become us, as I unveil them, as they become pure in heart.

"And those in great eternity said thus..." and what *did* they say? They are contemplating on death. You might think of death when you see someone go into the grave. That's not death—*this* is the grave. Everyone seated here seems so animate, so alive; these are the sepulchers of God. God is buried in every child born of woman, and that's the grave that these in great eternity contemplate. "And those in great eternity who contemplate on death said thus." Now listen to it carefully, what *did* they say? "What *seems* to be, *is*, to those to whom it *seems* to be, and is productive of the most dreadful consequences to those to whom it seems to be, even of torments, and despair, and eternal death; but Divine Mercy steps beyond and redeems man in the body of Jesus" (*Jerusalem*,Plt.36). And then the whole vision returns to its perfection: length, breadth, and height take on the original divine vision.

Come back to the statement that he is now saying. What did he say? "What *seems* to be." To Bill Donovan, it seemed that a Jew was a coward and he proved himself the bravest of them all in New Guinea. To Bill Donovan what seemed to be, is, to those to whom it seemed to be: the Negro was below him in courage, and in intelligence, and in everything—and he was his savior. When no white man came to save him, the Negro walked forward, threw him on the floor, and rolled him over, burning himself in the process, and saved him. And he overcame at that very moment all hatred. So go back, "What seems to be, is, what it seems to be, is, to those to whom it seems to be, and is productive of the most dreadful consequences to those to whom it seems to be, even of torment." Wasn't that torment? A man living with a prejudice, isn't he tormented? Anyone in this world with a prejudice, isn't he really living in hell? And doesn't he despair, can't get out of it? And it *is* eternal death… and they are contemplating on this eternal death. But, and this is our great comfort, the "Divine Mercy steps *beyond* and redeems man in the body of Jesus." He plots a play by which man overcomes his prejudice, where the walls of Jericho fall and the ancient evils crumble. And suddenly, he can unveil you, and that moment he unveils you, you see *him* who unveils you, and you become what you behold, one step higher. And then another play, and still another play, and we go on forever and forever becoming God; for God actually limited himself to man; he became man that man may become God.

So all of us in this world are one; there's only one. There's only one God; there aren't two Gods. As we're told in Zechariah: "And the Lord will be king over all the earth; on that day his name will be *one*, and the Lord will be one," only one. And he set up the only way in this world that he could reveal the oneness of us all. There is only one way that he could ever reveal that you and I are one. I answer to the name of Neville. You say "Neville" and I will say yes. Then all of a sudden I say "Charlie" and someone present, "Charlie," you'll say, yes, I'm here. And we seem so different, so distinct; and we are, we're unique in the eyes of God as separate visions of God. And yet I tell you we are one, we're actually one, because we're all being unveiled as *God*.

God only has one Son, only one Son, and that one Son's name is David. At the moment of the unveiling he unveils David, and then you see the relationship between yourself and David. And you look right into the eyes of David and he calls you Father; and you *know*, there's no doubt in your mind of this relationship, we are father-son. You go back into the ancient scripture and you read that "Thou art my son, today I have begotten thee" (Ps. 2:7). It's to David these words are spoken. And you know in the depths of your soul every being in this world will one day be unveiled in the presence of David and David will call him Father. If David calls *you* Father, and he's already called me Father, are we not one? There is no way in the world that God could ever reveal the *unity* of humanity save through a son. And so, "God so loved the world he gave his *only* begotten Son," not to walk with me as a friend but to reveal me to myself (John 3:16). God is unveiling himself in us: "For let us make man in our image." If I am the image of him, and *I am* he, then I *am* the father of his son. He can't make me less if he fulfills his purpose, and it's God's purpose to give himself to man; and so completely *give* himself to man that there is no one in the world, simply God and that man. And finally *only* that man: God completed the gift and he is God. So God becomes man that man may become God, and it's the unveiling process. And the only way in the world he can reveal the gift is through his Son. So we are told: "No one knows who the Son is except the Father; and no one knows who the Father is except the Son and anyone to whom the Son chooses to reveal him" (Mat. 11:27). So when the Son chooses to reveal himself, the relationship is Son-Father. It will happen to every being in this world.

So, until it happens we have our prejudices, we have our superstitions, we have our grand buildings and we're so proud of the buildings. But God sees the heart. So, "Blessed are the *pure* in heart, for *they* shall see God." We think a man because of his greatness in this world—he may be a very good soldier, a very good banker, a very good scientist, a very good and you name anything in this world, artist—and he need not be a good man. Well, God isn't seeing the status symbol on the outside, with the medals on you because you *are* a good scientist; and maybe you'll win the prize this year and get $50,000 from some great foundation, and the world will hail you because you did in the eyes of the world appear as a very good and great scientist. But God sees not the outward appearances; God sees only the heart. As we're told in the 16th chapter of the Book of Samuel, 1st Samuel, and they brought before the prophet the first son of Jesse. And he said to himself, Surely this is the Lord's Anointed—look at his height, look at the beauty, the greatness of this man. His name is Eliab: Eli means, my God, and Ab is father, so "my God is father," and surely he is the Lord's anointed.

The Lord said to the prophet, "I have rejected him; for the Lord sees not as man sees; man sees the outward appearance, and God sees the heart" (16:7). Then he brings another; I've rejected him. He brings a third; I've rejected him. And he marches seven before him; I rejected them. And then comes David, he said, "Rise and anoint him." So David was the anointed (16:12).

And then we come into the unfolding of the story. When Paul tells the story of David, he said, he put these words into the mouth of God, "Here is a man after my own heart" (Acts 13:22). So here he sees a man after his own heart; and so, you behold David (you are he). David is *his* Son, yet *you* are his father. For listen to these words, "the Son of man, who is called the Son of God"...but the Son of God is also God the Son, don't forget that. The Son of God is also God the Son, for "I and my Father are one." So he sets up a Son, called David, and he is your son, therefore, you are his father—and the Father of David is God. But *you* are the one that he brought out of humanity *called* David. David symbolizes the whole vast world of humanity, and he draws you out, and reveals himself, glory after glory after glory. It's himself being revealed.

So, as you are brought out you are the Son of God. Now listen to the words: "I will raise up after you your son, who shall come forth from your body. *I* will be his father, and he shall be my son" (2 Sam.7:12). So you're brought forth as the Son of God; for the Son of God is also God the Son, one, "I and my Father are one"..."though my Father is greater than I" (John 10: 29,30). For the thing symbolized in this world is greater than the symbol. So, I come symbolizing him who unveiled himself before me, and then I became him. Then he sent me back into the world, once more encompassed in my prejudice; and then he will tear it down, and unveil himself with a still greater glory, and send me back again. For there's no limit to the expansion of God unveiling himself in me, no limit. So Truth is an ever-increasing illumination, forever and forever. And every being in this world is one; there's nothing but God. God and God alone became us that we may become God; and he had set up the means by which he unfolds it in this world.

So I know we are purified that we may *see* God through the death of our delusions. When someone has numberless delusions... what is a delusion? Well, the dictionary defines it as a mental error, a false belief; especially that belief that is persisted in, that when one goes through it becomes, that's a fixation. Well, don't despair. Love them dearly, because God has plotted the means by which he's going to tear that building down. That building will crumble. Whether it be someone who thinks himself because he has a billion dollars he's better than someone else, and there are those who have it, God will tear it down. And don't despair when it crumbles. Someone who could not give them one penny to add to their fortune will be their savior; and then he sees that not the rich came to his support but the poor one. He will see. He may be prejudiced this day against rich people, you know. That's a prejudice too. That comes down. You can be very, very poor and you may have a frightful prejudice against those who *have* things; and those who *have* things, have no reason to save you will save you. That's how God plots it, that's how he plans it.

I speak from experience. When my father had the blow of blows in Barbados and no one came to see him because he was accused, wrongfully, but accused. Those who were playing it safe…no one came home even to say "How are you feeling, Joe?" Joe sat alone. And a man came, a very wealthy man, a very prominent person socially, financially, intellectually. He came to Barbados for his health years ago and made a fortune. But he came out as a perfectly trained gentleman from England; he was cultured, he was a great athlete, he was a Blue at Cambridge, he had all that it took. He was the only one that came home to see my father, and he said to Daddy, "Well, Joe, what can I do?" Well, he said, "I have all these children to feed and the servants to feed and I have no money." Well, he said, "What do you want to do?" He said, "All I know is simply what I've done before, a grocery business...just what I did before. I did a good business and I was falsely accused. They took everything from me by the false accusations, and if I had money I'd go back into the business and run it as I did before, successfully."

He went back to his office and he said to his people, "Mr. Goddard will open up in the next month or so a business and I want you to extend credit to the limit. Whatever he orders you fill the order and no bill must be sent to him. When he has it he'll pay." And so, we opened up a little business and he stocked us to the tune of about $40-50,000 in merchandise. We had no money, and when we sold it we paid him. And when he died and his son took over, if his firm had a match to sell and it was a cent more per box than any competitor, don't come near the Goddards. He and he alone sold us the match. And so, when, say five, six years ago, I know this much, they were doing with us in excess of $500,000 a year business. That was their initial investment. And so, if my father *had* any prejudice of the wealthy people of the world, for he had nothing as a boy, he certainly...that building collapsed and crumbled, that ancient prejudice, because one very wealthy, cultured gentleman came into his life and made it possible to once more start in a marvelous way.

So your prejudice need not be against a certain race or religion, it could be against wealth. Those who have none could be prejudiced against the wealthy and the wealthy may be prejudiced against something else, and it goes all over the world. These are the buildings spoken of in the 13th chapter of the Book of Mark, "You see these great buildings? I tell you not one stone will be left standing on the other but all will be thrown down" (verse 2). So, if today you have it, I know God has plotted and planned your redemption and no one will be unredeemed. And so, he will plot it and plan the scene by which the prejudice collapses in your presence and you fall in love with that formerly which you hated. And so, you actually fall in love with it.

And then eventually the whole veil is lifted and God's only begotten Son calls you "Father." You know, as he does it, you are not alone. He's going to call every being in this world Father; therefore, really, you are one with every being in the world. Then you understand the poet: "All things by a law divine in one another's being mingle." *All* things by a law divine. So every being in this world is actually interwoven. And so, when Dunne wrote the words: "I am involved in mankind. Every man's death is the death of me. Never send to ask for whom the bell tolls; it tolls for me." You read that something happened today across the water and someone was killed violently, don't ask for whom the bell tolls, it tolls for me. Well, I'm involved in mankind and every man's death is the death of me. For there's *nothing* but God buried in these graves in the world.

So "Those in great eternity who contemplate on *death* said thus"—and listen to it because it works in the most practical way on this level: "What seems to be, is, to those to whom it seems to be, and is productive of the most dreadful consequences to those to whom it seems to be, even of torments and despair and eternal death." Let us stop it there now. If it does this with torments and despair and eternal death, it will do it with joy and everything else in this world. So "What *seems* to be, *is*, to those to whom it seems to be." I wonder what the feeling would be like were I the man that I want to be? Suppose now that I had, and I name it, x-number of dollars a year...and I name it. All things being relative, suppose now I took just an outside figure, I had $35,000 a year. Well, living modestly as I do, wouldn't that be wonderful, $35,000 a year! Well then, what *seems* to be, *is,* to those to whom it sees to be, and is *productive* of that which it seems to be. If I dare to assume that I am it and walk this earth just as though it were true, if I could live just as though it were true, then I would prove that statement.

Now Blake claimed that these words were dictated to him by the Spirit of love who is God. Blake makes that bold statement and I trust him implicitly, "What seems to be, is, to those to whom it seems to be." But could I persuade myself that I am what at the moment reason denies? I'm taking this word "delusion" in a different manner, because "delusion" is to entertain a false belief, well, could this now prove true? Well, when a man may have a false belief that the Jew is not his equal, and until this thing happened he acted so that he proved it to his own satisfaction; and when he did it to the Negro, did he not prove it to his own satisfaction? Well now, we take the same principle: What seems to be, *is*, to those to whom it seems to be, and take it in a different light and prove it...though the whole thing will fade in the end. For in the end all will fade and only God remains. You will remain but everything else will go. All your buildings will collapse, whether they be made of gold, silver, precious stones, wood, hay or stubble. All will collapse, but *you* will remain, the builder.

So, I can now build using the same principle: What seems to be, *is*, to those to whom it seems to be. Well, can I not assume that things are as I would like them to be, for myself, for you, for anyone else in the world? And as I do it...a friend of mine this night before I came on the platform, he said he's been working on himself towards actually feeling the good of another. After all, he's working with others…it's up to him as a good man in his company to congratulate a salesman who brings in a big deal. But he said, "You know, in the past I must confess there was a certain envy on my part when I heard of a great sale on the part of another. I wanted to congratulate her or congratulate him, but I couldn't deny in my heart I wish *I* had done it. But when I could really let go and sincerely mean it, and say...I'm doing it all in my mind's eye; I didn't do it physically, I did it in my mind's eye, and really felt it. This past week a lady comes in having closed a $50,000 contract." Now, he said, "I know that's a tremendous amount of money for her, and I said to her, *thrilled*, I am not envious, I am thrilled that she could close that deal. In the past there was a reservation, I wish I had done it, and so my congratulations were not completely from the heart to the point where I was really pure in heart." But now he *knows*.

You can congratulate every being in this world for every good thing they do, because it's yourself. There's only one in this world, only one God, and one God became the seeming many. The stone became fragmented into unnumbered parts with different pigments. Some wear white pigments, some red pigments, black pigments, brown pigments; but only *one* in this world, all fragmented. And in the end, the Lord will be one and his name one. And may I tell you, that name, although the grand name is I AM, which is called Jesse, there is another name given to it, a glorious name, and that name is Jesus Christ. People don't believe it, but that name is Jesus Christ. It is I AM, granted, but if you read the story carefully he reveals the grand I AM—"I am the door, I am the true vine, I am the way, I am the life, I am the truth, I am the resurrection"—it's the same grand I-am-ness, but the name is a glorious name, and the name is Jesus Christ. Don't make a fetish of it, for he *became* you, he's unveiling himself *in* you, and when he completely unveils himself *you* are Jesus Christ. That's the story.

Now let us go into the Silence, and let us believe that what seems to be, is, to those to whom it seems to be. And may I suggest that this night you take the most glorious concept of yourself, I don't care what it is, make it *bigger* than you now even hoped to realize, because *all* things are possible to God. Whatever is your present ambition make it a noble ambition but make it *bigger*; and then try to persuade yourself, as we go into the Silence, that it is true. Assume the feeling of the wish fulfilled, and then view the world from that assumption—that you can see reflected on the faces of these imaginary friends that expression which implies that they see in you the man that you are assuming that you are. Now let us go.

* * *

Now first, may I call your attention to the book table. As you know, every book on that table I recommend. My books are there, my friend Freedom Barry's is there; any book on that table has my endorsement. And so, may I call your attention to it. On the way out please stop and look them over If you have one and you want to share your good fortune with another if you loved it, then you may get one for a friend.

Now, are there any questions, please? Yes, sir.

Q: (inaudible)

A: To repeat the quote, it is *The Gospel of Thomas* from the *Apocrypha* where man believes or women are taught to believe that they are secondary. Women are not secondary, because man is not a male and man is not a female. Man wears the garment of male and female, but man is the image of God. And so, no one knows man; man is the wearer of these garments, male and female. So as we are told in Timothy, "Woman will be saved by the bearing of *the child*." Not bearing children, as priesthoods the world over have tried to convey to womanhood...that's bearing children. Everyone in this world will one day go through a certain mystical experience who is now wearing the garment of female, where they will actually find and feel themselves male; and then, they will also know that they are man, wearing that garment. I speak from experience. Man in the resurrection is above the organization of sex, in the resurrection. We are told, that question was put to him in the most marvelous manner: Master, Moses in the law said that if a man marries, and dies leaving no issue, and has brothers, the brothers should marry his wife to raise up issue for the brother who died. Well, there were seven brothers, and the first one married, and died leaving no offspring. The second took her, and he died leaving no offspring, and the third, fourth; and finally seven of them married her, and they left no offspring. Whose wife is she in the resurrection? And he said, You do not know the scripture, for "the sons of this age marry and are given in marriage; but those who are accounted worthy to attain to *that* age, to the resurrection from the dead, they neither marry nor are they given in marriage...for they are sons of God, and sons of the resurrection" (Luke 20:28-36).

We're being prepared here to enter a new age altogether, where we don't need the relationship of male-female. It's a brotherhood, where we create out of our own wonderful Imagination. Everything is subject to our imaginative power. We don't need the divided image of male-female. We are man; and man is not a male, and man is not a female, because man is God. You're looking at his face, yes...to me when I looked into the face as it was unveiled before me, it's man, granted, but above the organization of sex. So, that book is not included in our canon but it's a glorious book. And I'll say to every lady, I know that my mother, my wife, my daughter, and all the ladies that I know in this world will one day confront David as David's *father*, not David's mother. He has no mother. And so, the most scholarly of all Biblical criticism is the *Encyclopedia Biblica,* and that gives no mother to David. And the manuscripts, the oldest known manuscripts mention no genealogy outside of a father whose name is Jesse. And the word "Jesse" is any form of the verb "to be"—I AM, that's what it means. So, "Whose son are you? I am the son of your servant Jesse" (1 Sam. 17:58). In other words, I am the son of I AM. He comes out of me, and so he looks at me, well, I am his father; therefore, he's the son of the being that I am...whoever I am. So when they said, "What shall I say?" "Just say I AM who I AM" (Ex. 3:14). He didn't say what it is...I am what I am, I am that I am, I am what I will be. So, he turns to me and calls me Father, and so he *is* the son of the being that I am, whatever that being is. So that's the name. No mother, just the father. So every being in this world, male or female, will one day have the experience, the thrill of thrills, to be called Father by God's only begotten Son (Ps. 2:7). And then he will know that he's God. There's no other way to know he's God unless the Son reveals it, for no one will know the Father unless the Son reveals him. So he tells us in the 14th of John, "No one comes unto the Father save by me." Any other questions, please?

Q: Your idea then is purification consists in ridding oneself of delusions?

A: Yes, yes sir, definitely. And yet, as I said, if it is a very difficult thing, don't despair. God has plotted and planned the way that that building, that ancient prejudice, will crumble. He will put you into the position where the one that represents that prejudice will be your savior, as it was in my friend's case, Bill Donovan. And Bill today, you couldn't meet a nicer person. You could hardly believe that he was that violent creature who fought all over Boston, and thought it marvelous to be always fighting, coming home with black eyes and all kinds of things. He thought that's the way that one should live—to prove yourself a man you must fight all day, so go into the street and fight. If he found a Negro, he would fight, if he found a Jew, he would fight, and come home to his mother with a black eye. But she was just as prejudiced as he because they were the best. First of all, they were Irish and they were Catholic. Well, you can't get any better in the environment of the Irish Catholic; that's part of the setup. So he had to prove to himself that that's not really God's only begotten child…that everyone is. And so, this thing happened to him. But he was big enough to tell me. For one night in San Francisco, last spring, I was talking on how man overcomes these strange delusions, and I was using stories. Then he said to me after the meeting, "Neville, are you free for dinner tomorrow?" I said I dine very early because I take the platform at 7:30. Well, he said, "I'll eat as early as you. You want to make it five?" I said yes. So he and Betty and I went off to a very lovely French restaurant, and then he told me this story, told me this perfectly marvelous story. When you meet Bill, you couldn't meet a sweeter, kinder person. His story is the one I told here the other day. He went off to Mexico, the boat went off to sea, and he re-enacted the scene as though it were now anchored safely on the beach. And then he plunged in, bravely, into this ocean, and here he is going to drown when suddenly a wave lifted him up, and he sees a boat that should not be in the area with three men aboard. He screams on the crest of the wave and they came and that's Bill. So you see, everyone is not only redeemable, everyone *will* be redeemed….they got him, took him out to sea, and brought back the little boat that was drifting away.

So this moral purity is not sexual, having to do with moral perfection. Because, the word "pure" in Semitic speech includes mind and emotion, and has no reference whatsoever to sexual morality or any moral perfection, none. It's a prejudice that God is seeing. Because, who is going to lay down the foundation of what is right sexually? What person in this world would dare to set himself up as the criterion of what is the right thing from a sexual point of view? To those who become celibate, either because nature made them that way, or they thought they could obtain the kingdom of heaven by *becoming* emasculated, and there are others who go through other forms of it—but it hasn't anything to do with any moral or sexual perfection, because, who is going to set up the standard? It isn't that at all. It's this strange, peculiar delusion that is a prejudice, a fixed, fixed false idea that will crumble. And God will see that it will crumble. As it crumbles he unveils himself. As he unveils himself, you become the one that you behold, so that's one more glory you are. So read it carefully in the 3rd chapter of 2nd Corinthians, I think it's the 18th verse, that wonderful unveiling of God, from one glory to another. And this is done by the Spirit, so no one can brag, no one can boast, because it's God and God alone who plots and plans the whole thing. In the end, we're all one. What a play! What a glorious play! That's why the cry at the very end, "Father, forgive them; they know not what they do" (Luke 23:32). They don't know because we are completely veiled.

But you take tonight's story: "What seems to be, is," believe me, "to those to whom it seems to be" whether we are prejudiced or you dream of good fortune. You dream of lovely fortune? What seems to be, *is*...believe it! I'm from a background where I'm a son of one who didn't have two pennies to rub together, and ten children to feed, and a wife, and himself, and a mother-in-law, and servants in the house, and not two pennies. But, "What seems to be, is, to those to whom it seems to be." So when he died five years ago, he could leave quite a fortune to his children. So that the speaker, if he so desired, need not work, if he so desired. But I'd rather drop dead this night than not do what I'm doing. The day that I'm not doing what I am doing don't let me just live on what he gave me, let me make my exit tonight. Perfectly alright, I know exactly where I'm going. But to remain here just because I could afford to eat and vegetate, I don't want that. I want to be here as long as I can do it. But the day I can't do it, just let me not vegetate; let me make my exit from this world. But he left me all that it takes to live graciously in this world of Caesar without raising a finger. Goodnight.

NOW MY EYE SEES THEE

1/30/1964

Tonight's subject, as you know from the title, is taken from Job: "I had heard of thee with the hearing of the ear, but now my eye sees thee" (Job42:5). And that is a promise to every being in the world. There is one divine event to which the whole vast creation moves and that event is to be incorporated into the body of God. God and God alone plays all the parts. And he's calling each and every one in his own good time and incorporates each, individually, not in any group, into his body. And you wear his body; it is your body, and you and he are one. This is the great plan of the world. If man believes it or not it really doesn't matter, because eventually he will experience it. So, in the scriptures, to *see* is to *know*, the same word in Greek. So when I *know* it, I know it only because I saw him.

Now we turn to one who is Paul. Paul had the grand event at the moment in time when no one was a greater enemy of the faith than Paul. Then he had a complete transformation of self and then he became the foremost apostle. An apostle is one who is called and sent. To be called *is* to be sent. Every one will one day be called. At that very moment he will be sent, sent to tell the story, regardless of what others will believe, because over the ages all kinds of things creep into the story and distort it. Now, here is the story of Paul being called. There's this discrepancy in the Book of Acts, which tells us first in the 9th chapter, then we have it in the 22nd chapter and the 26th chapter. In the 9th chapter, we're told that his companions who were with him that they heard the voice but they *saw* no one. Paul saw; they didn't see. In the 22nd chapter of the same Book of Acts, we're told that they didn't hear anything, they only saw the light. Then in the 26th chapter, we're told a light beyond the brightness of the sun descended upon Paul and his companions; not a word is said of anything being heard.

I tell you tonight, from my own personal experiences, the only one who heard *and* saw was Paul. It's unique...this whole thing is so completely individualized, no one but the one who is having the experience actually sees and hears anything. But our fathers through the centuries, they had to embellish it and put an intermediary between Paul and God. When we read his epistles he first states it in the Book of Galatians: If there is one thing that he was completely against was some intermediary between himself and God. He said, "Paul, an apostle—-not by men nor through man, but through Jesus Christ. When it pleased God to reveal his Son *in* me, I conferred not with flesh and blood" (Gal. 1:1,16). There was no intermediary between Paul and God, none whatsoever. And so, he said, speaking now of Jesus the Christ, "Even though I once considered him from the *human* point of view, I regard him so no longer" (2 Cor. 5:16). He was speaking only of the risen Christ. And said he, in Corinthians, the 9th chapter of 1st Corinthians: "Am I not free? Am I not an apostle? Have I not seen Jesus our Lord?" To him, the *only* qualification for being an apostle was to have *seen* the risen Christ, no flesh and blood being. You can walk with one who *is* that being, but that doesn't qualify you. It must be a complete unique spiritual experience *in you* when you see the risen Christ. "Am I not an apostle? Have I not seen Jesus our Lord?" No man sent me, no organization sent me; I *saw* him, and to see him is to be sent. So it is Paul's description of the conversion as we read it first in Galatians; then in the 9th and 15th chapters of 1st Corinthians; and then in the 4th chapter of 2nd Corinthians. Then he speaks of seeing the *glory* of God in the face of Christ. That's how you see him. God is Spirit; he can only be seen in his Son; but the Son and the Father are one. So you look into the face and there you see him. At that moment he embraces you and you become one with him, you fuse with him, and fusing with him then he sends you into the world.

And let me tell you my own personal experience of being sent. When you are embraced he sends you. Now these words are not recorded in scripture, but they should be recorded in scripture because the drama is identical for every one of us. Everyone will have the identical experience. There's only one play, one plot, one plan that God has devised to redeem himself, having fragmented himself—he is the eternal rock—-and he brings us out individualized as himself. And when I was embraced into the body of God, and made one with God, and wore his body as my own body, and then sent, the words ringing in my ear were these, "Down with the blue bloods." I came back unschooled, uneducated, wondering what is it all about? But the words you could never in eternity forget. I have forgotten so many things between that day back in the twenties and today in the sixties. So much that I have experienced in this world I have completely forgotten.

But these words are indelibly impressed upon my mind and I can't forget them. I didn't know the meaning of them until one day I came across the meaning of the words "blue bloods"—"Down with the blue bloods." It has always meant "church protocol; all external forms of worship," but all. No intermediary between yourself and God—no external sacrament, no external anything in this world—just you and God. There's only God. And so, I heard the words in my head ringing out. I was embraced by God; I am one with the body of God; and while I'm embraced and wearing his body that is infinite love, the words "Down with the blue bloods!" And then the words to me, right into my eye, "Time to act!" "God only acts and is in all existing beings or men." "Time to act!" was my command when I was whisked out of that divine society into this world.

So I know that someone tampered with that story as told in the Book of Acts. The Book of Acts was written by the one who wrote the Book of Luke, whoever he was. But between the writing of the original manuscript and our reception of it, there are those who tried to make it conform to their concept of what God ought to have done; and, surely, there must be some intermediary between man who is a villain and the saving of that man. So they called this one Ananias, and they speak of Ananias; and Paul never uses the name Ananias in any of his epistles. He speaks four times of his conversion, the same conversion, and never once mentions that individual, an intermediary between himself and the radical change in his being. But Luke mentions it twice. Here, Ananias comes in sent by God to one who is blinded by the experience to open his eyes that he may see.

So, "My eye sees thee." Everyone one day will see God, actually see God, and seeing God will become God. We always become what we behold. And God will call us in his own good way, and no one knows his secret of the call. When they're called, you stand in his presence and you ask no questions. You see infinite love. So when Blake said, "And love is the human form divine," I know from experience he's right, it is. It's the human form divine. You stand in his presence of infinite love. He embraces you as you are asked the question and you answer as you ought to answer it, and you will answer it that love is the greatest thing in the world. As he embraces you, you fuse with him and you are one with God. And there's nothing but love...nothing but God.

And then will come the most marvelous unfolding pictures of the world, that God's story, as told in the Old Testament, is true. Nothing thrills you more than when someone comes here who filled to overflowing with the eagerness to understand God's message will call me on the phone or write me, and then tell me these wonderful visions of theirs. One called this past week and said, "Neville, I met Jacob...but he's such a little one, he is so small, he's so tiny, he is so little." I will tell her, read the 7th chapter of Amos, the 2nd and 5th verses of Amos: "How can Jacob stand? He is so small!" Can you conceive of a child that can't stand? He must be very small if he can't stand. Today, they're precocious at the age of nine, pulling themselves up... nine months, I mean. At a year, if he isn't standing, "What's wrong with him?" But here, "How can Jacob stand? He is so small!" And all have been taught to believe that Jacob is a man, who gave birth to twelve sons, and they are the fathers of the whole vast world. Yet, in the Book of Amos, "How can Jacob stand? He is so small!" So she calls me up and she tells me, "But, Neville, he was so small. I met Jacob. No one told me he was Jacob, I *knew* he was Jacob. But, Neville, he is so small." Exactly what the Book of Amos tells you that he really is. The whole vast drama unfolds within the mind of man. There's nothing but God and his play is contained *in* man.

Another lady, who is here this night, wrote me the sweetest letter this past week and told the story of her four-year-old granddaughter. The granddaughter was then only four years old. She said to her, "Grandma, I dreamed last night. I dreamed I went away up into the sky, up to the sun, and I talked with the sun. And you know what? He has a face and he has hands and he has feet. And you know what, Grandma? His hands and his feet have magic. And then the big, big ocean began to talk and the ocean talked to the sun. Then the sun came down to the earth. And you know what, Grandma? He had legs, and he could walk, and he walked right over to me, and he kissed me on the cheek, and it was hot. Now isn't that a silly, silly dream, Grandma?" And how true that is! There is *nothing* but God in this world. Everything in this world is human, but people don't know. *Everything* is human. The sun is God and so is the moon and so is the earth and so is everything in this world. The day will come and you will awaken *as* God to discover there's not a thing in this world but God. There is nothing but God simply individualizing himself and expanding beyond the wildest dream from whatever he was prior to the decision to expand. Only God...nothing but God…so an ever-increasing illumination is the presence that is God.

So here was this child's dream. Luckily the grandmother recorded it and I have it at home in her own written word. Once she goes to school they'll tell her the sun is this huge hot body that's gradually burning itself out, because millions of so-called bombs, atomic bombs, are being exploded within it by its own power; and eventually it has no more left and therefore it will grow cold, and we, floating around it, will die because it will cease to be. ___(??) And they don't know that it has a face and hands and feet, and can come down to the earth and talk with the ocean, and then walk over to a child and kiss the child on its cheek, and the kiss was hot. And so, at her little tiny ___(??), knowing that the sun is away up there and it isn't a man, so, "Isn't that a silly dream, Grandma?" I tell you the whole thing is true.

This past week, a lady, who may be here this night, gave me a magazine based on faith. On the front cover and the back cover two lovely thoughts are printed. On the front cover, "Only the Imagination of man is vast enough to contain the immensity of space"; on the back cover, "Man's Imagination manifests itself in the Imaginations of men." Now, this is a magazine brought out, I think, quarterly, or maybe half-yearly, but, here, this perfectly marvelous thought that "only the Imagination of man is vast enough to contain the immensity of space." You think in terms of the sun—they say it takes eight minutes for light to reach us. And the fastest traveling thing in the world, so scientists say, is light—one hundred eighty-odd thousand miles a second. And you sit right here, whether you know it (never heard these words before), and you think of the sun, and there you are, didn't take eight minutes at all. Then they tell you that there are things away beyond the wildest dream of man that would take light-years, running into the unnumbered hundreds and thousands, oh, x-number of thousands of light years to reach it. So they tell you where it is, and you think of it, and there you are. So again, "Only the Imagination of man is vast enough to contain the immensity of space"; so that "All that you behold, though it appears without, it is within, in your Imagination of which this world of mortality is but a shadow" (Blake, *Jerusalem,* Plt.71).

And the day will come you too will have all these experiences. You'll meet Jacob and he is so small. "Jacob is so small! How can he stand?" And you think in terms of this giant of a man with his twelve sons and all these; no, these are states, all states of awareness. You and I must pass through the state called Jacob. I recall passing through the state where literally Jacob was a deceiver. Jacob deceived his father-in-law. He took cattle and put them at the watering time when it's time for fertilization, and then put poplar trees before their faces so that when they came to be sired they saw before them these stripes. And so, when they were sired, they brought forth striped offspring. He made a little bet with his father-in-law, Laban, that all the striped would be his and the spotted ones would be his; the plain ones would be Laban's and *only* the plain cattle. And so he deceived his father-in-law. He deceived his father, Isaac. He deceived his brother, Esau. He was a deceiving being. But to see God, his name had to be changed, so he wrestled all through the night. Not a night of twelve hours. We are wrestling through the night now. We've been wrestling for thousands of years, playing the part of Jacob, until that moment in time when he completes the wrestling and God changes the name to Israel, the pure in heart. For only the pure in heart can see God. And so, we look into the eyes of God and we become what we behold, where we're transformed from Jacob. And Jacob was always the little one, so small he couldn't even stand.

I recall when I was a boy six years old, five or six, my mother gave me a candy—-she had a lovely box of candy—-and she said, "Nev, you take this and then give this to Carl"—-my brother Carly. So I took my candy and I took Carly's, and she said, "Go and give it to Carl." Well, I ate mine before I left the room and it tasted so good I didn't have the strength to give Carly his, so I ate his. So you see I deceived my brother, just like Jacob deceived Esau. And I never told Carl that I had a candy to give him. Had I told him he might have cried and told Mother, or he might have forgiven me, he might have. At that age I doubt if you have the strength for forgiveness. And I didn't tell anyone, so Mother never knew I didn't give it to Carl. You see, I played the part of the little one called Jacob. "Jacob is so small! How can he stand?"

And she was so surprised when Jacob came into her world, this little child. So small she said to me on the phone: "But, Neville, he's so small." The very words she used, "He is so little." Well, the word in scripture is small. He is so little he can't stand. Well, he would have to be under a year and not be able to stand. And so, she is passing through these states where she actually is encountering God's eternal drama. The play is perfect and everyone encounters all these characters in eternity. And so when Job, at the very end—-there are forty-two chapters to *Job*—-and no one went through more hell than Job, the victim of the most cruel play when he seemingly was not really entitled to it at all; he did nothing to warrant this horror. And in the very end, when he complained and he complained and he complained, he finally, at the very end, he said, "I have heard of thee with the hearing of the ear; but *now* my *eye* sees thee." I've heard of him, but now I see him.

And when you see him, may I tell you, you will never, not in eternity, ever be able to describe him. Daniel tries to describe him in the 7th chapter, but you can't quite describe Jesus Christ, you can't. You look into this heavenly face of the Ancient of Days and he's Jehovah. That's Jesus Christ, as told you in the 4th chapter of 2nd Corinthians, and I behold "the glory of God in the face of Christ" (verse 6). You don't see God, God is Spirit, but you see him reflected only in the face of Christ. And you look right into this glorious face, and he asks you "What is the greatest thing in the world?" Automatically you answer, "Love" ___(??) "Faith, hope and love," the words of Paul. That is a great thrill, because Paul wrote that 13th chapter of 1st Corinthians and you're quoting Paul, the greatest and the foremost apostle of all. And he claims, "I am an apostle because have I not seen Jesus our Lord?" That is the one qualification for apostleship: "Have I not *seen* Jesus our Lord?" (1 Cor. 9:1). And then you quote Paul, and he, Jesus the Christ, embraces you; and you become one with him, and you wear his body and it's infinite love, there's nothing but love. And then you are sent and you are told, "Down with the blue bloods!" and "Time to act!" You go out knowing you must sever all contact with all organizations, but *all* organizations who think that they are going to acquire merit to get into heaven by attending service, by doing this, by doing the other, and all the outside rituals. "Down with the blue bloods!" that was my command.

Then, the one who sent me was infinite power, and Paul describes Jesus Christ as "the power and the wisdom of God." So I was brought before power, infinite power, and he said to me, "Time to act!" But what a command! Without using lips, without using any vocal chords, but I heard words immediately as he thought them. And that was the power of God. There was magic in the eye. Come back to Pammie, "And Grandma, there was magic in his hands and magic in his feet." I tell you, there was magic all over. Magic in his eye...he looked into your eye and not a word was uttered as far as a voice here goes; and you hear words in your own mother's tongue, the tongue in which you were born, that's what you hear; and hear it is "Time to act!"

You go out, and no organization, join none; make no outer effort to appease God, no outside effort whatsoever; no intermediary between yourself and God. And the day will come, you'll simply play your part and when God knows the time is right he will call. There will be no resistance. He will call you into his presence and you will look right into the face of Christ Jesus, which reflects the glory of God. There's no other way of knowing God other than in the face of Christ Jesus. You stand right in his presence, and you see him, and he embraces you, and you fuse with his body; and from then on you are one with Christ Jesus. So the words you understand, then, "He who sees me sees him who sent me."

So the Sender and the Sent are one, though you're veiled. And the body veils the being that you are. No one sees the being you are, for you are wearing a body that is a veil. The body is a veil, so no one knows the body you're *really* wearing. You know, but others do not know, and you can't display it to anyone's mortal eye. But you can display this. But you know "He who sees me sees him who sent me," for the Sender and the Sent are one. Then comes that moment in time when the veil is taken off for the last time. At that moment, you return to your eternal, immortal form—which was given you by the embrace of Christ Jesus—to become a part of the body of God. And everyone is destined to be a part of the body of God. So, "My eye sees thee."

But on this level, may I tell you, his every word is true. And while you wait patiently for "seeing," don't neglect the other levels of his being. For he tells us that whatever we ask in prayer *believing*, we will receive. Well, to ask, believing I must surrender myself to that state. There's a vast difference between speaking of a thing and surrendering myself to that thing. When I surrender to a thing, I think *from* it, I don't think *of* it. I view the world *from* the state if I surrender to it. So, whatever I ask in prayer, believe that I have received and I will receive. So I surrender, completely abandon myself, to the state. As I do so, I see the world differently. I see it as I would see it were it true that I am the man that I've just assumed that I am. And in that assumption I simply view the world and look at the world. So I must not neglect the lower level of God's truth, for he's given us these levels to aid us and to cushion us while we rise to that moment when he calls us and embraces us and makes us one with himself.

You take it this night, not only for yourself but for everyone that you know. And treat it lightly. Don't burst a blood vessel to make it so, treat it lightly. Someone asks anything of you assume that they've told you this very moment that they have what they want. Don't labor on it. *Believe* in God, God is your own wonderful human Imagination, so don't sit down and labor. Someone asks you something—they want a fortune, they want a job, they want more money, they want this, that or the other—if it's something that does not injure another if they want it, grant it! Whatever you are asked, if it is in love that you could grant it, grant it. Whenever you use your Imagination lovingly on behalf of another, you're actually expressing God, for God is love. So if someone says, "I want more money," why shouldn't he have more money? Certainly, more money, no matter what he has. If he has all the money in the world, if he wants more of it, you can grant that. He isn't going to hurt anyone if he gets it, not if you assume that he has it. Someone wants to be known, alright, if that's what they want. Who really cares?

I read this morning's paper...and three that I knew, one quite well; met him back in 1934 in New York City; in fact, it was he who introduced me to my dancing partner who was my dancing partner for thirteen years. And here, no one in this world that I knew of was more afraid of death than he. So he went to sleep and didn't wake. So at the age of sixty-nine they found the body in the bed. A very able playwright, he wrote many a Broadway hit, one lasted almost two years; many a TV program and many a moving picture he wrote. His name was Eugene Conrad. I knew him as Gene Conrad and Gene introduced me to my dancing partner, Amarina. But he didn't wake. He was out the night before with his wife and his friends; went to sleep, and Gene is gone. Gene never came here, never came to any of my meetings, because Gene knew the physical Neville. He wanted nothing of the experiences of the one who wears this garment. He knew the physical Neville and he knew the limitations of that physical body, all of its weaknesses, and so he wanted no part of it. This is the eternal story as told in scripture: Oh, we know him, we know his parents, we know his brothers, we know his sisters; and yet when Messiah comes no one will know where he comes from. Well, Gene wanted no part of that, because he wanted to believe in some miraculous being on the outside of himself. Not something on the inside which made him alive, first of all, that would slowly awaken *within* him and go through the entire story as told in scripture; every little detail would unfold into Gene, and it will.

But tonight, Gene is on the wheel and he's gone from this wheel into another wheel, the same wheel. And so, he will tomorrow read of one who had the experiences, but memory being very short he will not know he ever knew Neville. But he will know and read of the story of a man who actually had that experience that paralleled that which was told in scripture, and he will listen vividly. One day he'll be called, and because I'm already part of the body of God when he comes I'll look right into his face, and he and I will be one, all in the body of God. He doesn't know it now, but he *will* know it. Everyone will.

This morning's paper, Alan Ladd, he went to sleep and he didn't wake, age fifty, and so here, only fifty years old. He's made a hundred pictures, and was he interested in this? I don't think he was interested in this. Another friend of mine who came here twice last year—I knew him back in the days of Abdullah—and he came here, Robert Cummings, a very, very healthy person, a nice chap. But Bob doesn't come because this is not his cup of tea. It's something a little bit outside of what he would expect. But Bob and I knew each other well in New York City years ago. He is my junior but not by many years I assure you, in spite of his press agent. I'll be fifty-nine in a matter of days and Bob cannot be less than fifty-eight, in spite of what others will tell you. But at that age you would think that reason would tell you you're moving towards the inevitable and why not listen to the story as it has been revealed through one. Though you know this garment, listen to that which is actually speaking through the garment.

For what I tell you is true. I'm not making it up, I'm not composing; the whole thing *happened* to me. Everything said of Jesus Christ as told us in scripture I have experienced. That's why when I read the inconsistencies I told you this night, I can tell you of these inconsistencies. There's no intermediary between yourself and God. So when the Book of Acts brings in three, I know that someone tampered with the script, because in the letters of Paul himself, his epistles, he does not mention one intermediary between himself and God. His first letter, which is Galatians, he goes right out and says: The gospel which I preach is not man's gospel. It was not taught me, nor did I receive it from man, but I got it through a revelation of Jesus Christ (Gal.1:11). And a revelation to Paul was God in an act of self-revealing. He unveils himself, and that's how you *see* him. As he unveils himself, you become the thing that unveils itself before you.

And so I know that Ananias is an insertion. There's no reason for him whatsoever in scripture. So when I read these stories and I go back and I parallel it with what I've experienced, I know where, whoever the scholar was or the translator was. Because, after all, in those days they didn't wear glasses as we do to aid sight, and you could take one little letter and change the meaning of a word. For these scribes were simply working without electric light, without this aid, without glasses, and they were simply scribes transcribing, putting from one part into another what they thought they saw. They could have done it unwittingly. On the other hand, some did it knowingly, trying to make it conform to what they believed God *ought* to have said, rather than what he did say. But when you've had the experience and you *know* from actual experience, then you see, because to see is to know. And so, when you see it because you've experienced it, no one can thwart you. If the whole vast world rose this night in opposition to what I've just told you, it would make no difference to me whatsoever. I wouldn't hate them for it, because I would know each and every one who now opposes it will tomorrow meet me in the body of God, and I'll be there to greet them. I'll look right into their face and they'll become what they behold. The very being that now opposes will become…for I'll be one as I am now with the body of God. There is nothing but God in this world.

So may I tell you, you dwell upon what you heard this night...yes, that vision of little Pammie. As Blake said in the end of his wonderful vision, *The Vision of the Last Judgment*, and someone will say to you, "When you see the sun, do you see a big round guinea?" He said, "Oh, no, no, no, I hear a host of heaven crying out and singing 'Holy, holy, holy is the Lord God Almighty!'" That's how he saw the sun. Not as a huge luminous body radiating heat and energy, but he saw it as alive with angels crying to the glory of God. And so, little Pammie went a way into the sky and she talked with the sun. "And you know, Grandma, he has a face and he has hands and he has feet. And you know what, Grandma? The big ocean talked to the sun and then the sun, whose hands and feet had magic, came down to earth and talked. And you know what, Grandma? He also had legs and he walked over to me and kissed me on the cheek, and it was hot. Now isn't that a silly, silly dream?"

And may I tell you, you dwell upon it. Maybe in the not distant future you, too, will go a way up into the sky and talk with the sun. And may I tell you, she's right, he does have a face, he has hands, and he has feet and he ___(??). So everything in this world is God; there is *nothing* but God.

Now let us go into the Silence.

HE HAS PUT ETERNITY INTO THE MIND OF MAN

2/4/64

Tonight's thought is taken from the Book of Ecclesiastes, the 3rd chapter, 11th verse. This is considered the most disputed verse in the book. Man refuses to accept it because it doesn't make sense and man is a rational being. But those who wrote the Bible, or took it down I should say, were not writing rational thoughts. They were inspired and they were writing their vision. This entire book does injury to man's rational side, for to him everything is vanity, vanity of vanities, all is vanity. `No one knows who Qoheleth is, but he hints at it—and bear in mind this is a mystery—so the book opens with a certain claim, "The words of Qoheleth, the son of David, king in Jerusalem." The last chapter invites us all to leave everything and follow just the collected works of one shepherd, for the Bible tells us who that shepherd is. He is telling you who he is when he tells you "son of David," but it's a mystery, for in the scriptures there is no son of David whose name is Qoheleth. So in spite of certain scholars who try to say Solomon, there is no Solomon hinted in it.

But the verse that we are taking tonight, we have to go all over the Bible to support it. It is, "God has made everything beautiful in its time." That is denied by our reason: a child comes in deformed, mentally retarded, injured and, here, "God has made everything beautiful in its time." May I tell you, it's a true story; it's right in *its* time. Now we'll go on, "God has put eternity into man's mind yet so that man cannot find out what God has done from the beginning to the end." He's put eternity in man's mind. Well, again, man claims it can't be done. To understand what he means by eternity we must understand the meaning of the word Olem, for that's the word. Its interpretation can only be given if we know the real meaning of the word Olem. You pass a cemetery, Beth Olem (the same word Olem) and Beth means "a home, a house, one's eternal home" when one goes through that cemetery. But he doesn't mean that. The cemetery is earth. This world here is the cemetery called Beth Olem. He enters eternity here, that is, in his mind; everything here is in his Imagination, everything.

To understand it you must go back to the Hebraic mind who wrote it, who took it down. In Hebrew thought history consists of all the generations of men and their experiences fused into a whole. This concentrated time in which all the generations of man are fused and from which all things come is called eternity. Just think of it, a complete compression of every conceivable thing that man could ever do, all in just one compressed section of time. The Old Testament *is* that block. Every frightening thing in the world is openly described in the Bible. There isn't a crime that you read about in the daily press, not a war, that isn't openly described in the Bible. Talk about rubbing out a whole race, that's described in the Bible; a whole country, that's described in the Bible. And so, Blake made the statement: "Eternity exists, and all things in eternity, independent of creation which was an act of mercy." So here, in man's mind are all the things that it takes for man to be anything in the world that he wants to be.

Now, he tells us there is nothing new under the sun. He makes the statement: "What has been is what will be, and what has been done is what will be done; and there is nothing new under the sun. Is there a thing of which it is said, 'See, this is new?' It has been already in ages past. But there is no remembrance of former things, nor will there be any remembrance of things to come later among those who will come after," no remembrance whatsoever. Now he paints a word picture of what he himself has accomplished: great wealth. He amassed great wealth through his own toil and he knows he will die and leave it to one who did not toil for it. He says, "That is vanity of vanity." He built great buildings and he knows that they will crumble or go into the hands of one who did not toil. He sought out wisdom and became the wisest of men, but the end was like the fool, both turned to dust. He mentions all these things and then concludes it's all vanity.

Now bear in mind, the New Testament interprets the Old—it's not the other way around. These were inspired men. As we are told, "No prophecy of scripture ever came by the impulse of man, but men moved by the Holy Spirit spoke from God." So they aren't his words; he's recorded them. He's not trying to set up some workable philosophy of life. He has simply recorded it on a certain level where this block exists...all in the mind of man.

Now, let me define for you the word Olem. It does mean eternity if you remember what I've said concerning the Hebrew's mind and what history means to it. It contains all the generations of men and all their experiences, and *that* is called eternity. But the word is also translated "the world." It's translated "something hidden, something concealed, something out of sight, a secret; a youth, a lad, a *stripling*, a young man." These are all definitions of the word Olem. They're all right. Every one can be used in that statement. He did put eternity into the mind of man. As we quoted last Thursday a passage from this strange magazine: "Only the Imagination of man is vast enough to contain the immensity of space." Only the Imagination of man is *vast* enough to contain eternity and all that you could ever, all these combinations, bring out, and be anything that you want in this world. Yet he speaks of recurrence, and you might think that it's going to be a peculiar, monotonous recurrence. No, he means everything taking place took place and is going to take place, because you draw it out of this one block of eternity. But everything is in it, and you call the combinations and play them; but the end, as he sees it, is vanity. What are we waiting for, he's asking. We're waiting for something, because here is complete recurrence. No matter how rich you are you leave it behind to one who didn't toil for it. No matter how wise you are you leave it behind and join the fool in the same grave; and you join all the weak people if you're strong, all in the same grave. That all seems so vain and so fruitless!

So we must be waiting for something, and that was *concealed*. For the word Olem means "something hidden." What was hidden that he couldn't see? What was hidden from the prophets? Well, now listen to the words: "The prophets who prophesied of the *grace* that was to be yours searched and inquired about this salvation. They inquired what person or time was indicated by the spirit of Christ within *them* when predicting the sufferings of Christ and the subsequent glory." It was revealed to them they were serving not themselves but you. All these characters of the Old Testament were all *in you*. They were serving not themselves; they were serving you when the fullness of time arrived. No one knew when, so he asked, "What person or time was indicated by the spirit of Christ *within* them when prophesying this state?" Well, when the fullness of time had come, only when it came, could it be revealed that which was hidden in the minds of man.

Now, here is what is hidden. Think of Jesus Christ as the personification of God; just think of him that on his face you see the glory of God. So when you are told in scripture, God said, "Let *us* make man..." think of the Elohim, the gods, and together they form *one* who personifies *all*, that's Christ Jesus, think of that. Now, think of humanity, God's love, and *one* personifies humanity and that is David. When you see humanity, God's love, God's beloved—he's in love with mankind, with humanity—it's personified as a *single* youth. For eternity is youth, it's not an old man with a scythe. So when you meet eternity personified, you see David. When you meet God personified, you see him reflected in the face of Christ Jesus. So think of these two.

So the one now speaking—the son of David—why the son of David when in the New Testament he tells you that David calls you Father? We'll come to that. Yet he claims in this that he is the son of David, son of humanity. He is buried in man, in humanity; therefore, he has to come forth from humanity, and cannot deny he is the Son of man. But Son of man that comes forth, we're told, shall be Son of God. The words are: I will raise up from you (humanity) when you sleep with your fathers...I will bring forth from you a son. He shall be *my* son and I his Father (2 Sam. 7:12). So here, he's bringing forth from humanity which is David, a son. But the son that comes forth is going to produce the reversal of order that you find all through scripture: For man matures when he becomes his own father's father. So, who comes forth from David? Jesus Christ. "Christ *in* you, the hope of glory" (Col.1:27). He cannot emerge from me were he not now in me. Christ could not come forth *from* you were he not now *in* you. For you're told he's son of David—not *a* little boy called David that personifies humanity. When you meet David you're seeing the *personification* of the whole vast history that you have gone through, which is humanity. You're then his father when you meet him.

Now listen to the words as given us in the Book of Samuel, and three words are used in three verses, one after the other, and each word is Olem, translated differently. But first, a promise is made that the man who conquers the enemy of Israel will be set free—the father will be set free. So here comes the man who has conquered the enemy of Israel, the giant Goliath. The king said to his lieutenant Abner, "Abner, whose son is that youth?" and Abner replied, "As your soul liveth, O king, I cannot tell." He said, "Enquire whose son the *stripling* is." No one knows. So he's brought before the king with the head in his hands of the giant, and he said, "Whose son are you, young man?" and he replied, "I am the son of your servant Jesse the Bethlehemite." And now the king's order must be given and the promise fulfilled: The father must be set free. He confesses who his father is. His father, he tells you, is Jesse. Jesse means "I am." That's all that it means. The word "Jesse" is "any form of the verb *to be*"... *I am* (1 Sam. 17:56).

The day will come you will know why it is true God put *eternity* into the mind of man and man can't find it. He has put eternity in such a way that man can't find out what God has done from the beginning until the end. In the end you will; for as the end comes, there's going to be explosion after explosion in that wonderful head of yours, and the thing that was hidden in the beginning will come forward to confront you. Every one will confront you. An entirely different drama begins to unfold within you and the end of this world is at an end for you. The world remains...people think the world is coming to an end...it comes to an end for the individual. It doesn't come to an end for a group of people, like coming to the end of this world, burning it up. No, your world comes to an end when the final drama begins to unfold within you.

So, it was not given to the prophets to know, the prophets who prophesied of the *grace* that was to be yours. Grace is an unmerited gift, an unmerited good. In other words, it is God's gift of himself to you; you can't earn it. So they *heard* of this grace. For grace is mentioned in the Old Testament, too. You read it in Zechariah—in fact all through the Bible—but in Zechariah, they were about to put on the very top of the stone of the temple—the 4th chapter, 7th verse of Zechariah—and they do it amidst shouts of "Grace, grace to it." So the temple cannot be finished until Christ is brought forth from humanity. He comes forth singly, one after the other, the same Christ. And he only knows he is Christ when David appears to the individual from whom he comes, and David calls that individual Father. For in the Bible David calls him "Adonay," which means "my Father, my Lord, my God, the Rock of my salvation." So David comes out and he is youth. One of the definitions of Olem is "eternal youth," and when you see him he is an eternally young, beautiful, handsome fellow. It's David, a *single* man.

One night you're going to have this wonderful joy. You will see David in the distance, this radiant being, and when you approach, he is a multitude of nations. And then you know he summarizes and personifies humanity. You will see Jesus Christ and you will know he personifies the gods, the Elohim, all of us. Therefore, who are you when he personifies all? We are the Elohim who fell asleep for a purpose. We emptied ourselves of our primal form; and took upon ourselves the limitation of this that was hidden in the mind of man, in our eternal sleep having passed through this eternal death to awaken to eternal life; expanded beyond what we were when we emptied ourselves of the eternal form, and then took upon ourselves the limitation of the human form. He is not concerned with John Brown, Neville Goddard—these are parts of the eternal structure of this time-block. They are all parts of it, the whole vast world.

Have you ever had the experience of looking up and seeing on your mind's eye, on the screen of your face, inwardly, the block? There isn't a thing you can think of that isn't there and it comes out, it actually comes out and takes on a three-dimensional quality. You might be lost in it if you don't know what you're doing. You can become completely lost, like an insane person. But if you know what you're doing, you are in control of all as to bring them out of this concentrated block. And everyone mentioned in scripture is in that block, and you can bring them out in different combinations, different relationships, different, well, father-son relationships, man-wife relationships, any relationship. All the enemies in the world you can bring out. If you don't know what you are doing, it will scare you to death, because they become alive the minute you detach them from the block. They take on a three-dimensional reality, and become alive, and then they start. But if you know what you're doing, then you know these words also from Qoheleth in the 4th chapter, 15th verse: "I have seen all the living that move about under the sun, as well as that *second youth*, who is going to stand in his place; there was no end to the people; and *he* was over all of them. Yet those who will come after will not rejoice in him. This too is vanity and a chasing of the wind" (Eccles.).

Now, this is what I mean "he is over all of us." Take the block and fragment it,—as we are fragmented now, this is the fragmented block—and he is over all, animating all. The day will come you will have the experience and taste of the power of the age to come. You will take a section of that animated block and stop it; and it can't move—men can't move, birds can't fly, leaves can't fall—everything is frozen as though made of marble. And then you will release it from within you and it will move and continue to fulfill its purpose. After that, the faith you had before, which you would argue to support, you know now that faith is not justified through an argument but only through an experience. Now you know, you know what it means now to have life in yourself. For the purpose of it all, when the time is fulfilled and *then* you come forward from this block, you have now life in yourself. Until then you thought you had life in yourself. And your friends died and you buried them. You knew the day would come that you would die and they would bury you. You thought we were living beings independent of something on the outside. We had no idea that we were being animated from without until this moment in time as you begin to awake, you, too, taste of the power of the age to come. And tomorrow, you'll know that 15th verse of that 4th chapter of Ecclesiastes: "I saw all the living that move about under the sun, and that second youth who will stand in his place" and control. "Then I saw no end to the people; and he was over all of them. Yet those who will come after will not rejoice in him"—because they won't believe it. They will not for one moment believe that we are all being animated from without.

And yet, while we're animated we can choose and select if we know of these states. Without seeing the state you can still choose. You can choose the state of health, the state of wealth, the state of fame, the state of anything; and that state is personified in you when you see it. You can choose the state of poverty. So when Blake saw the block, he said to himself, now you know why "I do not consider either the just or the wicked to be in a supreme state, but to be states of the sleep which the soul may fall into in its deadly dreams of good and evil." So you have a deadly dream of being taken advantage of? You're right in a state. Someone doesn't like you? You're in another state. Someone likes you? You're in another state. And all of these are states and they're personified on the inside. If your eye would only open you would see it. But until the eye is open, you don't even know they are states and they're all hidden within you. So he has hidden eternity in the mind of man.

But the day will come that *second* youth...the second youth is Jesus Christ. David is collective humanity. Out of it, comes Jesus Christ and knows that he came out of man; but man is his offspring; man is his father. And man is forced by the personification called David to call him "Father." And he knows *now* that he is the Lord; yet no way of knowing he was the Lord until David appeared and called him Lord. For David is God's beloved: "This is my son, today I have begotten thee" (Ps. 2:7). That's humanity. He's in love with humanity. And now the gods are buried in humanity: "God became man that man may become God." Not the reverse, man didn't become God that God may become man; God became man that man may become God. He is pulling himself out of humanity, but individually when he pulls himself out. He pulls himself out of humanity and humanity is personified as David, so David appears before him, right out of his skull. It explodes like a real explosion and he stands right before you and calls you "Adonay," calls you "my Father." And only then do you know who you *really* are.

Everyone is going to have this experience, for the very simple reason God planned it as it would come out and as it would be consummated. For the very simple reason you can't earn it. No man can earn it. That's why we have today among our theologians the argument: Surely man can do something to earn it. You can't earn it. It was God's predetermined plan to actually sink himself in death. The mystery of life through death: "Unless a seed falls into the ground and dies, it remains alone. If it falls into the ground and dies, it brings forth much." And so God actually entered death's door, the human skull, and laid down in the *grave* of man, and shared ___(??) with man from within all of his visions of eternity, all of his nightmares, until the time is fulfilled. It must be fulfilled like a pregnancy. The child is conceived, but there must be an interval to fill time. And when that time is fulfilled, out will come Christ Jesus, for "Christ *in* man is the hope of glory." Were he not *in* man he could not *emerge* from man, and he has to emerge from David. So the Bible begins in the New Testament:

"The book of the genealogy of Jesus Christ, son of David," because that is prophecy. He comes out of humanity, but because humanity is the beloved *son* of God, it can't be the father of *God*. So, comes the reversal, and David automatically makes the statement, "My Father." And so, out of man comes God. And know "ye are gods"? Then bring my beloved Son before me and let me call him "Son" and let him call me "Father." And it happens exactly like that.

So, I hope you know what God placed in the mind of man. Buried in you is really eternity, but put in such a way that you cannot find out from the beginning to the end what God has done. Only in the end you will know. But God isn't taken by surprise. To God all events are present, including the end of all things, as told us in 1st Peter. The end of all things is before him now: He sees you as Christ Jesus. He isn't waiting for it; he knows the end. But you are immersed in the body of death for that purpose. So he sees not only all things coexisting, he sees the end of all things, and the end of all is Christ Jesus. "I am the Alpha and the Omega; I am the beginning and the end; the first and the last" (Rev.1:17;21:6).

So here, Paul tells us and Peter tells us, in fact, they all, if you read the Epistles: "Set your hope fully on the grace that is coming to you at the revelation of Jesus Christ" (1 Pet. 1:13). Revelation to Paul meant the unveiling of God, an act of God in self-revealing: he unveils himself *in* you *as* you. He set up a series of events, mystical events by which he unveils himself in you. So I cannot conceive of any hope that man should dwell upon more than that moment in time when the time is fulfilled and Jesus Christ unveils himself within you. Because Qoheleth said, I made money; I amassed more money than anyone in the world; I was the wisest of all men, and yet my end was like the poor man. My end, the wise man, was like the fool's and all these things were vanity of vanities, all is vanity. He knew tomorrow someone would come and build up much from the same block of time buried in the mind of man.

So tonight, if you believe me that everything is within you, you can single out the state of success. Well, how would you be successful? You wear it as you would this suit of clothes. You put it on and feel natural in the mood of being successful, just put it on. Just as God wears man, you wear the state and you can put it on. So you single out anything you want in this world and dare to assume that you are already that which you desire to be until the desire has been appeased. You don't long any more. You feel it, you feel natural. Now the time will fulfill itself in that too. All things take time. Time is a facility for change in experience; space is a facility for experience. But a change in experience takes time, so all changes take time. So you wear a change of mood and it's going to take its time. It may take a day, it may take a week, it may take a month. But that mood I now call (in Habakkuk) the vision. You visualize yourself by seeing yourself reflected in the faces of friends. They see you as the man you want them to see. Now, "*that* vision has its own appointed hour: it ripens, it will flower. If to you it seems long, wait, for it is sure and it will not be late"...not for its own appointed hour (2:3). And so the feeling of success has *its* appointed hour. For you change from not being successful into that which *is* successful. Alright, that shows you that time is a facility for *changes* in experience. But that now has its own little appointed hour. Don't you try to aid it. It's like a pregnancy. You don't aid a pregnancy after you discover that you are pregnant. In other words, one thing bear in mind, in spite of all the good men in the world who try to convince you that you've got to do something about it—all you do is make your selection and wear it. You were born physically by the action of powers not your own; you will be born spiritually by the action of powers beyond your own. You didn't have a thing to do with your physical birth. And you aren't going to have anything to do with your spiritual birth when the time is fulfilled, because God in you has impregnated you; he's one with you, and that pregnancy is taking place.

But the prophets didn't know it and they were confused. So this is what they said: "In the last days scoffers will come scoffing…and they will say, 'Where is the promise of his coming?' For ever since the fathers fell asleep, all things have continued as they were from the beginning of time" (2 Pet. 3:3). They didn't know how near they were to the fullness of time. And so, they will say, "Where is the coming?" They are looking for a man to come on the outside. No man comes on the outside. Resurrection is an event happening in this earthly experience of man the individual; it's right here. So when he comes, he comes *in* the individual. He doesn't come out of the clouds trying to conquer the world; he comes *in* the individual. And the drama as I have described it is true, just as I have told you, and it's all related to things told in the Bible. It's a true story, and the day will come *you* will be called to testify to the truth of God's word. That's all that you are going to testify to: Is it true? You will have the experience. You will go into the world and *testify* to the truth of his word. It's all true.

So this that is buried in you sets you free, really, even though it turns to ash. The greatest success in the world turns to ash, because he has to leave it into the hands of one who didn't earn it. But it doesn't mean you shouldn't do it. Why not select the best, even though you're going to leave it anyway. I know that I must leave behind me my library, but I'm enjoying it while I am here. And I hope I can name the ones that I would think would enjoy it the most when I turn my eyes from this sphere, and let them have the library. That it cost me a fortune and it's a lovely hand-picked library, yes,

I know that. But someone tomorrow will enjoy the library. And any stocks and bonds that I may have, I have a daughter, a son, and wife, so they will get them. I don't regret that. And so, what does it matter if you have to leave your toil and the amassed fortune to someone else who didn't toil for it?

But he [Ecclesiastes] regretted that, because he couldn't see the end. He saw only recurrence—this whole thing is going over and over and over—and when is it going to come to an end? Let it come to an end even though there is no real determined end. But there *was* an end hidden and he didn't see it. He knew by the words that he had received that he had put Olem in man's mind, he knew that; and Olem meant something hidden, something hidden away out of sight, something veiled, a youth. Well, what would a youth do in my mind? He didn't know that David was the collective humanity. He didn't know David would one day explode out of his Imagination and stand before him and call him Father. No one knew it until it first happened. And so, we are told: He is the first witness, the first who came from the dead, Jesus Christ. He rose from the dead, and came out of humanity, who, may I tell you, is dead.

Someday you'll see it and you'll stop them. You'll walk the street and you'll be able to arrest anything in motion and you'll know the words: "He was over all of them. I saw all living that move about under the sun, and then I saw that second youth who came to stand in his place, and he is over all of them." So then that second youth is born in you...because you are the Father of collective humanity, that's the second youth. For, the choice of God is always the second. First of all, you had Cain. He rejected Cain and took Abel. Then you came down and you had Isaac. He was the second, Ishmael was the first. He rejected Ishmael, took Isaac. Then you had Esau and Jacob. He rejected Esau and took Jacob. Manasseh and Ephraim... rejected Manasseh, took Ephraim. And all the way down there is a reversal of order.

So here comes humanity out of which Christ Jesus comes, and humanity *is* his father because he came out of him. For the words are: "I will raise up your son after you who will come forth from your body. I will be his father and he shall be my son" (2 Sam. 7:12). That's humanity, David. When the son comes out, David calls him Father. So who did God bring out? He brought out himself, so the son could then say, "I and my father are one" (John 10:30). He brings himself out of humanity and he does it individually. So you bear in mind, think of David as humanity. God is in love with humanity, and so in love with it he went in unto humanity and buried himself, laid himself down in humanity, in all the unnumbered Elohim. Then he comes out of humanity bearing the fruit of that long sleep of death. And now he returns to eternal life, expanded beyond that which he was when he emptied himself and buried himself in humanity.

So tonight, you single out a dream, a noble dream, for yourself or a friend. And trust it. Assume that your friend is telling you that he is, or she is, what they want to be...something that is lovely. Just assume it and feel natural in that assumption and see how it works. Because that block is completely interwoven and related. When you see it, it's completely interwoven: "All things by a law divine in one another's being mingle." But here they are completely congealed and you gather them one by one. Blake called this the house of Los, because he fragmented it; he saw them all in lovely objective forms like statues. You can too.

The other day my wife said in a vision of hers she saw panels at the back of the room. She didn't count them, but there were many, many panels and she was glued to just observing the panels. As she became lost in observation, just the panels, forms detached themselves from the panels and they came out into the room. Every one gave forth a form. At first it seemed to be a delightful thing, a very happy occurrence, something wonderful. The more it moved into the dancing form, the more it began to dance, the more she realized this is horror, this is sheer hell. And then for a moment... maybe she panicked for a moment...and then they all went right back into their panels and there they remained. You know what the word "panel" is in Hebrew? The same word as that which we translate "rib": And he took a rib and made something out of it. The word "rib," Zella, is panel. And so he draws out a rib and it becomes a living form. But it went back in when she lost control of her Imagination. She completely forgot how these things came out of sheer dead panels and became alive. Then she panicked, and they all went right back and assumed their previous patterns of that panel.

And the day will come you'll do it. Until that moment in time when you leave this age and leave it forever because it has accomplished its purpose: You wore it, you went through hell with it, and you came out of it expanded in consciousness. For God is truth and truth is an ever-increasing illumination. There is no limit to expansion; there's only a limit to contraction. There's no limit to translucency; there's only a limit to opacity. So when you come out of this opaque state, you'll be more luminous than you were when you entered it and more expanded than you were when you entered it. And then tomorrow, we, together as one being, yet without loss of identity, we will map the fifth act for a still greater luminosity and expansion of being.

Now let us go into the Silence.

* * *

Q: Do we have to come back to this earth experience?

A: You don't need it.

Q: Well, this recurrence…until we have all these experiences?

A: Not a thing dies in this world. The little flower that blooms once blooms forever. Everything is alive here because God is wearing it. But when he has accomplished his purpose, where he comes forth from it, and knows he is the father who sank himself into it by reason of his Son who calls him "Father," then he enters an entirely different age where we all enter expanded. We go back in our primal form, our pre-natal garment. But here, I cannot tell you how long. But it has its own appointed hour and it's not going to be late. Blake says 6,000 years, but who knows? This night you could be 5,999. You do not know. He claims it takes 6,000 years for the hatching-out process. That's what Blake said and he said it at least two dozen times in all of his works. He said, "I know it from my own experience." He, speaking from experience: "I walk up and down the 6,000 years and it's all before me—present, past and future seen." And he pleads with them "to listen carefully to the voice of the bard who present, past and future sees, whose ears have heard the Holy Word and walked among the ancient trees." And so he said that he actually did it and he knows it's 6,000—incubation 6,000 years. And the prophets wondered and wondered, and suddenly it happened. It comes like a thief in the night. So we have no spiritual doctors to look on our pregnancy and tell us when we may expect it. Because they're going to judge from appearances and think it should happen to what they consider the nice person, what they consider good by outward appearances; and someone in rags may be this night right on the night of delivery. But I cannot endorse the 6,000 years; I do not know from experience. But as far as this block, we don't leave it until we come out and come out as Christ Jesus.

Q: (inaudible)

A: ___(??) I'm not speaking of reincarnation. You never lose your identity, not in eternity. You could be a poor man or be a rich man and still be John Brown. You could be a known person or unknown person and still be John Brown. I am speaking of infinite states but worn by one being wearing it. You are identified, you are individualized, and you tend forever toward greater and greater individualization. You don't lose identity. The gods are known and we are known to each other individually.

Q: I should think that your state would improve. I don't mean in a material way.

A: But, my dear, states don't change, states are permanent. We, the occupant, move through states. For instance, this is California, I'm in Southern California. If I leave tonight for Chicago, California remains to be occupied by anyone who wants to live here. It remains permanent relative to Chicago, but I, the occupant, the pilgrim, I go to Chicago and then partake of all that Chicago offers. So, I move into a state and the state is unlovely, but I am the wearer of it. I am not transformed by the state I'm wearing. I am having an experience. But the being wearing it could tomorrow, observing what he's doing now is a foolish state, get out of it. So, many a person tonight who is a very, very wealthy person who would brag of his wealth, he could tomorrow, not knowing he's only in a state, find himself poorer than a church mouse...and wouldn't know he's in a state. My father had a saying, "Money doesn't care who owns it." Doesn't care who owns it.

Q: (inaudible)

A: No, it didn't begin...in the sense...for instance, they are always coming in. This is for hatching, and God is always entering his world to expand himself. He's *always* coming in. So it's not a mass exodus; it's an individual journey. As we are told in Isaiah: "I will gather you one by one, O my people of Israel." One by one, you're so unique, you're so altogether wonderful in the eyes of the gods who are waiting for you that you can't be gathered in groups. It's a rejoicing in heaven when that stone is put upon the temple, and they call it "grace, grace to it"—and you are it. And it's all a gift.

Q: Explain the statement you made "animated from without."

A: All right, there's a story told in the Book of John, the grand trial, that in a number of months we will enact it on Earth, and forget that it's only *portrayed* here. The drama takes place *in* man. So he's brought before Pilate and Pilate asks him a question, and he wouldn't answer Pilate. Pilate asks him, "Who are you?" and he wouldn't answer. He said, "So you will not speak to me? Do you not know that I have the power to set you free, or to crucify you?" And he answered, "You have no power over me were it not given to you from above; therefore he who delivered me into your hands he has the greater sin" (John19:9-11). It is from above. And you, tomorrow, will stand in the place of the second youth, and you will be in control, putting them through the paces, while they dream either noble dreams or ignoble dreams. But it's an animated wheel from without. And yet within it all, we are free to change states.

Q: Do you think that after man has laid down one garment here that he comes back and dons another right away, or is there a period of rest in between the wheel of recurrence?

A: First of all, we think that reality is confined to this Earth and it ends where our senses cease to register it. It doesn't. The world into which I go often and meet people who are supposedly dead, they are just as real and just as bigoted and just as limited as they were when they were here. I meet people...there is no transforming power in death, what we call death. You're going to meet people dreaming—you dream there as you dream here. We think this is not a dream, but *that* may be a dream. This doesn't *seem* to be a dream because the dream is so vivid it becomes objective. But when you are in a dream, and the dream is real, it's objective too. And when you return and contemplate the dream, you say, well, it *was* subjective because now it isn't objective. But while *in* it when you thought of this world, this would be subjective and that objective. Subjectivity and objectivity are wholly determined for the individual by the level on which his consciousness is focused.

And so, if my consciousness is focused there, well, I haven't transformed myself unless I change my state. Transformation in the true sense comes when Christ is born in man. And there are only two births spoken of in scripture—one here and one spiritual. One from below which is called the birth from Hagar; and one from above, called Sarah or called Jerusalem. Jerusalem from above and Jerusalem from below—one from the womb of woman and one from the skull of generic man—and so they speak of two births. But it would be no earthly good to me to cease to be Neville and become, well, some other being. I have met so many people in this present life ___(??) who played the part of Napoleon. Well, Napoleon was only a few years ago, and all these are my contemporaries and they all were Napoleon. Well, no wonder he went mad. They're all in it playing Napoleon. If one person told me in a letter a thousand years ago that he knew he *would* play Napoleon, or if someone told me, say, before I was born...but not all the people in my generation all played that one character, because we only had one Napoleon. We have quite a few in the madhouse, I know, but I mean only one in history. And they all played Napoleon. A friend of mine said to her husband one day, "You know, George, I just feel that I must have been some great lady in the court of Louis the 15th or Louis the 16th or 14th. I can just see myself now sweeping down the stairs." He said, "So can I, my dear, with a little pail in your hand."

Goodnight.

IN A VISION OF THE NIGHT

2/06/64

Tonight's subject "In a Vision of the Night," this title is taken from the 33rd chapter of the Book of Job: "In a vision of the night, when deep sleep falls upon man, while he slumbers on the bed, then he opens the ear of man and seals his instruction" (verse 15). Throughout the Bible, beginning in Genesis and going right through to Revelation, there are stories of the dream. It's man's contact with God. We're told in Numbers: "If there be a prophet among you, I the Lord will make myself known unto him in a vision, and I will speak with him in a dream" (12:6). In the beginning, the great dreamer who was sold into Egypt, one who was called Joseph—and they spoke of him as the dreamer: "Behold, this dreamer cometh" (Gen.37:19). It was his dream that saved the world from starvation, for he interpreted the dream. Most of us are past masters at misinterpreting the dream, but he understood the symbolism of the dream; and because he interpreted wisely, and Pharaoh acted upon it, then they could put aside in their fat years enough to save them from their lean years, when everything simply turned to dust. And so, we mustn't discount the dream.

But may I tell you, the night dream where you have no control over it is a parable. The earthly story of that parable is secondary to its meaning no matter how simple the dream is...if it is a dream. Not the waking dream; we'll touch that afterwards. The waking dream is the most wonderful thing for the control and the change of the circumstances of life...that's the *waking* dream. But the night dream where you're not in control and you simply are recording an unfolding drama, God is simply speaking to you through the medium of the night dream. Here we find that when Jesus was on trial just as Pilate took his seat to judge him a message arrived from Pilate's wife which read: "Have you nothing to do with that righteous man, for I have been much troubled today in a dream because of him" (Mat.27:19). Now, the dream is not related, in other words, it's not told, I wish it were. But it's not recorded what she dreamt, only "Have nothing to do with that righteous man, for I have been much troubled about him today in a dream."

Then we find in the Book of Daniel when the king wondered what was the nature of the dream and he said to him, There is a God in heaven who makes known mysteries, and he has spoken unto you, O king (2:28). And then he tells him how God spoke to him. He said, he's told you of the latter things. And the latter things are these, in a dream, in a vision of the night, that's how God speaks to man. When you put your head on that bed and you slumber and lose consciousness here, if you can recall it, God has told you something that really is important, *if* you can recall it. And the most simple thing in the world has meaning, deep meaning.

So, when I opened here last November, on my way back from New York I decided to give you a subject that—I knew I'd get the majority on opening night whether you ever came again or not, at least I could tell you what I found—and the subject was "We Have Found Him," the very one for whom the whole vast world is seeking. I found him, and he's true and he *is* risen; and he's rising in all of us. And so I tried that night to explain the great mystery of Christ. On the way out, I greeted many at the door, and one gentleman in particular—I knew exactly what he meant when he said it—he said, "I'll be seeing you sometime." But I knew in the depth of my soul what he really meant to convey: "If you ever see me again, you're lucky." That's what he meant. Well, I haven't seen him so far. I knew exactly what he meant: he was not going to allow me to interfere with his preconceived misconception of Christ. No, I could not disturb that misconception. He'd come for the law. For from this platform he heard the law, and through the hearing of the law and applying it he came from behind the eight ball where he owed a thousand dollars into eighty-odd thousand dollars with no investment, but no investment. Before he did it, his mother and his brother told him, "You mustn't go to that man; that isn't Christian." Because they go to their church, some denomination of the Christian faith twice or three times a week, and they sing all the lovely old hymns, and so, they're trying to persuade him not to go, not to go here, come with them. But he was desperate, needed money, so he came here, which in the eyes of the mother and the brother was simply coming to the devil. When he won the eighty-odd thousand dollars, then they forgave him, and all joined in rejoicing that because of their constant visits to their church, God was merciful and therefore sent it through him, even though it came from the voice of the devil.

However, since then I have been trying, as much as I can, to reveal to you the mystery of Christ. So let me share with you one of last night. It was a very quiet evening. I broke the pattern and looked at TV, a thing I rarely do, but I looked at that wonderful story of Abraham Lincoln and thoroughly enjoyed it. It ran ninety minutes, and then my wife and I discussed for another three-quarters of an hour; and then I turned in. So I must have been sound asleep before ten...it was a very quiet evening. And during the night, this is what God said to me. I found myself in an enormous ocean liner, huge ocean liner, and looking out to sea I saw an enormous fish the size of a dolphin. It didn't jump out of the water as dolphins do—if you've ever seen them, they simply play, they jump and go back into the water like the porpoise—but it did what the flying fish does. It jumped out of the water and sailed as it were for about a hundred yards, and then dove in again. Up it would come and then fly off for about a hundred yards, and dive in again. I noticed this behavior of this fish, it was a marvelous fish. So I turned to the passengers, I tried to show them the fish, but no one could see it. I pointed out the fish, I said, "Can't you see it?" No they couldn't see it. Then I turned to my wife, I said to her, "Don't you see it, dear?" She said, "No I can't see it." I said, "Watch my finger, I'll point it" and so I said, "Watch where I point it, at the very angle, and see if you can't see it." Then she said, "Oh, yes, *now* I can see it" and the minute she said, "I can now see it, yes" then I woke.

Well, Jesus Christ has always been symbolized as a fish, the big fish. In fact, the letters in Greek for fish gives us the initials of the sentence: "Jesus Christ, Son of man, Savior." That's exactly how it's spelled. The initials of the word in Greek give us the sentence: "Jesus Christ, Son of man, Savior." I knew that I have found him...tried to tell...God confirmed it in the depths. No one could see it. I was showing the fish and no one could see it. I wanted my wife so much to see it, so I turned to her, "Don't you see it, dear?" "No, I don't see it." And so, until she saw it I did not stop watching that fish as it came out, started, and then go down; he came out and started, playing all over on the horizon as it were; and finally, she said, "Oh yes, now I see it," and then I woke. So he revealed to me the truth of what I tell you concerning the mystery of Christ, for in all the books it is the great fish. The very last act, when he comes onto the shore and they are cooking fish, it is a symbol: he offers *himself* as the *big* fish to feed the whole vast world. He is the fish.

And so, I tell you what I've told you about the mystery of Christ is true. I certainly wouldn't fool you on so deep and tender a thing in the hearts of all of us. But I have found the *true* Christ, not the false Christ where hundreds of millions worship him. I found *that* Christ that made you alive, *that* Christ dreams with you, and will be with you until the very last moment when he awakens you as himself. That's the Christ of whom I speak. So I tell you, in the depths of your soul when it comes up in the form of a dream, you may not be able to interpret it but don't discount it. It's a story from God in the depths of your soul to you. And the day will come, it will get more and more clear to you, and you'll be able to interpret the symbolism of the dream.

But throughout...there's a little couplet, a little English couplet: "The fish fried was Christ that died." It's always meant much to me, "The fish fried was Christ that died." You find this all through the great poems and the great works of the masters, the story of the fish. They say that of all the symbols in the Catacombs the most numerous is that of a fish. On the Pope's crown you find the symbol of the Pisces, you find two tied together, so they understand the symbol. But whether they understand the significance of Christ or not that I don't know. But now, we'll take tonight in a more practical form where you can control it. It's the same Christ... if you control it on the surface of your being. Still you may go to bed, but don't go to sleep if you control it.

Let me share with you now the story told by a man that is respected the world over. He's gone now a few years, his name is Carl Jung. Well, Jung is among the great giants of the mind. If you name three, you could not omit the name of Jung in any list of three names when it comes to the understanding of the workings of the human mind, as a great analyst, a great psychiatrist. Well, he said, "One night I lay awake thinking of the sudden death of a friend whose funeral took place yesterday." He said, "I was deeply concerned, and suddenly I felt that he was in the room. It seemed to me he was standing at the foot of the bed, not as an apparition rather it seemed like an inner vision of him. And then, as I felt his presence there and saw him inwardly as it were, because of my work I had to do something about it, and so I explained it to myself as a fantasy. But then I said to myself, suppose it's not fantasy? You have no proof that it is or is not fantasy, why not give him the benefit of the doubt and credit him with reality?" He said, "No sooner had I made the decision to credit him with reality than he turned and walked towards the door. I am watching him walk towards the door; then he beckoned me to follow him. So I in my Imagination followed him, and he led me through the garden onto the road, and then he led me to his home, several hundred yards away.

"When we got to his house he led me in, into his study. Then he went forward, stood on a stool and reached up and pointed out a volume, a second book of a set of five. They were all bound in red. But he pointed to the second one on the second shelf from the top. He's standing on a stool. As he pointed to the second book, all bound in red, then the vision came to an end, and I remained pondering on this strange experience. It was so strange and exciting to me that the next morning I thought I must investigate, so I walked up to my neighbor's home and asked the widow whether she would allow me to go into the library and look up something, which she willingly granted. I got into the library and there under the book shelf is the stool, the very stool that I saw in my vision. I stood on the stool to reach the second shelf, and there were the five books bound in red, translations of the novels by Emile Zola. I picked the second one out to read its title, and its title was on death, *The Legacy of Death* was the title." Now, he said, the contents didn't mean much to me, but the title was most significant in connection with my experience, *The Legacy of Death.*

But in the entire story, as he tells it, the important thing for us, trying to control this power of the mind, our wonderful human Imagination which is Christ, was that sentence in it: "The minute I decided to credit him with reality then, and no longer fantasy, he turned and walked to the door, and he beckoned me to follow him." But he could not move while he entertained the thought of fantasy. But the minute that he credited that with reality then reality took shape, walked to the door, and beckoned him to come. He, in Imagination—the body is still on the bed—he, in Imagination, follows and he leads him through the garden, onto the road, and several hundred yards away up to his friend's home, his own home which he had just vacated through death. And then pulled out...by his finger pointed out the second volume. It *was* the second volume, it *was* on the second shelf from the top, and it *was* bound in red. And the stool was there. Well, that cannot be coincidence. A stool, the second shelf from the top, the second book in, in a series of five, and the title of the second to be *The Legacy of Death.* How can you brush it off as mere coincidence? You can't do it. So he assured himself of survival.

But in reading that, what impressed me...because I've always known survival, nothing dies as far as I'm concerned. So I know that nothing dies, so I'm not looking for assurance of survival. I'm not looking for someone to encourage me that those I love do not cease to be because they've gone through the experience that men call death. I am so confident of *all* surviving. God is a God of the *living*, not the dead. "I am the God of the living" said he, "not of the dead" (Lk.20:38). So everything lives in its form where it was at the moment of the transition. No transforming power in death. But, what impressed me was, it did not move. He entertained the thought "It's not an apparition, but in my work I must treat it and explain it to myself as a fantasy; and here I'm seeing it on the *inner* side of my being. It's not on the outside, but its objective to me from within; it's an inner vision of him. And then I said, No, I'll give him the benefit of the doubt, and so I will credit him with reality." He had no sooner said, I will credit him on the inside, I'll credit him with reality, than his friend turned, walked to the door and beckoned him to follow him. And he said, Alright, I'll explore, so in his Imagination he followed him. You can do it. You can go with it, and actually move from where you are right upon this floor, through the garden path, onto the road, and up the street. You can do it. Anyone can do it if you are willing to credit the thing with reality.

Now, it brings me to this. You sit down to change your world, you want something better than you have, and so you begin to conjure a certain scene that would imply the fulfillment of your dream. You begin to conjure it. The average person cannot control their mind long enough to go from A to B. If, for instance I assume that I am what reason denies and my senses deny, and at that very moment of assumption I think of all the debts and what people know me to be...I take it off. That doesn't fit, it's like a tight shoe, it just doesn't fit me; so I take off the assumption. If I could only *put on* the assumption! Now what's the next step? I assume that I am the one that I want to be. If it were true, my friends would know it. I wouldn't hide it from them. In fact, it should be so obvious if it were true that they should see it. Well, the next step, the B step, would be to bring them into my mind's eye and let them see me as they would see me were it true.

Now, what's the next step? Well, C...could they keep that secret? No, they would have to discuss it with friends. I would eavesdrop and listen to their discussion of the good fortune that befell me. And so I would listen..."Have you heard the good news?" one would say to the other. "You know what has happened to him? Who would have thought that he could ever get that?" Well, listen to it...then they tell a story. I'm conjuring the whole thing, I know I am, but can I endow it with reality and *not* say it's a fantasy? It's not an apparition, because not a person is before me, not a thing is before me, it's not an apparition. So, I would say it is fantasy, sheer fantasy, all conjured in my Imagination. But if I could say what Jung said, I will give it now the benefit of the doubt and credit it with reality; and the minute I credit it with reality, I'm believing. "Whatever you ask in faith, *believe* that you receive it, and you will" (Mat.21:22). That's the story.

So man, if he can only control his Imagination between A and B, doesn't have to go to C, just from A to B. Take the first step: You assume the end. The end is where we begin: "In my end is my beginning." So I assume the end, I *am* the man that I want to be. And were it true, I would be known by my friends first, so I bring them into my mind's eye and they see me. I let them see me. If I want to talk with them, accept their congratulations and not duck but really hold my head high and proud of what has happened to me; alright, accept the congratulations. And then I turn from that to the third step, and let them talk between themselves, and I'm listening. All of that is making it *real* to me. And then I go on in my wonderful state that it is true. I begin to make plans of the things I would do and am going to do now. And then, in this simple little drama I now credit it, I give it reality. And then see and test God: "Come test me and see if I will not open the windows of heaven and pour out a blessing so great you haven't room on earth to receive it" (Mal. 3:10). Come test me, test the Lord and see. As we're told, "Do you not realize that Jesus Christ is *in* thee?—unless, of course, you fail to meet the test" (2 Cor. 13:5). I hope you realize that *we* have not failed. And so, we must test it, and test it by giving it reality. I try to give it all the tones of reality, all the sensory vividness that I can muster. And when I do it, it works.

If I never hear from one who has asked help from me, it would make no difference to me. They may never come back. Because I'm told—I try to believe implicitly in my scripture—"Were there not ten of you? And where are the other nine? Only one has returned. Where are the other nine?" (Luke 17:17). So if the nine do not come back, that's part of scripture. They will accept it; it's going to happen so naturally in the lives of the ones who received it that they're going to say, "Well, it would have happened anyway." And so they do not come back to say thank you. And so I know that scripture is true and, therefore, one in ten will say thank you and the nine will not. Therefore, why look for them to ask...I never ask if it has happened, because to me it happened at the moment I did it. As far as I am concerned that's when it happened and I'm not looking to see confirmation. That's how it works.

So this is a controlled dream when you haven't lost it into the depths of the soul. So I teach the law in the controlling of one's Imagination, by simply conceiving a scene which if true would imply the fulfillment of the dream...*if* true. Now, you conceive it, enact it in your Imagination, then credit it with reality, and then let it go. Don't raise a finger to make it so, just let it go. I see faces here this night in the audience, many of you have proved it 100%, many of you. If you have failed in one little thing, you are not doubtful of the law because you have already proved it. You know that in some strange way you haven't in this peculiar incident done the thing that you should do; you haven't given it the reality that you should. Act upon it, see it vividly, enact it naturally, give it the tones of reality, and let it go. You can do it in the most detailed manner...and I do like detail. Don't say, "Well, he knows best, therefore, if he knows I should get it then let him be the judge." That's passing the buck.

Someone said to me, "Can I ask for a certain sum of money?" I said, "Certainly...for a definite sum of money." Well, she said, "My take-home pay would be so much and I want a hundred dollars net." Now this goes back many years ago, today, undoubtedly, she's making two hundred or more...I hope so. This goes back many years ago. She was in my Bible class in New York City, and she said, "Alright, what I will do, I'll conceive a scene" and this is what she did. She was a seamstress and a part-time designer, but mostly a seamstress—but she was sometimes called upon to do a little design work. And she averaged in the sixties, sixty-five, sixty-six dollars a week. But she wants to take home a hundred dollars a week, not sixty-six; and then have them deduct her taxes, she wanted to take home a hundred net. So she took up the envelope, and she could feel the envelope, she could hear it tear, she tore it, she shook the contents out, she could smell money, and she counted off the money, just counted it off. And to her that was real. This is on a Friday. On a Saturday, the phone rang—she lived at a hotel—and the phone rang and a lady called from the lobby asking her to come down and see her. She asked her, "What is it all about?" Well, she said, "I would like to see you. Your name has been recommended" so she came downstairs and it was sealed that day to start working for her the following Monday. And she said, "I want a hundred dollars to take home net." She said, "Alright, you'll take home a hundred dollars net" and she started at the figure that she had predetermined. It should have taught her a lesson now that she knows it, that she cannot anchor herself there. She can go up and up as far as she wants to if she knows it's a law. Because, "By him all things are made, and without him there is nothing made that is made" (John 1:3). Not a thing in this world is made save God made it; and therefore if God did it in this way, she knows who God is now. She tested him and found out who he is. He's not something in the sky. She knows the whole vast world is contained within man; it's not in the sky.

As we told you this past week, quoting this lovely magazine, *The* ___(??) *on Space*, that only the Imagination of man is vast enough to contain the immensity of space. So the whole vast world that you behold, though it *appears* without, it is within, in your Imagination, of which this world of mortality is but a shadow (Blake). So the whole vast world is contained within you. So give reality to anything that you imagine, for that's Christ in action. Your own wonderful human Imagination is Christ in action. Therefore, don't debase him, don't hurt him. You hurt him every time you use your Imagination unlovingly on behalf of anyone in this world or told of another what is unlovely. But every time you use it lovingly you're feeding him, actually feeding him.

So I say to you, you have a dream this night and you can't quite interpret it, alright. Still know that God so loved you that he talked to you. He talked with the medium of a dream. Sometimes it's so simple it needs no interpretation, but other times it comes in the form of a symbol. But if it comes in the form of a symbol, always bear in mind that the earthly story is *secondary* to the meaning of that dream. The dream is always a parable, always a parable, and a parable has one central jet of truth, only one. So, like last night, here comes the fish, this enormous beautiful dolphin. And I've eaten so many of them in my life, but you can't eat a whole dolphin. But if I took all of the dolphins that I've eaten in my life, it would be a school of dolphins. And so, I would eat...really, he said, "Eat my flesh"... so I did, I ate dolphin. But it's only the *symbol* of Christ. But it's a perfect symbol of him: He comes from the depth. What is a greater symbol of the depth than the ocean?

My first mystical experiences were with the ocean. When I was a child, a boy of maybe five or six, I would find myself at night…I knew exactly when it was going to happen, and it scared me to death. I would sit up in bed and hope not to go to sleep, but sleep would come regardless of my efforts. And so, my brothers luckily were with me in the same big bed. So I would get near one of them as I fell into the pillow. But then I would become the ocean, an infinite ocean; and then, not only was I the ocean but I was the wave on the ocean's back. The ocean would toss me, the wave. I was the ocean tossing myself, the wave, and catching myself on my own back, the ocean. It scared me to death. But I could tell the day it was going to happen. I could feel the feeling building within me, a mood taking possession of me, and that night I knew it was going to happen tonight. Well, this lasted all through the years until puberty, and then it vanished. But from my childhood, six or so, right through to puberty, and then the whole thing vanished.

My next mood when ___(??) was not an ocean, it was an ocean of light. That was when I turned twenty. I found myself this night...I was reading a book on the life of Buddha, and suddenly I woke and it was sunup, about eight in the morning. The light was still on and the book was on my chest. So I did a thing I never do, really—that was the first time I can recall ever having done it—read in bed. I go to bed to sleep. But this night, something was going on at the club. I was not allowed to participate because I was a guest of the manager, so I couldn't join the guests of the club because we discriminate in club life as we do in army life. You can't entertain the private with an officer...that's breaking protocol. And so, I was not allowed to dance among those who were members. So having not a thing to do, I took the book, went to bed quite early, and started to read. Next thing I knew it was eight, nine in the morning, and I hadn't turned in the course of the night because the book was still open flat on my chest. So I could not have turned and the light was burning.

So, then I threw myself into a deep trance—I didn't purposely do it—but in that deep, deep trance I became an infinite ocean of liquid light. There was nothing but myself. There was no buoyancy in the sense of a wave, just *living* light. The whole thing was alive and I am it. It had no circumference and yet I am it. And then when I came to, I remembered vividly the experience of the night. How long it lasted, I don't know. When I actually fell into the deep, I don't know. But I only know what happened in that interval. So what greater symbol of that depth of man than the liquid state, the water? Let it come down to the liquid state of golden, liquid, living light. But then in water what lives?—the fish. What could go deeper than the fish? So right in the very depth he symbolizes the Great God, and he's called the Great Fish, Jesus Christ. And when you think of the word fish in Greek and how the letters that spell the word yield for us the initials that when you take the initials it spells out "Jesus Christ, Son of man, Savior," that's no accident.

And so last night, from the depths of my soul came this revelation. Not that I had any doubt in my mind as to the truth of what I told you, for I have experienced it, but for those who may still have a question mark, who cannot quite see it. And what could drive it home to me? For my wife discusses these things with me all of the time; and in my vision of last night, I turned to her as a very last resort because no one could see the fish. In other words, no one could see the *mystery* that is the fish. And so I said, "Don't you see it, dear?" She said, "No, I don't." Then I said, "Follow my finger." I took the index finger and "Wherever I'm pointing it, that's the fish. You watch it now." Then I saw the fish come up, "There he goes," I pointed and she said, "Oh yes, now I see. Now I see." So she *sees* the mystery as explained. But you can explain it and explain it and hope that one sees it, and then you're not quite sure. Not quite sure if they say yes, but did they really see it?

Like the story we told you last Tuesday, the story that "he took eternity and put it into the mind of man" (Eccles. 3:11). How do you take eternity and put it into the mind of man? And then we took...so here's exactly how he does it. First of all, in the Hebraic world, history to them consists of the entire experiences of man, and all the generations of man, but fused into a single being. And that being, being eternity, has to be youth, for youth is eternity, not an old man; and that single being is David. The same word called eternity is called youth, called the lad, called the young man. And so, you turn to the Bible and you find these questions being asked: Who are you, young man? Inquire who is the lad? Whose son is that lad? (1 Sam. 17:56). The whole question is asked about the *father* by asking "Whose son is the lad?" Therefore, if I'm asking about whose son it is, I'm really trying to find out who is the father, because I have promised the father freedom. So I must find the father.

And so, I hoped when I left here that those who attended understood what I meant by David. David is the sum total of humanity. God's love is humanity. God loves man. And take all the generations of men, and all of their accomplishments, all of their experiences, and fuse them into a single man, you have David. So when you've overcome to the point where David appears and *you* are set free, you have actually played the parts; and so you now fall in love with humanity. For humanity fused together into a single being is David. And you are the father of David; therefore, you are the *father* of humanity; and humanity gave you birth. Through all of these troubles you came out of man, for he's born of man…and the very first verse, "The book of the genealogy of Jesus Christ, son of David" (Mat. 1:1). So Jesus Christ is *born* of man, as told you in the 3rd chapter, the 16th verse of Galatians: "And *your* offspring, which is Christ." He's speaking to man: Your *offspring* is Christ. Yet, when I bring him forward, because he actually begot me, and then comes a reversal of order, and he who seemingly was my father now calls me Father and he's my son. So humanity now calls me Father. That's the story.

But, it's a mystery, something that is not an easy thing to grasp. As I've said earlier that it's one of the most difficult things in this world to change the meaning of the event once certain interpretations of that event become fixed in the human mind. So, hundreds of millions who call themselves Christians have fixed in their minds the *event* called Christmas, the *event* called Easter...and that's the event. Well, now when you have the real meaning of it because it's unfolded within you and you experienced it, it's so difficult to change the meaning of that event after an interpretation, a certain interpretation, has been fixed upon that event. And so, they come clouded, like this man that I spoke of earlier. He's not to be disturbed. That is a fixed thing in his mind's eye. He wants no disturbance, because he might wake up tomorrow to find himself on the other side of the veil, and then I misled him. So he doesn't want to take any chances now because a man my age knows that he's nearer that side than he is this side, and so, he's taking no chances. But I'll tell you, what I've told you so far is true because I am speaking not from theory, I'm speaking from experience. And so, if you know anything in this world from experience because you've experienced it, doesn't really matter what the world will say, you *know.* Why?—because you've experienced it. So I know Christ is real, he's true. I know he's *risen.*

I also know he's rising in the whole vast body of humanity; but he rises *individually*.

And so, when he speaks to you this night, should he speak this night, record it simply. A friend of mine gave me a letter last Tuesday night. I have it with my other precious mail at home. When I went home before I retired I read it, and I was thrilled beyond measure. He said, "I quit the job yesterday"—that was the day before he wrote this letter—"so having no way to go for a job today...I had no desire for a job. I quit first, I wasn't fired; I just left the job. But I always rise early from habit, so at 5:30 I awoke, but I didn't get out of bed. There was no reason for getting out of bed, so I remained in bed in that sort of drowsy, dreamy state, not awake, not asleep, and then I heard a voice. It wasn't a deep sonorous voice but a lovely voice speaking to me, and the voice said to me, 'God knows the depth of your soul, and you will receive the promise within, that is, from 100 days to a year.' Then I wrote it down in a half dream state, and when I did wake I remembered writing something down. I picked it up and I read it: 'God knows what is in the depth of your soul and from 100 days to a year you will receive the promise.'" Well, he said, I haven't been able to think of anything but since!

I don't blame him. I don't blame him! What could you ask for in this world comparable to that? And he has no desire to take the platform and teach. He said to me tonight, "But I have no desire to teach." I said, well, you'll teach. So you want to be a musician? Tell the boys in the band...as they're dancing around you can whisper in their ear the message. Well, he'd tell it differently, we're all different, and so you can tell it in a thousand different ways. Blake had no audience; Blake told it in poetry. And so, he told the glorious story in his paintings, in his etchings, he told it in poetry. And he has grown bigger and bigger through the years. After 200 years since his birth to today, he is so *big* today he dwarfs all the people who lived in his age, and yet he was completely unknown when he made his exit from this world. And so, he told *his* story through the medium of the pen. I am trying to tell it through the medium of words from the platform and trying to leave a slight record in a written form. But you can tell it in your own wonderful way.

Another lovely vision was given to me, a different kind of a vision, last Tuesday night. This lady writes a letter, she said, "You know how doting grandparents are over their grand-children." She said, "My little boy"—whom I know quite well, I saw him this past summer, the previous summer, and he's just a tot, three years old— "you know they have playmates and they're very real to them. Well, he has two elephants and he tells me they're gray, and he talks to them, Mumbo and Jumbo, I think are their names."

Well, she said, "one day, it's raining, a very hard rain, so the mother said, 'C'mon, let's run to the car.' As he got into the car she slammed the door; he began to cry in a forceful manner, almost hysterics. She said, 'What have I done?' He said, 'You've closed the door on Mumbo and Jumbo; they can't get in.' So, she said, "I had to open the door and let the two elephants in, and then he placed them in the back of the car, and got them all nice and comfortable." So she said, "I don't want this again, so I better explain to him, in the future if the car is locked and it's raining they can get through the car, we don't have to open the door, so that the next time it happens this way at least they will understand and he will understand that they can make it." But they're so real to him until the little mind is closed around with the flesh. Hasn't yet closed, and so the minute it closes he will laugh at his own stupidity and others will laugh with him. Yet we are living in a fabulous world...and this little boy, only three.

Then she said, "I took him into the place that they rented for him." This lady, the grandmother, went to Hawaii and brought back some lovely Hawaiian music, and he wanted to hear the record. So she brought the records out and among the records she had among them my record, and she said, "It's Neville's record." He said, "I want to hear Neville's record. I know Neville." Well, he does know me, met me last summer. So she said, "But it's all talking and I have some lovely music here from Hawaii. Let us play the music." He said, "No, I want to hear Neville's record." So she puts on the record, and it came to a certain passage, he said, "Neville had a baby," just the most natural thing in the world for him that Neville, a man, should have a baby. And then, a few bars further on, where I held the child in my arms and called it by some endearing term, "How is my sweetheart?" he said to his grandmother, "Neville loves his baby." At the end of the record, he said, "Play it again." She said, "But no, you've heard the record." "I want to hear that record again." So he sits on the floor in a lotus posture like some little Buddha listening to the record, not really grasping it. And so, she had heard the record many times and she knows the record backwards. She got busy about the house when he said, "Shhh," with his hand on his mouth, "Neville's talking." So she had to stop what she had intended to do and come back and listen for the umpteenth time to the record. So these little children living in an entirely different world, but as they grow and the flesh closes around them they're completely shut out. And he has the Imagination to invite these two elephants right in. Maybe tomorrow's Republican, who knows?

But may I tell you, the story of Christ is true, the truest thing in the world. In fact, it is the only thing that is real. There is nothing but Christ, and Christ so loved humanity he actually *became* humanity, and he's crucified on the cross of man. He rose to fulfill the promise and he's *rising* in every one in the world. When he rises out of you, because he came out of you to fulfill the promise—"I will raise up your son after you, who shall come forth from your body. *I* will be his father and he shall be my son" (2 Sam. 7:12). But you're told, you will be his father because he's coming out of you. And then God speaks, "But *I* will be his father and he shall be my son." So he draws his son, himself, out of man, therefore, man gave birth to him. But when he comes out, man calls him "my Lord," "my God, my Father, the rock of my salvation" (Ps. 89:26). He comes right out of man and then the whole reversal of order takes place, and he calls what came out of him his own creator, which it is.

And so, you take the whole vast world, all the generations of men, all their experiences, and fuse it into a single man and you get David. Take all the gods that said "Let *us* make man in our image"—the Elohim, for that's a plural word meaning "gods"—take them all, the unnumbered gods, and fuse them into a single God, and you get Jehovah who is Jesus Christ. People don't believe it, Jehovah is Jesus Christ. They're one, and all of the gods are contained in the one God. These are all humanity, and fused into one man, it's David. All the gods fused into one God, you get Jehovah who is Jesus Christ. You dwell upon it. Last night it was shown to me so vividly, so clearly, all those who traveled with me in that boat, they couldn't see him, couldn't see the fish. But I was determined that at least one should see him, so I turned to my wife, "Can't you see him, dear?" "No." "Now you watch my finger and you watch it. I'm pointing at him. There he is." And finally she said, "Oh, yes, now I see him." When she saw him then I could awake.

Now let us go into the Silence.

* * *

Now first let me call your attention to the book table. The only books that stayed tonight are mine. I was waiting for my friend's book *I Do*, that's Freedom Barry's book, but it hasn't yet arrived. But on the way out, look them over and see if you would like a book.

Above all tonight, don't forget the importance of giving vision reality. For when he gave it reality and credited the thing with reality, things began to move. That is a man who is honored the world over. His books are translated into unnumbered different languages. You can buy them in any town. His works are in Chinese, Japanese, Russian, German, all tongues, that's how honored he is all over the world. And he's giving you his own personal experience.

Now are there any questions, please?

Q: Neville, in that vision of the fish, do you think Bill would be an aspect of yourself or Bill the person?

A: I took it to be one of the persons. I was trying with those who were moving with me. And it was such a vivid thing. First of all, it was a big ship. And Vishnu, the Hindu god of the ___(??) of the world, he, in the guise of a fish, led the ark of man to safety. And so, here was a fish. It's a savior in the guise of a fish, leading the ark, the ship. There were many chairs, and I was on the upper deck with a crowd of people, trying my best to make them see the fish...couldn't see it. I was determined to find someone and here was Bill; she couldn't see it, couldn't see it. "Don't you see it, dear?" "No" and then finally, "You follow me, just as I point, watch exactly as I point"...which is also indicative. I took my index finger of this right hand and I said, "Watch." I'm pointing correctly, "You watch it." She said, "Oh yes, now I see it." You've got to point it so directly and point it so clearly that the mind can see it. For every time Moses is read a veil hangs over their faces. Any other questions, please?

Q: ___(??) asking a little question on symbology. When Moses was working with the people and they made a mistake, or sinned, God brought serpents which bit or killed many people. Then immediately after that, Moses took the serpent as a sign of healing. What was trying to be conveyed there?

A: There's a false Christ and the true Christ, a false spirit and the true Spirit. Here, an obvious false spirit is alcohol, but it is spirit; and the true Spirit is Christ Jesus. The false Christ, in the form of the serpent... and yet Christ is called the *Great* Serpent. So, a serpent that moves up when Moses placed it on a rod—and there is a rod and that rod is your own spinal cord—and you, yourself, will move up that spinal cord of yours into your skull in the same way that Moses lifted up the serpent in the wilderness. But there are unnumbered false prophets in the world, and they are the false serpents that bite and sting and betray the world. That is spoken so clearly in Jeremiah and Ezekiel. These false prophets have gone into the world saying they had visions and they had not; where they talk of a vision that they did not have, and they concoct the vision, and then tell the world that they had a vision. They don't believe in immortality. They haven't the slightest concept of any Christ or God, but while they are here they're going to make hay on the superstitions of men. So they dress themselves up in all kinds of fancy robes, do all kinds of palaver before them, and they'll think, "There's a holy man"; and behind their backs get blind drunk, and do everything, always on the hidden side. If you drink, go into the bar and let the whole world see you. If you smoke, smoke as you walk the street. Whatever you do, don't hide it.

But these fellas would hide everything under the veil of secrecy and betray the world only for a dollar. There isn't a day you don't read in the paper across the country one of them picked up for playing a certain part where he should not be playing...the three fellas always being picked up. In fact, it's gotten to the point of amusing me now. They're all dressed as priests, begging money for their order, and they aren't priests at all. But they know they can get it wearing these robes. And they come before the judge, the judge gives them a nice tongue lashing and then discharges them. They go right out the same day dressed again. But that's only one little order of them. There's one chap here in the city who's always being sued for tens of thousands of dollars. And when he had his wedding, which really should be a funeral, when he had it, all these white doves released...oodles of white doves...a holy man. Six months later, some woman is suing him for $50,000 he took from her illegally. Another one comes up for a hundred thousand illegally...and this wonderful bunch of white doves. He's no better than Khrushchev with his white dove. When he wants to rub you out he has a white dove, holding it up. And so, that mentality, they are the false prophets who have gone into the world. And the Bible speaks of them.

If you know it, and you've actually heard the voice of God, and the whole drama has unfolded *within* you, then do not fear any man in this world. Tell it just as it happened to you. Eventually, after they go through the furnaces of experience, they will come out, because God will not condemn anyone. They'll come out from that phoniness. But what length of time, who knows? How vast, how severe the trials before they come out only God knows; which is merciful, because if he could see what he has to go through for the phony part he's playing, he would want oblivion, real oblivion. He wouldn't want immortality *after* the trials; he'd want oblivion now. But he isn't going to get oblivion. He has to go through the furnaces, because *all* will be saved. So there are false serpents and the true serpent. Who are the false serpents?—the magicians. As you are told, I quote tonight from the 2nd chapter of Daniel, he said, these are the words of the prophet Daniel, "No magician, no authority, no soothsayer can interpret your dream, O king. But this is your dream: There's a God in heaven who makes known unto you"...and he tells him that all of these fellas who were drawing little signs and all kinds of things trying to interpret the dream could not interpret the dream. They were the false serpents.

Goodnight.

GRACE VERSUS LAW

2/11/1964

Tonight's subject is "Grace versus Law." We're told in the Book of John, the first chapter, "For law came or law was given through Moses; but grace and truth came through Jesus Christ" (verse 17). Now the law spoken of is not our civil and criminal law. We speak here of the law of God. It hasn't a thing to do with the law of the land, as it changes from country to country. These are eternal laws, laws that Jesus interpreted for us. When he came he said, "I come not to abolish the law and the prophets; I come not to abolish them but to fulfill them" (Mat. 5:17); and then he interpreted for us the meaning of the law. He said, "You have heard it said of old, 'You shall not commit adultery.' But I say to you that any one who looks upon a woman lustfully has already committed the act of adultery with her in his heart" (Mat.5:27). In other words, the act was committed when men or a man *contemplated* the act. To contemplate an act that seems pleasant is all well and good. I may be inclined to do it if it seems pleasant. If I contemplate the act along with its consequences to myself and others, I may restrain the impulse. But I am told that's still not good enough. The very contemplation of the act was in itself the act. Therefore, we come to one conclusion: that causation must be imaginal. I imagined a state, and just to imagine the state was to be convicted of having performed that act. That's what I'm told by Christ's interpretation of the law as it was given through Moses.

Now grace is simply God's gift of himself to man. Grace is unconditional; you do not earn it, it's a gift, unearned, unmerited. No one can earn it. No one could be *good* enough to get it; therefore, all will receive it as a gift. Grace is the end, the end is God. So when the psalmist said, "Lord, let me know my end," for if I know the end then all that goes before it will then make sense. It gives meaning to everything that goes before it if I can see the end. The end may be far off in time, but do let me know my end, said the psalmist. Without knowing the end nothing seems to have meaning. All go towards the inevitable grave, but if I know the end, well, then I can sustain anything else in this world, I don't care what it is. Show me the end.

So this is grace and law. Let us turn, to make it a practical night, turn to the law, because I have told you week after week about grace. It comes in a strange, wonderful way, and you do not know why you of all people should be chosen at that moment in time to be given God's grace. As I've said before, the man who has received God's grace finds himself ascribing the entire process of his salvation to God's action. If he's honest with himself he will admit that he, himself, has had nothing to do with it whatever. Even his faith seems to be the gift of God. So I can tell everyone who will listen to me, you *will* receive it. Because I know as the speaker speaking to you I am no better than anyone who walks the face of this earth. Yet, I was called and given this gift of gifts: It was the gift of himself. We will not go into that tonight, for I've told you time and again how man knows that God gave himself to that man. There's only one way by which it can be revealed, and that is through his Son. When the Son [David] appears in your world and calls you Father, then you know by this relationship God succeeded in his purpose, which purpose was to give man himself.

But we turn now to the law, that you may prove it this night. I tell you, when you really believe, you can prove anything by this law...if you really believe. But man must believe. Believe what? He said, Believe in God. Well, who is God? "The eternal body of man is his (own wonderful human) Imagination, and *that* is God himself. That is the divine body, Jesus, Jesus Christ." [Blake] He sunk himself in man as man's own wonderful human Imagination. Can you believe that all things are possible to God? If you can answer yes to that question, well, then can you believe that all things are possible to your Imagination? You may say no to that. Well, then you do not really know who God is. You might put him on the outside. And may I tell you, if we fail, I have come to the conclusion why we fail—we make an effort, and there is *no* effort. If I really believe all things are possible to God and someone asks me anything now, I don't care what it is, and it comes within the frame of what I consider my code of honor, my code of decency. Don't ask me to hear that some enemy of yours is dead because you're asking the wrong party. If you ask me to hear that you have a marvelous job and you're gainfully employed, I can hear that. If you ask me to hear that you are feeling well when you're not feeling well, I can hear that. Don't tell me what the doctors said; I don't care what they said. Don't tell me what it looks like; I don't care what it looks like. Because I can turn to what I really *know* to be God and put the entire thing in his hand as it were, and with him *all* things are possible. So you receive a request. You *do* nothing about it...you don't sit down and burst a blood vessel trying to make something work. You simply accepted the request as something accomplished; accomplishing is done. Why do I know this? Because I've experimented.

May I tell you of all of the pleasures of the world *relief* is the most keenly felt—you think it over—of all of the pleasures of the world. I'll give you one simple little example. You have a child, the child is of an age where you allow the child to go out on dates. The child will say to you... as, you, a good mother, a good father will say, "When may I expect you?" Well, you don't want to curtail the activity, the fun, and they will say, "I'll be home before midnight." "Alright, before midnight?" "Right." So you sit up. So midnight comes, there is no child. One in the morning, there is no child. Two, there is no child. If you love your child, as we all do, the mind is a little bit anxious and so you sit and you're building up an emotion. Suddenly you hear the key in the door and what relief! In that interval if you're not in control and you knew nothing of this law, you thought of accidents, you thought of one who does not drink persuaded by the crowd to "be a man" or "be a woman" and have a drink, and you know because she doesn't or he doesn't drink, one could be like six, and so you think a *thousand* things in this world... until you hear that little key.

Well, that's what you hear before she even starts, before he even starts, because Imagination is spiritual sensation. Before you hear the physical contact you hear it just as though you heard it physically. And may I tell you (and let me repeat it), of all the pleasures of the world *relief* is the most keenly felt. And you can do that and put that into every aspect of your life. Go to bed tonight...and someone asks of you anything in this world, would they be relieved and would you be relieved if tomorrow you got a telephone call or a letter saying it worked? Could you be so concerned or be so interested that you would like to hear that it did work? Well, then this night when you go to bed, it worked...before you start the night in the deep of yourself, just that it worked. And this is the law that was given to us *through* Moses but made *clear* to us through Jesus. He interpreted the law. Read it in the 5th chapter of the Book of Matthew, from the 17th verse to the 48th verse, they all take one after the other and show you the *inwardness* of the law. It's not doing something on the outside. To this very day the whole vast world believes if I attend service, if I go through the ritual and follow the entire *outward* ceremony that I am really doing something; I am simply appeasing God wherever he is. And this one comes to show us *that* is not it at all; the whole thing is on the inside, it's what I am doing *within* myself. Am I clothing myself as the man that I want to be? Am I wearing the assumption that things are *already* what I want them to be? If I do it *that* way, well, then it comes to pass in my world.

So let me show you how I knew him. Go back to the greatest book in the world, the Bible. It is said of Moses—if you've never read it, it's the 12th chapter, the 3rd verse of the Book of Numbers—"For the man Moses was very meek"—not weak, meek—"more than all men who moved on the face of the earth." The man Moses was very meek, more than all men that were on the face of the earth. It is said of Jesus, and he said it of himself, "I am meek and lowly in heart." *Meek!* Now you and I in using the word meek we think of some beaten person, weak person, weak in character. He will simply fawn on others, he himself has no backbone, that's the way we think of meek today. It was not always so. This strange, peculiar, unfortunate association came to us through the ages; but originally it meant "to be tamed, as a wild animal is tamed." That's what it meant originally. It still means that in scripture, but priesthoods the world over have changed the meaning for us. But it still means what those who wrote the book meant it to mean to us who years to come will read it, "to be tamed."

So you take a wild animal and then you tame it. Or you take a wild tree and you tame it. "Behold this vine..." He said, "I am the true vine." I tell you, I AM is my own wonderful human Imagination, that's the *true* vine. But when I first heard that my Imagination was Christ Jesus it was an awful shock, because I always put him on the outside…never hoped that I could ever be good enough to face him, to meet the Lord face to face. I knew my weaknesses, my limitations, and I thought he lived and died 2,000 years ago. And you tell me that he's contemporary, that he's sunk in me as my own wonderful human Imagination? Well, that was really a shock! So I found him: "Behold this vine. I found it a wild tree, whose wanton strength had swollen into irregular twigs. But I pruned the plant and it grew temperate in its vain expense of useless leaves, and knotted as you see into these full, clean clusters to repay the hand that wisely wounded it" (Browning).

So when I found my wild, wild tree, my Imagination, I could feast on gossip, I could feed on everything that was negative. A little juicy this about someone who was big, and the bigger he was the more I would listen to the little piece that seemed so succulent. I knew some little weakness in that character that others didn't know, and I would read into that strength the weakness that I knew of him, and thought I knew more than others. So my tree was really wild. Then I had to go about *pruning* my tree and *really* pruning it, and bringing my ears deaf to every thing other than what I wanted to hear. So I would not lend an ear to the gossip, not lend an ear to all of the unlovely things that formerly I eagerly would listen to. So finally the tree that I wisely pruned repaid me. It knotted into full, clean clusters and repaid the hand that wisely wounded it.

So we are told in the 15th of John: "I am the true vine; my Father is the vinedresser. Every branch that does not bear, he takes it away, and every branch that bears he prunes it, that it may bear more fruit" (verse 1). The very thing that is bearing he cuts it and prunes it to get all into that one little cluster. And the branch that does not bear, takes the whole thing away. And so, our real vine is our own wonderful human Imagination. So we learn the law, how to operate it, how to really move into a place and assume that we are the man that we want to be. Move right into a state without the consent of anyone in this world, ask no one's permission. If I should really dare to assume that I am what at the moment reason denies, my senses deny, and everything in the world would deny that I could ever attain it, don't ask anyone's permission. Do you want it? Well, dare to assume that you are it and *relax* in that assumption, and trust God in his own wonderful way—which is your own wonderful human Imagination—to devise the means necessary to externalize that state within your world.

So here, the story of the vineyard, as we are told it in the 80th Psalm: And the Lord took a vine, brought it out of Egypt, and he planted it, having first of all cleared the way and prepared the way for the planting of the vine. And then it grew and the root went deep, and the plant spread all over the land. Hasn't it? Wherever there is a man in this world that plant is growing, because there isn't a person in this world who can't imagine. So that was planted; it came out of Egypt and he planted it. He prepared the ground for it—the ground is man himself. He's planted right in man and it's grown all over the world. There is humanity...the farthest north, the farthest south, both poles, there are people living there today. And it's gone all over the world, this plant.

So, then Israel asked him, "Why then if this plant was so precious to you, why do you tear down its walls? Because now as people pass by they feed from its fruit and then the boar from the forest he tramples on it." The boar is a wild pig; the wild pig takes and tramples on the vine. "Why did you tear down its protective walls and all the people who pass by it now they feed on it?" Well, can't you see it? He grows in every being in this world because everyone is saying "I am," and that is God. And everyone is imagining and that is the grand God-in-action, his son. So here, you planted it well, it went deep, it spread all over the world, and then you broke down its walls that the wild pig may trample upon it. The wild pig is simply the undisciplined and not the *meek* being. So you take your Imagination and you use it for all the unlovely things of the world. You can't help it. He had to break down the walls and let everyone do with it as he would, and use my back for all the stripes you would give it. As told us in the 53rd chapter of Isaiah, he took upon himself all the stripes of man, all the abuse of man, because you can't stop a man from imagining. Who knows but what in some woman this very moment in a dungeon, who feels herself abused because she was put there; and there she is in some dungeon, exercising her Imagination unlovingly towards others in this world. So Blake said, I would never be surprised to know that it was not some woman in the great dungeon who was treading out the wine presses of evil for all of the people of the world.

One night I was taken in vision, fully conscious, into a cave. Have you ever seen a hag? Well, wait 'til you see one...right into this cave and here was this monstrous creature, human as we are but monstrous. She would have put to shame the three in *Macbeth*, and there she was teaching her brood, all these strange creatures, teaching them the evil magic of the world. When she saw me at the door she said, "Man of God, what have I to do with you?" Well, she knew she was helpless in my presence; on the other hand, I had no right to change her from her task in this world. And so I simply stood at the entrance of her cave and there she was teaching all of the strange urchins of the world the *misuse* of Christ. And she spoke to me and called me "Man of God." As you're told in the first chapter of the Book of Mark, the demons knew him, no one else knew him. Always the demon knows him, for they are of the Spirit. And so, he silenced the demons and told them not to tell anyone who he was. Then he started his journey from city to city, for he said, It is for this purpose that I came.

So any of the evil spirits, when you enter in the world of Spirit they know you, exactly who you are, but they are powerless in your presence. On the other hand, you do nothing about changing them, leave them just as they are. They are taking this...the walls are down and they abuse the power which is Christ…for there's only one power. There aren't two powers in the world, God and the devil, there's simply God in the *wise use* of power and the *misuse* of power. So, Christ Jesus is the power and the wisdom of God (1Cor.1:24), but the same Jesus Christ is the power and the misuse of God. So when you do not know Christ Jesus, and you think he lived 2,000 years ago, and you pray to him on your knees as something on the outside, you do not know Christ Jesus. But if you know he's your own wonderful human Imagination, you will not allow one unlovely thought to cross that mind of yours. You simply prune the plant. Something is coming out, it's not going to bear good fruit, and you cut it off. You do not *allow* yourself to become involved and interested in the unlovely things of this world.

So here, in this grace versus law you can forget the grace, for it's coming your way regardless. When it comes I do not know. For we are told, "Set your hope fully upon the grace that is coming to you at the revelation of Jesus Christ" (1Pet.1:13). Set your hope fully on *it* above all things in this world, for by grace you are saved through faith. It is not your own doing; it is the gift of God. Not because of works...lest anyone boast. So no one can brag who receives the grace of God because you didn't earn it. It came in God's own good time, and no one has ever earned it; no one will ever earn it. But the end of all is the grace of God, and grace is the unmerited, unearned gift of God himself to man. So man gets it, and getting it then comes this wonderful revelation *in* man to prove to man he did receive the gift of God. And there is no other way in eternity that God could have worked it out for man, that man would know he really got it, save by that simple little statement in the 11th of Matthew where—and it's before he makes the statement, "Come unto me all of you weary and the tired ones"—he tells us the yoke is easy and his burden is light, that he is meek and lowly of heart (verse 28).

But before he makes this declaration he shows man what is going to happen. And this is going to happen to you. He said, No one will ever know it save the Son reveals it, for "No one knows the Son except the Father, and no one knows the Father except the Son and anyone to whom the Son chooses to reveal him" (Mat.11:27). And then he goes into this declaration, "All of you who are tired, the weary, the broken come unto me and I'll give you rest." If you really would come to me this night and take the rest, ___(??) I don't care what it is you want—make it lovely, make it wonderful—and dare to assume that you are it. Assume that you are and trust your own wonderful Imagination to do it. He'll do it. He'll do it this night or tomorrow, but he'll do it, in a way that you could never consciously devise. No one could devise the means that he will employ to externalize that which you have assumed that you are, or that which you have assumed for another. You can assume something lovely for another, without the other's knowledge, without the other's consent. And then when it happens you take no credit for it, you're only happy that it happened. And so, they not knowing that you did it or were in any way instrumental in doing it, you simply bask in the joy that it has happened. Because really in the end there aren't two of us, there's only one. We're so completely interwoven we're only one. There's only one Christ—not three billion little Christs running around the earth—*one sunk in all,* and that one sunk in all will *resurrect* in all.

Peter calls this grace "salvation." You read it in the first chapter of Peter, the 10th verse, the first Peter, 1st chapter, 10th verse. And he tells us it is all salvation, the grace was coming to man is man's salvation. And he saves, and he shows you how he's saved, and how man will know that he's saved by the revelation the Son will give to him; for the Son will call him Father. As the Son calls him Father, he knows now who he is which he never knew before. But he also knows that it's coming to every being in this world, so he can't crow. He cannot boast that he did anything to earn it. The thing was completely unmerited in his case. It would be unmerited in every man's case, so no one can boast in the end anyway.

So grace...and the most glorious use of the word that I've read in the Bible you'll find in the very end of the 2nd epistle of Paul to the Corinthians. It's the benediction of benedictions. It's the 13th chapter, the very last verse, the 14th verse. It's read in the Episcopal Church every Sunday, but I wonder how many of them really understand it if *any* of them do, including the minister. Here, this glorious benediction placed upon man: "The grace of the Lord Jesus Christ and the *love* of God and the fellowship of the Holy Spirit be with you all." What a benediction! "The grace of the Lord Jesus Christ"—-that's the gift of himself, when he's one with God. Then God is all love—-and "the love of God." And that brings a "fellowship of the Holy Spirit"—the Holy Spirit is God and God is Jesus Christ. It's really one being but presented in a trinity; not a trinity, just one being. The Son called David, who appears to *call you* Father, is simply spiritualizing humanity, and simply fusing him as a single being called a son, called David, who then calls *you* Father. It's the only way you'll ever know that you are the Father, one *with* the being spoken of in that benediction, God.

So, "The grace of the Lord Jesus Christ and the love of God and the fellowship of the Holy Spirit be with you all." If you took that this night and simply took it to bed and just dwell upon it, just dwell upon that one simple beautiful use of words in that last verse of the 2nd Corinthians, and just dwell upon it. The grace of the Lord Jesus Christ...and then all of a sudden you dwell upon it. Maybe tonight you might be a little bit hesitant to claim that Christ Jesus and your wonderful Imagination are one. You may, if you're raised in a Christian faith, you might think that's blasphemy. If you've been conditioned to believe that he's something other than you, you might really hesitate to do it, to think I don't want to blaspheme against the holy name. And so, it's a holy name. Sure it's a holy name, but so are you. You are a holy name. You're not some little thing that looked into the mirror. You are *wearing* this garment that you see in the mirror, but the *wearer* is one with Christ, and the wearer is your own wonderful human Imagination.

So tonight you dwell upon it and see if you can't produce in yourself the emotion of relief when you contemplate a state that you really want. Then use your Imagination, which is spiritual sensation, to hear what you would hear *after* the event or to see what you would see after the event…just like the child coming home when you hear what you would hear *after* arrival. But you hear it before she goes out on her date, so that you know, regardless of the seeming delay, she is putting that key in the door. You heard it; you heard it before she set forth. So the whole story in the Bible, I show you the end before you even leave home. So he shows Abraham the end before Abraham starts his journey into Egypt, and Abraham was sustained in faith by the end. He showed Job what he told Job, and Job could say "I heard of thee with the hearing of the ear, but now my eye sees thee" (Job 42:5). So he *heard* it; that's spiritual sensation. All of this is done in the soul of man.

So tonight suppose someone asks help of you. Turn the whole conversation around and have them tell you that they've got it. And go to bed relieved, because when they asked it of you, you weren't relieved; that's tension. Now turn the whole conversation around and listen as though they're calling you on the phone and telling you that they have it—no matter what it is, if it's within the code of decency, yes—and then go sound asleep in *confidence* that he who can do all things has done it. You simply have to rest your body now, so you're not going to burst any blood vessels trying to make it work. Leave that alone completely; just simply accept it, and then *let* it work. And may I tell you, it will work like a charm, without getting on your knees, without mumbling any words, without saying any prayers. That's prayer enough.

So you are told when I come to God I must believe that he *is*. Anyone who comes to God must first of all believe that he is and he rewards those who seek him. Read that in the Book of Hebrews, 11th of Hebrews: "Whoever would come to God must believe that he is and that he rewards those who seek him…and without faith it is impossible to please him" (verse 6). Would you please God tonight? You don't please him by giving a huge big sum of money to a church. That's no pleasure to God; that's pleasure to the priest who gets it, not to God. God is pleased with your faith. So tonight, when you go to bed and someone asked any help of you then feel that, that help has been granted. *That* faith pleases God and then God goes to work to produce in that man's life or that woman's life the condition that she or he asked you to help create in this world. And you do it without effort.

So I know from my own experience if I use *no* effort then it works. Not indifference, I don't mean indifference, I mean no *effort*. You accept it and you have such confidence in God that God *cannot* fail, and you simply accept it and say yes to the Father. Regardless of what was wrong with her, I don't care what was wrong with her—been in that state for the last week, two weeks or a month; it doesn't matter when they call you. They hadn't called you in the interval. At that moment they despaired and they called you. They tried this medicine, they tried that practitioner, they tried that one, and suddenly they call you. At that moment you don't ask them what's wrong. You called me, alright, thank you. At that very moment you turned the whole thing over to God without doing anything about it, just turning it over completely to God. And they will call you the next day or the next week or maybe they won't call you. One in ten calls. You're fortunate when three in ten call you. Nevertheless, it doesn't matter whether they call you to confirm it or not. You know it's done, and done it is, because you aren't trying to work it out in your own rational mind. You know it is done the very moment you accepted the call and said to them, I will take it. In that very moment when you completely accepted, the whole thing is done. I'm speaking from experience.

I know, in my own case, I do not sit down and try to work it out. I don't sit down and do anything about it. And from that very telephone call, I'm going right into my living room to discuss some other matter with friends who are present. Last Sunday night friends were here on their way north and we had a most delightful evening at home, had dinner, they went off about midnight, and the phone rang when we were just about to go to dinner. Well, that was no time for a long telephone discussion. My wife answered the phone and said "I'm sorry but I can't call Neville, he's now with his friends and we're just about to go to dinner." She understood, but she did say what she wanted: Will you please tell him for me that so-and-so is wrong with me and would he help. Well, she did, she told me…that's alright. We sat down. I didn't give it one second thought. We sat down and had dinner, and a heavenly discussion following dinner into the midnight hour. And then, today, around two, the phone rang and she thanked me profusely. She said, "I didn't get to the phone yesterday to call you. I could have done it yesterday because it worked completely as of yesterday."

Another one said to me tonight, she didn't, but her friend said to me tonight, "I spoke to the lady and something was wrong with her physically. It was seemingly something she did not remember doing to herself, but she had the evidence of it. And her daughter wondered why she called me instead of a doctor, for this is something for the medical profession, not for a man like Neville. But she called me instead of a doctor. So it taught not only her a lesson, but it taught the daughter a lesson, for within forty-five minutes it was gone. And she could do things that she couldn't possibly dream of doing had she gone to the doctor. I'm quite sure she would have been bandaged and she would not be walking. And so that was it. So, I didn't do anything other than accept the fact that I told her I would simply do my work.

Well, my work is simply to trust my Imagination *completely*. Whenever I go to bed at night, the very last thought, just as I'm about to retire, I think of those I would like to help and those who have called upon me for help. And all I do is just think of them. I know my Father knows before I ask him what was asked of me. And so, I think of them and I know exactly what they asked of me, I accept it *completely* that it's done. When it's going to be done, I don't know, and how it's going to be done, I still don't know. I only know I think of them, and thinking of them I know what they asked of me, and that was enough, and go sound asleep, completely oblivious of anything else. If I'm blessed that night with a vision, all to the good, a dream, all to the good; but the next day I don't think "I wonder if it worked?" I have complete confidence in my Father that it worked. Whether they ever tell me or not, I really don't care. I'm not seeking credit, I'm not seeking praise from them, I really don't care. Well, when they do tell me I can share it with you and it encourages everyone who comes here to *trust* God.

May I tell you again, God is your own wonderful human Imagination. He's not on the outside; he's actually sunk *in* you as your wonderful human Imagination. "Man is all Imagination and God is man, and exists in us and we in him. The eternal body of man is the Imagination, and that is God himself" (Blake, *Berkeley*). Trust it, believe it, and see how things work in this world. No matter what you are, what you're planning now to do, see that it comes within the lovely code of decency. We're living in a world where we're really a fellowship, this is a brotherhood. The very first words taught us in our prayer "Our Father" implies fatherhood, the first two words. He said, "I go to my Father and your Father, to my God and your God." Well, "*our Father,*" that's plural "our." "Our Father" implies a brotherhood of man. You can't get away from it if you believe the words "Our Father," the beginning of the Lord's Prayer. And so, I can't do it really to another; I'm doing it to myself. Whenever I seem to do it to another, I'm really doing it to myself. So God is one, and he's sunk in the seeming many; but the many are still one because one being is sunk in all, and that one being is your own lovely wonderful human Imagination.

But now, may I tell you, you can treat it, treat it lightly; don't treat it with effort. Effort would prove to me, were I the being I'm speaking of, that you don't believe in it...if you make an effort. Make no effort and it will work. When you go to bed tonight, really believe that your Imagination is Christ Jesus. I hope you believe in Christ Jesus as I do, that he's real, more real than this is real. This is going to vanish, the world is going to vanish, but he will never vanish. As we are told: "Lift up your eyes to the heavens, and see; they will vanish like smoke, and look to the earth it will wear out like a garment; but my salvation is forever, and my redemption shall never come to an end" (Is. 51:6). So all these things will vanish, but he will never cease to be. And he became you. Man was so loved by God that God became man that man may become God. And in becoming man he's man's own wonderful human Imagination.

So learn how to use the law. I come not to abolish the law, he said, not to abolish it, to fulfill it. And then he interprets to us the law, the *inwardness* of the law. That if you feel comfortable by going to church, go to church. If you feel comfortable by observing the rituals and the ceremonies, observe them. But, may I tell you, that's not what he brought to the world. He brought this and then told us that he was meek. Then, someone speaking *of* Moses—Moses didn't make the claim—it is said *of* Moses, he was *very* meek, more than all of the men that were on the face of the earth. The meek is the *self-disciplined*, a man who in spite of rumor can shut his eye to everything that would deny what he has now assumed. No matter what it is, he denies reason, he denies the evidence of his senses, and he gives to himself that inner glow that what he now asks of his Father is done. Are we not told, whatever I ask of my Father he does it? These are the words: I know you hear me, Father, for whatever I ask of you, you do it (John 11:42). Well, get to the same mood. Whatever I ask of him he does it; and he's not out there, he's right here as my own wonderful human Imagination.

So when I give you a technique, it's simply to work you into that feeling of the naturalness of it all. For if you were now desirous of going to, and you name it, well, then this night you would sleep there, wouldn't you? Well, then sleep there just as though you were there. That is accepting this technique, accepting this principle, and sleep in it. If it's not a spatial journey you need but a financial journey, move to the state financially and sleep in it. Just as you move spatially and sleep in it, move financially and sleep in it. Move socially and sleep in it. Whatever you would do, just move—it's a mental motion—and sleep in it, and accept it naturally, without effort on your part; and see how these things come to pass.

Then you'll get to the point, not a thing will phase you in this world. You will *love* all, but you'll put no man you see in this world on a pinnacle, not one. The day will come that you will accept no aristocracy but the aristocracy of Spirit, but none whatsoever. You let no one by his accident of birth wave some little flag before you to try to make you feel less-than, you don't. Allow him all the right to act that way but you don't respond. You go about your business simply doing good as you know how to do good, and lift up every being in this world. For we're all one, there aren't two; there's only one God. So in that day, we're told, "God shall be king over all of the land; and his name shall be one, and the Lord one." That we read in the last chapter of Zechariah, "His name is one and the Lord is one" (14:9). And that name, may I tell you, is Jesus Christ.

Now let us go into the Silence.

* * *

Now before we take the questions, may I call your attention to the book table. You'll find all of the books there that I have written; and any book on it undoubtedly is a book I myself recommended. I'm quite sure my friend Jack did not put one book there without first discussing it with me. Every book on the table I highly recommend, they're all part of my library. Are there any questions, please?

Q: There's so much talk about the bad effects of smoking. Should one keep on smoking and imagine that it isn't going to hurt you…

A: My dear…

Q: …or would you quit?

A: That's entirely up to you. My wife smokes all through the day. In fact, she lights a cigarette and goes out of the room, comes back, the thing is burned to the ground, lights another. She can't stand not seeing a lit cigarette in our house, so all day long there's always a lit cigarette. Really, she doesn't have to use more than one match in the course of a day, but she does because she lets it burn down and she lights another one. But she could easily, knowing how many are used in the course of a day, use one lit to light the other, because that's how...and it doesn't disturb me at all. Fortunately for me that her...today, filter tips, therefore they don't fall off the little thing and burn the carpet, so they go out before they can fall off. But I really don't know, I'm not a doctor, and man is not flesh and blood. Flesh and blood does not inherit the kingdom of heaven. So I would be the last one in this world to ask my wife to stop smoking. If she gets any pleasure out of it, smoke. They say that you have cancer...my mother died of cancer...never smoked one puff in her life. My father drank heavily, he was a two-quart-a-day man and he died at eighty-five. She died at sixty-one or two, and never drank and never smoked, and she died of cancer. My father didn't die of anything but sheer collapsing; eighty-five years old and that's all there was to it. Body simply collapsed. But he had nothing seemingly wrong with him, organs were alright, simply collapsed, died at eighty-five. And drank...oh did he drink! Very heavy drinker!

Here is Churchill, twenty cigars a day and about two and a half quarts of liquor. Did you ever read his menu for dinner? It's staggering.

Starts the dinner with two bowls of soup; then a big steak, garnished with the usual vegetables, and this he washes down with two quarts of champagne; has a big huge heaping of ice cream, all topped with all kinds of sauce for dessert; washed the whole thing down with two quarts of champagne. Then, he proceeds to his library with his black coffee and a fifth of brandy. That's dinner. He's been drinking all through the day...all through the day. He's now eighty-nine and he's not senile. The body is slowing a little bit, but why shouldn't it at age eighty-nine. But the man has lived so ruggedly all of his life. He didn't start this last month you know, this has been going on since he could breathe, practically. So I don't go along with all of these medical things at all. What are we trying to be, simply physically alert and then mentally gone? Look at all the great athletes of the world, try to carry on a wonderful conversation with them in the course of an evening, just try it. And suddenly you read this strong, big, strapping giant of a man who is a great wrestler or a great fighter, and last night he didn't wake; a little heart attack. Doesn't smoke, doesn't drink, he's a great athlete. You go to the beach over here in the summer and you see all these muscular giants, but open up a conversation with them... just open up a conversation with them.

Steinmetz came to this country, the only one allowed to smoke at G.E., and he smoked in every part of G.E., but put G.E. on its feet. When he came here they wouldn't let him land because he was a hunchback and they sent him off to Ellis Island, the little hunchbacked German. And this little hunchbacked German came into G.E a wizard. And what that man knew! But not for one second was a pipe ever out of this mouth; the only one allowed to smoke in all the labs. Because they couldn't take it from him…he was too valuable for anyone to lay the law down that Steinmetz should not smoke in a certain area. So, I'm not saying not to smoke, my dear. But one thing—and it was not Mr. Roosevelt who said it, he copied it or quoted it without giving credit—it was Thoreau who said it: "The only thing we have to fear is fear." I know he said that in his inaugural address, and today when anyone quotes it, they quote Mr. Roosevelt as the author. He did not originate that at all. This morning's paper, the thought of the day, the biblical thought of the day, and they gave Paul, in 1st Corinthians, 10th chapter, as the author of the thought; it wasn't so at all. The minute I read it I said no, that's the Psalmist, the 24th Psalm: "The earth is the Lord's." Yes he was quoted, so they quoted it as originated by Paul and that was the 24th Psalm: "The earth is the Lord's and the fullness thereof." But the minute you read it, if you know your Bible, you know it, yes, it appeared in Corinthians, but he was simply quoting the 24th Psalm. So I say, if you feel like smoking, smoke; you don't feel like smoking, don't smoke. I have a daughter, twenty-two, so far she hasn't acquired it; and for her own sake—not because of any health reasons—I hope she doesn't, but if she comes home smoking I'd be the last to tell her to stop smoking. So I really don't care, I don't care what people do. I don't like people to be hurt—and I don't mean suffer like having some ill effects and those things—-I mean to hurt people. I mean not only physically but mentally. I don't like people hurt mentally, where people are insulted and the insult was intended. It always hurts me when someone is hurt that way. Outside of that, what they do in their private lives, I don't care. Who's going to set themselves up as the norm, as what is right in this world? You live your life fully. But the end I tell you…I can tell you the end, the end is God. The beginning was God, the end is God: "I am the alpha and omega, the first and the last, the beginning and the end." So, the end is God's gift of himself to you, and no one in this world could ever stop it, no one. But if, in the interval, you find pleasure in a cigarette, well then, I don't know, I wouldn't tell you to stop it.

We tried Prohibition once, you know. It was an awful mess. Oh what a mess! So much bathtub gin, you never saw such quantities of it, and we made thousands and thousands of men who had no moral code whatsoever, made them multi, multi-millionaires. I read here recently that in 1926 there was a question asked of a magazine, "What individual—not what company or family or group—what individual made the most money in the history of this country in any single year?" And the year was 1926. Well, I thought, well, maybe Rockefeller, Mellon, or Ford...I mentioned all these names. I was so far afield. Then they gave the answer ten pages later, and this is by our government—this is not speculation, this is by our Internal Revenue Dept—and the sum of money that one individual made was one hundred twenty-six million dollars, and his name was Al Capone. That was not taxed. They got him on taxes afterwards for a very small little amount. But he had his hundred twenty-six million dollars, because he could not declare such money, so he made it and kept it. Al Capone. That's what Prohibition did. Well, he spawned thousands into the land who had no sense of values whatsoever, no code but the making of money, that's all that they cared. So Al Capone...if you saw his end...he went a little bit off, he was addlepated, and he couldn't carry on a conversation beyond an nth part of a minute. He was gone, completely gone, but he had his hundreds of millions. So I am not a moralist, really. I'm not here to give any moral code to anyone, but to interpret God's word as I see it, as it has been revealed to me.

Any other questions, please? Well, if there aren't any... remember the book table is waiting for you. And I'll be here on Thursday. Thank you.

THE POWER OF FAITH

2/13/64

Tonight's subject is "The Power of Faith." The most important Hebrew term for the word faith is "Amen," which signifies firmness, stability; but its precise meaning is "hold God trustworthy," to hold God trustworthy. And tonight I hope to be able to share with you what I have discovered about this fabulous power that is faith.

First, let us define faith as defined for us in the Book of Hebrews. This unknown author—some claim that Paul wrote it, but the majority of the scholars are not convinced; they feel it is not quite his terminology, unless he radically changed when he wrote this book—so it's an unknown author, one of the most profound books in the Bible. In the 11th chapter it is stated: "Now faith is the assurance of things hoped for, the conviction of things not seen. By it men of old received divine approval. We understand that by faith the world was created by the word of God, so that things that are seen were made out of things which do not appear" (verses1-3). Then comes the assemblage of witnesses. He first assembles seven, beginning with Abel, and then he summarizes this compound witness, and then he mentions another eleven. Then he summarizes it again.

But here in this statement speaking now of God—for when we speak of faith it's simply to hold *God* trustworthy—God becomes the object of one's faith. So here, "Without faith it is impossible to please him. Anyone who would draw near to God *must* believe that he exists and rewards those who seek him." Now, the best way to understand this is through a little story. A minister was calling at a home to make arrangements for the funeral of an elderly man. Although he was not a professing Christian he was highly regarded in his community. His widow, trying to persuade the clergyman of her husband's goodness, said to him, "Henry was a believer. He believed that God is. He's a believer; he believed that there is a God." Now she herself would never accept this definition of faith if it was applied by Henry to her. Suppose, for instance, during their married life she had asked Henry, "Henry, do you believe in me?" and suppose he answered, "Yes, Mary, I believe that you exist," would she be satisfied with that? So it's more than believing that God exists. So listen to the sentence carefully. People read just a little portion of it and they cut off the important part of that verse. This is the 11th chapter, the 6th verse of Hebrews: "You not only must believe that God exists, but that he *rewards* those who seek him." The existence in itself is not enough; there must be an activity. How could I know? I believe this exists [table] but I expect nothing more from it than to hold paper and pencils and anything I should put on it. That's not what I expect of God.

So I believe that God exists, but I must also believe that he rewards me if I seek him. So God acts; I must react. God speaks and I must say "Amen" to that. Well now, tonight I want something for myself or for a friend, how would I go about seeking God, having God act and I react? So I think of my friend and I see on my friend's face an expression which implies that they have what I want them to have. I see it right on their face. I listen as though we spoke to each other, and he or she, they are telling me what I want to hear. You may say, "Well, that's not God acting, that's Neville acting." I say to you, "I am doing it" and you will say, "Yes, I know you were doing it." I say, "No, *I am* doing it." What is his name?—I AM. Has he any other name? Oh, many names, his name is Father, call him Lord, call him God, call him by every name; but the name he *revealed* to man which must be a name forever and forever for all generations is I AM (Ex. 3:14). So I am bringing before my mind's eye the face of a friend, and I put on that face an expression implying the fulfillment of my desire for them. And so God is acting. I'm not separating God from myself, for his name is I AM. And so I bring it so.

Am I going to react now? I must now react to God's action. God acted, I'm quite familiar with the action, but it's *God* that is acting. "For God only acts and is in all existing beings and men." So he dwells in me as my own wonderful human Imagination. I know what I imagined...well, that's God. To believe in God is one thing, but to believe that he rewards me if I seek him is another thing, and that's where men stop, like Henry stopped. For Henry was a good man, Henry believed that there is a God and she thought that would pacify the minister, and maybe it did. For you could get from some Communist this night his belief, his confession of faith. And he said, "I believe there is a God." If you want all people to believe in God, you may be satisfied. That's not good enough. I must not only believe there's a God, I must believe that he rewards me if I seek him; and then put him to the test.

Now, I ask everyone here to put him to the test. I put him to the test; I put him to the test daily. He does not fail. If it seems long as far as I'm concerned, I *know* it is not long for what I've asked. At that moment that was the beginning of an action, and the action will fulfill itself in its own good time. I'm called upon to be patient, to be faithful, and simply await God's production. He's going to produce it. All I'm asked to do is to simply let God act. Well, God acted. I sit here tonight for the next half an hour, three-quarters of an hour...I will sit in the Silence and bring before my mind's eye some friend who is here, and carry on a simple conversation with him. God acted. So when I rise from there, did I react in confidence, in absolute faith? The opposite of faith is worry. Am I going to be concerned about results? Am I going to ask myself how is it going to happen? Well, then I'm worrying

Now listen to these words from the 4th chapter, the 6th verse of Philippians: Have no anxiety whatever. The words are, "Have no anxiety about anything, but in everything by prayer and supplication with *thanksgiving* make your requests known to God" or "Let all your requests be made known to God." Have no anxiety about anything. So you ask something...you say, "Well, the doctor said so and so." Well, I don't care what the doctor said. Well, the boss said so and so. I don't care what he said. I am told "Have no anxiety about anything, but in everything by prayer and supplication with thanksgiving let all of your requests be made known to God." So you sit quietly and now you're going to commune with God. Wait for God to tell you something? Don't you know who God is? How must I wait for God to tell me something? God is speaking to me every time I use my Imagination; for God is all Imagination and dwells in me *as* my Imagination.

So I think of a friend. As I conjure him before my mind's eye I represent him to myself as I want to see him. That's God's action. Now I must react. I've come to him and God would now reward me if I seek him. Well, I sought him and I found exactly what he's going to give me; for the expression on the face of a friend implies the fulfillment of what I want for them. Or, if the expression is not enough, I listen as though I heard words that I would hear and could *only* hear if things were as they want them to be. And so, I listen just as though it were true. And then I must not worry, for that is then the opposite of faith; and by faith all things were made; without it he didn't make anything. And how did he make it? He made all the visible things that I see out of invisible states. Now listen to these words from the 4th chapter, the 17th verse of Romans: "And he calls a thing that is *not* seen as though it *were* seen and the unseen *becomes* seen." He calls a thing that is *not* seen as though it *were* seen, and then the unseen becomes seen. So I bring your face before me. Alright, I can see your face; then I put the expression on it. I see that, but I don't see what it is implying. No one sees that. I can see your face, but what does it imply? It implies the fulfillment of your dream come true, all come true. But I don't see *it*; I only see that which it implies. Now I get the secret of God's creativity; he acts in this manner. I have found him…by him all things are made; without him was not made anything that is made, and I just did it.

Alright, a lady comes to see me—I do not know her from a hole in the wall—she said, "I had been recommended to you and I do not understand what you do." Well, I said, I just do nothing. You sit right there and I will sit here and you imagine that you are telling me you have found the lady that you are seeking. This was her request: "I haven't seen a friend of mine in over a year, and I'm anxious to see her, now what must I do?" I said, you sit there and you tell me mentally—don't scream at me—just simply tell me mentally that you have found her. I will sit just where I am, I will imagine that you are talking to me, and you're telling me you've found her. So when I say, that's enough or that's okay, we'll break the little mental conversation, and that's all that I will do. So she sat quietly for five minutes, I sat quietly for five minutes; I imagined she is talking to me and she is telling me she's found her. At the end of five minutes I got up and said, thank you so much. She said, "Is that all?" I said, that's all. Well, she wasn't at all convinced. She walked through the door, she'd never seen me before, and so that was all.

She could have told me within the week that she found her. But she didn't, she waited. And this is what happened. She inquired where her friend last was seen and they said to her she went off to Hartford, Connecticut. So she took a train to Hartford. She was having no faith whatsoever in what we did, because to her that was the height of stupidity. Off she went to Hartford. When she got there they said, yes, we know her, but she left for Boston. So off to Boston she goes. At the address in Boston, yes, they knew her, she lived here, this was her address, but she left here without leaving any forwarding address, and that's several months ago. So she returns to New York City. One day on 14th Street, shopping at Hearn's Department Store, she's walking by on the south side of the street. You come out of Hearn's on 14th Street, Union Square. Had she been five seconds early or late they would have missed each other. Because she was right on the button, they ran right into each other on 14th Street right opposite coming out of Hearn's Department Store.

How could you possibly have arranged it? She could not possibly have arranged it. She went to Hartford to spend her good money and time, Boston, her money and time, and returned disappointed. But we had planted the seed. I did not know *how* she would ever know that this person...alright, so she found her. She's walking down 14th Street and all of a sudden they bump right into each other in front of Hearn's Department Store. That's how it works. I could sit down and burst all the blood vessels of my brain trying to figure out for her what she should do. You don't *do* anything. God acts and man reacts; God speaks and we say "Amen." Amen is holding God trustworthy. That was his action. You act…I know I acted, well, that's God.

Is it arrogant? It's your own wonderful human Imagination, that's God. God actually became man that man may become God. And how did he become man? By sinking himself in man as man's own wonderful human Imagination, that's God. He so loved man he became man. And *in* man, can't you say "I am"? Well, that's his name. He has no other name, really. He does have fatherhood—that's the greatest name in the world—but that comes at the very end. Long before the Son appears and calls you Father you will use the name called "I am." Only in the very end are you called "Father." I tell you that you're Father, but it has to be revealed to you personally for you to *know* it. You must *experience* fatherhood, and only the Son can make you experience it. Until that day comes, use the name he gave us. For that same name will be forever and forever: "This is my name for all generations, forever and forever," and the name is I AM.

So I sit down quietly and I think of someone. At that very moment they may not respond, I may not hear from them. But do you know that at that moment, in some strange way, they thought of me. They may never sit down and write a letter and tell me, "At this very moment I was thinking about you." But they had to. They're all *in* me. So you bring someone up and you simply bring them before your mind's eye and you bless them. In what way? God blesses them because God *acts*. You bring them into your mind's eye and you see them as you want to see them, one who is happy, gainfully employed, things are just right. He could not ask at this moment in time for something lovelier. So you ask it for him, and then you see his face reflecting the fulfillment of that request. "Make all of your requests known to God." Well, God knows it. Don't *I* know it? Well, that's he. My own Imagination *knows* it; well, that's God. God is my Imagination, he's your Imagination. So when you *know* that, you do it *wisely* from morning to night.

Let me paraphrase that wonderful 13th chapter of Corinthians for you. It's the one on love. But now we'll take it and paraphrase it on faith. For you know the very last verse (which was asked me) and you've read it: "What is the greatest thing in the world?" and you answer, "Faith, hope and love; but the greatest of these is love" (verse 13). With that I agree, love *is* the greatest in the world. But in that trio faith is mentioned—-faith, hope and love. Love *is* the greatest, but faith is there...and these three abide. So we now paraphrase it: Though I speak in the tongues of men and angels, though I have all the prophetic powers of the world so that I know all the mysteries and understand all knowledge, though I give all that I have away, and though I give my body to be burned, and have not *faith*, I cannot please him. I said love—-I should say I am as nothing; without love you are as nothing—-but faith, without faith I cannot please him. Those who come to him must know that he exists, but before that is stated, "Without faith it is impossible to please him."

So if I gave all that I had…suppose that I had all the wealth of the world and I gave it to the poor. Suppose I offered my body to be burned while still living in it, as many Buddhists have done recently. Suppose I was so wise that I had all the prophetic powers of the world, that I could see tomorrow and play the game today based upon tomorrow, and knowing tomorrow's quotation on the market. If I knew exactly every horse that would win tomorrow...I was so prophetic I know every horse that's going to come in, and I knew it today. All I'd have to do is call my bookie (if I had one), have him go out and just simply bring the money back, I know it all. But suppose I knew all these things, and had not faith, I could not please him. He can't be pleased in any way save through faith. So he calls upon man, who is completely shut out from the next second—-he can't know exactly what's going to happen five minutes from now—because this [body] is a veil that blinds the being that he really is. For man is really God awakening. So God blinds himself with the garment of flesh, and with this blind upon him he has to live by faith. So we walk by *faith* not by *sight,* we're told.

Now, can I walk by faith? Alright, I think of someone...I don't have to sit down and really work it out. I don't consider the ways and means. You're told, "I have ways and means you know not of. My ways are past finding out" (Rom. 11:33, KJV). If they're past finding out what am I doing trying to unravel the ways by which I will realize my objective? So when this lady left my room, she thought, well now, this is the height of insanity. They told me to go and see this man, he seemed a normal person, but that isn't normal. So she goes through the door and the whole thing seemed to her a complete waste of her time. Yet a week later after her visit to one place, another city and back disappointed, she runs into her. How could you ever have arranged it?

A lady came to see me after completely exhausting all the things in New York City. She went to the police department first then she went to the detective agency, and paid a goodly price, to find the furniture that had disappeared while she was in Europe for almost a year with her children. She left her furniture and her apartment. She was paying the rent every month and yet when she came back there was no furniture. So she sought the help of the police department, she sought the help of the private agency, and they couldn't locate it in all of the things that they did in New York City. They went to the five boroughs, going to all the great storehouses, and they couldn't find any evidence of it. Then she came to me. She knew me well. She could have come first and saved herself time and money. No, she's going to take Caesar's way first. When Caesar failed, she came. She and I sat in the Silence and simply saw the furniture, and sat on it, and saw the lovely family pictures on the piano, and all the things where they would be were it true.

So one day she's coming out of a bank on Madison Avenue and there were rails—on Madison Avenue all things, sort of an old atmosphere—coming out of this bank and she sees these rails; and it reminded her of a very strange experience of hers years ago when she had a mental breakdown and they committed her. They thought she was violent so she was committed in a violent ward. So when she saw these rails it disturbed her. At that moment of being disturbed she turned south instead of turning north to her hotel. She went one block, she discovered her mistake. At the very end of the block, having discovered she was going south instead of north, she stopped, and as she was turning around to go north she sees a familiar pair of ankles. There they are. And just before the light turned green for her to cross the street, she sees, she looks at the face, it's her maid. And she goes and she holds the maid, and the maid begins to scream. She said, "I'm not going to hurt you. I only want my furniture, and I'm not leaving you, I'm not letting you go until you take me right this very moment to my furniture." So she hailed a cab and together they got into the cab and the maid took her to her furniture. The maid, in that interval, thought, well, this lady is always a little bit off, she will not know, so she'll disappear with the furniture.

And it all happened after all the police gave up and the private agency gave up; but not until they took her money, because she paid for that help, and then they couldn't deliver the goods. It was not contingent on finding it; it's simply putting in time. They put in x-number of weeks or months. If you want to pay for it, we'll try to find it for you. When you feel you can't give us any more, you can stop us, but we'll make the great effort. In that interval, we hope to find it. Well, they didn't find it. And how did she find it? By stripes coming down through the window...and so it reminded her of a most unpleasant past and it disturbed her. She comes out on Madison Avenue and turns south instead of turning north, and one block, because she was disturbed, there is the maid. See how God works?

So what happened? God acted. We sat on the furniture and there was no furniture. "He calls a thing that is not seen as though it were, and the unseen becomes seen" (Rom. 4:17; Heb. 11:3). You've got to learn to believe that God and you are one: "I and my Father are one...although my Father is greater than I." Believe it. If I and my Father are one, my Father can never be so far off as even to be near, for nearness implies separation. We either are one or we aren't one. So I and my Father are one, how can he be near? He can't be near; for God acts, well, how does he act? By putting my hand out? No, that's only compulsion. God acts in an imaginal manner, so my imaginal act is God in action. So I imagine a friend telling me good news, now can I say "Amen" to that? Can I, as he acted, can I react in confidence? For I must hold God trustworthy; that's the meaning of the word. Hold God trustworthy is Amen.

Another word used, which is not often used, but it's always translated truth, and that is Emeth—Aleph, Mem, Toph—that's translated truth. Well, what is a true judgment? Now this is called faith. A true judgment, said the world of Caesar, must conform to the external reality to which it relates, that's what Caesar said. I say, "Isn't that a wonderful plant!" and you say, "What plant? Now he's really gone." So there's a marvelous plant...and not one sees a plant...but I am seeing a plant, a lovely plant. And so, that's a false judgment, for it does not conform to the external fact to which my judgment relates. There is no plant, so that's a lie. So the word faith which is Emeth in another way is truth. So that's not true...but I still say I see a plant; and I live in the assumption that that was an act, God acted. All things are possible to God. And so, in my Imagination I saw a plant. Who saw it? Well, God acted. Can I accept it? Can I react? For God acts and I'm called upon to react; God speaks and I'm called upon to say "Amen" to what he said. So can I say "Amen" to that...that there's a plant there? If I can say "Amen" to it, well, then it's done. And in no time, and in a way I do not know and could not devise, someone's going to bring a plant. But they will say, "But someone brought it, it didn't grow out of the piano." Did I tell you it's coming out of the piano? They want me to bring it out of something.

Back in New York City I said, "Imagining creates reality." This professor, he teaches in some eastern college, and he said to me, "Imagining creates reality? Well, here is pencil, Neville, it's a yellow pencil. Make it red." I said, go and paint it, paint the pencil. Go in the back room and paint it red. You can make it red. "No, *you* make it red." "Did I tell you I'm going to *make* anything?" I said, everything is possible to Imagination. I can imagine it red. "But it isn't red." To you it isn't, I said, but it's red to me. I say it's red, and tomorrow maybe you'll lose this pencil and find one just like it, and you're going to find a red one. You go back to your college and teach them all your little things that you know concerning what Aristotle said, what Plato said, what all the others who are blind said. I am telling you only about the Bible, and the Bible tells me whatever I believe comes to pass…if I can believe it. Whatever I ask in prayer believing, the same comes to pass (Mark 11:42).

Well, can I believe it when reason denies it and my senses deny it? Can I give my belief sensory vividness and give it all the tones of reality? Well, *certainly* I can, I do it. I've gone all over this world when they told me I couldn't go, when I had no permission even to travel, no permission to travel from this country, or permission to get back into this country. I went out of the country and came back into the country by putting myself just where I wanted to be if it were true that I am there. And so, what's his name?—I AM. Well, can't I say "I am"? Well, is there anything impossible to God? *Nothing!* But man has to make that answer. Man may say, "Oh yeah? He can't grow a second foot if one is severed." So right away they think God can't do that. He can make me...he's already made four billion pairs walking the earth now, but he can't make another one. So he's made billions of pairs of eyes, but he can't make another one, not one single eye that you gouge out. He's done all these things but he can't make another one. And may I tell you, he *can.* I had that experience. I was lifted up on high and saw this fabulous world of imperfection, blind, lame, halt, withered, shrunken, and just as I was lifted up—and I did nothing—as I walked by everything was molded into perfection, as I walked by. Eyes that were missing came out of some strange place and molded themselves in the empty sockets. Arms that were missing came out of some strange reservoir and they came back and molded themselves into the empty sockets. And everyone was made perfect. When I got to the very last, this heavenly chorus sang out, "It is finished!" Then I came back to this limitation where I must live by faith. But I saw it.

Now, having seen another aspect of the power which will be yours and mine tomorrow, for I tasted of the power of the age to be. Where this whole vast world...if you took the human body with its billions of atoms and then fragmented it and each becomes a man...so if this whole vast world...just as God in this lady could take mankind and rearrange it to bring about the maid at the corner, rearrange the entire structure to produce the maid who knows where the furniture is. Well, someone is ill, can't he also rearrange the structure of the body in the twinkle of an eye? He arranged the structure of the macrocosm; can he not rearrange the structure of the microcosm? And so, who did it? All you do is simply act in your Imagination. You imagine that things are as you would like them to be, and they will react. The imaginal act was God. Don't say it was Bob doing it and John doing it and Mary doing it. Alright, it was God doing it; now let John and Mary and Bob react. And so, I react with pleasure.

So you are told, let me quote for you again, the 4th chapter, the 6th verse of Philippians, "Have *no* anxiety about *anything*"—what a statement!—"but in everything by prayer with supplication and with thanksgiving let all your requests be made known to God." No anxiety about anything! Now comes letting your request be known to God. Well, my request is that John has a wonderful job, gainfully employed and moving up, expanding, month after month. So I meet John in my mind's eye now, and John tells me he has the most wonderful job in the world. Well, that action was God. And so, he tells me; I react; I say "Amen" to that; the whole thing is done. I go to the end and then I don't raise a finger to get John the job. I don't call a friend and say, "You know John is in need of a job, can you help him out and steer him in the right direction?" I do nothing. I can't put my hand upon that ark and steer at all. Let it be steered properly by the imaginal act, for the imaginal act contains within itself the power and the wisdom to externalize itself.

So I can't do a thing about it. All I'm called upon to do is simply to react to God's action. But I know who God is. I have found him. Because, if by him all things were made and without him was not anything made that was made, I know exactly what I did. I recall exactly sitting with that lady in her imaginary wonderful room, sitting on her own furniture. That's *all* that I did. If she found it in this strange, unique manner, I know that I didn't aid her in the finding; I only sat on the furniture. If I'm sitting in her place on the furniture, and then it happens that the furniture comes in that place, and I'm invited there for tea and I do go and sit on that furniture, I know what I did. Now I'm told, "By him all things were made and without him was not anything made that was made." Well, I know what I did, so I've found him. I've found exactly who he is: He's my Imagination. My Imagination in action is God creating, and when I can react to that imaginal act and say "Amen" to it, well then, I know exactly what is meant in the Bible: "He is the yea to everything." He simply said yes to every imaginal act that takes place within him, confident that his Father who is himself can externalize it.

On this level, when I'm veiled I am shut out. When the veil is taken off, I am one with the Father in the true sense of the word; we aren't then two. And then you'll understand this fabulous mystery. I came out of this, and therefore that which comes out of this is its son, and this is its father. But that which comes out has been promised to be the father of this. Well, that's a fantastic thing! You mean I mature and I awake when I become my own father's father? Yes, I come out of this and therefore this is its father. I awoke *in* this and this is David. David is the sum total of all the generations of humanity fused into a single being that is a youth, called David. But *every* being is David. When fused, it's David. But individually, it's David. So that body is David. So I awoke in this body and I know who I am.

To you who may not understand it, when I say I awoke in my skull, don't think I was a little tiny thing this big, you know. I'm just as big as I am, and my skull, if I drew a straight line here, the skull is equal to the size of this area here. Because I stood up and walked around in my skull. The skull was just as big as this area here. All things being relative, I wasn't any little, tiny thing this big. I was the man that I am now, feeling myself just as I am now. So I stood up and walked around in the skull, the skull the size of this room. Then I came out. I woke in my own being, for this is David. I come out of David; and then five months later, David, the sum total of all humanity, stands before me and calls me Father. So man matures when he becomes his own father's father. For this gave birth to it. I slept in it and woke in it. And then you'll understand the words: "When your days are fulfilled"—which means when you're dead; that's a lovely way of putting it—"When your days are fulfilled and you lie down with your fathers"—that means when you're buried with the rest of them—"then I will raise up your son after you, who shall come forth from your body"—out from your body—"I will be his father"—who is speaking? God is speaking—"and he shall be my son." So I'm raising up out of David (the body) my own son. But he comes out of the body, therefore the body is its father; so he comes out of David.

Now listen to these words, Jesus Christ:—this is from the Book of Timothy, 2nd Timothy—Jesus Christ, risen from the dead, descended from David. "Jesus Christ, risen from the dead, descended from David, blessed forever" (2:8). Descended from David—you come out of this body, and therefore this that gave birth to it must be your father. And in spite of that, suddenly he appears before you and *calls* you Father. So I say, maturity comes to man when man, born of David, becomes David's father. So you're actually matured when you become your own father's father, and the father's father is God.

But while you are here in this world wearing this garment of flesh, you must walk by faith, and understand *why* you must walk by faith, and why you must react to God's action. God's action is your own wonderful imaginal act...that's God's action. So learn to discriminate and only act in noble manners. So you want to be successful? Why not! You want your friends to be successful? Why not! You want all the fellows that you know to be happy and successful? Why not! Well, then act in that way and say

"Amen" to it. Learn to say "Amen" to your imaginal acts, and then don't raise a finger to make it so; *let* it be so. And don't justify failure…but wait patiently. Simply let it be known to God, let all your requests be known to God. And you're known to God, because I know what I did—that's being known to God. How could I know something, and the presence men call God not know it if he's God? Well, is he all-knowing? Well, he knows what I imagined because he imagined it...because he is my Imagination. God became man that man may become God.

So now, this very moment, without any bursting of blood vessels, you simply think of someone and see them as you would like to see them; gainfully employed if that's the problem of the moment. If it's health, that you've never seen them *look* better, and they'll say, "Never felt better." Alright, that's *all* that you do. Say yes, say "Amen" to that imaginal act. Don't go home and call them up to see if it's working, just leave it alone, and in a wonderful manner that you do not know they will make it visible for you. They'll either call you, write you or some third party will say, "You know what? I read it in so and so, and you should see them" and then they will bring the good news. So it doesn't matter how it happens, it *will* happen. So don't go into any palaver.

I went to New York City two years ago, as I go year after year. I called a friend I hadn't seen in quite a while. And so I went up and I said, Is Mr. so-and-so in, Mr. x? and she corrected me, "Oh, you mean Dr. so-and-so." Alright, Dr. so-and-so. When I knew him he was not Dr. so-and-so, but now he has a little degree, not a medical doctor. She said, "He's busy." I said, "Well, I'll wait." "Well, he's giving a treatment and there are others waiting for treatments when he's through." Alright, I'll wait. Then I heard a voice coming through the door, "Infinite Mind is healthy, Infinite Mind is wealthy, Infinite Mind is so and so," and pouring word after word after word into this one sitting there getting all these words. And then the words came to my mind, if this man would only read the Bible, and go back and read, "Who by his many words hopes to gain the ear of God." They hope to gain the ear of God by empty words that he himself does not believe and the one who is paying him for that half-hour does not believe either. Just empty words, driving it into someone who is so anxious about tomorrow's job or tomorrow's rent, and sitting there all anxious, and this one, just words, empty words. Hasn't a thing to do with this simple approach to God. He's not out there and he's not dead. You don't have to scream at him. And so he's just simply bawling out someone about God being infinite in power, infinite in health, and infinite in wealth; and she came out of that simply minus whatever she gave him, and there was not a thing from the words. It doesn't work that way. You sit down quietly, imagine the loveliest thing in this world and say "Amen" to that. And then leave it.

Now let us go.

___(??) a section wherever recorded. You read it in the 11th chapter in the Book of John, the raising of Lazarus, and the words are "Thank you, Father," that's all that he says. He saw the end and could say "Amen" to that and the words recorded are, "Thank you, Father. You always hear me"... but I said it that they may know you sent me. The most effective words...you see something clearly in your mind's eye as you *want* to see it for a friend and then say "Thank you, Father!" with complete confidence that this is true ___(??) and then let it work.

Now are there any questions, please? Yes sir?

Q: Would you please recapitulate where you were talking about the word Emeth.

A: Emeth is truth—Aleph, Mem, Toph. Why should someone be called tonight and not another when judged by human standards the other is seemingly more worthy of that elective call? And I thought of the temple being broken, for the temple was destroyed. We're told in the 2nd Book of Samuel, the 7th chapter, Do not build a home for me; I will build one for you (verse 6). The word is house. And so here, if I took a jigsaw puzzle and the whole thing broke, but every little piece is unique and cannot be placed in any other part other than its part, it's unique, and God has to find *it.* He can't lose one little piece. But in the reconstruction of the temple that now becomes a *living* temple, instead of the former state of a dead temple, well, now all the stones are *living* stones in God's *living* temple that is eternal. So maybe at this very moment in time the piece that you represent can be fitted, and so you are called, because that's a living stone in the reassembling of God's eternal temple. Doesn't mean you're any better because you're called before the other fella. He hasn't come to that piece ___(??), and so that piece when he comes to it he fits right into this wonderful mosaic; for it is a living, living temple. And all are unique in God's temple, and not one can be displaced; therefore, "Not one shall be lost in all my holy mountain."

Q: In the statement of faith, hope and love, and love is the greatest, I've always related hope more to faith. Would you define what hope really means?

A: Well, you're told that no one hopes for things after you receive it. A hope that is seen is not hope, so hope can only be when it's not seen. I would put them...now they're not qualified faith, hope, love, because love is the greatest and it's named last in this. Now we don't go back and say hope, that's the next one, and then faith. If I were called upon to name the second, I would name faith, I would, because the world was created by faith. "By faith the world was created by the word of God," but by faith. Hope doesn't come into that passage at all. But everything is held together by love...and everything is love. It seems difficult to believe that the horrors you read about in the world that a God who created it all in love. And God *is* love. I stood in his presence and God is *infinite* love. He who created the whole vast universe is infinite love. But faith and hope abide with love, but love is the greatest of all.

Q: (inaudible)

A: Well, every piece that comes into God's presence is automatically purified. The true Israelite is called the pure in heart. "Behold this Israelite indeed in whom there is no guile." So no one can stand in his presence and not become him, for we become what we behold. But he doesn't draw into his presence until in *his* mind he sees the pure in heart. So he sought David "a man after my own heart." So he calls him. But he purifies the heart. Don't try to purify it. The heart becomes purified by the death of delusion, and man cannot work on his delusions and overcome them. A prejudice is a delusion. If you are against any race or nation or religion, you can't rationalize it, you can't justify it. And ___(??) a race of people because one individual of a race you dislike and think all of them are the same, it's stupid. Yet man who dislikes them can't seem to help it. But God will purify their heart: He will take a member of the race the individual dislikes and use a member as his savior. He'll be saved from some embarrassment in this world by a member of the race or the nation or the religion ___(??). I've seen it time and again. And so he could not have plotted the little play whereby he was put in a predicament, and then the only person who rushed forward to save him was a member of the hated group. So a man can't work upon his delusions, his present delusions. He always tries to justify them. And as Blake said, "Self-justification is the voice of hell." In hell there is no such thing as forgiveness of sin; it's all self-justification. A man justifies and justifies ___(??) justify it. He knew exactly what he did, but he doesn't know that you know how he's revealing himself. But he reveals himself by his attempt to justify his behavior.

Q: (inaudible)

A: ___(??) you are incorporated into the body of the one who called you, for you become what you behold. But to be sent, you must then at that moment empty yourself of the form that is yours—you *are* that being—and once more go into the world among men, and wear the garment of the slave, and play your part, knowing that this is the last round, and the time for your departure has come for you've been called. And you never return. I have heard people say, "I'm Paul come again." Don't believe it. "I am Jesus come again. I am this come again." Don't believe it. When you are called, incorporated and sent back into this world with the same identity that you had before being called, that's the slave body that you wore before you were called; but you came into your final form which is Jesus Christ, and you wear the body of Jesus Christ who is God Almighty, infinite love. But at that moment, to be called is to be sent. And then sent is your last round on the world and your time for the departure has come. But until that moment, you must wear the garment of the slave, and proclaim the gospel and represent Christ and instruct others in the way of salvation.

Goodnight.

THE LAST DAYS BY A SON

2/18/1964

"The Last Days by a Son," this is taken from the epistle to the Hebrews. It's an unknown author. Many scholars believe that Paul wrote it, but if you read it carefully along with the letters of Paul, you will come to the conclusion that it is not Paul. Whoever wrote it, the unknown author, certainly had one of the most profound understandings of this great mystery. And I say mystery advisedly, for most of us think it is history, human history, and it's not. In this you will see he is not speaking of Jesus Christ that the world thinks of when they use the words Jesus Christ. Yet he uses the word Jesus, ___(??) him first in the 2nd chapter, the 9th verse. But before that he establishes a *cosmic* Christ; he is speaking only of a cosmic Christ that is God himself.

Now listen to the words: "In many and various ways God spoke of old to our fathers by the prophets; but in these last days he has spoken to us by a Son, whom he appointed the heir of all things, through whom also he created the world. He reflects the glory of God and bears the very stamp of his nature" (Heb. 1:1). Here he establishes this presence. He reflects the very *glory* of God and bears the very stamp of his nature. If I say to you "Jesus Christ," were you a Christian you would think in terms of a being who lived and died approximately 2,000 years ago. If I say to you "Joshua," you would think of an ancient patriarch, an ancient prophet, the author of the sixth book of the Bible, but you wouldn't associate Joshua with Jesus, would you? You'd think they were two entirely different beings, Joshua and Jesus, and yet both words spell the same thing. Joshua is the Hebraic form of Jesus, and Jesus is Jehovah. You spell Jesus, Yod He Vau Shin Ion. That's how you spell Joshua. You spell Jehovah, Yod He Vau He. So why do they differ in spelling as to the last two syllables, the last two letters? Because, listen to it carefully, God in creative activity is called the Son. Infinite love in *unthinkable* origin is God the Father. Infinite love in creative activity is God the Son. Infinite love in eternal procession is God the Holy Spirit... all God...one God, not three Gods. But, God in creative activity is God the Son. The word translated "reflect"—he reflects the glory of God—that word can either mean "reflect" or "radiate." A radiation is a creative activity. It is this God, this infinite love that actually became us, every one of us. It is this God *in* man.

Now listen to it carefully, for when I use the words Jesus Christ I do not think of a unit, one little man born in an unnatural physical way 2,000 years ago, I do not. The being of whom I speak is not born in any physical unnatural way. He is born of flesh and blood. He comes into this world, clothed as *you* are clothed, in the most normal, natural conception, as I was conceived and you were conceived, in the same manner, in a family, a large family. And while walking the earth and he knows his real name ___(??). Well, Jesus Christ now is the name given to God in creative activity, buried in man, all men, the cosmic Christ. It's Jehovah himself that is buried in us. When we say "I am" that's Jehovah, and the word Jehovah is Jesus, same thing.

So here, when I speak of Jesus Christ...listen to the statement carefully, I take it from the last letter, the last chapter of Paul's letter to the Corinthians, the 13 chapter of 2nd Corinthians, it's the 5th verse: "Do you not realize that Jesus Christ is in you?" Well, if you ask that of the average person in the world and if they say yes, they don't really mean it, not really. For when they think of Jesus Christ they do not for one moment feel his presence, feel him *in* them as their own very wonderful human Imagination, they don't. If they begin to rationalize it, they may say to you, "Well, yes, I will accept that." But let them be honest with themselves, and when they think of Jesus Christ they see him as some historical character back in time 2,000 years ago. So the words are not contemporary with them at all. So when you read the words, "Do you not know, do you not realize that Jesus Christ is *in you*?" These are the words. Well, if you realize it, it's *that* one I'm speaking of this night. That is the one and the only concern of God the Father. God the Father is going to resurrect in you *his* Son. When he rises in *you*, you are he. He resurrects only Jesus Christ that is God himself. So the *grace* of God is linked with a specific event, and that event is the resurrection of Jesus Christ.

Now, there are many who believe that because of a certain experience they have experienced this birth of which I speak. Now, there are definite patterns that we follow in this birth. It's given to us so vividly in the 1st letter of Peter, the 1st chapter, the 3rd verse. Listen to it carefully, "By his great mercy we are born anew through the resurrection of Jesus Christ." You dwell upon it. By his great mercy we are born anew by the resurrection of Jesus Christ. But if Jesus Christ was once and for all resurrected 2,000 years ago, you have already then been born anew. And you have *not* been born anew. Therefore, it is simply the unfolding of the *cosmic* Christ in all, individualized as you. And when he is resurrected in you it begins the new age; a completely different age begins with the resurrection of Jesus Christ in the individual. It does not begin with the birth. The birth is the other side of the coin. It begins with the resurrection. No one has the birth prior to the resurrection. The resurrection *begins* Christianity, it begins on that note; but within a matter of moments after the resurrection comes the wonderful heavenly birth from above.

So, "In many and various ways God spoke of old to our fathers by the prophets." In what way? Well, he spoke in that 19th Psalm, the very first verse: The heavens are speaking of the glory of God; and the earth shows forth his handiwork. Today, our astrophysicists, through their telescopes and their trained mathematical minds look off into this fabulous world of ours, and they become excited...and the stories they tell us of this enormous display of the glory of God. Then, our geophysicists, they look down to the earth itself and what they tell us of the structure of this wonderful world of ours, made of one substance differently arranged in many patterns. A rearrangement of its pattern of one substance, and instead of having gold we have silver. Another rearrangement, we have coal. Another rearrangement, we have something else like gas. But one unit, one substance in a complex pattern produces this variety of things in our world, and our great scientists look at it. But he said, "That was secondary to his revelation by the Son."

"In many and various ways God spoke of old to our fathers by the prophets." And you can find it in the 1st chapter, the 20th verse of Romans, "Ever since the creation of the world his invisible nature, namely, his eternal power and deity, has been clearly seen in the things that have been made." Looking for his power? See it through the microscope of the great geophysicists or the great chemists today, and you see this power was *always* there. He tells us, "Ever since the creation of the world his invisible nature, namely, his eternal power and his deity, were clearly seen in the things that have been made." Well, you can't say that he turned from that. As Paul tells us in his very first chapter to the Romans, 1st chapter, the 20th verse, when you read it you transcend that view, and tells us now we transcend it when now the Son speaks to us.

The Son is not now this cosmic Christ. The Son...and he gives now the quote in 5th verse of the 1st chapter of Hebrews. For he bases his argument only on scripture, everything is based upon scripture, and so he either quotes or refers to scripture in every chapter of the entire thirteen chapters of Hebrews. He begins with two quotes: "For to what angel did God ever say, 'Thou art my Son'"? Or again, to what angel did he ever say, 'I am your Father, and you shall be my Son'"? To what angel did he ever say that? He's trying to tell you how infinitely great man is beyond all the forces of nature, including angels and archangels and all the beings in the world. For it was not to them that he came. They are his servants, we're told, the angels serve man.

Because God came to man, and *fused* with man, this infinite pulsing being that is God in action, which is God the Son but still God the Father. Only, when he is in action he's God the Son. For we are told, through him also the world was created. So when God goes into creative action that is called in scripture the Son, the cosmic Son. It is *that* that he's going to awake within you. And when he awakes him in you, you are not another—there is no change in the sense of I—only now you *include* within your being this cosmic being. But you are told he has given him the entire inheritance, to him all things are given; but your heavenly inheritance cannot become actual, or it's not fully realized by you, while you're still wearing this garment of flesh. When you take off this *after* you're resurrected, and may I tell you, in the Book of Luke it shows you so clearly it takes nine months to complete the entire mission, from the resurrection to the end, which is the ascension into heaven. Resurrection; birth; discovery of the fatherhood of God, which is yourself; and then the ascension into heaven, and it's only nine months. So the entire, I would say, missionary work required of the central character of scripture is given nine months in Luke, if you read it carefully. It's not any long, long years. All he's concerned with is that one, that little section of nine months. From his mightiest act which is to resurrect you, resurrect his Son, which is himself in creative activity. But when he resurrects his Son *in* you, why then you are fused with the Son and you *are* that being, and you rise in yourself. So resurrection is an event happening *within*, not on some outside place; *within* the life of the individual, within this *earthly* life of the individual. This all takes place right here.

So here, when I speak of the *last* days they are *these* days. Not when the whole vast world will be consumed, no. When your world, this age, has ceased to be and you enter on a new age, an entirely different world. Well, how am I clothed for that world? Listen to the words carefully, from the 3rd chapter of Philippians, speaking now of this cosmic Son, Jesus Christ: "He will change our lowly body"—and the word change literally means "refashion"—"He will change our lowly body to be like his." The phrase "to be like his" literally means "of one form with". That's what it means. "To be like his" literally means "of one form with his *glorious* body." So your *future* body is actually that of the radiant exalted Christ, not another. One body, one being, for God the Father, God the Son, God the Holy Spirit are one. And God the Son, which is a seeming certain aspect, which is only his creative aspect, became you, raises you to be one with him. So really in the end, you're not *less than*, you are *one with* the Godhead. Seems mad, doesn't it? But I am not speculating. I'm not asking any being outside of my own experience to throw light on it. I'm telling you exactly what happened.

Now our scientists tell us that only that which is scientifically proved can be relied on. Our scientists, not all of them, there are a few, like Alexis ___(??) who still remains a devout religious person, even though he did so much in the scientific world; and there are others who still remain willing to accept what they cannot prove through a test tube. But the majority of them, many scientists and philosophers, will not admit as explanation anything that comes from beyond or above this world of nature. If you can't prove it to them scientifically, then they will not accept it. And yet, I tell you there is not a test given in science today that must meet that *acid* test that this must meet if you will accept what the mystic must accept. The Old Testament is his frame of reference. You can have all the visions and all the dreams in the world, if you can't find the parallel in that book it's only a personal communication between the depth of your soul, which is God, and you. It's meant for *you*; it's not part of the great unfolding drama of God.

You go back and you read the ancient script for intimation and foreshadowing of that which you have experienced. If you can't find it there, then look upon it as a private communication between you and God, and try your best to ask for light to interpret it should it come in the form of symbols. It may come in a direct, simple manner and it needs no greater interpretation than your simple intelligence. If it comes in symbols, ask for light as to the meaning of these symbols. But if you don't find it in scripture, then it is not part of the unfolding play. The unfolding play must meet the most acid test. And I tell you from experience it begins with the resurrection. It's the exact opposite of the way man on earth thinks. Here, everything begins with birth. A man cannot be resurrected until he first dies and *here* it begins with the resurrection. So what is this death that we speak of, and in the next four or five weeks we are all really observing? That has *taken* place. Read it carefully in the 6th chapter of Romans: "If we have been united with him in a death like his, we shall certainly be united with him in a resurrection like his" (verse 5). So here we have the crucifixion is over. Everyone has been crucified with the *cosmic* Christ or you could not breathe. No one could cross the threshold that admits for conscious life unaided by the crucifixion of God, couldn't do it. But that's behind us.

But the real mystery begins with the resurrection. You walk the earth and do not think for one second that you are entombed. Who could think himself entombed? He goes to the cemetery and he sees sepulchers, he sees tombs; he knows he isn't there. He will say, yesterday they put some friend of his in one of them…but he isn't there. And he doesn't know the great mystery. He is walking in his dream...he isn't moving...in his *dream.* He is so sound asleep he doesn't know that he was placed in a tomb. And every child born of woman was placed in a tomb by that clothing of flesh and blood and completely encased in his skull. God's mightiest act, when he least expects it, will descend upon him, that *merciful* act, and arouse him. It will awaken him, and he will awake to find himself completely entombed and sealed in a sepulcher; and that tomb is his skull.

After the initial panic, he will come out, in the same manner that a child is born. But he doesn't feel a child, he doesn't feel himself any little baby, he is the same man, the same woman that he is now and was just one second before he was awakened. And when he is awakened he thinks it's a normal awakening, that's what he thinks. Only the intense vibration is something he's never experienced before. It hits him in his head, and he thinks, "This must be it"—not awakening, this must be death. It's the opposite of death; this is now really awakening unto life when he awakens *in* the sepulcher. You only put dead people in tombs, therefore, he must have been dead to be so sealed in a tomb...and the tomb is his skull.

It is only *then* that he realizes that he was all through these unnumbered ages *dreaming* in his tomb. And then he comes out; and then the symbolism of the first chapter of Luke begins. Then the whole thing begins to unfold and *he* is the one spoken of in scripture. He goes back into the ancient scripture now to find not only that which the New one tells...for the New Testament interprets the Old, not the other way around. The Old is a sealed book until the first breaks the seal. What is the name of the first one? We call Jesus Christ outside of it—because *everyone* who breaks the seal is Jesus Christ. There's only one Jesus Christ and there's only one God; and Jesus Christ is God.

Now, what is this ___(??) trying to show us? He speaks to me now not only through the *cosmic* Christ, he's going to speak to me through a Son, and he names the Son and where to find him in scripture: "To what angel did he say 'Thou art my Son, today I have begotten thee'?" and again, "To what angel did he say, 'Thou art my son and I am thy father'"? And then we go back into the 2nd Book of Samuel, the 7th chapter, the 14th verse, and there we find him. Did I have the experience? Well, then listen to it...and you begin to feel, well now, that all has taken place in me; I have just *had* that. You mean something written 3,000 years ago foretold, that foreshadowed the experience of last night? And you go back and you read it over and over, and you can hardly believe this whole thing is all about you, and that's all that it is about. The whole Bible is about God, only God. And God became us because he loves us, because God's nature is love. Yes, he's infinite power, infinite wisdom, infinite all these, but they are only attributes of God. God's *true* nature is love, infinite love, that's his true nature.

And God's real name now he's about to reveal to you through this Son. Now, who is spoken of in the 2nd Psalm, the 7th verse? For that's what he's quoting. He uses only scripture to support his argument, and that's what he quotes, the 7th verse, the 2nd Psalm: "Thou art my Son, today I have begotten thee." Well, these words are addressed to one called David...David. Now the next one, "And when your days are fulfilled and you lie down with your fathers, I will raise up your son after you, who shall come forth from your body. I will be his father, and he shall be my son" (2 Sam. 7:12,14). To whom is that spoken? Read it carefully. That's spoken by the prophet Nathan to David: "Go unto my servant David and say, 'When your days are fulfilled and you lie down with your fathers, I (the Lord) will raise up your son after you, who shall come forth from your body. I will be his father; he shall be my son.'"

You read it, but you haven't had the experience. And then one day this fantastic thing happens within you, and you begin almost to explode, and you do, something explodes, and here standing before you is David. There is no uncertainty as to who he is. I don't care what sculpture of David is now in the Vatican. I don't care what painter paints the David. Until you see him you can't paint him. And I defy anyone to capture the beauty of that David on canvas, that David in marble. You can't do it! He's radiantly beautiful! He stands before you and he is *the* David of biblical fame. He looks you right in the eye. He's just as described in the Book of Samuel, the 17th chapter...or the 15th chapter of Samuel, just like that (1Sam.16:12). And you have no uncertainty as to this relationship. And what does he call you? He calls you Father. And you know you are his father, and *he* knows you are his father, and you also know he is your son. You are looking right into the eyes of this spiritualized being.

Well, what is he? You didn't even know he was buried in you. You had no idea that was the thing that God in the beginning hid in man, as told us in Ecclesiastes: "And God has put eternity into the mind of man, yet so that man cannot find out what God has done from the beginning until the end" (3:11). The last days...in the last days when he is departing from *this* age and entering through the series of mystical experiences into *that* Age, clothed in the exalted body of Christ Jesus, the cosmic Christ; because he took my lowly body and changed it be like his glorious body. And so we are departing. So in the last days it will be revealed what God hid in the mind of man. And what did he hide?—David. The very word tells you: Olam. He hid Olam in the mind of man, and Olam means "the eternal youth"; it means "the lad, the *stripling*, the eternal youth." So eternity now is revealed not as an old man but this radiant lad. And he is God's spiritualized son to reveal fatherhood, because without a son there is no father. A son, there must be a father, and the son comes to reveal you as God the Father. So it's God's purpose to give every child born of woman himself, and no one will thwart God in his purpose. His purpose is to give you himself, as though there were no others in the world, just God and you. Finally, the gift is so complete when the Son comes before you, just you, because he so gave himself to you, you are he.

So when God rises in man, man is just like him. So you are told in the epistle of John, the 3rd chapter of 1st John, "It does not yet appear what we shall be, but we know when he appears we shall be like him" (3:2). Don't go looking for any being in the world as your leader. You are Christ Jesus; he's buried in you...because we are like him. And his sleep is so profound, which is now *your* sleep but you don't know it, that it is as though he were dead. And the day is coming—and it may be this night because who knows?—but I'll give you a cue as to how you will know when it is coming, and the Bible gives it. It tells of a peculiar famine that comes upon man when he's about to return to the Father. It's called the return of the prodigal son. What caused the prodigal son to come to himself and resolve to go to his father?—a famine. He was eating the husks; instead of giving it to the pigs, he ate the husks. And the world thinks it means husks of corn. No, the whole vast world is husks compared to the *reality* that is God. No matter how ambitious you are and how you realize all your ambitions, they all turn to dust. The rich man dies like the poor man, the wise man like the fool, the strong like the weak, and all is vanity, and vanity of vanities.

So this is husks. No matter how ambitious you are, you can realize it by God's law. But after you realize all of your dreams in this world, they turn to ashes, so they're called husks in the Bible. And when man grows tired of feeding on things that always pass away, that they wear out like a garment and they dissolve like smoke, then he changes the nature of his hunger. But *God* changes it for him. And the words are these, in the 8th chapter, the 11th verse of Amos: "The Lord will send a famine upon the land. It will not be a famine of bread nor a thirst for water, but of the hearing of the word of God"—a hunger so intense that nothing but *that* can satisfy it. It is not for money, it is not for greatness, not to be the president, not to be a dictator, not to be anything in this world that is known to men, but a *hunger* for the word of God. Not a thing in this world can satisfy that hunger but to *understand* the word of God, and the only way you understand it is to experience it.

Scripture must be experienced for man to see how truly wonderful it really is. You can analyze it as scholars do, you can take the grand exegeses and see this most wonderful display of words, what the original words meant when it was used, and it's exciting, it's thrilling, and you may know Greek backwards and Latin backwards and Hebrew backwards, and really understand it from the scholarly point of view. But you don't know scripture until you *experience* scripture. You get…all the scholars of world cannot by their learning extract the wisdom of that book until they experience it. They must *experience* scripture to know really what it is. So you can speak with all the tongues of men and angels, and know it in and out, but you don't know scripture until you experience it. And the day will come, may I tell you, *everyone* will experience it, for that is God's plan. "As I have planned it, so shall it be; as I have purposed it, so shall it stand" (Is.14:24) and no one in the world is going to change it.

So until that hunger comes, take God's law, and eat more and more of the husks, doesn't make any difference. You've been eating husks all of the time since you started the journey, and you will continue to eat husks until the nature of the hunger changes and it becomes the hunger for God's word. But only an *experience* of God's word can satisfy that hunger. So let no one tell you while the hunger is for this building or to join a club or to be some prominent person in the world that it's wrong. It isn't wrong. God gave it to you. You needed that kind of mood at a certain moment in time. He gave you that hunger, you feed upon it. Learn his law by which you can satisfy the hunger until that moment in time like the prodigal son, you turn around. And when you are brought in what does he give the prodigal son?—commanded the servants, "Put the *best* robe on him"—there is no second best in God's kingdom, the best robe. "Put the ring on his finger"—that's the insignia of being the heir to it all; and "put shoes on his feet"—for only the slave went barefoot. When you put shoes on him...but now he's free man. He has found David, and he who sees David, his father is made free, as told us in the 17th chapter of 1st Samuel. Anyone who finds the one who destroys the enemy of Israel I will set his father free (verse 25). So to be a free man you must be shod with shoes, for only those who are slaves go without shoes. This is all symbolism but it's beautiful symbolism.

So when the hunger comes upon you, real hunger, I would say to you the time is drawing near for the fulfillment of God's promise. He's promised you to give you a son that is *his* son; and when he gives you his son *as your* son, he has given you himself. That's the only way God could ever reveal to man that he has fulfilled his purpose to give himself to man is through the medium of a son. "So no one knows who the Son is except the Father, and no one knows who the Father is except the Son and any one to whom the Son chooses to reveal him" (Mat.11:27). Well, the moment will come in your life when the Son will choose to reveal you as his Father, and *his* Father is God. So in the end there is only God.

So when asked, "What is the greatest commandment?" the reply was, "Hear, O Israel: the Lord our God is one Lord" (Deut. 6:4). The Lord, spelt just like Jesus, it's Yod He Vau He, that's how you translate the word "the Lord." Yod He Vau He, we call it Jehovah, but so as not to mention the name, they translate it "the Lord." Sometimes Adonay is called the name, but it means the same. Well, in this case it was Yod He Vau He...you're going to say Jesus. The next word is Elohim; it's a plural word meaning gods. The first time it appears in the Bible, the very first verse, "In the beginning *God* created the heavens and earth"...that word is plural (Gen. 1:1). If you properly translated it, it would be gods...but God. Here is a *compound* unity. For in the end you will not lose your identity, I will not lose my identity, no one will lose their identity, and yet we are one...a compound unity, one made up of others.

So, "Hear, O Israel: the Lord our God is one Lord." Hear, O Israel, Jehovah our Elohim is one Jehovah, one Jesus Christ. Not *a* little man, but all are that *cosmic* Christ, the second aspect of divinity that is creating. So infinite love in creative activity is God the Son; infinite love in eternal procession, God the Holy Spirit—because the same thing is going to happen to every child born of woman, so it's eternal procession. So he makes the statement, "I will send the Holy Spirit upon you." Because when the Holy Spirit comes it's eternal procession of the same thing: It is resurrection; it is birth; it is the discovery of the fatherhood of God through the Son, David; and the ascent into heaven. So, the eternal procession—it doesn't alter the pattern.

If anyone has any doubt as to "did I really have the experience of being born from above," I say to you, were you resurrected? If you say no to that answer, then it is no to the other. You cannot be born until *after* the resurrection. It's an entirely new world. You're resurrected into a new world and born into that world, but the resurrection precedes the birth by a matter of seconds. But it does come first. If you haven't had the resurrection...and no one who experienced it could ever forget it in eternity. You can forget what you had for breakfast, you can forget what you had for dinner, you can forget the last telephone call you made and to whom, but you can't forget the resurrection. You can't forget any of these four stages, you can't do it. They are indelibly imprinted upon you and you can't forget them.

So no one need ask did I have it? Many of us in our anxiety and our eagerness to experience it will conjure in the mind's eye a certain experience of a child. We are eager...and who can blame anyone for being eager to have the experience...and we'll conjure it. It's a false birth. For the birth is so unique that it defies description. How are you going to describe it? I tried my best, I tried not to embellish, not to add to or take from, tell it just as it happened to me. As you're told in those five words in the Book of Luke, "They related their own experience." Almost the entire Bible could be wrapped in those five words; they told what had happened. When they told what had happened, it seemed like the words of an idle tale, and they did not believe them.

So it seemed like the words of an idle tale. For our priesthoods of the world taught us to believe that because Jesus Christ, *a* man, born physically in an unnatural manner, was resurrected from the dead, you who believe in his name and believe in him as a being outside of yourself, not buried in you, then you will enter the kingdom of heaven. May I tell you, don't believe it. Listen to these words, "Of all born of woman none is greater than John the Baptist; yet I tell you the least in the kingdom is greater than John" (Luke 7:28). I need not analyze it for you, it tells you John is not in the kingdom. Doesn't it tell you that? The least in the kingdom is greater than John, therefore, John is not in the kingdom. John belongs to this world and he was the most perfect born of woman. Wasn't born from above...born of woman. He tried to change his nature. He thought by a change of nature he would bring about the birth. Can't do it. It's wonderful to change from being violent to being kind, marvelous. And people will say, "But he must have been born again because look, I recall him when he was a thief. Look at him now, a gentle, kind, wonderful person. I knew him when he was violent in his reaction to everything. Look at him now, how loving he is. Surely he has had the spiritual birth." Not at all.

Listen to these words of William James, "The greatest revolution in this century was the discovery that man by changing his inner attitudes of mind could change the outer aspects of his life." Anyone can practice that and you'll amaze your friends. They all stand dumbfounded when they see you, the man that you are, as against the man that they knew. But it doesn't mean that because they see that radical change in your physical life that you have experienced the spiritual birth. That is something that is not shown on the outside. Hasn't a thing to do with what you are now doing on the outside. It's something that is a gift: It's the gift of God. And the grace of God is always linked with a specific event and that event is the resurrection of Jesus Christ *in you*. That's his grace. For when God gives you his grace, it is when he awakens himself *in* you *as* you.

For, Jesus Christ is God, believe it or not, and God is infinite love. Infinite love is buried in man. Yes, even the man this night who may be going to the chair, having in cold blood killed one or a dozen people. That being who could do such a thing, that dastardly act—still buried in that man that we in the world of Caesar will now exact from him a life for a life, and take his for the twelve that he took—buried in that man is the God of love. But, so sound asleep, and the nightmare of the being who is walking the earth is so intense that he is totally unaware of the presence in him of Jesus Christ. And may I tell you, Jesus Christ could not emerge from a man in whom he does not now exist, couldn't do it. What could come out of the ocean that is not now in the ocean? What could come out of man that is not now in man? So Jesus Christ is the *life* of man, he is *in* man.

And the day will come when God the Father who *is* Jesus Christ—but not in creative activity—Jesus Christ is God in creative activity; and it is *he in* man that will be awakened by that infinite, merciful act of God the Father, who will simply arouse him with the most intense vibration you will ever experience right in your head. And when he arouses him, it's *you*, *you* awake. The fusion has taken place. And then you know that wonderful mystery of the 54th chapter of Isaiah, "Your Maker is your husband" (verse 5). For bear in mind, through him ___(??) created the world. So "the Maker" is "he who created the world." This is God in creative activity, called God the Son. He is your Maker and he is your husband, the Lord of hosts is his name. And what must a husband do? We are told in Genesis he must leave all and cleave to his wife until they become one, not two. So here, you are his emanation yet his bride 'til the sleep of death is past (Gen. 1:24). He *emanates* man...that's his creation. He creates it by emanation, and then falls in love with his emanation, and cleaves to his emanation until they cease to be two, God *and* man, and *only* God. You'll become one with the being who cleaves to you. So when you awake, no loss of identity. But now you have inherited a presence. Aside from inheriting a kingdom you inherit a presence, and that presence is God the Father.

So this is what I mean. And the first three verses of that wonderful epistle to the Hebrews: "In many and various ways God spoke of old to our fathers by the prophets, but in these *last* days"—for the turn of the age is now to the individual who experiences it—"in these last days he has spoken unto us by a son" (1:1). And this son he gave all things. This son created all. This son which is himself reflects the very glory of God, and this son bears the very stamp of his nature. It is this son that is changing our lowly body to be like his glorious body, so that in the end the body you will wear will be one in form with that of the exalted Christ.

But, this night, if your hunger is on an entirely different level, take the advice of William James. He certainly proved it. He could have read this great advice in the Bible, but he was a great scientist, a great psychiatrist, a great philosopher. He taught at Harvard for years, his brother Henry wrote these fantastic books, and they were brilliant minds; but like all of these brilliant minds they don't really read the Bible. I saw in last week's *New York Times* that the Bible Society last year in 1963 distributed thirty-three million Bibles. That's one house, the biggest, granted, but only one house. Harper, Enroe, they publish Bibles, Schribner publishes Bibles, Nelson and Son publishes Bibles, all the big publishers publish Bibles; but one house, the Bible Society of America, distributed thirty-three million Bibles. Now add to that what the other parts of the world sold in Bibles. And then you will take all the best sellers of the entire year, put them all together, multiply them by a very large number, and they would only come to a fraction of the sales equal to that of the Bible. And yet, these best sellers, may I tell you, they are read, and the Bible, with a hundred million distributed, isn't read.

You give it to a girl at confirmation, or a boy; he's confirmed, and he thanks you for the Bible, takes it home and puts it where it gets dust. When one gets married, they go to their lovely Bible before they consult a priest, and he keeps that as a wonderful memento, that's all, never opened the book. And so, it's the most *unread* book in the world, and year after year it is a fantastic sale. If you take all fifty million in our land—for thirty-three in one house, surely the others would make it fifty million—and then take England, Australia, New Zealand, Canada and all the other parts of the world, France, Germany, all Christian nations, and see what there *would* be. And these books, I tell you, they're not opened. People who ride the subways in New York City if they have a Bible, know what they do? They put a cover on it. They're embarrassed to be seen, especially a man. A lady who had a Bible she wouldn't mind showing it, but a man on the subway with a Bible? He puts a false cover on it. He doesn't want anyone to know that he is so feminine that he's reading a Bible, the greatest book in the world.

And until man actually experiences the Bible he remains on the wheel of recurrence. So when the hunger comes to know the *word* of God which is the Bible, I say the time is drawing near for the promise of God to be fulfilled in that one who has the hunger.

Now let us go into the Silence for a moment.

* * *

We're supposed to close, you know, at the end of this month, that's by my contract, but I have an extension to the 26th day of May and then I close, and I will not be back here until the middle of October. I'm leaving on the 27th for New York to attend my daughter's graduation, and then we're going off to Barbados for a couple of months. Then my next stop will be in San Francisco in September. So I will not be back here until the middle of October. But I will be here through until the 26th of May.

Another point I want to make, these Tuesdays and Thursdays come to an end with this month. They have committed this room for Thursday night, and so we have to go back to our old stand of Friday night. So it will be every Tuesday and Friday beginning in March. Then I have scheduled the program for March and I would say five-eighths or three-quarters of it will be on the law. There will be enough of the promise woven into it, but it's going to be on the law, much of it, beginning with the very first one "Is Causation Imaginal?" We hope to prove to you with case histories and all kinds of proof that imagining *does* create reality. So, we have just a few left in the present series, and I hope maybe by Thursday night to have them for you. But, anyway, before we close the new programs will be out.

Now are there any questions?

Q: ___(??) man that thou has made him a little *lower* than the angels?

A: That's the 8th Psalm. The new translation does not. The word is Elohim; it is *not* angels. So, the translator of the King James Version could not bring himself to believe that God thought so highly of man that he would see him as *himself*. Because the word translated "angels" is the very word that is translated, the very first verse of Genesis, "In the beginning *God* created the heavens and the earth." And in the 26th verse, "Let us make man in our image" and the word is "and *God* said" and the word God is Elohim. That same word Elohim is now translated in the 8th Psalm as angels, the *only* place in the entire Bible. So the translator could not believe that man could be *that* dignified, *that* great in the eye of God. So the new translation which you'll find in the Revised Standard Version, "He made him a little lower than himself." For, to come here and take on the limitations of flesh and blood it would have to be lower than "infinite love in unthinkable origin." So, coming down and assuming the limitation he would have to empty himself; so God emptied himself of his primal form, his immortal body, and took upon himself the form of a slave (Phil. 2:7). That's what we're told. So he was not left as an angel. The angels, as told you in the very first chapter of the Book of Hebrews that we quoted tonight, are the *servants* of men…as the winds and the fire they are the servants of the

Lord and therefore servants of man. So man can say "I am," that's God's name.

Q: (inaudible)

A: The Holy Spirit, as we said, is infinite love in eternal procession. He said, "I will send to you the Holy Spirit. It is not for you to know the times or the seasons fixed by the Father in his own authority; but wait for the promise of the Father, for you shall receive power from above when the Holy Spirit has come upon you" (Acts 1:7). The Holy Spirit is active in all of this. The night that you are born from above, you have never heard such a wind in your life. I personally have not gone through a cyclone. I've gone through a hurricane, many a hurricane at sea and on the land. If a cyclone differs in intensity from a hurricane, I don't know, but I know what winds of hurricane force sound like. It doesn't compare to the wind that you hear the night of the birth, the night of the resurrection, followed by the birth. So that 2nd chapter of Acts, when that mighty rushing wind which they call the Holy Spirit at Pentecost, it is just like that. It comes like a rushing wind and you hear it, you are disturbed, but it is the Holy Spirit...his *presence* is there. And so he plays every part in the unfolding of this eternal drama. He doesn't vary it, one to the other; all go through the same series of mystical experiences as they are recorded in scripture. So the Holy Spirit, it is ___(??). It's simply another aspect of infinite love, but it's infinite love. God the Son is infinite love, God the Father is infinite love, and the Father and the Son are one. The Father, the Son and the Holy Spirit are one. They aren't three, they aren't many. It's this compound unity of ___(??), all of us together, to be one God. As told us in Zechariah, "And the Lord will be king over all the earth; on that day the Lord will be one and his name one" (Zech.14:9). And that name is Jesus.

Q: (inaudible)

A: No, I wouldn't put it that way. Just think of God, the 43rd chapter of the Book of Isaiah, "I am the Lord thy God, the Holy One of Israel, your *Savior*...and besides me there is no savior." Forty-third of Isaiah, "I am the Lord your God, the Holy One of Israel, your Savior...and besides me there is no savior" (verses 3,11). So bear in mind when I say Jesus I mean Jehovah. They're spelt alike. But Jesus—Jehovah in creative expression—is buried in you. That's his love for you. That's Jesus Christ in you, as told us in Corinthians, "Do you not realize that Jesus Christ is *in* you?" (2 Cor.13:5). Now, every minister of the world leads man *outside* of this inner being that is his savior, and tries to worship something on the wall. "Make no graven image unto me" (Ex.20:4); yet man goes around all day long making graven images;

and with the consent of the priesthoods of the world they sell these indulgences. They sell them, and people go home with them and think they have a holy image of the one. And "Make no graven image unto me" (the Second Commandment), none. But man will not obey that Commandment; he makes images after images after images. And you're told, "If anyone should say, 'Look, here is the Christ!' or 'Look, there he is!' believe him not" (Mark 13:21). And yet man still, in spite of that, points to this one as the Christ and that one as the Christ. Do not believe it if any man should ever say, "Look, here is Christ!" or "There he is!" do not believe him—in the 13th chapter of the Book of Mark—don't believe him!

ETERNAL STATES

2/20/64

Tonight's subject is "Eternal States." States...by states I mean states of consciousness and these are conditioned. Unlike the Promise that is unconditioned, states of awareness are all conditioned. You can't be in one state of awareness and expect to reap the fruit of another state. To reap the fruit of a state you must occupy the state, and any state in this world can be occupied. You are free to move from state to state, but man is not aware of it. The Bible teaches us how to do it. We are told, "Blessed is the man who delights in the law of the Lord, for in all that he does he prospers" (Ps.1:3). In all, not a few things but in everything that he does he prospers if he knows how to operate God's law. It's not as difficult as you've been told. In fact, it is *not* difficult; it just needs application on your part. Like all arts in this world there must be a certain method, and then there must be a certain practice and persistent practice, so that you actually master the technique of moving from state to state.

Now here is a story told us...and I'll tell you the story, and you go home and read it, and see if you do not see it through different eyes. The first one to really start the battle, who conquered, was Joshua. Joshua is Jesus. It's spelled the same way. It is spelled Joshua in Hebrew, and then translated into English it would be Jesus. Jesus and Joshua are Jehovah, same thing. So the battle starts, really, with Jehovah. It's the sixth book of the Bible. The first time that this thought appears in the Bible you'll find it in the 13th chapter of Genesis. It's the separation of Abraham and Lot. Abraham said to Lot, "If you go to the right, I will go to the left; if you go to the left, I'll go to the right. The choice is yours. So you take it, you take the first choice." And then he looked out at the valley, it was the valley of the Jordan, and it was well watered and so fertile and so real that Lot chose the valley of the

Jordan. Then Abraham went into Canaan, and then everything was given to Abraham.

Now when you read "the valley of the Jordan" you may be inclined to think of a place, the Jordan as a river, and a magical valley well watered by that river. Today if you hear the word Jordan, you think it's biblically... you think of a river in the Near East. That's not Jordan. If you have a concordance, you look it up. Here is the meaning of the word: "To descend; or, speaking of the individual, the descender." But we'll take it "to descend; to go down to a lower region; right down to the boundary; to the shore; to the enemy." These are the definitions in the James Strong's Concordance for the word Jordan. You go down; it's going down, right down to the boundary, to the shoreline, to the enemy. In the four gospels, the work of Jesus, his entire work, begins at Jordan. He goes right down into Jordan where he is baptized.

If you will see it through my eyes, right now this very room, this is Jordan. No water around, but this is Jordan. If I took you into my confidence and I told you exactly what I have in the bank, and what my obligations to life are as against what I have in the bank; what my income is over the years as against what my outgo is; if I showed you my social background, my intellectual background, my entire background, and completely confessed all these facts of life, I have led you right into my Jordan. That's my Jordan. Have I any ambition to transcend it? Can I get *beyond* the Jordan? Have I any desire to get beyond the Jordan? Well then, this is the story of the motion from state to state. It is all starting with the Jordan—looking at my world and seeing exactly what I have as against what I want in this world. When I know exactly what I have by looking at it honestly, I am right at the Jordan. So he doesn't evade the issue, he comes right into the Jordan, God himself, and assumes all the limitations of the flesh; blinds himself completely to all that he really is, and takes upon himself all the weaknesses, all the limitations of the flesh. So my reason dictates the facts of life and my senses affirm it, or confirm it. Here is my Jordan. And then I want to go beyond what I am, the man that I am, can I get beyond the Jordan? So that's the entire story.

Now, we are told Moses could not get beyond the Jordan. If you want to read it, in the 3rd chapter of Deuteronomy, he could not get beyond the Jordan. The Lord said to him, "Joshua, my servant, will do it" and so it was given to Joshua to go *beyond* the Jordan into the land that the Lord had promised. Now, these words are addressed to *you*, not to some being who lived thousands of years ago, these are your words, addressed all to you: "Wherever the sole of your foot will tread upon I have given to you." "Wherever the sole of your foot will tread upon I have"—listen to the tense—"I *have given* to you." Not something held in abeyance; when *you* tread upon it I have given it to you. Now comes a picture, "Prepare provisions; for within three days you are going to pass over this Jordan, to possess the land that I the Lord your God gives you." That's the 1st chapter of the Book of Joshua (verse 10). The last chapter, the 24th chapter, it ends, "Choose you this day whom you will serve, whether the gods your fathers served *beyond* the Jordan, or whether they will be the gods of the Amorites in whose land you now dwell." And they made their decision: We will serve the gods our fathers served beyond the Jordan (verse 15). That was their decision. Then he said to them, "You are witnesses against yourselves. You have chosen that you will serve the gods your fathers served." And then they answered, "We are witnesses" (verse 22).

Now, this is how I make my decision to go beyond the Jordan. It was taught me graphically back in 1933...always *beyond* the Jordan. I looked at my Jordan, and I didn't have a nickel. I had no bank account and I didn't have a nickel, and there was no one to whom I could turn to borrow any money. Why, five dollars in 1933 would be like asking for $2,000 today. Very few had five dollars. And what I needed at that moment nothing under $1,000 could do it. I wanted to go on a trip. I didn't have a job, living in the basement on 75th St. in New York City, overrun with cockroaches, I mean *really* a mess. Anything in New York City on that ground floor is just like that even in the best areas, but this was not the best area. I desired to go to Barbados, and I simply confided, I confessed to my friend Abdullah. As I confessed my limitations, my lack, everything, I was right down at the water's edge and showing him this wide stream that was Jordan, and telling him of a land beyond the Jordan. It was 2,000 miles away across water. And he said to me, "You are *now* in Barbados."

Now, we're standing physically together. He is not in Barbados, he is in New York City in his home on 72nd Street, and he tells me, I could touch him, that I am in Barbados. He would not discuss it with me after that day. I could not bring it up to ask him, "How am I going to go to Barbados?" He would not discuss it. I could not consider means *if* I am *already* there. How could I consider how I'm going to *get* there when I am *already* there? Wherever the sole of your foot will tread upon I have *given* you...it's past. "Are you standing in Barbados? Are you sleeping in Barbados? Are you preparing your ___(??) for Barbados? Are you seeing the world as you would see it were you in Barbados? Have you prepared this food? Have you seen the world as you would see it? Are you seeing New York 2,000 miles to the north of you when you sleep this night? How can you tell me that you don't have the money *to go* to Barbados when you *are* in Barbados? Well, if man is all Imagination, man *must* be wherever he is in Imagination, for man is Imagination itself. So are you now in Barbados? Well, you can't discuss with me how you're going to go there, the ways and means are not to be discussed because you've *gone* there. So you are in Barbados." That's crossing the Jordan, and only Jesus, Joshua, Jehovah could do it. Because Jehovah's name is I AM, the only prayer of mine that is answered is that which I am. If I must call with his name and his name is I AM, I don't say, "In the name of Jehovah do it, in the name of Jesus Christ do it, in the name of Joshua do it," or any other being. The only name that answers is I AM. So where am I? Well, I say, I am...and I name it. So here is the Jordan; and suddenly there is no Jordan, I'm on the other side. It's behind me now, I'm on the other side; I am dwelling in my wish fulfilled. I have changed the state.

So I've decided not to serve the gods my fathers served. Now, I'm a witness against myself if that's my decision. I will not serve the Amorites in whose land I now dwell: I dwell in the land of my senses. I refuse now to serve the gods of the Amorites in whose land I dwell. I can't deny I dwell in this land, but every moment of time I can cross the Jordan. And man has to *cross* the Jordan to dwell beyond it. That's what Abraham had to do. And so, he lived by faith, and the promises became his, not Lot. Lot was destroyed. He lived in Sodom and Gomorrah. The whole area, wife turned into the pillar of salt, and the whole vast place was burned. Abraham went out into a land he didn't know, all in Imagination, all in faith.

So you want...and you name it. You want more money, and you just name the money, I don't care what it is. God doesn't judge you. He has never judged anyone. It's man who judges, but God doesn't judge anyone because God is *infinite* mercy. And so, Jehovah's gift does not depend upon you doing anything to undo Jordan. You only go beyond it, that's what you do, because Jehovah is without money, without price in the continual forgiveness of sin. So one stands before you and confesses his limitation, he shows you his Jordan. Well, he tells you what he wants in place of what he has and he tells you of a land beyond Jordan. You say to him what my friend Ab said to me, "You are it now." You want a nice wonderful job that pays more than you ever earned before? You have it *now*. He looks into your face and he thinks you're mad. That's what I thought of my friend Ab, but I so respected him I couldn't tell him. I couldn't tell him that you're mad, you're insane, because I loved him. I respected him. And so, I walked away from him dumbfounded—"I am in Barbados!" And here I am walking the streets of New York City without a nickel, without a penny in my pocket, going back to my ___(??) on 75th Street. And I am in Barbados! And then in a way that I could never have devised I was in Barbados within six weeks, all as a gift. Three heavenly months in the island as a sheer gift; and returned to this country not only after having spent three months, at some cost to them, but brought back several hundred dollars in hard cash that they gave me when I got aboard the boat. But I didn't ask them for one nickel, not a penny. All was given because I went beyond my Jordan and lived in the state of my wish fulfilled.

So tonight, when you know what you want, you go beyond the Jordan. If you are right down at the water's edge...listen to the definition, "to descend to lower regions, right down to the boundary, down to the shore," and then the last word, we find, "the enemy." Who is my enemy? So when he comes out of Jordan in the Book of Luke, the first one that meets him is the embodiment of Jordan and it's called the devil. So here, Jordan is the enemy. So he now becomes personified, and so the personification of Jordan takes on the form of the monster that is called the devil, called Satan. He said, "You are the Son of God? Well then, turn one of these stones, turn a stone into bread." "Man should not live by bread alone, but by every word that proceeds out of the mouth of God" (Mat. 4:4). "If you are the Son of God, well then, stand on this pinnacle and cast yourself down." Then he quotes scripture, For did he not give his angels the command to hold you up, lest you dash your feet against a stone? "You shall not tempt the Lord thy God." Then he offers the entire kingdom for *his* wish. The embodiment of his senses is telling exactly what he is; for he took upon himself *all* the limitations of the flesh. He did not leave one little opening that he could see eternity and therefore be the being that he really is; completely shut the door on eternity and took on all the limitations and the weaknesses of the flesh.

Then, from within he began to apply his law, his divine law, wisely. As we are told in Paul's letters to Timothy, "The law is good if used justly." It is good if you use it justly. You can forgive every being in this world, and grant every request that comes within the framework of love. If anyone asks you this night to hurt someone for them, you have no ears to hear it. To injure someone, you have no ears to hear it. But if they told you the most horrible story about themselves, you can forgive them because they're only in a state, and so they're expressing a *state*. They just came from someplace where they stole. They did something that is horrible, something you hope that you would never do, that no friend would do, but you don't judge them harshly for having done it. You ask them, "What do you want?" Well, they would like to be free of this picture, alright, beyond the Jordan. You take them from where they are. In your mind's eye you put them beyond their Jordan into a state of joy, where they would never entertain the thought of taking advantage of another. And you see them through such eyes, right into the state of *beyond* the Jordan.

So Blake could say, having seen these infinite states and the infinite possibilities for man, "I now judge no one. For I do not regard either the wicked or the just to be in a supreme state, but to be every one of them states of the sleep which the soul may fall into in its deadly dreams of good and evil." It falls into a state. So, you and I are all day long, we don't know God's law; we're right down at the water's edge, at the shore, watching the Jordan. And there we stay...we can't get *beyond* the Jordan. It seems so wide and so deep we can't get beyond. But only Joshua was given the command to do it. If you read the story carefully, the battle was not completed, was not consummated, until the time of David. And so we are told, to him that conquers, I will give to him and grant to him to sit with me on my throne, as I myself conquered and am sat down with my father on his throne. And so, in the very end it is David who brings about the complete destruction of all these beliefs in things other than God. When he takes off the head of the monster, it is then he sets his Father free in the kingdom of heaven.

And so here, I tell you this day, *your* Jordan is just where you are now. If you're in the desert, you're right down at the water's edge, and that's your Jordan. In the desert you may be thirsty and dying of thirst, you want to get beyond this parched ground into some oasis. You've got to actually put yourself into the oasis, just as though you were there, and then believe and trust God implicitly to devise the means by which you are moved from where you were to where you are now *assuming* that you are. And in a way that no one knows you'll go there. I try to live by this morning, noon and night, but still wearing the garment of flesh I am always at Jordan. I must always make the journey *beyond* the Jordan. So every morning when I get up Jordan confronts me. The morning's mail brings not only requests for help, news from friends across the way, and bills. So every morning's mail there is a bill, which means you've got to face it, you can't duck it. You've been using the gas, using the lights, you've been using your department stores, and so because you have credit you take it. And so, all of a sudden you must confront the evidence, and here it is, comes the bill. So that's my Jordan. Now I've got to go beyond it and dwell with it all behind me as *paid*...not torn up and thrown away but all paid. And so, every day I'm at my Jordan.

So every day who goes to the Jordan and starts his wonderful work in this world? Jesus Christ; and Jesus Christ is your own wonderful human Imagination, *that* Jesus Christ. So when you say "I am," you're calling on the name of God. So you're told, "Whatever you ask in his name"—that's not a good translation—when I ask *in* his name, I ask *with* his name. To ask *with* his name for wealth: "I am wealthy." Not in words, but in the state I *feel* wealth. I put it on as I would a garment and *feel* it, and then allow it to hatch out in my world. No desire to pile it away because I feel insecure; no, that I can always cross my Jordan. If I know God's law, I don't have to pile it away for some rainy day. No, I can always cross the Jordan if I know God's law. So every morning you are at the Jordan, because you come right down to earth from wherever you were at night.

At night it may be some heavenly vision, a wonderful dream, some wonderful communication between God and yourself, where God instructed you and advised through the medium of a dream. But when you wake and the familiar things are on the wall and you know where you are, back to earth you come, right back down to the Jordan. You start your day there and from there you've got to go beyond the Jordan. So I will extract from you this day a promise, who would you serve? I'm not going to say you must serve the gods of your fathers; you may serve the gods of the Amorites. That's your choice. So choose this day whom you will serve. He doesn't say you *must* choose it; he's giving you the privilege of choice: Choose this day whom you will serve, whether the gods your fathers served *beyond* the Jordan, or the gods of the Amorites in whose land you now dwell. You're always in that land of the Amorites whenever you wake in the morning, and there is the Jordan. But the gods of your fathers, they are beyond the Jordan.

So if you now have a certain sum of money to meet in order to hold a job, you're a salesman, and so double it, treble it. You aren't doing it, God does it. Actually believe in him, so you can actually, as I told you earlier, you can say "Amen" to that. All of a sudden you think of something, you think of the person that you will be at the end of the month, when the report comes in and the sales manager sees the report and he congratulates you on what you've done. So you put yourself before him at that moment in time when he's going to do this. Then you start the day. But you are faithful to that ending; you saw that ending. Then in a way you do not know, instead of signing up, maybe, a hundred small accounts, you may settle for one. That one may not come till the last day, but it will dwarf the hundreds beyond your wildest dream. It doesn't have to be unnumbered little ones; you only want a big one at the very last day of the month.

So you go *beyond* your Jordan into that land that has been promised you. "Wherever the sole of your foot will tread I have given to you." What a promise! To actually feel yourself in it! I can't tread over there unless I'm saying to myself, "I am" and *that* becomes *here*. I must make there here to tread upon it. I have to make Barbados here. And if Barbados isn't superimposed upon New York City, no, New York City must move relative to Barbados. So if I actually brought Barbados here, then I've displaced Los Angeles. And where would Los Angeles be in my mind's eye if I'm standing and treading on Barbados? Well, I would see it to the west of me, approximately 5,000 miles. I mean northwest of me...not quite 5,000; 3,000 across the country and we are in the Atlantic and south by another

2,000 miles. So it would be 5,000 going around-about manner, but not as the crow flies, say 4,000 miles. So I would see L.A. as I think of it 4,000 miles to the west of me. So I'm treading then where, on Barbados, and wherever the sole of your foot will tread upon I have given to you.

So I will sleep this night viewing the world. As I view the world, I have prepared my provisions; these are my provisions I'm feasting upon. For in three days...now it doesn't mean three days, three twenty-four hour periods. Three is resurrection, for "on the third day the earth rose up out of the deep." It's like the eight; eight is a new beginning, a new day of the week. So on the eighth day he rose, but the eight was a new beginning. It was the first of a new week, of a new age. But three in the beginning of the creative power is resurrection, for on the third day the earth rose up out of the deep. So on what would be the third day of this vision—it could be in one hour, it could be in a day, it could be in three days, it could be in three weeks—but that means that then the thing that is unseen (for it's in the deep) you're going to bring it *up* out of the deep. It's going to be seen not only by you but seen by the world. For the earth, your earth on which you are now treading will rise up out of the deep.

And so, your Jordan will be behind you, but only for a while. Tomorrow morning the same Jordan will come back and your senses will be dictating to you what are the facts of life. So your senses and your reason every day of your life until you take this garment off puts you, everyday you start it right at the Jordan, at the water's edge. So you learn the art of moving *beyond* the Jordan to that land beyond the Jordan. And who does it? Joshua does it, and Joshua is the Hebraic form of the Anglicized word Jesus. Jesus can do anything because Jesus is Jehovah, Jesus is God; and when you say "I am" before you say John or Mary or Neville or any other name, before you put any little tag on it, *that's* Jesus. Now trust him implicitly.

So, where am I? Well then, view the world to see where I am, for I'm located by looking at the world. What I see mentally is only locating me. If I see you and on your face is an expression that you see in me the man that I want you to see, well, then you're telling me where I'm located in my own mind's eye. Now feed upon it, prepare your provisions, and in three days, I will take you into the land that I the Lord your God give you. In three days I'll bring it out, and so what you are now treading upon I the Lord your God have given you. It's all done the moment you start treading upon it.

So these are the infinite states. And not because you are worthy of it, forget the so-called worthiness, forget the so-called sin in the world the world talks about. No, he isn't judging you. The spirit of Jesus is *continual* forgiveness of sin. When you know that man is only occupying a state, you can easily forgive him. No matter what he's done he was in a state, and because he was in that state he had to express the contents of that state. A man feels sorry for himself; he's in a state; and things must happen in his life to make him all the more convinced that he had good reason to be sorry for himself. Because everyone must turn against him and make him feel that he is unwanted in this world because in his own mind's eye he was unwanted, or he felt himself unwanted. But that was only a state. He is wanted because he is as loved by God as any being that ever walked the face of this earth. So everyone can get out of a state if he knows he's only in a state. But strangely enough, when we are in these states they seem to be the only reality. A person who is in any state, elated or deflated, whatever the state is, he thinks it's the only reality; and everything else is simply like a cloud, that it isn't real, it isn't altogether something with substance only because he's not occupying it. And so I always felt that one of the great weaknesses of the world is the continual construction but deferred occupancy. They don't occupy it. One must *occupy* the state.

I tell you from my own experience, in '33, when I tried time and again to open up the discussion with my friend Abdullah, he just turned his back to me and walked right into his little study room, wouldn't discuss it with me. Then you learned afterwards he was teaching the most marvelous lesson in this world. You said you believed, you actually said you believed in God, and you took his word honestly. You're told not to change these words, in the 4th chapter of Deuteronomy, Do not add to or take from these words (verse 2). Do not add to them; don't take from them. What is the word? "Wherever the sole of your foot will tread upon that"—not something else—"*that* have I given to you." So, "You told me, Neville, you're in Barbados. Didn't you agree with me you're in Barbados? Didn't you say when I asked you whether you would serve the gods of your fathers who dwelt beyond the Jordan or will you serve the gods of the Amorites in whose land you now dwell? Right now you're poor and you couldn't go even on a bus, far less a ship, and you want a ship that takes you ten days at sea, and feeds you three times a day, and gives you all the comforts of a nice ship, right to Barbados. That takes money. So you tell me you don't have any of these things. Well, you're at Jordan. Now come, you're in Barbados. Now you're going to tread upon Barbados...that is beyond your Jordan. Now, are you faithful to the gods your fathers served, or are you now going to be faithful to the gods of the Amorites in whose land you now dwell? That's where you're dwelling right now, because you say you haven't anything. Well, then you haven't anything, remain just where you are." And so, he had no compassion on any of us. You either believe or you didn't believe.

And so, he was trying to teach us this wonderful art of moving from state to state to state. And when you catch on, you don't turn to the left or the right. Let the other fellow take the first choice. And so, Lot takes the first choice, he wants this wonderful fertile land, it's so green, so well watered, "I'll take this, the land of the valley of the Jordan." "Alright, you take that; I'll take the other one, the unseen one. I will dwell beyond your Jordan in the land of Canaan, a land flowing with milk and honey. I don't know it, but I'm told by the Lord it's a land flowing with milk and honey. I'll take that one." So Abraham, the faithful one, took the land that was unseen by mortal eye, and he lived in it, and then came the grand fulfillment of all of his promises. But they didn't come to Lot. So man wants security here, he wants to build more and more to feel secure against the so-called inevitable rainy day. And so, he *gets* his rainy day.

But may I tell you, every day of your life you wake and you're always at the shore, and that shore stretches out, and it's always Jordan. This is Jordan. But when you read the story, if you don't really read it with the eye of the mystic, you're going to think of a huge body of water where a man came, and they're all Baptists and they're all being baptized. And so they all went out and almost got drowned. No, there wasn't any body of water, hasn't a thing to do with any body of water. Although today there are millions of them who go in droves—we have them in Barbados too—and they delight in it. Sunday morning when you see a hundred or two hundred out to sea, all being dunked, all being pushed in, with lovely white robes—they come out like drowned rats, all of them, lovely white robes. That hasn't a thing to do with Jordan. Jordan is every moment of a man's life when man faces the facts, and he doesn't know where to escape. There's no place to go...here are the facts. You either meet them—well, you can't meet them if you don't have a thing—but beyond the Jordan you can meet them. That land is always the good land. So Blake said in his wonderful little poem, if you put the words into the mouth of a child, "Father, O Father, what do we here in this land of unbelief and fear? The land of dreams is better far above the morning star." Just imagine, "the land of dreams is better far."

So I had a dream. I didn't go to sleep and lose my dream. I had to stand right where I was and have a dream, a waking dream, and hear the sound of the coconut leaves on top of my mother's home, and actually hear it. For Imagination is spiritual sensation. So I know if I slept in that room I would hear that coconut leaf; and the window is open, and I would smell the tropical odors as they come through the window. I would see what I would see *only* were I in Barbados. And so I would think of the place where I lived only a little while before in New York City, and see it there, a way north, 2,000 miles north. And then in this treading out of the land I fell asleep. Falling asleep the three days came quickly. And the three days…and one morning a letter under my door, and here, a little draft fell out for only fifty dollars, but the letter said, "A ticket awaits you down at the steamship company. Go and get it, because we're all expecting you for Christmas." And so, I sailed on that lovely ship.

Everything worked so beautifully. I went in and got the ticket, and the man said, "I'm sorry Mr. Goddard but we have no space for you first class. But you can go third class until you hit St. Thomas, and then someone disembarks at St Thomas and then you can go first class from St. Thomas to Barbados." I said, "Thank you, I'll take it." So I took it. Went back to my old friend, Abdullah, I said, Ab, I've got it, they sent me a ticket. I didn't ask them for it. They sent me a ticket and they justified sending it in the most wonderful, sweet, loving letter why they sent it, and they justified it. He wouldn't talk to me. He said, "You are *in* Barbados. Not you're going to Barbados." Even then he wasn't going to discuss it with me. Then one word he did add, he said, "You are in Barbados and you went *first* class." Here, I'm going third class...and I'm in Barbados and I went there, it's all behind me, first class.

So forty-eight hours later I went down to the steamship company, we're sailing at noon, put my ticket in expecting to go third class, and the man, his name was Mr. Smith, he said, "Mr. Goddard, we have good news for you. We have a cancellation and so you're going first class." He wasn't surprised, that was the agreement. They agreed. To what would you consent? Would you be a witness against yourself? And then I answered, yes, I'll be a witness. And so a witness to God's truth...that's what you witness... that's the only thing you witness to in this world: God's word. God's word is truth, you're told. Well, is it true? Did you prove it? I proved it. Well then, you're a witness to it. Don't give me any argument how you're going to get there and how you're going to go there and what path you're going to go: You are in Barbados.

So now go and talk Christ and only Christ, and tell the whole vast world about Christ; that all things are possible to Christ. And so you go and you talk about it. You never tire of telling the world that he's as free as the wind if he knows God's law. So the law is simple. You ask no man's permission to use God's law. And so, blessed...a wonderful beatitude is pronounced upon the man who will delight in the law of the Lord, for in all that he does he prospers...not a few things but in *all* that he does. But bear in mind, tomorrow morning when you wake don't be surprised to find yourself getting out of your bed and your feet in the water of Jordan. It's going to be there again. But you know what you did, and so off you go again.

So I'm in Barbados and can't get out because there aren't any ships going from Barbados, for this was another year when the war was over. The war broke in the end of 1945, and the first ship out of there I sailed. Not thinking of return, I had no permission to come back into this country. I didn't have any of these things, but I'm off for Barbados. Then I'm told in Barbados there isn't a ship, not one ship before September, and I'm committed to a series of lectures in New York City in 1945 beginning the first day of May, and I can't get out. So again, I start treading the water. So I walked up the gangplank of a ship that I saw in the bay. Not that day, but I walked up. And then a little while later they called me, and they had a list that long of people waiting. They jumped me over the entire list and put me at the top, and never justified why they did it. But I walked up the gangplank, not alone, taking my wife and my daughter with me, and so we all sailed on that ship. So I went beyond my Jordan. My Jordan there was a list that long and there were only two ships serving this little island, along with another three dozen islands, and the demand in this island alone exceeds anything they could possibly ever take out in the next few months. Then we had Trinidad, St. Vincent, St. Lucia, Dominica, all the islands, to be served by these two tiny little ships. And so in spite of all their requests and their demands, my name was jumped in Barbados over all these and put at the top of the list. And I sailed and got in on time to give my series in New York City.

So I tell you, it doesn't fail. So you find yourself at the Jordan. Don't cry, here's the Jordan, alright, beyond the Jordan. You promised God…for the Lord is asking you a question, "Will you serve the gods that your fathers served—they served the gods beyond the Jordan—or are you going to serve the gods of the Amorites in whose land you now dwell?" And so, they all tell you, you're in Barbados, and you can't get out. That's where the Amorites are, right there, and you are in their land. But now you can get out if you will serve the gods of your fathers, and they dwell *beyond* the Jordan. So beyond this barrier was my place called New York City. So I went up the ship and then got off in New York City. That's exactly what I did.

So I say to everyone, you can do it. Don't think that one person in this world is more loved by God than another. Don't believe it. Because a man today that seems so kind and so wonderful, he is…he's only in a state. He's in the state of kindness, which is a lovely state to be in. A state of consideration, that's a state. One's in a state of horror, that's only a state. But the occupant of the state of horror is just as perfect in the eyes of God as the one in the state of love. These are only states. And so the occupant is divine, the occupant is Christ Jesus. It is Christ Jesus in man that one day will be awakened in man, and that man in whom he awakes will be one with him. So when he rises in us, we are like him and he's like us (1 John 3:2).

And so here, these are states. Tonight when you go to bed, be honest, look at your Jordan. If you like it, stay there, perfectly alright. If you're satisfied with the day, there's no reason to change it. But if you're not satisfied with the day, beyond the vision of today there is a state that is the solution of today's problem; you dwell in *that* state tonight. Then the words are, Provide or prepare the victuals, prepare the food that you are going to use. And the food is simply, it's all mental. So you look at the world and see it as it would be seen were you now the man that you're now *assuming* that you are. Falling asleep in that state, seeing the world as it would be seen were it true, you find yourself lifting it out of the deep. For within three days you will go across this River, and then you will enter the land that he gives you; and it resurrects, it comes out of the deep, the great earth on which you're treading. So this is something that everyone should practice.

Now bear in mind when you read the word prayer, well, what is prayer? Is it not defined in our concordance as "a motion towards"? Is it not defined as "nearness at, accession to, nearness at or in the vicinity of"? That's how it's defined, "at or in the vicinity of." So I want to be...and I name it. So I'm drawing nearer and nearer, and finally I feel I'm in it. How do I know that I'm in it? Well then, look at the world, mentally, and see if you are located properly. Because if you're in it, the world is a frame of reference and it should tell you where you are. If this very moment I suddenly begin to see the Empire State building before me, then I look to my right and I see a way down on 34th Street, why, that's the corner of Macy's, then I look over to the Eastside, well, if I'm looking at this enormous building and I can feel it, I must be there. Then how do I know I'm there? Well, think of Los Angeles, and I see Los Angeles in my mind's eye 3,000 miles to the southwest of me. And think of something else...then finally you're located. So you *must* be there if everything else is as it would be were you there. And then fall asleep. Then suddenly things begin to happen; radical changes take place in your life to compel that journey. So don't do it lightly, because if you do it lightly even to disprove it, you're going to prove it. And when you prove it, it may not be convenient to make the trip, but you're going to make it anyway.

That happened to me. I had no desire to go to Barbados in a certain year, 1941, but it snowed in New York City and in no time flat we had twelve inches of snow. And so, to get rid of the snow, I slept in Barbados. Just to be ___(??) I felt the warmth of Barbados. Got up the next morning, there were twenty inches of snow, so I'm still in New York City with my Jordan. And I'd completely forgotten it. Then came the summer and my wife and I made arrangements to go to Maine for a month, a little vacation in Maine. Sent off the check, sent off the request for our vacation in Maine, then came a cable from Barbados that mother was dying and there was no time to waste, come and come right away, come immediately. So my wife and I sailed in twenty-four hours. A ship was pulling out in 1941...and no British ship was going, no other ship was going because war was on. Well, we were not yet at war, this was the end of August, and so we got aboard the American ship, the Royal McCormick, The Argentina, this lovely big ship. And we were all lit up like a Christmas tree at night, so that no sub could mistake us for a British ship. Huge big American flag on the side, on both sides, and every light on the ship burning all through the night that they could not use that as an excuse and say that we were dark and they thought we were British and then sink us. So in four and a half days we were in Barbados.

I had no desire to go there. I went and sent my money off to Maine, got my whole thing done for Maine. But, you see, back in January when it snowed, in February when it snowed, I had lost myself in treading out the winepress, and those three and a half days came beautifully...but it took eight months. In eight months the three days came and what I was treading out being in Barbados came to the surface, and I *had* to go to Barbados. And it was not my plan. So I went to Barbados and got back, but it was not my plan. My plan was to go with my wife to Maine and have a lovely month in Maine. But that whole thing was cancelled because I, in February, treaded out the warm clime of Barbados, and slept in it just as though it were true.

So I say, don't do it lightly, because I speak from experience. I did it in a light mood to get away from snow, and then it happened to me. I got away from…the thing I wanted most was to go to Maine. I certainly didn't want to go home to see my mother dying, but that was the urgency of the call. The only thing that could have taken me away from my plan in Maine was just such an emergency. Any other request I would have thrown it out, but not when a cable comes saying that mother has no time to be with us any longer, and come now. Well, you couldn't fly, there weren't any planes. You had to go by boat, and luckily this lovely big boat was sailing in twenty-four hours. So off we went.

So I tell you, try it. Try it and try to master the technique of using God's law wisely. And every time that you exercise your Imagination lovingly on behalf of another, you are exercising this law wisely, any time you do it. So if the request is made of you tonight for anything that is not a murder or to hurt someone, it's good. And don't judge them, no matter who they are they're entitled to their request. They've confessed to you where they stand. For when they say, "I want so and so", they're telling you, I'm right down at Jordan, right down at the water's edge and I can't get across the Jordan. Take them across the Jordan in your mind's eye. Take them out of that state and put them into the state of their wish fulfilled in your own mind's eye, and you sleep in that state for them. And then you'll take them across their Jordan. So they'll get it when the three days are over. And those three days, it will resurrect, it will come out of the deep and they will have it. But the very next day they're still going to be at the Jordan. Every day of your life you wake in the morning, after your heavenly vision, to come down and start the day at the Jordan.

You will find there always will be those in the world, "If it is so, turn this stone into bread for me." I had that in New York City on this marathon. "You say imagining creates reality? Turn that yellow pencil into red for me." And so you always get it. If I said to him, this professional philosopher, that "Man does not live by bread alone," you know what he would have said? "What arrogance. Why he is quoting the scripture as though he actually said those words." And if I told him I did, he would have dropped dead. Who else could have said them but Jesus Christ? And who is Jesus Christ?—your own wonderful human Imagination. But if you don't know it, well then, he still said it anyway, but you were walking in your sleep then when you said it. If you don't *know* you said it, you said it as a sleepwalker.

But the day will come you will *know* you said it. For the whole book is about you. The whole vast book from beginning to end is all about you. There's no other being it speaks about other than God; and it's only speaking about God, and who do you think you are, a worm? All ends run true to origins. If your beginning is a worm, your end is a worm...and the scientists are right, little worms will get you...and so, you're only worms, maggots. But if your beginning is God, the end is God, for all ends run true to origins. So, if the origin is God, the end is God; and so you will awake as God if the origin is God. But if your beginning is a worm, call it by any other name, spermatozoa, it still ends as a spermatozoa, it's a worm. But I tell you your *origin* is God and your *end* is God.

Now let us go into the Silence.

HIS ETERNAL PLAY

2

Tonight's subject is "His Eternal Play." I call it a play because the end is predetermined, like a play. Paul speaks of it as a race, a game. He's concentrating on the second act. He said, "I fought the good fight, I have finished the race. The time for my departure has come. Henceforth there is laid up for me a crown of righteousness" (2 Tim.4:6). So he calls it a game; but a game has an uncertain end. Not a play—I call it a play only because the end is predetermined.

We start from innocence, we plod into experience, and we emerge as Imagination. These are the three stages. Blake placed them in his *Songs of Innocence* in this lovely dancing child on a cloud; then the *Songs of Experience* the child *under* the cloud; and then *The Marriage of Heaven and Hell*, where the child is above the cloud dancing in eternity. So he did synthesize these two states. But, we call it a play. I do not mean like an ordinary play where every word is committed and that you are fated. No, I do not mean it in that sense. We do not hide under the cloud of fate. And so, evil which you and I encounter—I'm not denying that we do encounter evil—but evil is not a condition imposed upon man by some malevolent deity. Rather it is a state of experience through which the soul of man passes in order that knowing good and evil he might achieve a more noble state, a condition that we call Imagination or liberty. For he said, the whole vast creation groans, waiting for the liberation, or the unveiling, of the sons of God; that we were not eager to enter this arena. For, "The creature was made subject unto futility, not willingly but by the will of him who subjected him in hope; that the creature may obtain the glorious liberty of the children of God" (Rom. 8:20). So there's a purpose behind it all; so we are inserted into it.

Now the play is given to us in the Old Testament. From beginning to end, the thirty-nine books, that maps the play. The New Testament interprets the play for us. Without the New Testament it would have no meaning to the Old. But the Old is the play. We open the book to read it, bear in mind that this is a *vision*, as we are told in the scripture. This is a vision when Elias speaks of the vision of Isaiah, Obadiah the vision of Obadiah, Nebo the vision of him. And when you don't use the word vision, you use the word "the word of the Lord came unto" and then you name the prophet. Well, "the word of the Lord" is the same as vision. "For if there be a prophet among you, I the Lord will make myself known unto him in a vision; I will speak with him in a dream" (Num. 12:6). So the whole from beginning to end is the vision.

But this is a vision unmodified by the conceptual mind. If you've ever had a vision, you know what I mean. You stand as a participant in the action. You may be the star in the drama when the vision begins within you, or you may be simply playing a minor role. But if you are playing a starring role, still the conceptual mind is suspended; it doesn't interfere and ask questions, you ask no questions. The most impossible thing is taking place before you and it seems not only possible, the most natural thing in the world that this thing should be as it unfolds within you. So the vision, really, is truth and this truth is completely untouched by the conceptual mind. It's completely set aside. For this experience belongs to a region that is deeper and more vital than that which the intellect inhabits; and because of this it is also indestructible by intellectual arguments and criticisms. You could bring all the criticisms in the world to one who has had the experience and he remains unmoved. You can't shake him, because *he* has had the experience. So the New Testament is beginning to *experience* that foretold in the Old, and this is the picture of the great drama. Now it doesn't mean that you and I inserted against our will for this divine end, which is God, that we must one time play an evil part and another time play a good part. No, that is what we are inserted into...all these are eternal states. So when I open my Bible I must always remember that the persons Moses and Abraham, Isaac, Jacob and all the rest are not there meant as persons as we are persons but they signify the eternal states of the soul—the states revealed to man in a series of divine revelations as they are now written for us in the Bible. So I'm not speaking of Moses as a person, Abraham as a person, Isaac as a person, or any other character in that scripture. They are all personifications of the eternal states through which you and I pass. As we begin the journey, at first it's innocence. You start from innocence, fall into experience, and emerge as a liberated being, as all Imagination, one with God.

Now, who is playing the part? "God only acts and is in all existing beings or men," all (Blake). God and God alone is playing the part. A man today who is simply so very poor he doesn't know where to turn, he cannot feed himself…you say, "Who are you?" He will tell you his name possibly. He'll say, "I am"...and he names it. And, "How do you feel, how are things going?" and he will say, "I am very poor." Before he said very poor he said "I am." You ask the man who is now rolling in wealth, "How are things going?" "Well, I'm very, very wealthy." Well, he preceded his very, very wealthy claim by "I am." The other did the same with his "very, very poor" claim. The same God, not two gods, there's only one God in this world. And that one God is given to man, and he reveals his name to man in the Book of Exodus as "I AM...it is my name forever...to be known by all generations" (3:14). There is no other name. So, knowing that God is playing all the parts, then I slowly begin to become discreet in my selection of the part that I will play. So no matter where I find myself in this world I now bear in mind I am only moving through infinite states. It is entirely up to me to select the states that I will play.

Now, let me share with you two experiences of two ladies who were here this past week. One lady, last Thursday night, left me a long typewritten letter, which I read when I got home. She said, On the 6th of February you spoke on a certain subject and you brought in Jung, Carl Jung, and you told an experience of Jung where he was contemplating the death of a friend whose funeral he had attended that day. And suddenly he felt the presence of the friend in his room and the friend is standing at the foot of his bed. But Jung being the brilliant mind that he is he said to himself, This is sheer fantasy. But he arrested that feeling and said, No, that would be sheer abomination on my part if this man is real. To say that my friend is not really standing there, it could be a horrible thing to do to him were it true that he *is* there. So said Jung to himself, I will now credit him with reality. The moment he credited the man with reality, the man became more and more real, and Jung could see him with the inner eye. He turned around and beckoned Jung to follow him to the door. Jung in his Imagination followed, followed through the garden, onto the street, and then several hundred yards away to the man's home, where he entered with the man. The man went into his library, got up on a little stool, reached up to the second shelf from the top, and pointed out four books bound in red. Then he pointed to the second volume of the four, and then he vanished. The next day Jung was so curious he went to the lady's home, asked the widow for permission to inspect the library. As he got in he saw the stool that he had seen in his vision, under the library. He stepped on it, and he saw the four books bound in red and then he went straight to the second volume, and it was *The Legacy of the Dead.* He said, "The contents meant nothing to me, but the title was most significant in view of the experience that I had the night before with my friend who had gone from this world." So here, *The Legacy of the Dead*...the man is trying to convince Jung in spite of his brilliant mind that we survive. He could make no further than that, that there is survival, not after unnumbered months waiting, for the man died the day before; he was buried the next day; and here the very day of the funeral the man appears to Jung. So all the so-called "you must wait three months, or three days, or three years" that meant nothing to an experience. The man experienced the presence of a man who could take him into his library and show him a book with a title that signified the reality of the experience; for here is *The Legacy of the Dead.* So the man had not ceased to be; he was the same man, there was no change in appearance, no change whatsoever.

So here, this struck the lady forcibly. She said, "You know, I've had many experiences like the one of Jung. It's an odd feeling because I'm a single lady, living alone, and then to find suddenly a man standing in my room. And some day, maybe, it could be an actual fact, and wouldn't I be surprised! Or maybe he'd be the more surprised," said she. However, she said, many a time I sensed the presence of a man in the room, and I see them quite vividly. But now the one I want to talk about is the story in which *you* appeared. And then she started telling me this, she said, "Last year I looked all over for an apartment. I was dissatisfied with my apartment, but because I'm French background I resent paying high rents for an apartment. So I refused to pay these extravagantly high rents...it's my French blood, she said. But I wanted a nice street and I knew the street I wanted, I knew the kind of apartment that I wanted, and what I wanted to pay for it. So I went out every weekend and looked, and got no results. I really labored. Then I said to myself, What am I doing? I go to the man, I listen to him, I have all his books. I shall now read and not go searching for any apartment. So I took your books and instead of going on Saturday, as I always did, with my paper all marked where I would go, I sat down and read the books.

Suddenly I read the books, all the way; every night for the week I read the books, and I didn't go any place. On Friday night, one week later, I finished my book and I retired. Between three and four in the morning I sensed the presence of someone in my room, and I said, before I looked at the presence, I'm going to have that presence smile. He must have something good to tell me. I will not have anything other than something nice and good. So I looked over and here you are standing at my bed, the same you that is on the jacket of your book. And then you turned around and I recognized you and you walked to the far corner of my bedroom. At that moment, I distinctly heard my door click shut. It was a definite closing of something, my door, but something came to a conclusive end, that it was so *definite* in the way it closed. So, I turned, I felt that I turned my head from you to the door. And then when I looked back, I said to myself, Before I look back, now Neville is gone before he could tell me the message that he brought for me. But, fortunately, when I looked back you were there, you hadn't moved at all. Then when you saw my eye you went to the far, to the very end. And then you went to a picture and from below the picture you seemed to take something, at least, I thought you did. But suddenly the whole area where you were became luminous. You were completely surrounded in light and everything was luminous. I could see you more vividly, the whole room was light. Then you took whatever you had in your hand and you went to a door, a big panel. It was so very difficult for you to move...you couldn't move it. It seemed so very difficult, but you kept on struggling with the door that you tried to open or to move. I said to myself, 'There is no door there...but there is a door. That picture is my picture, but it isn't hanging there...and yet, there it is hanging there.' Then you got my attention and you tried to show me how difficult this door was, then you vanished. This is on Saturday morning between three and four.

So the next day I didn't go looking. Saturday evening came, I thought I would either read the books again, or else I would read an evening paper, the evening news. So I took the paper and I turned to the section where they are renting apartments. I saw one on the street I wanted, and everything about it in the ad seemed to be what I wanted. Normally I would have gone straight to the telephone and called the apartment, but I didn't. The next day I called, and when the party said, You better come right over and see it, I said, No, I'll be over tomorrow, on Monday, at noon...a thing I would never have done in the month that I looked. I seemed so completely complacent, as though I didn't want it. It wasn't that, something possessed me, and I didn't go until Monday. At noon I saw it and I liked it, liked it immensely. The price was right and the street was the very street I selected. So I contracted for the place and I moved in two weeks later. And to my surprise, for the first time in all the apartments that I had ever rented there are two moving doors on a sliding something, she said, and it was most difficult to move them, in fact, impossible to move them. I said I must get someone to fix it or oil it or do something, because you can't move the doors. Then, she said, I started hanging my pictures. Then I saw this area, and after I took a picture, the very picture, and hung it there next to this panel, and got in my bed that night, I said, Why that's the picture... and there's the panel door. And what Neville did under that picture...there *is* an electric switch that floods the room with light, right under the picture where she caught him. So she said to me, "Neville, would you throw some light on it, other than the light you threw in that room? Did that something have to happen?" No, but she called...she read the books all through the week, began to apply it, and as you are told in that same book of mine, the latest book, *The Law and the Promise,* quoting Butler, Samuel Butler: "Who writes a book which others read, while he is asleep in bed, what knows he of the thoughts his thoughts are read? Now, which is the he—the he that sleeps or the he that even this he cannot feel nor see?" So here, you think of someone...and I tell you and I mean it the whole vast world is within you. She trusts me implicitly. She reads my books. She likes my books. This thing that she saw is within her. It's not contained here and only here. Every one of you, but everyone in this whole vast world, must be contained within you, but everyone. And so, the being that she saw standing in her room, I, the person called Neville, may I tell you, I'm totally unaware of having been present. I've been accused by many people of entering their rooms uninvited, but I'm totally unaware of it.

In New York City, many years ago, my friend, Alice Bentley—she's now gone from this world—she was a darling soul. Ouspensky and Gurdjieff all used her studio at Carnegie Hall. And Ali was just one wonderful person. Her name was Alice Bentley; we called her Ali-Ben. Ali used to walk the streets of New York without shoes with this lovely shock of white hair, long flowing Indian robes, and she was quite the character. But, people like Ouspensky and Gurdjieff and all of them arrived, when they came here, it was Ali's studio that they all used. And so one day, so this lady told me—she ran all the restaurants in the Wellington Hotel—and Ali told me the next day, after the event, she said, "Know what happened to me last night, Neville?" I hadn't the slightest idea. Well, she said, "You appeared bodily in the room and called this lady's name"—who was the manager of all the restaurants, and she lived at the hotel. I appeared in her room, so she said, and I said to her, "Ali needs money, and she must have it right away. I want you to go downstairs right now and take all the money you have in your purse and empty it right into Ali's lap." Well, she said, I spoke so convincingly that when I disappeared she thought this was some divine message; she went right downstairs to Ali, took all the money in her purse, and emptied it in Ali's lap. Ali thanked her profusely for the most generous gift. Ali *did* need the money...she owed rent. But I, with my conceptual mind, restrained as I am, I never would have done that. Never would I have even suggested that she help Ali. That's not my province in this world. But when truth begins to spring within man, unmodified by the conceptual mind, he can play any part. And so, when God sends his messenger into the world, it is unmodified by any conceptual mind, so he can be the perfect messenger to execute anything in this world. And so the God within her, praying for some light, some succor, something, and then all of a sudden she conjures one she trusts, and I became her messenger. And the suspended conceptual mind, I could stand boldly in the presence of a lady I didn't know very well, the wee hours of the morning, and tell her that she has to go right down stairs and empty the contents of her purse into Ali's lap. And so, that's how this *wonderful* world works.

This is a play. So you don't have to play the evil part. You don't have to play the good part. But you are ushered in *unwillingly* into this fabulous world of experience that you may know good *and* evil, and then rise above it all into a far more noble state; and that state I call Imagination. I call it the liberating state, because when man arrives at that point he is Christ Jesus. So the *end* of the play is Christ Jesus. The *end* is when the name is on your forehead. And what name is placed upon the forehead? You're told, "*his* name"...speaking now of the one who went through the battle, all the battles, and the Father's name. Well, the Father's name is I AM, and he who went through the battle is Jesus. So on your forehead is "I AM Jesus." Who else do you think played it? Through the entire journey only God is playing all the parts. So "God only acts and is in all existing beings or men."

So because God is one, whether you're left poor or rich, God plays both parts. You don't *have* to be poor. You can assume whatever you want in this world if you dare to trust God and hold God trustworthy, actually hold him trustworthy—he *is* trustworthy—knowing who he is: he's your own wonderful I AM. So assume that I am...and I name what I want to be, and then *thank* God for it. Trust him completely in moving you through the necessary states to bring me to *that* state into which I have gone and given thanks for. But these are infinite states and they are eternal, they don't come and go, and you can't change one into the other. The poor man never changes poverty into wealth. He leaves, he departs from poverty, and he enters a state that is permanent called wealth. When he departs from wealth and reenters poverty, he does not change the rich man into the poor man. He departs from wealth and enters the state of poverty. They're only states. And when we occupy the state we give it life and it becomes *real* within our world.

So anyone knowing this wonderful law can play the game. As Paul played it beautifully. He said, "I fought the good fight." And so, you and I *must* accept destiny, completely accept it, because we did it unwittingly. But finding ourselves in it, accept destiny. And may I tell you, when you accept it, you accept the conflict. You joy in the conflict. Know what a conflict is? It's not fighting against a man; it's a *mental* fight, I overcome and overcome and overcome. And so I rejoice in the mental fight. So finding myself at a certain state, I go right into it. There is the conflict, and I rejoice now in the *mental* conflict. So I overcome it by simply assuming that I am what this now denies that I am. I dare to trust God and dare to hold him trustworthy. And so, I will assume that I—well, that's his name, I am, and all things are possible to him—so "I am"...and I name it. And then I thank him, I say "Amen" to that state; and then allow myself to be pushed through all the necessary states, knowing that God is trustworthy and I'm *holding* him to that state. And so, I live in it, and he pushes me *into* that state.

In the end, I know I'm going to come out. As he said, "A crown of righteousness is laid up for me...for I finished the fight." Paul knew from the experiences which he recorded in Galatians that the fight was over, the race had been won. He kept, what?--the faith. Now Paul makes the statement: "For since, in the wisdom of God, the world did not know God through wisdom, it pleased God through the folly of what we preach to save those who believe" (1 Cor.1:21). So, all the wisdom of the world with the conceptual mind cannot find God. He can rationalize from here to the end of time. It's a mystery to be known only by revelation. God unveils himself in an experience, and then you know. But you can't sit down, no matter how wise you are…so he says, "Since, in the wisdom of God, the world did not know God through wisdom, it pleased God..." Well, what pleases God? We're told in the 11th chapter of Hebrews, "Without faith it is impossible to please him," can't please him without faith (verse 6).

And so, I will dare to assume that a friend of mine tonight has made the most wonderful, I would say, killing (if you want to use that word) in business. Wonderful! No hurt to anyone, mutual benefit to all. He has signed a contract or done something wonderful, and he is thrilled beyond measure. So I would assume that for him. If he calls me tomorrow or writes me next week or next month, I would not accept one word that is in opposition to what I have assumed. I heard it. I am still hearing it. I will continue to hear it until that which I heard and am still hearing is perfectly realized by my friend. So if tomorrow I hear that he's distressed, I will not tell God how to move him. He'll move him through all kinds of things if I remain faithful and hold God trustworthy. I will hold him trustworthy and he'll move my friend toward the fulfillment of that where I see him in my mind's eye.

So that is part of the play. And Paul is right by calling it a conflict. He calls it a fight: "I fought the good fight." And I will not quarrel with Paul. It *is* a play, but it's also a game. But because the end is predetermined I cannot altogether call it the fight. Because the fight, like tonight's fight, is most uncertain...as you heard the outcome. All the wise boys, all the wisdom of the world put it on one person because of a record, and the other fellow won. And so, this strange, strange...all the wisdom of the world means nothing in the eyes of God. The one fellow who won, did you see him on TV? He said, "Who is the greatest?" and he had his second say, "Cassius Clay." "Who is the prettiest?" "Cassius Clay." "Who is the biggest?" "Cassius Clay." "Who is the wisest?" "Cassius Clay." And he beat that into his mind's eye, and he said, "I'll take him before eight because I'm great." He's a poet. And all these things he weaved into his mind's eye. While the other was simply brawn, he was going to go along on sheer brawn, and the other fellow wasn't doing that at all.

Now we come back to another beautiful one told me last Friday night. This lady was here on Thursday, the 20th. She heard me once before when I quoted my friend Hallie(?) Smith at the Chinese Theatre. But, that was simply one Sunday morning when you have enormous crowds and so it was a quick meeting. I met her because I knew her mother and father so very well, it was a joy to meet her, but with the crowd moving you can't talk to her. But she was here last Thursday for the first time. Her mother drove her home and they discussed the meeting. Her mother said to her, "Did you like it?" She said, "Very much." "Do you believe it?" "I certainly do. That's what I believe. I believe every word of it." Well, the next morning they got on the phone again, again the conversation of the night before and the meeting. Because I was speaking of crossing the Jordan, that every moment of time man is at the Jordan; the facts stare him in the face and he's got to get beyond the Jordan. The only one who gets beyond the Jordan is Joshua, and Joshua's name is Jesus, and Jesus is Jehovah, and Jehovah is I AM. So I put myself *beyond* the Jordan, and assume that I am where I want to be, either spatially or in other states, like in a more noble state, that also you move into that state.

Well, she liked it. Then she said, "But Mother, I had the strangest dream last night." This is now the early hours of Friday morning. "This is what I dreamt. I saw a living serpent, small one, but very much alive. I picked it up and put it in my handbag. And then I woke." What a glorious dream! You see, the Bible recognizes only one source of dream: all visions and dreams proceed from God, all dreams. Now we go back to the great entrance into this world: from innocence, beyond the dream, into hell, the fires of experience, where man is called upon to embrace the fires and be consumed as its victim; and then rise from its ashes as Christ Jesus. But he has to completely embrace it, like the great moth, where the two moths went in search of their idol, the flame. They came back with uncertain intelligence—one thought it was hot, one thought it bright, but they did not agree as to what the flame represented. And a third, moved by sheer desire and true desire, rushed to the flame, and folded his wings beneath him, and plunged headlong into the sacred fire, until he became one color and one substance with the flame. "He only knew the flame who in it burned, and only he could tell who n'er to tell returned." He so became absorbed in it he could not return anymore; he rose as Christ Jesus. Couldn't discuss it on the level of the moth and the flame, he became the flame; and so, he rose as the flame, the light of the world.

And so, in this story, she heard it, she believed it. What did she believe?—that her own wonderful human Imagination is Christ Jesus. She heard *that*. She told her mother, "I believe that. I believe that that could save me from what I am, if I want to be saved from what I am...that if I really understood this, I could really apply it." And that truly is the state of the world. One's own wonderful human Imagination, that's Christ Jesus, that's God. So she so believed it that in the depths of her soul, unmodified by the conceptual mind, because in this world she wouldn't dare touch a serpent, anymore than you would. She would run from it or try to kill it. But she picked it up and put it in her handbag.

Now in the beginning, the serpent leads man out of innocence into experience. The word that we call "fall" is He Vau He, in scripture the root of the verb "to be", He Vau He. "To be" is, alright, the Self-Existing Being. The original meaning of that verb was "to fall, or to cause to fall." Here, to cause to fall...the one who caused the fall *also* fell. He caused the fall, and he himself fell. So, God himself enters death's door with those who enter, and remains with them through the whole furnace of experience, and shares with them all of their visions of eternity, until together they awake as one, and it's God. So the serpent has always been the symbol of Christ Jesus.

So she heard it, she believes now that Christ Jesus is her own wonderful human Imagination, that when it's said in Corinthians, "Do you not realize that Jesus Christ is in you?" now she knows that this Jesus Christ in her is her own wonderful human Imagination. So she sees him now *symbolized*, something alive, not a dead Christ, a *living* Christ. She picks up a *living* serpent and puts the serpent in her handbag, where all *valuables* are kept. For, whether you believe it or not, a handbag is part of a Western woman's equipment. She is undressed without one. I think that it's a horrible thing that our tax experts should tax a lady's handbag when you don't tax a man's pair of pants. It's another part of her wearing apparel. She puts everything into it that she considers of value—her car keys, her house key, her little notebook, her charge accounts, everything. It's part of the dress of the day. Without it some people feel undressed. So she has everything in it. Where she keeps her valuables she placed Christ. Now what she has to do is to prove she *really* believes it. But she does...from the depths of her soul she does. Now exercise him, because he only grows by exercise, and every time she exercises her Imagination lovingly on behalf of another, she is feeding Christ Jesus.

And that serpent will one day appear to her in the most glorious way. I'll tell you exactly how he will appear. One day, when the temple of her body is torn from top to bottom and then she stands divided, looking at the two sections of one body, she will see at the base of what would have been her spine, coiled, this glorious golden liquid light, pulsing and moving. She will know it is her Self, and then she will fuse by that knowledge, for we become what we behold. She beholds it and she becomes it. Then she, as it, will move up that spinal column of hers, right into her skull that is Zion. And she will be it: the one who fell is the one who will ascend. "No one ascends into heaven but he who first descended" (John.3:13). It is *it* that descended, your great Savior; and he descended, and is dreaming in you all the strange things of the world. So he went right down into generation, the base of the spine; and there he dreams all the dreams of eternity, all the creative dreams, by any name, all the sexual dreams, everything he's dreaming. It's Christ Jesus.

And one day, he turns around and what was down into generation becomes regenerated. All the currents of the body are reversed as he moves up into his heavenly world, leaving everyone to perform all they're performing and allowing all their dreams because *he* is doing it. And one day, you'll know these words in that 96th plate of *Jerusalem*: "I behold my deadly dreams of six thousand years dazzling around thy skirts like a *serpent* of precious stones and gold. I know it is my Self, O my Divine Creator and Redeemer." Right after he makes that bold confession, which he claims was dictated by the spirit of love, who was no one other than God, he then comes into the next line and he puts the words into God's mouth, and calls God, Jesus. Jesus is made to say, "Fear not, Albion (speaking now of humanity): "unless I die thou canst not live; but if I die I shall arise again and thou with me." So he comes down into generation from his heavenly state. He empties himself of his immortal form and takes upon himself the form of a slave, called man; and there he dreams with man until that moment in time when the fight is over, he's overcome the battles, and now the crown of righteousness awaits him as he moves up into Zion.

So this is the most glorious play. If you *know* it's a play and someone is playing an unlovely part, don't condemn him, pull him out of it. He doesn't *have* to play it if all eventually awaken as God. For eventually he's going to awaken as God *regardless* of what part he played. So, the only predetermined state in the play is the end. But within the conflict of the second act, which is the act of experience, you can play any part in this world. And in the end, all will be forgiven, because God is playing all the parts and God forgives them. But all these are the eternal parts. So this is a message of man: This being, sound asleep, moving through eternal death (this world), and awakening to eternal life. The story of the little seed falling into the ground, and unless it falls into the ground and dies it remains alone, but if it dies it brings forth much. It's the mystery of *life* through death.

So innocence...well, let me share with you a vision of mine. I once saw in this vision an infinite field of human flowers, beautiful flowers, big wonderful sunbursts, and every one with a human face. And when one moved, they all moved. If one smiled, they all smiled. If one frowned, they all frowned. They moved in concert, directed by some invisible hand. But they moved in concert. And I looking at them knew that I enjoyed more freedom than all of them put together; though I certainly was not as beautiful and certainly not in that state above the cloud or on the cloud, for I had gone down into generation. I was limited by the garment that I wore, the animal garment, subject to all of its weaknesses, subject to all its violence. And yet, in spite of these limitations of the human physical garment, which is an animal garment, I knew in my vision I enjoyed more freedom than all of them put together. They had not yet left the state of innocence and entered the world of experience. I was shown in my vision where I *formerly* was, one with that that moved in concert, and then unwillingly detached. For I did not volunteer, no one volunteers, because you are in a state of bliss, but it's an innocent bliss. And then you pass through the world of experience, and when you emerge you are as free, free as all outdoors, because you are liberated, and you are God. And you fly, like that angel in *The Marriage of Heaven and Hell above* the clouds, into that wonderful world and you dance as a liberated being.

But in the other, you don't, you move in concert. And you're beautiful and untarnished, unwithered, everything is perfect, but you're anchored, anchored to the ground. No flying around, no freedom whatsoever, but beautiful...waiting when that moment in time comes that God himself will subject you from that field of beauty into the world of experience. And you too will enter. And one day, like the little butterfly, or the little moth, you too will become so curious that you'll plunge right into the sacred flame. And then you'll be consumed as its victim, and you'll rise from the ash, but no one will see you because you're the flame. And you rise as the light of the world. So everyone will do it.

So I can share this vision with you. It's perfectly marvelous, unmodified by my conceptual mind. Because, had I seen it with memory of what I'd gone through, I would know the flowers could not be that human. I would know the faces, living wonderful fresh faces, couldn't be true. But you see, your reason is suspended when you have the vision, and it seems such a normal thing to see living childlike faces in a flower. And every one was a wonderful beautiful face, not one was unlovely, every one perfect, you couldn't improve upon it, it was perfect. And yet I knew inwardly I had more freedom than all of them put together. For, I, reluctantly, unwillingly was subjected to this futility. And then, passing through the great furnaces of affliction, exercising the being, as I found him slowly, to find he is my own wonderful human Imagination. It was he who subjected me, he who I didn't recognize. I sought him in everything *but* where he was. I sought him in the wind, in the earth, in the sunlight, in the lightning, and finally I heard him in the still small voice speaking from within: "That which I have done, I have done. Do nothing." And I heard the voice; it came from within; and then I did nothing, and what I had assumed within nine days it happened to me. I did nothing, he simply brought it from the depths of my soul and it happened. He influenced the behavior of everyone who could be used to make real that which seemed so impossible, so unreal, when I dared to assume that I am. And so, it came from within.

My friend may look for him in everything in the world 'til one day he's going to find him. And when you find him he's just like you. So if anyone should ever say, "Look, here is Christ!" or "Look, there he is!" don't believe him (Mark 13:21). Why? Because, although "It does not now appear what we shall be, we know that when *he* appears we shall be like him" (1 John 3:2). Just like him, because he's within you. So in that very twinkle of an eye he takes your lowly body and he changes it to be like his glorious body, to be of one form with that of the exalted Christ. Not something less than, one with the form of the exalted Christ, one with God.

So the play...it's perfect as a play because the end is predetermined. As you're told, he called us all to himself, and "Those whom he foreknew he also predestined to the conformed to the image of his Son. And those whom he predestined he also called; and those whom he called he also justified; and those whom he justified he also glorified" (Rom. 8:29). When you glorify in the Bible, you glorify with God: "I will not give my glory unto another." He can only give it to himself, therefore, when man is glorified, God succeeded in his purpose and gave man himself. Therefore, he has the glory that is God, and rises as God. So you are predestined to be conformed to the image of his Son, and the Father and Son are one when you rise.

But in this battle, in the conflict, you must accept destiny. Not your particular destiny...and say that the stars have consented unto your misfortune; they have not consented to your misfortune at all, nor have the teacup leaves, or the coffee beans, or the bones, or anything in the world. It is simply your choice. No matter where you are inserted begin to believe in God, and find him as your own wonderful human Imagination. Then become selective and get out of any place where you might have started life. And you can do it by holding God trustworthy. Go to sleep this night and try this. When you get flat on your back, before you lose consciousness, and your eyes are shut to the outer world, just think of this being that you would like to be. Don't be embarrassed. If it is something… that you want more income and considerably more, don't be embarrassed, don't think you're greedy. All things are possible to him, and he's right with you as you are contemplating the man, the woman, that you would like to be. Contemplate yourself *as* that being. And then in the most simple way say "Thank you." Just *mean* it. When you say "Thank you" it is always for something received, you know. I don't say "Thank you" in the hope I'll embarrass you into a gift. I say "Thank you" because you've given it. And so, I saw it clearly...I become what I behold...so I saw myself clearly as such a person, and then say "Thank you," meaning I'm holding God trustworthy. Try it, and see if you can't give me the most wonderful stories in the next few months, because beginning next week our series, five-eighths of it, is geared really to the law: How to use this law constructively to achieve *definite* goals in this world…so that we'll take it then as the race. But I tell you the end is predetermined, the end is God.

Now let us go into the Silence.

* * *

Q: Throughout the Bible we read that I AM, I AM, yet in Genesis it starts out "Let *us* make man in our image."

A: That is a plural word, Elohim. The word I AM was not revealed to man as the name of God until the 3rd chapter of Exodus, you'll find it in the 14th verse, the 3rd chapter of Exodus. Prior to that, God was known as The Almighty, Shaddai. He was known by other names. He still is Almighty, but as we go through the Bible he never drops the name I AM. But finally in the very end we find the name of Father given to him. In the 17th of John and all through the gospel of John, the greatest name that he has is Father, which name he also gives to us by giving us his Son to call us Father. It's the one way he has of showing man he's completed the gift of himself to man, because if he is a father then there is a son somewhere. When that son comes out and turns toward you and calls you Father, and there's no uncertainty in your heart that he is your son, and you know he's God's son, you go back into the scripture to find that, here, he promised him, his sonship. He said, "Today thou art my son, today I have begotten thee" in the 2nd Psalm (verse 7). And so, when that same being appears in your world and calls you Father, then you know who you are. So, the word Elohim in the 1st chapter of Genesis is God's creativity, it's plural. We are really the Elohim. But the grand commandment is "Hear, O Israel, the Lord"—that is Yod He Vau He called Jehovah—"our God"—that is Elohim—"is one Jehovah." So it takes all of us, the Elohim—it's a compound unity, one made up of others—to form the grand I AM that is God. Is that clear?

Q: This series of lectures is the first time that I have attended, and so I'm still a bit confused about using the Imagination in the way in which I understand you are telling us to. And what I am trying to say is, how can you use this Imagination with all of the senses when you are unfamiliar with a certain surroundings that you need to contact? Am I making any sense?

A: Well, for instance, let us make it spatially first and put it into other states. You take a spatial state, now if you were going to San Francisco then you know...(recorded over).

Q: You made a statement that you were going to have a certain thought about a friend of yours, helping him to sign a contract or something, I don't remember specifically. Do you mean to say...you also said, in conjunction with this, that if you would not hear any word that this friend had to say that is contrary to this positive thought. Do you mean to say that if your friend himself does not have this positive thought that by your mere thought can he get what he wants? Even though he himself does not...

A: Definitely, definitely! If I say it has to depend upon his acceptance, I am passing the buck. Because if all things by a law divine in one another's being mingle, then I have influence and I do it wittingly or unwittingly anyway. I don't ask my child's permission to hear good news for her. I love her and I hear good news for her. So, when she writes home, as all children do, "Oh, this is going to be a very tough exam, I don't know if I'll pass or not. In fact, it's in the lap of the gods and my teachers whether I even graduate!" I don't hear anything. So the last report card came in, beautiful B+s, A-s, and she's away up on the Dean's list. Well, they can't go any higher than the Dean's list. And so, she's an intelligent child, I know. She does make the effort. But I have never once waited for her to ask help. I love her. And so, eventually, you allow everyone, and ask no one's permission to love them. You know that wonderful poem? "He drew a circle that shut me out, 'Infidel! Scoundrel! A thing to flout!' But love and I had the wit to win, and we drew a circle that took him in." And so you take him in. You don't ask permission to take him in. He can shut you out if he wants to live in a little place all by himself. Grant him that right too. But you don't shut him out when he shuts you out. Eventually, ___(??). These little words in the epistle of John, "We love *him because* he first loved us."

Goodnight.

ALL ARE HUMAN

2/27/64

Tonight's subject is "All Are Human." In Blake's great *Jerusalem* he said, "All are men in eternity, rivers, mountains, cities, villages, all are human. And when we enter into their bosoms we walk in earth and in heaven, and when we enter into *our* bosoms we walk in earth and heaven; and all that we behold, though it appears without, it is within, in our Imagination, of which this world of mortality is but a shadow" (*Jer.*,Plt.71). That's difficult to conceive, difficult to follow, but I think I can throw a little light on it from my own personal experience.

It seems so difficult to tell a man that the whole vast world is himself made visible, that man is either the ark of God or a phantom of the earth and the sea. He either contains the whole of eternity within him, and truly is the *ark* of God; or he simply appears out of the nowhere, and he waxes, and he wanes, and he vanishes and leaves not a trace behind him, just like a phantom. So the choice is man's. But man thinks he is simply a little phantom. I tell you, you are the *ark* of God. You contain the *whole* of eternity within you, and what your destiny is, it's God. You are actually destined to become as he is, and it takes this whole vast wonderful world of ours to unfold it for us. As we are told, "As the Father has life in himself, so he has granted the Son also to have life in himself." Then he said, "Do not marvel at this; for I tell you that the day is coming that all in the tomb will hear his voice and come forth" (John5:26). All in the tomb will hear his voice and come forth. Well, Blake made something similar in a little comment in his book, the first book of *Europe,* he said, "The dead heard the voice of the child and began to awake from sleep. All things heard the voice of the child and began to awake to life." That this Christ child—and you always think of Christ as a little child, always as the child—and you hear the voice of the child, and all in the tomb begin to awake from sleep. Yet in a tomb they were called "the dead." They will come forth from the tomb; they will awake in the tomb and come forth.

Now here is this new concept that came with the first one who awoke from the tomb, awoke from the dead, to find himself entombed and came forth, and then he brought an entirely different concept of what man really is. Man was under restraint in the past. So we are told, Why do you live under restraints, under regulations? Why do you live as though you were still a part of this world, and why do you submit to regulations? That we read in Colossians, Paul's letter, the 2nd chapter of Colossians (verse 20)… because in the ancient world man had so many restraints if you read the 11th chapter of Leviticus, even as to diets. If a beast chews its cud and at the same time it has a parted hoof and the cloven foot, well, then you could eat it. But if it chewed the cud, like the camel, but did not have the parted hoof, then it was unclean. The pig did not chew the cud but it had the parted hoof. It was unclean; you must have both. And so, the hare, the rabbit, the badger, they chewed the cud. The hare does not chew its cud, but the ancients thought it did by the motion of the jaw. But it had the cloven hoof as it were, it was not a parted foot, and therefore unclean. And the unnumbered things in the ocean, if they had fins and scales, they were clean, you could eat them. But if they did not have fins and scales, you could not eat them, they were unclean. So the eel that today the French devour and love—I've had them and they are delicious—all the shellfish were unclean. They didn't have scales, they didn't have fins, so oysters, clams, our lovely lobsters, the shrimp, all that would be the unclean if you took the 11th chapter of Leviticus.

He comes and he tells us what goes *into* the mouth does not defile us. Not a thing that goes into the mouth defiles a man, only what comes out of the heart defiles him. And so, whether I eat or do not eat it means nothing in the eye of God. He tells us that there's not a thing gained by not eating it and nothing by eating it, it's all equal to the eye of God. Because man will one day discover he never really ate another...that seems crazy...he never really ate another. He never killed another. He never wounded another. There was only himself, the ark, containing all, and all were self-wounds and self-destruction, and he only ate himself.

Now let me share with you an experience of mine. One day I found myself at the top of a ladder, a very tall ladder, and I was alone as a man. At the base of this ladder was the jungle and all the animals of the jungle, the lions, tigers, everything that you would think of as a vicious animal, an angry animal, and they were really violent. You could see the river…these living growling beasts that they were. And I was afraid. I looked around and not a soul in sight, I'm all alone. Then, something in the depth of my soul told me—I didn't hear a voice but I knew—I knew that everything that I saw, the entire animal world, only reflected my emotional disturbance. The anger there was a reflection of the fear here, and my fears were mirrored in this moving, moving beast that was at the bottom of me. Then when I knew that, I lost the fear. As I lost the fear they became domesticated, like house cats, just domesticated cats, not angry lions and tigers and panthers and all that they were.

And then I went further, because I remembered what I once did by arresting in me an activity, which in turn arrested the moving panorama that moved before me. Not a thing could move when I arrested that energy in me, and I saw it stand still as though made of marble, made of clay. So I repeated it here, and I arrested in me that life promised: "As the Father has life in himself, so he has granted the Son also to have life in himself. And do not marvel; for you will one day hear the voice and those that are dead will come forth from their tombs." And so, I arrested in me this activity, and everything I saw one moment before *moving* stood still. Then I went down the ladder, and they were made as inanimate as this thing is here. They were dead; made of some substance, it could have been clay, or it could have been marble. But there wasn't one breath in the beasts that I saw, everything was dead. Well, where was the life? Had I eaten one of them, what life would I have eaten? Had I slain one and taken from it a nice piece of meat, and I consumed that meat, what would I have eaten? So I can only get from anything the life within it. Where was the life in it? Because I can't eat the dead thing, no one takes the dead or that with feet of clay anyway. You can only eat that which has life in it to get substance from it. Even if it's an apple, if it's a peach, anything in the world, it must first be alive. It can't be dead and decayed, and it can't turn to stone and you consume it and get anything from it. You can't assimilate that. You can only assimilate that which is alive. And so had I killed one of these and devoured it, what life would I have been eating? I saw that *I* gave it life. I could not have extracted from it anything other than I first gave it.

So the whole vast world that lives and moves in my world moves because I animate it. But I do it unknowingly. You are doing it unknowingly. You are making everything alive in your world, but you don't know it, for you haven't yet had the experience of stopping it to see it *is* something that is dead unless *you* animate it; that nothing is truly and really independent of your perception of it. That it moves, but you don't know it moves because *you* are animating it. And one day you are told of a certain law, that you could, without the consent of another, change the attitude of that being towards life, towards himself; and in changing his attitude, you could change the circumstances of his life. So you try it. You don't ask his consent. You simply represent him to yourself as the man, or the woman, that you would like him to be, and you're quite sure he would like to be it. And so, you don't confide, you don't take him into your confidence and tell him anything, you simply try it. Then when you meet him in the not distant future, he has changed his attitude towards life, and in that change of attitude he has changed the aspects of life. He has a change of environment, change of circumstances.

And so, you don't brag; you're just learning a lesson. Where was the activity to begin with? You are the ark of God, and the ark contains *everything*, nothing is missing from the ark. So you are either the ark of God or you're simply a phantom from the earth and the sea. By this, you know you're the ark, because he lives, seemingly, on the outside and he moves independently of your perception of him. Were he truly independent of your perception of him, a change of attitude in *you* relative to him could not produce in *him* a change at all, it couldn't. But it does! It produces a change; therefore, he must be truly *in* you. And we go back to Blake: "All that you behold though it *appears* without, it is within, in your Imagination, of which this world of mortality is but a shadow." So when Blake uses the word "bosom" he means Imagination, which he reveals in that wonderful statement, another passage in *Jerusalem*, that "*we* are ever expanding in the bosom of God, the Human Imagination" (Ch.1,Plt.5). So he calls the bosom of God "Divine Imagination," and we are expanding in Divine Imagination. What's expanding?—the *human* Imagination. And they do not differ save in degree of intensity, but not in substance, not in character. They operate in the same way, one is keyed low and one is keyed high. Keyed high, an imaginal act is an immediate objective fact; keyed low as we are, it's then realized in a time process. It takes time between the imaginal act and its externalization in the world. But it's still one, operating the entire world.

So you are doing it, I am doing it; everyone contains *all* in himself. And all that we behold, though it *appears* without and seems so completely independent of us, it really isn't. For I know that the night that I saw this thing it frightened me. I was scared by my own being, because it was simply myself made visible. That's part of the eternal structure of the universe. But I animated it. He said, "Eternity exists, and all things in eternity, independent of creation, which was an act of mercy" (*Vis. Last Judg.*,Pp.91-92). That act of mercy was the animation of that which exists. The whole thing exists, but it's dead, it's frozen, and then *you*, God, awaken it. You begin to animate it, and as you animate it you don't know you're animating it and it scares you. You are afraid of your own life, because *you* give it life; it has no life in itself. Only the Father has life in himself, and as the Father has life in *himself*, so he has granted the Son also to have life in *himself*. So you are that Son, but the Father and the Son are one; though the Father, at this level where we are called Son, is greater than the Son. So, "I and my Father are one, but my Father is greater than I." But I am moving towards that expansion where I and my Father are truly one (John 10:30).

But while I am learning and experiencing this wonderful thing I *must* go through, then at moments I am scared to death of my own creation. Didn't create the lion, I didn't create the tiger. They are part of the eternal structure of the universe. I didn't create this garment of hair called John Brown or Mary Smith; I didn't do that but I *animate* them. I animate everything in my world. But Mary Brown and John Smith are eternal parts of the eternal structure of the universe, and you simply animate them. And to prove you do do it you simply see them not as they now *appear* to you but as you would *like* them to appear to you and to themselves. You don't consult them, you don't take them into your confidence, you ask nothing of them, you simply do it; and persuade yourself of the reality of what you imagine relative to them, and wait in confidence. You wait in confidence, and then in this interval of time—because you're functioning on a lower frequency, you're down here, and this is the lower degree of intensity than were you raised to the height of the Father—so down here, you must wait in faith, confident that what you have done will come to pass. And then it comes to pass. As it comes to pass, you've discovered life in yourself. And the day will come when you take it off...you never know it completely while you are still wearing this garment, for this garment is also part of the eternal structure of the universe. You had to assume it and move above it, but trusting from within the being that you really are.

Now, what then endures? This is part of the eternal structure of the universe. What then passes away and what endures outside of the eternal structure that God has set up to bring forth himself as you?—love, love never ends. As for prophecy, it will pass away, as for knowledge, it will pass away; for our knowledge is imperfect and our prophecy is imperfect. But when that which is perfect comes, that which is imperfect will pass away. And so, when we are perfected in his own mind's eye...when the lowly being that we started as, just trying to make something move and it moved...but we didn't know we did it. We saw it move, and we didn't see any contact between the thing and ourselves. We didn't have a string, like a kite, but we know when we're flying a kite with the wind we can do certain things and we do know we are guiding the motion, or we feel we are. But we have no sensation of contact between the beam, say, a beam of thought, and we don't realize we're just as contacted with it as we are with the string and the kite. We don't know it. And so, it moves and seems to run from us and sometimes frightens us because of our attitude towards it. And it scares us to death...when it has no power in itself. All the power is in the mind of the one who is looking at it, and imagining whatever he is imagining when he looks at it. And the whole vast world is simply the animated structure of the world, animated by the percipient, and you are the percipient. So the only thing that really remains is love, because God *is* love. There is nothing but God and God is love.

Last night I spoke at one of these salons. That's one of those things that you get into occasionally, and you don't know why or how, but we all do it. And so, not a ___(??), so you got into it. And this nice couple, they asked me to tell them some stories concerning my mystical experiences. Alright, nothing pleases me more than to tell *these* experiences. And so, this chap said to me, "You mean to tell me that you actually saw God?" I said, "Yes, I saw God." Then he smiled a little sneer, snigger. Well, said he, "What is God?" I said, "Man...God is man. You may not believe it, you may think he's light and power and all these things, but I tell you God is man. And one day you will have the privilege of meeting God. When you see him, you'll be absorbed by him, because to see him is to become him. And so you'll be incorporated into the body of love, and you will know, regardless of the arguments of man, that God is all love, infinite love, and nothing but love. All things pass away, all the wisdom of this world passes away, everything passes away but love. Love never ends, never comes to an end, because God is love."

Then his wife said to me, "Are you Isaiah?" I said, What has that to do about it...am I Isaiah? I said, no, I'm Neville. "Isaiah saw God." Must I be Isaiah to see God? The pure in heart sees God, *only* the pure in heart sees God. So, if you're pure in heart—not in your eyes, for all of us in our own eyes feel that our ways are pure, all the ways of men are pure in their own eyes, but God sees the heart—and when in his eyes the heart is pure you are called. You have no choice. Because you don't know that moment in eternity when you were selected, and that little secret of God's elective love remains his secret. And you are called for incorporation, that's all. You'll be asked a question, you'll answer correctly; at the moment of the answer you are incorporated into the body of love, which is God. And let me repeat, God is man. That didn't sit with them at all.

And then, this lady asked a question, "Why if Jesus Christ is God, why did he cry out on the cross, 'My God, my God, why hast thou forsaken me?'" And then she quoted it as though it came from the Book of Luke. I said, no, it didn't come from Luke. It came either from Matthew or Mark or both, but certainly not from Luke, and not from John. Because they do not use that 22nd Psalm, they use...that is, Luke uses the 31st Psalm, and only the 31st is quoted in this last cry on the cross. It wasn't a cry. It was a complete surrender in faith; for the words are, 'Father, into thy hand I commit my spirit' not 'My God, my God, why hast thou forsaken me?' That is Matthew. That's when the great presence is presented as king. In Mark, he is presented as a servant. In Luke, he is presented as the perfect man. He would not cry, because a perfect man is made in the image of God, the pure in heart, so he doesn't. He knows God as infinite love. So, at the very last he knows the work is finished, and so, "Father, into thy hands I commit my spirit."

When it comes to John, John is God himself in the story as presented, and so, he presents Jesus *as* Jehovah. And so the last cry there is, "It is finished." To fulfill scripture, just prior to that, he said, "I thirst"...to fulfill the 69th Psalm. And so he thirsted and they gave him vinegar for his thirst. So he cried out, "I thirst." Then the very last words, knowing that it was finished, he said, "It *is* finished" and then gave up the spirit. So he didn't cry it. But the lady was insistent it came from Luke, because that very day she was reading Luke and she read it in Luke. Well, not to have the other guests be disturbed, I did what normally I really should not have done. But I thought for the benefit of all...because if I did not correct it, they would have gone out thinking, well, you see, he doesn't know what he's talking about, and one lady corrected him, and so *she* knew. So I asked the hostess of the place if perchance she had a Bible, and she brought out a lovely big red Bible. I said, Turn to Luke and turn to the 23rd chapter, for that would be on the cross. The 24th is *after* the resurrection.

So she turned...I didn't have my glasses with me, and when you're pushing sixty, you know, you need glasses, so I didn't have my glasses. So I said, I can't see this fine print...and some gentleman very graciously offered me his glasses, but I couldn't use them. He gave me the glasses, but I couldn't see anything then. Another gentleman, judging from appearances I would say many years my senior, and his fitted me perfectly. They were just magnifying, and so I could see, and I read it for her. She was, still I'm quite convinced, unconvinced. I said, I'm reading from the 46th verse, the 23rd chapter of the Book of Luke. When you go home, take the same Book of Luke and read it and you will see he never did quote the 22nd Psalm; he was only quoting the 31st Psalm, a complete confidence in his *surrender* to God.

So we think we know this great book, and we really don't know the book. The book is telling you what I've told you earlier: You *are* the ark of God. All things in eternity are contained in you; there's nothing but God; and you and God are one. That shocks people, as it shocked those last night...not all of them but the majority was disturbed. As the meeting...as it followed when the gathering after the meeting, from conversations that I had with so many of them following that, they were greatly disturbed. Because they can't bring themselves to believe that man is *that* great in the eyes of God. He's bringing out a Son. What do you expect him to bring out, a Son and not be like his Father? Suppose I'm bringing out a son and my wife says, "Oh, we had a child this morning," and I'm delighted, and I go into the room and she shows me a roach. She gives me a bug, a great big bug, and says, "I gave birth to this, this morning. You're the father." Now, wouldn't I be proud! That's exactly what man is doing with God. He said, "I will bring forth from you"—from man, and he calls man this wonderful David—and he said, "I will raise up after you" (after you're dead), and so, "When you lie down with your fathers, I will raise up from your body a son, that will come forth from your body. And I will be his father and he shall be my son" (2 Sam. 7:12,14). Then all of a sudden he brings out of David (which is humanity) what he's waiting *eagerly* for, *his* Son, the image of himself, and David gives birth to a roach? Can you imagine that? What would God do? Step on it. He'd step on it right away and call it, well, some miscreation and start all over again. Because if all that God could bring out of man, waiting eagerly for something like himself to come out of man, and it doesn't come out the embodiment of love but it comes out like a monstrous thing, step on it. And then you have eternity at your command, therefore, make it all over again. This time do a little better.

But God has done exactly what he planned. He is bringing forth from humanity his Son. He is bringing out of David, that's humanity, one glorious Son; it's you. When he brings you out, you're just like him. And, may I tell you, he's all love, nothing but love. There is no hate in God, no retribution. The cry on the cross, the very first words, "Father, forgive them"—if you read Luke--"Father, forgive them; they know not what they do." And then the second cry on the cross, he turns to the thief, he said, "Behold, I say unto you today..." You see, in Greek and in Hebrew there is no punctuation mark, in fact, no paragraph, no chapter, just one letter after the other, so our scholars had to break it and punctuate it. So if you take the comma and put it after "I say unto you," and that's the break, and then, "today you will be with me in Paradise" that changes the entire sentence. And yet they all do that. But if I take that sentence and change the comma, and say, "I say unto you today,"—I'm telling you today—"you will be with me in Paradise." I don't say you are going to be with me *today*. I'm telling you I have experienced it. I have experienced the Promise, complete, fulfilled, and I know my inheritance is the kingdom of heaven. I inherit not only the kingdom, I inherit a presence, and the presence is God. Because he gave me himself through the revelation of his Son, who called me what he calls him. He calls me "Father"; he calls him "Father." But he can't call both; we're one.

And so, I know I inherit a presence. I know when the time comes to take it off, automatically he has already changed my lowly body to be of one form with his glorious body, and the body that I will wear tomorrow is one with that of the exalted Christ. That I know. And so, when this happens, I will say to anyone, if a thief, alright, even though you are a thief, you're a cutthroat, you're a murderer, but I tell you, "You will be with me in Paradise." So his second cry on the cross, "Behold, I say unto you today,"—you put the comma there—"you will be with me in Paradise." I'm not committing myself that now, this very day, you're going to be with me; because, if you read the story carefully, he said, "Touch me not yet; I have not yet ascended unto my Father" (John 20:17), and that was forty days later. So either one is misunderstood or the whole thing is a lie, it's a contradiction. But if you take the comma—and the scholar had the right to place it where he felt the meaning would be—and so he thought after "you" if you placed the comma that would give the sense intended by the writer. It didn't give the sense. "Behold, I say unto you today,"—I'm talking today—"you will be with me in Paradise." So that's the story.

And then the third cry is a complete surrender in absolute confidence into the hands of his Father. "Father, into thy hands I commit my spirit," in confidence that this was intended, that we become one; for the spirit, everyone's spirit becomes one, and he's one with the Father. So when he goes to the Father, he *is* the Father. But, while he's here, clothed as we are clothed in flesh and blood, then, seemingly, he is not, and restricted to the limit of this region, this level of awareness.

So I say, all of you the whole vast world pushed out—everything is man made visible. Man has never killed another, he has never eaten another, he has never wounded another, because he only could hurt himself. I wouldn't say I wound a piece of clay. If I went in and I took a knife, I could disfigure a lovely painting, but I wouldn't say I wounded it. I could be some awful character and then take a knife and cut the lovely canvas, but I wouldn't really say I hurt it. But, if I gave it life and the thing became animated, it became alive, and then I put the knife to it, I would say I hurt it. But the thing that would make it alive would be myself, the perceiver; therefore, I'm really putting the knife into myself, but not yet *that* sensitive to feeling.

But the day will come, may I tell you, when what I just told you is true. I saw the entire world right before me and it was all dead when I arrested in me an activity that made it alive. I suddenly looked at it and it was simply dead. But before that, I was afraid, I was scared to death. I looked at it and it was all living, moving beasts, and I'm alone, no one to protect me, no one to comfort me, I'm completely alone. And then, something in the depths of the soul, I knew it, that if perchance I could only lose my fear of them, they would not be angry. When I lost my fear of them…these lovely kittens, that's what they were. Huge monstrous things...but kittens, domesticated. And then I went further and I arrested in me the activity that made them alive. Then I came down the ladder, walked right down to them and they were frozen, dead; not asleep, they were dead. They were only made of clay. Their life was in *me*, but I didn't know it until that moment before I started down. Because, at the very first moment of seeing them, because I saw them through my conceptual mind and my conceptual mind tells me that tiger is a very dangerous animal, and so is the lion, and so is the panther; and so, my conceptual mind modified that divine vision that I could have had were I not wearing the conceptual mind. So when I took it off as it were by remembering the being that I am, the whole thing changed and they were all dead.

So, had I eaten any part of them, or any part of the fish, I'm only eating myself. Because I'm only extracting, really, from that body, which is dead anyway, and it was only made alive by the life of me, so what am I taking back when I eat it? I'm only eating my own being as it were. So you're told in that wonderful second chapter of Colossians speaking of diets, it doesn't matter what you eat. Only do not use it as a stumbling block to others who are not yet awake. So don't brag about it. If they want to be vegetarians, let them be vegetarians. Don't brag about being able to eat all the things in the world without distress, don't brag about it. But *do not* submit any more to regulations. You're told, do not submit to regulations—all the regulations of the churches, all the regulations of the outside things of this world—don't. Why do you once more think of yourself, he said, as a part of this world? You're not a part of this world. You're wearing a part of the world's garment, and you're wearing it, but you're not the garment that you wear. You will have something that is coming out that is one with God; and your body is God's body, and the body is all love.

So we are told love never ends. Knowledge passes away, prophecy it passes away, for both are imperfect. But when perfection comes, when that which is perfect comes, that which is imperfect will pass away. And so, all that man knows today about gravity, all that he knows about the so-called structure of the atom, all that he knows about everything in this world will be as nothing; it'll pass away, because it isn't true. It is partially true and we get results with a partial truth. But when perfection comes all these partial truths will vanish, and they will not be so at all. And I saw that so clearly when I saw a bird in flight. If I arrested the motion of a man, which I did, and the lady walking through to serve food, and then she couldn't move one second beyond one nth part beyond. And I saw that so clearly when I saw a bird in flight. If I arrested the motion of a man, which I did, and the lady walking through to serve food, and then she couldn't move one second beyond one nth where I arrested her. And a man eating couldn't complete the action. He was drinking soup, so he took the soup up this way, and as I stopped him, he stopped, frozen, he was dead. And the waitress walking, she was dead. And the bird flying, it stopped in space but it didn't fall. And the leaves falling didn't fall any further when I arrested them. And everything was just as it was at that moment of perception. The leaves falling fell not, and the bird flying flew not, and the waitress walking walked not; everything that was in motion when I stopped it remained stationary. Then I went forward and examined it, and everything was made as though it were made of clay.

Then when I released that activity *in me*, what happened? They all continued to complete their intentions. The bird continued in its flight towards where he intended to go. The waitress came forward towards the table of four to serve as she intended when she came through that little door. The man drinking his soup, the hand that was stopped here completed the action and the soup went into his mouth. Everything continued as it was intended. But I stopped the intention, not there, in me. At that moment in time it had to be just where it was and I stopped it, and then allowed it to continue by an action in me. Well, if gravity is true, I mean absolutely true, not partially true, not relatively true, that bird should have fallen to the ground when I stopped it. For a bird in flight if arrested would fall. But, the bird in flight arrested, not supported by anything and still remained suspended in space, where is gravity? Where is the gravity of the leaf? Why did the leaf not come on down to the ground where it should have if gravity is truly an absolute universal law?

So I say, the time will come when all that man now knows...and you read it carefully in the 13th chapter of the Book of Corinthians, 1st Corinthians, 13th chapter. It's a hymn in praise of love. It simply states that love and love only is the everlasting of the world. Everything passes away. If I give my body to be burned and have not love, it is as nothing. If I have all wisdom and have not love, it is as nothing. No matter what I do in this world if I haven't love, I did nothing. Because, everything is going to pass away that man knows here; but it's love that he has here that will not pass away. Your love for your wife, your love for your husband, your love for a child, your love for a friend, your love for an animal, every expression of love is forever. So these loves *never* pass away...but what you now *know* is going to pass away.

You look into the mirror and you see your face, and you even catch it on a photograph, and you think, "I've got him now." Then look at yourself again next year, where is he? It all passed away, and you can't bring it back. You can go to the surgeon, have him cut you here, pull up a little place, but it doesn't look like what it did last year. And they go every year. I just saw where some very famous person in the East, she's an international lady—but like all of us we push the inevitable grave, and so, she's not far from it—but she's just gone to a surgeon for the nth time in London to once more have another little lift. A few more seconds, she can't smile. There's no more to lift. You look at it like this...you can't take any more.

I have played in the theatre with one of those. She had millions, and she was always taking a little lift, not only here but also here. Also making everything as she was when she was eighteen. It didn't work. Finally, the face couldn't move. It was simply completely filled. So, you see, all things will pass away, but *love* will not pass away. So, whatever you do in love know you are doing something that is permanent, something that's forever. So fall in love with anything, with a bird, a bird at home. If you have a cat at home, if you have a dog at home, if you can't find humanity to love, love something, because love is the only living permanent thing in the world because God is love. And everything else passes away.

Infinite power...you can call God's power almightiness, but that's not God, that's an *attribute* of God. When you see it, you see man, because all the attributes of God are men. When you stand in the presence, almightiness, it's man, no question about it, but it's not God. God is love. When you stand in the presence of God, infinite love, you don't have to ask anything, who are you? You ask no question. You stand in the presence of the Ancient of Days and he's all love. Yet you look here and here is infinite might and it's man; it's an attribute of God. Wisdom, an attribute of God... all this is an attribute of God. But love is forever, the only permanent reality in the world. So every time you exercise your Imagination lovingly on behalf of another, you know what you're doing? You're actually using the only reality in the world, the *only* reality.

Gradually you awaken, and one day you'll hear the voice of the child. You will hear him, and you will awaken him from a profound sleep. Where will you awaken him? He'll come forth from the tomb. And where is the tomb?--your own skull. One day you will hear the voice of the child in the depths of your soul, and then *you* who were dead will awaken from sleep. You will feel yourself waking from sleep, may I tell you. You had no idea you were dead, because you feel yourself waking and you can only wake if you were asleep. And when you are *fully* awake, you know now you must have been dead because you are in a tomb. It's the only way you know that you're dead, because where you are you are alone in a sealed tomb, a sepulcher. So are we not told in Luke—and they called the word by its real name, they call it "skull"—"And when they came to the place called The Skull, there they crucified him" (Luke 23:33). When they came to the place called The Skull, there they crucified him. And just the very next verse, he said, "Father, forgive them; they know not what they do." And then a few verses later on, "I say to you today, you will be with me in Paradise." A few verses later and he commits himself into the hands of the Father, "Father, into thy hands I commit my spirit." Then he gives up the breath, gives up the Spirit into the hands of God, for the journey is over.

And that will be played by every child born of woman; everyone is going to play that part. You can't avoid it, because that's your destiny. God has predetermined your end, regardless of what you do in between. I hope you play a lovely part, a beautiful part, but whether you do or not the end is predetermined; and the end is that God gives himself to you, as though there were no others in the world, just God and you. And so, the end is assured for all of us—even if you have murdered—but you've never murdered love. And so, the millions that Hitler murdered he really murdered himself, but he doesn't know it, hasn't the slightest idea. Stalin murdered millions; he murdered himself.

I know that you and I who have friends or relatives who were part of that awful story, we do not conceal that. We did not know that a friend was murdered. That friend was really never touched, for in him he too had life in himself. He animated his world. He was afraid of the rumors. He was afraid, as I was afraid of the animals. And before he was brought into that picture of the slaughterhouse, he didn't quite discover that his own emotions caused the disturbance that he saw. And so he couldn't quite arrest it, because he didn't know that he was animating the world and giving it reality, giving it life, by his own fears. And, as Job said, "My fears have come upon me." So, while he was afraid, he became all the more animated on the inside and all the more things became more stormy. Then it was too late, because he did not realize any relationship between himself and the thing that he perceived.

And so, when you one day have this experience, and may you have it tonight, you will see this wonderful world stand still. You'll know it stands still because in you, you made it stand still. You arrested an activity that you felt, and you didn't feel it out there, you felt it here, right in your own head. As you arrested it, everything froze, and you looked at it, and then you had no fear. Then you released it in you and they all became once more animated. You could keep them on the level of domesticated cats, or you could once more go back to your former state where you forgot, and once more they become violent as you become more fearful.

So I say, all men, all the whole vast world is man made visible; there is nothing but man because God and man are one. "Man is all Imagination. God is man and exists in us and we in him. The eternal body of man is the Imagination and that is God himself" (Blake, *Berkeley*., p.775; *Laocoon,* p.776). And when you go home this night, you try it, without the consent of another. Do it lovingly, though. Just bring someone into your mind's eye, represent him to yourself as you would like him to be, regardless of what he's done—I don't care what he has done or what he's doing—just simply be faithful to your vision of him. And to the degree that you are self-persuaded of the reality of what you've done, to that degree he will conform to it. But, bear this in mind and be comforted by it, were you functioning at higher intensities it would happen immediately. But we are not—we are wearing garments of flesh and blood, and we are insulated. Because we are, it's going to take an interval of time between your imaginal act and the fulfillment of that act.

Now let us go into the Silence.

* * *

Q: (inaudible)

A: ___(??) is the number of man. If you would tone 666, you would get 9. 6 + 6 + 6 would be 18; 1 + 8 is 9; and 9 is the number of man. Aleph, Daleth, Mem, and it comes to 1440 when you count. You take 1440 and you get 9. Aleph is 1, Daleth is 4, Mem is 40, and that spells Adam. And so, 144, whether it be 1440 or 144,000, you can add as many zeros as you want, and get that wonderful mystical number of 144,000 who will be saved and on their foreheads will be the name of both the Father and the Son. But the Father's name is I AM, and the Son in creativity is called Jesus, so on the forehead is "I AM Jesus." And that's you!

Goodnight.

OUR REAL BELIEFS

3/6/64

Tonight's subject is "Our Real Beliefs." I really want this series to be the most productive that we've ever had. By that I mean I want everyone present to really have a goal, a noble goal, and realize it, realize it before we close in May. May I tell you, you *can* realize it, I mean that seriously. So what do I mean by our real beliefs? Our real beliefs are what we live by. Real belief and knowing are one. When a man *really* believes, it's just as though he knows, it's tantamount to knowing. But I tell you, belief—I call it faith, I call it belief—it is not complete till it becomes experience. One must experience it and then they know it. Now you will hear the same thing tonight. Everyone present will hear exactly the same thing, but no two will hear it in the same depth. Some will hear it on the surface, others will hear it below the surface, and others will hear it down in the very depths of their being. It's where you live. As we are told, "The word came to them as it did to us; but it did not profit them, because it was not mixed with faith in those who heard it" (Heb. 4:2). They heard it and rejected it, but they heard it. It came in and went out. It did not receive acceptance by those who heard it, and so they instantly rejected it. Tonight, I hope you will not reject what I'm going to tell you. But that's your choice. You're free; you can accept it or reject it.

But I tell you, if I get through tonight and you apply it…because you are the operant power. I can tell you but it doesn't operate itself. If this very moment I ask you to think of a friend, just think of a friend, and now hear him tell you something lovely, something lovely about himself, about a mutual friend or about you, just hear it, do you believe that that actually took place? You may say, well, I imagined it, but it didn't *really* take place. I will tell you, the day will come, and I hope now, that when you imagine a state, before you have *external* confirmation of that state, to you it *is* as though you heard it externally, you know it; that this *internal* act is equal to the external confirmation of that act. You get to *that* point, because the difference between God and man is measured only in terms of this imaginative power.

If I would now speak of the *power* that is God—as we're told in scripture, it's revealed constantly as power, sheer power—3rd chapter, 4th, 5th, and 6th verses of the Book of Exodus—sheer power. Moses stands in the presence of power, but it's creative power. And the difference between God and man is measured by, simply, power. On this level, if I am on the surface of my being, only this is real, what my senses allow. But if I go deeper into my own being, moving ever toward the core of my being, who is God, then my imaginative act becomes externalized, quickly externalized, as I go deeper and deeper. On the surface it seems to take an interval of time, if I believe. If I don't believe, it never comes into some external form at all, never. Yet I'm living in a world not understanding it, not knowing what it's all about. So, really, the story that I want to tell you is trying to ask you, to plead with you, to buy your religion wholesale. Go to the Maker, go to the source; don't buy it retail with some man in between. No one in between you and the source, you go right into the depths and buy your religion wholesale by going to the source which is your own wonderful human Imagination, your own I-am-ness. That's God.

The story we told you last Tuesday of one whose name was Eddie... Eddie had the identical experience of the one recorded in the Book of Exodus, when he heard "Do not come up here." Read the words, the words are, "Do not come here"--read it in the Book of Exodus, 4th, 5th and 6th verses of the 3rd chapter of Exodus. And the Lord said unto Moses, "Do not come here." Then Moses hid his face, not in shame but in fear. He was afraid to look at God. So Eddie saw the symbol of God and he ran, he was *scared* too...the identical story. What did he hear? The revelation of God's name: I AM. He first heard it, "I AM"...no one in sight...then it repeated itself so loudly he thought it came from above. He looked up thinking it was some machine, maybe some helicopter with a P.A. system is broadcasting the name of I AM. There was not a thing in sight. And then the third, "Don't come up here!" Being curious he did go up there to the hill to confront a rattlesnake. Fortunately, it was not coiled to spring, it was simply a four-foot long snake all stretched out, the symbol of the creative power of God. But it scared him. It scares man, when man actually sees what really is in himself, that he is solely responsible for everything that's taking place in his world, solely responsible! It scares him. It's too much, until he goes deeper and deeper and hears the same word of truth but hears it in depth, and then he assumes full responsibility for all that is taking place within him.

So tonight, let me share with you a few stories. Several years ago, a lady—she's not here tonight; she's now on a new job, and it's taken her away for awhile—but when she heard it, that imagining creates reality, she said to herself, "Well, if that is so, I would like to go to Egypt." She had no money. She's never been a lady of means, always working, small sums of money, could never accumulate what it would take to make the trip. And so, the usual story, she told her dream, she didn't keep it to herself, she told it, nothing wrong with it. If you really believe it you can tell it. As you're told in scripture, "Go and tell no man, but show John." Show the world. Well, if you don't tell man *before*, will man believe you *after* the event? He may question your honesty, but if you tell him before the event then he is assured, because, actually, you have a witness to the fact you did tell it before the event. So that is also in scripture, "And now I will tell you before it takes place that when it *does* take place you may believe." For that is courage in the depths of the soul, where one knows the imaginal act is a fact at the very moment of the act, though not yet seen by the outer man. But not everyone has that courage and that faith in the imaginal act. So she told it, and, naturally, her friends criticized her, "It is stupid to go to that man, you waste your money. It's not religion, what is it? He is telling you that an assumption though false if persisted in will harden into fact? Well, that's stupid; it doesn't make sense." To them a true judgment must conform to the external fact to which it relates. So if I say, "Well, isn't it a lovely dog," and there is no dog to bear witness to my judgment, my judgment is false. So that's what they gathered from what she told that I am teaching... and so the whole thing is insane, it's stupid.

Well, the years went on—it's been seven years now—and this is what happened this past week. She got a job. She's a nurse and so the job moves around, she goes from home to home where the need is there. So she found herself in the environment or the neighborhood of a friend she had not seen or contacted in a year. She exchanged a birthday card and a Christmas greeting, with a little note on the card, but no telephone call and no other contact. Finding herself in the neighborhood she calls her. When this friend heard her voice on the wire, she said, "Oh, Jan, you can have it! You can have it!" She said, "Alright, alright, I'll take it. What is it?" And then this is the story. There was a party, a pre-Lenten party at the Hotel Hilton, some Mardi Gras by a Catholic society, the Joseph and Mary Society. There were door prizes. The major prize was a thirty day trip first-class, all expenses paid, stopping along the way at the Hilton hotels in the Near East, and, Egypt is part of the set up. The lady and her family had spent several months last year abroad, and had no desire this year to go abroad again. In fact, they had already arranged to go to New York City for the World's Fair, which opens in April. So a trip abroad is out. Furthermore, this ticket, this door ticket, only accepted one person, not a group, not a family. So that was what the friend said to her she would give her. Jan said, "Alright, I'll take it!" and then called me up to tell me the story, delayed, seemingly, seven years. She still now has the ticket if she wants it to the Near East, where Egypt is included, and she goes first-class, all expenses paid, but everything paid, because she believed. Maybe in the interval her faith wavered. Maybe she justified it by saying, "Maybe I don't want it" or in some strange way tried to explain it away. But it still, in its own good time, came to the surface.

I ask you not to throw your dreams away and see that they are impossible to realization in this strange drab world of external facts. Every dream can come true *if* I can get through to you that your Imagination is God, and that your imaginal act, when you think of a friend, carrying on a conversation, that is Jesus Christ in action. "Examine yourselves to see whether you are holding to your faith. Test yourselves. Do you not realize that Jesus Christ is in you?" (2 Cor. 13:5). If he is in you, then who is he? He is your own imagining. God is your Imagination; God in action is imagining; and God in action is Christ. Christ, as defined in scripture, is "the power and the wisdom of God" (1 Cor. 1:24).

So I tell you, everyone can realize if you *really* believe in Jesus Christ. One billion will say they believe in Jesus Christ, and cross themselves before a dead piece of wood or a piece of marble or clay or something other than a *living* God. The very being kneeling before these external icons...here is the king of Greece who just died, and they brought what they considered a holy icon for the man who has died. In the eyes of God a king is just like a servant, they do not differ. One's love for one is not greater than his love for another. To what extent have they heard the word of God and believed? So he's dying to bring a holy icon. It didn't work. He just saw the little icon, and so he makes his exit like any other person in the world. I hope that everyone here will find the *real* Jesus Christ. The *real* Jesus Christ is your own wonderful human imagining; that's God in action. The *real* God is your own wonderful lovely Imagination. When you say "I am," that's God.

Now let me share with you that which was given to me this past week by a gentleman, who is here tonight. He's written the most glorious story. I hope he keeps it up because they are exciting. I shared them with those who came home since I received his letters, and I will share them with you tonight. He's a writer, he writes for TV. He started three years ago on this show that has been running for three years, and he writes every third or fourth script. He said, "When I started, my price was $2,500 a script, and in two years my agent got it up to $3,000 a script. Then, a year ago last Christmas my mother came west, came from the east to visit us, and I told her what I received for a script, $3,000 a script, and she said, 'Well, I always assumed that you got $3,500 a script.'" She wasn't at all impressed with $3,000. Then he tried to explain to her that as far as he knew there was no writer in the field, solo writer, who got more than he did. He was getting $3,000 a script; she was not impressed; didn't disturb her at all. She still said that as far as she was concerned it was worth $3,500 a script.

Well, two months later the agent was called by the studio for a contract, a renewal of contract for the next year for the writer. Before, naturally, he would go to the studio, he would have to discuss it with the writer. So he explained to the writer he didn't think that they should ask for more. They moved up from $2,500 a script to $3,000 a script, and you shouldn't price yourself out of the business by asking for more. And so, the writer agreed. It was a nice friendly relationship between himself and the producer, so why ask for more and get out of the business? So, it was agreed. The very next day after this agreement a conference was held to discuss stories, a story conference. So the producer said to the writer, "Have you come to an agreement with the contract for the next year?" And he said, "Yes, I'm going to sign." He said, "Have you asked for more money?" He said, "No." He said, "You ask for more." He said, "But you're always complaining about the budget, it isn't big enough, and now you're telling me to ask for more." He said, "You ask for more money." Again, he said, "I don't want to price myself out of the business." He said, "You tell your agent to ask for more."

So when he went back, he called his agent, and when he told the agent to ask for more money, the agent thought he had too many cocktails for lunch. So, he said, no, I will give you the source, and he told him what had been told to him that very day at the conference. So the agent, now armed with this information that the very producer had recommended an increase, he called up the business office of the studio and asked for more. They simply blew their top, they screamed; and then very generously they said, we'll forget it, as though you didn't even ask for it, so that the nice relationship between the producer and the writer can go on as it has for the past three years. But the agent knowing the source was adamant, and so when he came out of that office he came out with a contract for $3,500 a script. So, said the writer in his letter to me, "My mother merely assumed that I was getting $3,500 a script, and so her assumption went behind the backs of all of us, the producers, everyone, and bore fruit." So then he said, "I called her up and I told her what I was getting for a script now. Then she started to seriously study your books." And he said, "A problem with Bertha, who has been with us twenty-five years, a most distressing problem, which I will tell you about at some future date. But may I tell you, last Friday it was completely swept out of her life."

"And now a confession is in order. When I first heard you I couldn't understand you; then I began to be afraid that I was going mad because I *could* understand you." Then he said, "I will explain that later." So, I am waiting eagerly for that explanation. But we are told in the Book of John, "He has a devil, he is mad; why listen to him?" You who have your Bible, that's the 10th chapter, the 20th verse of the Book of John. That is the chapter wherein he said, "I and my Father are one." He's just gotten through the previous, or the 8th chapter, by saying, "I know my Father. My Father is he whom you call God. But I know my Father and ye know not your God" (John 8:34,35). And for this they stoned him—stoned him with the literal facts of life—that's the stone of scripture. When you throw the facts at a man where the man dares to assume what reason denies, what his senses deny, then you, who will not go along with his depth, you throw the stones or the facts of life at him to deny the reality of what he is claiming by a mere imaginal act. And so, he has just gotten through making these bold assertions that, "I and my Father are one; and my Father is he whom you call God; but I *know* my Father and ye know *not* your God."

And so, this story...he said, "I didn't understand you...and then I began to fear a form of madness because I *could* understand you." For this teaching takes you into an entirely different world, where reason on this surface of the mind doesn't really prevail...that you really believe in the reality of what inwardly you are doing, and then it comes to the surface. If you don't tell it before and you tell it afterwards, they will question your honesty. If you take them into your confidence and tell it before, if you have enough faith, go about your business. If you don't, they will plague you and throw the stones at you. Every time they meet you they will say, "Where is it? You said you were going to have a certain home, a certain job, a certain sum of money, where is it?" And so, they are always throwing the stones at you, all the facts of life.

Now, here is something, and you listen to it carefully. It's a long letter, and he's bringing out certain points that might have escaped you. For here what we're trying to do is find out all the little facets of the greatest secret in the world, the secret of imagining. For as Fawcett said, "The secret of imagining is the greatest of all problems to the solution of which all should aspire, for supreme power, supreme wisdom, and supreme delight lie in the solution of this far off problem, this great mystery." And he has thrown some light on it. So if I can recall, it's a long letter, typewritten, four pages, but I will give you some of the highlights of it. He said, "When I met my producer three years ago, he was a very subdued and reserved sort of a gentleman." "Reserved," he said, "would be the right word to use to describe him, very reserved, so unlike the volatile enthusiast with whom I formerly worked. He was *very* reserved, in fact, he couldn't express the superlative in any way. In fact, his greatest praise was the word 'good.' You brought in a script and he would accept the script, and his highest praise was 'Good.'

"Well, I thought, I'm going to change this. So I lay on the bed and I heard him say to me, 'Great, just great!' Now, I hadn't started the script. I had just given him a script and he had pronounced the script 'Good.' I am now doing this on the next script, and I heard him distinctly. I went over and over in my audio setup as it were, so I heard him inwardly pronounce the new script as 'Great, just great!' And while I am lying there the phone rings...I haven't started the script...the phone is ringing and it's the producer. He is telling me that the script that he had formerly pronounced 'Good' was 'Great, just great!' Well, then he threw me a curve, because that's not what I expected. It was about the new script which I had not even started. So he not only threw me this curve, but someone had their lines crossed. So, right there I kept on now working a new, I would say, line for him to use, and I changed it from 'Great, just great!' to 'Terrific!' So here I am, I only heard one word, 'It is terrific!' Well, I submitted the script and that's exactly the word he used when he said to me, 'It's terrific!' and with the same enthusiasm that matched my imagining.

"Now I said to myself, two months later...every script I presented within two months it was either 'Great, just great!' or 'Terrific!' He didn't go back to 'Good' anymore. I said, now, I'm going to experiment again. So this time I'm going to make him say 'Absolutely sensational!' So I heard him say 'Absolutely sensational!'" Then he said to me, "What the hell, if you're praising yourself, why not get the best! So I'm doing it to myself, anyway, so why be modest about it? I'm doing the whole thing because he's only echoing it. So I said, 'Absolutely sensational!' So I finished the script, took the script into him, and he pronounced it 'Good.'" He said, "I almost fell out of the chair. It was not the role that I had written for him," and he said, "You know how authors hate ad-libbing."

I know what that means in the theatrical world. When the author writes a play and some actor thinks he knows more than the author, and he changes the script and he ad-libs, or maybe he forgets his lines and if he is smart enough he can throw a few words in, and he ad-libs. But, no matter how smart he *thinks* he is he doesn't flatter the author. The author feels he knows better than any actor what should be there at that moment. And so, he said in his letter, "You know how authors hate ad-libbing. So what could I do? The script had to be cut; so he gave me back the script to cut a certain portion of it. I took the script home, did all the cutting, and then mailed it to him. And I mailed it as a petulant child. I didn't even revise what he had said. But the very next day he calls and he said to me on the wire, 'It's absolutely sensational!'"

Now, this is a point I want you to pay strict attention to. He said, "You know, my experience with the producer disturbed me, *greatly* disturbed me. To hear or to occasionally think about this isn't so bad." By that he meant you'll hear that "All that you behold, though it appears without, it is within, in your Imagination, of which this world of mortality is but a shadow." Well, to hear that and to occasionally think about it isn't too bad, but when it seeps in and takes hold of you and goes deeper, and you realize that it's true! That that producer, who is so important in the production of this great series, who is spending such fortunes—he has it to spend, he allows it, he knows what he's doing, he's been successful, been running three years—and yet he had to actually utter the words that this writer is writing for him. And when he met him he was so reserved he never used any superlative and could never bring himself to praise a thing beyond the word "Good." And he raised him from "Good" to "Great, just great!", "Terrific!", "Absolutely sensational!" That's an enormous accomplishment in anyone's vocabulary when he began as a most reserved party. So when the individual writer now sees what he did with a man, he said, "You know, it distressed me. It distressed me for the simple reason I had to remake my world only as I remake myself; only as I could remake myself could I in any way remake the world...and what an undertaking!" But, he said, "I found a solution. I will not now think of myself x-number of years into the future. I am painting a portrait of myself. Portraits are not painted by one stroke of the brush. And so, I am taking it easy, and I start with the little things in my life, the little things, and I change them to make them conform to the portrait of the being I am painting of myself."

"I started with a simple thing. We have a cat, or we had a cat, and it simply clawed up the entire rug. All the rug was simply pieces of felt all clawed up. And so we delayed buying a new rug." Really, said he, "We were hoping that she would die. After all, she was fifteen years old and she seemed determined to outlive Methuselah. But, because she still was very healthy and she didn't die, we bought the new rug. Right away she started all over again to tear up the rug. For two days I said, 'Something must be done in my Imagination. I have proved it with the producer.' So I went to work in my Imagination and saw this cat in the backyard tearing up a mat that we had in the backyard for just such a purpose. On the third day, she was out in that backyard clawing the mat, and to the day she died she never once tore up our rug. Where is the destructive power in the world save in the Imagination of man!"

If someone heard that story and didn't believe it, they could this night have a cat in their house and they will say, "Oh, that was just coincidence in his case. It wouldn't work here, so I'm not even going to try it. That borders on madness, and no one wants to be mad." In fact, to say that you were once put away is like Leprosy; they don't want that, that you were once committed to some asylum. To go to a hospital because you had a pain and you needed an operation that's allowed today because everyone has them. But not everyone is put away for some mental, I would say, side issue. And so, in his case, he did it. The average person would have heard it; and who would believe that in their own home they, too, could make the dog or the cat or the bird or anything else conform to an imaginal act?

Well, having done *this* now he sees the power within him. He's now going to go all out. He knows he's done it; he has tangible proof that he's done it, and from now on he said he's going to actually be faithful to what he's found within himself. He's found Christ. The day is coming he will actually stand in the presence of infinite love. But before we stand in the presence of infinite love he presents himself first as infinite might. Throughout the Bible you can't find any basis to deny it: It is might, it's power and authority. From beginning to end when he presents himself it's sheer might, sheer power. Until one day, man will see that this power on this level, and on many levels below, resolves itself into infinite love; and it's man, and it's the being that you're moving towards, and it's God the Father. So here, in his own case, it scared him, or rather it depressed him… the thing that had such power was in man. And yet, it's no other place, it's *only* in man, because the power of which we speak, the greatest power in the world, really the *only* power, is your own wonderful human Imagination.

Now, the lady whose story I told first, Jan said that at this present job of hers this little boy came home from school, and the high winds we have been having took the aerial down and flattened it. It's still on the ground, she said. So she tried the TV and there was no TV. She tried it and tried it, and there was no TV. The little boy came home and she said, Oh Lord, he's going to be so disappointed because he's back from school and he wants to see the TV. So he goes straight to the TV, he turns it on—he saw the aerial flattened—then he put his two hands on the top of the machine, and just put them there. She said to him, "You know, there's going to be no picture." He said, "Oh, yes there will be. That does it." She said, "What does it?" He said, "My Imagination; I just imagined it. It'll work." He came back, got in front of the picture with Jan, and here comes this beautiful picture.

Now, Jan couldn't do it, and yet she knows this principle. But she's an adult now. We become adulterated as we grow in this world. The little child could actually believe that that power in his hand was all his Imagination: "It'll do it." And Jan told me over the telephone, because she's working and can't come here now, that the little boy only put his hand on it and swore that here would come a picture; and the picture came to Jan's amazement but not to the boy's. He sat there and looked at it and Jan sat there bewildered, the one who has the thing now to go to Egypt.

Now, to come back to the gentleman's story. He said, "I saw an ad of a Swiss record changer, so I went over to my electronics dealer and I told him that I would like one. He said, 'They aren't in the country and it will be, possibly, a few weeks before they get here, but we have eleven orders so far, would you like to order one?' He said, "Yes, I'd like to order one," so he ordered one. So he said, at the end of the month he received a bill for $375 for the changer. Well, he hadn't received the instrument, so he called up the office. They apologized and said that the girl mistook the order for a sale. And so, we have bad news for you, said the girl, it will not be here before three or four months. But they corrected their mistake. It was not a bill, it was simply an order they had misinterpreted. He then said to himself, I will now look around the house, and spent three days, instead of writing, to see where he was going to put the outlet for this machine. When he decided where he was going to put it, he called the electricians to bore a hole through the wall to put in a cable for this changer. Now he said, "I will need a stand for it, so I went out looking for a stand. Went to all the places... one salesman said, 'What kind of a machine have you because you don't like these stands?' So he told the nature of the machine, and the man said, 'If you have one it's a miracle, because there aren't any in the country, and they won't be here before three or four months,' which was only confirmation of what the agency said.

He said, "Alright, I can't find the stand, I will design one." So he designed the stand and had it made. When the stand came and he placed it where he intended putting the machine, he said to himself, "I will now see the machine on it," which he did. He said, "Now that I have the machine it's only fair to pay the bill," so he sat down and wrote the check out and sent the check off to the electronic firm for his $370-odd in full for his machine. Two days after this they called him to say, "We have your record changer." He wondered why? There were twelve of them on the list. The man only received four in his shipment of an order of twelve. This friend, who wrote me the letter, said, "Well, it could be that I sent my check in advance, because I paid for what to me was before me in my Imagination, it could be that. On the other hand, I'm not asking questions, why he gave me the first one in and why he jumped me from twelve to number one. However, I have the machine. And now my next problem is this, it's a very delicate, complicated, sly, tricky thing, and so I am now trying to imagine myself smart enough to operate it." So that is a story of using your imaginations.

I say faith...as we're told, "We understand that by faith the world was framed by the word of God." Well, you know who God is now: Your own wonderful I-am-ness, that's God. He's framing his world, but it takes faith. To hear it without faith it won't work; to hear it mixed with faith it will work. If you sit down, as he did—he said, "I lay on the bed"—you can sit right here and carry on this inner mental conversation from premises of fulfilled desire—for thinking follows the track laid down in one's own inner conversations. You control the nature of the conversation and see to it that it's not an argument; it's simply from wishes fulfilled, regardless of the nature of that wish. You carry it on in the inside. Some are better at the video; they can see better than they can hear. But I find hearing so very, very easy, and I'm not a musician, so you don't have to be musically inclined to really hear. I appreciate music but I don't play. I don't understand music, in the true sense of the word, I simply appreciate it. Yet, I can hear it vividly. A man's voice...let him speak for one second, let me get the tone, then put upon that tone any word I want to hear and I hear it as though he were here.

Now, how long it takes for what I have heard him say to come to pass, I don't know. As we tell you in that story in the Book of Habakkuk: "The vision has its own appointed hour. It ripens, it will flower. If it be long, then wait; for it is sure and it will not be late" (2:3). So, one seed grows over night, another seed takes a month, another seed takes a year. As in birth a child comes into this world nine months, but a chicken comes out in twenty-one days. So everything has a different interval of time between conception and birth in this world. So what determines the nature of that interval I don't know, but have faith that it is *sure* and it will not for its own sake be late. Not for its own nature will it be late. So the child comes out in nine months, it isn't late for a child, and if a chicken comes out in twenty-one days, it's not late or early for a chicken. That's the interval of time between that moment where it was fertilized and properly nested and then the moment of breaking the shell and hatching.

So here in our case, apply it and you *will* in the next few months—I'm only here for three months, not yet three months—and you'll be able to tell me the most fantastic stories in the world. Because you couldn't start with anything more behind the eight ball, to be a conservative gentleman, who would never beyond the wildest dream go outside and exclaim something is really "Absolutely sensational!" It's so against his nature. A thing is good... that's good enough. You're being well paid for it. You got 2,500; then you got 3,000 for a script; and every three weeks you're bringing one in because it's a half-hour show, it runs weekly; so, every three weeks you're getting a check for 3,000, and now you're getting one for 3,500. And yet the man, I'm quite sure, like all writers he's not contracted to write only, and *only* for that. If he has time outside of writing these scripts, there are other outlets for his talents as a writer. He's not confined to that. And therefore the man who is not given to exploding, he made him explode, and raised him gradually to "Great, just great!" to "Terrific!" and then the final explosion. And he said in his letter, "It's the warmest and the friendliest of relationships between us."

So I ask you to do the same thing. I don't care what it is in this world: know what you want, conceive a scene implying the fulfillment of that dream, and then inwardly carry on these mental conversations from the premise of the fulfilled desire. If you can see at the same time that you hear, like a TV set, alright, put them together, it's better. But if you can't really visualize, and not many can visualize, you will find the audio very, very simple. But when you begin to visualize, may I tell you, it's the most thrilling thing in the world, to be able to actually see. Just like this...to be in a dream awake. It's like being in a dream, only awake. And so when you break it and return to this level where it hasn't taken place, you have no fears, you have no doubts. The whole world is a mask. You know you saw it. You're still seeing it in your mind's eye now; but you actually saw it, and you heard it, and so it *must* come to pass. *You* saw it and you heard it.

And so, if you meet someone who is passing through sheer hell, and they ask of you anything, they're in your world, single them out, and hear them tell you that they have what they sought, just as though they have it. And then let it go. Don't raise a finger to make it so. Don't get on the phone and call a friend to ask the friend to intercede, to help you out. Don't do a thing! Just simply believe in the reality of your imaginal act; because if you go to the *end*, then you can't concern yourself with the means to that end. That would deny the end, by any means that you would even entertain to aid the birth of it, because you went beyond pregnancy right into birth. And so, you saw it and you heard it; now leave it alone and let it work. May I tell you, it *will* work. Then you will find God. And when you come to the final grand, I would say, the last stretch, the final stretch, when you're going home now, really going home, leaving behind you this world, this age altogether; then will come one after the other the most fantastic mystical experiences where everything said of Jesus Christ *you* will experience. And you will know beyond all doubt who Jesus Christ really is: That he truly is supernaturally born, born out of the skull of a man; how he discovers the fatherhood of God; and how he ascends into heaven. Everything said of him happens to you. And then you know how true the story is, how altogether fantastically wonderful scripture is when one experiences it.

And so, I ask you to join with me in testing this greatest of all mysteries. Put it to the test. Start with something simple. The average person who would have a destructive animal like a cat wouldn't consider that a simple problem, and yet in forty-eight hours it was resolved. But one point he made, when the man told you, he used the words, "He expressed himself when he said to me 'Terrific!'—he expressed it with the enthusiasm that matched my imagining." The world is only response, infinite response, it's an echo, and the whole vast world only echoes. So, what echo in this case? When he said "Terrific!" you can see what the writer's imaginal act was. He actually caught a mood that was really forceful, so when the word "Terrific!" came through, it wasn't simply "Oh, I think it's terrific," he exploded with "Terrific!" to equal the imaginal state of the man who made him say "Terrific!"

So, catch it and feel it, and use your Imagination as a great actor would. He has to put himself into the part and play it. And to the degree that he *feels* it he gets beyond the footlights. If he doesn't identify himself with the character that he's trying to depict, he never gets over. He has to *become* the character. And so this one became the character of hearing the actor whose lines he wrote, and the actor was given a line to say, you say "Terrific!" "And now listen carefully, because you've got to say it as I am directing it: I don't want any little 'terrific,' I want you to really give it. And so I will now give you the mood that I want you to adopt." And so he gives the mood, and the word comes through exactly to match his imaginal act.

His use of words fascinates me, because not everyone understands the baseball language when he said, "He threw me a curve...something entirely different. It wasn't what I expected. That was the script that he already read and pronounced 'Good.' I don't want that, I want him to pronounce this new statement and say that it is really great, 'Great, just great!' of the new script. I haven't even started the new script, and you used my words but you sort of predated it. You went back in time and called it the other script." And then the man comes back and *actually* calls it, but after he changed the word from that to "Terrific!" That's really discovering how you use your Imagination. But if you don't, and you think it's just on this level, you will never get off. I want everyone here to really believe it and try it.

If I take from you this night—if you're here for the first time—and I've taken or shaken your belief in a personal God outside of yourself, a personal savior outside of yourself, I don't apologize, because I know it is true what

I've told you. I'm not theorizing; I am speaking from experience. So when I take this platform and tell you that I *know* the reality that is God, I wouldn't care what the whole world would say about it. When they say, "You don't mean that God *truly* stood before you, or you stood before him, and you looked into the face of man? I said, Yes, I did…and it *is* man. I AM is Spirit, but it needs man, its perfect form, to really express anything in this world. It assumes the form of man. So when you see I AM in form, the form is man. Just like the little girl who told her grandmother, "You know what? I went up last night in my dream right up to the sun. And you know what? He had a face. And you know what? He had hands and he had feet. And you know what? The ocean, the big ocean...(tape ends.)

WHO ARE THE CONDEMNED?

3/10/1964

Tonight's subject is "Who are the Condemned?" We're told in the Book of John that "God sent the Son into the world, not to condemn the world, but that the world through him might be saved" (John 3:17). And then it goes on to tell us, "He who *believes* in him is not condemned; he who does *not* believe in him is condemned already, because he does not believe in the name of the only Son of God." So here we see it starts, the whole thing starts with believing in him. Everything follows that, just believing in him. Well, who is this presence that I must believe in?

There are a billion Christians in the world and they all will claim if you ask the question, "Do you believe in him" and you told them you meant by "him" Jesus Christ, they would say yes. One billion would say yes. But I am quite sure they do not really believe in him—not the "him" of the one I speak, not Christ. And I am speaking with a certain authority, because I've been sent to tell you. No man gave it to me; I'm not ordained; no man gave me anything to tell you. God himself sent me, and tell it I must and will even at the risk of many thinking that I am mad. But I'll tell you who this presence is, and if you believe in him you'll be saved from any situation in this world...if you believe in him.

Well, let us now see who is this presence? Can we get it from scripture? In the Book of John, one is supposed to be speaking, and this is the one speaking, and you might think it's a man outside of yourself speaking to you if you were addressed. He said, "You are from below, *I am* from above; you are of this world, *I am* not of this world. I told you that you would die in your sins, for you *will* die in your sins *unless* you believe that *I am* he" (John 8:23,24). When you read it, to get the depth from it, this must take place in you. It's a conversation between the rational mind, addressed as "you are from below," and that which is above the conceptual mind, the presence defined as I AM. It's something entirely beyond the reasoning mind that is controlled by the senses, the conceptual mind.

So this drama takes place; this dialogue is within man. And so, "I told you, you will die in your sins, for you *will* die in your sins *unless* you believe that *I am he.*" Well, do you believe in that presence? Do you really believe that the Christ of scripture is your own wonderful human Imagination, your own wonderful I-am-ness? If you don't, you are already self-condemned. No one condemns you. He said, "Who condemns you?" "No one, Lord, no man, Lord." He said, "Neither do I condemn you." If no man is condemning you, then I can't condemn you, for the simple reason man only bears witness of your own self-condemnation or your freedom. When men point the finger, it is because you have pointed the finger at yourself. And you do not know who he is, and so one is sent to tell you who he really is.

When you read these words "I am he" at the end of that sentence—"unless you believe that I am he"—here we have a cryptic formula that recalls Exodus 3:14, "When you go to them, just say to them I AM has sent you." Then we turn over to Deuteronomy, the 32nd of Deuteronomy: "See now, I, even I, am he, and there is no God beside me; I kill and I make alive; I wound and I heal;" I do all these things, "and there is none that can deliver out of my hand." Read it in the 32nd of Deuteronomy, the 39th verse, No one can deliver out of my hand and I do all things. And then we turn to the 43rd and 45th of Isaiah: "I am the Lord your God, the Holy One of Israel" and "Beside me there is no God." There is no savior besides this I AM.

So you must be the judge, I can't judge you, do you believe in him now? Or do you have a mental picture of a being on the *outside*, who lived 2,000 years ago, who addressed the Pharisees and the Jews of the day and told them, as something external to himself, that if *you* don't believe that *I am* he, well then, you will die in your sins? You can't see the mystery that way. It's either you see it in the depths of your soul between your own being; it's a dialogue between the outer man and the inner man. And when you really believe in this inner man, your own wonderful I-am-ness, nothing is impossible, and then things are revealed to you that startle the reasoning mind.

Let me share with you an experience. I've told you in the past that you're only wearing a garment. This is a garment whether it be a so-called white garment, a black garment, a yellow garment, a red garment. They're only garments, but I am not white, pink, yellow or red. I am Spirit, I AM. Now I have told you in the past my closest intimate in this field of mine was

Abdullah. He and I studied…I studied with Abdullah for seven years in New York City, seven days a week. We were inseparable. Ab was an old man when I met him, he was then about ninety. He was born in Ethiopia of the Negro race in the Hebraic faith. That was his background. I was born as you see this garment (I've worn this from birth) in the Christian faith. And we were inseparable. He taught me scripture as I never heard it from my mother's knee or from my minister or from anyone who taught me the Bible before. It became a book that was alive to me under the guidance of Abdullah. Well, here is a man, you look at him, here is a Negro, this brilliant, wonderful gentleman. Never once for one moment made any other claim, he would only say to me, "I picked up this garment ninety-odd years ago in Ethiopia." He always described it as a garment that he wore, just a garment.

As William Blake, the great mystic poet has said that when he first..."when once he did descry the *immortal* man that cannot die." And then he addresses in the form of an epilogue to what he calls the ruler of this world, Satan, the ruler of this world, the doubt of this world; and then as he put these words into the mouth of one addressing Satan (this doubt) that he does not know the garment from the man: "Thou really art a dunce," said he, "and dost not know the garment from the man." A man looking at a man sees a man as the thing he's wearing and doesn't for one moment discriminate between the wearer and the thing worn.

Well, this morning, in my usual ventures in the mind, here I found Abdullah. Ab is gone from this world now. Here stands before me—and Ab was my height, I'm 5'11"—Abdullah stands before me a man not over fifty years old, about 6'5", in a Caucasian body. And here is Abdullah before me, no loss of identity, no change of identity, but this majestic figure, and he and I were discussing this theme of tonight. Then he showed me a little instrument with a tape, and then he said, "Now as you know, Neville, it only echoes; that's all that it can do. That's the world, the world is only mechanism, it's just mechanical. The whole vast world, the eternal structure of God's eternal world, all these garments they're just as mechanical as that. And now, you're not going to speak into it, you're only going to hear, you're going to listen, and what you listen to will play back there. What you listen to and hear from within you, as you actually hear it you'll play it back there." I thought of this party, that party, that party, and whatever I thought of and the very things I heard as I thought of it, and then he played it back coming from that tape. Not a word voiced from my vocal chords, just inwardly imagining that I am hearing the sound of a certain friend's voice, and here comes this mechanical echo playing back.

Well, here was this majestic creature, Abdullah, 6'5 at the least towering in this sheer majesty, and here, what he never wore on earth. So I say I saw him in his primal form. He could have presented himself to me in an Oriental form; he could have presented himself to me any form, because all races are at his disposal. For when one rises into the spiritual world all things are subject to his imaginative power. And when I first met Ab and came into the place, he said to me, "You are late, Neville." Called me by my name; never saw the man before. He said, "You are late, Neville, six months late." I said, "I am late? I never saw you before, how do you know that I am late?" He said, "The brothers told me you were coming, and so you are six months late. For six months ago they told me to expect Neville, Neville's coming, and you mustn't leave the city until Neville has received all that you must give him. When you go, he must carry on." And here was this man...I never saw him before...I couldn't remember him. Then he said, "You have no memory, but it'll come back, it'll all come back." And then for seven years, as I told you earlier, we were inseparable. For he taught me Hebrew, and taught me the scriptures, both ancient and modern, or rather, the Old and the New; and I began to experiment with this strange, peculiar power *in* man, which he taught me was Christ Jesus, *nothing* but Christ Jesus, the power and the wisdom of God (1Cor. 1:24). God is your own wonderful I-am-ness, and Christ was that *in action.* I-am-ness in action is Christ; God in Christ reconciling the world to himself. And so, unless one believes in him he is condemned, completely condemned. Why is he condemned? Because he can't get out of what he is.

And now we come to Blake. And then, Blake in his wonderful thought to his friend, Crabb Robinson, Blake said to Robinson one day, "There is nothing like death. Death is the best thing that can happen in life, but most people die so late and take such an unmerciful time in dying, God knows their neighbors never see them rise from the dead." You see, Blake had this strange use of words, and he gave an enlarged meaning to words. So, you say something died; you think, well, now we put it in the grave. No, *we're* in the grave, and we are in the grave of what is now our problem. And so we won't believe in him to get out of it. For he is the resurrecting power, he can pull us out of every problem in the world. And so, if I now believe that I am poor, unwanted, this, that and the other, if I believe in him I am pulled out of the grave, and my neighbors will see me rise from the dead. But if I don't know this, I take such a long time disengaging myself from the state that I seem *never* to rise from the dead.

Well, how would I rise from the dead? By this simple little technique that I've told you over the years now: When I know what I want to be, I simply assume that I am it. But I'm not dumb, and so if I were it I would share my good fortune with others and I would tell them, and they, in turn, would talk to me and tell me, as a friend, how they rejoice because of my good fortune. So now I carry on a mental conversation from the premise of my wish fulfilled, carry it on with them, and listen carefully until I actually hear the sound of their voice within me. Physically they may be in Timbuktu—I don't care where they are physically—the fact that I bring them in my mind's eye and carry on with them this mental conversation. Then, in a way that I do not know in my conceptual mind, the thing happens, and I'm resurrected from my former state, which was a dead state, into this now new living state.

So Blake was quite right. But he said, "There is nothing more wonderful than death"; then he observed that man trying so hard to get out of poverty and getting all the more into it like quicksand. He's trying to get out of something but going all the more into it, because he doesn't believe in Christ Jesus. He'll go to a church and pray to some saint on the wall, and light a candle, and do all these things on the outside. But he doesn't believe in Christ Jesus. If he *really* believed in Christ Jesus he wouldn't go any place. Wherever he stands...it could be at a bar with a drink before him and maybe two in him...and simply shut out the bar completely, and carry on a mental conversation with a friend who is not physically present from the premise of fulfilled desire; and *that* is believing in Christ Jesus. Because wherever such a man stands is holy ground. He's actually standing on holy ground because he's one with Christ Jesus. He is walking in the company of Jesus, and no matter where he goes in this world he is actually one with him. And *this* is believing in him.

Now, the question is asked: "How can men call upon him in whom they do not believe, and how can they believe in him of whom they've never heard? And how can they hear of him without a preacher? And how can there be a preacher unless he is sent?" So "Faith comes from what is heard, and what is heard comes by the preaching of Christ" (Rom. 10:14,17). There's nothing else to preach, the preaching of Christ. You have a problem? You don't know what...it's a mechanical problem, so it's a problem. He is the solution of all problems. So you carry on a mental conversation with a friend that it's solved. And maybe tomorrow you'll have an accident in your lab, a *seeming* accident, and the solution is the result of the accident. It has happened all over the world. I am told that vulcanization is the result of an accident. Something spilled on the stove and whoever was there at the moment discovered vulcanization. That most of our so-called grand inventions are simply the results of a seeming accident in the lab. But either knowingly or unknowingly one believed in the solution of its problem. And so, he was believing in the solution to the problem, and he believed it. He didn't go to some other party or some outside thing; *inwardly* he believed it *could* be found and he found it.

Well, you now actually take it and test it. You're called upon to test Christ, test him and see (2 Cor. 13:5). You test him in this simple, simple way. I saw it so clearly—of course, I've been teaching it for years since I met Ab—but last night he came into my world, just as real as you are now, in fact, more so. And may I tell you, in eternity you will never lose your identity, not in eternity. Though God became you and that's the stamp of identity, and when you awake you are God, and yet you do not lose your identity. But in this world into which you go you are God and all things are subject to your imaginative power. And you can clothe yourself at will in any sex. He could have presented himself without loss of identity in the female form, in that form of the Oriental, in the form, as he did last night, of the Caucasian, in the form of a Negro, in any form based upon what he wanted to reveal to me. But he came in that form to confirm what I've been telling you, that you do not lose identity and that you're not black, white, yellow, pink or any other color, you're God. God became man and God is man.

God *really* is man. God is human. People think he's a big light and force and power. Yes, he's all that, he's infinite power, almightiness, yet he's man. To stand in the presence of God as almightiness, and to know it, it is almightiness, and it's man. And to stand in the presence of God and it's infinite love and it's man. Then to read *The Divine Image* of the mystic Blake where "God appears and God is light to those poor souls who dwell in night; but does the human form display to those who dwell in realms of day." Then he goes on to take it apart for us: "And mercy has the human heart, pity the human face, and love the human form divine, and peace the human dress." And to stand to confirm that, to stand right in the presence of infinite love and know it is the human form; it's the human form, and he looks you right in the face, and then embraces you, and you are *fused* with the body of God. You become one with the body of God, without loss of identity. So all of us, the three billion and more of us, will not lose any identity only raised to the nth degree of majesty, with no loss of identity. With a power at your command where you can clothe yourself at will in any sex, in any racial form, or even without form if you so desire. But your face is still pity, infinite compassion on that face, and the heart, infinite mercy, and the form itself, love divine.

So, you be the judge of yourself, let no man judge you. Who are the condemned? Tonight, do not leave this room condemning self. Be like the woman taken in adultery. The law says (the law of the world, the law of Caesar) condemn her by stoning her to death. And so he rose within himself—for we are told he is bent and down on the sand when condemnation took place, and he was writing on the sand—and then when he rose, what are the words? They said, "Who are you?" He said, "Even what I have told you from the beginning. And when you have lifted up the Son of man, then you will know that I am he" (John 8:25,28). When you have lifted up the Son of man, you'll know I am he. And that's a true story. The day will come you'll have that experience, and you will find yourself looking at living, living golden light, and it's alive, very much alive. As you look at it, from the depths of your soul you will know, *I* am it; and then, at that very moment of the knowledge you are it, you fuse with it, and then you are lifted up. Then you will know the words, "As Moses lifted up the serpent in the wilderness, so must the Son of man be lifted up" (John 3:14). In the same manner in which the serpent, which always means the departure of Israel from Egypt, when man is departing from this age and leaving it forever behind him, but still leaving it in its present frame. *He* departs, the spirit that is now God, for he became one with God. So he's lifted up in the same manner that the *symbol* was lifted up in the darkness of Egypt, the departure of Israel from Egypt. So when the individual is called out of this age into *that* age, where he's *completely* free, but completely set free, then he's lifted up, just like the serpent. And you're told, "In that day, you will know that *I am he.*" And you do, you look at it, and you know I am he; and fusion takes place; and then I AM goes up right up into Zion, into the skull.

So tonight, *don't* condemn yourself. If *you* don't condemn yourself, no man in this world can condemn you, they can't do it. If you don't want to share with them at the moment what you're inwardly desiring and planning to accomplish, well, don't share it. But *don't waver.* You carry on these inner conversations, always from premises of fulfilled desire, and do not waver in the outcome. Be *adamant* about it! And no power can stop it from coming to pass; they can't stop it. You try it and you will know from your own personal experience that it can't be stopped. Because all things are possible to God, and God is in Christ Jesus reconciling the world to himself. So *I am* in Christ Jesus. Christ Jesus is God in action; imagining is Imagination in action...same thing, same thing. You read the scripture carefully, you come to certain words and take your time to look up the word in the Concordance, you see it means Imagination. The active part of Imagination is imagining, and therefore that is God in action.

Now, like the speaker, if you were raised in the Christian faith as I was raised, you too held a man on the outside and thought him to be Christ Jesus, didn't you? Well, now you can say this to almost every person in the world. They're startled when they hear it. It comes straight from scripture, from the New Testament, but if they've never heard it in this manner they're really startled: "From now on I will regard no one from the *human* point of view; even though I once regarded Christ from the *human* point of view, I regard him thus no longer." You know who said it?—Paul. You will read it in his 2nd letter to the Corinthians, the 5th chapter, the 16th verse. "I once regarded Christ from the human point of view; I regard him thus no longer." He saw the light; and then he died. And so, in this wonderful letter of his, the previous letter, the 1st letter to the Corinthians, he said, "I die daily" (15:31). He discovered the art of dying. So he didn't die once in the lifetime, he died daily. "I die every day" he said. So today I have a problem, and as long as I have that problem, well then, I'm alive to that problem, and the problem is alive to me, and I'm keeping it alive, for life is in *me*, not in it. And I, by occupancy of that problem, I animate it and make it alive. Now I must detach myself from that *state* which is now a problem and attach myself to the solution of that problem. And doing so, I die to one and live to the other. So he said, "I die every day." Every day he's faced with a problem, and now he knows how to die by giving up one state and entering another state. And he makes the state that he enters alive. Why?—because life is in himself.

Here, this past week, you must have seen a daily paper, our scientists... there are two schools of thought: Some believe that there is no life outside of earth, and others believe there's a possibility of some life, maybe on the moon, maybe on Mars, maybe some other place. But they are equally divided. Some believe there is no life outside of earth, as we understand biological life; others believe that there is life and let us go and seek it, even if it takes $50 billion to prove or disprove. I'll tell you from my own revelation—I didn't know it before it was revealed to me—*life* is an activity of imagining. Everything is dead, and were it not that he who occupies *this* garment has life in himself nothing here would live, everything would be dead. Just like garments are dead, but they seem to be animated when you put them on and start walking. And so, these physical garments are just as dead, and you put them on and start walking, and so they *appear* to be something alive in themselves. They're *not* alive in themselves. They are alive only because you, the occupant, you are alive; you have life in yourself. And they can start from now to the end of time and they aren't going to find life outside of an activity of imagining. I don't care what they do they aren't going to find it. "As the Father has life in himself, so he has granted the Son also to have life in himself" (John 5:26); but nothing else is alive, it's all dead, the whole vast world is dead. And this is the cradle of God's grand experiment to actually bring himself out and to give life to that which he brings out, life in itself. It's all here.

So in one little book called *Man and the Stars* by Sir James Jeans, and someone asked him that similar question: Why do you think, as an astrophysicist, that little earth, this tiny little speck—you couldn't even see it; were you on the sun you couldn't see the earth it's so small. You could see the sun, because it's so vast from the earth, but were you on the sun you couldn't see the earth; it's such a tiny little speck—what makes you so arrogant to believe that you, because you're a man, that this thing called earth is so unique in this fabulous universe of God? If there is a God, said the scientist. You know what Jeans said to him? He said, "Have you ever seen the attempt of man to reproduce himself under a microscope? There are just as many potential sons in that one explosion of a man in the attempt to reproduce his image as there are in this fabulous display of light in the universe, just as many, and only one comes out. All the billions that are present under that microscope, they cease to be, and one comes out. Well, *this* is God's grand creative explosion, and only *one* comes out. It's the earth: the only thing that has all that it takes for this biological experiment, this wonderful creative darkness that is the earth, for a divine purpose." That was Sir James Jeans.

Well, he has a vast following today, and this chap at Harvard who's been bringing up this recently, he denies we will find anything outside of earth that you would call life, as we understand life. But I'll tell him, if he'd only listen to me, he's not going to find it any place outside of his own Imagination. And the day will come he'll walk this earth, as I have done it, and then at that moment stop it within him, and everything stops. Not a man could move, not a bird could fly though they were in flight when I stopped it, not a leaf could continue falling though it was falling when I stopped it, and looked at it and it was all dead, but I mean dead. Not suspended animation; no, dead, no breath in it, for the breath wasn't there. That was an animated body and the animation was within me in my own Imagination. And then I released that activity in me and it all continued moving once more again.

A great drama, which you will hear enacted but not understood when the great trial rolls around this month. For 2,000 years they've been reenacting this drama, and the words are asked, "Do you not know that I have the power to release you and the power to crucify you?" And he answered, "You have no power over me unless it were given to you from *above*; therefore he who has delivered me into your hand has the greater sin" (John 19:10). Now, what is the "above"? He just got through telling him, "You are from below; *I am* from above. You are of this world; *I am* not of this world." So from that grand presence within, this is animated, and so, I'm playing a drama. Alright, *no one* can take me and arrest me were it not within me. I allowed it, and that something in the depth of myself allowed it, and it takes place. If you know this and believe in him, you're free. So, you know the truth and then the truth will set you free (John 8:32).

So, who now is the condemned? God sent the Son into the world not to condemn the world but that the world might be saved through him. "He who *believes* in him is not condemned; he who does *not* believe in him is already condemned, because he does not believe in the *name* of the only Son of God." The name is not Jesus. Name means "nature." The *nature* of this Son of God, he doesn't believe in it; because *Jesus* is the Father. The world doesn't know that; they can't believe that. They speak of Jesus, Jesus being Jehovah, the grand I AM, that's Jesus. If you spell it in French, you might get onto it: Je Suis. Spell Je Suis and you get Jesus—a little "i," drop the "i"—Je Suis is "I am" in French. And so you spell it out in the Latin form, you're going to get I AM. So that is God. "Go and tell them I AM has sent you" (Ex. 3:14). Who is speaking?—the Lord of the universe!

So he said, "Where is your Father?" He said, If you really knew me you would not ask that, because you could not really know me, in the true sense of that word, and not know God, for he and I are inseparable—that's what he's telling them. And so, "When you see me you see him…when you see me you see the Father (John 12:45, 14:8). So don't ask me to show you the Father, for I and the Father are one, that's what he's saying. In the depths of the soul, one; he *is* the Father. So that is not the name of the Son. The name, in this case, is the *nature* of the Son of God, which is an inner livingness, an activity of your own wonderful human Imagination.

So, my plea to you, if you were trained as I was trained, listened as I had to…first I had to die to all of these beliefs and so completely die to them, I did not know how to explain that to my mother. I didn't want to hurt her, didn't want to hurt my father; they were trained as I was trained. And then to confront those that you love dearly! And you cannot enter into the conversation that formerly would be a normal part of an evening's discussion, for you took for granted the historicity of the Bible, and now you can't take it at all. It's a mystery. It's not secular history at all, it's divine history. The whole thing is unfolding in the soul of man, and everyone is destined to play all the things claimed of Christ Jesus: To be supernaturally born as he was supernaturally born; and to be one who discovers his own Fatherhood, one with God the Father; one who is lifted up in the same manner that he said, When you lift me up, then you'll know that I am he. And it will have everything recorded about him actually transpire in the soul of yourself, and the whole thing then becomes something very personal. And you know it is true of every being in the world. When it begins to unfold, the end is in sight, and then you are departing from this age into that age already prepared for those who are being lifted from this age. But *all* will be lifted from this age.

Therefore take the story...nothing is more important than that the story of Christ Jesus should be heard and responded to. In the Book of John it is underlined that necessity of hearing; one has to hear it. So go and preach Jesus Christ not as secular history. Go and try to the best of your ability to unfold for anyone who will hear you the *mystery* of that story, because everyone is going to have it. And so, you will be supernaturally born, not through the womb of woman; that's a natural birth. You will discover that you have no father to this birth, no mother: You're *self*-begotten. And then you're a father. And then comes the tangible proof of your fatherhood because a son appears. Now you know exactly who he is and he calls you, Father. All the generations of humanity plus all of their accomplishments, their experiences, but everything, fused into a single youth; and that youth is eternity. but yet it's human, his name is David, and he calls you, Father. Then you know—then, but not before—who you really are.

So the question is then asked of you in the depth of your soul, "Where is your Father?" and you answer, If you knew me you wouldn't ask because you'd know who I am, if you really knew me. Then who are you? Even what I've told you from the beginning, that's what he answers. Even what I've told you from the beginning, and now you don't know me, said he, but I'll tell you just what I was from the beginning. And then, everyone will then meet in this eternity, all fused into one body, without loss of identity. And that body is the most radiant body that you could ever conceive, and it's God the Father, and *you* are he. All one, and not *one* lost in all God's holy mountain. Not one condemned ever by God. He is not a God of retribution; he's a God of infinite love. And so *none* will be lost and all will be raised to the nth degree of beauty, of perfection, majesty and every attribute of the world you can think of raised to the nth degree, and that's you.

Now tonight, put this to the test. You put it to the test tonight in the things of life, like a better job and more money on it, a better home, more security, everything in this world that you want. Don't ask anyone if it's possible. You do it just by inwardly carrying on the conversation with yourself from the premise that it's done, and see it happen in your world. But don't forget how it happened. You take this discussion with someone, they may say to you, "Well, you know, it would have happened anyway." And then comes the great accuser of the world, the great doubter of the world, but he knows nothing, the doubter of the world, because he doesn't know that you're not the garment that you wear. The doubter of the world and he thinks that your exit from this world through the gate of death is your final departure for all time. But he doesn't know who you are. He thinks that when you came into this world you began for the first time. He doesn't know who you are: you came *from* God and you return to God.

And while you came into this world, it didn't really matter what was the nature of the garment that you picked out, it didn't really. Because, wherever you picked it up, regardless of the race, the nation, you only picked it up for educative purposes, to hear of Christ Jesus while you walked the earth and of the *real* Christ Jesus, and then test it. And then while you're walking this earth, then without notice to you a sudden unfolding within you of a series of mystical experiences which ___(??) you to leave it. And you're leaving this world forever, but still leave it behind you for those who are being woven into it for the same educative purpose.

Now let us go into the Silence. And let us imagine that someone is talking to us and telling us either of their own good fortune, which we want for them, or else they are aware of *our* good fortune, and as a friend they are present to congratulate us. What would they say if they really were your friend and they heard of your good fortune? How would they express it? Well now, let them express it and you listen carefully as though you heard them. They are compelled to meet you as that being and express what inwardly you have heard them say. When they express it, it's because the thing has already happened, and they are fully conscious of it, and as a friend they simply joy in congratulating you. Now let us go.

* * *

___(??) they are all marvelous stories. I hope you will keep it up. So now he has the technique perfectly because he heard. First of all, he gave us three decided techniques. The first was feeling, when he felt the policy in his hand, and although no one else could get a policy in the area where he lived, he got the policy. Out of the blue it came, without any increase in any surcharge. Although it was a friend it was all resolved. Then came the visual concept. He used it to see the green where there was no green, only mauve decayed marble. When he saw green, out of the nowhere a total stranger became the means to move away the little fence and then put it where he had mentally seen it. So he had the sense of touch; he had the visual sense aroused. And then with his producer, where he could take a man who could never express himself in the superlative, could only express his joy by saying "It is good," and how he raised it from that limited state that a thing is "good" to "Great!", "Very great!" or "Just great!", and then "Terrific!", and then finally to "Absolutely sensational!" So he took a man who could not go beyond the expression of "good" when he approved of something and raised that man's ability to express himself more generously...all by hearing.

So again he confirmed Blake's definition of Imagination: It is spiritual sensation. For he distinctly heard the man's voice—not just *a* man but *that* man—very definite about the man he wanted to hear and what he wanted the man to say. So he heard it, and the man repeated it in the next breath really. So all these things he shared with us were exciting stories. I want to thank him from the platform, and hope that he will continue to favor us with more of these wonderful stories. And everyone present, you're invited to experiment and then write me a letter, and give me the permission to tell it. If you want me to know it but there is something in it you would rather not be broadcast, just state it. That you want me to know that it worked but you would rather not have the thing told, I won't tell it, I promise you, only with your permission. So you write me. But first of all, experiment.

Now are there any questions, please?

Q: (inaudible)

A: My dear, there's nothing greater in this world. Good...it's a conversation that takes place in the depths of the soul. You can't get anything deeper than I AM: it's the center of the universe. So when you hear it, you hear it from within. But quite often it seems to be to the individual who heard it as coming from without. But it's not really coming from without at all. The drama of the I AM in the Book of John, the gospel of John, is simply a series of I AM sayings, right through the entire gospel, because he's presented as God himself. So you find all the grand I AM sayings in the gospel of John. So thank you. I'm glad that you heard it. As is his friend, the writer...I call him his friend because such relationships can develop into very nice friendships though they are worlds apart socially and intellectually and financially. You can still have friends with every level in this world; you don't have to have them on your own level. Quite often they can't become friends; they're rivals. But this could be a very good friendship. He heard the grand voice and he thought it came from without. Then he heard it repeated a second time, and then a third time. And even the symbol of the presence was the one that scared him, as told us so clearly in the Book of Exodus. And so, when he looked, he hid his face because he was afraid of God and he was afraid to look at the symbol of God… though he heard the voice coming from the depths of his soul.

Now are there any questions, please...any other questions?

Q: Would you explain about the unjust steward and his master commends him?

A: You hear that question? First of all, it's a long one and that's the theme I will use for "The Rascal." You'll find it in the coming series...a clever rascal, for that's the title I gave to the unjust steward. But far from being an unjust steward it's something that you and I are invited to emulate:

to be just as unjust as he and falsify the record. Don't go into your office and falsify the physical record, because as you do it, you will know you run the risk of being put away and you're doing it to yourself if and when you get caught. But you falsify the *mental* record; that's what all repentance is. Are we not told this is an evil generation? Therefore, on this level, I would be the eyes of an unjust steward.

Q: (inaudible)

A: Abdullah? Lived to be over a hundred and had one consuming desire, to put the body back where he picked it up which was in Ethiopia. The last time I met Abdullah was about eight years ago in New York City. About seven years ago I met his secretary and she voiced that request of his, and said he was planning to return to Ethiopia. I haven't seen or heard from Abdullah or the secretary since. I know he's gone from this sphere. I know now that when I see him he is wearing his primal form, which is completely under the control of his imaginative power. It was Abdullah who first taught me how to "die," like he said to me back in 1933, "You will die but not surely die." Well, that seemed like so many idle words that I would die but not surely die. And he was telling me the great truth that I could not at the time grasp. Because when he told me this I was a strict vegetarian, teetotaler, celibate; I was everything that did nothing...that was Neville. Whatever man would do normally I didn't do it; therefore, he said to me, "You know, you're so good you're good for nothing." And then he said to me, "You're going to die." So I went to Barbados, still all these restrictions, and I came back from Barbados three months later and I hadn't one restriction on me. And I can't tell you to this day how it happened—came back drinking wine and liquor and enjoying it. Tried to smoke, couldn't enjoy it when I tried it. And all the others that I tried I enjoyed. And so, that was my Ab. And he would always say to me, "The brothers came last night and what the brothers told me to tell you"—always referred to the divine society as the brothers. He really took it in the most wonderful manner: "*Our* Father," therefore the fatherhood of God would imply "*our* Father" the brotherhood of man. And so, the exalted men—made to have gone through this vale of tears, which is called death, and resurrected from it—are part of the divine society, therefore, the brothers. And he never referred to them in any other way than the brothers. The brothers told him I was coming and I was late.

And the reason why I was late, the man who suggested to me that I should go there to hear him was a man that I didn't trust at all. He went to Fordham University in the hopes of becoming a priest and he flunked in his third year. His father was a rumrunner in the days of prohibition, and died and left him an estate, the only child, of two million dollars. And he proceeded to lose the entire two million in the first year on Wall Street. So I had no confidence in his ability to do anything. So when he told me he met a man that I *really* must hear, I postponed and postponed and postponed the going. And one day I ran out of excuses, and it was a Sunday evening, and he said, "Now you have no more excuses. I know you have no dates, so come with me." So I accepted. Ab was just about to start when I went through the door and so I took the first chair, not to disturb the twenty who were present. Ab was sitting in a huge, big chair, and he came right over, called me by my name, he said, "Neville, you are late, you're six months late." So I was stunned. The man knew my name and could tell me that I was six months late. And it was about six months before that that David, his name was David ___(??), asked me to come and hear a man called Abdullah. And from that day on I never failed, I was with Ab daily. ___(??) but I can't, I have to pay rent here. But he would never take a dollar from me.

Goodnight.

THE LAW OF LIBERTY

3/13/1964

Tonight's subject is "The Law of Liberty." In this present series I'm asking everyone to try it, test it, and then share with us the result, that I in turn will then share with others what you have proved by this wonderful law of ours. Lord Lyndsay once said to a group of clergymen, "You ministers are making a mistake. In your pulpits you're arguing for Christianity and no one wants to hear your arguments. You ought to be witnessing: 'Does this thing work?' Then share it with the rest of us." And so, that's what I'm asking you to do, share it. I tell you it works. We have found that which the whole vast world's been seeking and it works. But you'll not know it by just hearing about it. To be convinced you must test it and prove it, and you *can* prove it.

Now we turn to the great book, the Bible. You judge to what extent you accept it, the testimony of Jesus. For we repeat here, night after night, that it's very important that we hear the testimony of Jesus and respond to it. So then I make the claim here, quoting Blake, that "All that you behold, though it *appears* without, it is within, in your Imagination, of which this world of mortality is but a shadow." And I mean that literally. This is not just a lovely poetical thought duly expressed by Blake; he meant it literally. And so the Bible makes this statement—you will read it in the 6th chapter of the Book of John. It's really called the chapter of secession, because in this chapter a bold claim is repeated throughout the chapter, and in the very end they seceded. And the statement that caused it was this, "No one can come unto me unless the Father who sent me draws him; and I will raise you up at the last day" (verse 44). And then we are told he asked a very simple question, "And suppose you saw the Son of man ascending into heaven?" (verse 63). There was no response; no one believed him. And then he said, That's why I told you that no one can come to me unless it be granted him by the Father, no one. And then he said of the evangelist writing the story he is now editorializing and so he said, And Jesus knew from the first who those were who did not believe and who it was that should betray him (verse 64)—knew it from the first who did not believe and who should betray.

Now we read the story carefully and he said, he repeats it again, "No one can come unto me unless the Father who sent me draws him." Then we are told that many, at this point many of the disciples turned back, never to walk with him again, never to go with him again. Well, who are the disciples who turned back? They couldn't go all the way; they came part of the way but they couldn't go *all* the way. Now no man judges you, for the drama is taking place *in* us. We hear the testimony, we hear it either from a platform or we read it in the book or maybe we have the experience, but to what extent can we go all the way?

We are told that there is a law, the law of the identical harvest; that "Be not deceived; God is not mocked, for as a man sows, so shall he reap" (Gal. 6:7). And then we are told, "And the Lord said, 'Let the earth put forth vegetation, plants bearing seed, and fruit trees bearing fruit in which is their seed, each according to its kind'" (Gen. 1:11). No variation, each according to its kind. Now, I think the whole vast world will accept that, in the vegetable world; and they'll come into this animal world and accept it, that doves produce doves, men produce, men and women produce, well, men, really. And so, we can take that law in the natural world and see that it does work. Can we step beyond that boundary and take it now in the mental world? Can we now actually perform a mental act, an imaginal act, and observe the working of it? And then admit when we see the fruit that the imaginal act was the seed planted by us, and the thing now we see reflecting it is really the offspring or the fruit of it? Can we accept it? Well, we may. I trust that everyone here will accept that. I think that the majority of you will; that's why you're here. But can you go further and say no man, and this literally now, "*No* man can come to me unless the Father who sent me draws him; and I'll raise him up at the last day"? Can you go *that* far?

Well, they couldn't go that far. They could go as far as relating an external event to an internal imaginal act. But they could not believe for one moment that encountering a total stranger in the world, and that stranger comes in to play a part in my life, that he cannot come *unless* my Father draws him; and I and my Father are one. I am the Father and the Father in me, so that no one comes into my life and plays any part in my life but what I am drawing him, good, bad, or indifferent. He just can't come. Well, man isn't big enough as yet to accept that widening circle. Can't quite stretch it out *that* far to encompass the whole vast world; and that everything that is happening in his individual life he is the cause of it. He can't quite relate these events when they are touched by living beings in the world to anything that he inwardly has ever done. He can't believe one moment. But I say, you be the judge whether you believe it or not. For he said, "I know every one from the very first." Why did he know every one from the very first? Well, who is he to do all this? Are we not told, "What person knows a man's thoughts except the spirit of the man which is in him?" (1 Cor. 2:11). But who's the spirit in you? I tell you it's Jesus Christ. "I've been crucified with Christ: it is not I who live, but Christ who lives in me." Read it in the 2nd chapter, the 20th verse of Galatians. I have actually been crucified with him and it is not *I* who live, but Christ who lives in me. So the spirit in me knows from the beginning whether I believed it or not.

As I sit here this night, do I believe it? To what extent would I believe this law of liberty, where not a thing that is happening that I didn't cause, not a thing in my world? Well, who betrayed me now? I knew the one who would betray me. But no one can betray me unless he has my secret, but no one. You can't betray a man unless you know the man's secret. And to know the man's secret you have to be in the spirit of that man. So who could betray a man but himself? So, "No man takes away my life, I lay it down myself...the power to lift it up and the power to lay it down again." No man takes away my life. So he knew the one who would betray him and should betray him because he *is* himself. He is self-betrayed. He knows the secrets to the point where everything is happening in his world because he is the sole cause of all the things that he encounters, that he experiences. There is no other cause. He knows that. And so he's betrayed the creative experience within himself. He knows what is the cause of it. He's found it in himself: his own wonderful human imagining is the Christ spirit in him that really is the cause of the phenomena of his life. And so now he is self-betrayed. He will share it with the world, but who will accept it? He'll tell it to the world and so men will themselves judge to what extent they will go with it. But when he comes to the statement that no *man* can come unto me except the Father who sent me draws him, we draw the line at that.

Now let me share with you what's been given to me. The gentleman is here tonight and this is his story as given me last Tuesday night after the meeting. He said, "Last week I was having serious difficulty with a story. I was satisfied with the dialogue, the scenes were all right individually, but for some reason or other I just wasn't satisfied with the story. So Sunday morning, realizing that the story was the problem and not my treatment of the story, I did this. I put myself into the shoes of Robert Louis Stevenson and then I imagined how he must have felt after he had written a *good* story. Then, I went back and put on my own shoes and tried to match that feeling which I had imagined to be Stevenson's feeling as he felt having produced a good story." That was the technique that he employed.

He said, "All this happened while I was taking my morning walk. When I came home, I began to list point by point to my wife of what I thought was wrong with the story. And then, point by point as though someone standing behind me and prompted me, and suddenly the solution to each point came into my mind, just as though someone was standing behind me and thought of it. And the whole thing came into my mind point by point." Now he said, "I should add that while I was gone my wife had imagined 'Wonderful things are happening, wonderful things are happening, wonderful things are happening!'" He said, "I'm quite sure that your wife would understand that when a man is at home day in and day out, a woman has to use generalizations, sweeping generalizations. So she would understand that because my wife and I spend twenty-four hours a day, seven days a week; we're on the same place." And so, he, the writer, uses his home as I do with my home.

So, with that confession off, he said, "About an hour later I was in the shower and I was pleasantly recalling an experience of six years ago... recalling this thing that happened six years ago...when a story was being, or seemed to be, dictated to me in a like manner, the thing that just happened, that someone standing behind me and dictating the story of the past hour. And it seemed six years ago, as I recalled the story that this happened in a like manner: some presence dictated, or seemed to dictate, the story. And then, it hit me like a sledge hammer. For the story of six years ago, that same character in the story of six years ago was Eddie. Identical, down to a T, it was Eddie.

And then, if you weren't here when we told the story of Eddie, let me now tell you the character that he conceived six years ago. He said, "He was mildly insane. Well, you know, Eddie was committed to an insane asylum for those who were *mildly* insane." He said, "The character was periodically picked up and released by the police. Well, the police picked up Eddie and when the asylum wouldn't take him back, the police didn't want him, and so the police released him." He said, "For plot reasons, I gave the character a limp in the right foot, the right leg—so had Eddie a limp in the right leg." He said, "The people of the town of the character treated him in the way that the people in my neighborhood treat Eddie. The character lived in a tent outside of town; Eddie lives today in a tent up in the hills of Hollywood. The character wore the kind of clothes, the same clothing that Eddie wears. The character had a fascination with atomic fallout. In fact, he perpetrated a hoax upon the town and almost scared the daylights out of them and they wanted to lynch him. Eddie has the most unusual fascination for atomic fallout and tells me he has a pipe that when he rubs it with some other piece of metal he can cause atmospheric disturbance on any part of the earth. And it disturbs him, because he feels his misuse of this pipe which he calls his "space needle" is the cause of the unrest in parts of the world, like Cypress for instance, so he's had to restrain himself. He has currently buried this pipe on the desert, which, said the writer, is perhaps safer than where he usually keeps it, under my house." And so, the same intense interest. But, he said, "This is the amazing similarity between these two—-that the feeling I have always had for the character is identical to the feeling I had for Eddie."

Now, he said, "I didn't tell this story to my wife immediately, I wanted to test it, and so I began to tell her and describe to her a story of a character. And I purposely omitted the limp in the right leg, because had I said it she would instantly have thought of Eddie. So I didn't mention *that* characterization. Then, I omitted completely from my vocabulary the use of the words 'unwanted' and 'rejected' which, by the way, in describing this character, he felt himself unwanted and rejected. But in spite of these omissions, she said to me, 'You're talking about Eddie.'" And then, said he, "I was stunned that my wife from a description of a character I conceived six years ago could see in that character, and not see *that* character, that I'm talking only of one character she knows is Eddie. So I really signed this letter "worried" for the simple reason having written all my life I've created some characters that I'm in no hurry to meet in the flesh." So everyone has done that.

Then he goes on, "So I quickly turned to your book *The Law and the Promise* and re-read the chapter on 'There is no Fiction.' And now, said he, with this off my chest as it were, I must say something good in favor of an outside God and candles; for in my present state of mind I think that really such a thing, an outside God, will be more comforting than to be the God creating all these things that are coming into my world when I reflect upon the characters, as a writer, I have conceived and projected on the screen; characters that I don't really want to meet in a hurry, not in the flesh." Then he said, "I hope you will keep this letter in a safe place, because if I ever want proof for insanity I would have it. You keep it in a safe place and the day I need it to prove my own sanity, well, there is the proof."

For here, this one, this gentleman has gone all the way. And is willing now from his confession in this letter to admit that the character Eddie, that seemingly came by accident after a great rain storm; that all the cars were washed in the neighborhood and Eddie had no job for the day; and thumbing his way up the hill, possibly to where he lives in his tent, this gentleman very kindly gave him a lift, and the friendship began there.

Because outside of this friendship which he said is the same intense feeling he felt for Eddie that he had for his character and he always had for the character, they have no social meeting point. They do not travel in the same social circle, intellectual circle, financial circle, yet there was a closer feeling, I'm quite sure, towards this Eddie than he has towards maybe nine-tenths of those who move in his circle. And he created Eddie. So I say, that everyone...you may not recognize the character. Maybe you're not a writer and have written to the point where you can remember an actual character that you created out of the nowhere, and had it produced, and saw the production yourself, and moved others to see the character. But he remembered. And then he ran into the flesh and blood character that he conceived six years before.

So the 6th chapter of the Book of John, "No one can come unto me unless the Father who has sent me draws him; and the last day I will lift him up." I'll raise him up at the last day. So I told this gentleman exactly how he's going to raise him up. The day will come...and the last day doesn't mean the last day of twenty-four hours. It means the last day of the journey from the cradle to the grave when it is your last time around, and you're not on the wheel of recurrence anymore. And when that last phase comes to an individual he will have this experience. When he least expects it, no one ever told him about it; and maybe when I tell you now you'll forget it and scripture forgets, so when it happens it will come as a very wonderful pleasant surprise, because you have no memory that you heard it from my lips. But while you don't know about it, you never read about it, no one told you about it, and one night—or it comes in the day; in my case it always seemed to come at the wee hours of the morning—and so you'll be suddenly twisted from within yourself, like a corkscrew, and through your skull you'll go. And you'll be clothed in the most glorious body of fire and air. It is that luminous...you need no stars, no sun, no moon to illuminate your path. And a heavenly chorus will call *your* name, whatever your name is, and they will pronounce the name and say "He is risen." Not "he" is risen but the name, say your name is John, "John is risen!" "John is risen!" they'll repeat it; and then this chorus will sing out, the most glorious heavenly chorus will sing *your* praise because *you* have been risen.

And then you will come upon a sea of infinite imperfection, human imperfection. The limp of ___(??) will be there, the blind, the halt, the withered, everything you've conceived, all taking human form; and they're waiting for *you*, their redeemer, to redeem them. And as you glide by, you seem to glide by, every one will be transformed into the image of perfection. You do not raise a finger to make it so. Blind people become those of perfect sight, the deaf hear, the limp, the halt, the withered all cease to be what they were as you pass by. And when you come to the very end and the last one is finished and all are perfect, then the same heavenly chorus will exult and ring out, "It is finished!" the last cry on the cross. And then you, for unfinished business, return here to complete it, to tell it, maybe to leave it in a more permanent form, in the form of a picture or a story. But you will tell it in a more permanent form than you yourself at that moment experienced, for that's forever as far as you're concerned. But you will tell it for the benefit of others; and scream it out as it were; return here to complete the few remaining years, for your end is at hand.

Everyone had to be raised that you would create. Everyone had to be transformed into perfection to conform to you when you were lifted up. At that very moment you were perfect, and so as you walked by you molded them in harmony with the perfection springing within you. And you do it without effort, without taking thought; you're above the conceptual mind. You're not concerned about these people, you simply walk by knowing in the depths of your soul it is all perfect; and everyone is reshaped and molded in harmony with that perfection springing within you. So you're told, "If I, if I be lifted up from the earth, I will lift all men up." I will shape them and transform them.

And so no man came save I called him. So, if I call Eddie with a limp... and then memory served me well, I am taking a shower and suddenly I'm pleasantly recalling a story of six years ago and while I recall it and dwell upon it, suddenly it dawns upon me...for I've been walking around these past two years in the company of one that I myself created, and I didn't recognize him. Here is a man in my own world and for two years he's been in my life and an intimate of my world, but I didn't recognize my own creation. For that's what the world does all day long. It draws only its own, but doesn't recognize its own creation. No man cometh unto me save I draw him, for "my Father and I are one." So he can't come unless my Father draws him. He can't come unless *I* draw him, for I and my Father are one. And so, I am drawing every being into my world, good, bad or indifferent. So when I think *he* is wrong and he crosses my path morning, noon and night—"he's no good, you can't trust him"—where in my world can I go back to that moment of mistrust in me, when I really couldn't trust myself. I couldn't, I was afraid of my own behavior if given an opportunity. If I thought I could get away with it, I might. I need not be an author to sit down and write the story; I could enact the story. I could walk through a store and if no one really had eyes upon me and I thought they didn't, I might contemplate with pleasure an act that if caught would be quite embarrassing to those who love me, I might. If in the past I ever contemplated that, someone's going to cross my path and come right into my world and will play that part right in my world. I may condemn him for it, but in condemning him I'm condemning myself, because he *is* my very self bearing witness to my own creation...bearing witness.

I told the story here once many years ago. It was a very intimate story and I told it certainly not to fill any ego here, but to encourage every person in this world to forgive every being in this world. Because *you* are the cause of the behavior of everyone you're observing in this world. And I told it in the most intimate manner because it struck home forcefully. And I was severely criticized by the audience for it, and criticized the following month by the wife of the gentleman who brought me to this town to give a series of lectures. She said, "Neville, I thought that was very, very unbecoming, and so many have criticized you for it. They've written me letters and I can't tell you of the many letters I have received that are very, very critical of what you said from the platform." I said, "I didn't say it for any purpose other than to show everyone that *they* are the cause of the *mis*behavior of others that they condemn. *They* are the cause of it." And so, I tried to explain to her that it was not condemnation of the person. I was putting myself...*I* was the *cause* of her arrest, the *cause* of her *actions.*

And this is the story. I was married, separated for fifteen years; no divorce and no final separation; no legal separation but separated. I was married at the age of eighteen, father at nineteen, separated at twenty, and then for the next fifteen years we lived our separate lives and only saw each other when she dragged me into court for nonpayment of alimony. That's the only time we ever saw each other. I always came out of the court with a reduction, always, one after the other. So, seven times before the judge and seven times it went down, this way. So, finally, she knew "Better not take him anymore, there's not a thing else to get." She'll get nothing the next time. And so that was the picture. So I told that story and all these things are happening.

And one day, I knew I wanted to get married to a certain party, who's now the mother of my daughter. But I had all this entangled personal life—not separated legally. You can't get a divorce in New York City save but on one ground—the most archaic law in the world--therefore, nothing but collusion goes on in the divorce courts in New York City. For the whole thing is forced upon man because of this archaic law. However, I wanted my divorce. And then she was told by a very close intimate friend of mine that I wanted that divorce and to really leave town, get out of town. But my friend didn't want me to get a divorce and marry the girl that I eventually married. So I thought, alright, I will now apply this law, and I slept as though I were happily married to the girl who now bears my name. And at the end of a week, my dancing partner who I thought was the one who had really told her to fly (and she was) came to me and told me that she looked upon me as a brother, just a brother. She could never marry me, because it was not that feeling towards me. Well, that made me very happy.

And then, the other one was gone now, never to be found again so the world would think. But I still slept in the assumption that I was happily married. One morning the phone rang, I answered the phone, it's the court, courtroom calling, "This is the federal building." I said yes? "Are you Neville Goddard?" Yes. "Are you the public speaker that goes by the name of Neville?" I said yes. "Well now, you better be in court next Tuesday morning at ten." Well, I was too sleepy to ask why. And so, next Tuesday morning just a little before ten, here, the phone rings again. "Are you Neville Goddard?" I said yes. "Why aren't you in court? Didn't we call you last Tuesday to tell you to be in court today?" I said, "Why should I be in court? What's wrong that I should be in court, I haven't been subpoenaed?" Then said this party over the wire, "You're a public character and reporters are always in court and they love to get the story into the papers, and the papers today." But I said, "What's wrong?" They said, "Your wife happens to be on trial, and so if you would come on down and maybe you could throw some light upon this."

So I went on down, got into the courtroom just in time to see them bring her into the dock as it were. Three judges came in, took their positions, and then someone whispered to one judge, and then the voice said, "Is Mr. Goddard in the courtroom?" I said, "I'm here." "Would you take the stand?" I got sworn in, I'm under oath. "Maybe you could help us, throw a little light here." And so I took the stand. They asked me if we were the same religious faith. I said, "No, she was born a Catholic, I was born a Protestant. But that's no problem, she is not a practicing Catholic and I'm not a practicing Protestant. So there's no problem there at all." And then he said, "Well then, could you throw some light?" I said, "First of all, she's eight years my senior and you know my age, therefore, you must know her age. She's undoubtedly passing through some emotional disturbance and so when a woman is passing through such states, well, they can do any irrational thing. What she's now charged with, I am quite sure she has never done it before. Even if you have the evidence to support it, I still think she's never done it before. I will swear she will never do it again. I ask you for my son's sake, who lives with me, that if you've got to sentence her, therefore, the law says sentence her, but then be merciful and suspend it."

He said, "I've never heard a plea in this court of mine similar to that in all my years on the bench, from a man who has nothing to gain by this merciful plea of his, when he really wants a divorce. Because we have all that evidence before us taken from your wife when she was in jail this past week waiting for this day of trial." He said, "I'll act upon your recommendation, Mr. Goddard. I now sentence you to six months and suspend it. Don't you ever come before me again." Mary met me in the lobby, she said, "That was a very decent thing for you to do, Neville. Give me the papers." I said, "I don't have any papers with me...come home and I'll give them to you." We rode up together, first time in these many, many years we were closer than seeing the judge and the bench. We rode together to my hotel and I gave her the papers I had not been able to serve for unnumbered months. Gave her the papers and got my divorce uncontested.

So I told that story to say that I caused her to do what she did. Had I not assumed that I was free to marry the girl that now bears my name she would never have done these at all. And so, she goes into a store and for the first time in her life she picks up something that she hadn't paid for, and someone saw it. And so, it was a silly thing, but, nevertheless, she did it. And that's what brought her into the city so I could find her. And she was moved to ask me to give her the papers because I pleaded for her. And so having done all this, who actually was the culprit? I was the culprit. She came right into my world to play a certain part, to grant me my freedom. I'm speaking of the law of liberty. And so, should she be condemned for acts when I, the unseen author, wrote for her? I didn't write it out by sitting down and writing the part for her, but I determined the behavior of that part, that she had to do something in order to melt her to take the papers from me. And so, I told it only to show that don't condemn anyone. You and you alone are the author of the things happening in your life.

And therefore, would you condemn a man...this gentleman writes into his script a limp in the right leg. Here comes a man with a limp in the right leg. He writes everything into an imaginary character and he isn't imaginary at all. You can't distinguish between what the world calls imaginary and reality, you can't; this is all one. And so, people could not go beyond a certain limit...and so you could say, well, I will assume that I am what I want to be and things happen in my world like this. But don't tell me now that I actually created her in that part. I did. And so, many departed never to walk with him again, never; and so, he turns now to the twelve remaining, he said, "Would you go also?" Peter answered, "To whom would we go? You have the words of eternal life; and we believe, and have come to know that *you* are the Holy One of God" (John 6:68). Well, to whom is Peter speaking? He isn't speaking to another. Whoever is the character written in this drama as Peter came to that position within himself.

It's the most difficult thing in the world to accept. For, this is the cause of secession. They seceded at that moment because they will not accept the fact that they are actually the cause of these things that are living and moving in their world, some crippled, some limited, some maimed—-and they're the cause of it? They will *not* accept it. He said alright. They left him, never to walk with him again. And then Peter said, "Well, to whom to go? You have the words of eternal life. These are true, and now to whom would I turn? For you know we have believed and we have come to know you are the Holy One of God." Know what? Turn back now to Matthew and you see the answer. "Who do people say that I am?" "Some say John the Baptist, some say Elijah come again, some say Jeremiah, and some say a prophet of old." He doesn't respond to that. He asks another question, "But who do you say that I am?" and Peter becomes the spokesman, he answered, "Thou art the Christ, the Son of the living God." He said, "Blessed are you, Simon Bar-Jonah! For flesh and blood has not told you this, but my Father who is in heaven" has revealed it (Mat. 16:13). Well, who is the Father in heaven? He said, "I am the Father. When you see me, you see the Father." Well, who but the Spirit in man has revealed what Christ really is? No prophet come again, no reincarnation but man *has* Christ within him. And he's awakening more and more and more.

So the gentleman who wrote the story concerning Eddie said, "You know, up until now I really wanted to wake up and tried to wake up. But *now* I'm trying desperately to go to sleep again." In other words, he doesn't want—-but he really doesn't mean it—-he doesn't want what he just discovered, this *enormous* responsibility, to be responsible for the characters that he has created. And they're all walking the earth, and one after the other will enter his circle and become an intimate. And one that he really is very fond of, one that he created and endowed him with all these strange things, a peculiar mental unbalance, and a limp in his right leg, and unwanted by society, and looked down on by the neighborhood, put him in a tent and ostracized him from society, and made him unwanted and unwashed, and, well, repellent in many ways. All these things he does for character and then falls in love with the character. So you can see the words, "Father, forgive them; they know not what they do" (Luke 23:34). They're playing all these parts because imaginative men and women are writing dramas. And the world is forever falling under the spell of imaginative men and women. No matter what the world will tell you, they're always falling under the spell of those who are writing intensely with emotion.

So today you try it. I hope—but the judgment is yours, don't tell me—but I hope you can go all the way. And don't tell anyone if you go all the way, because the Spirit in you he knows whether you can really go all the way or you'll turn back tonight and take only a portion of it. But even a little portion of it, take it. So there's a law, the law of the identical harvest: "As a man sows so shall he reap." Regardless of what it appears to be really, you'll reap it. And you'll find in the end everything is simply bearing witness to man, of what man is doing. As Blake said, "I went to heath and the wild, to the thorns and thistles of the waste, and they told me how they were beguiled and driven out and compelled to be chaste." And you would not believe for one moment that Blake is telling us that the unwholesome suppressions of the normal natural urges of the animal body that we wear are the cause of the thorns and the thistles of the waste. The society has clamped down upon all the normal natural urges of the human animal body—for these are animal bodies that we wear—and by putting a clamp upon the *natural* urges, then come thorns and thistles of the waste. And what botanist will believe that? He doesn't believe that for one second and he thinks he's going to kill them by some insecticide or some other kind of thing, and he goes out and burns the things. They'll all come back, as long as man walks the earth who can impose these restrictions on growing healthy bodies...and we call them moral laws. There isn't a thing in this world but man, because God is the only reality, and God is man, and man is God. So "Man is all Imagination. And God is Man and exists in us and we in him. The eternal body of Man is The Imagination, and that is God himself" (Blake, *Annotations to Berkeley*; *Laocoon)*.

So I tell you, whether you be a writer as this chap writes and undoubtedly writes remarkably well to earn the kind of money he earns from his own confession. And so, he writes it, and luckily he could spot it. But he lived with it for two years before he realized it was his own creation. But now what *he* did to rectify this problem of the story, ___(??) being a writer, he took a great imaginative writer—anyone who could write *Dr. Jekyll and Mr. Hyde*—alright, you certainly have an ideal in *that* when you take Robert Louis Stevenson, and you can put it into the feet, the shoes of this imaginative writer—and then right behind him someone who is Stevenson. He caught it by a mood. You can tell by the mood that you wear who you're going to meet in this world. You wear moods and they come. And he caught the mood. He wondered what would the mood be like, what would it be like? Asking who? He's asking what would Stevenson feel, how would he feel, after he finished what he considered a good script, a good story? And having caught that mood, then he said, I got back in my own shoes; and then I tried to match my own feelings to what I had imagined Stevenson must have felt. And so, when he got them mated...and when two agree as touching anything in this earth, it shall be established for them in this world if two agree. But he called the one with whom he wanted to agree in moods, and then, as though someone stood behind him and dictated the solution of every point as he brought the point up, they all came into his mind. There'd be no problem for this man, a writer, to sit down and bat it out *after* they were all solved in his mind. Then taking his shower and feeling very happy about what just happened, he very pleasantly recalled an experience six years ago. And while he's contemplating it, like a sledge hammer on his head...who would have thought he'd been walking around with his own creation two years and didn't recognize him? And he didn't want to spring it on his wife. He thought, "I'll test it first before I spring it on her." And so, he described the character, leaving out very pertinent things like the limp in the right leg and the use of the two words "unwanted, rejected," and leaving out things that would give her the cue, she still would spot the character was Eddie.

And so, *that* story you can take to heart. Tonight, what would it feel like? If you want money, well, make yourself one who has oodles of it. What would it feel like to him, if he really wants money? Because many have it without any thought of money, but if someone *really* wants money, what would it be like *after* he really went over in a big way? And then you try to match your feeling to that which you've imagined he *must* have felt when he made what he considered the big killing. Match the *feeling*...and then just match it and see what happens. Just try it. What we're doing here, we are experimenting, because this is the greatest problem in the world. As Fawcett said, "The secret of imagining is the greatest of all problems, to the solution of which everyone should aspire." First of all, infinite power is in it, if you unravel it, infinite wisdom and infinite delight. So if it contains all of these and we can unravel the problem, then why not try it?

So we're asking everyone to try it and then share with us that I, in turn, will share as I did this night with this gentleman's letter. Again, I repeat, I hope he keeps it up and shares with me that I, in turn, may share with you these perfectly lovely facets of this great diamond. For if he could put his imaginary feet into imaginary shoes, and feel what the great Stevenson *must* have felt when he was satisfied with the story, then take the shoes off and put on his own shoes, all in Imagination; for he's taking his morning's walk when all of this is going through his mind. And people walking by will see a man walking by and possibly ignore him, not even have a second thought, or they might wonder what's in his mind. But no one but the Spirit of that man would know. Who would know for one moment that *Stevenson* was walking by? But while he was wearing the shoes of Stevenson, Stevenson was there, to the point that were you sensitive, you would not see the man that was there that his wife would see, you would see Stevenson. You really would, because "all things by a law divine in one another's being mingle." And so, they aren't outside in space or outside in time, they're only as far away as you allow them to be.

And your moods can call them, any being in this world. You can call anyone who has been gone for unnumbered centuries call him by feeling that you are he. Put yourself into his shoes and call him. Then, if you have a problem, share the problem. You'll have the same sensation someone is standing behind you and prompting you so that point by point the solution is given to you, it crowds right into the head. If you believe that Blake who died in 1827 could really solve a certain problem for you, feel the presence of Blake. Because they're not pushed out, as the world would think, say in time back to 1827. He certainly is not in any little grave in England; no one is there. And so, they are only as far away as you let them be. So he went back and read the chapter on "There is no Fiction" and discovered he, the writer, and very humorously when said in his letter, "Having written all my life I have created such characters I assure you that I am in no hurry to meet them in the flesh." But it doesn't matter, the day will come you will move out by a spiral motion when you least expect it, and without effort walk by and redeem every one of them. Every one we were given for the ___(??) play here, because they are created either wittingly or unwittingly. And so, I ask you to join with me, put it to the test, and don't delay with your letters, bring them to me just as many as you possibly can that I may encourage others to try it too.

When you go home, read this chapter, the 6th chapter of the Book of John. It really is the secession chapter: They all departed, never to walk with him again, and only the few remained. And he turned...and they said, "Where would we go? You have the words of eternal life. We have believed you and we have come to know"—it didn't come over night—"we have come to know you are the Holy One of God." But the Holy One of God is God himself...you come to know it. But you're not talking to a man: You've found a creative presence *within* yourself. And although the world will try to make you feel that the creative presence is a power—speak of it as "it," don't personalize it—oh yes you do. It's *yourself* you've found. Aren't you a person? So if Christ is in you as the creative *power* in you, you are doing it and you're a person, therefore, Christ is a person. So he said, "Is your Christ a person?" He always talks about Christ as a creative power. He's not only a person, he's the *only* person. He is the heavenly man...you are finding in yourself that heavenly man, the man that cannot die, the immortal you. Now when you find him, don't let him go. Let everything else go, but don't let him go. So when Paul writes to Timothy, he said, "I know *whom* I have believed"—not what—whom, and he's speaking now of Christ. And yet he defines Christ as "the power and the wisdom of God." Having defined it as power and wisdom, he *personifies* it, personalizes it. Because it's *himself*...

that's what he found. He found it in himself. You'll never find him on the outside.

And so, to what extent this night you can go with the testimony of Christ Jesus? Can you go all out and say that no man, no woman, male or female, can come unto me unless my Father who sent me draws him? And I will raise him up at the last day…leave that section alone…that's going to happen anyway. But to what extent can you accept that testament that no one can come unto me unless my Father who sent me draws him? And I and my Father are one because I am in my Father and my Father is in me, can I go that far? And then go all out, that not one being in this world can cross my path that I did not call? Those who come more intimately into my circle, they're really things I have been dwelling upon. You start dwelling upon the so-called tyrants of the world and forming in your mind's eye, you'll find he doesn't really live in Russia, he lives right next door, comes right in. And then you wonder how to get rid of him. You've been creating in your mind's eye a certain something, and it comes right into your world. You draw them as you draw them out of a panel.

Now let us go into the Silence.

* * *

Q: Who is the woman in "Revelation" who has the moon under her feet?

A: Everything in scripture, from beginning to end, is all about you. Not the garment that you're wearing, but you, the wearer of that garment. Everything from beginning to end is your real auto-biography. Much of it you have not yet experienced, but it is still yours to re-experience, therefore, truly an auto-biography. At the moment you may read it as biography, but don't think that it's of another; it's all about you. The most insane revelation will prove itself true; one day you'll experience it. It's all about you. When the child was brought forth and it was quickly caught up into heaven, you'll have that experience. The child will vanish from those who will try to destroy him. And all the destructive powers of the world are still begotten by you, all in the state of dream, when man was sound asleep. So you are that being. I hope tonight you saw who Judas was. Not some being who betrayed what the whole vast Christian world believes to be their Lord. No one could have betrayed a man unless he knew that man's secret; and no person knows a man's secret but the Spirit of that man which is in him. So who is Judas? The word Judas means "the praise of Jehovah." Judas is praise. But man thinks the drama took place 2,000 years ago. It's *taking* place, all here. He said, "No man takes my life, I lay it down myself." If no man takes my life, then what are you blaming him for? I laid it down in every garment that moves upon the face of the earth. "Unless I die, thou canst not live. But if I die I shall arise again and thou with me" (Blake, *Jer.*, Plt.96). And so, he became man that man may become God, and he did it voluntarily. You can imagine, well, that's Christ, that's the power of God. And it is personified— though a power because you're a person, therefore, it is a person. Every evil act in the world needs a man as an agent, therefore, it is man. Every noble act needs a man as an agent, therefore, it is man. So it's all personified. So scripture personifies the powers. Yet that's right; they are powers, they are personified.

Q: What is the symbolism of the two thieves on the crosses at the crucifixion, one on the left and one on the right?

A: We're coming to that in the not distant future right from this platform. But we answer some claim that man is constantly robbed by looking back or looking forward. He's so concerned about what he did and what he's going to do, what he formerly encountered and what he hopes to encounter, that he omits the everlasting present which is I AM. So Christ defines himself as "I AM the way, I AM the truth, I AM the life, I AM the bread of heaven, I AM the true vine, I AM the resurrection"... all *present*. But man goes back and thinks of him as something past and hopes to meet him some time in the future...and it's ever-present. He's only in the present, so man is robbed by two thieves that he walks with all day long, because Christ is crucified here in the present. I have been crucified, "I am crucified with Christ, and it is not I who live but Christ who lives *in* me"—he's present, and his name is Jesus, and it's I AM. The word Jesus is Jehovah, and Jehovah is Yod He Vau He, and it's defined as I AM. So, my thief to my left, my thief to my right...I'm always looking to the past or future and omitting the only reality which resurrects, which is the present. And *only* what *I am* ever reaches heaven; only what I am am I putting out. So don't wait to assume that I am what I would be because reason denies. Ignore reason, ignore the facts of life, and dare to assume it, because all things are possible to I AM. So the two things are with us morning, noon and night. We wonder..."I wonder if I did the right thing at that cocktail party last night? Did I say the right thing? Did I make the right impression?" And we worry all through the night, "Did we really do it?"—that's a thief. And now, I'm invited to one tomorrow, "I wonder if my tongue will be tied or do I have a nice dress? Will I have time to go to the hair dresser?" and all these things and concern about tomorrow when it's only today, it's now, this is I AM.

Well, I see my time is up. So do test it and share with us in the written form your results. Thank you.

I AM CALLED BY THY NAME, O LORD

3/17/64

Tonight's title is taken from the Book of Jeremiah. It's the 15th chapter, the 16th verse: "Thy words were found, and I ate them, and thy words became to me the joy and delight of my heart;"—and then he tells the results of eating these words—"for I am called by thy name, O Lord, God of hosts." He found the words, he ate them, assimilated them, and then it produced this knowledge that *he* who ate them, who assimilated them, is actually the very being that is the cause of all the phenomena of life. The whole vast universe was himself pushed out, that everything was created by him, and he didn't know it until he found the words. Then he ate them, and having eaten them he assimilated them. And that's what you and I are called upon to do. We take food in, and we assimilate what we can build into our system, and then we reject what we cannot use.

Well, the Bible is the same way. We have taken the vehicle that conveyed the instruction for the instruction, and we have mistakenly taken personifications for persons, and the gross first sense for the ultimate sense intended. And so, like food, you take it in; and then the system discriminates between what it can use, what it can assimilate and build into its system, and what it must expel, what it must reject. And we read, so we're told, And they read from the law and they read it clearly. This is the Book of Nehemiah, 8th chapter, 8th verse: And they read it clearly; so that they heard it with understanding. When they heard it with understanding, well, then they could discriminate and reject the instrument that conveyed it, and then accept what it conveyed, the kernel, the life essence of it as it were.

So tonight, our story is "I am called by thy name." Now what is the name? Well, we are told the name of the strong tower, and the righteous man runs into it and is safe. I will respond, I will answer all who call me by my name. He will answer everyone who calls by his name. Well, now how will I call this night? Because I'm also told, "Whatever you ask in my name, I will do it," anything that you ask in my name I'll do it. That you'll find in the 14th chapter of the gospel of John (verse 13): "Whatever you ask in my name, I'll do it"...but find out the name. Well, now there are millions this night asking in certain names and they're not getting any response, so it may not be the name. What is the name? Either then the promise is a lie, or they haven't the right name.

Now, in the Bible, a name, whether of a man, an angel, deity, regardless of what it represents in scripture, it simply in some wonderful way reveals the character of its bearer. So if Moses who claims that he had a revelation of the name of God is going to impress the elders with what he claims that he heard and what he saw, he has to know the name. And so, he said, this is my revelation, it came to me in this form: "I AM has sent you"...When I go to the people of Israel and they insist on a name, what shall I tell them? "Just say I AM that I AM. And when you go say I AM has sent you," that's all. Now, is that the name? I tell you it *is* the name as told us in the 3rd chapter of Exodus. It's not only my name, it's my name forever, my name for all generations, forever and forever...just I AM (verses 13-15).

Well, how do I call upon I AM? If the God I worship has the name I AM, then it seems to me that only through what I am can I worship him aright. So how can I call this night on the name? So you can call me Neville and I respond. If I walk down the street and I hear the name John I don't turn around. If I hear the name Neville, I will stop and respond because that's my name; for I am told, if he calls upon my name I will answer him. If he doesn't call on my name, I can't respond. I can only respond to my name. Well, how then will I call upon God's name? His name is I AM. Well, I put it to the test. And I tried unnumbered ways, putting it to the test. The name is I AM, that's what we're told. In scripture the word is Jehovah; in the New Testament that same I-am-ness is spelled Jesus. But the word Jesus doesn't respond, the word Jehovah doesn't respond; I AM does respond. But *how* does it respond?

Here comes this day a letter to me (he's here tonight) he said, "I'm from the Midwest. My mother and brother have had nothing but physical problems, I mean, health problems. He came out of the 2nd World War emotionally disturbed and he's been in and out of the Veterans' hospital, well, constantly, really. He's always taking these psychological treatments. For four years I made a little plan, I called it my mailing program, and I mailed them what I called metaphysical literature for four years, hoping that they would read it and would have a change of attitude towards life and bring about a change in themselves. For the medical world seemed not to help; they got no help from the medical world. So I thought, well now I'll get this and call it my program, my plot. Well, at the end of four years I heard you, and then I stopped it, I stopped sending them books, which I didn't realize until only two weeks ago that they never even read one of the books. As they came they threw them into the ashcan. But I didn't know that until two weeks ago when a neighbor of my mother from the Midwest came paying a visit to the West Coast, and she told me as the mail arrived, books right straight to the ashcan. So they never once read a book... in keeping with what Ben Franklin said about books that were given. He said that people seldom read a book that is given to them, and the best way to spread a thought is to charge a modest price for it. Don't *give* a book; charge a modest price for it and because they've invested they read." But this was not an investment on their part. The son sent these books week after week in the hope that in some strange way the mother would read them, the brother would read them, and bring about in themselves a change of attitude towards society, which they didn't.

So he said, "What I did was this. I couldn't reach them by sending them gifts of books, and having heard you, that the whole thing is myself—didn't have to depend upon my mother reading a book or my brother reading a book—*I* could do it. So I assumed full responsibility now to produce a change in them, though we are hundreds of miles away, no physical contact save by letter. I took a letter in my hand, a mental letter in my mental hand, and I could actually see—he used the word "actual"—I could actually see my brother's hand writing and then I read what I wanted to read when I opened that letter, that 'I am feeling much better and Mother is much better than she has been.' I read it over and over in his handwriting. On the morning of the 24th of February, last month, I received a letter dated the 22nd from my brother, word for word." Because he actually told me what he said, and then he quoted from his brother's letter, not one word, not a comma was out of place"...that this letter is coming across space, saying to his brother here. He said, "May I tell you, Neville, not in ten years have I had anything but a negative letter from my mother and my brother, not once concerning their health condition but a negative state. And here in three weeks...I did it for three weeks, every day, and quite often several times in the course of the day. When I thought of it I simply repeated it. At the end of three weeks this letter came, and the following day, one from my mother. This is what she said, 'I have not felt better in fifteen years'—from the two that were simply hypochondriacs."

He said, "I know now imagining *does* create reality. I don't have to spend my money sending them books to get them to read it. All I need is the desire on my part to help them, and then it becomes my responsibility. And so, I simply went to the end. The end was a letter in my hand where I could actually see my brother's handwriting and then read the contents of that letter as I wanted to read it. So I actually wrote the letter that I read three weeks later. It was written in my brother's handwriting but I dictated that letter. The whole thing was all within me. So I know today I can support this claim: imagining does create reality." So that's the name. "Call upon my name." Who was doing it? And I said to him...he said, "Well, I am." And he would have told me, but he said, "I told no one. I kept it as my secret, I never confided to anyone. I just said I am hearing from my brother."

So he was calling on the name, the only name in this world that responds. The name Jesus?—yes, it's the most glorious name in the world, but only when you know the name, what it means. Jesus actually means "I am" if you know how to spell it. It's spelled Yod He Vau Shin Ayin—Joshua—you break it down Yod He Vau Shin Ayin. There's a definite reason for the Shin in the name. A Shin is a flame, a fire, and an Ayin is an eye. And so Yod He Vau He would be Jehovah. But the name in an active state, which is called Jesus, is "God in action"...same thing. Do you believe in Jesus? "What do you think of Jesus?" someone asked Blake and he said, "Jesus? Why he's the only God, but so am I and so are you."

If I tell you this night that *you* are Jesus, would you be embarrassed? Are you going to bend your head in shame or think that I am blaspheming the name of God? I mean it when I tell you that you are Jesus. You don't know it yet but you *are* Jesus...that God actually became man that man may become God. The day will come—I hope it's tonight—but it's coming to every child born of woman; then they will know who they are. And in the very end—because the story of Jesus is all about The End, hasn't a thing to do with your social world, anything here at all—it's all about The End. Eschatology is the only story of Jesus. So he comes only to fulfill scripture: The End. And what was that End? That God so loved man that he actually gave himself—for he and the son are one—he actually gave himself to man because of his love of man. He became man and lost himself *in* man. But when he actually gave himself to man, bear in mind God was father, so if someone who is a father gives himself to me, but completely gives himself to me, well, then I must be a father. Regardless of my sex, regardless of my position in this world, if he succeeds in his purpose of giving himself to me, and he who gave himself to me was a father, then I must be a father.

He has it all planned out, how to reveal to me that he gave himself to me. And so he reveals it in his Son. There's no way in the world that God can prove to me that he gave himself to me save he has a Son that is his only begotten son. Then that only begotten son, in the depths of my soul I see him; and I know he is *my* Son, and he calls me Father. I know he is my son and he knows I'm his father. There's no way in eternity that God the Father could ever give himself to man and convince man to whom he gave himself that he succeeded in his purpose of that giving of self to man unless the son reveals the gift. So out of the depths of the soul of man comes the son, and the son is David. So a riddle is asked in the Book of Proverbs, the 30th chapter of the Book of Proverbs: "Who has established the ends of the earth? What is his name and what is his *son's* name? Surely you know!" (verse 4). So we're told we know. Well, where is he? In the depths of man is the son. He's called Olam in scripture and Olam means "the eternal youth, the eternal lad, the eternal son" (Eccles. 3:11). The question is constantly asked, Where...who is he and who is that son? "Whose son are you, young man?" Whose son is that stripling, whose son? (1 Sam. 17:56). And then no one knows. No one will know until he appears in the depths of the soul of the individual to whom God now reveals his purpose: You see the son and the son calls you Father.

So what is his fabulous name? The name is I AM—for purposes here on earth it's I AM—but in the end you will know the meaning of these words, and all will become king. Who? "The Lord will become king over all of the earth; on that day the Lord will be one and his name one" (Zech. 14:9). So you and the other three billion or four billion of us in this world will one day have the satisfaction of knowing that God fulfilled his purpose in you. You will see God's only begotten son and he'll call you Father (Ps. 2:7). Well, he's already called me Father. So if he calls me Father and he calls you Father, then you and I are one. Without loss of identity we're the father of the same son. Then we understand the great mystery of this compound unity where "Hear, O Israel! The Lord our God is one Lord" (Deut. 6:4). The I AM our I AMs form one I AM.

So the whole vast world, all are aware of being. So if I'm aware of being, I say "I am"...and you are aware of being so you say "I am." But you think you differ from me because I respond to Neville and you respond to John or some other name. But gradually we're moving towards one name, for "in that day the Lord will be one and his name one." So I'll tell you that name: In *that* day, your name is Jesus—self-born, born out of your own wonderful being, brought forth, and you're Jesus. Because Jesus is the Father of the only begotten son of God, "When you see me you see the Father." "How can you say, Show me the Father? When you see me you see the Father" (John 14:9). And so, did not David call me Lord? said he. "If David in the Spirit calls me Lord, how can I be David's son?" (Mat. 22:42). Well,

David called me Lord, called me Adonay; he called me "my Father." So if he called me Father, how can I be David's son? And so he reveals himself as the Father..."for he who sees me sees the Father." Everyone will have the experience of being called by David, Father, and then you know who you are.

So I say Jesus...you *are* Jesus, but you haven't yet remembered. He said, this is my name forever, not only forever but that all generations... thus all generations shall remember me by that name. And that name when you come right down to it as a sound, it's Jesus. In a practical sense it's I AM. I am writing a letter. What letter? I'm not going to tell you now. I'm writing a letter, it's coming from my brother. I'm writing another letter, it's coming from my mother. And they're telling what they haven't told me in ten years, because they're always complaining about how horrible they feel. But now I'm going to make them tell me they never felt better. And so, my mother's going to write me a letter. Here's the letter in my hand and she's telling me she hasn't been better. And I thought ten years...she changed the script somewhat because she told me fifteen years, but my memory went back ten years. I can't recall when she wasn't complaining, and so I thought ten years was long enough. She tells me by her own letter fifteen years. My brother tells me he has never felt better, that everything is perfect, and I haven't received a letter of that nature in ten years from my home in the Midwest. And to discover through the grapevine...a lady comes west, or someone comes west, who just saw them and said that every time when the mail came bringing your gift of a book, right straight to the ashcan…didn't even open the book...right into the ashcan.

Well, I have those, too. I must confess I do the same thing with a few things. I have some Jehovah's Witnesses who are determined to convert me; and I get all kinds of letters from my ex-wife—she sends me these magazines from something. Well, I look at it, I thank her profusely, then tear it in half and into the ashcan. I do the same thing there, too. So I must confess in this way I have acted in the same strange manner. I have no time to read it; it's called *The Watchtower* or something. But I'm not on that kind of watchtower. This is a different kind of watchtower that I'm talking about here, where there's only God, and God is your own wonderful human Imagination. That's God.

Tonight you can test it, as this gentleman has tested it. As every story I tell from this platform bears witness to the fact that imagining creates reality. There is no other God. God actually became man. And the end is in God's control. No tyrant is going to change it. If the bombs began to fall now, they aren't going to change the outcome. God planned it as it is and as it will be consummated, and no power in the world is going to change it.

So the whole vast world is responding to the activity taking place in us. And much of it is confusion because we don't know the name of God. So we go to church, we light candles, we do all kinds of things, and call upon a name; that isn't going to help at all. You could be right in a bar, if you're ever up against the sixth glass and not quite sure what you're seeing, and carrying on an inward conversation with self from premises of fulfilled desire—and in a way that no one knows it will come to pass. Hasn't a thing to do with your outer behavior, your activities, what are you doing on the inside?

So we are warned time and time again. You've heard it said...well, I'll tell it, said he, if you look on anything lustfully you've committed the act (Mat. 5:28). For that very act of feeling *was* the act. Whether you restrain the impulse following that ___(??) makes no difference, you did it. In the very moment of contemplating a thing with pleasure you were doing it. Well, you contemplate the receipt of a letter with pleasure. I received the letter and oh, what wonderful news! Contemplated with pleasure...that's lusting. Not just a physical lust after a woman or a woman after a man, but to lust after the receipt of a letter with contents bearing witness to the fact that this imagining creates reality. And then wait for it, it will come. His took three weeks. What is a matter of three weeks? Three months? May it come in three seconds! It could come...I've had it happen while I was in the act of doing it. I've had the phone ring to disturb my meditation and I hadn't even completed it. I was doing it and hearing it *vividly* when the phone rang, and I'm answering the phone to hear confirmation of what I'm doing on the inside.

All depends on where you are, on what level, because there's no difference between divine imagining and human imagining save in the degree of *intensity*. So if I withdrew long enough or deeply enough, then I'm more intense. And so, if I really withdraw, if I shut out the entire world, and then I start going into the depths of myself to hear something, then I'm more intense (so the phone rang). But if I don't, I'm disturbed by the noise and I'm concerned about other things, well, then I'm not withdrawing enough. It still works, but then it takes a little longer time. Like putting on a little single light under the pot, it will boil eventually, but you could increase the flame and boil it quicker. And so, the whole thing is within us.

So when the Bible speaks of God, they're speaking of Jesus and they're speaking of your Imagination. When Blake speaks, say for instance, of the great Poetic Genius, to him God was the Poetic Genius. And you say, "Well, I'm not a poet." You aren't? Have you ever had a dream? Do you know any poem in this world comparable in structure to a dream? Think of anything in this world...take a Shakespeare, the world's greatest in the use of words, or take a Blake, do you think anything that Shakespeare every wrote could compare to your dream? You take a dream and the structure of the dream, everything falls out and in perfect order, and the conversations are in perfect order, not one word misplaced, and every character speaking just as they should speak, and the whole thing is unfolding, and you're doing it, aren't you a poet? There isn't a poem in this world that can compare to a dream. And the whole dream unfolds so vividly before the mind's eye. You also are not only the author of the dream, you also throw yourself into the character, you are part of the dream too. It may be the major character, it may be a minor that you are playing, but you wrote it, wrote the whole thing. You dramatize it and externalize it, and actually, well, you directed it. The whole thing took place in you.

So when Blake speaks of the Poetic Genius as Divine Imagining and he calls Divine Imagining, Jesus, well, can't you imagine? That's Jesus. But if you think for one second that's being blasphemous, no, it's not blasphemous. You dwell upon it. Tonight you dwell upon it. You sit there and think noble things about others and expect it to come back to you just as you've imagined. That's Jesus doing it. And don't be ashamed of it, for the day will come, you will not be called, possibly, Jesus, but you will be called Father by the very one who called him Father. Then you'll know who you are. If he calls you Father and he called him Father, are you not Father? Well, who did he call Father? He called the grand I-am-ness Father.

So I say to you, eat the words. He said, "I found your words and I ate them"—-I assimilated them. I expelled all the things I couldn't take in, like the instrument that conveyed the story. So, alright, I will take that, I'll take the kernel and discard the husk. And then they became to me, "Your words became to me a joy and the delight of my heart." Why? What did they produce in me? What, as I assimilated them, what did they build? They built this knowledge that "I am called by thy name, O Lord God of hosts." You mean when I read the Bible and actually assimilated it I discovered the whole book was about me? Yes! I discovered the whole book was about me. That he who brought me into being as it were as his emanation so loved me that he cleaved to me and wouldn't let me go until he actually fulfilled his purpose to give me himself. And he, being God the Father, and I being his wife, his emanation, that he cleaved to me and wouldn't let me go until I actually became one with him. When that was completed, that union had to result in a child, for this is male-female. God the Father, as we're told in the 54th chapter of the Book of Isaiah: "Your Maker is your husband; the Lord of hosts is his name" (verse 5). And so, my Maker is *my* husband, I'm his emanation, and he cleaved to me until this dream of life comes to an end. It's called death...until this death disappears…then I am he. Well, this union must result in something creative and that is a son. So he brings into my world his son, but by then I am he, and so the son calls me Father.

I am telling you what I know from experience. I'm not speculating, I'm not theorizing, these are not opinions. I never heard it from a man. I was never taught it. It came by the revelation of Jesus Christ. When I least expected it, it happened to me, and it happened in such a marvelous manner. I can say to everyone: Do not despair. I don't care what you have ever done, the love of God is so intense and so great he isn't going to leave you. He has made a pledge to cleave to you and he is not going to let go until he has transformed you into himself, and you are he. And so when it is done, you will have to confess that it's grace, it's a gift. You could not have earned it. No man in the world could earn it; he isn't good enough. Therefore, because he can't earn it he can't brag about it; it's simply a gift, the gift of God. Grace is simply God's gift of himself to man. When he succeeds in giving me grace, then he gives me himself; and so when he gives me himself he has to give me his son. He can't be a father, giving me himself, and leave me barren. He has to give me his son or he didn't give me himself. If he is a father, then he has to give me fatherhood. If he is God, he has to give me God-ship. He has to or he didn't complete his purpose. So whatever he is when he pledges himself to do something, then I must be it. If his pledge was to give me all that he is, whatever he was before, I must become.

And so, the fatherhood I am, and if that name, that holy name is Jesus. Well, you may laugh or may walk out of here never to return again, it makes no difference to me. I am he. I'm the same man, Neville, but I am he, as you are he. You don't know it and I know it. I know not because I earned it; I know it because it was given to me. I didn't earn it, no man can earn it, it's a gift, and because it's a gift everyone will get it. So don't be embarrassed. When you see him, infinite love stands before you. And in the end there is only one body, strangely enough. You are embraced and incorporated into the body of love and it's your body. It's infinite, not in space, it's human, very human, but it's all love; infinite in wisdom, infinite in power, infinite in every sense of the word and it's your body, never again to be divorced from it. For that body is cleaving to you until you fuse into it, completely incorporated into the body of God, and that body is Jesus. Because you're one with the body you are he—not a little portion of it, the whole, the fullness is in you.

But here, for our practical purposes, I want letters after letters. I want you to take it this night and just try it...just what the gentleman did. He tried the outside affect, we all do that first, and so he tried to reach them by gifts of books, and they didn't even read the books. Four years of spending time and money and they all went into the ashcan. Then he stopped after he came here—he hasn't been coming here too long—but he heard what you heard, and then he decided that the whole responsibility was his. He isn't going to blame his mother, he isn't going to blame his brother, he isn't going to blame anyone, and he isn't going to try to change them through physical, external means. He's going to change them because they are all himself pushed out. He assumed full responsibility for the world in which he lived. So if the whole vast world is myself pushed out, I'll change any aspect. For did not James say, the greatest revolution in this century was the discovery by man that by changing his own inner attitudes of mind he could change the outer aspects of life? So he didn't argue with others, he only changed the inner attitudes of his own mind. And so he did it by holding a letter, which he was reading, as having come from his brother and having come from his mother; and that letter came at the end of three weeks. A complete radical change of attitude on their part because there was first a change of attitude on his part. He didn't expect the same kind of letter that he did for ten years. He radically changed it and expected the response. If this world is only response and I am the cause of the response, well, then get about the business and do something about it. We are the operant power. It can't operate itself, we are the operant power. And so, if my whole vast world is my Imagination made visible, that "all that I behold, though it appears without, it is within, in my own wonderful human Imagination," and that this world that seems so objectively real and so completely independent of my perception of it is only reflecting the activities taking place in me, well, then *do* something about it.

So I'm asking everyone to do something about it and then write me. Tell me what happened, how you did it, as this gentleman did. It only took him two pages—not on both sides of the sheet—one page would have done it. In just two simple pages in longhand he told me the story I told you tonight. And now I say to him, not a thing in this world can stop you but you. You're in business, go to the top. Go to the end—hold the end in your own mind's eye. Hold it in your hand if there's something you can hold in your hand implying the fulfillment of your dream; hold it in your hand as you did the letter. If it's a contract, hold a contract. If it's a bank book with a certain statement, hold it...if it's the morning's paper bringing you the news you want. Do you think that's crazy? You can do it. Tomorrow's news can be determined by your own wonderful...it's done anyway by your wonderful human Imagination. In spite of all the conflicts of the world, try it. Don't say, "Well, now suppose he operates differently." You'll give him power that doesn't belong to anyone in this world save he. The story is: I am he. Where is he? I am he. So don't think *he* can do it because *I am* he. He will only reflect what you are doing.

So you are the whole thing. It seems an awful responsibility…but it's true. And in the end, you are the very being that became you. He became you in love, he will raise you in love, and you will discover that you are the being that did the whole vast world. So you try it. But above all, please share with me that I in turn may share with others your wonderful use of faith. The first thing to do with faith is to begin to live by it. The very first thing, just begin to live by it. And it's faith in his name, and his name is I AM. If you take a concordance and look up the word "name," it's the most exciting search in the world through the sixty-six books, the name "name," and see where it goes, and how he leads you to only one point: confidence in I AM. Not in some other being—no intermediary between yourself and God—because Jesus, you think, is the intermediary. No, Jesus is your own wonderful I AM...that's Jesus, that's God. He *is* God. He's God the Father, and he became man that man may become God. So he's dwelling in man.

This coming fortnight we're going to have all over the Christian world stories of his resurrection, stories of his crucifixion, and the same thing's going to happen this year that has happened in previous years—the story will not be properly told. It isn't ___(??). This is the great mystery of life through death. He gave himself to me, completely gave himself to me, and had to die like the little seed must die to be made alive. He died in me; he's buried in me in the tomb, the only tomb into which he was ever placed, my skull. When he awoke *in* my skull I was he, the same being, I was he. And so, the only place where he's ever buried is the skull. And when he comes out, all of the things told you of him you are going to experience, everything said of him you are going to experience. And the whole thing is only The End, the last days. That's all he's come to reveal, because all prior to that was preparation. He's only concerned with the eschatological concept of life: The very last days when he awakens in man.

So tonight, let me quote it in a simple, simple way. You sit quietly and now forget what you even did one second before. You may be ashamed of what you did; God isn't. You've been made to feel that you did wrong, or maybe you did wrong in your own mind's eye. But don't think for one moment because you did something that you thought wrong or society may judge you harshly for, that you are not now worthy to call on his name if you know his name; his name is I AM. The night before you could have been plastered, the night before you could have done a thousand things of which you may be ashamed. It doesn't stop you from getting the response from God if you call on his name. So you sit quietly, close your eyes (just to aid your attention), and then construct a simple—the simpler the better—the simplest little scene which implies the fulfillment of the dream. The holding of a piece of paper in your hand from a certain character, and that's what you want, and it reads as you want it, well, that's it. You want to take the hand of a friend, congratulate the friend on his good fortune, that's it.

You want to see the ring on a finger of some friend who is anxious to be happily married in this world, that's it. Whatever is the end implying the fulfillment of the dream. And all you do, you do it naturally and simply; as you do it naturally, give it tones of reality, sensory vividness; and then open your eyes. Then hold God trustworthy!

God is your own I AM. Who did it? I did it, I was doing it, well, you're saying "I am, I am doing it"...that's God. Now hold God trustworthy. He's infinite in power, infinite in wisdom, and so we can do it. This conscious reasoning mind can't do it; that was suspended when you actually called upon the name of God. You come back and you wear this conscious reasoning mind, alright, wear it, it's a good mind, nothing wrong with reason. But you try this. If you get results—and you *will*—then it doesn't really matter what others think, does it? For if we have evidence for a thing, does it really matter what the world thinks about it? If I can produce results by a way that seems insane and seems crazy, it doesn't matter if it seems insane if I get the results.

So I am called by thy name, and your name is my name, and the name is I AM. Not some little thing on the outside; there's nothing more central than I AM. If this very night I slept any place in the world…,and by using my Imagination I could sleep wherever I wanted to sleep in Imagination, couldn't I? Would it work? Yes it will work. I've done it. You ___(??) awakened there. How could I go there in the flesh? You *will* go there in the flesh. Things will happen to compel a change in your world, to compel you to make that journey if you sleep in Imagination elsewhere as though elsewhere were here; because I AM can never be other than here. I don't say I am there; wherever I am, it's here. And so, it is always first person and present...right here. So I can make here Moscow if I so desired. Then this would vanish and I would actually feel it to be Moscow here. Who is feeling it?—I am. That's God, and all things are possible to God. Then, in a way that Neville, the conscious reasoning mind, does not know, he'll be compelled to make the journey to fulfill that command of God.

So do it in this light and you will *not* fail. And you'll send me letters, because I do really want the letters to encourage everyone here that this thing works. It proves itself in performance.

Now let us go into the Silence.

* * *

Q: (inaudible)

A: The question is...first of all, this is a story told last Friday. A gentleman who is a professional writer writes the story of a friend of his today by the name of Eddie. He's extremely fond of Eddie. He met Eddie seemingly by accident two years ago, to discover suddenly last Sunday morning, while in the shower, as he personally recalled an experience of his six years ago when a story was dictated to him in a similar manner, the story that he had that very week dictated; he felt the presence behind dictating, prompting. And then, the whole thing flashed into his mind: Why that central character of the story of six years ago is identical with Eddie of flesh and blood. Here, this character of fiction is now wearing flesh and blood. So he reread the story in my book *The Law and The Promise*, called "There is no Fiction" (that chapter). So he discovered that all of the characters that he as a writer created over the years actually are walking around this world in flesh and blood. He hasn't met all as yet, but, said he, "There are many that I have written that I have no desire to meet in the immediate present. Not in the flesh, anyway!" Well, it doesn't really matter; we've all done it, anyway. Without being a professional writer we are having these characters.

For instance, I know a man in New York City, he didn't know Mr. Roosevelt, didn't know him at all, but he delighted...every morning when he shaved, he would spend, say, ten minutes shaving that face of his, a young man, thirty, and I said, "What on earth prompts you to do a thing like this?" He said, "You have no idea, Neville, what a joy I get out of it! There's no show on Broadway that could give me the kick that I get when I look into that mirror and tell Roosevelt off. I'm looking in the mirror and I'm telling him what I think of him. I say, 'Who do you think you are, king? This is America, a democracy. We don't have any kings. So you want four years in the White House? And your four sons are they going to be all princes now? Are we going to have this royalty?'" I said, "What are you doing this for?" He said, "Oh, but Neville, what a joy, what a kick I get!" I said, "After all, you're building a character." Now, he doesn't write. This man hasn't written, but he was carrying on a mental conversation with something that he despised. Well, Mr. Roosevelt is gone from this world; never met the man, the man never met him; but he will meet a character that will make Roosevelt look like a bunch of roses to him. I mean these are the things we do in this world.

And so, you single out...here, this is the year of politics, and so you are either for or against, this year. All the things we are for...and then you are going to take the other fella in your mind's eye and you're going to tell him off. You're going to carry on these mental conversations with him and say everything that is unlovely. You're going to spend the most time on the one you don't like and little time on the one you like. Man should be for, not against. The morning's paper, you can tell the editorial policy of a paper by the things they're against. They'll tell you exactly who they're going to vote for. Read the columnist in any paper and you see the policy that will capture that paper. They're against; they're not for. But you be *for* in this world. You single out what you want; let them go their way. Vote, yes, certainly vote. Vote *for* someone—don't vote against someone—and vote for him, if you want to vote, and you should. I think you should if you want to vote, vote for someone. But don't waste your precious time in carrying on these mental conversations with the opposition; you're only enlarging them and building characters in your world that you must tomorrow encounter.

But, may I tell you, in the end, all will be forgiven, in the end all is forgiven...all. You could make lame people in this world, blind people, all kinds of people. In the end, you will confront them and in the twinkle of an eye all will be made perfect. Every one of them will be transformed into the beauty that they should have been in the beginning, that you disfigured them by your arguments and all of the things that you did. But in the end, you will confront them, an infinite sea of human imperfection. As you walk by—because in that moment you have been lifted up, and the heavenly chorus sang out your praise and called you by name, that you are risen—and as you walk by, gliding by in this glorious body, this immortal body of yours made of fire and air it seems, and as you walk by everyone is molded into perfection because you are perfect. Then you understand the words: "Be ye perfect as your Father in heaven is perfect. You must be holy because I, the Lord your God, am holy." And as you walk by, every one is made whole. So in the end all is perfect. But while we are struggling to awaken to the realization that our own Imagination is God, we create such strange, monstrous things.

So to come back to your question, "What should he do?" Were I he, I would do nothing. He wrote them; they sold. He'll be called upon tomorrow...he doesn't have to conceive all the stories. Maybe when he goes to the conference, I don't know, I'm not a writer, so when he goes into conference and they say I want a story and this is the plot, as a professional writer he has to take the suggestion of the producer, whoever is responsible, and he has to conceive and put it into these things. Like Shakespeare gave us these fantastic things...but what characters! Were I Shakespeare walking this earth, I wouldn't undo one thing that he's done; they're so altogether marvelous, every character. In fact, we speak of Shakespeare's four hundredth anniversary, and

I think of the great ones. You take a Dickens...do you know that his characters are better known than Dickens? They're all alive, and don't you meet them? Haven't you met Scrooge? Who hasn't met a Scrooge in this world? He's far more alive than Dickens. Dickens as a character... maybe he wasn't pleasant, I don't know, maybe I wouldn't want to have a dinner party with him...but I enjoy his characters. I wouldn't mind having them to dinner, quite a few of them, not all. And so these characters are alive and they're all people in the world. You meet them. And one can play so many parts. You could be the most protective, loving husband in this world, and in the office you're a devil. And yet at home you could be to her all that she desires as a husband. So we're all characters ___(??) anyway. You hear them all day long, they're doing ___(??).

Are there any other questions, please?

Q: (inaudible)

A: "And I, when I am lifted up from the earth, I will lift up all men unto me." And that's an actual true story. The day will come you'll be lifted up, and I'll tell you exactly how you will be lifted up: in a spiral motion. You'll go up like this...and you don't even know, you simply are taken up that way through the top of your head in spiral motion. A heavenly chorus will sing your praise as you are lifted up, call you by name, and pronounce "He is risen!" calling you by name. And the chorus will sing it out, unnumbered voices, but what heavenly voices! Then you will see an infinite field of human imperfection and they're all waiting for you. Not just idly waiting, they're waiting for you because you are going to redeem them. You will glide by in this immortal body of yours, a fiery, airy body. It's luminous—you don't need a sun, you don't need the moon, you illuminate your world because *you are* the light. As you walk by, gliding by, every one is made perfect as you go by. That chorus comes in at the very end and it swells in the most glorious exultation: "It is finished!" the last words of the cross. And when it exults "It is finished!" then you crystallize once more in the body of clay for unfinished business, which unfinished business is to tell it—to tell and testify to the truth of Jesus Christ, the only reality in the world.

But the churches have completely misunderstood the mystery of Jesus Christ, and talk about him as a being of flesh and blood. What a man in whom it first appeared did for a job on earth is irrelevant—that he was a carpenter, a mason, a banker, a writer, it's irrelevant. He's not talking of that. The whole story is simply taking place in the soul of that being. If you read it carefully the experiences were not witnessed by anyone other than himself. And he was not what they were looking for. They were looking for some majestic being to come out of space as a conqueror who would lead Israel (who had been crushed) into some victorious campaign and enslave those who had enslaved Israel. That was not Messiah at all. So they knew him, they knew his background, they knew this, that and the other. Doesn't matter what you know of a man, the weaknesses of a man. Who isn't weak in this world? The body is weak. Spirit is willing; the flesh is weak. No matter how strong it is it's weak. ___(??) weaknesses, our little links that are weak. And so, if you know the little weak link you can always point the finger and say, "What, he? How can he be chosen?" Well, it wasn't his choice, God chose him. God made the choice. And so, if God chooses, well, then it's God's secret of election. No one knows it. But those who know you well and know you intimately can always point the finger at your weaknesses...they know you.

I have those who wouldn't come near me because I am a divorced man. If I was not divorced and kept twenty on the side, perfectly alright, nobody would know it, so they would come. I'm keeping no one on the side for multiple reasons. But I was once divorced, therefore, that right away that's anathema. I know that. My podiatrist in New York City this past summer, past fall, here I am sitting in his chair and he is taking care of my feet. He said, "You know"—he calls this lady by name, a very prominent lady, you'll all know her if I told you, I won't tell you, very prominent—"she's read your books and she's trying to convert me. I'm a Jew. She's trying to convert me to her way of thinking, which happens to be—without any offense because it's a marvelous concept and nice positive way of thinking—which is Christian Science. Well, she's a Christian Scientist and she's trying to convert me, the Jew, to Christian Science. I said, Well, I'm a Jew. My father was an orthodox Jewish butcher, and we were raised in a strictly kosher home. Though I don't maintain a strict kosher home, I still consider myself a Jew. But I do go to a man who is a friend of mine—and his name's Neville—when he comes to town. He happens to be in town at the moment, so I'm going to all of his lectures." "Oh," she said, "I've heard of that man. I have his books, the books are alright, I've read them, they're alright, but I wouldn't go near that place." He said, "Why?" She said, "Well, because the man was divorced. Not only divorced but I also heard that he lived with a woman for years before he married the girl he's married to now." And so, my friend Hal not understanding the picture of life, he tried to justify my behavior. He said, "Well, can't you forgive him? God is merciful. If God can forgive, can't you try to be like God and forgive, too?" I said, "Hal, why do you say that? Am I in need of her forgiveness?" Of all the things in the world! So she wouldn't come near my meetings because I was once married and someone told her I lived with a woman. Well, really, every husband lives with a woman!

Goodnight.

GOD ONLY ACTS

3/20/1964

Tonight's subject is "God Only Acts." You may be familiar with that statement from Blake, "God only acts and is in all existing beings or men." We're told that what is impossible to men is possible with God, if we can only find *God*; for what is impossible with us as men is possible with God. I am confident I can locate him for you right this night. And it's very simple. There are unnumbered things that you and I can think of that are truly impossible with us, *unnumbered* things you can think of them. Now, could you imagine the thing that is to you impossible solved? Can't you imagine it solved? Think of something that you cannot, I defy you to think of something that you cannot imagine. Think it over. And so you say, I can't go because I haven't a passport. I can't go, say, to Russia. They wouldn't allow me to go to Russia. I couldn't get a passport. Can't you imagine that you have a passport? Can't you imagine that you've been to Russia and that you're back? You may say, well, that's a lie; there is no evidence to support that imaginal act. But can't you imagine? Can you imagine it? Well, that's God. That's God in action.

If you can imagine, all I ask you do now is to hold God trustworthy. You've found him, you've found something that can imagine anything in this world, well, that's God. For with him *all* things are possible, and with men there are unnumbered things that are not possible. So you found in *yourself* a power that makes everything possible. But all God intends from us is to accept the imaginal act with faith, that's all. Faith is being loyal to unseen reality. You remember what you did, that's an imaginal act. All it takes from us now is to be loyal to that imaginal act. For through faith we made all things. An imaginal act is one thing and that's self-determining, that's causative. Everything on the outside moves under compulsion, but everything, and no one really knows the unseen, hidden, causal act. Once in a while you can trace it...the individual may be able to trace it back to something that he did. But between the imaginal act and its unfoldment in the world, in this whole vast world, unnumbered things come out, all contributing. And much of it we condemn. We condemn this act and that act and that act, and harshly condemn it. But it all is moving towards the fulfillment, the bloom of what each in the Silence did back here. And yet we sit in judgment of all the unfolding picture of that act, right up to the bloom of the act.

Now let me share with you a story that was shared with me. About two weeks ago or three weeks ago I told you a story—it was unfinished, it wasn't yet completed—about the lady who had carried this tremendous burden on her shoulders as it were for twenty-five years, and suddenly, that very day, it was washed out of her life, completely washed out. But I didn't know the nature of the burden; it wasn't yet told me; in fact, it wasn't yet told him. He just wanted me to know, to encourage me to encourage you of this story. Well, this is the story. It's all about his mother, who lives in St. Louis; that's, maybe, 1,500 miles away. So take that in to consideration when you hear the story.

She has a very important position. She is executive secretary to an organization similar to our Bowl here. You might have seen these great shows in the summer. They produce...every summer twelve musicals are produced, and you either take them, or you've read about them, or you've heard about them. And so, she has been, and still is, for many, many years, executive secretary of this organization. But in spite of the glamour of the job and all the wonderful things she enjoys on the outside of her home... because in that capacity, and as I'm told in his letter, that one of the great status symbols in St. Louis is to be a member of that board. And so, they all love her, all respect her, they all admire her, and she enjoys their friendship, and so all the lovely social graces and friendships are hers *outside* of her home. But in her home, she's not been able to entertain any of these people who entertain her. Because twenty-five years ago, her father, just moving like the old man of the sea, fell. Well, being her father, she didn't want to do anything to simply dispossess him as it were. He said, "In a strange and wonderful way he is a very remarkable man, because not very many men have reached the advanced age of ninety-five without ever having done one day's work in his life." Well, that happens to be her father, and he said to me, "a remarkable accomplishment, ninety-five and not once ever having done a day's work." So there he sat.

Well, when he became aware of my books, the first thing he did, he packed off a set to his mother, in the hope that she would read them and apply the technique as described in the books. When she came home this Christmas, he discovered she hadn't really applied it and he would like to know why. Well, she confessed she could see no out to this but death of her father, and if she applied it in the way that the book teaches, she might produce a death, and then she'd have to live with that on her conscience for the rest of her days. And although she would love the freedom of living alone in a nice lovely home, where all things were lovely, she still would persist in this horrible sacrifice and carry this burden rather than face the only out that she could think of, that the man would die.

Then he told her the story that he heard from this platform, that when I found myself in love with the girl who now bears my name, I was terribly involved. I mean, so many complex facts confronted me. I had a dancing partner the world thought I should marry and everyone thought I should marry her. I was not yet divorced from my first wife, and yet here I'm in love with this girl. Well, I knew I could not be happy in this relationship of marriage if it caused any distress to my dancing partner. Yet, I postponed and postponed the joy of mine by not *doing* something about it, not acting. One night I said to myself, "If I am now blissfully happy in this new relationship of marriage, then it could not be really a happy state if I knew that my dancing partner was injured in any way by this act of mine. So I will simply forget all of that and assume that I am blissfully happy, which would include that she's happy." I did it night after night for six nights. And then she confronted me and told me she didn't know how to tell me, she didn't want to hurt me, but I was to her like a brother. She couldn't think of me in terms of her husband and that she had found a doctor—she mentioned his name, a friend of mine, a very dear friend of mine—and that she and this doctor had been, well, lovers for the longest while and that she hoped one day to marry him, and she thought I should know it now. Well, here I had been going for the longest while not wanting to hurt her and she not wanting to hurt me, and we both robbed each other of the joy that was really in store for us.

So he told his mother of this story. He said, "I saw in her eyes a certain glimmer of interest, so I said it over and over in the hope that she would actually apply it. But she didn't tell me when she left here that she *was* going to apply it. So what I did was this, I imagined that she had done it and done it successfully. So I imagined that she had applied this principle towards that end and that she had been most successful in the application of the principle. Then a telephone call came that…she didn't mention what the father did, but he did something to outrage the neighbors. It was something that really outraged the entire neighborhood. And then, she said to him, "I must make a decision," and her decision was to move. Then he said to her, "I've decided, too. I'm going back to my home fifty miles from here, from which I originally came." Then came a letter, which he enclosed to me, in which he told me that she saw the place—he has a beautiful room, and she saw the meals he's having, and so he has wonderful meals and living in a beautiful room. Now for the first time in twenty-five years without the man dying she can have her own lovely apartment and do what she's been wanting to do for the last twenty-five years.

So, you see, you hurt *no one* when you apply this law and really *act*. "God only acts and is in all existing beings or men." So he has found God, definitely found God, for he found the cause of the phenomena of life. And back here, I think he knows it tonight, that whatever that grandfather did, whatever he did—he could have done something that if he were not ninety-five could possibly it would go very hard with him today—he may, I don't know. But you know who did it?—the one back here. He wasn't quite sure that the mother did it, and so he was taking no chances, and so he imagined that the mother had imagined herself in this new wonderful place, and that it was successful. And so, now that thing was *causal.* and everything that had to take place to bring about the fulfillment of that imaginal act *took* place, including a man performing some kind of an act or saying something or doing something that outraged the neighbors. Now you judge the act and the old gentleman would be harshly judged, and yet he was compelled. For every outer act moves under compulsion, and that compelling force is in man as an imaginal act. It's the only creative force and that is God. "By him all things were made and without him was not made anything that is made" (John 1:3). So you've found God in that wonderful act; therefore, why go elsewhere when you've found exactly how this thing works? When you know what you want, you hurt no one; you simply go to the end. But, may I tell you, you may cause many things to be, well, on the surface, to be very distressing. Not to you alone but to others, and sometimes never to you. But that's why in the end you'll understand the words, "Father, forgive them; they know not what they do" (Luke 23:34). For everyone is acting in a way he doesn't really know why he's doing it. He thinks he initiated it; he doesn't, he's under compulsion, because someone removed not only in space, removed in time, is treading out the winepress and they're only instruments to bring about the fulfillment of that unseen imaginal act.

So here, he has shared with me that I in turn may share with you. I am convinced that if you take me seriously and do it, I will get before I close on the 26th of May one hundred percent. I will have everyone who could testify to the truth of God's law, I mean that seriously. I don't mean ninety-nine percent, I mean 100%. If you treat it seriously and *act*:

"God only acts and is in all existing beings or men" and if he starts with the premise that with men things are impossible but with God *all* things are possible. They couldn't understand how a rich man, who is denied the right to enter the kingdom of heaven because he couldn't—"it's easier for the camel to go through the needle's eye." And then they asked him, "Then who can get the kingdom of heaven?" His reply was, "With men, it's impossible; but with God all things are possible" (Mark 10:27). So now you know that you can't conceive of something…no one can tell you something that you can't imagine. No one has ever gone to the sun, but can't you imagine it? No one has ever gone beyond the sun, beyond our sphere into some other sphere altogether, but can't you imagine it? There's nothing you can't imagine, therefore, all things are possible with God. Therefore, God *must* be my capacity to imagine...that's God. And if I try it and it proves itself in the testing, then I have found him. I try it again and it proves itself in performance, so I have confirmed that I have found him. Then I share it with others and they try it and it works. Then we have found him, haven't we?

So I say, we can get from this group here 100% success that you can actually testify to the truth of God's *law*. I'd be satisfied and thrilled if one percent could testify to the truth of God's Promise. But that is unconditional...not a thing you can do about it, it just happens. But you can do everything about testing his law, because his law is conditional: We are the operant power. For when it comes to his Promise...that is something that thrills me beyond measure when I hear anyone confirm the Promise. So now let me share with you what was given to me in the same letter. He said, "Last week I began to write you a letter." He was going to tell me how about a month ago he met God. He said, "It was then, at that meeting, soon after that meeting, that I began to write to you. But my experience in meeting God is not identical to yours. First of all, there was no meeting of an infinite might, only love...a mixture of light, joy and love; that was the mixture." He said, "Unlike *your* experience it was not a person, but fuse with it I did. And after so many years of being confused, it was a thrilling relief to be fused, for a change." So he met God. Even though he didn't see God presented in bodily form, he was fused with God. You know what fusion is? Where things are gathered together and actually gathered together as though by melting. That's an actual experience: you are fused with God and no power in eternity could ever put you apart. Read the 8th chapter of the Book of Romans. No power in the world could ever, after such a fusion, ever bring about a separation of you two (verse 38). And therefore, when we are fused with God we have the same body, that same glorious body of God. And, here we have unity and equality in diversity. He and I do not look alike, we're both men, I'm older, but we do not look alike, and yet we are both fused with the same body of God.

So here we have equality in that body, we have union in that body, and yet diversity. That's the great mystery: when all are gathered together, one by one, not collectively but one by one into the body of God. And eventually *all* will be in that one body, and it's our body, and the individual's body. That's your resurrected glorious body. You can't describe it. In this man's case it appeared to him as a mixture of light, that's right, of joy, that's certainly right, of love, absolutely right...so all mixed together. But it was not a person. It did not come and present itself in bodily form. In my own case, it was just as described in the 7th chapter in the Book of Daniel, the Ancient of Days, right before me. Clothed as he's clothed, looking just as he's described, and I'm presented to him as described in that book (verses 9, 11). And the very open book as described in that chapter was present. Only three characters stand out in my mind; there were others, but three stand out. Infinite might...and they're sitting in what I would call a carriage drawn by the most glorious horses. And then, a woman, an ideal, like an angel, like a recording angel, writing at a table and an open book, as told us in the Bible. She wasn't composing, she was recording, the most glorious angelic being but woman, just simply recording. Then I'm presented to the Ancient of Days and it is infinite love.

In this same chapter, they speak of the animal, the beast that was slain. It doesn't tell you *how* it was slain. That was an experience of mine that came about the same time. It wasn't the same night, but whether that experience preceded this presentation or followed it, it was not too long before or after. But *that* was the beast. And may I tell you I'll share with you how the beast is slain. It is not said *how* the beast was slain, but love that night slew the beast. For here, I found myself in the presence of the most horrible monster, and then I looked up and this glorious being, not unlike the recording angel of that vision of the night. The same person, really, only this one was standing and looking at me; and this one was down below and calling this glorious creature "Mother." As this hairy animal, hair from the head to the toe, like an ape, and the hair was reddish, sort of a reddish brown, and as it called this glorious woman, "Mother," I banged it. And then it kept on calling it, "Mother, Mummy," and I pummeled it, I was so annoyed with it. And it gloated. It spoke and it gloated in my blows, violent blows, as though it were a masochist. It simply loved to be beaten.

And then, something on the inside of me, from the very depths of my soul, knew—I can't tell you I heard a voice—but I *knew* that that was my creation and so was she. Both are my creations. She embodied every noble thought that I have ever entertained, and it embodied every ignoble, horrible, monstrous thing I have ever entertained, and both were my offspring. I knew that if this monstrous hairy beast had no right to exist, that I was the cause of its existence. I pledged myself—there was no one to whom I could turn—I didn't pledge with another, all with myself. I swore to myself that if it took me eternity I would redeem it. I had no sooner made the decision to redeem it, regardless of the cost to me in pain or in time; and when my decision was made—without anyone looking on, so it was all within me—before my very eyes it melted.

I have never in my life felt such compassion for anything as I did for this. No hate, nothing but sheer compassion, that I could bring into this world such a monstrous thing and allow it to live when it really shouldn't live. I didn't kill it in the sense of cutting off its head. I had compassion for it. And because it was the embodiment of all of my misspent energies, as it melted before my eyes leaving not a trace behind it, all the energies that I saw embodied there came back to me. They actually came through me. I have never felt so powerful in my life. Everything that throughout the centuries, how long I don't know, unnumbered ages went into this monstrous creature. Invisible to me with my mortal frame of it, it whispered into my ear repetition of the deeds that fatten it, on which it would grow. So any opportunity to "take advantage of" would be encouraged by the whispering of this unseen monster that I, myself, had created. And every attempt to be noble in my world came, and encouragement would come, from this noble creature that I had created. And so, at that very moment then I discovered what I had done with sheer energy; for I gave it life, I brought it into being. It was my dweller on the threshold, and I faced it one night and sheer compassion wilted it, and it melted before my eyes and vanished. But in vanishing, all the energies—they weren't dissipated—they returned to me who had put them into that horrible monstrous form. So the beast spoken of in that chapter...and you'll find it in Revelation, you'll find it in many chapters. The open book you find in many chapters, all through the Psalms, Isaiah. These are true visions.

And so, he did not see the human form, but he was fused with the same being, for that being is love. When you fuse with it, the joy is beyond the wildest dreams. So he felt joy and life...you can't measure the life. For, "In the Father there is life, and as the Father has life in himself so he's granted the Son also to have life in himself" (John 5:26). So fusion with it; the Father, he's become the Son who is one with the Father, and, therefore, has life in himself. So I can say to him, that in this fusion there is no Jew, no Greek, no slave, no free, no male, no female, only one in Christ Jesus. And all the powers of the world can not ever divorce you from that fusion. He's one with it.

So I can't tell him the thrill that was mine when I got that letter and began to read it. He said in his letter—which is irrelevant for the evening but still it's part of the picture—he was writing a story when his wife happened by and said, "Oh God, what, another letter to Neville? You want to monopolize all the meetings?" She said, "Read it." She didn't say it unkindly...at least, not too unkindly...and so, he said, "I promised at the moment that I would delay writing any more letters for the next few weeks. But Mother's note came this morning and because I had mentioned it to you in a previous letter, I thought I should share with you the conclusion, and that you tell others as I have told you." So I want to thank him and I want to ask her, please don't stop him from writing anymore letters!

So everyone, I want to get the letters and really get them in. I say everyone can bring me letters on the condition, which is the law. I hope most of you can send me something comparable to that fusion. For now that's done, they could shoot him now, chop off his head, and they can do nothing to separate him from the love of God. He was called into that state; he didn't earn it any more than I did. What was God's secret of his elective love that night when he was, about a month ago, when he was called? He was called and he saw love, only love, for God is only love, really. But the love is so ecstatic you can't deny the joy that is with it. And you can't deny the life that you feel when you are fused with it, you can't. But in that union, oh, what joy! what life! So all of the qualities he expressed perfectly.

I still say to him, it may be this night, who knows, that you will see him, presented just as the 7th chapter of Daniel presents him. Just as Daniel presents him that's exactly what he looked like to me. And then you are that Son of man who is brought and presented to the Ancient of Days. The recording angel, yes, she's there. Infinite might, yes, he's there. They do not look alike, but you can't deny infinite might when you stand in his presence. It was infinite might who sent me, and the words ringing in my ears were the words, "Time to act." Time to act...I had to discover *how* to act. It was time to act. "Drink no more water; take a little wine for your stomach's sake and your many afflictions" (1 Tim. 5:23). I had been absorbing, absorbing, absorbing all the psychological truth I could get by attending all the lectures, reading all the books, and going mad trying to adjust the conflicts with all the so-called different aspects of Truth. And the words are, "Drink no more water; take a little wine for your stomach's sake and your many afflictions." Certainly wasn't to take wine in a physical sense—although I must confess I enjoy it—but that was not the suggestion. Wine is how to apply it. You've been absorbing the psychological truth; that's symbolized by water. So I filled myself 'til I almost became waterlogged. And now, don't take any more, start to apply it by drinking a little wine: put it into practice.

I then *had* to put it into practice, and putting it into practice I found God. For if by him all things are made and without him was not anything made that was made, and I found out what I did and how I got something in result, well then, I've found him. I tried it again and it worked again. I kept on trying it, sometimes a long delay, sometimes shorter. I can't quite bring it down to the point of why the delay, other than it's not a delay, it is simply the seed takes a different interval of growth, interval of time. One would come over night, one would come while I'm doing it, and some would come the next day, the next month, the next year.

But, looking back, as I told you a week ago tonight, a story from which I have ___(??), and I tried to explain that night that *I* was the cause of her misfortune. The things she did for which she was criticized and sentenced and suspended, *I* did it. Had I not done the imaginal act, she would not have done what she did; and if she did do it, she would not have been discovered in the act. But she had to be discovered because she had to come forward that I could serve her with papers. She was hidden in the eight-odd million people in the city of New York. There are over eight million. Buried in that enormous crowd, how are you going to find her when she leaves her address and gives no forwarding address? But she *had* to be found even as like a needle in a haystack. She had to come out of hiding, because I had performed an act. Performing the act I compel her to perform a certain act for which society condemns her. So, who did the act? I did it. And so, I only told the story to show you, don't judge anyone harshly. You may be the very one treading the winepress that is causing that act, then you now sit in judgment and condemn. But when you awaken you will say exactly what is said on the cross, "Father, forgive them, for they do not *know* what they do." They're all moved under compulsion. You awake, you are moving from the inside, and that's self-determining. You know exactly what you are doing, and you watch what you are doing on the inside, and you do it constructively, lovingly. But even a loving act as it was in his case—he loves his mother and wanted her to be free of a burden. He didn't want that grandfather to die, but he wasn't concerned as to *how* the mother would be set free. But he knew from the story that you've heard that if he felt her *joy* in her new home that something would happen without hurt to her. Well, the old gentleman did something that outraged the neighbors. And that she said to me..."Mother has not yet mentioned what he did, and as far as I'm concerned it doesn't really matter what the old gentleman did. He could have done one in a thousand different things that would have caused the neighbors to rise and in some great fiery __(??) against him." It doesn't really matter. But the cause of whatever he did was fifteen hundred miles removed in an imaginal act of a son who so loved his mother he wanted her to be free from this horrible burden that she'd carried for twenty-five years.

So I tell you, everyone do it and then share with me. But bear in mind God only acts and is. He is not a passive spectator at this passage of history, he is the supreme *actor*, the *supreme* actor. So in everyone God is acting, and he's acting every time you sit down and imagine a thing with faith. That's how God acts. If you imagine and think, oh, well, that that's nothing, that isn't real, well then, you've already cancelled it at the very moment of saying that it was unreal.

Do you recall the story we told you quoted from the great Carl Jung that only when he credited the fantasy with reality did the thing work? For you who were not here, Carl Jung who died in '61, and the book came out in '61, which is really a form of biography. And this night he was contemplating the death of a friend whose funeral he had attended that day—the man had died suddenly without warning the day before and was buried that very day—when Jung, in his bed, was seriously considering the man and his present state. Whether Jung believed in the afterlife or not is irrelevant to the story. But he's contemplating the friend and suddenly he senses the presence of the friend at the foot of his bed. As a great scientist he said to himself, "Well, I know ___(??). I know, I went to his funeral, the man is dead so he can't really be here." Then he arrested his thoughts. He said, "What right have I? Wouldn't that be the most abominable thing to do to a friend! If the friend were here, and I treated him as though he were not, and I was indifferent to him, wouldn't that be a horrible thing to do to a friend! So now I will credit him with reality." And so the minute he decided to credit him with reality and assumed he was there and real, the friend became very, very real in his Imagination, turned around, walked through the door and beckoned him to follow, which he did. As he followed through the door the friend went through the garden and he in his Imagination followed onto the street. And then the friend walked several hundred yards up to his home, where now only the widow lived, and he, in his Imagination, followed the friend. He went to the friend's home, the friend went right through the first room into his library, mounted a little stool that was there, up to the second shelf from the top, and pointed out four volumes bound in red. Then he pointed to the second volume. And then, as he pointed to the second volume—and that was the one he wanted to bring Jung's attention to—he disappeared. And, of course, Jung broke the spell...back on his bed.

The next day, he physically went to the home and asked the widow for permission to see the library. As he entered the library here is the little stool that was in his vision of the night before. He mounted the stool and there, second shelf from the top, are four volumes in red. He picked up the second volume and its title, the title of it *The Legacy of the Dead,* Zola's translation into the German, Zola's work translated from the French into the German. But it was titled *The Legacy of the Dead.* That's all the man wanted to convey to Jung. Jung, the great giant in the mind, might believe that with the dissolution of the brain there is no man. He might, because Freud believed that and he was Freud's great student. So many psychiatrists believe that without the brain there is no being, no entity; it vanishes with the dissolution of the brain. How they can conclude that I don't know, but many of them do. Well, Jung might have been on that verge. Well, here is a man who is dead now—he went to the funeral—he returns to convince him of the reality of a *post*-death state, and takes him to the place and points out a book where the title bears a great significance, *The Legacy of the Dead.* And so, Jung could take that in 1944, I think that happened; but he would not allow it to go into print until after his death. He died in '61 and the book came out in '61 after Jung himself had made his exit from this world. So the story is that when he gave reality to the so-called unreal state it became so real it could guide him to show the reality of an after-death state. So if you would now imagine something and give to it a same credit of reality, the thing would then become embodied and become real in your world. You can't take an imaginal act and treat it as unreal. Take your imaginal act and treat it as reality. Really believe it's real and have faith in the unseen reality, that it will externalize itself in your world.

So you take it and try it. And trying it, I know from experience you'll prove it. And then, if you're not the one in ten, or if you're not the nine, I should say, you'll write me a letter. Because not everyone who gets it ever writes a letter. And may I tell you, it doesn't really matter how well you write. If you just can barely print but you can't express yourself in writing, tell me in the first person. I want to hear it that I may in turn share it, as I've been sharing this gentleman's story with you. But when I read the beginning of that letter...and he started the letter that he may explain to me how a month ago he met God, and then drew the story so vividly. It was not a parallel of mine—although I did meet infinite love and permitted myself to speak from that—he met love only. It wasn't infinite might. That doesn't matter. Might is but an aspect, an attribute of God. God is infinite love. Almightiness and omniscience they're only attributes of God. But God himself is all love. So you are fused not with almightiness—that's an attribute he'll use—you're fused with the reality and that's God. So he's right, he was *fused* with love. And when you're fused with love you can't deny it's a delight, sheer joy that is present, and the sheer life that you feel... life in yourself.

Now having had that experience I can prophesy for him: All the things that I have told in my books that I've had as mystical experience happened *after* that experience. And so, he can look forward to all these experiences. Where he'll come upon a scene like this and he will know, for now there's life in him, and he will arrest an activity in him and arrest as it's seen on the screen. He will arrest it and not a thing can move while he holds it still within him. Then he'll release it; then all will continue on its way. And he will prove for himself that he has life in himself. That's going to happen to him, as surely as I'm standing here. For everything that I have recorded happens after the fusion with God. Early dreams as a child, they were all preliminary, preparatory; but that was really the beginning of it all, that fusion with God.

And the night that I was called and brought into that state I certainly didn't expect it. If anyone had told me that very day of coming in the very presence of God and seeing God as man, I might have smiled, I might have. Therefore I can't blame anyone who smiles when I tell them that I met God, and God in presenting himself to me presented himself in the human form. And that the human form is truly love divine, it's all love. And the fusion is so intense it's a melting right in him, without loss of identity. So, every one of us will be one day united in that body, so we will have union *and* equality and diversity…no loss of identity whatsoever.

So you hear this night that God only acts. I do not know your background, not all of you, your religious background, what you believe in. As far as I am concerned, *true* religion is really a devotion to the most *exalted* reality of which one has experience. So this experience of this gentleman with the fusion with God is something he could *never* forget. And no priest in this world, or rabbi in this world, could in any way divorce him from that union. He will listen like a gentleman, occasionally, to any argument they have to present, but they could never persuade him to give up the notion. It's not a notion. This is a reality beyond anything that one who has not had it could ever conceive. So you couldn't present any argument to divert a man after the union with God. You will allow any argument, listen to it carefully, but you can't listen to the point of being deflected. First of all, you can't get out of the union; you're part of God. Fused with God, you could never in eternity ever be separated from God. There's no power in the world that could do it, because God is more powerful. And no power could take you out of the body of God, after you're invited into it and fuse with it.

So tonight, you take that. At least one person here, others have told me too, they're all coming towards the grand, really, the *only* end, which is the fulfillment of God's promise. But, that you must wait for and wait for it patiently. He said, "Wait for the promise of the Father." Just wait, because you can't earn it. When it comes it's a gift, a complete gift. And then all the other things, they'll come with it. But in the meanwhile, his law being conditional, you need not remain as you are if you don't like what you are for one second beyond hearing the law. You can take the law this night knowing who God is. If God is doing it and all things are possible to God, well, then it's done. I don't care what it is, it's done if it's all God doing it. If a "little" you is doing it and you take someone you know, can't do it. But the minute you know that imaginal acts are God's acts; that God actually became you that you may become God and that you are all Imagination; and God and you are one, therefore, if he actually became you and he acts *in* you—the only thing *in* you that is completely…that you could say all things are possible to it, is your Imagination. You can't think of anything in this world outside of your Imagination that you can say of it "with it all things are possible" because almost everything else is impossible.

You think of the things that you would like to do, and how many things are impossible if you take the little you of flesh and blood; but take yourself as Imagination, can't you imagine anything in this world, but anything? If you can imagine it and actually accept the imaginal act as fact and wait in confidence that the imaginal act has all the power necessary and the plan wrapped within itself to externalize itself. And while he was here, 1,500 miles away, this imaginal act was taking the old gentleman and making him do something that would outrage the entire neighborhood. The old gentleman and his daughter would be totally unaware that an unseen imaginal act was cause of his behavior. Because they would say, "What on earth is he doing?" Or, "what, in a household of that sort, with a daughter who is so gracious and so noble, and to have a father like that, how could he possibly do it?" We would judge him harshly. The real culprit, if there's a culprit, was hidden 1,500 miles away. And he did it through love. He so loved his mother he wanted his mother free and be separated without killing the grandfather.

And so, you do it this way. Do it in love. Every time you exercise your Imagination lovingly on behalf of another as he did, you're mediating God to that other. And so, he mediated God to his mother, and only that act of the grandfather would have forced her to the decision. So she told him, "I have to make a decision and I'm going to move." Then he comes forward and says, "I'll make a decision, too. I am moving, I am moving back to my home of my origin, really, fifty miles from here. Well, that's near enough, isn't it? I mean, you're not the only ones ___(??)." Fifty miles is a long way to walk at ninety-five years. And so she can go visit him and see him, and leave him just where he is with his friends. All the meals are good, she said in her letter, for I read her letter. He was very gracious and loaned his mother's letter to me, and just as I've told you what he told me the mother told him. And he need not be that curious to find out what he did...that is unimportant. Whatever he did he outraged the people to the point where something had to be done, and a move was in order, and the move became a fact.

So, I'm asking you to take me seriously. And when you sit down this night in the Silence or when you go home and you are with yourself and gathered together and you imagine anything, do it lovingly. Of a friend, do it lovingly and believe it's *done*! That's God in action and with God all things are possible. You don't have to aid it, leave it alone. It's going to actually move itself through all, and all things being interwoven they will take anyone in the world that it can use to embody itself. And, therefore, forgive all when you become the man or the woman you want to be. All those who seemingly tried to oppose you on your forward motion were aiding you, but you didn't know it. Therefore, forgive them all in the end. A bird couldn't fly unless opposed, a fish couldn't swim unless opposed, a plane couldn't take off, you couldn't walk, nothing in this world could really move unless opposed. So if you have opponents, then they're only playing the part. Because you dared to assume that you are the man, the woman, that you want to be, they had to come to give the necessary opposition. Without that you wouldn't move.

Now let us go into the Silence.

Q: (inaudible)

A: ___(??) a noble, noble end. It need not be for yourself, it could be for a friend...(tape runs out.)

JESUS OR BARABBAS?

3/24/64

___(??) John is my favorite, really. So in the 18th chapter of the gospel of John, Pilate is speaking to the Jews. And he turned to the Jews and he said, "You have a custom that I should release one man for you at the Passover; who would you have me release, the King of the Jews?" And, they cried out, "Not this man, but Barabbas!" Then he adds, "Now Barabbas was a robber" (verse 39-40).

Now, we know nothing of any such amnesty as a custom. It is not attested outside of the gospel. You can't find it as a custom at all; therefore, it's a mystery. We have to start digging for the mystery, for it's not a custom. And so we are told, just like an aside, Barabbas was a robber. So you have to start searching the scriptures to find out what is this robber, where is he? Now, listen to it carefully—also in John, you'll find this in the 10th chapter of the gospel of John—"He who does not enter the sheepfold by the door but climbs in by another way, that man is a thief and a robber; but he who enters by the door is the shepherd of the sheep. The gatekeeper opens to him; the sheep hear his voice, and he calls his own sheep by name and leads them out" (verses 1-7). Then we are told, "They did not understand what he was saying to them, and so he said to them again, 'Truly, truly I say to you, I am the door of the sheep.'" They didn't understand him. Any attempt to acquire anything in this world without the consciousness of the thing that you would acquire makes you a thief and a robber. The consciousness of health produces health; the consciousness of wealth produces wealth. You could inherit this very night a million dollars. Without the consciousness of wealth you'd spend it, you'd waste it; in fact, it would vanish from you. You can't hold it. You can only hold that which you are aware of being. So the story is a revelation to man.

Now you pass judgment: "Without me you can do nothing." Honestly, nothing? That's what we are told. "If you abide in me and I abide in you, then you will bear much fruit, but apart from me you can do nothing" (John 15:5). So you pass judgment, will you accept it? May I tell you, you are not going to find him outside of yourself. Tonight, there are in this country of ours, well, hundreds...how many millions? One hundred ninety million they claim? Well, take the world...they claim a billion Christians are in the world. I hate to be harsh in my judgment, but I don't imagine that an nth part of an nth part of one percent have accepted Jesus. They think they've accepted him, but they haven't, because they have some image of a being on a wall, or some being in their mind's eye that they turn to mentally as Jesus. And that's not Jesus. Jesus is your own wonderful human Imagination. When you say "I am," that's he. Will you trust him? No, I trust another Jesus, well, then you don't know Jesus. By him all things are made, and you can easily find him if you accept that claim: "Apart from me you can do nothing."

Alright, here is a simple story told me this week. A man remembers the place in Denver where he slept, and by his own confession in his case history as I received it yesterday morning, he said he slept in a basement, next to a deep freeze. And so, he didn't tell me why he wanted to return to Denver...just to experiment...and so in his Imagination he slept in the same basement next to the deep freeze. Just one night he assumed that he was there. Physically he was here, but in his Imagination he slept there. The next day was Sunday, so he called on a friend, and while at the man's table the man turned to him, casually, and said, "By the way, how would you like to go to Denver? We're going to Denver to visit my brother and how would you like to make the trip with us?" A gift! The very next day another party said to him, casually, "How would you like to go to Denver?" Of all the things in the world, two invitations to go to Denver! He, in Imagination, occupied a state and the state is Denver, and then in twenty-four hours, one invitation, in forty-eight hours, the second.

Who did it? "Apart from me you can do nothing"—well, hasn't he found Jesus? Then who was Jesus? Wasn't Jesus his own wonderful human Imagination? Well, who was doing it?—apart from him you can do nothing. If I saw you reading a book, well, who's doing it?—Jesus. I am reading a book; apart from me you can't read a book; apart from me you can do nothing. You can't be anything other than through the consciousness of being it. And so, will we accept Jesus? It's the only Jesus in the world. I don't care what the world will tell me, *that* is Jesus. He creates everything in the world, and apart from him you can do nothing. "If you abide in me and I abide in you, then you'll bear much fruit." If you do not abide in me, then you're severed from the vine, for "I AM the vine."

So here, the trial takes place, and "You'll have me release one, and who will you have me release, the King of the Jews?" They said, "No, Barabbas." So they chose Barabbas, and Barabbas rules over them to this day. On one level you take it that way. On a deeper level, when you come to another portion of John, he said, "Now that you have found me, don't let me go but let all these go." And, therefore, if you don't let *me* go, well, then you've released the robber from consciousness...on another level. But on the level that we treated here this night, man has chosen Barabbas and he would not accept as his leader, as his God, Jesus. No matter how many statues you have of Jesus, how many paintings you think you have of him, you've never really seen him until you see him; and when you see him you see yourself. That's the grand I AM. And the day will come you'll meet him—you look right into the face of yourself, beautified, glorified beyond your wildest dream, and it's self. That's Jesus.

And so, you either accept him or you reject him. If you reject him, then you've made your choice and you've taken Barabbas, Barabbas the thief and the robber. Man tries morning, noon and night to become other than what he is conscious of being and he can't do it. You could this night simply assume that you are the man, the woman that you want to be...just a mere assumption that you are it. Then looking into the face of others—mentally, of course—and let them see you as they would see you were it true—do *nothing* to make it so but nothing—and it will become so. You will actually grow into the character that you've assumed that you are, whether it be a rich man, a poor man, a wise man, a fool, anything in this world. You choose it, you choose the man, the woman that you want to be, and dare to assume that you are it. If you dare to assume that you are it and sleep as though you were, well, then you will become it. And then you have found him.

How did I find him? Well, "By him all things were made and without him there's nothing made that is made" (John 1:3). So if you become it, then you've found the maker of the thing that you become; and you've found Jesus. You've found him as your own wonderful, loving, human Imagination. And, may I tell you, I use the word loving advisedly, for when you meet him he's infinite love. Everything in the world that you thought, well, inanimate and not alive, and certainly if it was alive, indifferent to all that's taking place in the world, and one day you have an experience where it isn't so at all: It's all love. But everything in the world is love, and it's all God, and God is your own wonderful I-am-ness.

So tonight, you pass judgment on it. You can accept it or reject it. I know you would find it difficult to have such confidence in *this* form of Jesus, in this reality that is Jesus. It's so much easier to lean upon another, to get on that telephone and call a friend, have the friend do it for you, or call a teacher, or in between, the doctor, the dentist, someone else...but not self. And so, to actually assume full responsibility and take the whole thing upon self, and call that Jesus, it's so much more difficult. But may I tell you, eventually you're going to do it. Everyone will accept the only Jesus, and that's the *only* Jesus. There is no other and there never was another, in spite of the one billion this night who believe in another.

And so, the one of whom I speak this night, you'll find him if you look carefully and dig. You'll find it. All was told in the gospels. So I ask you to believe in this Jesus. I've found him...would like to share it with you, share what I've found with you. As you're told, he who sent me, I'm just like him. He who sees me sees him who sent me; and he who receives anyone I send receives me. He who receives me receives him who sent me. Then you get right back to the one who sent me. Well, how could I be sent by myself? I *am* sent by myself. I am then self-begotten? Yes, begotten by myself. And the being that I really am is the being that in my blindness I thought lived centuries ago and lived elsewhere, and he wasn't there at all. I'm not saying it's the easiest thing in this world to accept, but accept it you will one day if you have not already accepted it. My hope is that you will accept it, if you haven't so far, accept it tonight. Let your judgment be: I will accept the King of the Jews. The King of the Jews?—well, who is he?—I AM. When you go into the world, "Go and tell them I AM has sent you" (Exod. 3:14).

So sit quietly and prove that I am he. When you do it, you'll prove it and no power in the world can stop you from proving it. Having proved it you are free of all idols. But man has made of Jesus the grand I AM, have made of him an idol. You don't believe in the Lord Jesus and be saved. Well, the word Lord is I AM. Believe in the I AM that is *my I am* and be saved...you and your household. But man when you use the word Jesus, he always thinks in terms of *a* man, living elsewhere, or who lived 2,000 years ago. He never thinks of Jesus as I AM...and that's how you spell the name. It's really Yod He Vau Shin Ayin. The Shin is put into it for a very good reason. Rather than Yod He Vau He, it's Yod He Vau Shin Ayin. Shin is a consuming flame which enables every man in this world not only to create but to unmake what he's made. He makes something. If he had to live with it forever, then he couldn't unmake it. So a Shin is put into the name of the creative power of God. For Yod He Vau He is God, I AM; but I AM-in-action, which is imagining, a Shin is in the name. The Shin is a consuming flame—its symbol is a tooth. A tooth crushes, it consumes.

And so, I make something; I don't like it now; I want to unmake it. Were it not that I contain within myself a Shin, I couldn't unmake it, I couldn't undo my mistakes. But I can undo *all* my mistakes when I know who made the mistake. I made it, I can unmake it. So a Shin is in my name. The last one is an eye, an Ayin, and that is an eye. I see clearly what I want to see, in spite of the facts of life, and if imagining creates reality, well, then I can create. I don't have to limit my vision to the facts of life; for I make facts, I create facts. So he creates all the facts of the world by knowing who he is.

So I will now say, will you release Barabbas and hold onto Jesus, or will you now pick Barabbas and reject Jesus? That's entirely up to you. No one in this world can force him on you, because, really, in one sense of the word, real spirituality is the gradual transition from a God of tradition to a God of experience. And so, when you have the experience you know that's all there is to it. You don't have to turn to anyone in the world to ask them, "Did it really work because I did so and so?" Ask no one, try again and see.

Now the same gentleman who told me the story of Denver, he writes of a lady. Because of an age condition she couldn't get a job, couldn't find a job because you're beyond a certain age limit. So she turned to him and asked him to help. He said, "It only took forty-eight hours. I simply imagined that she told me that she had a job, a good job, and she liked the job. In forty-eight hours she was employed and now working for the Civil Service." He said she said to him before he imagined, "Should I lie about my age?" He said, "No, don't lie about your age, they'll find out. They have ways of finding out. Tell them your age, just what you are. I don't care what they tell you about your age, you tell them exactly how old you are." In forty-eight hours she was working. Yet prior to that she was turned down, turned down, turned down. All that he did was simply he imagined that she told him that she had a marvelous job and she loved it, and they loved her, the entire office staff. That's *all* that he did.

Well, "If apart from me you can do nothing"—and who is speaking?—Jesus—well, then who is Jesus? What did the man do? If I said to him, "What are you doing?" "*I am* imagining that she has a job." Well, he told me Jesus is doing it, but he didn't use the word Jesus as the world thinks... but he did, because Jesus is I AM. And so, in everyone Jesus is buried, but everyone. We carry him within us. Within our bodies, we are told, we carry the death of Jesus. That's what we are told in Corinthians (2 Cor. 4:10): "In our bodies we carry the death of Jesus." Because man is unaware of him, and that of which I am unaware doesn't exist for me. A thing has no existence for a man save through the consciousness that he has of it. So the man is totally unaware that he is carrying the actual death of Jesus within him; that he bears on his body the marks of Jesus. He said, "Henceforth let no one trouble me; for I bear on my body the marks of Jesus." But if I don't know it, well, then it doesn't exist for me. I could read these words over and over, say, in Galatians (6:17), but if I don't know it, if I haven't had the experience that I actually bear on my body the marks of Jesus, well, then I don't know it.

So, I can tell you, and maybe you yourself can read it, but you have to experience it. So we are gradually moving from a God of tradition which is the false concept of God to a God of experience where man experiences God; and then he knows. And then you find Jesus, and having found him, do not let him go. "Now that you've found me," he said, "let these go, but don't let me go." This takes place in the garden prior to the trial. So they come out with staves to find one in the darkness of the night. They can't see him because this is a dark night. He said, "Whom do you seek?" Well, "We seek Jesus." "*I am* he." These are the words; I'm quoting, "I *am* he." Didn't say I am Jesus…I am he. And so they all fell to the ground. Now, you can't conceive of hundreds of people hearing a man from the dark say, "I am he," and that all would fall to the ground, would they? The shock was so great when man discovers it he mentally falls to the ground. The whole thing is taking place *in* man. I can't believe it, for Mother taught me that this was a little boy who was born unnaturally; God came into the world in this peculiar, marvelous way; and that he rose to manhood; then died for us; he was sacrificed on a wooden cross. That's what she taught me and that's what I believed. That's what I was flogged for when I went to school, because I misquoted a passage of scripture, and so, beaten unmercifully by some sadist. But, that's not the story.

And when I heard it, I heard it from the lips of one who was not born a Christian. I heard it from the lips of one who was not in the Caucasian race, he was a Negro. Here I actually heard the *mystery,* Christianity. But what a blow to me! Everything that I believed in tumbled within me. I represented that crowd seeking Jesus, and I thought I would hear from him something comparable to what I heard from my mother, and it wasn't. The shock was so great; whatever I held within me that was dear all fell to the ground. I had to rebuild my world from ashes practically, and then gradually begin to believe in a *true* Jesus, and prove it. He said, "Come prove me and see. Come test me and see" (2 Cor. 13:5). So, how could I test him? Then you start to test him. For could I imagine that I am what at the moment reason denies, what anyone would deny that I could ever become, and dare to simply assume that I am it? Not that I'm *going* to become it, that I am *already* that being, and sleep as though I really am? And then, in a way that I could not devise, that I'd become that being? I actually mold myself into the very likeness of the being that I dared to assume that I am. Becoming it…then I've found him.

Then, when you began to discuss it, wise men tried to dethrone you. Two years ago, back in Barbados, my two nephews came out from Cambridge. They just recently graduated in medicine. We were discussing on the beach and one, Michael, said to me, "Uncle Neville, you don't believe in Jesus?" I said, "Michael, I believe more in Jesus than one hundred million people who claim they believe in Jesus. Put all their beliefs together, it would not equal my belief in Jesus." "But, Uncle Neville, you say that as a man that man wasn't born from a woman called Mary." I said, "But, Michael, I am Mary. I am Mary." He said, "Uncle Neville, how could you be Mary?" "I am Mary, I am Mary and birth to Christ must give. I have to give birth to Christ; I am Mary. And so, I've found him. And I was actually blessed because I gave birth to him, actually became him. I didn't give birth to something other than myself, Michael, I gave birth to myself. I actually gave birth to my own being. And then, when I gave birth to it, I discovered who I really am. For the one that called him, ___(??)of the great mystery, the same one called me Father. Therefore, who am I, Michael?"

He said, "What you're telling me doesn't make sense, Uncle Neville. You're telling me, without using these words, you're going all around the circle to try to tell me that you think you are he?" I said, "I don't have to think it, Michael, I am he, but so are you. But you don't know it yet. You don't know it yet and you're denying him, although you think that you have found him. And you think...you have six years at Cambridge, and your brother Roger he has six years at Cambridge; you married two lovely girls—one an ardent Catholic and one from Scotland, I dare say a good Presbyterian—-and the four of you really believe in Jesus and your Uncle Neville doesn't believe in Jesus. But I have found Jesus, the *living* Jesus. Not something that died 2,000 years ago but something that is alive in all of us. But you've got to find him. And so, I will tell you about Jesus, if you will listen, and then you pass judgment. You either accept *that* Jesus or you reject him, it's entirely up to you." And we had these lovely discussions on the beach. But I left him unmoved, completely unmoved. He has to go through...he's a doctor and he knows that you go into the lab and he makes up his little potions and he simply gets results today and maybe not tomorrow under similar conditions. One day he's going to find Jesus, because everyone must find him. When he finds him, he believes in him. "Believe in the Lord Jesus and be saved, you and your household." Take your whole household with you and save them by actually turning only to Jesus, and Jesus is your own wonderful, loving human Imagination...that's Jesus.

So you find him, and when you find him you test him. As you test him and he proves himself in the testing, you try to share with others what you have found and hope they will listen. Listen to the words: "One was on his way from Jerusalem armed with letters to all the synagogues that if he found anyone along the way who were the people of The Way, he would bring them bound into Jerusalem. And on the way, looking for people who belonged to The Way, he heard a voice and the voice said, 'Saul, Saul, why persecutest thou me?' Who are you, Lord? And the voice answered, 'Jesus'" (Acts 9:4). But Jesus in Hebrew is Joshua and Joshua is I AM. He heard it from the depths of his soul, the being from within himself. And they were the people of The Way…alright, go back and read the story. How is The Way defined in scripture? He said, "I am the way." The way to what? The way to everything in the world but specifically to the Father: "I am the way; and no one comes to the Father, but by me" (John 14:6). You can't possibly come to the Father save you come by me. And so, who are you?—well, I AM.

The strange part about it, when you meet the one Son who calls you Father, his name in scripture was I AM...the name was Jesse. So you see you can't come to the Father but by me. Well, who are you? I am, I am he. So "I am the way, I am the truth, I am the life" revealed. I am everything, but I am the way to all things. And I am the truth. So if I am the truth, then truth need not be confined to facts. A true judgment need not conform to the external fact to which it relates. That's a piano, I know, but I may desire something in the place of the piano. I must begin to see in my mind's eye what I want to see there instead of a piano. If I persist in seeing it, I'm not going to go mad, someone's going to come in here and say, "You know, we're going to change this entire place." And they think they initiated the desire to remove the piano and put the flower that I'm seeing there. They will take full credit for the change in this room when they are only executing the imaginal act of one who was persistent in that act, and just didn't accept anything other than what he imagined. So they go forward and change the things to conform to someone imagining, and that one imagining has found his Christ. He's found him and he isn't going elsewhere.

So tonight the great trial is on, this whole week, and they'll tell the story this coming Friday. I know many a wet eye will be in the churches this Friday, because I, myself, as a boy when they dramatized it as they did they always made me cry. So they dramatize the story, three hours this coming Friday, and if you are emotionally given to life, you will cry too the way they dramatize it. But that's not the story. They should cry for the one billion who have rejected him and they think they have accepted him. They have not accepted Christ. If they accepted him, they wouldn't make all the preparations to defend themselves as they do. They would simply know that he is love, *infinite* love. And the day will come you will have experiences that all who have found him have, and they will find everything speaking love, but everything...without the aid of mescaline, without the aid of any artificial, I would say, injection. You don't have to.

One day you will actually look at this room, or look at the street, or look at any place, and suddenly the whole thing comes alive to you. The whole thing will come alive. Even though after the experience it goes back to its normal, you can never forget the experience—the whole thing was alive. When I say alive, it was communing and it was all love. The so-called inanimate things, all love. You and I were placed here, as Blake said, "Put on earth a little space that we may learn to bear the beams of love." We can't bear them yet. We are put here a little space to *learn* to bear the beams of love. For the day will come that you are one with the whole vast creative power of the universe, and you *are* it. You'll see the whole thing was made out of love; there's no other substance in the world. But while we're in it, so much of it seems horrible.

So, I'm asking you today to go back and read it and bring in your own verdict. For *you* are the Pilate, and *you* are Jesus, and *you're* Barabbas; and the drama takes place *in you.* So as you read the story let the whole thing take place in you. Will I ___(???) Barabbas as the world has done, or will I take now Jesus? And so, hold on to Jesus and then live by him morning, noon and night. Walk just as though you were he...don't be embarrassed. Now, for what was he condemned? We're told in the scriptures ask the question, what was it? He said, "Why do you stone me? For what good work do you stone me?" and they answered, "Not for any good work but for blasphemy; because you, being a man, make yourself God" (John 10:32). Aren't you a man? Well, that was what he was stoned for—blasphemy, because being a man he dared to make himself God. For he said, "I and my Father are one...and my Father is he whom you call God; only I know my Father and you know not your God; and my Father and I are one" (John 8:19; 10:30). So they took up stones to cast at him. Not stones from the street but all the facts of life. For they knew exactly where this man, who dared to claim that he is God, where he was born, they knew his entire environment, they knew the family life, everything about him. And he dared to make this bold claim, and so, for blasphemy he was stoned with the facts of life.

For he claimed he was not of this world. The day will come you'll have an experience which is not in this world, an experience far more real than anything here. You will know you are not in this world. Your earthly father, yes you honor him, you love him, but you know he's not your father. And you can't point to anyone who is your father; you have no father. You're like Melchizedek: you have no father, you have no mother, you have no ancestors, for you're one with the cause that is the origin of all; therefore, you have no ancestor. Because, actually, the only one that could call you Father was the one that God said, "You are my son" (Psalm 2:7). If he called God Father and then he called you Father, and God has no ancestor, then who are you? You're one with the origin that caused it all to come into being.

So isn't that blasphemy? Isn't that the most arrogant claim in the world, a simple, little you, man? These are the words, "I stone you for blasphemy, because you, being man, dare to claim that you are God." Who else can claim it? And so, you don't talk about it. This is all a mystery. It's all written in our scripture for us that man, really, suddenly becomes aware that it's all about himself. It's not about someone else, it's all about himself. He goes back and reads it. He can hardly believe it until the visions begin to appear within him, and one after the other confirms this impression that he is the one spoken of in scripture. And then the entire thing unfolds within him, word after word, and then he knows that the whole thing is true. But it's true of everyone in this world. And so, go and tell it in the hope that they will accept it.

So when the one heard it, "Lord Jesus, have I been persecuting you?" and then the voice came from within him, "I am he." So he then stood in the presence of a judge. This one, well, this judge was now a king, King Agrippa, and he said to him, "Why should it be thought incredible by any of you that God raises the dead?" He had the experience; for he tells us in the very first chapter of Galatians he had the experience. He said, "When it pleased God to reveal his Son in me, I conferred not with flesh and blood" (verse 16). So the Son was revealed *in* him. Doesn't name the Son, but the Son revealed *in him* was David, and David called him Father. Then he knew the ancient scripture for the first time. He went out to persecute all the people belonging to The Way, for he didn't quite know the definition of The Way was "I am the way." So he thought there was some little ism gathered together, and then when he had it revealed to him—for it pleased God to reveal his Son in me and when it pleased God to reveal his Son in me, I conferred not with flesh and blood. To whom would I go? So, you will have it, everyone will have it.

But in the meantime, believe me. Don't believe in Neville, believe in Christ within yourself. Believe in your own wonderful I-am-ness. Believe there. Accept him one hundred percent as Lord. Believe in the Lord, the I AM, my I am...and be saved. Saved from what?—saved from anything that now is my problem. If I am unemployed and an employment is my solution to my problem, believe I am gainfully employed. If today I am unwell and a state of health is my solution to my problem, dare to claim, as told us in the Book of Joel: "Let the weak man say, 'I am strong'" (3:10). While he's weak, let him say, "I am strong" and let him persuade himself that that claim is true. Tomorrow or the next day, the not distant future, he begins to radiate the health that he *dared* to claim that is his. Well, he calls upon whose name? He called upon the name of God, because he was saying, "*I am* strong!" That's what we are told in the Book of Joel. Let the weak man say, "I am strong"; let the poor man say, "I am rich"; let the unknown say, "I am known" if that's what he wants in this world. And everything comes into his world because he's called upon the only name that can respond and create in this world. There's no other name under heaven by which man is saved save *the* name. Well, in the scripture, when you read it the name is Jesus. But get it into your mind the word Jesus actually means I AM, that's what it means. So this night, when you go to bed let your prayer be simply an internal communion with self, and dare to clothe yourself in your assumption just as though it were fact and live in it just as though it's true. May I tell you, it will become true.

So the choice is man's—Barabbas or Jesus—just as simple as that. And the world has rejected Jesus even though a billion claim that they've accepted him. That's why I told you the story of my two nephews...and I speak for all the family. I had my two brothers in New York this past November—one is a doctor, the father of these two doctors, and the other one is the head of all the businesses. Well, we didn't get into deep discussions, but at intervals we would. But Lawrence, the doctor, and Victor, the businessman, they can't go along with me. Yet they wanted to see every church in New York City. I saw more churches this past November. I went to all churches, lovely feeling, all of them pealing out lovely organ music, everything was lovely about it. But I didn't feel any different when I came out. But they loved to just sit in the silence and drink in something lovely, perfectly alright. But I went from church to church, Catholic churches, all the Protestant churches, every kind of church, and so they loved it. But we didn't get into the deep discussion concerning what these things represented.

I took them to St. Thomas' church, this glorious painting, these glass stained windows, beauties! On one side, looking north, tapestries, and I said to my brother Victor, "You see these tapestries?" "Yes." I said, "You know, behind them are the most glorious stained glass windows, but the tapestry hides them." He said, "Why?" I said, "Because a man who has built so many churches in this country, who gave them, his name was Rockefeller (this was the first one who made the billions) and he had a fight with the bishop of this church (this is St. Thomas' church). His home came right up against the wall, the north wall of the church, St. Thomas' church, so he built a spite wall, built it right up to the very top of St. Thomas' church. Couldn't stop him, it was his property, his money, his bricks, and the whole thing was blocked out so not one little ray of light could enter that church from the north. But when you look to the west...the glorious burst of light; when you look south...all these lovely lights coming through the stained glass windows. But here, they couldn't have that blackness—because you saw the glass but not a thing coming through--so someone gave these beautiful tapestries. But it should all be nothing but sheer beautiful light coming through.

So here, he built a lovely church on Riverside Drive. Riverside Drive and 125th Street is this wonderful church that Rockefeller built. But he left a Will that no one can break, for the old boy has been gone for years. His son couldn't break it and his grandsons can't break it and their sons can't break it. He so left that Will…that wall cannot be brought down; and so, all was done in the name of Jesus Christ, for he was a good Baptist. He gave millions and millions to the Baptists. He's a good Baptist. The bishop is the head of the Episcopal church, St. Thomas' on 53rd Street and the ___(??). So here I tell you, let us find the real Jesus. Victor didn't find him in that church. And when I told the story to Vic, he said, "Well, I always thought much of that man. I admired him as a businessman, but now he's gone all the way down in my estimation" because he saw what spite could do. Yet he died believing he was a believer in Jesus. Never found him.

But now don't you die from this little sphere without finding him. If tonight you're disturbed, you take it under submission, take it home with you, and sleep on it, and feel the nearness of Jesus as your own wonderful human Imagination. I can't begin to tell you when you accept him in the true sense what begins to happen within you. You become alive, something in the head becomes alive, and you can feel it. May I tell you, long before the experience of the birth from above, I began to sense something alive in my skull, actually could feel a pulsing, a pulsation alive in the skull. You could feel it move up and move down, move all over. At night you go to bed...that lovely sensing something alive. I dare say you can call that spiritual pregnancy. And so, all of a sudden when I least expected it, the event happened as recorded; and not a thing changed, just as told in scripture. Well, if he is the only one who is born that way, and I know I was, then am I not he? And when you duplicate the same experience, are you not he? And if only Jesus is born that way, haven't you found Jesus, because you've found him as your own I-am-ness. Because when you awake, *you* are awake; and you come out, it's *you* coming out. Then three men come and take away the body, and the body's all taken away, and three men are there. You know the three men of scripture and there they are. Every symbol is true and perfect. The wind that you are told in the 2nd chapter of the Book of Acts (verse 2) that same strange unearthly wind is present. So when you go through the experience, the identical experience, are you not he?

There's only one—-that's I am. You can say it in the depths of your soul, just say "I am"...that's he. But now begin to believe it. And then you test him and he proves himself in the testing. What chance would you put it down to—a man sleeping only in Imagination in Denver just as a joke? But he sleeps there, next to the deep freeze in the basement, and then casually calls on a friend the next day, and the man turns to him without prompting and asks him if he'd like to make the trip to Denver, that he's going to see his brother.; and then the very next day another invitation to go to Denver. How could you cast that aside as a mere coincidence? That's not! You can try it tonight. I tell you, I tried it and I don't ever do it any more just as a joke, because whenever I do it it's going to work. When I least expect it I'm on my way to fulfill that journey…when I don't want to make the journey. I am moved under compulsion, for outer moments are compelled; it's the inner motion that is self-determined, that is causal. All the outer motions are all under compulsion. And so, I don't want to do it now and make it real—and then tomorrow, when I don't want to go be moved by compulsion, I had to go. So don't treat it lightly, for he will hold you not responsible for it, and he doesn't care because he's doing it. Who's doing it?—your own wonderful human Imagination.

Tonight you bring in your verdict. Don't tell me, just sit there quietly and say, "I will accept that Jesus" or "I don't accept it. I prefer the one that my mother taught about, the one that I have at home in a book, where I can look at the picture of something." So if you want that Jesus, alright, I wouldn't take him from you. Go on with that Jesus until you find the *living* Jesus. That's why you're told, "It does not yet appear what we shall be, but we know when he appears we shall be like him" (1 John 3:2). So always ask yourself, Do I look like him in my mind's eye? No? Well, then he hasn't yet appeared, because when he appears you're going to be like him. You're going to see exactly your own being magnified and beautified to the nth degree. That's the being.

Now let us go into the Silence.

* * *

___(??) Jung's book, a few copies I noticed tonight before I came on. And then my books are there. If there's any other book you would like that's not displayed, you ask them to get it for you and they'll get it for you. On your way out stop and browse.

Now are there any questions, please? Yes, sir?

Q: In the third lecture you quoted, "And God became"…I'm trying to recall exactly what it was… "God became man and was no more?" or something of that nature.

A: No, I said, God became as we are that we may be as he is. God became man that man may become God. That is told us in the story: "He emptied himself and took upon himself the form of a slave." That thought is told us in Philippians (2:7). And so, he empties himself. In other words, people will ask, as I have been asked, "How can you claim, how can you conceive of a cosmic Christ as personal, or a personal Christ as cosmic?" My answer to that is the 8th chapter of Romans, "The whole vast creation waits eagerly for the unveiling of the sons of God" (verse 19). And so, it's really the plan and purpose of the whole creation.

God actually became you as you are seated there...or you couldn't breathe. He will not in eternity leave you until his purpose is consummated; and then he can't leave you because you're going to be fused with him. When you are once fused with God no power in the world can "un-fuse" you, can't be. You cleave to her…you are God's emanation, my emanation, yet my bride, until the sleep of death is past. So the sleep begins in the second chapter: "And God caused a profound sleep to fall upon man" (Gen. 2:21). It's himself. And he slept, and then came an emanation, called his wife, his bride—we call it Eve. You are Eve; you are the bride of the Lord. As told you in the 54th chapter of Isaiah, "Your Maker is your husband, the Lord of hosts is his name" (verse 5). If you have a husband, then you are the Maker's bride. Therefore the emanation is called the bride, and he cleaves to his emanation, his bride until they become one flesh, one being.

So that's the purpose. You must leave everything...but you do not leave your emanation. He so fell in love with you—it's all love—that he cleaves to you, his love, his beloved, until you become one. You're going to be fused. So one day, you'll be fused, and after you are fused you can't be un-fused. Not in eternity could you ever be un-fused after the fusion. And you fuse always with love. But love, in the way I use it, includes everything—all the powers, wisdom, might—but love. And you're fused with love. At the moment of fusion you've never known such joy, such delight, in your life, never. You cannot from then on be un-fused. You can truly say, "He who sees me sees him who sent me," because we are fused. You may not like the way he looks, but it's true nevertheless, because we can't be un-fused anymore.

You, Bill.

Q: What is the meaning, Neville, of the statement—I don't know if I have the exact words here, "No greater love hath he than he who lays down his life for his friend"?

A: No greater love hath any man…well, that's told us in the Book of John, too. "He who would lay down his life for his friends...I call you hereafter not slaves but friends. No greater love has any man than a man lays down his life for his friend" (John 15:13). Well, you are that friend and God laid his life down for you. He actually became you. No one could cross the threshold that admits to conscious life unaided by that death of God. He actually became you, in the extreme sense, because he completely forgot who he was in becoming you. And then he awakens when the work is completed, and that is completed at fusion. Then after fusion comes the unfolding of these marvelous mystical experiences, all recorded in scripture, as a unique birth from above and an ascent in the form of a serpent. You waken to find that, really, the tomb that they're all talking about this past year, the great religious procession into the Middle East to find it and they all claim they found it, isn't there at all. The great tomb in which God himself entered that is death's door was your skull. That's Golgotha. One day you will awake and you awake to find yourself entombed. But you'll come out without the help of anyone, no midwife, come right out, self-born out of that tomb.

So we're going to celebrate it this coming Easter. That's the beginning of it all, really. But resurrection apart from death has no meaning. It begins with that mightiest act, the awakening in the tomb, and then you come out. And everything is true. As you're told, they've taken away my body…"they've taken away the Lord's body and I do not know where they've laid it." Well, then you took one little look and here is the body out of which you've just emerged. You're attracted by the wind; you look back and in the twinkle of an eye it's gone, the body's gone. So the story is true, they remove the body. In that one little diversion the body is gone, but in its place sat three men. They come to bear witness, to see this event; for they were told and they came to testify to the truth of what the angels had said. But they can't see you because you are Spirit, more real than they are. So they come to find the *sign*, that's all. And then we are told, told, in spite of all the signs that he did among them, they still did not believe in him.

___(??) You could just take all of these stories that I have told, and I tell you it only happened because men and women used their Imaginations lovingly to do it. I've printed forty in one book; I could have printed a thousand. Had I printed one thousand and I stated quite clearly in every one this is done not by any little magic, this is done because this individual did this all in her Imagination or in his Imagination, so that the cause of everything you read here was all taken back to Imagination; so you read a thousand case histories, you will still say "I don't believe it...it would have happened anyway." If you printed a hundred thousand case histories, they'll say, "No it couldn't be." So you're told in the Book of John that in spite of… although he did so many great signs among them yet they did not believe in him. The number and character of the signs did not evoke faith. If you read the story of the Bible in the Book of John carefully, you will notice that the entire teaching of Jesus, as John tells it, rests upon faith and unbelief in him, one or the other. You either accept it or you don't. But all the teachings of Jesus in the Book of John rest on faith or unbelief in him. Either he believes or he doesn't believe.

Yes, Art?

Q: Would you repeat that a true judgment need not conform to...I didn't get the last part of it.

A: I said a true judgment need not conform to the external fact to which it is related. That's a piano, and so I tell you that's a piano, then my judgment is in harmony with the fact. But if suddenly I am seeing a door there, then that must be hallucination or some idle thought of mine because it doesn't conform to the facts. So I say a true judgment need not conform to the external fact to which it is related, because to me truth depends upon the intensity of imagining. If I can imagine intensely enough, someone will come in here and say that shouldn't be here. Or, maybe, the club people will want it elsewhere for some other purpose and then put in its place what someone is imagining ought to be here.

Q: How do you ___(??) this imaginary ___(??)? For instance, you said that you have to live or feel the consciousness of what you want. But if you're working on a problem of human relationships for an expression of love, and then you find yourself, unconsciously at first, just boiling because it's going the wrong way but yet you've been trying to imagine?

A: Well, at least you're honest about it. And so, if you admit that you know this thing ought to work—"I've been doing it but it hasn't worked"—well, at least you are aware. Well, keep trying. He said, "Lord, how often must I forgive him?" He said, "Seventy times seven." He thought only seven; he said, "Seven times Lord?" "I didn't say seven; seventy times seven." Well, seventy is the numerical value of the sixteenth letter of the Hebrew alphabet, which is an eye, an Ayin; and seven, numerical value of the seventh letter, which is a sword, a Zayin. So you see it until the eye becomes single. You don't see anything else for that individual other than that. But it comes. Because it hasn't worked as yet, you still don't listen to him. When he comes he will not judge by what his eyes see or decide by what his ears hear, when he comes. So when he comes to your mind, then you're not going to judge by what the eyes see or decide by what the ears hear, when he comes.

So this is the one the whole vast world is looking for. And you're told he comes in the form of a little child and a little child shall lead them. This is from the 11th chapter of Isaiah. And so, when he comes, this one from the stem of Jesse, and Jesse is the father of David, so when he comes to confirm your fatherhood he isn't going to judge what his eyes see or decide on what his ears hear. He will only see what he *wants* to see; he will only hear what he wants to hear. He will remain faithful to what he wants to hear and to what he has heard until what he has heard is externalized, for he's creating reality. He's inserted into a world, but he isn't going to accept it as fatal, as final. He's going to change it to make it conform to his ideal, to his dream. If we didn't do that here, we'd still have a wilderness. But our forefathers, as Robert Frost so beautifully brought out, he said, "Our forefathers did not believe in the future, they believed it in." He said, "There's nothing more creative in man than to believe a thing in." So if they believed the mere passage of time would change this fabulous continent, then they were simply believing, and let the thing be wilderness. But no, they didn't believe the passage of time would make any change. They had to believe what they wanted in this world and believe it in. So they went to the end and believed in the end. Then men followed them, took their ideas, their dreams and brought it to pass. So nothing is more important for a man than to believe a thing in.

So your case, my dear, don't give up. Keep up until finally it works. When it works, you've found him. And then you have the satisfaction and a comfort that no one in this world without such a Jesus could ever have, no one. Because, you see, wherever you are he's there too, he's present. He's never too busy to take care of your wants, your needs. And so, wherever you go he goes with you: I'm with you always, even to the ends of this time, end of the age. "I am with you always, even to the end of the age" (Mat. 28:20). I don't see how you could tell it more plainly than you read it in the gospel of John.

Q: And also, he said, I'm closer than your hands and your ___(??).

A: Certainly, nothing is closer than the center of your being which is I AM. You can take out one lung, either one, and live, either kidney and live. Portions of every vital organ can be chopped away, and many vital organs. A spleen, you can take it out ___(??) and portions of those you say you must have, you still live. As far as the members go, chop the whole thing off and you still live. But you can't chop off I AM. That's center, that's God, that's Jesus.

Q: Neville, ___(??) and one of the things that worked so well with us that I'd love to hear you say it again, because it sparked and it ___(??) and that is when you explained about the inner conversations, laying the tracks, remember that?

A: Um huh. Well, there is one chap, Tom, who certainly is a living example because nothing would remove these things from his skin... (tape runs out).

LIFE THROUGH DEATH

3/27/64

___(??) it starts with the crucifixion and ends with the resurrection. But today unnumbered millions attended service and they were taught the story or told the story of God dying to save man. Hundreds of millions undoubtedly attended. I know I did it year after year for unnumbered years, taught the same story, the same cry on the cross. It's so very difficult to change the meaning of an event once certain interpretations are given to that event and become fixed in the public mind. So here, this event was so fixed in my mind I must confess it was difficult to dislodge it, and only revelation could really dislodge it. And so, I hope I can share with you my actual experience in the hope I can dislodge from you that fixed idea that has become fixed in the public mind, and put in its place that which came to me by revelation. You'll find it in the Bible, it's all in scripture; but, unfortunately, although we read the book over and over, we seem to fail when we try to find the one of whom the prophet spoke. We can't find him. We're looking for him in time, although we are told that he's not in your time, it was not for your time. It's for the time to come that this prophecy was made.

So let us now look at it—and you follow me closely—and if you can't remember the words that I'm quoting, I'm quoting from the Book of Romans. You go home and you read the first six verses of the very first chapter. It's Paul's longest letter, his book, or rather, his epistle to the Romans. He starts it with this note, he said, "Paul, a servant of Jesus Christ"—that's how he starts it—"called to be an apostle." Let us stop right there. We'll take the entire few verses...we'll take the first great revelation: "Paul, a servant of Jesus Christ." Nothing is said in scripture of Jesus Christ having servants. The word, really, properly translated is "slave"—a slave of

Jesus Christ. So he confesses in the beginning, Paul, a servant. You've been led to believe, and I was led to believe, that anyone who ministered on the Christian faith, who was a priest, who's a teacher of the Bible, is a servant of Jesus Christ. That's not the interpretation.

Now we turn over to another letter of his, to the Philippians, the 2nd chapter of his letter to the Philippians: "Jesus Christ, though in the form of God, emptied himself and took upon himself the form of a servant, and being born in the likeness of man. Finding himself in the form of man, became obedient unto death, even death upon the cross" (verses 5-8). Paul is confessing that he has discovered the *wearer* of the garment that is Paul. Listen to the first few words, "Paul, a servant of Jesus Christ...Jesus Christ being in the form of God...emptied himself" of an infinite splendor "and took upon himself the form of a servant, and being born in the likeness of men. And finding himself in the form of men, became obedient unto death, even death upon the cross." So Paul is telling us that he discovered the wearer of the garment that he was calling all along Paul, the servant of Jesus Christ.

Now he goes on, Called by God himself and set apart for the gospel of God. And now he tells us what this gospel is. The gospel of his son who was born according to the flesh, born of David; on the human level descended from David; on the spiritual level according to the Spirit. Here, he was designated Son of God, but he tells us *why* he was designated Son of God: By his resurrection from the dead, designated Son of God by his resurrection from the dead. You are wearing the same being, or the same being is wearing this garment. When you say "I am" you named it. I am Neville. You say I am John, I am Robert, I am Grace, I am Mary, so you say I am so-and-so. And you may just as well write this letter and say, "John or Mary, servant of Jesus Christ"; for I am now the slave being worn by Jesus Christ. Now, as I move across the surface of this world, going from experience to experience, at one moment in time I am going to be designated Son of God. Why?—by my resurrection from the dead. I wasn't born that way through the womb of my mother. I didn't know it, and mother didn't know it, my father didn't know it, my brothers didn't know it, no one knew it until it happened in me. So walking across this world, having all the experiences of normal man, one day it happened. And so we are told, he was designated Son of God by his resurrection from the dead. You aren't born from the womb of woman as a Son of God; that's the descendant of David.

Now we are told this came to man, as he tells us in these first six verses, it was given to man through his prophets in the holy scripture. His promise to man came through his prophets in the holy scripture. Well, where did it come? I start reading the scripture and go back to find, if I came out of David as a man, and you came out of David as a man, where was David ever promised that something coming out of David would in some strange way be adopted as the Son of God in full power? So you go back and you read all about David, and you find that it is said to David by the prophet Nathan. And Nathan said to David from God that "The Lord God has said unto me to say unto you, that when your days are fulfilled"—when it is the end as far as this world goes—-"when your days are fulfilled and you lie down with your fathers, I will raise up your son after you, who shall come forth from your body. I will be his father and he shall be my son" (2 Sam. 7:12). Here is man, humanity. On the human level we all came out of David. David is the personification of all the generations of man. So we all come out of the human level, on this human level, out of David. And while we walk the earth wondering, "When is this promise ever going to be fulfilled?" "For ever since the fathers fell asleep all things have continued as they were from the beginning" of the world. So, when, O Lord, when? And we all wait, expecting some peculiar thing to come out of space, and it doesn't come that way. Suddenly one day it comes. It comes in the unique way that no one ever suspected, and to this day they still don't expect it.

So, this day hundreds of millions were told the story incorrectly. They were told of a man, born of a woman; came into this world as the Son of God from the womb of a woman; and then he was crucified on a wooden cross for the redemption of humanity. It isn't so at all. Everyone is the cross that God is nailed to, but everyone. Paul, a slave of Jesus Christ—and Jesus Christ is your own wonderful human Imagination, your own wonderful I-am-ness, and you're nailed on it. But you don't know it. So you walk the earth misled, all are misled, battling everyone in this world until one moment in time, just like a thief out of the night, it happens to you. Now go back to the story told this day. He was placed in a tomb that was hewn out of a stone in which man had never yet been laid: It's your skull. No one was ever laid there but you. It's an entirely new stone completely carved out all for you. And God entered that stone.

Now let us show you the difference between survival and a hundred thousand people die in our world every day. A hundred thousand every day, but none cease to be, all survive. But survival is continuity; resurrection is discontinuity. Now here is the story. Possibly you've had this experience. I know many who have had it, but I will now quote one. No one need know who she is or who he is or they are, because it's a story that many have had. I have told you in the past that every dream is a parable. Its earthly story is secondary to its meaning. But every dream is a parable. And God speaks to man through the medium of dream; he communicates some profound message to the individual. So an individual finds himself clothed in the garments of those who walked this earth 2,000 years ago. Then someone comes towards him...he thinks it may be a play and so he treats it lightly. The man points a gun at him and he said, "Go ahead and shoot." So he shoots and it goes right through his brain and he falls. At the very moment he falls he sees the thing on the floor, just like a costume, and he has survived. The ridiculousness of the whole thing that he hasn't been killed yet here is the body with the bullet through its brain.

Now, two thousand years ago there were no guns. Right away you can rub that out, the literal story, you can take it apart. There was no gun powder known then. So he wore the costume, yes, of, say, 2,000 years ago. Purposely the depth of his soul is trying to show him something. It could not be reincarnation, because 2,000 years ago you could not have been shot by any bullet. We didn't have bullets. We didn't have guns. Well, what is the central jet of truth in this story? Survival is continuity. There was no change in the consciousness of the one who saw the event. He rose and he saw the body that was just blasted and, in the eyes of the world, dead. He came out of it a living being but the identical being that he was one second before. You can discount a bullet; there were no bullets 2,000 years ago. No such thing as, well, dynamite 2,000 years ago. We didn't know it. But he finds himself in an ancient world, so it's trying to show him regardless of unnumbered deaths in this world, there is continuity.

But tonight I am speaking of discontinuity. It's an entirely different picture and everyone is destined towards discontinuity. And resurrection is God's mightiest act, the one act that sets it apart from all other acts, and reveals God as a God of the living, not the dead. We all become sons of God by God's mightiest act, the act of resurrection. So we are told, "He was designated Son of God by his resurrection from the dead." No one comes into this world from any holy womb in this world as a physical womb, no one—all of this is descended from David. So forget the story as told this day of Mary's son, and know the being that is really here, present in this audience tonight, wearing all these garments. And you may say...use your name, don't say Paul, whatever your name is...and "from Paul"—you say from John, from Robert, from Neville—"a slave of Jesus Christ," because he, the Jesus Christ in my own I-am-ness, emptied itself. Being in the form of God, it emptied itself of this wonderful splendor, and took upon itself the form of a servant, or a slave, and being born in the likeness of man, and finding itself in the form of man, it became obedient unto death, unto death upon the cross (Phil. 2:7). And this is the cross.

May I tell you, I have had the experience of the crucifixion, and it's the most ecstatic state in the world, the most glorious sensation in the world, no pain whatsoever. For this night I was one of an unnumbered crowd walking toward some invisible Mecca, the fulfillment of God's promise, all together an ancient world too, all dressed in Arabic costumes. A voice out of space came and the voice said, "And God walks with them." A woman at my side questioned the voice—no one saw the face; we all heard the voice—she said, "If God walks with us, where is he?" The voice replied—we all heard the reply—"At your side." This woman in her Arabic costume turned to her side, literally, looked into my face, right into my eyes, and then she became hysterical it struck her so funnily. And she asked, "What? Is Neville God?" and the voice replied, "Yes, in the act of waking." Then the same voice, but this time in the depths of my soul, heard only by me, by no one else. She heard the reply to her question: "Yes." That would have been true of anyone at her side. If Grace is at her side, Jack at her side, Bob at her side, anyone, the question would have been yes. We're *all* in the act of waking.

And then, in the depths of my soul I heard this voice and it said, "God laid himself down within you to sleep, and as he slept he dreamed a dream. He dreamed..." and then I knew the completed sentence. I became so emotional that I began to waken, but in the waking process my hands became vortices, my head a vortex, my feet vortices, and my right side a vortex. I was nailed by these vortices right upon this body. I woke on my bed in New York City thrilled beyond measure, for I was one of this infinite sea of humanity moving towards, I would say, an invisible goal. I called it Mecca, then, because we were all like Orientals, moving towards what would be in that Arab world the world of Mecca. We're all moving towards it...and that was my vision to share with the whole vast world. I was the same being then as I am now, no change in identity. Any more than the one who was shot through the head had any change in identity. So that after this event takes place you are still that same being.

Now let me share with you what I mean. This happened years ago, many years ago...and then four years ago, back in 1959, this intense vibration at the base of my skull and I began to awake. Now the voice I heard that night "Yes, he is God in the act of waking" and I began to awake. Well, morning after morning I have awakened in this world in my fifty-nine years; I am quite conscious of waking every morning and I thought this was a similar waking, for it was waking, no question about it. I began to awake. As I became fully awake and alert in a way I've never known before, I am in my skull. Now, today, if you were in church you heard the story: "And when they came to the place of the skull, there they crucified him." I awoke within my skull. My skull, if I can put it, put it the size of this area of the stage. I am standing in my own skull, but there is no opening, no eyes, no ears, no nostrils, no opening; it's completely sealed. But the vibration began at the base of my skull. I'm completely awake. I've never known such alertness in my life, but I am completely sealed in the sepulcher of the skull. It's the tomb in which I who wore this body am now laid. Then I began to move and I did it without knowing consciously, I did it automatically, and I pushed at the base of the skull. Something rolled away, just rolled away, like a stone, and then I came out, head down, inch by inch by inch, of this skull of mine.

When I was almost out, I pulled the remaining portion of me out of my skull, and for a few seconds I lay on the floor. Then I got up, looked back and saw that out of which I came. It ___(??) the size of this; it was the normal size of this body now, on the bed, ghastly pale, ghastly pale. And then a wind, an unearthly wind holds my interest from the far corner of the room. As I looked over, only took me a few seconds, wondering if this thing is so strong it will blow the whole place down, an unearthly wind; as I returned to my focus on the bed the body is gone. Now, here's the story. They went to the tomb and the body was gone, and they said, He is risen… but the words seemed to them the words of an idle tale and they did not believe it (Luke 24:11). The body was gone! I personally did not see anyone remove it but it is gone; but in its place sat now the witnesses to the event, three men. You're told in the story as you read it in Luke that they sat at both the head and feet of where the body was—for there is no body—but where the body was they sat at the head and the feet.

I didn't know what's going to happen now. I could discern all of their thoughts. I'm so alert I can see thoughts; there's nothing concealed, everything is to my mind like an open book. And then the wind disturbs them, as it disturbs me, and one got off the bed and started towards what seemed to be the cause of the disturbance, where it originated. He hadn't gone more than two paces when he looked down and then he announced, "It's Neville's baby." The other two asked, "How could Neville have a baby?"...that's an impossible statement. He doesn't argue the point; he places the evidence on the bed. It's a little child, a little babe wrapped in swaddling clothes. I lifted it, looked into its eyes and asked, "How is my sweetheart?" It smiled the most heavenly smile, and while I'm looking at this heavenly smile, the whole thing dissolves.

Now go back to the 1st of Romans: "I've been set apart," said he, "for the gospel of God that was promised beforehand through his prophets in the holy scripture" (Rom. 1:1-2). So you go back and you search the scriptures for intimations and foreshadowings of this event. Is it in scripture?—for they're looking for it in some peculiar strange way—and you come upon the passage where it *is* in scripture. The question is asked… aside from that which is said of David, when he comes out of David, he's going to raise out of David a son that will come forth from his body, but (he the Lord is speaking)—"I will be his father and he shall be my son." But now *this* incident...and you go back and you read it: "Can a man have a child?" He doesn't wait for the response and he goes forward now, "Why then do I see every man"—not *a* particular man but every man; this is a prophecy for all men, and by men it means humanity, male-female—"Why do I see every man with his hands pulling himself out of himself, just like a woman in labor? Why does every face turn pale?" Then it goes on, never has such a day been seen in all Zion.

Never has such a thing been seen in Zion, because no man can understand it, no man can appreciate it, and all would deny it until it happens in the man. For he foretold this by his prophets in the holy scriptures. The prophets who received it didn't understand it, and they asked the question, "O Lord, when, when is it going to take place?" They were told, "It is not for your time but for our time." The time had not yet fully come for this germination to take place, to unfold itself in man. So you go back and you read it. You who want to read it go back to Jeremiah, the 30th chapter, and read the story in the first two verses, down, say, to the 6th and 7th verse. Read the entire six or seven verses where the prophet was told to go and ask, in fact, he's asking the question, how can it happen? So it happened *in* man. Not in Jerusalem on the surface of this earth; it happens in this body in every body in the world.

Now comes this great event this coming Sunday and the world will be told that he is risen. They will look in the hope of his return and they don't know how he comes to man. His return is: He's coming to man, the resurrection is taking place. The crucifixion is over, everyone has been crucified with God, everyone. There isn't a child born of woman who has not already been crucified with God. As we are told in the 6th chapter of Romans: "If we have been united with him in a death like his, we shall certainly be united with him in a resurrection like his" (verse 5). See the difference in tense: We *have been* united with him in a crucifixion, in a death like his; now, we *shall be*—see the change in tense—we shall be resurrected with him in a resurrection like his. We shall be one with him, a union with him in our resurrection with him, because we are sons of God through our resurrection.

No child born of any woman in this world by that birth no matter how holy it is—you could call it a eugenic birth—well, that's not a holy birth. *Every* birth is holy in the eyes of God. I don't care how the child was conceived; every child conceived is God conceived. But that is the descendant of David, the human form, the slave that God then assumed. While God walks the earth, unknown even to himself that he is God, then he is born from above by a way foretold by God through his prophets in the holy scriptures. And when it happens to man, man is dumbfounded. He's the same man. He hasn't changed his relationship to society. He knows he's the same husband, the same father, the same son, the same brother, the same friend, he knows he is. But he walks with this knowledge of what has happened to him. Having studied the ancient scriptures he sees in the scripture all the foreshadowings, all the intimations of that which now he has experienced, and he's dumbfounded.

He sees now that the prophets when they foresaw it, their vision was, like all prophets, foreshadows; and they saw as present what was future, they saw as near what was far. And then we go on the far journey and while we're on the journey, like a thief in the night, it comes to us suddenly. And then we know now— to go back to the scripture—we are departing from this world. For this is not continuity anymore, this is discontinuity. So the question is asked, "Whose wife will she be in the resurrection?" The answer comes back, "In the resurrection they neither marry nor are given in marriage" (Luke 20:35). You do not know the scriptures or the power of God, for he is now a son of God, all because he's a son of the resurrection. No more a part of this world that moves upon its wheel, and therefore not a thing changes in this world; it is simply continuity.

If you've had the experience of continuity, to see the body drop with a bullet through its brain and see no change in self, you'll know the difference between survival being continuity and resurrection being discontinuity. Because then you go back to the form that you emptied yourself of, when you wore for educative reasons the garment that is a slave. These are the slave garments and every male in this world, every man in this world, female in this world, these are garments that God wears. As he puts it on, he first must empty himself of his infinite being, his glorified form, to assume the form of a man, and walk the earth as a man for educative reasons in this educated darkness. This, believe it or not, is very important for in this contraction of infinity to a point where it can't contract any more, which is this slave, it expands its luminosity, it expands its glory by such contraction. There is no limit to translucency, but there's a limit to contraction and the limit is the garment that God assumed as a slave when he put it on by first emptying himself of the being that he really is who is God.

So you read it and he confesses it is Paul who had the experiences. For Jesus Christ is the I-am-ness of every child born of woman. It is Paul who is telling you the story. It is Paul who is confessing the great secret of Christianity. And so tonight at sundown the Jewish world is telling the story of their freedom, their freedom from slavery. The freedom from slavery is always associated with the serpent rising on a pole. Tonight, they may not tell it that way, but they ask four questions, there are four glasses of wine, and there are four of everything on the table. They don't really answer these questions correctly at all. The four is a symbol, just a symbol. The four is a door, the Daleth, and the Daleth is I AM. Well, Daleth is the door; he said, I am the door; don't come in or try in any way to come in (in any other way) save through the door. "I am the door" (John 10:9). And the fourth letter of the Hebrew alphabet is Daleth. It's the symbol of the door and he tells you "I am the door." No one tells you that at Seder tonight. No one tells you why the fourth was the fourth son who was Judah, praise. No one tells us.

Tonight...a story came to me this past week. It's one of the most delightful stories. The man is here tonight and if anyone can end his letter to me as he did...he said, "Forty years ago in the state of Washington, I was then seventeen years old and while saddling a horse on our farm, we had a wheat farm, the horse just simply stepped on my big toe, and my big toe was injured seriously. I not only lost the toenail but it ruined or injured the root of that toenail and from then until this past few months I had an odd nail. It wouldn't grow in as a real nail, only a piece of it would come in. It was always sore and a very bothersome thing in my foot, this part of a nail. For forty years from the time I was seventeen until today." He confesses he's fifty-seven. He said, "I read your book *The Law and The Promise*. I saw where a lady who was injured at a very tender age went back in time and replayed it where she was not injured. So I went back and saw my toenail as it was before it was injured. I did it every night for only three nights, and then in a couple of days after I stopped it I noticed a little yellowy goo around the nail, and then the nail came out, and a complete new nail came out, and for the first time in forty years I had a perfect big toenail."

Now, he ends his letter this way, "But, Neville, what amazed me is this, for so little I was given so much!" If you could only catch that mood...that's Thaddeus, the tenth disciple. He's only mentioned in the disciples; not a thing is said about him. So few people are so faithful. He could close his letter to me by saying, "But, Neville, what amazes me, for so little I was given so much." He only did it and it cost him nothing to do it. Three nights he saw what he saw when he was seventeen years old, forty years ago. He saw it and accepted that as the norm for that toe. A few days later something happened. A little goo, he said, a little gooey matter appeared around the nail, it came out, a new nail came, and it's a perfect nail. Now he has a perfect nail and he hasn't had one in forty years. But I love his ending of his letter: "So much for so little." Well, what is the divine measure in the Bible—pressed down, shaken together and running over. That's how God gives to man for his "little." So you and I, only a little, and then he brings it back multiplied a thousand-fold.

So I tell you, this great mystery is the mystery of life through death. God died that you and I would become alive forever in his presence. Now listen to these words from Hosea, it's a promise made by the prophet, dictated to the prophet by God: "And after two days he will revive us; on the third day he will raise us, to be alive in his presence" (Hosea 6:2). After two days he revives us; on the third day he raises us to be alive in his presence. Well, the third day from today is Sunday. In the mystical language it is the eighth day, for the Sabbath is the seventh day; the Sabbath is tomorrow in the Hebraic world. So, Sunday is the first of a new day, a new week, and it's called the eighth, the sign of resurrection. But three is also resurrection, because on the third day the earth rose up out of the deep. So on the eighth day he brings up his son and he redeems his son. And everyone will be redeemed and all of us will be wearing that body that God himself wears, which he emptied to become us. It was God and God alone, God himself, who emptied himself of his infinite hu-form, his divine form, and took upon himself the slave of John Brown, Neville Goddard, and all these in the world.

He wore it, and after two days...two days does not mean two twenty-four-hour periods. All that happened to you happened in the tomb. Everything happened in the tomb and in the tomb you were buried. Then infinite mercy, divine mercy turned death into sleep, and so you slept. So everything that happened and is happening now is a dream. Everything in the world is a dream while you are entombed in God's holy sepulcher, which is the skull of man. If you don't think it is a dream, ask the man who wrote me the letter. He only imagined that. He saw in his Imagination what he knew he experienced when he was seventeen years old. Before the great mare, and he called her Pansy, he said, "I was standing on a plank and she dropped her big foot onto my big toe, and the plank was so rigid that it was simply the whole weight of that foot came on my toe." And so, he only imagined and that's a dream, isn't it? That's a waking dream. And so today he has the tangible results of this dream. Now he has a nail, a perfect nail, having not had one in forty years.

And so, I say it *is* a dream. And the whole thing that happens to man on his pilgrimage of 6,000 years takes place in the second day. That second day is when man is entombed, which tomorrow the Christian world will now relive as Saturday, which is to their calendar the day before the resurrection. So, on that day before the resurrection—and they tell it as a twenty-four-hour period; no, it is the six-thousand-year period—he is crucified and entombed at sundown. And sundown tomorrow night ends the 6,000-year dream of man. They will come early in the morning and they can't find the body, because they're looking for it where it isn't. For the body is *in* man. And when he awakens, it will be taken away and he, himself, who wore it will not even know how it was taken. Because it was so well worn and beautifully worn by him, it is in the eyes of God divine; for it played the perfect part while he wore it. It was taken away and he was invisible to those who came to bear witness to the story.

So who then was the little child that was found? Is it not Isaac? So in the ___(??) tradition it is stated that Isaac is not to be thought of as begotten of generation but simply the forming of the unbegotten. God is forming himself; he, the unbegotten, forming himself in us, in this sepulcher, the skull of man. And when his job is complete and to his satisfaction it is perfect, it is his image, well, then he awakens that image which is himself and it's you. "Let us make man in our image" and when the image is perfect and alive, just like him, that it can wear his glorious form, he awakens it in that sepulcher. He awakens to find himself completely entombed, and did not know for one moment in his entire pilgrimage that he was ever entombed or ever asleep. And then he awakens and he comes out, and here comes the fulfillment of the promise—I will give you one, you call him Isaac (which means "he laughs"), you hold him in your hand and he laughs—and the whole thing is completed.

So the prophecy of scripture is brought to its fulfillment in this series of experiences. So I tell you it is from death to life, rather than from life to death, as we experience it on this level of our being. And so, in these three great experiences the whole mystery of Christianity is contained. So remember, 100,000 this day made their exit normally. I hope that they all know—of course they now experience it—there is no death. Survival is automatic. But survival is continuity. I am speaking this night of God's mightiest act, which brings about a *discontinuity* and breaks this invidious bond, and brings us out as his sons. So listen to the words, he was *not* designated Son of God by his birth from the womb of woman, in spite of what the churches taught you (Romans 1:4).. Read it carefully. The earliest Christology accepted that. It was only in the later centuries that the churches organizing around the mystery that they did not understand then claimed it to be something that happened when the little child was born. No, it happened when he was born from above, and the birth from above comes on the heels of his resurrection. For resurrection comes first in a tomb; and he comes out of a tomb, so he's born from the grave, his resurrection from the dead. He's resurrected in the tomb and he comes out of the tomb. No one speaks of a woman's womb as a dead spot. But anyone who awakens in his skull to find himself entombed would know it's a place where only the dead are placed, so he comes from the dead. It's the mystery of life through death: The mystery of the little grain of corn...unless it falls into the ground and dies, it remains alone, but if it dies, it brings forth much.

So God buried himself in us, and then we dream, and in our dream we have the illusion of motion and travel all over this vast, wonderful earth of ours. One day we awake to discover we have never really left this place. So when I was told, many years ago, you do not move in waking any more than you move on your bed in sleep—it's all a movement in mind. You only believe you moved in waking as you believe you move in sleep. Well, then I woke, and how could I understand when that very day I had dates that would take me out of my apartment in New York City? I was on the road traveling around, and yet here is the voice telling me, "You do not move in waking any more than you move on your bed in sleep." That I do not move on my bed in sleep that's obvious. I get up in the morning, I'm still in the bed after an experience of vast travels, but now he compares that to this—that I think I move. And so, when I awoke in my skull to find myself in a tomb, I realized that the voice was telling the truth. Even though tonight I'm going to drive home and tomorrow travel around, I still must know the whole thing here is taking place in a dream. And so the great Shelley was right: "He has awakened from the dream of life. 'Tis we who lost in stormy visions keep with phantoms an unprofitable strife."

Now, you learn what that gentleman who told me this story tonight has already learned. You can imagine something that was injurious forty years ago, go back and see it as it ought to have been seen through the forty years. Don't do much! He said, "I did so little and received so much." Treat it just as lightly as that, and see how you can dream all these lovely things into being. For it *is* a being.

Now let us go into the Silence and dream nobly.

* * *

___(?? Jack has all of my books and books that I recommend.

Q: ___(??) these cycles ___(??) and I read the Mary Magdalene all through the rest of the story. I didn't quite recognize it at first...

A: May I tell you, after you've had the experience you will still, through habit, think as you thought before the experience. You find it so difficult to believe that you really are the being that the experience convinces you that you are. You are still human, with all of the weaknesses, all the limitations, and you can't bring yourself to believe that such a marvelous thing that has happened to you really means what it does mean. You find yourself hesitating to make a claim, almost being very self-conscious in your discussion of it, because you still want the affection of others. And there aren't any others; these are all garments that you wear. There's only one Jesus Christ, and so when he awakes in you, individualized as you, it's the same Jesus Christ that awakened in me. And so, he's wearing that garment and that garment, and that garment and the other garment. But there's only one God. You find it difficult even to discuss it, especially in a social gathering, so you don't recognize the being that you really are. You toy with the idea, you go to, you ponder it, you dwell upon it. It seems too good—that's what the gentleman said, "So much for so little." What have I done to earn it?—-you see that you've done nothing. And so I mean it seriously when I tell you that I cannot, when I reflect upon it, for one second can I assume that I did anything to earn it. It was grace, grace and still more grace.

Q: What is your interpretation of the saints? The Bible speaks of saints.

A: Saints? Well, you're told, all eventually are destined to be the saints. But it's not the saint that man makes. Today our religious bodies name someone as a saint based upon their investigation of what happened in the interval. But no man can make a saint. You're automatically, by your birth from above as a son of God through resurrection, you're whatever in the divine mind a saint means. Whatever it means you are, for you're the Son of God in full power. That's what the words are in this translation: "And he was designated Son of God in full power by the Holy Spirit by his resurrection from the dead." So there's nothing beyond the full power. You rise into a world which you find completely subject to your creative power, and that creative power is your imagining. So none will be better than the other; in fact, if you really love, you wouldn't want it. I would feel embarrassed to think that he loved me more than he loved my mother, I really would. I would think that if I met her and I was more in her eyes more glorious than he had clothed her, I would be embarrassed, knowing what she has meant to me. And so, you aren't going to be more than another, but nothing less than another. And none can lose their identity in the body of God. All perfect in the body of God, wearing the body of God.

Any other questions, please?

Q: Neville, the significance of the crucifixion and the resurrection...what significance does the youth of Christ have? For example, as a twelve year old he spoke in the temple.

A: The youth of Christ? What significance does the youth of Christ have if it's resurrection right after crucifixion? From crucifixion to resurrection, what significance has the youth? Well, the youth is simply when man has the resurrection, he is like a babe he is so bewildered. He talks of nothing but, just like a child, and simply ponders it and it grows in him. So the understanding of what has happened to him grows in him. So we're told, the ___(??) for the Lord was upon him and he grew in wisdom and in the fear of the Lord. It has happened but it is so overpowering that it will take him eternity to fully digest what has happened to him. That he was taken off the wheel of recurrence and lifted by a divine, merciful act into the kingdom of heaven where he inherits not only the kingdom but he inherits the presence that is God. So, how can you take it in all in one grasp? You can't do it. It comes to me later, but later. Someone would write me a letter and the letter throws light on something that I'm reading in scripture.

Well, the time is up. And then after tonight we go back into a norm of the law. So we'll start next week. I'm quite sure the subject, whatever it is, will be on the law. Please send me your letters and tell me how you use it and how wisely you used it. I hope you have fantastic results in your world. So, 'til next Tuesday. Thank you.

THE NEW AND LIVING WAY

3/31/64

Let me tell you, I think I do tell you from time to time, no matter what the title is, I am talking about only one thing, really, and that is your own wonderful human Imagination. And I call your human Imagination God. The eternal body of man is our Imagination. In scripture it is called Jesus. Man misunderstands it and limits it to a little being, one being who lived and died 2,000 years ago. But that's not my concept of Jesus. My concept of Jesus is that of God, and my concept of God is that of the human Imagination. "Only the Imagination of man is vast enough to contain the immensity of space."

And so, tonight, we ask the question concerning this new and living way: Can any man go forth where his Imagination has never gone before? I will answer that, no he can't. Therefore, tell me the greatest story ever told, if you know it, so that I may walk with you in Imagination. For I cannot walk there with you through faith in Imagination, I can never get there; so you tell me if you know it from experience best of all. If hearsay and you believe it, that will do. But don't mislead me. Tell me the story, the greatest story ever told. That is the story as read in the gospels, that's the story. Read the story in the Bible, from beginning to end, but it comes to a flower in the gospels. If you tell me that story and I can respond to it and go with you, I am walking in Imagination with you, then I can go there. But no man in this world would ever go forth where his Imagination has not gone before, no one. So if you know the story, share it with me, and we can take it on many, many levels. So I'll show you this new and living way.

A new book came off the press I think this week. I can't recall the title. The author is Bill Donovan, the great attorney. He represented Colonel Abel, the master spy, a few years ago. He was the lawyer for the defense.

Abel, as the testimony brought out, was the arch-spy for Russia. He was not a traitor; he was a spy in the true sense of the word. Prior to his trial the Rosenbergs were tried on less evidence and executed. Both paid the ultimate penalty, but they betrayed their country. This man Abel did not betray his country; he worked *for* his country against what his country considered the arch-enemy, America. But the testimony against him was mountainous, and Bill Donovan knew he was defending a man who was guilty as guilty could be, he knew that. But in the end, this was his plea. He turned to the court and asked the court not to execute the prisoner—-he was found guilty—-but to sentence him, well, maybe to life, which he received. Then this is what he said, "In the not distant future we of America may want to exchange him for one of equal importance in Russia...one of equal importance."

It is said the courtroom burst into hysterical laughter at that peculiar plea, and a columnist dubbed him a Red or a Pink or some other name, because he dared to plead this case for this arch-enemy of this country. Well, he received a life sentence, Colonel Abel. Three years later it was Bill Donovan who was the one who negotiated the exchange, and he exchanged this arch-spy Colonel Abel for Lieutenant Powers, who was shot down over Russia. We would have given anything to get Powers alive and consciously alert to find out how he was shot down. For until then no one brought down our U-2 planes, and we were photographing the entire Russia from altitudes that we thought they could never reach. We weren't quite sure but what it could be some mechanical defect and the plane simply faltered in the air and came down, but we didn't know. He had all the orders to destroy the plane, destroy himself—he was paid well for it—to blow his brains out. He didn't blow his brains out and the plane wasn't destroyed, so what did the Russians do to bring him down? Was it from the ground? Was it a plane even higher than ours? What did they do? And we would have paid anything. Well, the price we paid was Colonel Abel.

Where is the origin of the entire drama? Isn't that in Bill Donovan's Imagination? When Bill Donovan pleaded this case with passion to the point where the whole court exploded in laughter, he still got his point over to the point where they took his plea under submission and brought in, well, a judgment based upon his recommendation: He asked for life rather than execution. And three years later we did have the man that Russia wanted badly, for he was their top spy, as we understand or thought. I hope he was the top spy! Well, we got all these things on him and they said the evidence was mountainous, so that Donovan could not possibly plead any innocence; everything was so obvious. But he could ask for mercy. The court granted mercy in the sense of not killing him. They put him away for life and three years later he was the instrument that negotiated between the two countries and exchanged Colonel Abel for Lieutenant Powers.

So I say this is a living way...a new and living way. I ask you to think carefully before you imagine anything. For the interval between your imaginal act and its fulfillment may be longer than you could remember, and because you can't remember, you deny the harvest that is your own harvest. You planted it. Were it not that this book is out now, and even though the book is out (came out this week) I question seriously that Bill Donovan believes that his imaginal act was causative. He thought himself a very smart, wise lawyer, and he still is, but he doesn't for one moment trace that plane coming down in Russia to anything he did in that court in New York City three years prior to the event. Man will not accept the testimony of Jesus. This is the testimony of Jesus: "You have heard it said that any man who lusts after a woman"...or that no man should lust after a woman…"but I say unto you, any one who lusts after a woman has already committed the act with her in his heart" (Mat. 5:27). Well, the word heart, the word mind, the word Imagination are one in this drama. He's already done the act. By the very act of imagining that, he has performed that service, that act. He has committed it.

Now, take it down to every level in this world. And so, you put yourself into a court and you perform this imaginal act where you can see yourself actually exchanging this man for another man. And they want the other man so badly the country will be very happy they didn't shoot him, that they had him to really offer as the prize for the one we needed badly. And so, I ask everyone here to watch carefully how you imagine anything. For all day long you are imagining things, and the interval between the imaginal act which is the sowing, and the reaping of that act may be longer than you can imagine what you did; and so you deny your own offspring, you deny your harvest. You can't recognize any relationship between it and you. Now, if you can walk with me that far, we can take you beyond that.

And so, the testimony of Jesus must be heard and responded to; for faith is response to revelation rather than discovery of new knowledge. Yes, you can go into labs and find out about the most fantastic things and hear it told and love it. You see the explosion of it, you see the demonstration of it and you love it. But that is not the faith of which the Bible speaks. The Bible speaks of a faith that comes in response to revelation, and the most fantastic revelation in the world is the revelation of God, put into the story of Jesus Christ. Can one believe it? Now, churches have distorted it. They've told the most fantastic story that is not the story of Jesus Christ. It is *not* the story. The whole story is our own wonderful human Imagination.

So now, we go back this night to the title, taken from the 10th chapter of the Book of Hebrews. In this 10th chapter we are told that there is a new way, a living way. First of all, it starts off by inviting us to enter into the Holy of Holies, "the sanctuary, by the blood of Jesus, the new and living way, which he opened for us through the curtain, that is, by his flesh" (verse 19). That's what we are told. We go into the very presence of the Holy of Holies, right into the presence of the Ancient of Days, by his blood. And this we do through a new and living way; not any dead sacrifices. We don't kill animals; we don't destroy anything and offer it in the hope that we could enter the Holy of Holies. No sacrifice, no external sacrifice at all. It's all something new, a new and living way, by something that is the blood—the blood of whom?—the blood of Jesus. And he did this in a new way, through the curtain. Then he tells us, he identified the curtain with the flesh of Jesus.

Well, what is it? I can tell you that experience from experience. I am not theorizing, no man taught it to me, I never read it in a book outside of the Bible. But before I went back into the Bible and read it, I experienced it. So I can tell you this new and living way into the sanctuary, into the Holy of Holies, and yet by his blood. There will come a time after the series of events of which I have spoken time and time again. It is said when he gives up the Spirit, there was tearing of the temple; and the curtain of the temple was torn from top to bottom; and the earth quaked; and all the stones were split, every rock was split. You read it and you wonder "What is it all about, something in the Near East?" For there were no Christian churches. The only temple he knew was the temple of the Jew; everything was the temple of the Jew. So what was this temple? The only curtain we know of was the curtain that hides the Torah. Behind the curtain is the Torah, the holy word of God, his law, and in some places he spoke of the ark behind that wonderful curtain. Now he identifies the curtain with his body, the author of Hebrews does: Through the curtain which is his flesh.

Well, I'll tell you what happened. A bolt of lightning out of your skull will split you in two, from the top of your skull to the base of your spine, and every section of your spinal column will be actually split in two. And then you will look at the base of your spine and you will see living liquid molten gold; it's alive, just gold but a living gold. You will know as you've known nothing before that I am it. As you look at it you know you are it. And then at that moment of knowing you fuse with it; and *as* this living blood of Jesus you go up in a serpentine manner into the Holy of Holies, which is your own wonderful skull. That's the blood of Jesus and Jesus is God and God is your own wonderful human Imagination. The drama takes place in you.

Everything, listen to the story carefully, all the testimony of Jesus, for everything to which he testifies you are going to experience if you will accept it. You cannot walk beyond where you've gone in Imagination, and so when you hear the testimony, you're response may be negative and you will not accept it. So I ask the question, "Can any man go forward where his Imagination has not gone before?" And the answer is no. So you listen carefully and then you respond. If you say, "I'll walk with you, I'll walk that far with you, but I can't go any further. That is as far as I can go with you; beyond that, leave me right here. I'll go back and hold onto these things that seem so much more real, and so I'll hold onto the things around me. But I won't go that far." And so, listen to it. It's the most fantastic story that man could ever hear, for it's the story of God. It's the story of you. How *you* awaken into the whole being that is God, for there's only God. For in the end, the Lord is one and his name one; there aren't two, just one, and you are that being. If you hear the story, respond to it positively, then you can walk as far as you've heard. If you haven't heard the story, you can't venture beyond what you've heard, for no man can go forth where he has not walked in Imagination before. And so when I hear a story or someone tells me something else, as I hear it I am walking with him in Imagination. Turn on the TV, I may deny it or accept it, but I walk with him in Imagination. And everything is one's Imagination. There's nothing but one's Imagination.

So the story must be heard, and having heard it, it must be responded to, either negatively where you deny it and reject it, or you accept it. So it's entirely up to us to accept it if we really want to walk as far as the story will take us, which is the new and living way, right through the curtain. And the curtain is one's own wonderful—it isn't this [body]—I saw this split. But surely when I woke in the morning to find this body still knit together and no scar on it, it could not have been this. This is but the shadow world. So Blake in his wonderful *Jerusalem*: "I know of no other Christianity," said he, "and no other gospel than the liberty both of body and mind to exercise the divine arts of Imagination. Imagination the real and eternal world into which we shall all go after the death of these vegetable, mortal bodies of ours." Then he asked, "What are these gifts, these treasures of heaven that you and I must lay up for tomorrow, are they not all mental gifts—the arts, the literatures, all these lovely mental gifts of the world." He said, the apostles knew of no other gospel, only the arts of Imagination.

Well, when a man could come out and he could bring about the... and the book is in print, you can buy it tomorrow...where he confesses his argument, and then you see the facts as they followed three years later. He himself did not relate the fact to an imaginal act. He was simply a shrewd, wonderful lawyer. But yet in scripture we are told...don't...the whole thing is mental, causation is mental. It is not physical; the physical moves under compulsion. The self-determining motion is all mental, it's all in us; it's not on the outside. And try it. All you need do is just simply try it and find the new and living way. It's all in us. You can take anything in this world…a gentleman (I don't see him here tonight) he said to me last Friday night, "My brother said to me, 'You mustn't go or you should not go to Neville anymore,' and the reason given is this, 'You went to Neville for an increase in business. Now we have so much business that we haven't time to fulfill it, so don't go any more, wait awhile.'" These are his own words. He said, "I don't write letters but this is my...you want a testimony? You want to prove to yourself and the people who listen to you that imagining creates reality? Well, my brother said to me, 'Don't go to Neville anymore; not yet anyway.'" Well, he isn't here tonight and he comes here all the time, but he said, "We have so much business we haven't really time to fulfill the business, and the purpose for going there in the first place was to get business, and now we have more than we can take care of." So that was his letter, given to me verbally.

So I say you *can't* fail because imagining is God and there's nothing but God. Every imaginal act is a causative act. But you may not have done it with feeling; you may not have done it in a prayerful manner. And by prayerful I don't mean any holy manner, because "to pray" is to move towards, to accede to, to get near the object of your affections, something that you really intend to have in this world. So the word prayer is defined as "motion towards, accession to, nearness at, at or in the vicinity of." Well, if today...like the chap whose story we told last week, he wanted to prove this law—he's done it numberless times—but he wanted to prove it, and he actually fell asleep in the assumption that he was in Denver in a bakery that he knew so well, next to the deep freeze. And the very next day, on Sunday, seated at a table, a friend of his said to him, "How would you like to go with us to Denver? I'm going to see my brother." Well, how can you simply rub that out as coincidence? And the very next day, a second party invited him to go to Denver. He could have been invited to go to Alaska. He wasn't going to Alaska—Denver, exactly where he wanted to go. And he slept in his Imagination in the assumption he was physically there.

Well, isn't that praying? To pray is really "to want *intensely*." In fact, a definition in my Concordance, my biblical Concordance, for "lusting after" is pray; and this is how it's defined, "the superimposition of time, place or order with passion." The superimposition of time, place or order with passion: to superimpose Denver upon Los Angeles so Los Angeles ceases to be in my Imagination and I'm really in Denver. And to see that I really have superimposed to the point of displacing Los Angeles, I think of Los

Angeles, and then I think of Los Angeles in my Imagination as I would see it relative to Denver; and there I sleep. And so, I did it with intensity, I did it with feeling, I did it with passion. So I displaced Los Angeles as I put in its place this superimposed state called Denver. And that's praying. He got it in twenty-four hours.

All I ask of anyone here is to try it, just try it, and you'll see a new and living way. Eventually you'll be able to take the whole story; and the whole story will lead you straight into the Holy of Holies where you're in the presence of God. You will know God to be man. As Blake brought out so beautifully, "Thou art a man; God is no more. Thy own humanity learn to adore." He *is* man. The world will say, "How can God be man? God is some impersonal force." I tell you from experience God is man and you stand in his presence and he's infinite love, in spite of all of the horrors of the world. And so, one day you will know the truth of that 13th Corinthians, the 1st Corinthians, that although you have all the gifts of the Spirit but have not love, you are nothing. And it's just as simple as that. So you could take this wonderful law and go as far with me as earning billions and owning fortunes in this world, go as far as that in the use of the law, but you have not love, you have nothing, but I mean nothing. If you own the whole vast world and have not love, it is just as nothing. It's as simple as that.

But the day will come, you will hear the story and you'll go as far as you've heard—if your response to the story was positive, that you believed me; and one day right straight through the curtain into the presence of the Holy of Holies, into the sanctuary. And when you're brought into the sanctuary, there is the Ancient of Days that is the embodiment of infinite love. It seems strange that such a being (man) that I could say of this man that he created the universe; and that only this man which is only Imagination personified is vast enough to contain the immensity of space; and *that* man's Imagination manifests itself in the Imaginations of men. That you perform an imaginal act here and don't concern yourself as to which individual in this world or how many in this world will be used as instruments to externalize what you've imagined. Leave it alone, because we are one and all things by a law divine in one another's being mingle. So leave them alone. You simply remain loyal to your imaginal act, *confident* in this presence that you really are. When you say "I imagine," that's God.

Just wait. If you wait a day, as my friend Ward waited a day, and the invitation to Denver. This man Donovan, he waited three years for a man to be shot down over Russia. If I told him this night that you shot down Powers, were he bigger than I he'd slap me in the face. And yet he shot down Powers, using an extension of his arm called a Russian soldier…if it came from the ground. Or if it came from a Russian plane, he used that, for he imagined it. He was a very brilliant, and still is a brilliant, brilliant trial lawyer, and yet, he cannot believe for one moment that causation goes back to his own wonderful dramatic feeling (imaginal act) in that courtroom. And if there is no other cause, you can stand right here, just right here, and imagine yourself the lady, the gentleman that you want to be. And then looking into the faces of your friends, all in your Imagination, and allow them to see you as they must see you were it true that you have become the man, become the lady, that you want to be. Then trust that imaginal act implicitly. And that is holding God trustworthy.

You hold him trustworthy because he is faithful to his promise. He told me that if I lust after someone without the physical confirmation of the act, I've committed the act. I may lust and restrain the impulse. I may contemplate the act along with its consequences and feel that I might be discovered in the act, and so the consequences I want to avoid. But I am told in this story that's not good enough. To actually imagine the act, regardless of the restraint on my part having considered the consequences, was not good enough: I performed the act. And so, you imagine the act of anything, that you're wealthy, you imagine that you are wanted, you imagine that you are contributing to the world's good, you imagine that you are a great…and you name it, and you actually feel that you are. You don't think in terms of the consequences. That's an act in itself, well, then you are going to get it. And when you get it it's going to carry with itself certain obligations to society. You may not then enjoy the obligations that come with the birth of that imaginal act. Sometimes tremendous responsibility goes with wealth one has imagined, and they want the wealth without the responsibility. But it will come together if you are willing to completely accept the birth of what you really have created, recognize it as your own offspring, your own harvest, and take it.

Then you will know this new and living way. It comes straight through the curtain of the flesh. And in one moment of time, when you least expect it, you will realize the depth of this story, how true it is in depth. For your whole body will be shattered; and it's not this, it's that eternal you torn. Why? I can't tell you. The moment I get it I'll tell you. I only know what I've experienced. I only know that it parallels what I was told in scripture I would experience *if* I believed that I am he. For if this body that is torn is identified with the flesh of Jesus, and it was my body that was torn, wasn't that the flesh of Jesus? And did he not say, "I am the way"? Well, I know exactly what happened to me. So I knew exactly what I'm told, that "I am the way." So don't divorce yourself from Jesus; don't divorce yourself from God; don't separate yourself from God. That the human Imagination..."the eternal body of man is the human Imagination and *that* is God himself, the divine body, Jesus" (Blake, *Laocoon,* P.776).

And so, take it all together, and don't put them apart—-that's Jesus, and I'm a little me, and that is God who is his father—don't. That's what the churches taught for 2,000 years. It hasn't a thing to do with the great story, the story of God actually becoming man that man may become God; burying himself right into man and then transfusing, transforming man with himself by lifting man as his own being. And there is a path by which this is done, and this path is told us in the story of Jesus: his birth, his discovery of fatherhood, his ascension into heaven, all these, one after the other takes place in the Imagination of man. Well, when you feel it, it feels so physical. When I was severed in two, it felt like my body physically was severed in two. When I felt that infant, it was something physical in my hand. When I saw the witnesses to the event, they were physical. This is all man, there's nothing but man in this world. Because why? God is man, and there's nothing but God. And so, when you look into the vast world, the whole vast world is man and you are that man.

But how far will you go with me? I hope you'll go all the way. I hope that you will take this story as I have told it in the *Promise,* and read it over and over, and go with it. Some will go no farther than the law. One chap (he never comes here any more) when I wrote the book I sent him a copy because his wife was so kind in helping with the typing. He got me on the phone and he said, "You know, Neville, you've written an excellent book up to the end of the law, and then it became a spoiled book by the addition of the Promise." He can't take the story; he'd have no part of it. You can't discuss it with him. No matter how you try to show him, he will not listen for one second, but he will take all concerning the law. That's why I've told you in the beginning by asking a question, "Can any man go forth where his Imagination has never walked before?" No! So this friend of whom I speak he can't go forth, he can't go beyond the law, because he will not listen and respond positively to the story as recorded in scripture. Yet he trusts me implicitly. He feels I've told the truth, but he feels it's hallucination, because that's the whole vast world. You go back and you show him that in the scripture long before you physically came into this world it was written there. Well, how can your experience parallel what was written there 3,000 years ago and what was told by the servants of the Lord, called prophets; that these things would happen to man when the fullness of the time had come, when everything had been ripened, ready for hatching out, then it would start to be hatched out? But he will not believe it.

So, there may be many here this night who can go no further than the law. And so because of that, we've got to bear that in mind and night after night, week after week, come down to a certain level where everyone can benefit from whatever is said from this platform. I tell you the same living way. Sitting here this night, you do not need the assistance of anyone to become the one that you want to be. All you need to do is to hear the story and respond positively to that story, and that is that your Imagination is the being spoken of in scripture as Jesus Christ. Will you believe it, that your Imagination is he, that's Jesus Christ? And with him all things are possible and that by him all things were made, and without him was not anything made that was made, you believe that? You believe it of Jesus Christ? Some will say yes; others will say, no, I can't believe it of him; I believe it of God. But they won't believe that Jesus Christ is God...they can't go that far.

Well, alright, go back...you believe it of God? If you say yes, alright, will you now believe that that God that you believe in, and by him all things were made? You say yes to that. Well, do you believe that that is your Imagination? If you hesitate there, well, then we can still go a little bit. Then come down, are some things possible to your Imagination? You may get a certain acceptance there, and you start from there, and try it in a little way, in some small wonderful little way. And then from then you start moving up and you go farther and farther and farther, and one day you'll take the entire story and go the limit. Then you'll find that the God spoken of in scripture in the very beginning when he reveals his name as I AM—and that's my name forever, to be known forever by all generations—-then you will find out who he really is. You'll repose on him then until the morning of the grave when the stone is rolled away, and you will know that he is your life. I AM life! "I am the way, I am the truth, I am the life" (John 14:6).

So you repose on it, you sleep on it. You sleep every night on I AM, don't you? Who goes to bed and who gets out of the bed? You say, "Well, I am getting out of bed, I'm going to bed." Well, repose on it. For when you go to bed at night, you repose on God and you sleep on God. And the day will come, that morning of the grave when the grave is opened, and you awake. Who's awakening? You say, "Well, I am awakening." Well, that's God, and so God will awaken that morning (Psalm 78:65). How many years I do not know? Blake claims 6,000 years in his own case. So how long you've been going in the journey, I don't know. But you will repose on God and God is saying to you, I am your life, and I am the only way, and I am the truth, and there is no other way in the world. So you repose on him night after night. You wake in the morning, you're still with him, and you go through life not knowing that you really are the being spoken of in scripture as the one called Christ Jesus.

And the day will come...and when you read it the whole thing becomes so luminous. Who would have thought that the blood of Jesus was this living pulsing golden light? Who would have thought that man is truly washed in the blood of the lamb? That he actually enters it and knows that blood of Jesus to be himself? And the life is in the blood, you're told. So you go into the blood, and it's you; and then like a serpent you ascend into the Holy of Holies, no loss of identity. You know that the story of the blood is true; the story of the temple being torn in two, that's true; and the whole thing was true. But it is so unlike what the churches have told you in the past and still today tell you concerning this greatest of all stories. They've separated God from man and put him up there to be like something other than what you look like. And may I tell you, when you see him, you *are* like him. Whenever you meet him, you are like him. He actually became you and took upon himself your limitations, and raised you to be just like him, and you are like him. That's the story.

So this new and living way...if you want to check it, you'll read it in the 10th chapter of the Book of Hebrews. You understand these words of Paul from his 2nd Corinthians, the 5th chapter: "From now on we regard no one from the human point of view; even though we once regarded Christ from the human point of view, we regard him thus no longer" (verse 16). And Paul means exactly what he has said. Don't try any interpretation; he means exactly what he said in the 2nd Corinthians, the 5th chapter, "From now on we regard no one from the human point of view; even though we once regarded Christ from the human point of view, we regard him thus no longer." And so, no one on the outside would he ever judge by. He was looking for some Messiah to come in a peculiar way, some majestic way, and that's not the way he comes. He comes from within. He may come in one that you would never judge. Because if you judge externally, you judge his situation in life, you will think he should come from this noble family or that intellectual ground.

Here, I heard only a few months ago where before Aldous Huxley made his exit from this world he called himself a humanist. He and his brother Julian and a raft of others, and they had this little ___(??). They claimed they should now limit this exploding population to the intellectual crowd. In other words, stop all production save through this one channel, which they would decide (the intellectuals) who would bring forth tomorrow's intellectuals; therefore, they called it the humanist crowd. Can you imagine that?

And so, Paul discovered that you couldn't judge anyone, because here you will see someone who is very poor, unknown, unwanted, and in the eyes of God he is so close to complete awakening that his value, compared to all that Aldous would think, well, you couldn't compare them if you took his worth in the kingdom compared to those that man on this level would judge as worthy. So listen to the words: "You see John the Baptist? No one born of woman is greater than John the Baptist; yet I tell you the least in the kingdom is greater than he" (Mat. 11:11). And yet today we have cathedrals built to John the Baptist and we call him a saint. We call him Saint John the Baptist, and we have cathedrals, and here in the Holy Scripture, "The least in the kingdom is greater than he"—-stating quite openly he is not in the kingdom. Not that state of consciousness...that is the rough state, against everything, a complete against-ness of things. He didn't eat meat, he didn't drink wine, he was simply in the rough state. All his clothing, we are told, which is all through, representing how the mind is formed as it were. He was simply against everything in this world in the attempt to be a very holy man. And here comes one who did not abide by any of these outside things at all, and he said, "He who is the least in the kingdom is greater than John." Yet we've gone blindly on "sainting" this one, "sainting" that one, and putting ourselves up to judge who has entered the kingdom.

Listen to the story carefully and if you've had the experience, doesn't matter what the world will tell you. You only get in, in one way: "Except you be born from above you cannot in any wise enter the kingdom of God" (John 3:3) and "As Moses lifted up the serpent in the wilderness, so must the Son of man be lifted up" (John 3:14), in the identical manner; and you're lifted up by the blood of Jesus; and so you are saved. You are told, "I will enter the Holy of Holies by the blood of Jesus, a new and living way, through the curtain, which he has opened" (Hebrews 10:19). The word opened literally means "inaugurated"—which he has inaugurated through the curtain that is his flesh. And so when you go through and your whole being has been cut in two, you know the flesh of Jesus. So you don't separate yourself from Jesus, don't separate yourself from God, you don't separate yourself from this grand mystery...it's all you.

But how far would you go, I can't tell you. Listen to the story and you be the judge. If you respond positively, well, then you can go as far as you can respond. So now let me in closing again remind you by asking the same question we asked in the beginning, "Can any man"—I don't care who he is, how wise, how foolish, how great, how little—"can any man go forth where his Imagination has never walked before?" No. So let your Imagination walk as far as it possibly can by hearing the story from one who has experienced it and walk with him. Because if you can walk with him—-it may not be tonight or tomorrow night—but if you can hear it and walk with him in faith that this is true, you will wait then patiently and in confidence that one day you will experience it. Then you will go as far as that. And the day will come, you will go to the very end and you will awake.

And who are you?—God. Seems incredible! You will awaken one day and you are he; and you will know the words "I am he."

Now let us go into the Silence.

* * *

Q: (inaudible)

A: Did you hear the question? "It's expedient that I go away." If he doesn't go, he cannot send the Comforter known in other verses as the Holy Spirit. Again let me say, do not divorce the Holy Spirit (one aspect) from God the Father or God the Son...they are *one*. It's all one, in different functions. And so he said earlier—not tonight but in previous lectures—that infinite love in unthinkable origin is God the Father; infinite love in creative expression is God the Son (still infinite love); infinite love in eternal procession is God the Holy Spirit, the constant outpouring of the gifts and creativity of God but still infinite love, which is one basically. If I told you the story and dramatized it, and then I say to you see it mentally as a play, as told us in the 3rd chapter of Galatians (verse 1): "O foolish Galatians! Who has bewitched you, before whose eyes Jesus Christ was publicly *portrayed* as crucified? Let me ask you only this: Did you receive the Spirit by the working of the law, or by hearing with faith? Are you so foolish? Having begun with the Spirit, are you now ending with the flesh?" So "portray" is to represent vividly and as alive as you possibly can, whether you do it in drawing, in painting, in literature, in acting. For in this case it's acting. So it was portrayed, a drama was put on the stage as it were, call it the world, where a man deliberately and consciously plays the part as told us in the Apochryphal gospels, called the *Gospel According to Nicodemus.* You can read it in the Apochryphal gospels that that drama was deliberately acted like a play on Broadway. Now, he said, you saw it portrayed, and you saw it, and you heard it, and you believed it. You saw the spirit behind the play, it had a message, now, are you looking for something material, a man, something in the flesh? Didn't you see the spirit behind the play? That's what he's asking.

Now, suppose now you see this play and you believe this is God, and God is saying to you to whom he shows the drama: Now I must depart…I must actually depart from you, because I am *in* you. This presentation that you think is something other than yourself will now depart, for I am he. Well, everyone looking at it is saying "I am." So he departs from something external and detached from those who are in the audience, and they now can't see him; but he is nearer than he was when he was seen, nearer now than hands and feet. And wherever you go, I am there. If you take the wings of the morning and you fly to the ends of the earth, I am there. If you go into hell, I am there. Because, now that the physical picture has departed, the invisible reality which is your own life is present; and I am your life. So he departs; that Spirit of holiness will be upon you and in you, and *is* your life.

So the whole thing is dramatized. But having heard the story as something external to the one who heard it, he keeps on thinking it must be something other than this, it must be some being, and he wants to make an idol of the great mystery. And he does, he succeeds in making them. But it's really all within us; it's taking place *in* us. And I know it's a frightening thing in some respects and disturbing, and then when it happens to the individual he's startled. It seems the most fantastic thing in the world that it could happen to him. He knows the limitations of his flesh, he knows the limitations of his being, and he can't believe that he could have been elected, for it's all by election. And he cannot discover the secret of God's elective love. That why, at this moment in time, he, of all, was selected and put through the paces of these fantastic mystical experiences, all recorded in scripture as having taken place here in the flesh. Then he discovers what the real flesh really is. That the curtain spoken of that was torn is the flesh of Jesus, that's what we are told in the 10th chapter. And then he discovers that *he* was torn and it was *his* flesh, and that flesh is the flesh of Jesus; then he knows who Jesus is, and knows now who the blood is...what it is. And now it does make alive, and through that blood he entered the Holy of Holies. For you're told, Let us enter the Holy of Holies by the blood of Jesus. Well, it was to him living, liquid, pulsing, golden light. He became it and then he *did* enter the Holy of Holies by it. He fused with the blood of Jesus. Now he sees an entirely different picture. He doesn't see the personalized individual man called Jesus. Now he regards no man after the flesh. He doesn't care where they're born, how much money they have, how famous they are; that doesn't impress him at all because he's looking at no one after the flesh. He doesn't know when they are veiled as they are in these little garments of flesh how worthy they are in the sight of God. So he isn't judging anyone. Someone today could be tomorrow's headline that maybe he died or maybe he got married or maybe he is unwell, and he's so very prominent they've got to make a big headline out of it. But he isn't going to judge anyone by such headlines because he doesn't know behind that veil to what degree he is close to the awakening as he's called by God. Some unknown

___(??) in the world, completely unknown, could be this very moment being called and elected by God. So God presents the play and departs.

Now in this wonderful Book of Hebrews, it's the only book in the entire Bible that refers to Jesus as the apostle. He's not called an apostle in any other book, and in this book no one else is called an apostle. The apostle, in this case, is one who not only is called and sent, he is the one who sends himself armed with the authority to speak in the name of the person who actually sent himself into being. For he always claims now "I am," and he speaks in the name of God. So he's actually armed with the authority to speak in the name of him who dispatched him; so he said, "When you see me, you see him who sent me." And no other place in the scripture is he called an apostle, but here he's called the apostle; and the high priest not after the rabbinical order but the high priest after the order of Melchizedek, one who has no father, no mother, therefore, God. No background, no genealogy, only God.

Any other questions, please?

Q: When Paul had this experience on the road to Damascus, wasn't he fighting this story of The Way when it happened to him?

A: As you read the story in the Book of Acts he was. He was an ardent student of the Old Testament—-there was no other Testament—-and he abided by the law literally, by the letter of the law, so the story goes. He is blinded by the vision. He could not go back on the experience. What a man knows from experience he knows more thoroughly than he knows anything else in this world or than he can know that same truth in any other way. Paul was told it, but he didn't know it to the extent that he knew it after he experienced it. And he was blinded, we are told; the blinding was so intense it produced a physical blindness in Paul. Then Ananias came and said he was sent by the very one who had blinded him to now untie the eye as it were. So he resisted it. I'm not saying that if you resist it this night that you may not in spite of your resistance, having heard the story and you're fighting with it, that it gets the better of you. Because, in the story everything said was paralleled by something prophesied in the Old Testament to what he was seeing unfold before his eye in the drama. He would not relate it to anything of the Old Testament; but everything...he said, I've come only to fulfill scripture...and "scripture must be fulfilled in me" (Luke 22:37). And so beginning with Moses and all through the prophecies, all through the psalms, he interpreted to them, in all the scriptures, the things concerning himself. But they would not believe it. If I say to anyone—-I've said it time and again and I've gone out on a limb and told it in print—-that everything said in the gospel concerning this miraculous birth, I have experienced; the resurrection, I have experienced; the ascension, I have experienced; the descent of the dove, I have experienced. But I can't prove it to anyone if you ask me for physical proof; for the drama does not take place here. And yet, it was all physical in the same sense that you felt it to be a physical drama as you were experiencing it. So the word translated "flesh" is truly flesh, without the skin, it's so much but only the real flesh. That's how real it is. So there's not even a thing to touch to stop it from its sensitivity. Flesh minus the skin it's so much the real flesh of a being. And I've had all of these experiences, but how can I prove to anyone? Therefore, you hear the story and you respond, you either say no to it or yea to it. "For all the promises of God find their yea in him." You either say yes to it or you say no. And at a certain point you really don't care. You tell it as best you can, as often as you can, but you really don't care, you simply tell it. You're called upon to tell it. You've been sent to tell it. You were called and sent, and you go and tell it as it happened to you. But the most difficult thing in this world is to change the meaning of an event after certain interpretations of that event become fixed in the public mind.

Well, today we have one billion who call themselves Christians and fifteen million who call themselves Jews who have heard the story differently, so they aren't going to believe it. Especially when someone comes and he's all dressed in robes of authority, and so these robes right away change the mind of the perceiver. And he sees the robe; he endows it with an authority that it doesn't possess. And he sees the robe come and it frightens him because the robe believes, or, at least, it claims to believe it has the power to excommunicate him. That's said in scripture too. He said, You know what they'll do to you? They will kill you and they will excommunicate you, and this they will do because they know not the Father, nor me (John 16:1). He's telling anyone who claims himself to have the right of excommunication he is doing it because he knows not the Father, nor me. Read it carefully. You read that in the Book of John. They will put you out of the synagogue; they will excommunicate you, and they will even kill you and think they do God a service. This they do because they know not the Father. They believe in God, fatherhood ignored. They haven't had the experience of the fatherhood. They don't know who the Father is, and to this day they still call Jesus the son.

Goodnight.

HIS OWN CREDENTIALS

4/3/64

Tonight's subject is "His Own Credentials." When anyone aspires to hold public confidence, they must begin with their own credentials, that is, they must speak from experience. Then it will be said of you what was said of the central figure of the gospels. They were astonished at his teaching and they said, He speaks as one having authority and not as the scribe.

Now this is a gradual transition from a God of tradition to a God of experience. Tonight I can tell you what I have discovered, but I can't persuade you to accept it one hundred percent. It will come. You'll try it, it will prove itself in the testing, but it takes time for a man to give up his belief in an *external* God. And so, from this platform we identify God with the human Imagination and in doing that we close the gap between God and man. And so, tonight you may allow the gap to close and then test it. If you do, you'll get the result. But I'm not promising that tomorrow you will not depart from this God that you find tonight. You will simply...it's too much, it sounds so great, so overwhelming you can't believe that this thing really is true. So you try it again, and gradually, as you try it and try it, then God himself will unveil himself within you. It's called in scripture revelation. But Paul said, "The gospel that I preach is not man's gospel. Nor was I taught it, but it came to me through a revelation of Jesus Christ" (Gal. 1:11). And revelation to Paul was an act of God in self-revealing.

So here, we turn back to the ancient scriptures, the Psalms. You and I will read the words and you might think they are said of someone else. For by the word of the Lord the heavens were made…this is the 33rd Psalm: "By the word of the Lord the heavens were made, and all their host by the breath of his mouth. Let all the earth fear the Lord. Let all the populations of the world," every man and woman in the world, "let them stand in awe of him" (verses 6, 8). And now he asks why, like you would ask why, why should I fear the Lord? Is he not a God of love as the psalmist told me? And here is the psalmist writing again, so why should I stand in awe of him? Why should I fear him? And he tells me why, "For he spoke, and it came to be; he commanded, and it stood forth" (verse 9). Well, I certainly should respect that power. For the word translated fear means "reverence," means "to revere, to respect." And so, I must respect a power that is so creative. It only speaks, and it comes to be; it commands, and it stands forth.

Well, here is a simple story. This will amuse you...I got it in the morning's mail. He isn't here tonight...he comes on Tuesday...but he said, several months ago the wedding of his nephew was announced for the 23rd of March; that was the day of the wedding. His sister-in-law, his brother's wife, came over to explain the family into which her son was going. She said, "You know, the mother of the bride-to-be is quite a snob. She doesn't think they're good enough for her, and really quite a snob in every sense of the word, that this boy should not come into their family." But, nevertheless, it was all done and they were getting married the 23rd. When the sister-in-law left, this chap who wrote me the story said to himself, "Wouldn't it be fun just to put her nose out of joint"—meaning the mother of the bride-to-be. So he said this is what I did, I said, "Wouldn't it be marvelous if my sister-in-law wore a Don Loper dress." Well, now you ladies would know what the Don Loper dress is. I had to ask my wife, so she put me wise concerning a Don Loper dress. And so, he said himself, "I'm going to see her in a Don Loper dress." Well, "Came the day of the wedding and she wore a very pretty blue dress," and he said, "she looked very pretty in it; but I thought to myself it certainly wasn't wedding-ish for a member of the wedding party." "So the next Saturday, after the wedding, she called to say hello to Mother, that is, she and my brother. She said, 'You know, I felt myself a little bit underdressed but I said to myself, "I'll be damned if I cannot wear a Don Loper dress to my son's wedding."

Now, she thought she initiated it. She thought she had originated the entire thought. Then my friend added a little after-line, "Undoubtedly it was the least expensive model, but, nevertheless, it was a Don Loper." Then he said, "Now I see why you stress it constantly that all of us should be so very, very careful to invest our thoughts rather than spend them, because everything that you do you're going to reap." So he reaped it and it was fun. I wouldn't blame anyone for having that little something in them to get even if "your child isn't good enough." You wouldn't be human if in some strange little way you didn't do something just like that. It didn't offend her, didn't hurt anyone, but he proved a point.

Now, who did it? My friend did it. Well, did he fulfill scripture? For it said God did it, he spoke, and it came to be; he commanded, and it stood forth. Could that be the same presence spoken of? Certainly, there's only one God, only one creative power, and he found it in himself as his own wonderful human Imagination. But I am not going to swear that he tonight will not go back through habit to the God of tradition. It takes a little while to move, to grow up, and spiritual growth is a gradual transition from the God of tradition to the God of experience. When you experience it over and over, then you too will speak with the authority that he speaks of in scripture.

Then another one came in the morning's mail. This chap said that he works at the airport. And so he felt quite inspired, and he was reciting to himself the 2nd verse of the 2nd chapter of Habakkuk. He said, whenever I go over there, I go down to the very end of the runway, a place where I usually go to meditate. There's an old gate there, and it's almost like a friend of mine. I lean against it and dream; I lean against it and think all kinds of things. Well, two fellows had asked me to aid them in getting promoted and getting more money. Well, he said, my position in the company does not warrant making this decision. I have no power to promote them or to raise their salary, but I could do it in my Imagination. And so, in my Imagination I saw the two fellows being congratulated by the entire staff on being promoted and receiving more money.

Well, a few months later, the first one was called in to be interviewed, and strangely enough when he entered the office to be interviewed who was the interviewer but an old friend of his. And so, the old friend instantly raised his present salary on that same job, that when he accepted the promotion it would automatically carry with it a bigger salary than that promoted job would carry. By taking the present job and raising the salary for it, when he now accepts the promoted job, it would carry an automatic bigger salary. And, one month later, the other one was promoted with an increase in salary. Now he said, "Neville, all I did was simply put into practice what you teach. I imagined that my two friends had what I was powerless to give them. I have no position in the company that would allow me to promote them or in any way raise their salary. But I could do it in my Imagination and that I did with the result that here today they are working. They're all being congratulated. I called them up to ask them if they liked the job and they are ecstatically happy on the job."

Now that is simply identifying God with your own wonderful human Imagination, closing the gap between God and man, and trying to keep it closed. Because it's not the easiest thing in the world, for you and I have been conditioned from the cradle to believe in some external power. We can't bring ourselves to believe that by the word of the Lord the heavens were made and *that* Lord is the same presence in us when we say "I am"... when I can't even make a nail. How could I bring myself to believe that by a word uttered in faith the heavens came into being and that being that brought them in to being is one with my own wonderful human Imagination? That's difficult to accept over night but it gradually comes. When it becomes now a vision, an actual experience, that's when the thrill begins. All that is said of him in scripture you will experience. Everything said of him you're going to experience. At first to you with the experience it's a mere presentiment, a mere strange foreboding, is it really true? But then when they become rapid and you can come through one after the other, it's an absolute certainty. At first, a mere presentiment; because you can't believe that you, this little you, born of a woman, who will die in this world in a few short years, and that *this* you, that you don't even know the thing that has been happening to you, that how could it be you when you are taught to believe that it applies to someone 2,000 years ago?

Listen to these words of the 40th chapter of the Book of Psalms, "And I said, 'Lo, I come; in the volume of the book it is written of me; O my God, I delight to do thy will; thy law is within my heart" (Psalm 40:7,8). Here is an *inspired* man, because no prophecy ever came by the compulsion of a man. He didn't sit down to compose it, but men moved by the Holy Spirit spoke from God. So they didn't understand what they were writing; they were writing under inspiration. But the time of the fulfillment of it was not yet. So here in the 40th Psalm, suddenly it dawns upon him that in the book itself it is written of me. And I thought all that I received in dictation was of another being, a being I always referred to as "the Lord" or as "my God" or by some other name. It could not for one moment be me. And then it dawns upon him: in the book it is written of me. And now he sees the whole law spoken of is in his own heart, and now he delights to do the will of the Lord. And now he tells us, "I have not restrained my lips. I have not kept it a secret in my heart. I have told it to all the congregation." Let them hear it and let them now respond either negatively or positively. But I told it to everyone who would listen, because I have found him. And so, you find him as your own Imagination and then you tell it; and while you are still struggling with yourself to convince yourself this thing is so good, so marvelous, it's really true...because it doesn't come over night. When a man finds himself making only a mental adjustment, and by that change in mental attitude he changes his inner conversation, because the change commands it and compels it; and then an outer world appears to conform to that inner change within him. Well, he tries it again and it still proves itself. He tries it again. Now he tries it with others, without their knowledge, without their consent and it works again. He wonders, "What is this strange power?"

Well, I was taught to get down on my knees and say the Lord's Prayer, and make some mental image of a being in space that would be listening and would hear. And so, at the age of seventeen I didn't have the courage, regardless of how tired I was and how late I came home, to go to bed without first getting down on the floor on my knees and saying the Lord's Prayer. I just recited it quickly because I wanted to get to bed. But I didn't have the courage to break that habit. I didn't understand it. "Our Father which art in heaven," we all would say, but it didn't mean anything to me. I had my own earthly father. I did believe...always believed in a God, but until I found him he was always an *external* God. But I couldn't conceive that he could ever see in me anything. So all the arguments in scripture take place in us. When you read that they say to him, "Well, we know your parents, we know your brothers and sisters," that part of it is not taking place on the outside. That's taking place in the mind of the one who has had the experience. He knows he does better than anyone else does, as you do. "What man knoweth the Spirit of a man but the Spirit of that man? What man knows the *things* of a man but the Spirit of the man?"

So then, this thing happened in him, and he was born differently. Yet he knew the physical birth took place, for he saw himself clothed in flesh and blood. And then a new birth took place within him and he knew that was foretold, that was prophesied. So he goes back into the ancient scriptures and finds the parallel passage. And now the argument starts in him because he is making a claim that is fantastic. It's opposed by what he knows to be true concerning the outer garment. And so, *he* is saying, I know my father, my mother, my brothers, he names his brothers, I know my sisters. And so, it is *he* carrying on the argument within himself. And so when we are told the father against a son, and a mother against the daughter, a mother-in-law against the daughter-in-law, this is not an argument taking place on the outside. It's the ancient against the present. He has made the discovery now. And so, it's always the father against the son, the mother against the daughter, the mother-in-law against the daughter-in-law, and not any relationship on the outside: It's all *in* man. And so, the father represents the ancient traditional concept of life. And suddenly, I've found that everything in that book is about *me*; it's *not* about something on the outside at all. And the battle is on, and it's yours until I overcome the war within me. So I can then face the whole vast world and it makes no difference if they listen or not because it's overcoming you. So then you will speak with an authority that you could not speak with before, because now you speak not only from a conviction, you speak from experience. You aren't theorizing anymore. This is no theory; this is something that you know because you've experienced it.

And so, this is the story of speaking with your own credentials. As Paul said, "When it pleased God to reveal his Son *in* me, then I conferred not with flesh and blood" (Gal. 1:16). To whom would I turn? What person in this world that has not had the experience or heard of the experience in the way that you've heard it here could throw any light upon the experience when someone is dumbfounded? How could they? They will tell you as they told me, many a doctor has told me, "Why, Neville, it's a strange hallucination." I said, would you define it for me? Well, they just use words without any meaning, they can't define it...just a vivid dream. Well, a man can refer to this as a dream because he's never had a vision. A vision is truth unmodified by the conceptual mind. You're raised above the limits of this world altogether; but it's just as real as this, only more so, and things unfold one after the other.

So when you return, it's not a dream. I dream nightly, but visions come at long intervals, especially the visions as recorded in the gospels, beginning with the resurrection, then the birth, then the discovery of the fatherhood of God, then the ascent into the Holy of Holies, and then the descent of the dove. They come at intervals, stated intervals, the first great four: two the first night, one on the heels of the other; and then five months later the second, the discovery of the fatherhood of God; and then four months later, comes the ascent into the Holy of Holies; and then three years later, the Holy Spirit descends in bodily form as a dove...the identical experience. So when these happen, you have no more doubts in your mind. If in the beginning you thought that this could only be a peculiar self-induced state, you have no doubt *after* the other, one on top of the other.

So here, believe me. Take this thought this night: Identify God with your own wonderful human Imagination. Close the gap between the two—not God *and* you, just say just God or just you. Go on now. And having found what this presence did (your Imagination) you go out determined to put it to the test. As you're told, "Come test me and see...if I will not open the windows of heaven and pour out gifts so great you haven't room on earth to receive them" (Mal. 3:10). What, "Do you not realize that Jesus Christ is in thee?--unless of course you fail to meet the test!" (2 Cor. 13:5). So here, we are speaking of a test of faith, really.

So when we are told, "Stand in awe," it doesn't mean...well, the word awe, as far as I am concerned, is an emotion that comes when you contemplate the sublime. How would I contemplate God having discovered him to be my own Imagination? You can. You're told, "Worship God...for the testimony of Jesus is the spirit of prophecy." Well, how do I worship

God? Worship means "to count worthy," that is, worthy of observation. So you sit down quietly and you turn your attention *inward* and you become attentive to what is happening now. You notice a miracle taking place because you can think of someone and you see them. And that's crazy. You can think of something else and you see it. You can listen and you hear what you want to hear. Well, who is doing it? So here, all of a sudden you realize *who* is doing it. Well, if this presence in you is doing it, haven't you found him? So that's worship. You're counting worthy of observation this presence within you. At first you see no one. You see only the people that you think of. You see the scenes you think of. But the day will come that the presence that's doing it all will take on human form and stand before you, and then you will *know* God is man. You will see God and you will know he's infinite love. God *is* man. People don't believe it. I hope you do. As Blake said, "Thou art a man, God is no more. Thy own humanity learn to adore" (*Everlasting Gospel*). And then you know the most beautiful little verse, only one verse, *On the Virginity of the Virgin:* "What ere is done to her she cannot know, and if you ask her she'll swear it so. Whether it is good or evil, none to blame; no one to take the pride, no one the shame."

I'll give you a vision of mine. To see the universal man, just one man, and to see that you and I that seem so solidly real, all these garments, they are only the outer skin of that heavenly man, all these; and *you are* the heavenly man. You have the experience of being the skin made up of all the generations of man, constantly changing through the event called death, like the serpent shedding skin, all being shed; yet the It itself remains being re-clothed, the new generations; and yet it is both; and *you* are that heavenly man. A sensitivity in that man, you can't describe it at all; because as the man you can get below the skin and see the being that you really are, that living being. But I tell you whatever is done to this virgin is spoken of as "that heavenly man." And then I saw the sign come before me in big block letters "virgin pure," and I looked so closely to be sure I was reading it correctly, "virgin pure." And then comes the vision and the actual experience: I *was* that man, with all the sensitivity, and clothed as skin by every being that walked the face of the earth. And then you know the oneness of all, the unity of all.

So I ask you, take it seriously. Try it. Try it this night for a friend. Maybe you have no urge to change your world. But someone in your world could be changed for advantage and you try it for him, try it for her, try it for them. Because it is God *in* you that can speak and it comes to pass. Just as you're told, he spoke. Fear him because he spoke, and it came to be; fear him standing ___(??), why?—because he just only commanded, and it stood forth. And so Tom only commanded, "I'll put her nose out of joint. I will see my sister-in-law wearing a Don Loper." And then seven months go by. He mentioned something to his sister-in-law. He doesn't suggest it that she could act upon the suggestion. She thinks she did the entire thing and justified it, when they met the summer after the wedding, by saying, "I said to myself, well, I'll be damned if I cannot wear a Don Loper dress for my son's wedding" and that's how she justified it. She felt that she was a little bit under-dressed, but that's all right, it was a Don Loper. That's all there was to it. That's all that he asked.

Undoubtedly, she's not a lady of means and maybe she never wore one before, and may never wear one again, but Tom, knowing the law, he can always keep her clothed in Don Loper dresses. Doesn't take any couturier in the world, they could all be used. That's what they're there for, to sell dresses. And if you want to clothe your sister-in-law better than she has been clothed, you can do it, without her knowledge, without her consent. I've seen people doing all kinds of things, but after they do it they still don't believe it worked that way and they will say, "It's just my luck," or "That was simply luck." Well, you know what the word luck means? Luck is a name given by those who have no faith to the works of faith, that's what luck is. There is no such thing. It's all the outpouring of these imaginal acts of men.

So you act with faith and no power in the world can stop you. The man had no power to change the position of two men. He couldn't increase their salary. But no power in the world could stop him from doing it for them and he did it with results. Now today, if he's here tonight, I hope with his eyes and ears wide open he will close the gap even more, and keep on closing that gap to find there aren't two of you. You can say "I am he." In all the scripture it's simply "I am he." "But who are you?" "I told you, 'I am he.'" "But you haven't told me this day." "Oh, yes I have." "Well, who is your father?" "Well, my Father is he whom you call God; but I know my Father and ye know not your God." And after that comes the argument and the argument is taking place within you. For, I'm speaking from experience. It wasn't easy to discover this and overnight to fuse to it. It wasn't, because the very next day you had an unpaid bill and no sums to meet it. Yet, you found that your Imagination is God, can't go back on that discovery, and yet your anxiety now postpones the day of the harvest. You can't quite bring yourself to actually imagine the end, because the need is now, urgently, now. And so, you postpone the closing of the gap until finally you'd rather die, be cut in pieces, than go back on the discovery of the one and only God. The one who is your own wonderful human Imagination, that's God. And don't think I'm robbing you or taking anything from you. In fact, if I took anything it would only be the idol that you've kept alive in the place of the living God.

So when you go to bed this night, just *worship* God. Close your eyes, just turn on the inside. You might see ___(??) glorious light, golden liquid light, moving around your head and moving off into space, like a man blowing a smoked cigar. Only this is living light, something that comes out of your head this way, it forms circles, and goes off in puffs from your forehead. You simply become entranced with it all. And then you could turn away from it to something else. But think of any friend this night, and in confidence, and hold God, which is your Imagination, hold him trustworthy. Trust him implicitly to bring it to pass; because this is your word, you spoke, and it comes to pass. You're speaking the word when you imagine something in faith. You must imagine it in faith. As we are told, many heard it, but it was not mixed with faith in those who heard it, therefore they did not get the results. They heard the same word in the Book of Hebrews, but only those who heard it and received it with faith got the results (4:2). And the others were called "the children of the wilderness," because they kept on moving through the wilderness. They wouldn't stop for one moment to turn in and worship God, and prove his existence, and his nearness, and the oneness with God. The day will come to every one of us, because not one can fail.

Now, we are called upon to set our hope fully upon the grace that is coming to us at the revelation of Jesus Christ. Set your hope fully upon this grace, and grace is God's gift of himself to man, directly, no intermediary, none whatsoever. There's no intermediary between you and God. When you read the story carefully you will see that no one ordained ___(??), no bishop, no elder, no president; he has no intermediary. In fact, he repudiates all institutions, all customs, all laws that interfere with the direct access of the individual to his God. No one in this world can be between yourself and God. Call upon a friend if you feel that the thing is too pressing ___(??), call a friend if you trust him to believe that his imaginal act relative to you is true, then call him, call her...because we're all one anyway. But don't believe for one moment that intermediaries are essential to your access to God. It's all God. And God became man that man may become God.

If I took this night some other form of God from you, I don't regret it. Because only as we die to these gods can we find the true God, the living God, the real God. And I can't tell anyone the *thrill* that's in store, the actual thrill. It's morning, noon and night thereafter. You sit no matter where you are and you dwell upon this loving kindness that has been shown you by the very being that you really are. You dwell upon it...just can't think of anything but. And it goes on for years. This thing started with me before I found the principle. I found the law; well, the law thrilled me when I got results, marvelous. But when God began to *unveil* himself within me on that morning of the 20th day of July, 1959, from then on I could think of nothing but. Yes, I had to fix certain things, but it doesn't really hold my interest very long. I go back and ponder this greatest of all things, best of things, and then try to tell it to as many as will listen that it's going to happen to everybody. And no one differs in the eyes of this being that I saw, and *was* when I saw it, this universal man that is one man, living being, allowing everything to be done *to* him by man's misuse *of* him.

For he's all Imagination and my misuse of my Imagination hurts this very sensitive part of me. Wish I could share with you the sensitivity of that part. It responds quickly and allows everything that you do to it. "So what ere is done to her she cannot tell, and if you ask her she'll swear it so. Whether it's good or evil, no one to blame, no one to take the pride and no one the shame." For in the end though what we have done be like scarlet, it'll all be washed just as white as snow. Doesn't really matter, in the end all things will be washed white as snow. And *you* will be the God that in your darkness you worshipped as another than yourself. So when you read the Bible in the future—I hope you do it daily—try to get the mood that the book is written about you: "In the volume of the book it is written of me." He didn't know it. And then his heart jumped for joy, he said, "I delight to do thy will." But he couldn't believe that this whole thing could really center in him, centered in you as an individual.

There's another letter I got this morning, but it's too long because there are so many dreams in it. It's perfectly wonderful. I want to thank you, if you're here. You tell me you come quite often. That letter came...I read it with great, great interest. I have it on file, but it's too long to take up from the platform tonight. Again, let me appeal to all to test it and then share with me by giving me your letters that I, in turn, may tell those who come to encourage them. Your faith, my faith, together will encourage all. If I can just share one, two or three stories a night based upon actual experiences. I don't want anyone manufacturing these stories. Please don't manufacture a story, tell me exactly what you did, what was the objective, how you applied it, and how it worked, that I may have your letter on file that I can turn to it. I don't imagine you'll ever question my honesty, but I would like your letter on file so that if someone should question that I can bring the letter out. So you write and take me into your confidence and share with me this use of this greatest of all laws; for there is no other law.

So tonight, you can start with the man you are, with the woman you are, and change yourself completely by the use of Imagination. You have no one to whom you can turn for promotion? Alright, you don't need him. No one can give you a raise? You don't need him. No one who can dress you properly? You don't need him. All you have to do is use your Imagination to dress yourself properly, and you give yourself promotion, and do all the things that you really want to do. Except do it first in Imagination and then you'll do it externally.

A chap came to me in New York City and he said, "Neville, I want to make"…and he mentioned a sum of money. He was an engineer, but he never really made big money, but always held responsible jobs. I said, "Where do you want to work?" Well, he said, "There's a firm on Madison Avenue," and he named the floor where they operate. I said, "Would you go there if you got the job?" He said, "Yes, until they send me overseas. They always do things all over the world, but until I receive my appointment I would go there every day." I said, "Now in your Imagination get on that elevator and go up, feel the thing ascend, get off at the floor, go in the door, hang up your hat, and sit at your desk. That's all. That would imply if your hat is hung up now and you're at the desk you're working there." In one week he got that job, with a salary he had never dreamed of before.

Unfortunately…and yet not unfortunately because we all have our exits from this world at appointed hours, he was on the job and simply died. He was only there four years and one day, heart attack...young man, fifty-six years old. But that's alright. He lived fully, and before he made his exit here he discovered a creative power within himself. So he and his wife and daughter always came to the meetings, and before he made his exit the three of them found God. If the blow was so great that it turned them aside to another god, I don't know. Some people, you know, turn aside and think they should not have done that; it displeased God and then God took me, or took my husband from me. They think of a God of retribution and I have found the God of love, infinite love, no retribution whatsoever. And so, he was simply called at the appointed hour.

But I could take these and multiply them by the dozens, the hundreds, yes, I'll go into the thousands, of these stories. And one seems more fantastic than the other. But we are told, in spite of the number of the signs that he gave them and the character of the signs, they still did not believe him. They still did not believe him. I can talk to many...this night before I came out I got a call from New York City. This lady got off the plane last night and called to ask me to help a certain very dear ___(??). Now, at a distance she wouldn't mind if I was called. But when I meet her in the flesh, in the month of July, in Barbados, she couldn't possibly credit me with the power to change a condition in *her* life that someone else that she trusts implicitly as a doctor would feel it's going to take time, and this can't work this way, it may never work. And so, to turn to something you can't put your hand upon. You're trying to touch God, but you can't touch him. He's just like quicksilver and he hides himself in his own creativity. He creates something and hides himself in it...just like quicksilver.

So here, this night, just go into the Silence and imagine the loveliest thing you can imagine of someone ___(??), and when you break the Silence believe in the reality of what you have done. And don't expect a long interval of time between what you've done and the fruition of it, believe that it's done, just believe it's something *now*, and it will come out.

Now, let us go.

* * *

Q: Does it help in any way to have many minds with the same faith on one thing rather than one? Can the one by itself…?

A: Did you hear the question? Does it add to have many minds work on one thought or just the one mind itself? Well, in the end there's only one. I don't feel that you can add strength by getting a crowd about it, I really don't. It's simply faith in the imaginal act by the individual who is performing that act; and if I turn to others, hoping the crowd will do it, well, it's a lack of faith on my part. This man did not take anyone into his confidence. He simply did it for his sister-in-law and would not even suggest to her it would be nice *if* she got it.

Q: (inaudible)

A: ___(??)..."and pray to your Father who is in secret and your Father who is in secret will reward you openly." So you are asked to enter the closet alone and shut the door of the senses. Go right here, ___(??) and close out everyone in this room; therefore, you close each door of the senses on everything here, and you are in communion with your Father who is your very self.

Q: (inaudible)

A: Can the Imagination extend the appointed time of death? If I go back to the Bible, I would have to answer in the negative. "There's a time to be born and a time to die, a time to laugh and a time to cry, time to plant and a time to reap" and we have all these in the Book of Ecclesiastes. Because of this fixed frame that is called a play that the author of my fate and finisher of my fate does not allow me to alter the fixed frame. But he gives me great freedom within the framework of his plot, of his plan to give me himself; for his purpose is to give me himself *directly*. He inserts me into this framework and really there's no death. But I mean our exits from the stage and our entrances from the stage the Bible tells me they are fixed. That's what it tells me.

Q: (inaudible)

A: "For my own sake I do it, for my own sake, for how shall my name be profaned? My glory I will not give unto another" (Is. 48:10). Can't give it to another! He has to make you himself, and when in *his* eye you are *perfectly* made, then he gives himself. His *glory* is himself.

Q: (inaudible)

A: If you read it carefully, it's the most cruel experiment on an innocent being, and that's man, my dear. Therefore, Job was completely innocent of any guilt whatsoever. But he didn't know God. He started off in the beginning with everything in the world—possessions, ten children, beautiful daughters, wonderful sons, a nice wife—and then comes one blow after the other. His friends depart from him, they all begin to leave, and then the sores come, everything comes. And then in the end, he's made to say in the very last chapter, "I have heard of thee with the hearing of the ear, but now my *eye* sees thee" (Job 42:5). He wasn't convinced of the reality of God until the very end. For he spoke only from the cloud, he spoke only from some concealed area, and then he wouldn't even speak to Job. And Job knew that he was innocent and said that if I would have the pleasure of standing in his presence to defend my innocence, for he knew if he stood in the presence of God he would be God. Because man becomes what he beholds, and only the pure in heart can see God. Therefore, if he could stand in the presence of God, that would imply he was pure in heart, and therefore that in itself would be a fusion with God. So he asked God to please let him come into his presence and plead his case. But in the end, "I have heard of thee with the hearing of the ear, but now my eye sees thee." And then you see him, and then there are no more doubts in the mind of man who sees.

Q: On the one hand Jesus is saying, "I am the way, I am the life, I am the resurrection"; then on the other he prays "Our Father." I can't...

A: The fatherhood of God is revealed through his Son, and only through his Son, *only* through his Son. He said, "I go to my Father and to your Father, to my God and to your God." He establishes this point: Don't think for one moment he's telling the world that I differ from you. I have found the fatherhood of God. "I and my Father are one." "When you see me you see the Father." And what revealed me as Father? God's Son revealed me as Father, for I saw him, and he called me Lord, called me Father. And I knew it. There was no uncertainty in me when he called me Father. I knew he was my son. It takes the Son to reveal the Father. "No one knows who the Son is except the Father, and no one knows who the Father is except the Son and anyone to whom the Son chooses to reveal him" (Mat. 11:27).

So one night, an explosion and standing before you is this eternal youth; it's David, and he calls you Father. Well, he's already called me

Father. The scripture is, call *Paul* father. These who claim they are awake he must have called them Father. It's part of the unveiling of God in man. Therefore, when he calls you Father, though you answer to the name of Bill and I answer to the name of Neville—and I have a child and you are not that child's father, her name is Vicki—but I also have a child, a Son, and one day you are going to know that *you* are his Father. And I won't be envious. We are one. But you will not know that unity of being until the Son who revealed me as Father also reveals you as Father. And so if you are the father of my Son and I know I am, well, then are we not one? So, "In that day the Lord will be one and his name one." That's what we're told in Zechariah.

So, all will know the same Son as their Son, and there will be no envy because we will be the Father. He's taken us to the Father. He said, "I am the way." To what? Really to everything, but specifically to the Father. So follow this way and you'll be led to the Father. And when that moment in time is right for you, you have an explosion and standing in your room, in your presence, will be David, the eternal youth, Olam. "I have put eternity into the mind of man, yet so that he cannot find out what God has done from the beginning to the end" (Eccles. 3:11). And that that he put into the mind of man and hid it so that man cannot find out is Olam and Olam is the eternal youth. Eternity is a youth; it's not an old man. And so, that's that 2nd Psalm, I have begotten you, today I have begotten you: "Thou art my Son, this day I have begotten you" (verse 7). These words are addressed to David, to Olam, the eternal youth. But when he stands before the king and the king wants to find out the *father* of that child; he's not interested in the child. The child is this grand child that brought down the Philistine, Goliath. He said, "Whose son is that youth?" Nobody knows. "Well, inquire whose son is that *stripling*." Nobody knows. So he turns to the son himself, he said, "Tell me, son, whose son are you?" and he answers, "I am the son of thy servant Jesse the Bethlehemite." Well, the word Jesse is I AM, that's what it is; the word Jesus is I AM. And so, David did call Jesus "Father." But in scripture Jesse is the father. But it means the same thing: it's I AM. Because, he's promised to set the Father free, not the Son.

The Son is concealed in everyone and the Son has to make the Father free. So if it makes you free, that father's free. He made this father free. He makes all the fathers free, and in the end, altogether they form the one God, the one Father. Is that clear?

BE MASTER OF THE MOOD

4/10/64

Tonight's subject is "Be Master of the Mood." First of all, I want to thank you for your perfectly wonderful letters. Another windfall this week...one gentleman enclosed eight pages thick, another six, a lady two, and so it goes. Perfectly marvelous, really! The gentleman with eight said he only started coming here when I returned this past November and gave me this perfectly wonderful epistle. Tonight we will tie them in—not all of them, we can't use all—but tie a few with the deep part of the story which is taken from the 42nd Psalm, and how we read the Bible.

First of all, we are told the three-fold cord is not quickly broken. The first strand is that which anyone who can read will discover when they read the story. What you can't read you can listen to the story, and the one who can read it for you can tell you. If he can tell it with understanding so you understand the story, that's one strand. Then there's a second strand—for that is simply a story, but it's secondary to his meaning—and you try to extract the meaning of the story told. Then you must put it to the test because you are the operant power. If you can take what you extract or think you've extracted and test it and it proves itself in performance, you have the second strand. And the third comes by revelation, and you'll find every passage of the Bible autobiographical. Every chapter of the Bible will be seen eventually in an autobiographical manner.

So we'll take the 42nd tonight and show you how it is seen after one has had the experience as an autobiographical chapter: He's experienced it. On the surface it's called a Maskil. Well, a Maskil...there are thirteen Maskils in the Psalms...this is the second of the thirteen so called. A Maskil is simply special instruction, that's really what it is. Unlike all the other psalms, read the Maskil, you'll find that they are telling you something very, very deep. And don't let go, just read it, and ponder it, and simply scrutinize it carefully, for it has something very profound in it. That's a Maskil.

Take the Psalm, a psalm of loneliness, and here it is trying to give us instructions concerning the overcoming of loneliness. So here, as you read it, everyone suffers eventually, if not in the past or today, some time in one's life they have a sense of loneliness, where it may be through the loss of some human company. But in this case it isn't, for the beginning of it is a thirst for God that nothing in this world can satisfy but an *experience* of God. You could be among millions of people, and he's alone, because he can't be entertained by things outside of himself; he wants to find God. And so, here in this thirst…he said, "As the hart panteth after the waterbrook, so panteth my soul after thee, O God. My soul *thirsts* for God. When will I come and behold the face of God? My tears have been my food day and night, while men say to me and they say continually, 'Where is your God?'" (verses 1,3). And so, here is this bruised body as it were. The scoffers knowing his interest in God, his belief in God, and he can't prove the existence of God, and they throw it up at him. He has not a thing to prove the existence of God, the reality of God, yet he cannot quench the thirst with anything that happens on the outside. It's a *thirst* for God that only an experience of God can satisfy.

So here, first of all, he confesses his own sorrow, and then he tries to urge his soul to find rest and hope in the certainty of God. But he himself is not sure of this reality of God. He believes in God, he hasn't had the experience of God, so he's urging his soul to really find rest and hope in the reality of God. So he makes the statement, "Hope in God!" after he tells himself, Why is this soul of mine cast down? "Why art thou cast down, O soul? Why are you disquieted within me? Hope in God; for yet again I will praise him, he who is my help and my God." Then he gives us a cue. If you can take tonight as one of my friend's said in a case history, maybe totally unaware of what he did, but he was using this Psalm. So in this he gives us a cue: that in his self-communion I find no rest, I cannot in some strange way find the peace that I seek; then I could by consultation with the past find it. And so he said, "These things I remember, as I pour out my soul" and then he itemizes the things that he remembers. The first one he remembers: "How I went with the throng, and how I led them in procession to the house of God. And then the crowds, they were gay crowds, and they sang these songs of praise and thanksgiving and it was a multitude—not just a few—a multitude keeping festival" (verse 4). He remembers that, so he claims. But that was not the satisfying experience that he wanted of God. And everyone wants it.

Well, here I'll tell one story and how this gentleman used this unwittingly. For if I cannot by self-communion find the peace that I seek then I can employ this communion with time, consultation with the past. So he writes this story. I can only take three of his stories. The first one, he said, "I wanted really seriously to have my son say to me, 'You're the greatest dad in the world!' and so that night before I retired I simply imagined that I heard his voice and he said to me, 'You're the greatest dad in the world!' I did it twice. I told no one and then dropped it. On Christmas morning when I opened the presents, and opened my son's present to me, he had bought it himself with his own money, a present he wanted only for me. It wasn't something that could be shared with my wife, just my present. It was a gold-plated cup on a wooden bowl and on the wooden bowl there was brass for some inscription, and on it he had it inscribed 'The World's Greatest Dad!' Now, he said, he kept it to himself. He didn't mention it to anyone, not even to his wife, just simply inwardly he imagined it. He assumed that he heard it, told no one, and did it twice.

Then he said, "The same month of December, I went to the grocery store and as I went through the door here was a friend of my son. This chap is called Gary. He was selling mistletoe. He didn't look very happy about it, and so I said, 'Gary, how are sales going?' He said, 'They aren't going very well.' When I got outside by myself I went into the Silence and I heard my son say to me that Gary sold all the mistletoe and he made a profit of fourteen dollars." So, he said, "I can't tell you why I picked out fourteen dollars, other than the boy is only twelve and I thought fourteen dollars profit was good for this time. It's enough for a lad of twelve. And so I just said, I heard my son say he sold all the mistletoe and he made a profit of fourteen dollars. Well, two days before Christmas when I came into the living room I noticed among the decorations some holly, and I inquired, 'Well, where did the holly come from?' My son said, 'Well, Gary had some left over and he gave me some holly.' So then I asked, 'What happened to the mistletoe?' Oh, he said, 'He sold *all* the mistletoe and he made a profit of fourteen dollars.'" Well, now these are two.

Now this is where his consultation with *time* comes in. He said, "At my home looking from my dining room, I could see in the past a beautiful landscaped hillside, about a quarter of a mile away. And then the neighbor next door grew bamboo, and the bamboo came up six to eight feet above my hedge and blocked off completely this lovely view of mine. And all the benefit I got from the bamboo, when the wind blew I got all the leaves. And so, I didn't want to do anything about it physically or say anything to my neighbor, but I sat at my dining room table—again I did not tell anyone what I am doing or what I did—but I saw the past. That is, I saw that hillside as it used to be seen by me, sitting just where I'm sitting now. I saw it clearly in my mind's eye, because I closed eyes to the obvious, and in my Imagination I recalled the scene of the past and felt satisfied in seeing that same wonderful, beautiful scene of the past. Ten days later when I came home my wife said to me, 'Have you heard the news?' and I wondered, 'What news?' She said, 'Our neighbor is going to cut down the bamboo.' Well, in the immediate present the neighbor took down the bamboo. And, he said, strangely enough, it was so detailed in keeping with my image, where mine would go over now and take my vision and put it over the fence. There is still bamboo out there, lots of it, but only the bamboo that blocked my vision, only that was removed, in keeping with exactly what I did seated at my dining room table." Then he goes on and gives me another five perfectly marvelous ones.

But here, these five prophets, he's telling us to consult with the past. He said, "These things I remember" and they're only joyful things among the things that he remembered, not one sad note in the things remembered. So if I by communing with myself cannot dispel the loneliness, then I can just fall upon another aid and remember something lovely in my life, something perfectly marvelous, and once more consult with the past and put myself into *that* state; for I'm just moving from one state into another state. And so, that's what he did in this third case history.

But here's another one...and you watch this because you must get *intense* about it. A gentleman, who is in the audience tonight, he writes this, that he finds...of course, he's an artist and so maybe he has to fire his Imagination with some peculiar twist, as he said, a negative twist. And so, "This is what I do. I stand in a long line for a deposit in the bank and the very last, and I'm annoyed. I'm annoyed that I have to wait in this long line to make a big fat deposit. And so I get a kick out of my own annoyance, because I'm annoyed that I have a big fat check in my hand to deposit at the end of this long line." He said, "That's the twist in my mind."

"And so, I'll go back eight years. I was new to TV eight years ago. And so, one day I discovered my house needed painting when at the moment I didn't have the funds for a real job of painting the house, and so this is what I did. I imagined the house painted. I was annoyed with the painters at the window; they could see me taking a shower. That annoyed me that they could look right on me and see me taking a shower. And then I saw and could smell the wet paint. Then I took my hand, all in my Imagination, and put it on the paint. I didn't trust the sign and it *was* wet. So I got more annoyed that I had paint on my hands." Well, he said, "The very next morning after I did this, I had written a pilot which was under consideration back East, so I called my agent and I asked the agent if he had any news about the pilot. He said, "No, but I was just about to call you because" (he mentioned this person by name) "he just called me and asked me if you would take twenty-one thousand dollars cash for your residuals? Well, he said, "At the moment, I didn't know I had residuals. I was so new in the business I didn't realize I had residuals coming from things already shot. But this man appeared, bought out his partner (he's a producer undoubtedly), he bought out his partner and was trying to buy out everyone connected with this series and hold it all for himself; and was trying to get it for fifty cents on the dollar. So my agent said to me, 'Knowing this man's attitude towards money and how he operates, I'm going to suggest that you take this $21.000 and just run like a thief... because, just take it, take the twenty-one thousand.' So, he said, I did, and to my knowledge I don't think anyone else in the series ever received anything from their residuals. But he said, I was so new in the business I didn't realize I had residuals. So the house was painted."

So he annoys...if you want to, get annoyed. If it will make you annoyed to put your hand on wet paint when you can't afford the paint...but if you put your hand on wet paint, the paint must be there. And if you're going to get annoyed because you have a long line waiting for a deposit of a big fat check, well then, if that will do it, intensifying your imagination, then do it. For the thing is to get your Imagination worked to the point where it becomes *real* to you. But he did it and he made it real. He used his sense of sight—he could see the man watching him while he was taking a shower. He could smell the paint, that's another sense. He could *feel* the wet paint, that's another sense. And with his very annoyance took these senses and raised them to the nth degree. And then it worked and worked quickly. So in twenty-four hours there was twenty-one thousand cash waiting for him which he took.

Now this is a cute one. I hope she's here tonight. But she wrote, she said, "I'm a grandmother and last fall I made arrangements to go to the South Pacific and to the Orient. So I said to my little granddaughter, two years old, 'What would you like Nanny to send you?' Well, she discussed it with her mother and together they came up with this request, a kangaroo, but a stuffed kangaroo. I said, 'Alright, a stuffed kangaroo.' So when I got to Australia I looked at all the toys and I didn't like the kangaroos, so I sent her a little polar bear. I wrote the mother what I had done. So when the mother read the letter to the little child, only two years old, she said, 'I don't want a bear! I want a kangaroo!' In the meanwhile she had been talking all the time about her little kangaroo. She told her mother, her friends, anyone who would listen to her only about the kangaroo.

So when this lady came back, she heard anew that her granddaughter was greatly disappointed in this little bear, in fact, wouldn't want it, really. But the bear hadn't yet arrived. Two weeks later the bear came and the little girl didn't want it. She would have not a thing to do with it. And forty-eight hours later, a package addressed to this little girl arrived, it was a stuffed kangaroo. And the little girl said, "I *knew* that Nanny bought me a kangaroo." The grandmother said to me in her letter "I never did, I never bought a kangaroo for her. I only bought and paid for one thing and that was the little bear. Now while I was gone, she in her Imagination only accepted the kangaroo." So six thousand miles away some stock clerk is trying to explain the loss of a kangaroo, and the culprit is a little two year old girl right here in the city. And so, these are the stories that came in the week's mail, all sheer fantasy, all based upon this conscious use of one's Imagination to create reality. But we are the operant power; it doesn't operate itself. When you know what to do, well, then you do it.

Now we go back to the great Psalm. He paints this most wonderful story of something that he remembered, this thing he remembered. "These things I remember..." and then he said, "as I pour out my soul." And he starts with joining this enormous crowd and he led them: "I led them to the house of God." He led a procession to the house of God, and they were all joyful, singing praises of gladness and thanksgiving to God. And then he saw this enormous multitude, a huge multitude in a festive light, keeping festival. I tell you, the day will come and you open that Bible and look at it, you will be looking at it through the eyes of one who experienced it. That's autobiographical. This comes first, long before the kind of experience he wanted. But not a thing could satisfy him; he wanted an actual *experience* of God. But in this you don't *see* God. He wants to *see* God, he said, "When will I come and behold the face of God?" That experience you do not see God; you only hear God's voice.

And so, in this wonderful festive mood where there are unnumbered, you can't number them, multitudes, and all moving towards the house of God, this wonderful sanctuary; and you, having the experience, you will lead them. You will actually be the leader, the dominant character in that entire drama. And you will hear a voice and the voice is the voice of authority, the voice of God. And the voice will say, "And God walks with them." One of the crowd of this wonderful gay, praising crowd will ask the voice—you don't see the face—"If God walks with us, where is he?" And the same voice will come back, "At your side." And this one, who is only a projection of yourself; the whole vast world is yourself made visible—and this one will only respond and echo that which is taking place in you. Because the voice is now going to answer...because she is going to look right in your eyes and she's going to call you by name—the name that you respond to here, John, Robert, whatever the name is—and she's going to say, "What? Is Robert God?" And the voice will respond, "Yes, in the act of waking." And she'll be hysterical. You now why? Because *you* are, you can't believe it, it is too great. You can't conceive that you really *are* God in the act of waking. And so, she had to respond in kind; because you doubt and so she has to doubt. And she only reflects that theme, not concern so much as unbelief that is so great.

And then the voice will speak from the depths of your own soul and this is what you will hear: "I laid myself down within you to sleep, and as I slept I dreamed a dream. I dreamed..." and then you will know the end of the sentence: he's dreaming that he's you. That's why all of this is taking place. He's taking you towards his holy place. And you will wake with an experience of the crucifixion. Your hands, your feet, your head and your side will be whirling vortices, each a vortex; and you will be nailed upon this body; and awake on your bed where you had left it when you started the journey. So when you re-live that you will see it autobiographically—whole thing is talking about your own experience.

Ten years later will come the experiences the psalmist wanted. But bear in mind, he wasn't asking for it, because the psalmist only received the dictation. As we're told in the Book of Peter that no prophecy of scripture ever came by the impulse of man, but men moved by the Holy Spirit spoke from God. So men are organized by divine providence for spiritual communication, and these are called the prophets. They take it down, not knowing what they're taking down. So on one level you can read the story and much of it doesn't make sense. Then you read it and read it and try to extract its meaning, and that's when you take the meaning extracted, and put it to the test, and make it prove itself in the testing—as the gentleman proved it without destroying anything. He didn't ask the neighbor to cut the bamboos down; the neighbor had the impulse so he thought. But the neighbor's desire to cut them down originated in the vision, the imaginal vision of his neighbor, who saw clearly, sitting in the dining room where before he was obstructed by these, well, about six or eight feet tall bamboos above his fence.

Now, here is another one. ___(??). This gentleman writes me that in 1933 going down the Danube from Vienna to Budapest that he fell in love with the sight of Budapest, the lights of the night, and pledged himself that someday he would have a view just like that. So when he came back to America he came straight to California and sought a home that would have a view comparable to this view; and he found one in the hills of Hollywood. He bought it for the view, just for the view. Well, he said he lived there for years and recently someone planted poplar trees, and they grew up to the point where they just were blocking his lovely view which he lived for. Well, he saw the view and not the trees. He said, "Neville, did I misuse my

Imagination? Was it selfish of me? The trees died...not all the trees, only the poplar trees that blocked my view. Every tree in that area that blocked my view they died." And he had an orange tree and, for reasons not explained to me, the man chopped the orange tree down. Now, he said, "I just noticed another little tree planted and the leaves are coming out. But knowing what I did with the poplar trees, I'm not concerned." He said, "I know having had the experience of God that God can't kill God, and God being love, God can't kill love. It only rearranges the furniture of the mind and lets something come in to conform to the structure of my imaginal act. For you can't kill love. And God created all things, as we are told: 'Never would you have made anything had you not loved it.' And so, you don't kill the tree when you burn the tree. You don't kill anything as you *think* you destroy it, really.'"

So that was blocking his view...and this thing in his mind's eye was so vivid when he came down the Danube on his way to Budapest, and that vision of Budapest was to him so thrilling that it influenced his choice of a home. Then to have someone block it, he couldn't stand it. So he, too, went forward and communicated with the past: He saw the city as he always saw it. He would have no trees block it, and so they died. He didn't ask the man to cut them down, and that could have been an argument, because they grew on the man's property, not his property. That could have started some unpleasant conversation. And so, without asking anyone's permission he saw clearly that clear, wonderful vista that he's always enjoyed.

So when you go back and when you read it, see it in three levels, like the ark. The ark is built on three levels. On the lowest level is where man's senses, with intelligence, can read the story. But bear in mind that the story is like a dream. For these were taken down practically in a dream state. And so, every dream is a parable, for these are all parables. But the story is secondary to the *meaning* of the story, so you get the meaning. Don't change one word of the story as it is. If it's a good translation of the original text, leave it, for you're going to experience it. And that's the depth.

One day you will experience this enormous journey toward the house of God, and you will hear the voice, and you will know, with a thrill you've never known before, who you are! For you are destined to awake *as* God: for the voice will say, "Yes, God...in the act of waking." Then the voice will speak to you from the depth of your own soul, and you will hear it, and pass through the sensation of being nailed on this cross of flesh and blood. Then will come all the others; for you are told, "Now we're going to go up to Jerusalem...and *all* that is written about the Son of man will be accomplished." I am going to Jerusalem. That's where you're headed when you find yourself in this enormous crowd and all that is said of the

Son of man—-that's you—-will be accomplished as you start this journey. By the time you get there, it *is* all accomplished. What was accomplished there in that grand city? It's birth. Weren't you resurrected there? Who was resurrected there? That's where he's resurrected. And was it there that you saw David? It was David; it's called the city of David. And all these things will unfold within you.

But here, on this mastery of moods, it is so important that you actually observe yours and use anything to get out of a bad mood, but anything at all. If you want to use an irritation, like you're in a long line waiting to put in a huge big check, use it as an irritant if that is going to get you out of the mood of want into the mood of affluence. Because if you can deposit a huge big check and annoyance goes with it, just be annoyed. Not a thing wrong with that. And so you want to have it painted and you can't afford it, and then you put your hands on wet paint and you get annoyed, then put your hand mentally on wet paint and get annoyed. And so, he has that quirk. And so, he's creative and yet maybe he needs that peculiar quirk of negation to spur his Imagination to create, maybe he does. But if you can use that… that's a contribution of that to each who will accept it…to bring here and share with me what they did. And then you can use that and apply that to business. If something annoys you in business, it's so big that you didn't have time to handle it, would something annoy you? If the oil for ___(??) that you could fill, well, then get annoyed. It's far better that way than not have any oil. And so, you take this and apply it wisely. It's a simple, simple technique.

But I tell you the story of the lady who sits for one week and bathes herself emotionally with the feeling that she had security. "But I have security!" and she feels the way she would feel *after* she has confirmation of what the feeling is implying. Then one day after her six days of vigilance she gets confirmation that she receives now $540 from this fixed annuity and then her Social Security. For she's entitled to it, so together she has over six hundred dollars a month for the rest of her earthly days. She just spent the winter in Barbados. She called me long-distance, she called me this past week, to bring me news of the family in Barbados. And that was an extra gift that didn't come out of her $600 a month, because she couldn't afford that for the time she spent in Barbados. But he who gave her this money, that pays $540 a month, said to her, "I'm going to give you for a Christmas present your two months in Barbados, and that would mean I'm going to pay all expenses, including your hotel and your transportation." So that was additional.

She has *accepted* that way of living now. And this lady before this never earned more than seventy-five dollars a week at any time in her life. Now that was a mood; that was a controlled mood. She was simply a receptionist in a beauty parlor. And so, before she left for work in the morning she took her morning tub, as she told me, and while seated there she would feel the way she would expect to feel *after* she had confirmation that she had financial security. She bathed in it as it were. Then on Saturday night of that very week she was informed by this man who did not entertain this thought until Wednesday of that week. She started on Monday morning and this man had said to her all through the years that he knew her: "I will never give you a nickel, so don't look forward to any money from me." They were friendly, they were friends, but he always said to her, "We have had fun together. I've paid for all the expenses in this world, like the theater and all these things. That's all you're getting from my world."

And she believed it until I said to her the previous week, "Don't you read my books? Go back and read the story of a lady in the book called *The Law and The Promise*, and turn to the chapter called "Moods." That lady was just about your age, she is fifty-six, and you tell me sometimes you're fifty-five, the next time you're sixty-five, I don't know. So I would say you're both the same age. So you go back and read that book. But if you don't have time to read it, let me tell you what she did." So I told her exactly what the lady did. This is now on a weekend. The following Monday morning she began to put it into practice. So I made it very, very clear to her, you are the operant power. Knowing what to do and doing it are two entirely different things. So she did it religiously for five mornings. On Saturday night he said to her, "I don't feel like going out to dinner tonight, suppose we have dinner sent upstairs?" and so they had dinner sent upstairs. And then he told her, "I took one look at you Wednesday night and I said to myself (calling himself by name) it's later than you think." So the very next day he went down to his factory in Pennsylvania, called in his legal department, and said to them, "I don't want any if, ands or buts. I don't care what it costs, I want so much money, $540 a month paid to this lady, and I want it now! I don't want it next year; I want it to start immediately!" So he figured out all that it would cost, after the lump sum of money. He said, "But your taxes alone will be $28,000." "I don't care...it must be tax free. This gift is a tax-free gift, so add the $28,000 to it, whatever it costs for this lady's age to receive for the rest of her earthly days. And furthermore, the money is a gift in the sense she does not have to pay it back to my estate should she precede me in death. She can throw it away. She can will it to a kennel. She can will it to anyone she wants in this world. It is *her* money, but she cannot touch the principal while she lives. I put that proviso only to protect her, because I know when someone has that sort of principal, someone will know of it, and then get it from her. So that is one proviso: she cannot dispose of principal while she lives. But she can give it away or tear it up in a Will of hers when she's gone from this world. And so, he paid the $28,000 extra to make it tax-free gift.

That's a mood. If you haven't read that chapter, it's the chapter called "Moods" in *The Law and The Promise.* You catch a mood...and what would the feeling be like were it true? Well, then ask yourself the question, "Suppose I had so and so, well, what would the feeling be like if it were true?" Then you catch the feeling and you put on that feeling as you would wear a suit of clothes. You know, if you really put on a new hat for the first time, you think nobody knows it's new, but *you* think that everyone knows it and you feel uncomfortable in that hat until you wear it. Well, the feeling of affluence when you don't know what it is, is so new a feeling that you feel just as uncomfortable in that feeling as you do with a new suit on. You walk down the street...and a man buys a new suit for the first time, he has to walk around in it for a little while, and he actually has the mood that everyone knows it's new. He feels uncomfortable in that new suit until he breaks it in, like a pair of new shoes. Nobody really knows or cares if you have a new suit, but *you* care and you know, and you wear it until it seems natural. Well, you wear a mood until it seems natural, and when it seems natural it has taken root, and it will grow and bear fruit in your world. So these are the moods. You can make a mood very natural in a little while. But you must wear it.

And so, you just dwell upon it and see how...you read the Bible and each chapter is telling you that below the surface is a message for you to increase your joy in this world. Don't change it, leave it just as it is; and one day you're going to experience that message in the depths of your soul. For, who on looking at the 42nd Psalm would think for one moment that it's self-communion that's done it? So he communes with himself in this Psalm. And it didn't work…he communed with himself but he didn't feel the relief that he sought. And then he took up time, past time, and then he said, "These are the things I remember"...and *then* there was a *joyful* remembrance, everything about it was happy and joyful. He tuned in on it and said, I will seek and praise the Lord, even though at the moment the soul cannot and the soul is cast down. "Why are you cast down, O my soul, and why are you disquieted within me?" Then, asks you to have hope, "Hope in God," and then try to repose and try to find some rest in this hope. Because, first of all, he asks you to *hope* in God long before you hear him or you see him or experience him. And then try to find rest in that hope and that sympathy of God...and some day you will. So I never despair when someone tells me he's an atheist, makes no difference, one day he will have the experience of God; and it doesn't make any difference now what's said after the experience of God. Khrushchev will one day experience God, Stalin will one day experience God, and in the end all of their hands dripping in blood will be washed clean. No matter what he's done, it will all be washed clean. But today, he *brags* about the fact that there is no God. He says there is no God therefore it makes it so.

But I tell you, I know from experience not only there's God but God is love, infinite love, so you can always approach him. And the day will come there's no one to approach because he has completed his gift, and his gift is to give you himself. Not some little piece or part of him, he's going to completely give you himself; that you can't then commune with him, you *are* he. It's self-communion from then on. And yet it doesn't rob you of the joy of knowing that infinite presence that once embraced you and made you one with himself. And you knew by that experience the joy of wearing the divine form of light; for love truly is the human form divine, and you once had the joy of wearing it. And you know, although you can't see it and mortal eye can't see it, still it will never detach from you. You are incorporated into that human form divine. An eye can't see it but you feel it. And you've never been, I would say, at any time unaware of the fact that you wear it. From the very moment you are incorporated into it, you are fully conscious of the fact that you wear this form. And things seemingly, well, they may be more sensitive than man, but many a bird has sensed it, many an animal has sensed it, and made you fully conscious of the fact that they are aware of it. And you can't even breathe it because it doesn't make sense to any normal person. But then, something that is actually a flying being, a bird, and that bird will be arrested in its tracks. That makes it very, very conscious of the fact, fully aware, of the being that you are, and then you're ___(??).

I've had it happen time and time again, even to a little thrush. When I lived in Beverly Hills, this little thrush, every day of its life—I was there ten months—it would bring me its gift. Its gift was a sprig, come right up, follow my steps, look at me first to get my attention, and then drop it before me. Then one day it got what it wanted. It wanted to get into my house and so I let him. It walked around, perfectly tame, and then I opened the door and out he went again. But not one day did it fail to bring me a gift. The gift was to him a marvelous gift, a sprig. I didn't feed the bird, I didn't encourage it, I didn't feed it, but I was fully aware of *its* knowledge and what it knew.

So Blake made the statement, "How do we know but every bird that cuts the airy wind is an infinite world of delight closed by our senses five." He was not alone in his vision of the bird, the bird world. Victor Hugo saw it and described it beautifully. Many a mystic sees it and describes it beautifully. But we think they are just simply birds. And every bird that cuts the airy wind is an immense world of delight closed by our senses five. Man has no idea what is prepared for him when the gift is completed and his eye is opened and he's wearing the human form divine. But in the meanwhile, use these moods wisely. Take any person and put yourself in a good mood relative to them, help them. Help every being in this world and do it lovingly, costs you nothing. Get into the mood that someone told you good news concerning himself, wonderful news; and don't wait for confirmation, believe in the reality of that imaginal act, and go your way.

There's a lady tonight in this audience, I haven't seen her in the longest while. In fact, I often encourage her not to come. She comes alone, comes from a far distance, and she finds driving at night not the easiest thing in this world. But I know this problem because her husband had it, and every medical doctor confirmed the other doctor, that this open wound in his side could never heal. It could never heal! He'd been going back to the hospital from time to time for further treatment, but everyone assured him that it would never heal—no tissue would grow, none whatsoever. Two months ago she said to him, "Now look here, let us stop this nonsense. You and I know this principle, we know how it works. You look into my eyes and you see the expression on my face when I know that that thing is cured; and I'm going to see on your face when you tell it." And he went to work doing it and he did it daily. This was religious practicing. He said to her here recently, "I've got to go to the hospital. Call up and make a date for me today. This thing will not stay in my side." So they made a date, went to see the doctor, the family doctor, he took a look at it. "Why isn't this remaining in the side?" Then he examined it, x-rayed it, he said, "This is a miracle! No one is going to believe this but tissue has grown, that's why it can't remain in. And you don't need any operation to clean up what is there now. We can leave it just as it is. The tissue has started to grow in the most marvelous way, and not a thing can remain in there because the tissues will push it right out. It's all growing." And he's had that like a thorn in the side of Paul, a constant reminder of his own mortality. Now the doctors saw it and the x-rays confirm it. There's a new case history ___(??). Well, isn't that marvelous! All by the use of Imagination!

So I ask you to simply treat it naturally but seriously, and believe when I tell you that an imaginal act creates the fact. And all day long you and I are creating all the confusion in the world or the joy in the world depending upon what we experience. Just like the little girl, 6,000 miles away, simply caused some person to fill an order that wasn't there. That's exactly what she wanted and it came.

So I'll hold the other stories for the next time. But still because I have so many now, don't stop. Write them and write them and write them that I may share them with everyone who comes here. I want them by the hundreds. I have a few more weeks left and I still want as many as I possibly can get confirming the truth of what I'm talking about here.

Now let us go into the Silence.

THE MYSTERY HIDDEN FOR AGES

4/21/64

Tonight's subject was taken from Paul's letters: "The Mystery Hidden for Ages and Generations." Then he tells us what the mystery is. He tells us the mystery is "Christ *in* you, the hope of glory" (Col. 1:26). Well, through the years, through the centuries, man is taught to believe that Christ is something other than himself. He's been taught all kinds of things about Jesus Christ. Yet the author of this book, in another work, defines Jesus Christ as the creative power and wisdom of God. You'll read this in his letter, his first letter to the Corinthians: "Christ the power and the wisdom of God" (verse24). Well, what is one's power? What is one's wisdom? I tell you, it's your own wonderful human Imagination. That's your power, that's your wisdom. We are told, "All things were created by him and without him was not anything made that was made" (John 1:3). The Bible recognizes only one source of dreams and that one source they call God. And Paul calls God's creative power, Jesus Christ.

This morning's mail brought me two very interesting letters. One is too long to discuss tonight, but I'll just give you just the end of it. She said, "I had a vision. I saw before me the Bible, bound in maroon, and on it I saw the titles; and the first was 'The Way' and then 'The Story of ___(??),' and then 'The Bible'...all three on the book. Then, a few days later, the visions returned, this time with a single title, it was the Bible, and it was titled 'Adventures of Me'; the whole book 'Adventures of Me.'" I wish I could tell you about the letter but there are four very large, very closely spaced, typewritten pages, so I can't discuss it tonight. But it's perfectly marvelous.

Another came, and this gentleman said it suddenly came to him that the purpose of life is simply to learn how to create. Well, I couldn't agree with him more to that. That's exactly what the purpose of life is, to learn how to create. Now, you listen to this point that he drove home. He said it was the most thrilling thing to him! He said, "There's a world of difference between using creative power to achieve certain goals, and using goals to develop creative power." You dwell upon it. One is man; the other is God. God took death...the whole vast world was dead...he took death as a challenge and turned death into sleep, and sleep into his own being that is a creator. Infinite mercy: That is, God turned death into sleep. And then he gradually turned this sleeping being who dreams (if you are asleep you dream) so he turned death into sleep; and then the horror, the despair, the everything in this world; and finally he awakens the sleeper; and the sleeper is himself, the creator. That was his challenge. So he took a goal to develop *further* his own creative power.

But we are allowed while we are here to use our creative power to achieve a specific end... perfectly alright. But there is a wide difference, a world of difference, between using creative power to achieve a definite end and using an end to develop this creative power, all the difference in the world. So it fired him as a creative artist and he shared it with me that I, in turn, may share it with you. And it is, really, all the difference in the world. So you can take a goal this night and if you want to have a home or a bigger home, more money, more of everything in this world, you can do it. That is, you take your creative power and use it towards the achieving of a definite end; that is the dreamer working. Then you take an "end" and use it to develop creative power, that's God in operation. And God took it by taking death...he took death and God himself entered death's door; and laid down in the grave of death which was man; and then began the wonderful dream while encased in death, confident that his predetermined plan would have to be fulfilled. His predetermined plan is the mystery of the Bible. The whole vast Bible is about this mystery; the gospel is the mystery, the whole Bible is the mystery.

Now let us take just pieces of it, because you can't cover it in any one evening. We couldn't cover it in a year. There are sixty-six books in the Bible. Any one would exhaust the year, and there are sixty-six. But we'll take pieces of it, because we are told that those who studied it carefully, they sought and sought and sought, and they could not find in him the Christ of whom they wrote and whose coming they foretold, they couldn't find him. So they enquired what person or what time was indicated by the spirit of prophesy within them, called the spirit of Christ, when indicating the sufferings of Christ and the subsequent glory (1Pet. 1:11). They couldn't find him. It's all promised in scripture, but they couldn't find him. They were looking elsewhere; they were looking for something on the outside. No one suspected that the thing prophesied was coming from the inside.

That Jesus Christ foretold in scripture...not by the name Jesus but the name Jehovah, for Jehovah is "the Savior of the world." But the word Jesus means "Jehovah saves," that's what it means. So no one thought in terms of something coming from the inside. They didn't know that God himself entered death's door and laid down in the grave of man, confident that his purpose would be realized; that he would transform death into sleep; and a dream would start, a horrible dream, the dream of confusion, the dream of war, conflict, the most horrible dream in the world. But gradually he would transform this dreamer, and then awaken him, and he would be God. So the whole thing is simply God.

Now, what are we told are the signs? They're all signs. There are signs to watch for when the dreamer begins to awake, definite signs. The promise is made in the 15th chapter of the Book of Genesis. But we are told even to this very day when Moses is read a veil lies over their minds. Now, you might say that was written 2,000 years ago. It's the same thing today, our scholars are no nearer to this picture than they were 2,000 years ago. They're still trying to rationalize God's picture. You can't rationalize it; it's a mystery. So when Moses is read a veil lies over their minds, because in the 15th chapter of the Book of Genesis the promise was made and it was unconditional. It was not a covenant between two where one could violate it and break the contract. It was unconditional. God made a promise, but no one understood the nature of that promise. It was made seemingly to an old man. He was an hundred years old and the promise was: You will have a son. Your present son, which is completely denied in scripture, will not inherit your kingdom; but you will have a son—it's not yet born—you'll have one and he will be your heir.

But he was then an old man, a hundred years old. Well, no one knew the symbolism of a hundred, that it was "the back of the skull." The letter is Qoph and the numerical value is a hundred. So it was told to him when he was a hundred that he would have a son—it would come from his skull. But it isn't spelled out. This is a mystery, you don't spell it out. So when the question was asked, "Why do you speak in parables?" he said, "Unto you it is given to know the secrets of the kingdom of God, but to those who are without it is in parable" (Mark 4:11). So this is a parable, this is the dream of God, where he dreams into being his plan of salvation for every being in this world, but every being. So everyone will be seemingly old. He now painted a fantastic journey, a journey into a land that is a strange land where he will be enslaved, he'll be ill-treated; but the promise is: At the end you'll be brought out and you'll be heir to a fabulous kingdom. He didn't know what that kingdom was. The kingdom, may I tell you, you fall heir not only to a kingdom but to a presence, and the presence is the kingdom:

You inherit God. So we are told, "They should have no inheritance; I am their inheritance: they shall have no possession; I am their possession" (Ezekiel 44:28). You inherit God! He became you and gave himself to you; and finally, after this fantastic journey of a horrible dream you awaken as God. You inherit God and you possess God. God is all creation; God is the creator of it all.

So when my friend writes me this wonderful letter, I want to thank you, because it is true. Let me share it with you: "There is a wide, wide difference, a vast difference, between using this creative power to achieve a specific end and using an end to develop this creative power." So you can take the most stubborn thing in this world as an end and then use it to develop your power. And gradually something begins to awake within you, and the child is born. So here, we are told a child will be born. It is called Isaac meaning "he laughs" is what it really means. When you look at it, if you're a scholar or any person in the world, you'll simply ignore it and yet the thing is literally true. It's exactly like that when it happens. When it happens to you it happens suddenly, in an unknown room, a guest room in an unregarded inn. He comes ___(??) into the world, to signify the coming of the awakening of God in you. God begins to awaken in you. He told you the first sign that he would give you is that of a child—his name is Isaac. He will come unnoticed into this unobserved guest room in an inn that has no value whatsoever. He'll come just like that. When suddenly he awakens within you and comes, as far as I'm concerned just as you're told in scripture, just like a thief in the night, unobserved, unexpected. It wasn't expected this night. It comes so quietly and it comes so *within* you that that's not the way you expected Messiah to come, he doesn't come that way. But he comes that way.

And so, God awakens *in* man as man's own wonderful human Imagination, and that is Jesus Christ. There is no other Jesus Christ. He awakens in man and when he does, other signs will follow to show you that God is one and his name one. As we are told, "He will be king over all the earth; and his name will be one and the Lord is one" (Zech. 14:09). If he is a king and he has a son, the son should be a prince, shouldn't he? Now listen to the words: "I will raise up David." I will make him a prince among men. "I will make him a prince forever." That's what we're told in the 34th and 37th chapters of the Book of Ezekiel, I'll raise him up. Well, if David who is now dead is raised up, isn't that now alluding to the resurrection of the historic David? May I tell you, it is exactly like that, for when he is raised up—there are unnumbered thousands of David's in the world—when you look into David's eyes there is only one David that you know and he is the historic David, the David of biblical fame. But he's not king, he's prince.

You are told, "I'll make you a prince forever"...for *you* are king. "For, the Lord will become king over all the earth; and the Lord will be one and his name one." For if he is your son he's prince, for *you* are king, Lord over all the earth and your name is one.

So one by one it happens. So in the end there's only one man and his name is Jesus Christ. It seems a fantastic story…only one man. But contracting our infinite senses we behold multitudes, nations, unnumbered nations; expanding, we behold one man. So in the story of Paul...and Jesus appeared, and Paul beheld the Lord and saw his form, the form of a man; then, as a man, a man conversed with man in ages of eternity. He beheld Jesus and called him "the Lord," and then he saw his form, and the form was man. Jesus is simply universal humanity. Everyone that awakens is Jesus Christ. There's only Jesus Christ. We go back to the story: "I tell you a mystery, a mystery hidden for ages and generations…Christ *in you* the hope of glory" (Col. 1:26-27). Not Christ outside; Christ *in you* is the hope of glory. I tell you a mystery, he said, "Great indeed, we confess, is the mystery of our religion" (1Tim. 3:16). It's a mystery, something not to be concealed but something that is very mysterious in character. How could one man contain all of humanity? And yet I speak from experience—it's true: One man contains the whole.

The day will come that you will be absorbed, embraced by Jesus Christ; and at that very moment you are forever Jesus Christ because you wear his body of love. It's only love, nothing but love, and so you feel infinite love. And you're never divorced from it. But there's work to be done, and so you are sent to tell the story of love: How God became man that man may become God. And so, in that moment of being sent there are pains to be suffered, to be endured, disappointments, all kinds of things; but never for a moment do you entertain the thought you are ever separated from the body that incorporated you into it. You're one with the body of Jesus Christ, it's *your* body, and in the end all will wear the same body. That body is the body of love. Then we'll understand Blake's vision of it: "Mercy, Pity, Peace and Love is God, our father dear, and Mercy, Pity, Peace and Love is Man, his child and care. For Mercy has the human heart, and Pity a human face, and Love, the human form divine, and Peace, the human breast" (Blake, *The Divine Image*). This is how the Divine Man is clothed. In the end everyone is completely incorporated into the body of God; and that name, for his name is one, is Jesus Christ.

But if you are taught to believe that Jesus Christ is a unique little individual born 2,000 years ago, and that's it, something set apart, you don't know the mystery of Jesus Christ. Jesus Christ is the creative power of God, and God is all love. The creative power of God he gives to man;

therefore, what does he give man when he gives power to man? The power that God gives to man is the power of his own love. I saw it so clearly in my experience, that only to the degree that man can really fall in love can he really exercise true power. And this is *creative* power. And so, this friend who writes this letter to me is perfectly right. It came to him like a bolt out of the blue. He said, "This is the most exciting thing that's ever happened to me: that the purpose of life is to learn how to create." This is educative darkness...it's to learn how to create, how to create imaginatively. Then he saw that wide distinction between man's use of the creative power and God's use. Man uses it…perfectly alright, use it that way, take a definite goal and use your creative power which is your Imagination to achieve that goal. That's man's use of it.

God's use of the same power is to see a goal and not to use it to achieve that goal, just that goal to develop his creative power. He took the limit of contraction which is death and then took that as a challenge to develop his creative power beyond whatever it was when he conceived this fantastic play in four acts, because there is no limit to the *expansion* of the creative power of God. When people speak of absolutes, I don't go for it. There is no absolute, because there's always an expansion of the creative power of God, always an expansion of translucency. There is a limit to contraction, yes, but not a limit to expansion; a limit to opacity, but not a limit to translucence. Therefore, it must ever be expanding in this world. And so, the creative power took the limit upon himself and the limit is man and man was dead. Took the very limit upon itself which was opacity; that is called in scripture, Satan. Took the limit of opacity and then broke through with his creative power; transformed death, first of all, into sleep; and then to awaken the sleeper as himself; and make God.

So this is this great mystery as told us in scripture. And Paul uses the word no less than eighteen times, all through his letters he's always referring to the mystery of Christ. So when you read the story of Christ you may think there's no mystery attached to it. One came into this world born unnaturally, and you're told he was born without a father. Don't believe it! He was born without a mother. He was born of a father who became the one he would form in this world. In the 13th verse of the first chapter of John, speaking of this unusual birth: "He was born not of blood, nor of the will of the flesh, nor of the will of man, but of God." He was not born in any physical way whatsoever. He was born of God, out of a grave called the skull of man where God himself entered and laid down in the grave of man which is the skull of man. And then he came out of that as man, and you are he.

But you cannot realize your divine inheritance so long as you are still wearing this garment for educative purposes to tell the story to everyone who will hear it. So while you walk still clothed in flesh and blood, you cannot fully realize your inheritance, for your inheritance is God. "They should have no inheritance; I am their inheritance. They should have no possession; I am their possession." So when you inherit the kingdom, you inherit God, for you inherit all the creative power of the world. What do you need with something that is already created when you can create forever and forever? And there's no need of holding onto anything, because you are a creator. You inherit creativity when you inherit God. So they should have no...read it in Ezekiel..."They should have no inheritance; I am their inheritance. Give them no possession; I am their possession" (Ezek. 44:28). So everyone possesses God, inherits God.

So this is the story of the great mystery of Christ *in you* who is the hope of glory. So the day will come that you will know that you and I are one, because he gives us the prince. He shall be a prince forever, and he shall be among all a prince. Now in this world of man we think of a prince, say, of some lands of the world who still have princes; and they speak of him as the prince of the land, and the people might refer to him, if they don't understand any better, "their prince." No, in this case, he is the son of God, because God is king, and a prince would be the king's son. "And the Lord will become king over all of the earth. On that day his name will be one, and the Lord one." So we're all being absorbed into one body, and, may I tell you, I have seen it. When your vision is contracted, you see the whole vast world as nations, and when it is expanded you only see one man. May I tell you who that one man is? You are! You look at him, you can't...well, it's the most thrilling sight in the world! You contain the whole of humanity, the whole vast world contained within one man when your infinite senses are expanded.

So when my friend wrote this letter, I thought of Blake in his early part of *Jerusalem*, he said, "I must cerate a system or be enslaved by another man. I will not reason and compare. My business is to create." That's the business of everyone who awakens in this world: to create. I will not compare, I will not reason what they did, I will simply create. And so, I must create my own system of creativity. There are infinite aspects of how you use this power to create. And so, he is perfectly right, that the purpose of life is to learn how to create. That's why I ask you night after night to share with me one little aspect that you discovered that you actually use...how you created it. Whether it be from the male, I mean, the man's side or God's side. So you wanted a home, what did you do? Did you irritate yourself to possess a home or to dispose of a home? How did you do it? Share it with me that I may share it with others. What did you do? Because this is creativity and there are infinite facets of this power of creation. And the power of creation is Jesus Christ, it's the only Jesus Christ in the world, and that is your own wonderful human Imagination.

And so, this mystery that has been hidden for ages and generations and now revealed to man, it is called in scripture, "Christ in you the hope of glory." The hope of glory! Now listen to the words: "And now, Father, return unto me the glory that was mine, the glory that I had with thee before that the world was" (John 17:5). He's asking for a glory. What glory? How does God give glory to you when you awake?—he gives himself. Listen to the words, "A son honors his father. If I then am a father, where is my honor?" Where is my honor? A son honors his father—this is the last book of the Old Testament, the Book of Malachi, the very first chapter—"a son honors his father" (verse 6). Well, *if* I am a father, where is my honor, where is my son? For the son honors the father. Bring me my prince that I may know that I am king. And so, "The Lord will become king over all the earth." Well then, if this is really true, and you really succeeded in giving me yourself and you are king, and you are Lord, and you are father, then where is my son?

And then he brings the son. Then he brings the son by an explosion. For you are told in this 34th chapter, he's going to raise up David. Now if you read Ezekiel and you take it chronologically, David is dead; therefore, if I'm going to raise up David, I'm going to raise David and resurrect David from the grave, am I not? So you are going to resurrect David from the grave. Where is the grave?—my skull where I experience it. The whole thing takes place in my skull; the whole drama takes place in me. So he picks David and he brings David out of my skull. I felt it; I felt the explosion when he raised him up. And then there was no doubt in my mind when I saw David, the David; *the* David of biblical fame. Not just *a* David, *the* David. I have two nephews and a nephew's son who are called David. In fact, in our family I think there are all kinds of David's. And in my circle of friends, my friend who brings me here every week he is David. I have so many friends...it a marvelous name. But when you meet this David, *the* David, there is no doubt in your mind when you look into his face that he is the prince, the Son of God, and he calls you, Father. You have no doubt you are his father and he is your son.

So he will raise up David to be a prince among men. As he raises up David, he automatically reveals that he has succeeded in his purpose, which was to give himself to you. So in the end, everyone will have the experience. And therefore it can only be one man, and that one man has one name, and his name is Jesus Christ. You are Jesus Christ as these things unfold within you, for they unfold as a pattern that he hid within Christ, as you are told, according to his purpose, which he planned in Christ before the foundation of the world (Eph. 1:9). He planned it and he hid it as a plan in Christ before the foundation of the world. So then the whole thing unfolds like a scene.

So this is the great mystery of life through death. He took the challenge to take death, turn it into sleep, and then after the dreamer dreams the dream of life, awakens the dreamer, and the dreamer is himself. Then by this act, this creative act, God has expanded beyond what he was when he created this fabulous universe. There is no limit to the expansion of the creative power of God. I can't conceive of anything more stale than an absolute. There would be no challenge, no challenge whatsoever. In this world of ours, courtships, love affairs, these are challenges, aren't they? You go into business, that's a challenge—there's no assurance that you're going to succeed. When you meet her for the first time or you meet him for the first time, there's no assurance that this is going to culminate in a romance. It could, but you don't know. That's your challenge. So everything is a challenge in the world. And the whole vast world is a challenge for God. Were it not so, it would be horrible. You mean the whole thing has to be cut and dried because he's absolute? No. So you go back, and let me once more quote the words of my friend that there is a world of difference between using creative power to achieve a definite goal and using a goal to develop creative power. You dwell upon it, you just meditate upon it. It's all the difference in the world.

So I'm not minimizing the use of it from the side of man, we're man. We're living in this world and limited in our exercise of this power. So use it on this level. But don't for one moment neglect to contemplate and to meditate the other use of it, because you're moving towards that point where you are God. For you're going to, tomorrow, not just build a home or more homes, you're going to take the ultimate challenge as you will see it. And tomorrow, as the poet said, "Be patient, our playwright will write in some fifth act and explain to us in some fifth act what this wild drama means." So be patient. In the meanwhile, listen to these words of Blake: "And in great eternity, those who contemplate on death said thus, What seems to be, Is, to those to whom it seems to be, and is productive of the most dreadful consequences to those to whom it seems to be, even of torments, despair, eternal death; but Divine Mercy steps beyond and redeems man in the Body of Jesus" (*Jerusalem*, Plt.36, Ln.50).

Everyone by exercising his talent on the level of man is creating worlds, destroying worlds, conquering nations; and so it's sheer torture and despair. But at a certain moment of his exercise of talent, Divine Mercy steps beyond and redeems him in the body of Jesus; for divine mercy is Jesus Christ himself. And he incorporates you into his body, and from then on you're one with and you *are* Jesus Christ. So all of your sins have been washed white, all of your sins have been forgiven, everything you did in the exercise of your talent on the level of man. And so, you use it on the level of man, and then, while you're maybe going wild in the use of it or misuse of it, divine mercy steps beyond and redeems man in the body of Jesus. So everyone will be, and consciously so, Jesus Christ.

So this is the mystery hidden for ages and generations: Christ in you who is the hope of glory; and the glory is you wear the body. It's your body—no little piece of it, it's the whole thing. It's your body; you contain the whole of humanity. All of humanity will be contained within the body, and it's your body, and you wear it, and it's *a* man. That seems mad, but it's true. Then your senses will be extended and expanded, and you only see *a* man. When they are contracted as we are to the limit of opacity and contraction, we see multitudes of nations. I saw it so clearly, I saw the whole vast thing as a man. And then, contracted senses, and it broke into unnumbered and fragmented pieces; and then nations appeared and all the parts of nations. Then, an expansion of my infinite senses, and then all the nations formed one man. And that man is infinite love. That man embraced me when I answered correctly, "The greatest thing in the world which is love." Because I answered that way, he embraced me and incorporated me into his body; and then sent me to tell the story, but not with any loss of what happened to me, as a part forever of the body and wearing the whole body. It is the body I wear when this thing drops and they say he's gone and he's dead. But death then is swallowed up in the victory that is ___(??) because I have that body. It's my body, it's your body, because in that body, whether you know it or not, we now live and move and have our being. But tomorrow you'll consciously wear that body, and it is the body called Jesus Christ.

Now let us go into the Silence.

* * *

___(??)book table you'll find *Living Time* there. ___(??) books that you ordered. I'm quite sure that they've been received by now. Jack told me last week that you ordered some books, that some of them had arrived. So if you ordered a book, just stop by and ask if it is there. Meanwhile, look it over and Nicoll's *Living Time* may I recommend. It's a perfectly wonderful book. Now are there any questions, please?

Q: What is the translated meaning of the word "David"?

A: David is "the beloved." It's "the door." He said, "I am the door"; Daleth Vau Daleth; "the beloved", really. Read the 7th verse of the 2nd Psalm, it's told so perfectly where it is addressed to David: "Thou art my son, today I have begotten thee." These words are addressed to David, the Son of God, God's gift of himself to man; for when he succeeds in giving himself to you, you become the father of David. Because in that 2nd Psalm it is addressed to David, "Thou art my son, today I have begotten thee." And so, then David appears in your world, and when he appears, he'll come right out of your skull. Let no one disturb you, if you drop this night in the eyes of man and you're no more in the eyes of man here, you still haven't ceased to be. The skull of which I speak isn't physical. We must spiritualize the mission of David, and it is in that spiritual you that David is contained. He will one day come out. Whether this body drops now, is consigned to the flames or not, there you will see David. And he's just as he's described in the Book of Samuel, he's beyond description as to beauty. Sheer majesty stands before you. There is no uncertainty in you as to who he is and the relationship: It's David of biblical fame, and he's your son. Because he's your son, and I know already he is my son, then you and I are one. This is the grand unity spoken of in the 17th of John: That they be one as we are one; I dwell in them and they dwell in me...and my prayer is that they be one (verses 5,11), He's praying for the unity of mankind where all become the Father; and if we are all the *one* Father, the Father can't be a father without a child, and that child is David. So all become the Father of the one; and therefore the joy when the whole play is over and the curtain rings down upon this fantastic drama; and God has succeeded in his purpose to expand his creative power beyond what it was when he determined to transform death, and convert it into a sleep; and then the sleep into life itself, awaking life.

Any other questions, please?

Q: Neville, is there any recognizable point between that death and sleep? We know the waking point, but the sleep point and the death point?

A: My dear, I don't really think I could answer that. I know that we all seem so much alive and so awake...and one's dream would tell you... you'll have an experience, say, of this nature. Suppose I would share with you an experience of mine...so that you know that certain things are different. You're out, but you don't know that you are out because you are conscious, you're alive. You're still bearing the same name, whatever your name is, that's your name. So Lucille is the name... and you're out. But memory is serving you a very good purpose and showing you these things are not normal. What are taking place here do not normally take place, you know that. But as far as you are concerned you're alive and as real as you've ever been to yourself before, but things are a little bit different. You say to yourself, "Maybe I'm dreaming."

But reason tells you, you are not dreaming. This is too real, this can't be a dream because you can stop and rationalize, and do things, and argue with people. And so, as you begin to wonder and think you're dreaming reason steps in and says you're not dreaming. But yet strange things are happening that do not normally happen in this world. Then you say to yourself, "Well, maybe I'm dead, maybe this is an afterlife state. I'll go to Jim and ask Jim if I died." And then you will say to yourself (I'm speaking from experience) and you'll say to yourself, "Well, this is irrational, I couldn't talk to Jim. Were I dead I couldn't communicate, because I couldn't ask him if he buried me." And so at that moment you'll say to yourself, "Come on, Lucille, wake up!" This is a fantastic reality, how are you going to awake from this reality? And it's going to be a terrific struggle, may I tell you, but you'll do it. You'll feel yourself tearing yourself apart to wake from this very, very real state to find yourself once more on the bed in this world. No one ___(??) thoughts occupy you after that. How the devil am I going to wake up from this one, because *this* is solidly real, *that's* solidly real, and it took a tremendous struggle to awake from that into this? But you will know when you come back that this that seemingly is more rational and more stable, that things have continuity, how am I going to awake from this? Goodnight.

THE FRIEND OF SINNERS

4/24/64

Tonight's subject is "The Friend of Sinners." I think you will find this a very interesting subject. It may be difficult, but you'll find it interesting. We are told, "Call his name Jesus, for he will save his people from their sins." We're told in the same book, the Bible, there is only one savior, and that savior is Jehovah. Before me no God was formed nor will there be any after me. I, I am the Lord and beside me there is no Savior. It is I who blot out your sins and remove your transgressions. You read this in the 43rd of Isaiah (verse 3). No other Savior. So he must be the one spoken of in the Old Testament as Jehovah, and he is. The word spells the same thing and means the same thing.

So let us tonight see it in a practical light. You and I are inclined to believe that if something is wrong with us it's caused by something on the outside—maybe our circumstances of life, our surroundings, something, but something on the outside. And yet, the Bible teaches that all of our troubles spring from sin. But you've been taught to believe that sin is the violation of some moral code. The Bible doesn't teach that. The Bible teaches that man sins for want of faith in "I am he." "Unless you believe that I am he, you die in your sins" (John 8:24). That's what we're taught. So, it's want of faith in "I am he" that is the cause and the only cause of sinning, and sin is the cause of every problem in the world. I don't care what you name it, regardless of the nature of the problem it simply is it results from sinning.

Now let me share with you two stories that came to me this week, one from a lady, one from a gentleman. I have just seen the gentleman enter, I haven't yet seen the lady...oh yes, she's here. So we'll take her story first. She said, "Having heard you I took thirteen goals, and by the application of this principle I achieved *every* goal in detail just as I had envisioned it." But the story I want to share with you is this—she didn't tell me what she took as goals, having heard me she took thirteen—she said, "Now I'm working on two. They seem more difficult because they are so long in standing, they go a way back in my life; and because of a conditioned mind maybe I find it more difficult to overcome the two. But the thirteen that I simply fixed, I quickly realized them in detail." But, she said, "Recently I was sitting in the Silence, simply reflecting on my thoughts, and suddenly you appeared in my skull, lifelike, not a little thing, simply a lifelike figure. And you looked directly at me and you said to me, 'May I tell you, you are looking at your problem instead of the wish fulfilled.'" And then she said, "It seemed so real to me because you stood in my head, but you were lifelike, that then I heard myself say in answer, 'You are right!' And so my meditation ended."

Let that be a warning to you. If you don't want some uninvited guest to come into your Silence and disturb your meditation, then be faithful to God's word. If I use, today, the terminology that differs from scripture, it's only because of the year 1964. I am not changing the word of scripture, for in scripture we are told, "Whatever you desire, when you ask it in prayer, believe you've received it and you will." If I have taken that thought from the Book of Mark, the 11th chapter of Mark (verse 24), and I have put it into what is to me a more understandable, modern expression—"Assume the feeling of the wish fulfilled"—I haven't changed the thought behind it.

And so, another thought comes to mind. We are told in scripture that no man understands or knows the things of another save the Spirit of that man who is *in* him. No man knows the things of another save the Spirit of that other who is in him. Well, I appeared *in* her, did I not? She saw me in her skull she said. These are the words, "You appeared in my skull, lifelike." Are we two or one? Did I not know the secrets of her heart? Did I not see that she was actually looking at the problem rather than the wish fulfilled? And if no one knows the things of another save the Spirit of that other who is in him, then are we two? If she has not yet become aware of the fact that she is God the Father by reason of the Son who reveals it to her, and I *have* already become aware, it doesn't mean that we are not the same Spirit. There's only one Spirit, there's only God. And so, I was in her in her skull. Is that not where he is crucified? Is it not there where he resurrects? Does he not awaken *in* the skull? Is it not out of the skull he comes to be born? Is it not from there all things take place?

I tell you, Christianity as the world *should* understand it is the story of simply awakening, then being born, and then ascending, just like a seed. A seed awakens in the ground, and it splits the ground when it awakens. It awakens in the ground and as it starts to come forward to be born it breaks the ground; it comes through granite. I've seen a little tiny seed come through the sidewalk. You see it all the time, not just a little crevice that is left between blocks but actually through the granite, through the cement. It will break it and come right through. And so, the seed is planted in the earth—the earth is man, man's the earth—and as it is planted and becomes alive it becomes awake, it begins to awake, and as it awakes it starts moving up. As it moves up it breaks that earth, and it is born. Then it starts ascending, moving towards the heavens as told us in the 4th chapter of the Book of Daniel (verses 10-12).

So here, she tells me the story that only recently, sitting in the Silence, reflecting upon her thoughts, suddenly I appear in her skull, lifelike, not some little miniature. And this lady is an artist, so when she speaks of being lifelike she speaks of a live model, because this lady is an artist who draws and paints from live objects. Yes, still-life too, but live objects. And here I appear as a live model. She knows the man and I look directly at her and I say to her, "May I tell you, you are looking at the *problem* instead of the *wish fulfilled.*" And to her the thing was so alive and real, she agreed, and heard herself answer, "You're right!" So here is this story I share with you. We are one—the being in you is God; and you are God, I am God, everyone is God. You'll find the whole vast world contained within yourself. But he who is awake in the entire unfolding picture will speak the words to *you*, because you and he are one; and you simply begin to listen as he tells you where you are going wrong—you're not abiding by the word of God. For "sin" is simply disobedience, not obeying the word of God. Well, the word of God is: When you know what you want in this world, believe that you have it. If you don't assume the feeling of the wish fulfilled, you are not *abiding* by the word of God. And so, in this moment, she is not asleep, she is sitting in meditation, she is fully aware of what she is doing, and while she is reflecting on her thoughts, suddenly this thing happens in her skull.

Now, another letter came, came today (he's here tonight), he said, "Two months ago I sat and deliberately conceived a scene." He said, "I'm very fond of flying in jets and so I conceived a scene of flying in a jet, but then I included my family, my little daughter, eight years old. And so I imagined that my wife and my daughter and I were simply animated, all excited because we were going to go someplace. Then with all the animation around and the excitement of going someplace, I then jumped from that little episode, one little scene, to the airport where at the terminal I am explaining to my daughter the excitement of flying on a jet. Then, from the terminal I am on the jet. I am only talking to my daughter, and I am speaking to Lynn and I am telling Lynn of the scenes below as we take off. As the jet takes off, I am explaining the entire structure below. And that's it. Three little episodes: getting ready for a journey, then the terminal, and then the flight as we take off…that's two months ago.

"A month later I said to my wife, 'You know, April the 3rd is Dads' and Daughters' Day, and so I'm taking off with Lynn, just the two of us, and she and I will have the whole day together.' My wife thought that was an excellent idea, to go off, just you and Lynn." So came the 11th day of April, which is called Dads' and Daughters' Day (which I didn't know until today) and so they got up early and they're all dressed and they started off to have breakfast on the outside. No breakfast at home...this is going to be a whole day where they'd have fun on the outside. He said, "I hadn't the foggiest idea what I would do with Lynn for the whole day. I knew I had plotted it and planned it, but I didn't know what to do with her. I thought I could go to a movie after breakfast, and then we'd fly to the beach, and then we'd have lunch. And so, I started off with Lynn and I'm driving down the San Diego Freeway, and right on the freeway the most overpowering thought possesses me: go over to the airport and fly to San Diego. I couldn't resist the impulse; it was something that completely controlled me. So off to the airport I went. My wife had a date that day with the hairdresser, so she went her way, and just Lynn and myself went to the airport.

"We flew to San Diego, then I took a taxi to the zoo, and she and I took in the entire zoo, everything the zoo had to show. Then from the zoo we walked a half mile up to the Fine Arts Hall. After having seen that, I was dead tired. My feet just wouldn't move I was so tired and my feet were so sore. So having driven from the airport to the zoo by taxi I thought we'd get a taxi and go back to the airport. But no taxi in sight! So I turned to a lady and said, 'Can I get a taxi?' She said, 'You wouldn't find one...if you do see one it's already occupied. But three blocks from here, three very long blocks, there is a booth; you may call for one.' He said, I wouldn't move three feet I was so tired! And so at that moment I had the impulse, I've got to do something, can't stand here. So he said, Well, I turned to Lynn, I said, 'You know, Lynn, let us now play the game we are getting into a taxi. Let us actually put ourselves right into a taxi and start for the airport.' She said that she really loved these things and she delights in it, so she actually entered into the feeling of getting into a taxi. Together they did it. He said, 'Within a minute a Yellow Cab came by, I hailed him, he stopped to say that he had a fare, there were four people waiting for him at some other point, but he would get in touch with the base and have a taxi for them in no time flat.' In a matter of moments, he'd called in, and a taxi came, and off they went. But, before this taxi came he had the impulse, he was so tired and so sore of foot, he said, 'Well, I've got to start towards the phone booth anyway,' and the minute he entertained that thought, he said, no, he denied it completely, denied what the woman said about you can't get a taxi, and did what he did.

Now, you've heard the word in scripture, you've heard it from the pulpit, you've heard it all over the world: antichrist. You've heard it, you must have heard antichrist. Well, in essence antichrist is only an idea or a person in history who denies the Christian mystery. The Christian mystery is simply "imagining creates reality"; and all that is told in the story concerning how Imagination is born, how he awakens, how Imagination awakens *as* the being in whom he awakens, how he's born, how he discovers the fatherhood of God, and how he ascends on high. And so, at that very moment when he rejected the idea of walking up to put in that call, he rejected and turned his back upon the devil called antichrist. There is no other devil. Antichrist is only the individual or the idea that would deny the truth of the Christian mystery, this great story as told in the world. So that very moment he turns back and once more called upon the great mystery, and with his daughter they entered into the taxi. Then within a minute here comes the other taxi right straight towards them and said, "I have a fare waiting for me, they're a foursome, and so I must go. But I will call the base and have a cab sent to you."

So sin by definition is "missing the mark." Anyone in this world who has a mark, an objective, a goal in this world who fails to realize it is sinning. And so sin...a man sins *only* for want of faith in I am he. So we are told in the 8th of John: "I have told you that you will die in your sins unless you believe that I am he." Before me no God was formed nor shall there be any God after me. I, I am he, and beside me there is no Savior. I, I am he who blots out your transgressions and remembers your sins no more. There is no other being. So you meet one in this world, you think you are saving another or helping another, there is no other. This whole vast world is yourself fragmented. The whole vast world is yourself completely fragmented.

Did she not see me in her skull? Now, the world will think that I am at home on my bed, and physically I was; but being awake to this great mystery I could speak the word to her, which was really not another, it's myself; she and I are one. Now that she has made me aware of that which on this level I was not aware, the two things that she now finds difficult they are *my problems*, because she is my fragmented self. And seeing within me this being who now becomes aware of this inner self, I can now quite easily imagine that she has what—in her letter she told me that "don't tell it from the platform, these are simply for you and you alone"—and so it's easy now to hear that she has what now she desires, because, really, I am not doing it for another. There is no other. "Before me there was no God formed...

nor shall there be any God *after* me" (Is.43:10). There is no such thing as a twosome in God. It's fragmented into unnumbered parts, but all will be gathered together, and only one God. For he'll become one, king over all the earth, and on that day his name is one, and the Lord is one, not two; and that is called in the scripture, Jesus, which means, really, I AM. So everyone is awakening to the being that really *is*, which is the only God. So call him Jesus because he will save his people from their sins.

Now we are told, "Against thee, thee *only*, have I sinned, and I have done that which is evil in thy sight, so you are just in your sentence, and that which you've done is justified" (verse 4). You read that in the 51st Psalm: "Against thee, *thee only*, have I sinned." Man thinks he sins against another; there is no other. He only sins against the being, I am. So he would like to see you in some better light and he *doesn't* see you in some better light, "Against thee, and thee only, have I sinned." Not you the one he wants to see in a better light, but against himself. He hasn't yet learned the art of repentance. The earliest scripture, which is Mark, begins on the note, his first proclamation: "The time is fulfilled, and the kingdom of God is at hand; repent and believe the gospel" (1:15). Repent seems to be a prerequisite for any change in this world of ours, and repentance simply means "a radical change of attitude towards life."

So I see you and you tell me what you would like to be, and if I simply become indifferent and I don't persuade myself that you *are* the one that you have just voiced that you would like to be, it is *my* sin, because I am now sinning against myself. "Against thee, thee only have I sinned." For I have just seen a fragmented portion of my being in *want* of something... and there's only one God: "Before me no God was formed, nor shall there be any after me." Alright, so he turned to me, that portion of myself, and said he would like a better job, he would like more money, he would like a measure of happiness that he's never enjoyed. He's made me *aware* of that aspect of myself of which I was *not* aware; because I dwell in him and he dwells in me, we are one. Well, if I now become indifferent and do nothing about it, just simply go my way, then I have sinned. At the moment of becoming aware of his need, I should represent him to myself as now the embodiment of that which he would like to be, and persuade myself of the reality of that imaginal act.

And to the degree that I am self-persuaded...like the gentleman who simply played three scenes... here, all in his Imagination, he's now excited he's going off on a jaunt with his daughter. He includes the wife only in the first scene of three, and she does, she leaves the house with them, but she has to go to the beauty parlor. But in the two scenes that follow he only has his daughter, Lynn. And so, in the second scene it's the terminal where he's all excited they're getting ready to go. And then in the third scene, he's in the plane, they're airborne, and he's describing the land below to a little girl eight years old. These are the three exciting scenes. He said in his letter, "The reason my wife didn't join us, I didn't include her in the second and the third scene. I had no reason for excluding her; I would have loved to have had her. But, strangely enough, since I have heard this story of Imagination, when she and I get together and start to discuss, she's always trying to bring up to me the facts of life as against these things of Imagination." Well, he said, "I do to her what I did to the lady at the Fine Arts building—she told him what she said about the cab—I didn't hear her. And so, my wife talks to me about the facts and I don't hear her. And I love her dearly, I'm passionately fond of my wife, I love her dearly, but I don't hear her. She wants to convince me of the reality of the facts of life, and I will have none of it.

"I simply went on this thing...but strangely enough I was not only airborne, I was landed. I was in the zoo, I had almost completed the zoo, when suddenly it dawned on me what I had done the month before." For this happened to him in actual fact on the 11th of April. It was a month before that he set the whole thing in motion...that's how short our memories are. Between doing it and realizing it he had completely forgotten. He went right through the entire thing like an actor stepping on the stage; and he forgets. Well, he has to, to be a good actor, he must forget he's acting and lose himself in the part. Well, so he was the author, he wrote the scene, he directed the scene, he became the actor in the scene; and then stepped upon the stage and completely forgot that he was the author and the director, and thought himself only an actor, and, well, very well rehearsed. So you and I play the same role in this world. You can be anything in this world that you want to be if you know who God is. And you can't sin against another; you can only sin against God. And so, our sin is simply the lack of faith in I am he. You will believe in everyone else but "I am." You will call this one, or write that one, or get in touch with someone else in the hope that *they* can do it; and the only being that can do it is "I am." So you are told, "You will die in your sins unless you believe that I am he."

This is a mystery, a fantastic mystery. But the day will come that you will discover as the lady had by her story, discovered that I am not another. I stand here and talk to her (she's here tonight), I talk to her. She's a very gentle, tender lady, and she'll wait and I'll shake her hand, we go downstairs occasionally together, but she thinks I'm another. I hope tonight she knows I am not another. When you saw me in your skull, that's where God awakes, that's where he's crucified. And so, he spoke to you using the mask of what you know to be Neville. He used the mask—the mask is the personality, the persona is the mask—and so he puts on the mask and tells you, "Yet this moment you are not really obedient to the law, because I see that you're looking at the problem instead of the wish fulfilled." And so, everyone must have an objective and see it clearly in his mind's eye, and see it *fulfilled.* Then, from then on, regardless of all rumor, remain faithful to that end, the wish fulfilled. And he never sins then.

And so, he comes into the world to save man from sin, that's all. He comes *not* to call those who are righteous to repentance—not the righteous, those who are complacent, but the sinners to repentance. And so I say, and I say time and again, religious faith must be tested. It *must* be tested. If it isn't tested, it becomes some simple, oh well, emotionalism, "creedalism," call it by a thousand names. It's some liturgy where some outside ceremony takes place rather than putting it to the test. You *must* put it to the test. Religious faith must be tested as much as any other should be tested, such as my intelligence should be tested. If I go on a job, give me an aptitude test; test me to see if I'm qualified to fill the job. You'd do that. Well, religious faith should be tested in the same manner.

So we say "imagining creates reality," that's the foundation, and then try to show you in numberless aspects how it works. And then ask you to share with me what *you* did and how it worked with you, and then I can tell others what you did. Then we become richer this way, on the same principle, imagining is creating reality. Well, if I make that bold statement and you prove it, tell me how you proved it so that I can tell another. I have proved it time and time again. I live by it. I try to live by it, and if I forget what I do this morning in my imaginal act, I know regardless of my lack of memory it's going to come anyway…that tomorrow it will come up. I may not even recognize my harvest, but I cannot encounter something that I did not bring into this world. Because, God is not mocked; be not afraid, be not ashamed. "God is not mocked; as you sow so shall you reap" (Gal. 6:7).

And so, you sit in the Silence and you plant it, and then it comes. It may take a day...in the gentleman's case it took a month. In the lady's case, there were thirteen case histories. She didn't tell me the nature of the case history or the time interval between the actual doing and the actual reaping…she didn't know. I hope some day she'll share with me the thirteen that she simply mentioned as thirteen objectives that she realized in the most minute detail. The two that seemed at the moment to stick with her she confesses that they go back in time; and because they go back, and they've been over a period of years, they seem to be more of a problem. But may I tell her, it's no more than the thirteen that you realized so easily if you'll treat it in the same manner.

And so, the friend of sinners is called in scripture, Jesus. If I could only convince you that *you* are Jesus, you may not know it but you *are* Jesus. There is *only* Jesus in the world. God became man that man may become God; and there is no other God; there's only *one* God. Jesus *is* God. He's buried in you; and say "I am," that's Jesus. But you do not know it. But the day will come you will know it by a series of events that I have, night after night, told you. Because, when these begin to unfold within you it has come through the earth called man. One of her visions (which is a very lovely vision) she says, "Sitting in the Silence—-this has happened to me now three times—-the first time it happened I saw through my skull a crack." Lovely vision! "And it was so exciting I wanted to...I knew something wonderful, more wonderful than anything I've ever experienced before was going to take place. I felt like pulling myself through it. And then the whole thing vanished. And the second time it happened, a crack, but this time in another part of my body; from my solar plexus right through to the heart, another crack. Then the third time, in the skull again but the crack deepened." May I congratulate you! You are the earth. The word Adam means "red earth," doesn't mean anything else. And God became man, Adam, and then he planted himself in the earth called man; and while in this earth it grows, it stirs, and becomes alive. As it becomes alive it cracks the surface of the earth, and all of a sudden you will see through from below; there'll be light. You will crack it and crack it and crack it, and finally you'll come out. When you come out you are Christ Jesus. There is *only* Christ Jesus in the world. So everyone in this world is simply God awakening, God unfolding.

So to sin...you don't sin because of any so-called violation of a moral code. You have an objective in this world and you fail to realize it, you're sinning. You will change your objectives when you know we are only one. You will have no objective of hurting any being in this world when you know we are one. You'll have no objective of getting the better of another when you know we are one. You don't need to get the better of anyone in this world; there is no other. You simply have objectives. You need money? It need not be at the expense of others. You need a bigger home, a more secure future? Not at the expense of another! You simply have the objective in itself, and take your mind off the problem, and try not to solve it by thinking and rationalizing it, go to the solution of the problem. And then dwell on the wish fulfilled...not how you're going to do it, where's the money going to come from, how you're going to get it—just dwell in the end. And the end is where we must all start from: "In the end is my beginning."

I start in the end. That was shown me so vividly a couple of years ago where I saw this fantastic story. I was taken in Spirit into this palatial home, and here I saw this family, two generations and a third, they spoke *of* a third, but the third was the oldest, unseen by the eye of man. He had gone from the world, but he left a fortune that they now enjoyed. It was well invested, and they lived on this fortune. They would speak of this one who had made the fortune and they called him Grandfather. They said, "Grandfather used to say while standing on an empty lot, 'I remember when,' and then he would paint a word picture for this lot and paint it so vividly that those who listened to him saw the structure rise in their mind's eye. He never thereafter thought of this place in any other way other than the end that he saw, so he would always say, 'I remember when this was an empty lot.' And to him, he's standing on an empty lot but it was no longer an empty lot, it was simply the structure he desired. And you can do that with everything in this world. So I awoke, it was a little after three in the morning, and I took my yellow page and I wrote out my vision. Went back to bed and re-dreamed the dream, but this time *I* was Grandfather. I had so completely absorbed the message of the vision that I stood in the same mansion, and I told the others that I would stand here and I would remember when this was...and I painted building after building in my mind's eye. I was that grandfather. This vision was revealed to me by the depths of my own soul. We are told in the 41st chapter of the Book of Genesis that if the dream is doubled it means that the thing is fixed by God and will *shortly* come to pass (verse 32).

So the dream need not be a dream where I am not in control of it. The dream could be as we sit here right now and enact it vividly, break it, and five minutes later, go into the same scene and enact it. That's a waking dream. That's affirmative. If it happens twice, we are told, in the 41st chapter of Genesis, it means that God has fixed it and it will shortly come to pass. So you do it twice, do it *vividly* in your mind's eye, and let it happen. It will happen! For I saw it so clearly, that the secret of it all is to go to the end and live in the end, the wish fulfilled; and then if you break it, go back into that end, do it again. Then God has done it. But you say, "What God? I did it." But you said, "But God did it." Well, who did it when I say I did it? What's his name? Well, his *real* name is I AM. Well, who is doing it? If you ask me in the midst of something I'm doing, wouldn't you say to me, "What are you doing?" Would I not answer, "I am"...and then tell you what I'm doing? Well, I called upon his name when I did that: I am imagining that I am now...and I name the thing that I think I am. And so you ask me again, and would I not answer, "I am doing so and so"? But you said, "God did it." Well, God's name is I AM; he has no other name; and so, *I am* doing it.

Doing it in this light, see how it works. If it works, does it matter what the world will think? There is no other world than yourself-not-yet-gathered together. The whole vast world is yourself pushed out, because "All that you behold, tho' it appears without, it is within, in your Imagination, of which this world of mortality is but a shadow"...a shadow reflecting the activity taking place in your own wonderful human Imagination (Blake, *Jerusalem*, Plt.71). And so, his only name is I AM. Put into a sound where you can call it, it is Jesus. And so when you are told, "At the sound of Jesus all knees should bow," alright, bend within you to the *power* that is within you, which power you really are. Look upon it in that sense…that's the only awe you should feel.

So the friend of sinners is seated here this night if you know how to forgive sin. It's a challenge to every person in this world. When you meet someone in want, represent that one as he would like to be, and persuade yourself that he is. It tests your ability to enter into and partake of the nature of the opposite. For you see him in want, and you persuade yourself that he is affluent; and then you leave him, physically, but you do not leave that image of him that he is affluent, and you walk in that state. To the degree that you are self-persuaded that he is that which you have assumed that he is he will conform to it. Don't try anything to make it so. Call no one to do it, ask no favor, leave him just as he is, because you dwell in him. As the lady brought out, she saw me in her skull. I *am* in her skull. Not in eternity can she throw me out, she can't get rid of me; I am in her skull.

Because I awoke a few years ago, I am in the skull of every being in this world, but especially those who hear me. Those who hear me, I am awake in their skull, watching if they are faithful to the law, the law being: Assume the feeling of the wish fulfilled. For, "I came not to destroy the law or the prophets but to fulfill them." So far, as far as the Promise goes, I have fulfilled it. As far as the law goes, I have not destroyed it. I've only changed the words to make it more, I would say, palatable in the year 1964. So if I told you that when you sit down to pray...maybe you don't want to pray...that you must now believe that you have already received what you are asking for in prayer (Mark 11:24). And maybe like today in this world of ours they are trying to rub out the word God or the word prayer in our schools and in all government offices, I can still get around that. Without using the word God, without using the word prayer, I can say to the atheist, "When you know what you want, assume the feeling of the wish fulfilled." Well, they can't rub that out of school, because I'm not using the word God. Well, who is assuming it? He doesn't know that God's assuming it, because he will say to me, "Well, I'm assuming it" and I won't tell him at that moment who "I am" is. That comes after. So I get around this objection to the use of the word God. Because, he is offended by the word God, and he's offended by the word prayer, offended by the word religion, and so we get around it.

So "I've come not to destroy the law or the prophets, not to abolish them, but to fulfill them." And so, you will never in eternity rub me out or get rid of me. If you shot this body now, you still can't get rid of me, because *I am* in every being who walks the face of this world. So as John Dunne said, "I am involved in mankind; every man's death is the death of me. Do not seem to ask for whom the bell tolls; it tolls for me." Every man's death has to be the death of me, and every man's life must be my life, for I'm involved in mankind, as *you* are. We're one, we aren't two. So everyone is completely interwoven. So you ask favors of no one. When you hear an aspect of yourself in need, do it, just simply do it, because you're doing it to yourself. "When you do it to the least among one of these, you do it unto me." Get the mystery? "When was it you were hungry and I didn't give you? When were you thirsty and I gave you no drink? When were you in need of shelter and I didn't take you in? When were you in need of raiment and I didn't give it to you? When you did not do it to the least among one of these, you did not do it unto me" (Matthew 25:35-40). And so, they are looking for one being to come that they could really fawn upon...no, every being in the world... you're buried in every being in the world.

So I will say to this lady (who is here this night) I have heard it, having received your letter, and will continue to hear what I have heard until what I have heard you will echo. You will echo it because I am doing it unto myself; because, I, as you, do not want the two things that you mentioned in the letter.

Now let us go into the Silence.

* * *

___(??) attention to the book table. All the books ___(??) although mine are there and any other book there I have and love.

Now are there any questions, please? None?

Q: You described sinning as missing the mark, and it seems to me to be a lot of teaching in the Bible that encourages one to live to a moral code, a code of mercy, or ___(??) teaching of Christ. How would you reconcile this with your description?

A: Well, I would reconcile it...if you read the Sermon on the Mount, he said: "You've heard it said of old, 'You shall not commit adultery.' But I say unto you, anyone who looks lustfully upon a woman has already committed the act of adultery with her in his heart" (Matthew 5:27). He shows us the *inwardness* of the law. Until that moment and even until this day people look upon the law as something you do on the outside. That if you look lustfully on another and you restrain the impulse because you contemplated the consequences along with your lustful act, you might think, "Well, I didn't commit it." He's telling you the very act was committed in the lust. And so, if you take the Sermon on the Mount...he takes the entire Torah and puts it into a new Torah: It's not enough to restrain impulses on the outside. Because, I could restrain the impulse to steal because I not only would like what appears to be good there, but I don't like the consequences. When I contemplate the consequences along with the act, I restrain the impulse; but he tells me it wasn't good enough. And so the whole drama becomes a *mental* drama: The battle ground of God is the mind of man.

Q: He's still laying down a code.

A: He's laying down a code...it's entirely up to you...I acquaint you with the law and then leave you the choice and its consequences. I can't have any person in this world a puppet, an automaton. If you must be good, then you're no earthly good to God. If you could make a mistake and suffer the consequences of your mistake, I could bring you out into the kingdom. But if you couldn't make a mistake, not allowed to make one, and you *had* to be good based upon a certain code, well then, you can't be used creatively. He said, "I have made *everything* for its purpose, even the wicked for the day of trouble" (Proverbs 16:4). So, he uses everything, but he uses it creatively.

A thing we brought out last Tuesday night disturbed a few friends of mine, who called me on the phone, and they said they drove home to the Valley and they were discussing it. Because, I was simply quoting what a gentleman wrote me, and he said, "It came to me like a flash out of the blue that the purpose of life is to create" and then said he, "Man uses his creative power to achieve certain goals, while God uses goals to *develop* his creative power." And he said, "This is an entirely different orientation: one is man creating, the other is God." I agree with him one hundred percent. Yet I will encourage every man until he awakens *as* God to use his creative power to attain definite goals in this world—that I would encourage one hundred percent. But when we all awake, and it's the one being once more unified, and once more integrated, we will, because we took before we became fragmented the most fantastic goal: to develop our creative power. And that goal that we use to develop our creative power was death. God took death and then turned it into sleep; and then after a process of a nightmarish dream awakened the dreamer which was himself. And by that process, by turning death into sleep and the sleep into God, he developed his creative power beyond what it was when he started this drama.

Because, the world will speak of God as absolute...I cannot conceive of an absolute. There would be no room for growth, no room for expansion. So I would say that translucence and expansion is forever and forever and forever. Truth, to me, is an ever-increasing illumination. And so, God took upon himself a certain limit of contraction which is death, a limit of opacity, of unbelief, absence of light, and then turned it by his mercy into sleep. And so, in the very beginning of Genesis we're told, he took man which was dead and caused a deep and profound sleep to fall upon man (Gen. 2:21). There's not anything in the Bible where man as the sleeper was awakened until Jesus Christ; and then we are told he is the first fruits of those that rose from the dead (1 Cor. 15:20). He said, "Awake, you sleepers and *rise* from the dead" (Eph. 5:14). And it's all God, because God took upon himself that constricted state called man, and then turned it by his mercy into a sleeping dreaming being. And as a dreamer we can dream the most fantastic, nightmarish things in the world. And having dreamt it, he then in a terrific *act* he awakens the dreamer. The waking of the dreamer is resurrection; then the dreamer comes through and it is birth. Then the dreamer having been born, as you're told, and the favor of the Lord was upon him...and he grew and grew in wisdom and understanding. He grows like the tree, the Tree of Life, forever and forever.

So I would say to everyone, *use* your talent. I hope you'll use it *lovingly*, because, may I tell you, you can't really hurt another, it's only self. It's your fragmented self the world over.

Q: In John 8, where it referred to "you will die in your sins" does this indicate then the word, in the place of the word "die," you could put "sleep"? You will sleep in your sins?

A: You remain, yes, you continue missing the mark. Because, if sin is missing the mark, which it is by definition in the Bible, and then I don't change by repentance—for repentance is to change radically my attitude towards life—but if I don't bring about a change of attitude, I will continue in my present attitude and perpetuate the conditions of my life. So, I have told you, said he, that you will die in your sins unless you believe that *I am he.* So if I don't believe I *am* that which I am seeking, I continue to believe that I am that which is falling short of what I'm seeking. There's only I AM in the world. There's nothing but! Thank you.

THEY DID NOT DIE

4/28/64

Tonight's subject is "They Did Not Die." It is possibly the most difficult subject to discuss, but I'll do my best. We turn to the greatest of all books, the Bible, and so the Old Testament really is prophetic history: Everything in it will come to pass, everything. So we turn to the 51st chapter of Jeremiah, the 39th verse: "While they were *inflamed* I prepared a feast for them and made them drunk, till they swooned and then they slept a perpetual sleep and did not awake, says the Lord"...while they were *inflamed.* The word translated inflamed is a "self-imposed trance" really—to become so completely carried away with a story that is being told me that I'm completely inflamed, I'm entranced. And so, the feast prepared is the story told me: I'm being told a story of transcending myself, and I'm feasting upon it. Then I feast upon it until I swoon away, I am drunk; and then in this state as I swoon away, I sleep a perpetual sleep and do not wake. That's the story. You who have your Bibles you can check it, it's the 51st chapter, the 39th verse of Jeremiah.

Now, I know from my own experience that nothing dies, but nothing dies. The little flower that blooms once blooms forever; and yet in this world of ours everything seems to come into being, it waxes, it wanes and it disappears, everything. So we see things constantly dying. They're born and then they die. And yet, I can tell you from my own experience that nothing dies. So tonight we'll take this and try to take it, in the limited time, from different angles.

The Bible begins, "In the beginning God..." this is Genesis; the Book of Genesis ends on the note "...in a coffin in Egypt" (Gen. 1:1, 50:26). All ends run true to origins; the origin is God: "In the beginning God...in a coffin in Egypt." The word translated coffin is also translated ark, and so

Blake said, "Man is either the ark of God or a phantom of the earth and the sea." I say man is that ark that contains God and God being all that there is, everything goes into the ark and the ark is man. So, "In the beginning God...in a coffin in Egypt." But the one placed in that coffin is called Joseph, and Joseph was called the dreamer: "Behold, this dreamer cometh" (Gen. 37:19). Now, the Bible recognizes only one source of dreams: All dreams proceed from God. So, Joseph is the prototype of God. So the dreamer is put into a coffin which is man, in Egypt. But he exacts from the sons of Israel a promise that they will not leave him there; they'll bring him out of Egypt into that which was promised by God before this journey started.

Now, the Bible itself ends on the note (in the end of Revelation)—omitting the very last verse which is only a benediction—but the very last verse of the actual end is "Come, Lord Jesus." These are the words...so, "In the beginning God...in a coffin in Egypt...Come, Lord Jesus." We are told in the New Testament, in Colossians, in Corinthians, that Jesus Christ was raised from the dead, the first-fruits of those that slept. So here something is placed in the coffin and it seemingly is dead; and the first awakening is called Jesus Christ, the first-fruits of those who slept. So, Come, Lord Jesus, come awaken us from this dream, this fantastic dream where we are fighting with demons.

A very great Irish mystic, poet, painter, essayist, his name was George Russell, but he's better known to us as A.E. He chose the initials A.E. He wrote a book called *The Candle of Vision* and in this book he reveals his mystical experiences. The one I would like to use this night he called *The Many Colored Land.* He said, "I will not tell you where I saw it, but saw it I did. I will not tell you *where* I saw this." And then he describes what he saw: "A hall vaster than the largest cathedral, and its pillars made seemingly of living, pulsing opal. And between the pillars were thrones and they faded into the very end. On these thrones sat divine kings, fiery crested. He said, I saw one who wore the crest of the dragon, another, as I can describe it, said he, it seemed to be plumes of fire, and they stretched to the very end. At the far end was a throne higher and on it sat one greater than the rest, a light like the sun glowed behind him. On the floor there lay a dark figure and over this dark figure two of the divine kings waved their hands. And as they waved their hands over this figure, head and body, fire came from the body where the hands moved, like some strange moving fire; or he described it as jewels, scintillating jewels coming from the body. Then, out of this body came a figure as tall, as glorious, as radiant as those who sat upon the thrones. Then he awoke to the hall, and then he became aware of his divine kin and raised his hand in greeting. Those on the thrones leapt from their thrones with hands lifted in greeting to the one who had returned from his long dark journey. Then altogether they moved and vanished into the light." Then he woke here in this world.

It's the most perfect picture that I have read concerning this descent into this world. You're only here for a purpose: to play a part. You are here to increase your creative power. You are *not* a being born in this world at all. But in this descent, when you were entranced from on high, you would have the experience of birth and of death. So, many years ago I wrote a tiny little pamphlet and I closed it with this thought, that "This universe that we study with such care is a dream, and we the dreamers of the dream, eternal dreamers dreaming non-eternal dreams. One day, like Nebuchadnezzar, we will awaken from our dream in which we fought with demons, to discover that we really never left our eternal home; we were never born, have never died, save in our dream" (*The Search).* That nothing in this world, I don't care what they will tell me, passes away. But you and I are not the thing that we are observing or at the moment that we experience. And this goes for everything in this world.

So now let me share with you on different levels what I know from experience. Back in 1944, at a Bible class in New York City, a lady who lived with her mother, she was then forty-five; she wouldn't marry because she thought, "Well now, if I marry I don't think a husband would want to take on the obligation of my mother. I would not leave my mother for any man in this world." So she refused marriage and she and her mother lived together until the mother died. At the Bible class, she said to me, "Neville, I just can't tell you...my whole heart has gone out. Mother's gone and my house is empty, my world is empty." I said, "Do you want to see your mother? If it would be any consolation to you, to prove to you your mother hasn't gone, you want to see her?" She said yes. This is Monday night, my classes were held on Monday night. I said, "Alright, this is Monday, it is now the following Monday and you're in this room now and you're telling my Bible class that you met your mother, and that your mother hasn't died; there is survival in this world." I said, "Will you do it?" She said yes.

The following Monday, she rose in my Bible class and she said this to the audience, she said, "I did it Monday night, Tuesday, Wednesday and Thursday. The wee hours of Friday morning I began to awake and I found myself out of my body. I knew that because I looked back at the bed and there is the body. At that very moment my mother is coming through the door. Well, it didn't seem strange to me she was coming through the door, but that was not as interesting to me as the body. So as mother came through the door, I completely forgot that she was dead, the purpose of what I was doing, and so I said to my mother, 'Look, my body!' She said to me, 'You're just as stupid as ever.'" Because her mother would not come to my meetings, and her mother always disapproved of her daughter coming to my meetings, because her mother was a nice, orthodox Christian, and she thought that I was leading her daughter astray by teaching her a Bible along this line—this was simply the devil's Bible. So, as the mother said "You're just as stupid as ever," a little dog came into the room, and she bent down and began to fondle this dog. She smothered the dog with kisses and affection, and then it dawned upon her, "Why, this is my dog that died five years ago." At that moment, she became so emotionally disturbed that she snapped and found herself back in the body.

Two years later, I came west and received one morning a cable that my secretary who served me faithfully—he was like a brother to me—had died. And so, we went back and I took care of his funeral. He never really attended the Catholic Church, but he was born in the Catholic faith, and his sister that he never saw, and really heartily disliked, but she insisted that Jack should have a Catholic funeral, so we abided by her decision. So we went up to Haverstraw, New York, and he had the perfect Catholic funeral, where the sister went by and kissed the dead body, and they all went by and kissed it, and did all these things. Well, if that is par for the course or not, I don't know, but that's what they did.

Well, I have a sister-in-law, my wife's sister, she's a pillar of the Episcopal Church in Jersey, and I think she loves me dearly for one reason, because I take good care of her sister and our child. So being a good father and a good husband, she will tolerate my way of making a living. She doesn't go for it; she said, "I don't believe one word that you say, Neville, not a word. Immortality is simply the extension of oneself in children, in their children and their children. But immortality, as you teach it, I don't go for it." I said to her, "How can you say this when you are a Christian? Don't you know the foundation stone of Christianity is the fatherhood of God, the brotherhood of man, and life everlasting? And you can't rub out one stone. If you rub out one of these foundation stones, the whole building will topple. It's the fatherhood of God, which you find in the words "our Father", and the belief in the revelation of Christianity is eternal life. You can't rub out one." She said, "I will not believe one word you say"...said she.

Well, six or seven months after my secretary died, one night I was out, consciously, just as I am here. Al (my sister-in-law) came into the room, and my secretary who was then so-called dead six or seven months he came into the room. She said to me, "I still don't believe one word you teach, Neville." Then I said to her, "How can you say that when you see Jack?" She said, "What has he to do with what you teach?" I said, "Don't you know that he died six months ago?" See, she's not consciously out, she is in a dream state, so she's not aware. Well, when I made the statement all of a sudden I can see her face begin to show a certain memory image, and she begins to bring back the knowledge that he *did* die six months ago. As she's looking at Jack and Jack is here solidly real, I said to her, "I'll show you how real he is." I said, "Jack, come over here." So Jack came, and I put my hand on his thigh, and the thigh was as solid as this. I said, "You see, my hand doesn't go through his thigh. He's real, he's solidly real." And with this, Jack did this to me [slapped his hand away]. He said, "Take your hands off!" just what he would have done were he here. There was no transforming power in death... the same Jack, on the wheel of recurrence. There is no death, but there are wheels within wheels within wheels in this world.

Then the scene shifted from that moment and the most pleasant, I would say, few years that Jack had on that little wheel (he died at the age of fifty), so in fifty years the most pleasant experience was in Florida when he managed some little citrus grove of a hundred fifty acres. He managed it on the basis of so much per month and then if a profit, he got a profit. But he was living in the open and he just loved it. So the scene shifted and there we are in Florida and he's throwing grapefruit at me. I caught a few, and then she said, "Where is my grapefruit?" At that very moment, my little girl, who was then only about four or five years old, she said, "Daddy, time for breakfast" and I snapped it and was back in this world on this wheel. There are wheels with wheels within wheels, and nothing dies.

So the purpose of it all is to awaken the dreamer. "In the beginning God...in a coffin"—this is the coffin and this is Egypt. "Come, Lord Jesus"—the first-fruits of those who rose from the dead. Come that promise in me that I will not leave you, for I exacted a promise from the sons of Israel they would not leave me in Egypt; they would take my body out, out of Egypt, and bring it into the Promised Land. So, I am asking to come Lord Jesus that he will take me—the being encased in this coffin, in this ark where all things are contained—and awaken me. Christianity is only the awakening, that's all that it is; the awakening from this age into that age. So, man thinks while he is on this wheel that we are moving towards the inevitable climax of good in this world. The climax has already occurred with the words "It is finished." "It is finished" is simply the end of one age and the beginning of a new one, a new age that is marked by the resurrection. So we are resurrected from this age into an entirely different age.

But we came into this age...just as A.E. saw it so clearly and so vividly, that here, this dark figure entranced on the floor in this opalescent, scintillating world, where these already resurrected divine kings dwell. And these sons of Israel would not let him remain there. He's entranced and he's dreaming this world, for the dreamer was the one embalmed and put in a coffin in Egypt, for his name was Joseph. "Behold, this dreamer cometh." And they took him and sold him into Egypt. Then Joseph died; and they embalmed him, and put him in the ark "in a coffin in Egypt" (Gen. 50:26). But the verse before the very end of the first book, the Book of Genesis, the verse before the end, he exacts the promise: Do not leave my bones, my body in Egypt. Bring me out and take me into the land that was promised. Then comes…the next book is Exodus. So the seed plot of the Bible is Genesis. It's also the great, I would say, introduction to this unfolding picture.

So here, when I say nothing dies, I mean it seriously. You're on a wheel and the wheel is perfect. You can't change it; you get off the wheel. And may I tell you this night what is the secret of getting off the wheel: It is revision. Revision is repentance. Repentance which I call today revision, for repentance simply means "a radical change of attitude towards life." Then you break life's invidious bond and turn the circle, the wheel of recurrence, into a spiral of ascension. You turn it right into a spiral and conquer Zion, or the home of God. So David built in a circle and he built inward at one and the same time; and to accomplish this unusual strange architectural feat, it could only be done if you built in a spiral (2 Sam. 5:6-9). And now I'm speaking from experience: By practicing revision you don't allow anything in this world to be as it is. If it isn't pleasing, you change it; therefore, you will not, when the wheel turns, you will not come back to that point. You've changed it. It will not return to that point. It will return in the form of a spiral and instead of being in a circle of recurrence when the wheel turns, you are turning on the spiral by changing one event in your present recurring circle.

Now there is a lady here this night (she and her husband) and three weeks ago last Friday she said to me, "I lost my father, my father died." I told her without explaining in detail what you've just heard what I did with the lady in my Bible class twenty years ago. She came back two weeks later and I said to her "This is Friday night, you go forward in time one week, it's still Friday, and you reflect upon the thrill—for of all the pleasures of the world relief is the most keenly felt—so you feel the relief that is yours because you know beyond all doubt, from actual experience, that your father lives. He hasn't died, he survived." She didn't come back for two weeks, but she could tell me on the seventh day, which was the night of the Thursday of the following week, in vision she met her father. So she knows now beyond all doubt that the father hasn't died, she knows it. Took one week to prove beyond all doubt—not going through a medium, no medium tells her or tries to persuade her—she knows—she had the experience that her father lives.

Well now, a gentleman wrote me a letter that I received today. To show you how this works, he said, "A friend of mine was out of work for quite a while, so I simply applied this principle towards him. In the past, I've applied this principle of imagining towards many things, but it happened so naturally I thought it would have happened anyway, and so I put it down to coincidence. But in this case, my friend being out of work, I applied it, and he got a job, a fine job. It meant going to New York City, or rather, going off to Connecticut and be trained for the job, to be trained in a month. Then the next thing I heard that they filled the job—-someone in the East got the job, and so they didn't complete it here. I felt a bit disappointed. Then I remembered the story of revision, so I revised it. I revised the entire thing that I heard about my friend and saw him in the job. Then came Friday and I thought I'd give a little party the following day, thought I'd call a few friends in and have a little fun. I called a friend of mine, and he was busy, he couldn't come, but he was curious and asked me, 'Who are you having?' I mentioned this friend of mine who had been turned down on this job. He said to me, 'You'd better call him right away because he's leaving on Sunday for New York City.' I said, 'Did he get the job?' He said, 'Yes, a better job. He was turned down on one; then they called him back through the same agency and gave him a better job. Now he's leaving on Sunday for New York City to be trained for one month in Connecticut and then back to the job." Now, he's not here tonight, but his letter came to me today.

So I can tell you from experience we are on wheels, wheels within wheels within wheels, and no one knows that they play this part over and over and over again. You won't break life's invidious bar until you start repenting, and repenting is simply revision. The first proclamation in the earliest gospel is: "The time is fulfilled, and the kingdom of God is at hand; repent, and believe the gospel" (Mark 1:14). To repent is to radically change your attitude towards life, completely change it, no matter how factual it is. So the job isn't his, he's been turned down, somebody else got it, and it's 3,000 miles away, and you can't argue with them. I will not accept it! I will see my friend in that job. I will persuade myself that he has the job. And when I call him on a date, he's leaving not...he's leaving on Sunday. I'm calling him on Friday asking him for a date on Saturday, and he's pulling out Sunday, and he's pulling out Sunday to be trained in the East. That is breaking the wheel of recurrence and turning it in to the ascent, the spiral.

That's exactly what David did when he conquered Zion. For above, we are told, only the blind, the lame and the halt were necessary to keep him away forever. And so, unlike all the others who tried to storm it from without, he went up the water shaft in a spiral. You go up the water shaft in a spiral by practicing the art of revision. So if I gave nothing to the world in my fifty-nine years so far, I have given the art of revision. It isn't new, it's simply repentance. But repentance, after the years of misuse, is like a ship at sea with barnacles. It should be taken in and scraped, because, today, repentance in the world means "remorse, regret." After unnumbered centuries of believing that repentance means "to feel regretful and remorseful," that was not the original intention, and never was and still is not. It is simply a radical change of attitude towards life. And so, I discovered it. It wasn't new. There is nothing new under the sun. As we are told: "Is there a thing of which it is said, 'See, this is new'? It was before in ages past. But there is no remembrance of former things, nor will there be any remembrance of things to come after among those who will follow later" (Eccles. 1:10). Because they are on a wheel, and the wheel is so vast there are wheels within wheels within wheels.

Well, take this wheel: In 1901, these two educators, Miss Mobeley and Miss Jordin...Miss Mobeley was principal of St. Hughes College at Oxford—and Miss Jordin was vice-principal—who when she resigned the principal-ship then Miss Jordin became principal. They came from a long line of educators; therefore, they were schooled in observing and knowing how to really observe carefully what they're supposed to pass an opinion on. Well, in 1901, they made this trip to Versailles, and when they returned after their vacation in Versailles they wrote an account of their experiences, and they paralleled, they duplicated each other. You could superimpose one upon the other and they fitted. It was not what they should have seen in Versailles. While in Versailles in 1901 they both slipped in time and went back to Versailles when the queen was there, just prior to the execution. They saw the entire picture, the costumes of the people, what they wore, what they did, the little bridge that is no longer there, and their account was so accurate that the French government made a thorough investigation of what they said they saw as against what today the French government presents as factual, and they rearranged that picture to conform to what they saw by investigation. The little bridge that was not there they replaced; the costumes that were not worn they replaced; because a thorough investigation proved that their vision of what they actually saw was the true vision of that period. It hadn't passed away.

If you could now slip in time into any part of this constant turning wheel, you would see things as they are always. When Sir William Ramsey, the English scientist, took doses of ether under control, and he had his secretary give the dose, and then record what he was observing and experiencing. Then he observed that "I now see a man delivering coal, and it seems at the moment that he is delivering coal because someone ordered coal. But at this level of withdrawal he is not delivering coal because someone ordered coal, it seems to me that he is the eternal part of the structure of the universe. At this moment in time he is *always* delivering coal." You dwell upon it. At this moment in time, that part of the structure of the universe is always delivering coal. So at this moment in time, this thing here is always saying what it's saying. But you break the circle, and you come out into the spiral, and leave this age and enter an entirely different age.

Hamlet remains to be played. It's the four hundredth year of the great Shakespeare. Hamlet has been played for four hundred years, and they've come and gone as actors playing the part, but Hamlet, the internal structure of that creation of Shakespeare, remains. Actors come and they play and they go, they play and they go. The actor goes on...and the actor is the one that is called God in scripture. The actor is the one that was entombed and put into a coffin in Egypt, and this is that coffin. So I am playing parts, and then comes a moment in time where I reach the end of my long dark journey, and in that wonderful structure my brothers are waiting, waiting, passing over this dark body of mine while it is entranced on the floor of that heavenly structure. And as they pass their hands over the dark body they awaken the fires within it and split it. That cloven pine is riven and out comes a being as tall, as glorious, as shining as those who are seated on the thrones.

Everyone comes out in the same manner, for I exacted before I was entranced a promise they would not leave me entranced. I would dream the dream of life. I would take upon myself the limitations of death, and then dream this dream of being born and dying, and having nothing and having something, and being wanted and being unwanted, and being hurt, and being severed, no eyes, no arms, all these I would dream. But don't leave me in the dream. Awaken, awaken, me at that moment in time when the dream is complete, because if I complete the dream I have increased the power of my creativity. And I will join with my brothers, my heavenly kin, and then as I awake and become awake in the room, I will look around and see those I've always known, and seeing them, raise my hands in salutation. They will leap from their thrones with their hands greeting me and together into the one body called Jesus Christ. Only *one* in all this fabulous world.

So, all of this is the dream and nothing passes away. It remains fixed, a fixed structure animated by the dreamer. As he dreams he animates it, and the whole thing becomes an animated world because of the dreamer that is God. So the Bible begins, "In the beginning God..." and ends, "Come, Lord Jesus." But the seed-plot of the Bible being Genesis, the end of Genesis is, "And he was embalmed and placed in a coffin in Egypt." The word coffin is the same as ark, and this is the ark where all things are contained. He takes everything in, in a creative manner; so that they will reproduce he takes them in, in pairs. So that everything, all the animals, everything goes into the ark because God is in the ark, and there's nothing but God. So the power to create and multiply beyond my wildest dream is contained within this ark, this coffin that you see here.

But above, that no one sees—not out in space but in the depth of the soul—those that I actually extracted a promise they would not leave me in the ark. They watch carefully, and when the dream is coming to an end they pass their hands over my sleeping dark body. From it come splits in the body and sparks come out, like scintillating jewels; and suddenly out from the dark body emerges a being as tall and as glorious and as brilliant as those who were seated on the thrones. I recognize the place, for that was where I was entombed and recognize my kin, my divine kin. And I know the end that was promised me; for we come out of God *as* God. We are the Elohim. You are the Elohim, not some little thing on the outside. So when the Elohim said, "Let us make man in our image," he assumed the limitations of man for the expansion of his creative power. So as Jung brought out in his book, and when he saw himself in deep meditation, he said: "Aha, so he is meditating me, and when he awakes from his dream, I will no longer be." May I tell you, when you awake from the dream this age will no longer be to you, but you, the dreamer, will be simply expanded beyond what you were when you began the dream. Not a thing is lost; all is gained.

Now, do you know the meaning of the word ark? The primal meaning of the word coffin is "to pluck, to gather"...that's the primary meaning of the word. You'll find it in your Concordance: "to pluck, to gather." So by assuming the limitations of death and dreaming of the horrors of this world, I pluck and gather a far greater power to create than I could if I did not descend to this limitation. So that's the meaning of the word ark, the meaning of the word coffin.

So here, "In the beginning God...Come, Lord Jesus." So the cry to the whole vast world is "Come, awaken me from this dream." For it seems that man so entranced has told you—let me quote it once more, the 51st chapter, the 39th verse—"While they are inflamed I will prepare for them a feast and make them drunk, until they swoon away and sleep a perpetual sleep and not awake, sayeth the Lord." The sleep is so profound it seems forever and forever. "I make them drunk"...who makes them drunk? It is God. Well, this is God making the statement. What is this inflammation? It is the inflammation...in the normal translation is called "heat," that is, in the King James Version. It's the heat like the heat of an animal. When an animal is in heat, the neighborhood is disturbed. The whole neighborhood is disturbed when an animal is in heat. They come from afar and everything is disturbed when she is in heat. So in the King James Version it is heat; in the Revised Standard Version the same word is translated inflamed, means the same thing. While they are inflamed: when I am inspired with the story.

For he's preparing me a feast, and what is the food? When he was asked, "Haven't you eaten?" he said, "I have food you know not of. My food is to do the will of him that sent me, his plan, his purpose" (John 4:32,34). I am feeding upon his plan, his purpose. I am so inflamed with this plan of expanding my creative power that I swoon and appear to others as though I am drunk; which is now repeated in the 2nd chapter of Acts when Peter said, "We are not drunk" when they were feasting upon the plan of God for expanding his own creative power. It left them in a swoon and the swoon was a sleep, like a perpetual sleep from which they would not awake until God in his merciful act awakened them. But he extracted a pledge from himself: He would not be left in Egypt in this coffin, he would be awakened.

And so, A.E.'s vision, he said, "I will not tell you where I saw it." I wish he had. But that's his privilege, "I will not tell you." But if you have *The Candle of Vision*—it's out of print but go to the library. It's beautifully written, it's simply...it's all in prose but it's poetry, and it's all based upon what the man actually experienced. It's a small little book. I called his son up in New York City and asked him if he had extra copies and anything that A.E. wrote; and the son was delighted that I mentioned and remembered his father, but, he said, "I'm sorry, I don't even have a copy of it myself." I can hardly believe that, and yet, when I think of it I don't think my son has one book of mine, so it doesn't really matter. I'm quite sure that if I went to Barbados, as I will in two months, and asked my son for a copy of anything that I have written he couldn't produce it. He's not interested.

And so, I called young Russell, the son of George Russell, and asked him for any copy that his father had written, for he wrote some lovely novels, all based upon this strange, wonderful use of Imagination. But the one I quoted this night is *The Candle of Vision*. He begins it...in a very little note that precedes the entire work he quotes from the Book of Proverbs and the Book of Job. In the Book of Proverbs it is said, "The Spirit of man is the candle of the Lord" and in the Book of Job it is said, "And when his candle was lit upon my head, by its light I walked through darkness." So he takes these two passages from Proverbs and Job and puts them in the first page, and then starts his own wonderful mystical experiences. So the book is called *The Candle of Vision*. I had two copies and I gave one to my friend Freedom Berry in San Francisco. Because he is doing this work, if I had any extra copies of anything that I loved, I would give it to him that he may be encouraged to simply go and keep on expanding.

Now let us go into the Silence.

* * *

Q: Where is the theory of reincarnation?

A: Where is the theory of reincarnation? The Bible doesn't teach it. You are in that profound state, on high, dreaming this dream of life, and when you awake you simply expanded your creative power. But you were never any of the garments that you played any more than Lawrence Olivier was ever Hamlet. He's played, possibly, every character that Shakespeare wrote, but he remains Lawrence Olivier and he was never Richard III, which I saw him in the other night. He was never Hamlet and I've seen him in that. He was never any of the characters that he's played. So reincarnation is not taught in scripture. And as we are taught in a rabbinical principle: what is not written in scripture is non-existent. I have never had any experience where I was anyone other than the being that I am. At that moment when I became aware that I am the father of God's only begotten son, whose name is David, I was still the being that I am. So don't be concerned with the garments round about, means nothing. You re-shuffle them and make them conform to dreams as you decide you want life to be. So you simply ignore facts, revise it, and then turn your wheel into a spiral.

Q: I just lost my sister, Neville. Will I ever see her again?

A: Certainly, my dear. But you are the same being that I spoke of this night in the depths that is dreaming. See, in the resurrection there is no giving or taking in marriage, as we're told in scripture. They asked him, they said, Master, Moses said that in the law if a man dies leaving no offspring his brother should marry his widow to raise up seed. Well, there were seven brothers, and one married and died leaving no offspring; the second married her, he left no offspring when he died; and then the third and the fourth and so on, until finally they all married her leaving no offspring. And then she died. Whose widow is she in the resurrection? And he answered, "You do not know the scripture. In this age there is marrying and there is giving in marriage; but those who are accounted worthy to attain to that age neither marry nor are they given in marriage, for they are sons of the resurrection" (Luke 20:27-34). The resurrection means they are lifted out of this wheel of recurrence into an entirely different age, for they die no more, they are now sons of God, sons of the resurrection. So that when you awaken from this wheel of recurrence you'll be one with the Elohim because you are one now. You are *now* the Elohim who contracted himself into the coffin called man to dream the dream of life, and when you awake you'll simply be an enhanced God, still the Elohim.

Q: When you find yourself with quite a difficulty...I'm not familiar with this teaching...?

A: My dear, first of all, as you're seated there, now say "I am," just say it. That's God. All things are possible to God, *all* things. Don't turn to the left or the right, just God. Hold God trustworthy. So assume that I am...and you name it whatever it is. Now when you assume you are it, for confirmation of that assumption look mentally at your world and see your world mentally reflect the reality of what you've assumed. If a friend of yours would know your good fortune after it is a fact, then mentally let your friend know it. But don't tell them physically. Live in that assumption and your assumption if you persist in it will harden into fact. Is that clear?

Goodnight.

A CONFESSION OF FAITH

5/1/64

Tonight's subject is "A Confession of Faith." The Bible really is a confession of faith, a confession put in the form, I may say, of an anthology, for they are the collected sayings of one shepherd given through his servants the prophets over the centuries. But the book has been culled and culled, as you can see from the *Apocrypha*; for at one time they were all part of the canon of scripture. Before the 4th Century A.D. the epistles of Peter and the epistle to the Hebrews and the Book of Revelation they were not included in what is now our canon of scripture. But if you take it as it is today—and it has been in this form since the end of the 4th Century—it really is a confession of faith in the form of an anthology. But faith is not complete until it becomes experience.

And so, we have a hymn of praise for faith given to us in the Book of Hebrews, where he took all the witnesses beginning with Abel and he came all the way through, all living by faith. They received the promises of God, but they did not receive the thing that was promised. There's a vast difference between receiving the promise and receiving that which was promised. The time was not completed for them to enter what we speak of this day as the new age or the kingdom of God. But he defines faith for us in the 11th chapter as "the assurance of things hoped for, the conviction of things not seen." Then he tells us that the whole vast world was framed and created by the *word* of God. The word of God is called "the truth" in scripture. The seal of God consists of the three letters in the Hebrew alphabet, Aleph, Mem and Tau. If you put them together they spell truth, Emeth. It's the first, the middle and the last letter of the alphabet. So we are told in the Book of John, "I have taught them thy word. Thy word is truth" (7:14,17). He comes only to bear witness to the word. His every act is simply foreshadowed in scripture. No one is concerned in the scripture as to whether one is a good carpenter or a poor carpenter, whether one is rich or poor, for scripture is something entirely different. It simply is God's word and everyone is destined to *experience* scripture. And so, then faith becomes experience; faith is fulfilled in the experience of scripture.

Tonight we'll take a statement from the Book of Hebrews and one from Luke. In Hebrews it's the 12th chapter: But now you've come into Mount Zion, the home of the living God, the heavenly Jerusalem...where the assembly of the first-born are really now entered into heaven, and here you find the spirits of just men made perfect, here you find a judge who is God of all, and here you find Jesus, the mediator of the new covenant. See that you do not refuse him who is speaking— that's in the 12th chapter of Hebrews (verses 22-25). The one speaking in this chapter is Jesus Christ, the *risen* Lord. There you find the entrance into the book of those who are raised from the dead, and they're called the first-born of those who slept; there you find the spirits of just men made perfect; and we're told it all takes place in the new Jerusalem in Mount Zion which is the home of the *living* God.

When you read it you wonder, "What is it trying to tell us?" Well, let me share with you my experience. We go back now to the 12th chapter of Luke. Here we are told that everything in this world is forgiven but one—which is unbelievable because to a merciful God *everything* is possible and *everything* is forgivable—but we are told that the sin against the Holy Spirit is not forgiven; it is the eternal sin. But it doesn't leave us there, as Mark does, the 3rd chapter of Mark, when Mark makes that statement Mark leaves us there and there is no out. But not Luke, Luke is more developed as to this mystery. And then Luke turns our attention to that one moment in eternity when it's possible for man to sin against the Holy Ghost by adding the words, "And when they bring you before the synagogues, before the rulers, before the authorities, do not be anxious how or what you are to answer or what you are to say; for the Holy Spirit will teach you in that very hour what you *ought* to say" (verse 11). The very little word "ought" is your freedom to stand in the presence of the one who is speaking and refuse to make your confession of faith after having been supernaturally prompted what to say. For you are told what to say...not audibly...but in that very hour when you stand in his presence you are actually being prompted, supernaturally prompted what to say. Now listen to it carefully, "Do not be anxious when you stand in his presence how or what you are to answer." Well, if I am to answer, someone must have asked me a question. And so, do not be anxious how or what you are to answer or what you are to say. So having answered, I'm also going to make a statement: for while in that very hour the Holy Spirit will teach you what you *ought* to say. So when you stand in the presence of this one, defined for us so beautifully in the 12th of Hebrews, I can't conceive of anyone not actually automatically answering the question that is asked you.

So this is what will happen to you. As you're told, he was taken in spirit, just as you're told in Isaiah he was taken in spirit; they all were taken in spirit, and you *are* taken in spirit. You have the sensation of a long, long journey, that's the sensation, yet it's completed only in a matter of moments. But you, if you would analyze the feeling, it's a feeling of an infinite journey. And you are taken in spirit, you don't see your ___(??), but you are brought into this heavenly council. As you are told in the 82nd Psalm, "And God has taken his place in the divine council; in the midst of the gods he holds judgment." Well, who are the gods? The spirits of just men made perfect, they're the gods. You are the gods. And when you enter that society you meet men, and you're brought into the presence of the one who you're told not to refuse, the one who is speaking. You're told that those who are born from above are now being enrolled. You will see the most glorious angelic being with an open book and a quill pen. Now, what is directed, I do not know. I only saw what I'm now describing. I saw this angelic being sitting at a desk with a quill pen, an open book, and here was motion. What was recorded I do know. But you're told in Hebrews that *these* are enrolled in heaven. Who are enrolled? Those who are called the first-born from the dead, those who are born from above, and they are enrolled. You actually see it.

Then you are brought before the one that is speaking now. You stand in the presence of the *risen* Christ, the Lord of hosts. You can't describe him, save that he was encompassed in light, infinite light, but it's man. The words of Blake may speak to your mind, Don't humble yourself—if you humble yourself you humble me—for you too are man and God is no more. You stand in the presence of man, infinite in love. That's the one feeling that you feel coming from him, infinite love. Then he asks you a very simple question, "What is the greatest thing in the world?" And maybe after that moment, in your conscious reasoning mind, you never fully understood it or even accepted it, but you don't hesitate to answer. And you answer in the words of Paul, his 13th Corinthians, because he did for love what the writer of Hebrews did for faith. And so, he said, the greatest thing in the world is love: "Faith, hope and love, these three abide; but the greatest of these is love" (1Cor.13:13). That's what you're going to say. And as you say it, the risen Christ will embrace you; and from that moment on you wear his body. No mortal eye can see it but you are incorporated into the body of God, and you feel a joy and an ecstasy that you can't describe in words. Then from that, you are sent on your mission, for to be called is also to be sent. And as Paul said, "Am I not an apostle? Have I not *seen* the risen Christ? Have I not seen the Lord Jesus Christ?" (1 Cor. 9:1). So to have *seen* him is to be qualified for apostleship. The word apostle simply means "to be sent, one who is sent." So as you are embraced and become one with God you are then sent to tell the story that all may hear it and then respond to it. That's why it's so very important that the testimony of Jesus should be heard by all, and then let them be the judge and respond to it. Reject it or accept it.

But I tell you, every word of scripture you're going to experience. But you accept it first purely on faith, and you walk blindly led only by faith. You do not receive the promises until the end of a certain journey. But the door is open now and has been since the first one who was raised from the dead. Everyone is being called, called one by one, into that divine council; and while you are there you will encounter all of these things that are mentioned in the 12th chapter of the Book of Hebrews. You will see the men. They are giants, not in height but giants in power. The first one that I saw was the embodiment of infinite might, but a man. I felt in his presence that if he desired he could destroy the earth. I felt he could destroy the universe. I felt the embodiment of infinite might in the presence of that man...and it is a man…the spirit of a just man made perfect. I met others. I met infinite love...that's God himself. But, mercy was present, peace was present, all these attributes were present in the form of man. And I mingled with them and I moved among them—they're all men, the spirits of just men made perfect. The children preceded that motion and they were simply perfectly heavenly children. So everything recorded that seems so silly on the surface you are going to experience. That's why I can tell you from experience the book is true.

On this level of ours, you take the same faith that led the patriarchs and move it in our world to better the environment in which we live. Now what do we mean by living by faith? He said, they endured as seeing him who was invisible, that's what they did. Well, you and I endure as seeing *that* which at the moment is invisible. Seeing what?—the success that you see. When I walk by sight I go my way by the objects that my eye sees. If I leave here tonight and suddenly the streets are not what they were when I came in and the signs are rearranged or gone, or the buildings are gone, I am quite sure that we couldn't find our way home. We must have some familiar objects, stable objects, to lead us that we see them by the eye. So I know my way when I walk by sight by objects that the eye sees.

When I walk by faith, I know my way by objects that only the *mind* sees. And so, when I want to walk by faith, I set up in my mind's eye objects to lead me. The objects are the faces of the friends that I call my friends, who would sincerely rejoice with me if they learned of my good fortune. Then I let them know of it. I see the world as I *want* to see it, not as it is here to be seen. So I rearrange the structure of the mind; and then I remain faithful to it—as the patriarchs remained faithful to their invisible being. For we are told in the 11th of Hebrews that Moses endured as seeing him who was invisible. He was told about him, as Job was. And Job said, "I have heard of thee with the hearing of the ear, but now, in the very end, my eye sees thee." He was faithful to the end, and then he saw the being who predicted the moment in time that he would actually stand in his presence. And Job went through, as you know, the proverbial hell, but he was always faithful. He never once complained, but he did not feel for one moment that this pain that he endured was justified. And in spite of that he still believed in God. He believed in the Promise. So the Promise is to all of us that God one day will give himself to us, individually. That's called grace in scripture...and grace is God's gift of himself to man. So when he embraces you he gave you himself. All that he had he gave you in that one moment that he embraced you. If he is the king of kings, he gives you that honor. If a king has a kingdom, he gave you the kingdom. So you will inherit with that embrace not only a presence but a kingdom. He doesn't take back anything. He gives you his most precious possession: He gives you his only begotten son as *your* son. Not as your companion, to walk as a friend, but he gives you his only begotten son as *your* son. Therefore, he gave you fatherhood in that gift. He gives you *everything* that he has.

Now, you are sent into the world to encourage all to be faithful and endure as seeing him who at the moment is invisible. And to prove to them that you are on solid ground you explain to them the nature of faith, that faith is "the assurance of things and the conviction of things not seen." So I would put it in these words, faith is simply loyalty to unseen reality. So you tell me what you want in this world and you name it. You want to be successful and you name what you mean by success. I'm not here to judge you, just to guide you, to tell you, well alright, if you really want to be successful, *assume* this very moment that at this moment now you are *now* what you want to be. Take the dream and wear it as you would a suit of clothes. Now, see the world as you would see it were it true. Now that's the invisible you. Now you walk faithful to this *invisible* you. But make it natural, wear it just as you would wear any apparel in the world, and as you wear it, it becomes more and more you, more and more natural. And you can tell it in your dreams. Your dreams will change, because your dreams will reflect the mood that really dominates you, because the dominant mood really spells out the individual. That mood to which man most often returns constitutes the man's truest self. So if I return constantly in the course of a day to the mood of success, at the end of a couple of days it's a *natural* thing. I don't have to come back to it as often. Then, in a little while, I take it for granted. It's the most normal, natural thing in the world thereafter.

Let me tell you a story of my brother, which I told a friend tonight. We started after a disastrous failure in a way back in 1919...started from scratch with borrowed capital. When my brother and father, who were then partners together, owed the bank 5,000 dollars they were concerned, they were worried. This past November in New York City, discussing with my brother Victor, I said, "Vic, what do you owe the bank?" Oh, he said, "I presume a million and a half." I said, "You owe a million and a half?" "Yes, always owed a million and a half. That's their money, their rent money, and our rent money to them. And so I need money to turn the wheels of industry. But today, owing them on every day of the year 1,500,000 dollars I'm not as concerned as I used to be when I owed them 5,000 dollars. No concern whatsoever."

And it brought to mind a story, which is a very true story. He's gone from this world now. He was mayor of Hamilton __(??), a little island in the Indies. He started from scratch washing bottles in a little store. But they couldn't import bottles all the time so if you brought your bottle back you got a penny for it; and he had to smell the bottles to see that you didn't put kerosene in that bottle before you brought it back, for these bottles were used for rum. Well, he was a very ingenious lad and he rose to be the mayor of the town. He owned the biggest hotel and parts of other hotels. So during this period that we called Prohibition in this world, there were nine indictments against him in this country, because he was running as much rum as would float the country into this land of ours, all on the eastern seaboard, had his own ships, had everything else. He bribed this mayor, bribed that mayor, and they all would come down and count the pieces that he brought ashore, because these mayors got two dollars a case, and they weren't taking his count for it. They would come down and count the cases and each got their two dollars in cash per case. It ran into millions.

Well, he had to be financed too. And so he went to the local bank and he raised money to finance this project. The banker one day said to him, "Ronnie, did you know you owe me an awful lot of money." He said, "Are you worried?" "Why, certainly I'm worried, because you owe me more money than we are capitalized for." Well, he said, "You're worried…there's no need for both of us worrying." He had one person worried so he didn't worry, while Ronnie did all the money for him. Now, Ronnie applied this unwittingly. He never saw failure. He couldn't conceive of failure. He started, as I told you earlier, without one nickel in this world, but he lived in the assumption that things were right. And with nine indictments against him in this country the day that Prohibition went out this country tore the nine up and he was as welcome in this country as you are. For, he came and left as he wanted after they tore the nine indictments up; for they only belonged to that age of Prohibition.

So I tell you, faith—read it in the 11th chapter of the Book of Hebrews, "Things that you see were made from things that do not appear." If one could only keep that in mind. The success that you want is made from things that you do not know in this world. It is not made from your friends. Don't depend upon one friend in this world. Don't depend upon anyone, just...it's all *in* you. The whole vast world is yourself pushed out, and so, if you know that the things seen were made from things that are *not* seen, then you will take off from there; and you will know that imagining and faith are the stuff out of which man fashions his world. You can start wherever you are and fashion anything you want in this world. So when you walk by faith, you walk by objects only the *mind* sees. If you insist on walking in the natural way by sight, well, then you walk by objects that the eye sees. Your friends will see you as they now see you, and you'll never get beyond it if you don't *dare* to assume that you are other than what you *seem* to be. You must dare to assume it and be faithful to it, be loyal to this unseen reality, and then day in and day out it becomes more and more natural. After awhile you will know what I'm talking about concerning proving it here on this level, and then be blessed with the proof on the depths of the soul.

But I can't tell anyone what a thrill it is when you are taken in spirit into the divine society. Because you read it in a book, but you can't believe, as most people can't believe, that God is man. It's a stumbling block. No matter when I speak or where I speak there's always someone to challenge my right to say that God is a man. "You dare in this modern age of 1964, of nuclear energy, to say that God is man?" Well, I'm speaking from experience. I stood in his presence. I can say exactly what Paul said, "Have I not seen the risen Christ? Am I not an apostle?" Did he not send me? I *saw* him, therefore, that was the qualification. And the words ringing in my ears then are still ringing in my ears, and the command was "Time to act!" Therefore, if you say you believe this. then it's time to act. Don't say I believe it and not act. For, I'll tell you, there's not a thing in this world that tests one's belief better than action. Action puts belief to the acid test. For if the belief isn't strong enough to effect action then it can't move anything in this world. So if I say I believe, then I will act upon it. I will not sleep this night in the assumption of being the man that I was today if I didn't want to be that man. I would *dare* to assume that I *am* the man that I want to be, though at the moment everything denies it. If I don't *act* that way, well then, my belief or my claim isn't really great enough.

Now, people will say who know the Bible, "Did not James say that faith without works is dead?" Granted, he did say that, but he did not propose that we substitute works for faith. Works are the evidence of whether the faith we profess in this world is alive or dead. If it is alive, you'll act; if it's dead, you'll simply give it lip service and do nothing about it. You will say, "Imagining creates reality. It's a lovely statement. It causes arguments if you're at a social gathering." And so, you can have that as some little thing as a toy. But I'm not speaking of a toy, I'm speaking of the force of creation in this world. It *does* create reality, but if I really believe it I will act upon it.

So when I was commanded to go and tell the story of Christ, the words in my ears that were ringing from the one who embodied infinite might were the words "Time to act." And the words that preceded that, that have disturbed so many people, were the words "Down with the bluebloods" because we have a certain association of bluebloods that we think it means the socially prominent. Hasn't a thing to do with that, because in heaven the only aristocracy is the aristocracy of the Spirit. Hasn't a thing to do with flesh and blood, because no one can inherit the kingdom of heaven with flesh and blood; because God is Spirit but *man*; and you are Spirit, just as solidly real as you seemingly are here, but you are Spirit and you are man. You stand in the presence of man and you look around and there are only men.

So when you hear these words "Down with the bluebloods," don't think for one moment it means that you destroy any of the lovely fruits of this world...not a thing about it. The bluebloods is simply "church protocol." You do not need them. Leave them alone. But you don't need it; you don't need any external worship, any external form of worship or ceremony or any outside creed. The whole thing comes from within. So I have never gone out to disturb any group, I assure you, and yet these words were my command. And so, they came back in the late 1920s. I was not more than twenty-one or twenty-two when this happened. I have never been a disturbing influence in any group. I might disturb your mind as I go by you, but not if you're satisfied with a certain thing. I never invite you to leave a certain church to come here, nor would I invite you to leave a certain group to come here. But the protocol being spoken of is simply church protocol—anything that is on the outside that you think in some strange way God is looking out on you and will accept that in lieu of *acting*. No, he wants you to *act*. He wants you to create, for God is a creator; and his sons must be as creative as he. So we must create and create and still create again.

So, this is a confession of faith. And one day, I swear as I stand here, the joy is beyond measure when you are called. The night you are called you do not know; you haven't the slightest idea. You go to sleep as you would sleep this night, not expecting anything, and suddenly you are picked up in Spirit and you are carried seemingly forever. Then you come into this grand, wonderful gathering of the gods. And when he holds you, because you've answered correctly, you did *not* sin against the Holy Spirit. For the Holy Spirit prompted you by asking the question. Now, I do not say that everyone will be asked the same question. But I do say, regardless of the nature of the question, the answer you will know, for the Holy Spirit will teach you in that very hour what you ought to say. And because he teaches you what you ought to say, you're prompted by some supernatural power which is the Holy Spirit, you will say it, and because the answer is correct he will embrace you. The moment he embraces you, you fuse with God and you never become un-fused again. You're one with God forever and forever. When you're time is up here and this little flesh and blood garment is taken off, you awake there. And *that* is the being that you are. It seems incredible but it's true.

And may I tell you, you don't earn it. You don't earn it, it is a gift, therefore, you're going to get it. And secondly, don't think that you've got to fit yourself to receive it, just act. I'm quite sure that Ronnie who violated all of our laws that we ourselves violated when he ran unnumbered cases of liquor into this country. He violated all the laws of this country, but there wasn't an American who wasn't violating the same law. Unless, naturally, you were an extreme "dry" and many of them were, but on the whole we did not want the Volstead Act. It was against the grain of the country. And so he simply fed America what they wanted and made millions doing it. But I am quite sure that in the presence of God he is not unclean because he did that, I'm quite sure. No one can tell me that they feel in their heart that they're qualified to stand in his presence and be embraced by him, and be incorporated into his body as himself. So I know today that fitness is the consequence not the condition of his grace. The minute you are embraced you are fitted. You weren't fitted prior to that, yet you were called. So man is called. And what is the secret of God's elective love I do not know. But we are called in order, not in groups; we are called singly but in God's own order. For he is building his new Jerusalem, building it out of these *living* stones that *we* are. And he...his body is that great Jerusalem, that creative power that can create anything in this world.

So to come back to that unforgivable sin, I can't conceive of it. I can't conceive of anything impossible to God. And a merciful being that God is, I can't conceive of a thing that his mercy could not forgive. So we're pointed to it, and Luke leads the way. Mark doesn't. When Luke adds what he does to that statement, it throws light on it. So when you are brought before the synagogue, before the rulers and the authorities, do not be *anxious* how or what you are to answer. Right away he tells you you're going to be asked something. Don't be anxious. Why? Because in that very hour the Holy Spirit will teach you what you ought to say. So he does give you the freedom of choice to say no, or refuse to speak, or give the wrong answer. Because, you *ought* to say what you've been prompted to say, but you need not because you're free. So you are warned again in the 12th chapter of Hebrews, So when you stand before him, he who is speaking, do not refuse him (verse 25). Don't refuse him, the one who is speaking. Well, who is speaking? The previous verse tells you who is the one speaking: the risen Christ. You stand in his presence, he is the one asking the question, and you stand there, and you answer him, and then he incorporates you into his body.

So here you take it this night and take it in hope. As you're told, "Put your hope fully on the grace that is coming to you at the revelation of Jesus Christ." It's coming! Can't stop it! Put all of your hope on that grace. But in the meanwhile live by faith. Ask a friend "What do you want in this world?" and don't raise a finger to make it so for him. Don't call your friends and tell them to help him; you do it, do it in your mind's eye. And if they are a thousand miles away or ten thousand miles away, still do it. They aren't 10,000 miles away in your Imagination, they're right here. I get a call from Barbados, well, physically that would be 5,000 miles from here, but they're not. I could talk to my sister as though she were here. I could talk to my father, who is gone, as though he were here. I talk to my mother. In fact, my memory of my mother has been quite a guide in much of my behavior. First of all, I don't think that mother would approve, well, that stops me; because I know she isn't dead, and I know she isn't 5,000 miles away, and I know she's as near as to me as my thought is to her.

So, I know when I think of mother that her attitude towards my behavior guides me, because I know what she'd expect from her son. She used to tell us when we were little children and the word Goddard had no meaning whatsoever in the island—no social standing, no financial standing, nothing, no intellectual standing—and when we were little tots and mother was raising us, we could ill-afford the little things that we had to have. If you did something that displeased her, mother would say, after she corrected us, "Have you forgotten that you are a Goddard?" Well, she shamed you that you forgot you were a Goddard. She made the name important. It had no importance whatsoever, had no significance, but you walked in the consciousness of being a Goddard. With the result having built that into your consciousness, they are the biggest business people in all the islands today. That is in all the...that's nearly all the islands...definitely in Barbados, and now St. Lucia, and St. Vincent, and they are the tops as to name and industry. She *made* it important. And quite often she didn't have to go beyond shaming you, "Have you forgotten that you are a Goddard?" Try it with your children. Make your name, which they bear, an important name. And then actually you can spare the whip by simply recalling their memory to the fact that they have forgotten the importance of their parents and, therefore, the importance of themselves.

And so, if you treat those who are gone from this world as though they were here, and you respect their opinions, and know that they can see you as I see you now, then you would not do many things that, well, without that consciousness you would do. Because I know that she would disapprove. I know my father would disapprove. I know that he had a certain attitude towards life that you could not criticize any woman in his presence. A man, yes, you could say what you want of a man, but he would not allow anyone of us to say anything that was not noble concerning a woman. He just wouldn't stand for it. And that happened even when we were all grown men with our wives and children. He disapproved heartily of any criticism of woman. He always put woman on a pedestal. To the very day he made his exit they were something different in his life. If something obviously was not right, he would rather not discuss it. No matter how obvious it was, he just wouldn't discuss it. He built that into his mind's eye.

And so, I say to everyone, try it. Walk by these internal guides, for we have guides. The internal guide is the same you use with the external guide of the eye. You walk home by objects that you know, and you walk to your objective in life by the inner object that you know. Along the way you're going to meet this one that you know well and they will congratulate you on your good fortune, and as a friend you will accept it and be gracious about it. Then the next one will congratulate you and you will congratulate them because you want them to be equally progressive in this world. We can take everyone in our circle and lift them up in the inner circle of the mind seeing them as we would like to see them. And may I tell you it will work. If we have evidence for a thing, does it really matter what our critics say? It doesn't really matter if we have evidence for it. So we can test God's law. We can test the power of faith and when we test it and prove it, well, then we'll live by it. If someone asks us what is the secret, you tell them. If they don't ask us, well, we need not shout about it. But, if they ask we'll tell them. They may not believe it, but you can tell them. I know my father told me the very first day he heard me in New York City, we came home after the lecture in the morning and he said, "Boy, I agree with every thing you said this morning but one." I said, "Alright, tell me. You are a success in life. In my eyes you're a great success. So what is the one?" He said, "You told them this morning that when they meditate close the eye. No, don't do that, just partly close it. Just close the lid but don't completely close it, and then you can see better. You can see exactly what you want to see if you only partly close it. If you close it completely, then your mind wanders." And so, that was his advice to me.

But I couldn't laugh at my father for the simple reason he had proved it. He started without a nickel and his goal was success in *this* world. He had his own ideas concerning religion, concerning family life, and he held them up very high. But in business he started from scratch. When he was thirty-nine he could give us what he did, and when at eighty-five when he made his exit from this world had you come in the next day and offered to buy out the enterprises, you couldn't come with less than five million and get even a carrot. And he did that for us by simply not closing his eye. Every morning he would sit after breakfast and see exactly what he wanted for the day. He would carry on all of his transactions and bring them out successfully. Any contract he had pending for the day, he'd get it before he left home and saw the whole thing at the end. Now, whether he did it unknowingly or someone told him, I don't know. But I know in my own case, after my first lecture that he heard, he said to me, "Everything you said is true but one. Don't tell them again to close the eye, just partly close it, and then they see exactly what they want to see and carry on conversations with that scene from the premise of exactly what they want in this world, and believe it." He was a very faithful man to this belief.

So now, as we go into the Silence, I'll close mine because I've grown accustomed to it. But try my father's technique. I can close my eye and see exactly what I want to see. But maybe others are helped by his technique. As I say, I can't laugh at him because he proved it. And if he had evidence for a thing it doesn't matter what others think. We will stick by what we know based upon experience.

Now let us go into the Silence.

* * *

Q: ___(??) of Rachel dying in childbirth?

A: I really don't know.

Q: (inaudible)

A: The first-born is disclosed in the 1st chapter of Revelation: He was the first raised from the dead, the first-born of those who slept. You'll find that in the 1st chapter (verse 5). So the first- born...he's speaking of an entirely different age, when one leaves this age, the wheel of recurrence, and enters that age. Everyone who enters that is the first-born.

Q: (inaudible)

A: ___(??) it seems this way to us, but no, "All that I behold, though it appears without, it is within." Well, you're told in so many passages of the Isaiah story, in the 6th chapter of Isaiah, and he beheld him. Moses saw him face to face and talked to him as a man talks to a man. Jacob saw him, wrestled with him through the night, and said, "This is the place of God." He called it Bethel, or the house of God. And so, it's not a unique thing. Everyone will see him. And everyone, I'm quite sure, is going to see infinite love and you'll stand in his presence. If you say you die, you die only because in Jacob's case it gave the cue: his name was changed from Jacob to Israel. He could not remain Jacob and see God, because to *see* God is to be transformed. And whatever you were prior to that, you're not the same being. You appear to others to be the same being, you answer to the same name, but you are not the same being; because you cannot rub out that indelible imprint that has been made upon you. You can't forget the sensation of love that was yours, the ecstasy that was yours, and it haunts you. And so, you are not the same being.

Now, I didn't say one of these things to my father. When I went home to my father in 1933— I left there in '22—I'm sitting on the veranda with him one day, a minister calls, and this minister is an old friend of mine as a schoolboy. He went his way and became a minister and came to America. So he came home to see me to discuss, and, naturally, we got to discussing the Bible. My father turned to me in the presence of the minister—I had never discussed it with my father before—and he looked at me, he said, "You know, son, you are an apostle." Well, at the moment I did not accept my father's judgment on *that* score, for I still hadn't...I couldn't bring myself to believe the significance of the experience that happened some years before. But he was very, very familiar with his Bible, and he knew that having seen the risen Christ and having been sent that that in itself would imply, whether you know it or not, you have been sent. And you can't be sent and not be one. But people will say, Well after all, the man has been married twice, he has children, he drinks, eats meat, he does all these things, how can he be one? If you go back to the book you see he came eating and drinking; they called him a drunkard and a glutton and he liked all the harlots. He was a friend of all the sinners and the harlots and the tax collectors. And so, you point these things out in the scriptures, they get annoyed, they don't like that. Because man has a strange concept about what is a holy man. What is a holy man? (tape runs out...)

THE CLEVER RASCAL: THE UNJUST STEWARD

5/5/64

Tonight's subject is "The Clever Rascal." This is taken from the 16th chapter of the Book of Luke. There's a story told there of an unjust steward. There's a very rich man who had a steward and charges were brought against the steward that he was wasting his man's goods. So he called the steward and told him to turn in his stewardship, for he could no longer represent him. The steward went out and got all of the debtors and asked each in turn what they owed his master. "The first one said, 'One hundred measures of oil.' He said, 'Sit down and write, quickly, fifty measure of oil.' Then he said to the second, 'How much do you owe my master?' He said, 'One hundred measures of wheat.' 'You sit down and you write eighty.'" And so, he falsified the entire record of his master, making friends for himself. For he felt, I am too weak to work and too proud to beg, and so by doing this I'll make these friends of mine, so when I'm fired from my job they will know that they are in my debt. For I gave this one fifty percent of what he really owed, and that one twenty percent of what he owed; and so at least to this extent they are indebted to me. When his master heard what he had done, the master highly commended him for his prudence. Then he said to those to whom he told the story, 'Make for yourself friends of the unrighteous mammon. For if you are not faithful to that unrighteous mammon, who will trust you when it comes to the real riches of the world?'"

Now, a parable has a central jet of truth and the outer story is secondary to its meaning, what it really tries to convey. He is not recommending the man who stole his master's goods or falsified the master's records; it's a story. What is its meaning? That's the important thing. And what are the real riches against the so-called riches of the unrighteous mammon? Well, the *Encyclopedia Britannica* defines for us the word righteous as "equitable, just, right thinking," therefore "unrighteous" would be the opposite. It would not be just, it would be unjust. It would not be right thinking, just the opposite of right thinking.

Now, what is right thinking? If today I reflect on the activities of the day and I have a hundred percent recall, I would have a perfect record of what happened today. If I had a perfect recall, that when we had dinner, for instance, I should not only know what I ate but the order in which I ate it, the chronological order. Did I take this piece before that? Did I take a sip of coffee with the meal or after the meal? Everything in the day—the mail as I received it, as I opened it, not only as I opened it, my reactions to the mail—everything should be perfectly recalled if my memory is perfect and I have a hundred percent recall. So memory is the conservative aspect of imagining. So I recall the day; that is right thinking, that's righteous mammon. But I don't like what happened today, and I'm invited to emulate the unjust steward and simply recall the day and simply revise every little aspect of the day that does not conform to the day as I wish I had encountered. That is being unjust, that is right thinking. I am completely changing and modifying the whole day to make it conform to my wish fulfilled. I am invited to emulate the behavior of the unjust steward; for if I do not do it in this way, if I am not faithful to this unrighteous mammon, who will trust me with that which is real in this world?

Now, what is the "real" in this world? He is telling us by that statement this whole vast world would be really unreal. But I am learning to cut my mental teeth and spiritual teeth on the unreality: Getting a home when I can't afford it, increasing my income when seemingly I haven't the talent, bringing in all kinds of things in my world. But this is a world that wears out; it wears out like a garment, and the whole vast world, including the stars, they are fading and dissolving just like smoke. But, there is a *real* world...and if I can't be faithful in this world with unjust, unrighteous mammon who would entrust me with the real riches of the world?

Now, sixteen years ago I had an experience which I recorded in one of my books, called *Awakened Imagination*. I've only seen it once in print and it came after my experience. That is, it was printed thousands of years ago, 2,000 years ago, but I did not know of this book. It was given to me after I came out in print and I told my story. The book is *The Apocryphal New Testament as Compiled by James* and in it is a story told by Joseph, the father of Jesus Christ. As told in this story, Joseph had this strange experience the night of his birth, where everything stood still. The heavens stood still, the shepherds walking walked not, and the little lambs drinking drank not, and the water flowing flowed not, everything stood still. Then all of a sudden everything moved on in its course.

Well, that experience was mine sixteen years ago, when suddenly I slipped in time and went back in time, say, 200 years, and came upon a scene of a wonderful lovely gracious dining room. It was in the eastern section of this country. I could tell from their clothes, from the setting, everything was simply New England. Then, at that moment, I knew that if I could arrest within me an activity which I felt, that all that I now perceived within the focus of my vision would stand still, it would all freeze. And so, at that moment, I arrested it, and my head jelled, it became solid. At that moment, I, the perceiver, I was awake and I could change my attention, but within the focus of my vision everything froze. The diners who were dining dined not. One young lad, about twenty-two years old, bringing a spoon to his mouth froze, and he couldn't move it one moment beyond where I froze him—father and mother on both sides, and his brother to my...his brother's back to me, so the two boys and the father and mother. A waitress coming through the door and as she started walking she froze and she couldn't move. A bird in flight, it froze. The little leaves falling, they froze. The grass waving with the wind, it froze. Everything froze. I examined the whole thing, it was all dead. The life was in me! And when I released that power within me, that life in me, then everything continued on its course. The boy completed his action of bringing the soup to his mouth. The waitress completed her action of walking to the table to bring the second course. The bird that was arrested in flight continued in its flight, and the leaves falling fell. Everything moved as it intended when I arrested the intention.

But across this country I am always asked, "Did the four diners and the waitress were they aware of being frozen?" But I have no way of telling, I couldn't answer. I only know that I froze it in myself. I couldn't tell whether these four and the waitress walking towards the table were aware that they were frozen, I didn't know. From here to New York City and across the country—I gave lectures in Milwaukee, Detroit, Chicago and all over San Francisco, all the way down—I've told this story and someone would always ask that question. And I was unable from experience to answer and to tell that I know that they were dead. I thought they were all dead. I looked at them, they were dead. The bird should have fallen if our law of gravity is true. The bird should have fallen, for the bird in flight, if arrested, would fall to the ground. But it didn't, it was simply arrested. Space was frozen; everything was frozen so it couldn't fall. But I could not answer their question intelligently.

Well, this past week, a lady, who is present here tonight, told me this story. It only happened to her recently. She lives in the Palisades and she hears the ocean and can see the ocean. These are her words, she said, "Neville, I had this experience, but it was from the negative side of yours. You were the operant power, you stopped it. I didn't stop it; I was on the negative side: I was stopped. Suddenly, someone or something turned me off and I was nothing but literally nothing." She was aware, because she could not know she was nothing unless she was aware of being nothing. "They turned me off and I was nothing. There was no sound of the ocean, but nothing, everything was dead. Then whatever turned me off turned me on again and then everything became alive."

Now, that's the power that I call the *real* riches of the world. So if you are not faithful to the unrighteous mammon, who will entrust you with the real riches of the world? You think about it. If this very moment some tyrant in the world who wants to conquer, say, this marvelous land of ours and enslave it for their own personal gain, if they had such riches and did not have the heart of love, they could turn us off; and then that's like simply wiping off the slate, wiping off the blackboard, and then rewriting the script as they would intend. Then, when they turned us on again our intentions would be completely changed, even if that intention was to walk willingly—and think we were initiating the urge to walk—into the ocean beyond our depth. We would think this is what we want to do, like the lemmings do. Do they not by the hundreds of thousands just move towards the ocean and all become, well, they all commit suicide? They do it year after year as they seemingly reproduce so many. Then suddenly they all start moving, these little animals, and move toward the ocean and all commit suicide. Who turned them off and then turned them on with a different intention? Instead of reproducing themselves, the slate was wiped clean, and then a new script was put on it, and then the lights turned on once more.

Now listen to the words, "In him was life, and the life was the light of men" (John 1:4). In him was life, and the life was the light of men. We go now to the epistle, this is the 1st John—that is, I just quoted from the first chapter of John—we go now to the first epistle of John, "He who has the Son has life; he who has not the Son has not life" (5:12). If you have the Son, you have eternal life in yourself. Life in yourself is the light in men, and you can turn it off and turn it on. But I doubt that anyone would ever have life in themselves until he's embraced and fused with love, for what would he do to this fantastic world if he had life in himself not moved and guided by love? Can you conceive what man could do…to turn off, as the lady was turned off and everything stood still? There was no ocean...she can hear it from her window from her home, she can see it from her home, but it was all still. There was no ocean. The ocean was simply frozen as though, well, a lake frozen. It was just simply still, the atmosphere still. And she said in her own words, "I was nothing, but literally nothing." She was aware of being nothing. And then someone or something, whoever turned her off, turned her on again and suddenly she became someone, became something.

Well, I had the positive side of that experience, so I can say to this lady you are on the verge of moving from that side to the positive side. You have to have the negative side first. It's only God, the operant power, operating on himself; and it's God, her own wonderful being, operating on himself *in* her. So it was he who turned off what he loves more than anything else in this world, his emanation, which is this lady. She is his emanation, his love, and he will not in eternity leave her until they cleave and become one flesh, one being. So he operates upon her and shows her the power that he intends one day to share with her when they become one. That power she will then exercise…and you will turn it off or turn it on.

So then Blake said, "Eternity exists and all things in eternity, independent of creation, which was an act of mercy," so now you put yourself into this mind, that everything is aware of being ___(??), but everything; and it is simply an act of mercy that now turns the light on, and animates it, activates it; and then through this activation brings out what he loves more than anything in the world. Brings out himself, his own emanation. Haven't you seen these ships up in San Francisco—as you go from San Francisco and take a ride into Sacramento—and they're all in mothballs? Hundreds and hundreds of ships deactivated, dead, completely dead. They could tomorrow if the order were given be activated and once more become alive. People would go aboard, ___(??), things would come aboard, all things begin to move, these ships, thousands of them all in mothballs. Blake saw these and he called them "the halls of Los." He implies that everything *is now*. The Bible tells us that, the 3rd chapter, the 15th verse, of the Book of Ecclesiastes: "That which is, already has been; that which is to be, already has been; and God is seeking that which is lost, or which has gone astray." What's gone astray? He sent himself into the entire structure and he is extracting himself, his creative power. His creative power is called in scripture Christ Jesus. Christ is defined in scripture as the creative power and wisdom of God. It's the wisdom of God (1 Cor. 1:24).

Now, listen to this carefully, taken from the Book of Proverbs, the 8th chapter: "God created me at the beginning of his way, the first of his acts of old" (verse 22). Before he brought forth the heavens, before he brought forth the earth, before he established anything, "I was beside him, like a little child" (verse 30). Now, this little statement "like a little child," the King James Version takes that same word, one single Hebrew word, and all scholars have put it into a phrase. "I was beside him, like a little child" is the Revised Standard Version. The King James Version takes that same word, a single word, and gives it this interpretation, "I was brought forth, I was brought forth by him." Can you imagine that? Here, he doesn't say what was brought forth, "I was brought forth by him." The English Revised Version gives a still different interpretation of the single word. I'll tell you what the word is, the single word that means "faith" which is called "Amen"—-Aleph, Mem Nun—is the word translated as "I was beside him, like a little child." So you go to your Concordance and you look it up, and it says simply "*faith*, moving to the right hand of God." Not "moved" to the right hand of God. What did he bring forth first of all in the world? He brought forth faith.

I encourage you to use the unrighteous mammon that is faith. As you exercise your right, your talent to rearrange and falsify the record of the day and make tomorrow conform to the falsified record of tonight—so tomorrow is not the record of today; it conforms to your falsified record—you can only do it by faith. And then, one day, he'll be born. Who is born? Faith is born. He's called Jesus Christ. Born of whom?—born of God. Well, did you give him birth? Yes I gave him birth. Well, then who am I? That's what you ask yourself. So you're told in the 3rd chapter, the 16th verse of the Book of Galatians that man must give birth to Christ, and that the promise was made unto Abraham and to his offspring. It does not say "offsprings" referring to many, but to offspring referring to one: "And to your offspring which is Christ." So Christ is the creative power and the wisdom of God, summarized in one little thing called "Amen." It stands beside him in the very beginning.

So, man is put into these wheels that are already completed. Everything *is*. "Eternity exists, and all things in eternity, independent of Creation which was an act of mercy" (Blake, *Vis. Last Judg.*, P.614). So man is inserted into a wheel and there are wheels within wheels. And may I tell you, there is no moral order in this world, only an order of nature to which both man and beast are subjected. So let no one tell you there is a moral order in this world. We are subjected to futility, as told us in the 8th of Romans: "The creature was made subject unto futility, not willingly but by the will of him who subjected him in faith." Why? He was subjected in hope that this creature that is so subjected will once more be extracted and be set free from this world of corruption, and become once more a child of God; the child being his creative power, where he increases his capacity to create by the experience of inserting himself in this world of futility.

So everything *is*. There isn't a thing that is impossible to God because the whole thing is done. Every man in this world, no matter who he is, he could be any kind of a man he wants to be in the world because he *is* all that is his potential. He now can select the kind of a man that he would like to be; although at the moment when he selects the kind of man that he would like to be reason tells him that he could never be it. Forget what reason tells you and exercise faith, and become now faithful to the unrighteous mammon. Simply represent yourself to yourself as the man that you want to be, and be faithful to it.

Now let me tell you a little story. We have a pine tree in front of our house. The last two days the gusts of wind thirty, forty, fifty miles an hour...right...not more than, say, six feet from my eye, on a little branch, doves are nesting. Well, I've been watching them. A branch above is banging one of these two doves all through the day, from above. One from below is knocking the tree out... sometimes it goes up, seemingly five, six feet. But whoever is nesting is sitting on that nest in spite of the blows, and the other one, the mate whether it be male or female brings a worm and feeds the one on that nest. You would think the impulse of a bird when they get a worm is to swallow it. No, it has a mission. The mission is not to swallow but to bring it to the mate who is hatching out something. This is a world for hatching. As it was revealed to me so clearly, the whole vast world is for hatching out: And you do it through faith. So she with all the blows or he with all the blows on its little head, and all the bouncing all over the place—-for these gusts have been fantastic in the last forty-eight hours—-it still hugs that little nest. Regardless of all the blows and all the wind, there it is in faith that what it is keeping warm is going to come out.

Now in the Book of Habakkuk: "The vision has its own appointed hour; it ripens—it will flower. If it be long, then wait; for it is sure and it will not be late" (2:3). Not late for the idea. How long it takes a little dove to hatch out an egg, I don't know. A chicken, alright, twenty-one days; a little sheep, five months; a horse, twelve months; a man, nine months. So we have different time intervals for hatching out, but "at length for hatching ripe he breaks the shell." So you hatch out. You're the dove. You're hatching out something, and if it doesn't work by tomorrow, so what, regardless of the blows of the day. So this little beast, this little dove, here it is sitting on a nest and these terrific blows on top of it. I can see it, I look outside and here is the thing coming on the little bird, and then something comes from below, then its own little branch is flying all over the place. But it doesn't leave that little purpose: Its purpose is to hatch out.

Well, we are the dove. We are this Holy Spirit that is God. We conceive an idea that seemingly is impossible, and so we too form our little nest. Our nest is simply to assume that we are what *now* we want to be, and we do assume it, that mentally we are seeing the fulfilled desire. See it reflected in the faces of our friends. See it reflected in society. See it reflected the whole vast world over. And regardless of the blows of the day, regardless of the gusts that come, the rumors that come, we simply hang on to what we are hatching out. Not a power in this world is going to stop it, it *will* come out! One after the other we bring them to this world of ours. Then, if we are faithful with this unrighteous mammon, the day will come, we will receive the Son. He who has the Son has eternal life in himself; he who has not the Son has not eternal life.

But let us first prove ourselves faithful with the unrighteous mammon. And then will come the day we'll be given the power to stop and start what is forever; for all this is forever, all these are the characters of God's world. You are not anything that you are now wearing; you are the wearer, the actor. "God only acts and is in all existing beings and men." The actor is God. The costume…alright, call it Hamlet, call it Neville, call it John, call it any other name in this world, all these are the characters that God created. They're almost...you could call them resultant states of his first creative act; and then he buried himself in these costumes and plays the parts.

Let no one tell you there's any moral order in this world. There's only an order of nature to which the whole vast world of man and beast and birds and animals and everything else are subjected. They're all subject to it. Then he has to bring forth the first inkling which God brought forth and that is faith: "I'm the first of his acts of old...before he brought forth the universe I stood before him as a little child." And the word translated "as a little child"—I stood beside him as a little child—is Amen. The Hebrew word Amen simply means "faith." In its essence that's Amen. So he brings it forth first, for by faith he created the universe. "Faith is the assurance of things hoped for, the conviction of things not seen" (Heb. 11:1). "By faith we understand that the world was created by the word of God, so that the things that are seen were made from things that do not appear" (verse 3)... all from the invisible reality.

So, you simply single out the man, the woman that you want to be and assume that you are it, regardless of what the world will tell you. Then live faithful to this unrighteous mammon; because reason tells you that you are not and memory tells you that you've never experienced this, so you are falsifying the record. But we are encouraged to falsify the record. You read it carefully, the 16th chapter of the Book of Luke. And so, the rich man called his steward and highly commended him for what he had done by falsifying the record to make friends for himself of the unrighteous mammon. Well, the word steward originally meant "a ward of the sty," in other words, a keeper of the pig. The pig has always been the symbol of the redeemer and the savior of the world, so the keeper of the savior of the world. Well, who is the savior of the world? We're told in Isaiah, the 43rd chapter, "I am the Lord your God, the Holy One of Israel, your savior...and besides me there is no savior" (verses 3,11). So, if I am the keeper, if I am the steward of the sty, the steward of the mystery of God the savior of the world, and he tells me "I am the Lord your God, the Holy One of Israel," then I am the keeper of the savior; and he is my own I AM. If all things are possible to God, now start on this level and then serve faithfully the unrighteous mammon. Just try it. Righteousness is right thinking; unrighteous is seemingly wrong thinking—I am not faithful to the record. But I will not be faithful to the record, I'll change it. If I am faithful to the record, I am simply not competent forever and forever and forever. The purpose is to make me a creator like my Father, he creates. I can't create if I can only observe automatically that which passes before me.

So, nothing passes away. The past hasn't really passed. I slipped into it and having slipped into it 200 years ago, it is still taking place. The diners who dined 200 years ago are still at that very moment in time dining. This moment is taking place and will forever take place. It cannot pass away. This little building will go, you and I will make our exit from this world, but this moment in time is clothed as it is now clothed and cannot pass away. The building will go, certainly, bigger buildings will come here, and you and I will make our exit from the scene. But the scene is caught in time and that section of time is forever, and you can't take it away. Tomorrow in which we think we go it is *taking* place. It's not going to be created; it is all done. Read it carefully in the 3rd chapter, the 15th verse of Ecclesiastes: "That which is, already has been; that which is to be, already has been. And there is nothing new under the sun." It is all here, and you and I only become aware of increasing portions of that which already is.

So, becoming aware of it ___(??) is simply, change it. I know it is taking place, and we are automatons until we practice this wonderful art of falsifying the record. I call it revision. The Bible doesn't use the word revision, but I try to make it more understandable to our section as it were. They speak of it as repentance. Repentance is a radical change of attitude towards life, but a radical change. Well, if today I reflect on the day and my recall is fairly good, if I recall the day and a portion of the day is not a very pleasant thing, well then, at the moment of recall change it. I'm saying to someone, "What do you owe my lord?" My lord is my own consciousness. "Well, I owe him so much." "Well, then sit down quickly and modify it. You don't owe him that much at all. Make it fifty percent." "And how much do you owe, one hundred percent? Well, make it eighty percent."

There are certain things in my life that I can't possibly change more than fifty. You meet a man with one foot missing, and you know in eternity he hasn't a foot that is missing, but at the moment you can't quite bring yourself to believe the foot is going to grow, so you can't forgive him one hundred percent. But you can modify it and say, in spite of the handicap of a foot gone or an eye gone, he still can be successful and happy and in love and being loved in this world. So the absence of a foot doesn't make any difference. So you can modify it to a certain degree. There is not a thing in this world you can't bring down to some degree. So in one case he gave it fifty percent; another case he only gave it twenty percent. But you can take everything in this world and to some degree improve it by lopping off some little portion of it, if only five percent. And so, at the end of a day, take your day, bring it into your mind's eye, try to get as perfect a recall as possible, and then play the part of the unjust steward. Then, forgive it, completely forgive it: that's not so and so, so and so happened. And may I tell you, it works like a charm, just like a charm.

Here's a simple little thing. My brothers are great humorists. I think they are. So they were late in sending me my check. I'm 5,000 miles away...so they say, "Oh well, Neville doesn't care, forget it." So after all it is my money. I have a portion of the stock. They should have held a board meeting five months ago, for the fiscal year closed the end of September of last year. So certainly after the closing of the businesses the end of September they should have decided what kind of dividends they're going to pay. Well, they didn't. They have all the money they need and they take it for granted I have all the money that I need, so "Forget him, he's 5,000 miles away and he can't complain. And if he does, so what does it matter, we are too remote to even respond to his complaint." Then finally my brother Victor became aware, "Well, after all, we shouldn't do this to Neville, so we will simply send him a check." So he sent me a very lovely big check last Saturday, but he had to get his little humorous note into it. He dictates this letter to his secretary, mind you, of all the people in the world, and then here comes this letter with the check enclosed, and he said, "Because of your dire need I'm sending this check off to you," this draft.

So a friend of mine only a week before (how God works)...only a week before a friend of mine who works for RCA, and he always puts into the mail, almost daily, some little thing that the salesmen bring him. It's a choice little morsel. He mimeographs it or has it photographed, and then he makes multiple numbers of it and sends to his friends. Well, this one that he sent to me was a man standing at a bar with a huge big mug of ale, a bulbous nose, and no pants, and here he is, a picture of him with a big smile on his face, holding this huge thing in his hand, and no pants on him, and the caption of it is, "Good heavens! I've forgotten my wallet." So I took this and I wrote my brother on this little note, a thank-you note, and told him he must be psychic. He must be psychic because I didn't get my wallet, and now he's filled it for me. See, all these little things…I never would have thought of such a thing, but my friend sent it only a week ago. Usually, you read it, you laugh and you tear it up and throw it away, but for some reason or other I kept it. I kept it as a little piece of paper on which I could answer my brother and thank him for filling my wallet for me. So you see, let us falsify the record.

This whole vast world is for one purpose: for hatching out. It's for... really, this is educative darkness, and the purpose of life here in this world is simply to exercise our talent which is God, our own wonderful human Imagination, and simply learn the art of image making. The art of image making...you simply, well, what do I want in this world, not only for myself but for my friends? Well, they may not even want it, but you think it's lovely, want it for them. If it's a loving gift no one returns it. If the gift is unlovely, they should return it, and you who offered the gift will be stuck with it. But if it's a loving gift and should they stupidly return it, you would not be unwilling to accept it, you the giver. Therefore, give only the loving things in this world.

And be just like the little dove that is now being pummeled from above and below and all over the place. But she and he are faithful. They're being fed. Are we not told: Are you not more worthy and you are worth more than five sparrows...and not a sparrow falls but your Father knows it? Are you not of more value than the sparrows? Well, the little dove is being fed, whether it be the male or the female, they don't get off the nest. Whoever is there the other one brings food and gives it, and they remain faithful to their purpose which is to warm and to hatch out that little egg. And of all the birds I know of the dove is the most careless in the making of a nest. They don't make good nests. They almost drop the egg on a piece of leaf. They expect in some strange way...other birds will build a nest and do it beautifully, but not a dove. That's why they use the symbol of a dove to descend upon man the one that he loves, the one who has his favor, and to smother him with kisses because he brought forth Jesus Christ. He brought forth the symbol of his faith, for Jesus Christ is faith— that is the word "Amen"—who stood beside him in the very beginning, because he couldn't make a world without faith. "We understand that by faith the world was created by the word of God" so he had first to bring forth faith. And so, everyone must bring forth the child, the Christ child, and the Christ child is your faith. Therefore, when you are born from above, it is symbolized in the little infant wrapped in swaddling clothes which is Jesus Christ. You bring him forth, symbolizing your faith.

Now let us go into the Silence.

* * *

Q: How do you get that faith?

A: Sir, how do you get that faith? That's a marvelous question! He said, "Lord, I believe; help thou mine unbelief" (Mark 9:24). Believe in the reality of your imaginal act. It's an imaginal act that is the egg that you really drop. Warm it and keep it aglow to the best of your ability. So I call faith loyalty to unseen reality. To me it's a good definition of faith, because when a man says he is loyal, he says I'll take this woman to be my wife, well, the pledge is through thick or thin. You just have to protect her. Well, you must be loyal to the best of your ability to that pledge, and she makes a similar pledge. So loyalty is a marvelous word, loyal to our country, that no one should be able to take any one of us as Americans and drive us to betray our country. So you're loyal, I mean, you're beyond it. No one could even approach you if you're loyal to the country. You don't have to fight for it to defend it with words and these things; you're loyal to your country, your feeling about it. Well, you're loyal to an idea. You assume that you are or that a friend is what you would like to be, or what you would like him to be, and then you remain loyal to the unseen reality until the unseen becomes seen. It will…if you are as loyal to it as that little tender bird this night is loyal to her duty, which is to bring what she is sitting on out into an animated world. So practice, practice and still more practice.

Any other questions, please?

Q: In reference to the pig being the symbol of the savior, how does this then relate to the prodigal when he was eating with the pigs?

A: Did you hear that question? The pig is the symbol—you can find it in any great book of symbolism—has always been the savior, the redeemer of the world, the symbol of it. The prodigal went prodigal, spent all of his money, and he was feeding the pig, that was his last job, and eating the food that belonged to the pig. He was really a steward in the extreme sense of the word. To share with you, Tom, for you haven't been here since I had this experience...and a few years ago I had this vision. I found myself one night fully awake in an enormous display of flowers and plant life. It was closing time, dusk, and I was alone, and I knew that everyone had gone from the place, and it would not be open for a little while and so I must be going too. Just as I started toward the exit I saw a little pig, a little runt, a small little fella but perfectly healthy, but very, very small. I said to myself, I can't leave him here unfed, unwatered, I must do something about it. So there was a table, maybe the height of this, and I took branches and I took flowers and I took all the green things that I could find. I made a little bed for him. Then I said, "If he gets hungry enough he will eat of the flowers. They may not be the best kind of food to feed him, but he will still survive until someone comes in and finds him." And so then, as I did the best I could with what I had, as flowers and leaves and so on, then the thing changed suddenly, like turning over a leaf, and I found myself in an enormous supermarket, every conceivable kind of food displayed.

In the supermarket, my brother Victor, who runs all of our businesses, he was there, my daughter Vicki, she was there. Suddenly as I looked down here is the pig. But the pig had grown about four or five times its size since I last saw it. But it was rangy, it was thin, and obviously not well fed. It should have been better fed in the interval between the discovery of the pig and the present moment of the pig. So I went right away and I got a bag of meal, and I started to mix it with water. My brother Victor came by and he said, "What are you doing?" I said, "I'm mixing some food for my pig." So he had a bag and from the bag he took three or four handfuls of a very thick white gravy and he gave substance to the meal. I thanked him for adding substance to it, but I knew it would take me quite a while to mix it so that the pig could eat it. So I said to my daughter Vicki, I said, "Go over there and bring me a little package of crackers." She said, "Daddy, what will I use for money?" I said, "You don't need any money, all of this belongs to us. Everything here is ours, so ask no one any favor, just go and take it." Well, there was a huge pyramid of crackers, and she instead of taking one from the top took one from the bottom and dislodged...the whole thing fell as she took it. It exposed a little light, a little single four or five inch candle that was lit. I said to her, "Don't touch it, and don't build the pyramid any more. That's my light. It must never in eternity be put out. The candle now shines upon my head and by my light I walk through darkness; for the light of man, the Spirit of man is the candle of the Lord. And that's my candle, so don't build it and conceal it anymore." And with that it all dissolved.

So between finding the symbol of the savior of the world which was a pig and then the interval afterwards, he had grown. But he should have been fed by me better than I had fed him. I did not take every opportunity that was presented to me in the course of that interval to feed him. Well, when do you feed him? Every time you exercise your Imagination lovingly on behalf of another you've done it unto me. And so, where's the glass of water? When you did *not* imagine something lovely about another; I was thirsty and you didn't give me a glass of water. When you did *not* imagine something lovely—I was in need of shelter and you didn't take me in, I was in need of raiment and you didn't take me in. So every time an individual exercises his Imagination lovingly on behalf of anyone in this world he is feeding the pig.

Goodnight.

SPEAKING FROM EXPERIENCE

5/8/64

Tonight's subject is "Speaking from Experience." There's a conversation that takes place in the Book of John between Nicodemus, a member of the Sanhedrin, and Jesus. It's the 3rd chapter, and he said to Nicodemus, "We speak of what we know and bear witness to what we see, but you do not accept our testimony. If I tell you earthly things and you do not believe, how can you believe if I tell you heavenly things?" So here is one who is a member of the Sanhedrin, the highest order in the Jewish faith, and he came at night asking certain questions. Now he did not really ask... he called him "rabbi"...and Jesus admitted the fact that he was a teacher (that's what a rabbi is); and then proceeded to instruct him concerning a great mystery and said to him, you must be born from above, "For unless you are born from above, you cannot enter the kingdom of God" (verse 3). And he replied, Can a man who is old enter a second time into his mother's womb and be born? And this was answered in a strange way, he said: "That which is born from the flesh is flesh, and that which is born of the Spirit is spirit" (verse 6). But unless you be born from above, you cannot enter the kingdom of heaven. "The wind blows where it wills, and you hear the sound of it, but you do not know whence it comes or whither it goes; so it is with every one who is born of the Spirit" (verse 8).

Then he goes on after the next interruption. This turns into a discourse, really, began as a dialogue and finally the whole thing is moving into a discourse, like an argument. Then he said, "How can this be? You, a master, a teacher of Israel, and yet you do not understand this? I tell you, as Moses lifted up the serpent in the wilderness, so must the Son of man be lifted up; no one has ever ascended into heaven but he who descended" (verses 10-14). All this is compact in a few verses, which you will find in the first few verses of the 3rd chapter of John. He takes it literally, on a physical level. The Greek word translated "anew" or "again" or "from above" is Anothin. Scholars claim that you can give no other meaning to the word, especially when you read the context, than "from above, begotten of God, begotten from above." That birth can be considered either from the father's side in which case the verb is "to beget" or from the mother's side in which case the verb is "to bear." The word here is from the father's side: "to beget"; it's "begotten from above, begotten of God."

Now I tell you from experience this is *literally* true. He thought you couldn't take it on the physical level, it could not be literal; but he explained that which is begotten; that which is born of the flesh is flesh, what is born of the Spirit is spirit. Nicodemus didn't understand it, he just didn't understand it. Because, what man in this world *could* understand it unless he had the experience or he believed the one who had the experience? So here, the story is literally true. He's speaking of an entirely different age, an age that is *not* this age at all; where one must have a body equal to that age to exercise a power completely unknown to any man or by any man in this world; an entirely different thing where he's exercising a creative power that is the power of God. So he has to have a body to exercise that power, to use that power, and this body comes from his birth from above.

Now he makes the statement: "I came out from the Father and I came into the world; again, I am leaving the world and ascending to the Father" (John 16:28). In these four little phrases he admits of a pre-existence: "I came out from the Father..." Well, to come out from the Father is to die. Like a prodigal son he departed from his Father and the Father thought him dead, thought him lost, and said, "My son who was lost is found; he was dead and now he is alive again" (Luke 15:24). So he admits in that departure, "I came out from the Father," that he died. "I have come into the world," that's incarnation. "Again, I am leaving the world and ascending to the Father" and this is also *literally* true. Man finds it difficult to understand, but in the course of the evening we will explain it from actual experience.

Well now, let us get down to this level, from experience. I have asked you to join with me and share with me your use of the law, that I in turn may encourage everyone who is here to use the law lovingly to *expand* their world and make it a wonderful world. Because you can be anything in this world that you really want to be if you're willing to be vigilant, to be faithful to the assumption that you are already such a person...if you're willing. Well, a gentleman wrote me this past week and he said, "On Sunday when we discussed, you reminded me of something that in the interval I had forgotten, that when I discussed possible stories with my producer...and he gave me all these stories…I went home boiling I was so mad. Because I knew I could conceive of many more wonderful stories than the stories that he suggested. I was so mad when I got home, I just simply raged. And I said to myself, audibly, screaming it out—my wife didn't hear me—but I went upstairs and to the mountains I spoke, 'I don't have to write for TV, I can write for Broadway shows, write for Broadway plays, I can write books, I can write for pictures. I don't have to write TV scripts!' "And then I thought, well now, I'll take his most stupid story, but the most stupid of all the ideas that he gave me, and then I'll work on it." So he said, "I gave him the challenge. And so, that story that I worked on was nominated for an award that year. Of all the stories that I've ever done, it was the one story nominated for an award as the best story of the year. It was his most stupid story but it was a challenge. So you reminded me on Sunday that a challenge is necessary in this world. So on Monday morning I felt calm and passive, and I was walking on my usual walk, and I was in a mood of "thanking Father" when suddenly I remembered what you had said the day before, on Sunday, about a challenge when I took the most stupid story and developed it into what was nominated for an award. And suddenly I heard the loudest, the most authoritative voice I have ever heard before. Never heard anything as loud as this, with such authority, and I heard it from the depths of my soul; and it is saying to me, and this is what it said, 'Feed me with challenges! How else can I grow?'" You think it over: "Feed me with challenges! How else can I grow?"

As I've told you, God actually became man. Man is the *limit* of contraction, the *limit* of opacity; there is no limit to translucence, no limit to expansion. But he took upon himself the limit of contraction, which is man, called Adam, and now Adam has to feed him with challenges that he may create, that he may expand his creative power. For the purpose of the whole thing is simply to create and to develop one's creative talent, one's creative power. So, "Feed me with challenges! How else can I grow?" You wouldn't think that God is growing. God grows, God grows forever and forever. God is truth and truth is a *limitless* expansion, forever and forever and forever. So it simply comes down to the limit of contraction, assumes the challenge that it can give, and then creates.

He said, "I came out...and the day before I had a story which my producer accepted and liked, and instantly I threw it into the ash can. I want a bigger and a better story, more alive, something more vital, and in one hour I had it. I took the challenge!" And then, in a very sweet way thanked me for reminding him of what he had told me about this stupid story that he developed to the point of receiving at least the nomination for an award. But, in the interval he had forgotten what he did with that challenge. And now he said to me in the letter that a challenge changes man's consciousness from the passive state into the active state. It's the most wonderful thing in the world to lift man's consciousness to higher and higher levels, a challenge in this world. So I ask you to take what he has given to me, which I am now sharing with you, and use it, and then grow. In growing, God grows. It's all God; God is playing all the parts. So he very generously gave me in letter form his reaction to our conversation on Sunday, which tonight then I can share with you.

Now, he knows this now from experience, for he got his story in one hour. And a truth that man knows from experience he knows more thoroughly than he knows anything else in this world, or than he can know that same truth in any other way. For instance, I tell you the story and you believe me. Alright, so you believe me, but you don't know it as you will know it after you've tested it and you've proved it in the testing. So what you know from experience you know more thoroughly than you know anything else in this world. So today he knows that a challenge took his consciousness and turned it from the passive state into the active state; that he had the courage to take a story that was already accepted and liked by his producer and discard it, and in one hour come up with a story infinitely better than the one he had discarded. He had the courage to discard one already accepted. Well, that was already money in the bank when you're getting that sort of money for a half-hour script; but he discarded that and took the challenge, and then rose to a higher level. So I share it with you. You take the challenge.

Now, another lady (she is here this night) and she said this past week to me, "I was talking to some friends and I said, 'You know, I remember when...' and as I said 'I remember when' it dawned upon me, these are Neville's words, the words he used to describe a vision of his. And then I said to myself but I am not *using* it. Here the man shared with us his vision and I haven't used what he gave me. He *gave* it to me! I'm now talking to my friends telling them 'I remember when' and I myself have not done it." She said, I've just written a letter to my landlord to explain to the landlord that I would be unable this month to meet the rent on time. I'll pay, I've always paid, and I will pay, but this month things are difficult. I cannot pay this month, that is, not on time. Then suddenly 'I remember when'...then she began to remember when she cleaned a motel room, a hotel room, a private home fourteen dollars a day. Then she lost herself in the mood 'I remember when', therefore, that implies she's not doing it now. The phone rings and a former employer who formerly employed her at ten dollars a day employed her that day at fifty dollars a day. He said, "You put in your bill as long as it will take you to organize a certain something (which she did not explain in her letter) and it's fifty dollars a day for the work you're going to do to set this thing in motion." I remember when...

As I've told you, that vision was so clear to me, just as clear as this room here, when I slipped. I'm on my bed here in this city, and suddenly I am in this huge mansion on Fifth Avenue, one of these enormous sixty and seventy-room mansions. And there were three families present, one was grandfather, one was the next generation, and then the third generation. Grandfather was invisible, but the other two generations they were present and always discussing grandfather. And they would say...I heard them, I came in, in Spirit…and I heard them discussing grandfather, who made the fortune that they now enjoyed, the mansion and the income from this entrenched wealth they were now enjoying; but they themselves did not make it. They told the story of grandfather and grandfather said while standing on an empty lot, "I remember when this was an empty lot" and then grandfather would paint a word picture of his desire for that lot, and paint it so vividly that everyone saw it as grandfather saw it. That's how he made his fortune: He lived from that moment on in his wish fulfilled. "I remember when."

I woke, it was about three in the morning, and I wrote the entire vision out. Then I went back to bed and re-dreamed the dream, but this time as I re-dreamed it *I* was grandfather. I had so completely absorbed the message that I found myself in the same mansion with the same people and I told them that I remember when I'm standing on an empty lot, "I remember when this was an empty lot." Then I would paint the word picture of my desire for that lot and paint it so vividly, so graphically they *all* saw it. And then I woke. Well, the 41st chapter of the Book of Genesis (verse 32) tells us that if the vision is double, the doubling of the vision means this, said Joseph to Pharaoh, that God has fixed it and it will shortly come to pass. God has fixed it. This is fixed now if the vision is doubled. God has fixed it and it will shortly come to pass. So I shared it with you. And now, this lady has been coming faithfully over the years, but like all of us, we hear it, it's a thrill at the moment, but we don't carry it into action. She didn't apply it. But the very day she *applied* it the phone rings and she is offered fifty dollars a day, not ten dollars a day. So it was a challenge. She took the challenge that "I remember when I only earned ten dollars a day."

Now you can take that same thing, "I remember when my income was only"...any kind of income, a thousand dollars a week, you can make that. You think it's crazy? *Nothing* is impossible to God. Feed me with challenges, how else can I grow? That's the story of God to a friend who is here this night. Feed me with challenges, how else can I grow? And so, if your challenge is that you want...and you name it. I know in my own case, when I was opposed by my teacher in elocution it was her opposition to my voice and her statement that I could never in eternity earn a dollar using my voice; and she used me as the guinea pig, one of a class of forty, and she made me step forward, and then pointed her finger at Neville and said, "You see Neville? Listen to him. He will never be able to use his voice to earn a dollar, so just watch all that he does, listen to him, and avoid it." I am the only one of the class of forty using a voice and thoughts behind it to earn a living, and the other thirty-nine are elsewhere. What they are doing, I don't know, but not one of them ever entered the theater, not one. Not one entered any other part of life where the voice would be used, and she was the great teacher of elocution. But she challenged me...and that was *my* challenge. I would not allow myself to waste my father's 600 dollars. He could ill-afford to give me 600 dollars to go to a dramatic school for six months and then come out and be a failure. I knew in my heart I couldn't do that to him, and so I just would not allow it. So I say to everyone, everything in this world is possible if you will now accept the challenge. Because, who is accepting it? *God* is accepting it, because God is your own wonderful human Imagination...that's God. God actually became man that man may become God.

Now, we'll take you through the book from now to the end of the series (the 26th of this month) and show you how the book is so true, every word of it is true and literally true on deeper levels of the soul. Here is a friend tonight (he's in the audience) and this happened last week. You've heard this story time and again of the crucifixion and the voice that said, "Behold, I say unto you today, you will be with me in paradise" (Luke 23:43). Well, this lad (he's just a lad) he found himself in vision in a theater, and here was this huge big screen. To the left of the screen is a cross almost his height or a little bit more than his height. Then a man suddenly appeared out of nowhere, walked to the cross, turned around and faced the audience, and then stretched his hands out, and fused with the cross. Then a voice said, "I say unto you today, you will be with me in Paradise...for a little while." I can't throw any light on it...but at least he's honest and he's telling me exactly what he heard. And when a vision breaks into words then deity is present. The very presence of deity is confirmed as the vision breaks into words, as told us in the 3rd of Exodus (verse 4). Here from the bush…and suddenly the vision breaks into words and the very moment it breaks into words, the revelation begins: "Say I AM has sent you" (verse 14). And the presence of deity is always confirmed whenever the vision breaks into words. So in this case the vision broke into words. Now what that tag-line is, which is not recorded in scripture, "for a little while," I do not know. He wrote me this letter just a few days ago and I do not know, it has not been revealed to me why the tag-line. But it's obvious what the first part of it is, "Behold, I say unto you today, you will be with me in Paradise." But why "for a little while"? Yet it does tell us that because of the instant, or rather, forever expansion of God, all things are only for a season. It's always a growth and a growth and a growth, forever and forever. So he has shared that with me and I have shared it with you.

But I tell you from my own experience everything in scripture is true. I have had almost every experience that is recorded in the gospels concerning Jesus Christ, from the birth through to the very end...every one. I have not had the story of Lazarus, no, I haven't had that one. But I've had the dove. I've had all the stories of scripture as recorded. They take place in the soul of man; they don't take place on the outside at all. For it is said of him, We know where this man came from, we know his origin, and when the Christ comes no one will know where he comes from. So they rejected him because they knew his origin. But when Christ comes, so they thought, he will emerge in some strange mysterious way. And he does, but he comes in a mysterious way *in man* that man himself did not know.

Now listen to the words that we started off with the meeting. He tells us he's only talking of things that he knows: I tell you what I know and bear witness to what I've seen, and you will not accept my testimony. He's only testifying to what he's actually experienced, what he's seen, and they will not accept his testimony. "Now if I tell you of earthly things and you will not believe, how can you believe if I tell you heavenly things?" So he tells them earthly things—all the signs of earthly things; all the signs of health; transforming a man who's poor into a man who is rich; a man who could not sell a material into one who sells all that he can write; a man who was unwell into a man who never felt better in his life. So he transforms all this, and they will not believe what he tells them of how he did it. He only did it in his Imagination, for he said, "Whatever you ask for in prayer, believe that you've received and you will"; that's all that you do (Mark 11:24). Well, if he could convince himself of the reality of what he's now imagining, then it should externalize itself if that principle is true. Well, it did. But he told them *how* he did it. They couldn't believe that; they wanted some other kind of a trick. And he's telling them that this is *all* that you do: When you know what you want, believe that you have it and you will have it. And if one can get to that point of belief, then everything would come into this world based upon the great law of Israel.

So he recited the entire story for them. In the 78th Psalm the whole history of Israel is recorded. He said, "Lend me your ears"—or let me have your ears, your understanding, your attention—"and I will open my mouth in a parable and speak in dark sayings as of old" (verse 1). And then he tells them he will tell them all the things that the fathers said that everyone should hear, and then carry it on to the next generation and the next generation and the next generation, and all the unborn generations, all the wonders that God wrought. And the very end it comes to David, in the very end of this very long chapter the 78th, which is a chapter by Asaph and Asaph means "the gatherer." He gathers all these things together. We have twelve psalms by Asaph, the 73rd through the 83rd. And then the 50th, and that 50th is the one where: "If I were hungry I wouldn't tell you; for the earth is mine and all that is in it. The cattle on a thousand hills they're mine" (verses 10,12). And were I hungry I would slay and eat, why should I tell you when it's all mine? That's the first psalm that he gave us, the 50th. Then he gave us the other eleven, the 73rd through the 83rd, and the name simply means "to gather together." He gathers all the traditions, all the stories of the fathers, and he tells them to the next generation, and tells them to tell it to the next generation and keep on telling it until one day they experience it.

And so, we tell you, and then one after the other has an experience. The one this day was the cross; he's experienced it. He knows how true that story is. But what are we told in scripture? "Oh you foolish Galatians! Who has bewitched you, before whose eyes Jesus Christ was publicly *portrayed* as crucified?" Isn't it a drama vicariously done? "Before whose eyes Jesus Christ was publicly portrayed *as* crucified. Let me ask you only this: Did you receive the Spirit by the working of the law, or by hearing with faith? Are you so foolish? Having begun with the Spirit, are you now ending with the flesh?" (Gal. 3:1). It takes place in Spirit, not in the flesh. No one was crucified physically. Yes, undoubtedly in this barbarous world of ours tens of thousands of men undoubtedly by some tyrant, some sadist, were crucified. But that's not the story. The crucifixion is in Spirit, and I know from my own personal experience it *is* in Spirit, for I was; and it's the most glorious sensation in the world. You can't conceive of the thrill, the joy when the vortices nail you to this garment; when each hand, each foot, side and the head become a vortex, and these vortices, six of them, nail you to this body. And the thrill! It's sheer ecstasy when you have it done, and you hear the words which means God's presence is here. And then God speaks from the depths of your soul: "I laid myself down within you to sleep, and as I slept I dreamed a dream. I dreamed, yes, I dreamed that I'm you." He's dreaming that he's you.

Now to come back to our friend: "Feed me with challenges." I'm dreaming that I'm you; I'm your very being, your own wonderful I-am-ness is God. Now, God can do anything, all things are possible to God, so feed me with challenges, how else can I grow? And so be bold enough to take something that you have written, that you have presented, that was accepted and liked, and you know that's money in the bank, and throw it in the ashcan, not good enough. And then take a challenge, something more vital, something more wonderful, something more thrilling and write it, and in one hour get it. Get something far better than what you're quite willing, just for money's sake to accept, because there's money for you.

So you take it this night and take a large sum. If anyone had told me when I worked at Macy's for, what, eighteen dollars a week and did everything in the place for eighteen bucks, if anyone told me then that I would in the not too far future be making five hundred dollars a week, why, I would have laughed at them. But I did. One day I quit Macy's. I don't mean fired. I was fired from Penney, J. C. Penney. So I worked for J. C. Penney and they gave me twenty-two dollars a week, and one day they fired me. I asked them why, what have I done that's wrong? They said, "Nothing wrong, but we have an economy in this country that when things are slow we let people off. You've been working here for a year and a half, and so we just simply have to economize, and so you have to go." I said, "Where I come from you fire a person because he's done something that is wrong… that if I've stolen or if I've done something that is wrong causing the company loss, fire me, but don't fire me because of certain strange trends in this world." "But that's how we operate," they said to me.

Well, they thought, well, this man, he's a boy and he's stupid and he's foolish, we'll give him a letter, and send him over to Macy's. So they did. He wrote me a little letter and sent me to his friend who was the employment agency at Macy's, so I moved to Macy's and gave my little letter. They said, "We can't start you at any twenty-two dollars and fifty cents a week, we'll start you at eighteen." So alright, I have to pay rent, so they started me at eighteen. So I worked there for a year, and one day I said to myself, "You're getting nowhere fast, still making eighteen dollars a week, and doing everything that they ask you to do because you don't want to be fired." So I had the courage to quit without a nickel in my pocket, and six months later I was making five hundred dollars a week as a dancer. Went off to England; five hundred bucks a week. I never danced in my life before, save ballroom dancing. I told my dancing partner when she said "Can you dance?" "Certainly I can dance!" She said, "Alright, let me see." Well, I said, "I danced with someone else, I'll dance with you." And so, that's how it started. So off to England; we got a hundred pounds. In those days, a pound was worth four dollars and eighty-four cents, not today's two, eighty; and I got a hundred pounds a week dancing in London for three months... from Macy's eighteen dollars a week. So I say, you take a challenge, you simply throw yourself out completely and walk on the water, and either go down and drown, or simply live better.

So here, I am speaking from experience—I am not theorizing—when I tell you I've done it. I have taken God's word just as he told me, and then stepped right out and did it. When no power in this world could have taken me out of our Armed Forces, God took me out, with an honorable discharge. No power in the world could have taken me out, but God took me out. I simply assumed that I was out and slept night after night in the assumption that I am home as an honorably discharged civilian. In nine days, the very man who refused it called me in and then discharged me. Then I was on my train back to New York City. So again, I'm speaking from experience, I am not theorizing when I tell you that God can do anything in this world if you'll trust him. Hold him responsible, hold him trustworthy. And so in your wonderful field this night, dream the most noble dream in the world for yourself and for others. Take a challenge, a real challenge, and then fall asleep in the assumption that you are already such a person, and then let it work. It'll work, work like a charm. Not one person in this world need you call or write to ask to help in any way. If a thousand are necessary, a thousand will respond; and you don't have to seek the thousand, they'll come. Whatever it takes will come.

So here, in this speaking from experience, he said his brothers did not believe him because they knew him. He said to them, "My time has not yet come, but your time is always here" (John 7:6). Now there's a *profound* statement and who will believe it: "If I tell you earthly things and you won't believe it, how would you believe it if I told you heavenly things?" Your time is always here, he said, but my time is not yet come. You know what it means? This whole vast world of ours is forever, just as it is now at this moment in time. What took place last year, in the month of November, on the day of the 22nd of November, is always taking place, forever and forever in time. It is always taking place...everything in the world is taking place on this level. So your time is always here, but my time is not yet come. He's telling you of an entirely different world, with a different use of power, different creativity, where man is lifted off this world of recurrence and he enters *that* world that is creative, one with God. But who understands it? If you did not slip in time and see that it hasn't passed away, that the present is not receding into the past, this present is advancing into the future…the future has already passed? It's a wheel. You're only coming upon phenomena that's already old, and therefore "your time" is always here but "my time" has not yet come. Then he repeats it and he uses it a little bit differently, and he said, "Not yet *fully* come." He knows he is moving into an entirely different world because he's had the experiences foretold in scripture.

And so, all these were foretold: the birth; the awakening; the descent; the discovery of the Fatherhood; the ascent; the dove—all of these are the signs of one's departure from this time.

So when Paul made the statement that "The time of my *departure* has come. I have fought the good fight and I have finished the race, I have kept the faith. Henceforth there is laid up for me a crown of righteousness," he knew from the experiences in himself (2 Tim. 4:7). For he said in his confession in the Book of Galatians, "When it pleased God to reveal his Son *in* me, I conferred not with flesh and blood" (Gal. 1:16). It *pleased* God! What a statement! What pleases God? If you read the Bible carefully, only one thing in this world *displeases* him—-you read this in the 11th chapter of the Book of Hebrews—-without *faith* it is impossible to please him (verse 6). So you can't please God by any act of yours if it is not an act of faith. So, challenge me, bring me challenges, how else can I grow? Have confidence in me, in my ability to create, and bring me a challenge, something *big*, something terrific! How else can I create? So without faith it is impossible to please God. So when he said, "And when it pleased God to reveal his Son in *me*, I conferred not with flesh and blood," he confesses that the Son was unveiled *in* him and he saw the mystery. Then he asked all those who listened to him to look upon him as a steward of the mysteries of God, for they all awoke within him.

So tonight, *please* God. How would you please God? Take the most fantastic dream that is not yet realized, that seems impossible, and then hold God trustworthy. Assume that you've realized it and hold him trustworthy. Challenge God to use his creative talent to create that dream in your world so that you have experienced it. That's how you please God. So, when it pleased God...and so through faith one day he will take the veil and tear it apart; and then unveil within you the series of mystical experiences which series will reveal to you who you really are. For when it's unveiled he's only unveiling himself. He's reached the end of his creative power, what he intended when he contracted himself and became you. So he *uses* you, puts you through all the furnaces in the world, because you and he are one, you are his contraction. So when this comes to the end you awake as God. Everyone eventually will awake *as* God.

So here, let us take what others have given us and in their generosity use it. My friend was wise enough and generous enough and modest enough with herself to say while she was telling the story it dawned upon her that she had never really tried it, "I remember when"; and yet the very moment she tried it, the phone calls, and she's getting fifty dollars rather than ten. And so don't just hear it, put it to the test. This chap who wrote, and got all that he wanted, a nice acceptance and a feeling that the man liked it, and then threw it in the ashcan, "that wasn't good enough." And then he took a challenge and in an hour the whole thing inflamed his mind and so he was raised from the passive state into the active state, and the whole thing came through in one hour.

I know in my own case, I brought back a manuscript that thick from Barbados, 1946, and while at sea this vision happened. Here I was lifted up and I saw this fantastic sea of humanity, and when I walked by they were all transformed from their unlovely states into the most perfect, most beautiful states imaginable. I took my manuscript and tore it up and threw it away. Didn't even bring it back with me, and I labored on it for months. I spent five months in Barbados. And so, I labored on this manuscript and I brought it back, thinking I'd have a nice manuscript for my publisher. After this experience I took that manuscript and threw it overboard, didn't redeem one page of it. And then, in one hour—of course, it isn't a long thing, it's a little tiny pamphlet—but in one hour the whole thing poured through me. I sat down and wrote the whole thing in an hour and then sent it off and it was published. It just came that fast. I couldn't possibly have gone to press with what I'd brought back after five months of labor. This whole thing just came like fire, and that had to be it. Just a little tiny thing called *The Search*, but it poured out. And if you ask my wife what she thinks of all my books, the first one she would pick is *The Search* because it came that way.

The same thing is true of *Your Faith is Your Fortune*. I took care of a doctor; he was a dope fiend, a *brilliant* surgeon and told me that when he was under the dope he did his best surgery. For seven years he had this most fantastic private hospital with about a dozen doctors under him. Then he took the needle and became a victim of his own practice. And I took him. Because he was a very prominent doctor they allowed me to do what I could with him. So with the consent of New York City's head of the dope ring, that is, the Police Department, they allowed me to take him to a hotel. So I did, and took him there for two weeks. He was stark raving mad. If you left him for one second, he's in the nude, down the hallway, on the street...and we're on the twentieth floor. So this day, watching him, I was completely ____(??) just watching him, because he was on the bed. I didn't know what he would do the next second. Here I am with my yellow papers and pencils and I wrote *Your Faith is Your Fortune*. It came out in a matter, I would say, forty-eight hours, the whole thing, talking on the inside. The voice is talking and dictating, and everything is being dictated, and came out that way. So *Your Faith is Your Fortune* is simply from the depth, I only put it down. I wasn't concocting it, it simply poured out, the whole thing poured out. When I took the manuscript and turned it in to my chap to correct it, there was practically nothing, not a thing he had to do with it...simply poured out...all because I took the challenge to take care of a friend who was a dope fiend. And Scotty was a wonderful man, grand fella, but he simply became the victim of his own practice. So I watched him, and while I'm watching him and getting more and more sleepy—because day in and day out you just can't get any sleep—and so, suddenly this thing began to pour out of me. And I could hear the words in the depths of my soul, dictating, something on the inside talking. I simply wrote down what they were telling me. And *Your Faith is Your Fortune* came that way and *The Search* came, after five months of labor on a large manuscript, which I discarded.

So my friend is sharing this with us this night: "Feed me challenges! How else can I grow?" So tonight you take a challenge as we go into the Silence. Take the most wonderful challenge, and then hold God trustworthy. Now let us go.

* * *

Now are there any questions, please?

Q: When the Bible says, "In my father's house there are many mansions," um, I'm trying to understand when you say everything is here and we move into those states. For instance, you have moved into a state as a lecturer, haven't you?

A: Yes.

Q: And a Kennedy has moved into a state when he was shot. All these states are here, like the many mansions, is that right?

A: Yes.

Q: So if we move into poverty, we have moved into that state, or we move into richness or illness we've moved into that state?

A: Granted.

Q: And they're all right here?

A: The thing is to become selective. You don't go into a restaurant and say, "Bring me a dinner," you say, "Bring me a menu" and then you order. You're going to pay for it and you want proper service. If he throws it at you, you're going to complain because you're paying for it. You go into a place and you order a dress. You don't say, "Bring me a dress," you become selective, and you go through dozens and dozens of dresses. Then you pick out the one you think that you need to fill your wardrobe. And so, you may need a brown. They have the most beautiful blues in the world, but you don't need at this moment a blue dress, you want a brown to complete the wardrobe. So you look through stacks and stacks of dresses and you find what you want. Yet they're all there. Everything is here, and man must become selective and discriminating in every thing that he does in this world. The more discriminating he is, well, the better. You simply select it and you move into it. They're only states, infinite states; but you move from one state— leave the state alone for someone else to enter if they want to enter it—and then move into another state.

Now, we think we're going to change poverty in this land. You can't change states, can't do it. If you took all the money in the world, divided it up equally, in twenty-four hours Rockefeller would still be rich and the other fellow would still be poor, go right down again. There used to be a lecturer and he had a system, he had a huge big glass bowl and he'd fill it with all kinds of nuts. He had walnuts and other kinds of nuts, all kinds of nuts. And then he would take the bowl and he would say, "Life is like this: it's a constant rhythm, you can't stop it." And he would take the biggest nut, the big walnut, and put it at the very bottom. He would show it to you in his hand and take it and put it right at the very bottom. But he said, "You can't stop life" and he started shaking this bowl and in no time up came the walnut, the big walnut, to the very top again. And all the little fellas…of course, he had a wonderful line, he would say, "I hear someone squeaking down below" and he would say, "The little one down below is saying, 'You started me there in life. If you'd only start me at the top I would be alright. Well, so you started me at the bottom; start me at the top.'" So he goes all the way down to the bottom of the bowl, brings a little nut up, puts it obviously before all eyes at the very top. But you can't stop life; life is a rhythm, it's a shaking, and the little fella will go all the way down to the bottom. So why pick out the little one? Pick out something noble in this world, something grand in this world, and remain faithful to it.

Goodnight.

WHAT IS HIS NAME?

5/12/64

Tonight's subject is "What is His Name?" This is taken from the 30th chapter of the Book of Proverbs. It's a riddle and you and I are challenged to unriddle the riddle. Now, last meeting we told the story of a friend who heard this voice from within him speaking with tremendous authority, and the voice said to him, "Feed me with challenges. How else can I grow?" Well, the Bible has asked us to unriddle the most fantastic riddle in the world. I know—if you will believe me—I can share it with you this night, I have unriddled it not by labor, not by speculation, by sheer revelation. You can't conjure revelation; it simply happens in its own good time. But the riddle is this: "Who has established all the ends of the earth? What is his name, and what is his son's name? Canst thou tell?" (verse 4). So there is the challenge, to give the name of one who established all the ends of the earth, and also to give his son's name.

Now we are told to search the scriptures, search them diligently, for if it is not recorded in scripture it's nonexistent. So search it and search it over and over, for there are so many names given in scripture for the creator of the universe. In the very first verse we have the word Elohim: "In the beginning God created the heavens and the earth." Is it Elohim? In the very first chapter, the same Elohim: "Let us make man in our image." That's Elohim. Then we have the word El Shaddai, "God Almighty." Then we have Adonay, "my lord." Then we have the great secret name of Jehovah or the Yod He Vau He, defined for us as I AM. And we have all these names throughout scripture, and we're called upon to name *the* name and then name his son.

Well, in the very question a part of the answer is given. Read it carefully or listen to it carefully, "Who has established all the ends of the earth?

What is his name, and what is his son's name?" That should give you the cue right away. It isn't asking us how this universe was created, by what process, but *who* created it and for what purpose. But if I ask you, "What is his name?" and then the second question is "What is his son's name?" I have pinpointed it. Isn't he a father? Isn't that a father? Isn't that the ultimate name that you're seeking? It isn't God, it isn't Elohim, it isn't Jehovah, it isn't any name, it's Father. "What is his *son's* name" is the cue to the first question "What is his name?" Because the second one pinpoints it: "What is his son's name?" To have a son is to confess you're a father, and so to say I'm a father is to admit of the existence of a child, to prove your own creative power. Your creativity is in the offspring, so right away we see in it a father-ship relationship somewhere.

Now, Jeremiah makes the statement—-and the word Jeremiah is defined in many ways, but here are three wonderful definitions of it—"Jehovah hurls; Jehovah will rise; Jehovah will loosen the womb." That's what the word means by definition. He hurls, he will rise, and he will loosen the womb. Then Jeremiah is made to say: "Thy words became to me a joy and the delight of my heart. ...I am called by thy name, O Lord, God of hosts" (Jer. 15:16). He discovered that he was called by the name. Now mind you, he was hurled into a turbulent state, but he knew as he was hurled Jehovah will rise. He hurls himself into this world of confusion, but he will rise, and he will loosen the womb. If he loosens the womb, well then, I can come out, I can be born.

Now only the indolent mind will really fail to rise to the challenge of a riddle. But I warn you if you will accept it, I'll tell you this night if you will accept it, it will save you from losing your way in the tangled speculations that pass for religious truth. That all over the world, they don't mean to mislead you but they're speculating—they haven't had the experience. You'll find unnumbered denominations and that goes for even the biggest of the organized groups, they are speculating. So here we find these words in the Book of Matthew, "Take my yoke upon you." This "Take my yoke upon you" in Hebrew is a very common rabbinical expression, the yoke of the law, which means "the studies of scripture." So he's asking you to take *his* yoke, his knowledge of scripture based upon *experience* and not upon speculation. He's asking you to exchange your yoke, your present inherited yoke, based upon the speculations of the priesthoods of the world, for *his* yoke which is based upon his own personal experience of the answer to this riddle. So, "Take my yoke upon you, and learn from me. My yoke is easy, and my burden light" (11:29).

Now in this 11th chapter of Matthew (and it's all crowded together) he said, "Thank you, Father, Lord of heaven and earth, that you have hidden these things from the wise and the prudent and revealed them unto babes... for such was thy gracious will" (verse 25). And then he invites one to listen and accept his yoke. Now he makes this statement (it's all wedged right into this marvelous claim that he's going to make) he said, "No one knows the Son except the Father, and no one knows the Father except the Son and anyone to whom the *Son* chooses to reveal him" (verse 27). He's asking you to take *his* yoke, his actual understanding of the scriptures based upon his personal experience; and defies anyone to name that Son. You could name... he always reveals the creator of the universe as Father. He doesn't speak of him as some other being, just Father, and he speaks of Son. And the world has taught you to believe that he is the Son. And so, the priesthoods of the Christian world will tell you Jesus Christ is the Son of God, while in the story, if you read it carefully, *he* confesses he *is* God *the Father.* He said, "You want to see the Father, Philip? He who has seen *me* has seen the Father; how then can you ask to show you the Father? When you see me you see the Father" (John 14:9). But he confesses no one has seen him, that is, they have not *grasped* him. They see the outer garment, the mask, the persona that he wears, but they can't see the wearer of the mask. But when you see me, if you ever can grasp me as I tell you the stories, said he, then you've seen the Father. So do not ask to show you the Father; he who has seen me has seen the Father.

And no one asked him then concerning the Son, no one. So because no one asked him concerning the Son—if I am a father, well, then there must be a child—so he brings it up. He said, "What think ye of the Christ? Whose son is he?" They answered based upon tradition, "The son of David." Then he replied, "Why then did David, in the Spirit, call him Lord? If David thus calls him Lord, how can he be David's son?" (Mat. 22:42,45). The word translated Lord is one of the words for God, Adonay, which is used more often than the word Jehovah, because Jehovah is the sacred name, Yod He Vau He, and so they used Adonay in place. Even though you see it in the script Yod He Vau He, the translators will concede it, and put Adonay in its place. It's the closest to Yod He Vau He. And so, he was called Adonay. Adonay means "my lord," but that's an expression used by every son of his father. You asked the son of his father and he referred to his father as Adonay, my lord. And so David then is playing the part of *son.* So David in the Spirit, not in the flesh—this is a drama of the Spirit—and David in Spirit calls him Adonay, calls him "my Father." So if David thus calls him Father, how can he be David's son? So he establishes the riddle, he unriddles the riddle, and tells you who created the universe, who established it, who sustains it, and who is his Son.

Now, that is in conflict with the rabbinical concept and the priestly concept today. They will not accept that at all. They teach you that there's a presence called God, something *outside* of man that created him, and that man in some strange way is simply begging a favor of this creator, and that he's promised to redeem man. Man and God are really one! But in this mystery, it was done for a purpose: to extend his creative power. By putting himself into this complete contraction called man, he could then unravel a mystery which was *predetermined.* It isn't worked out as he goes along; the whole thing was set up in the beginning. It is God's intense nearness that makes him invisible to us. Were he not so near...he's not even near, because nearness would imply separation; therefore, it's not near, he actually *is* the very being in search of the answer to the riddle. In fact, the whole vast history of humanity is nothing else than one long wrestle with this infinite riddle.

And so, man having organized around the mystery not understanding it and rejecting it as told in scripture…for *he* told the story if one would read it carefully. But now, if I read it as I was taught it, I would be influenced by my teacher; and my teacher would have made me believe that a presence called God, where he is they didn't know, therefore, they couldn't convey it to me. But then they taught me of a being called Jesus Christ, and he was born as I was born. Maybe a little differently— he didn't have a father, not an earthly father, his father was God—but I had the earthly father. She was something different, something unique, that's what they taught me, that she brought forth a son, and she didn't know a man. I believed that and believed it all the way through until I began to wrestle with the riddle, wrestle with life. And then certain visions disturbed me.

And then came the vision of visions: the discovery of the Father. I hadn't the slightest concept of the meaning of that statement: "No one knows the Son except the Father, and no one knows the Father except the Son and anyone to whom the Son chooses to reveal him" (Mat. 11:27). I read it, as you read it, and my school master in his own limited way tried to explain it and only added to confusion. I had no light thrown on it whatsoever. Then came that moment in time, to go back to Jeremiah, "Thy words became a joy and a delight to my heart…*I* am called by thy name, O Lord, God of hosts." I am actually called by your name? Yes, called by my name. Well, my name is Neville and that is certainly not the Lord, God of hosts. Your name is Robert, your name could be Mary, name could be anything, but that's not the Lord, God of hosts. So, how could I be called by thy name, which is the Lord, the God of hosts? Suddenly he tells us the name means "Jehovah will rise, Jehovah will loosen the womb." Well, he *did* rise in me; and he rose in me and he loosened the womb, of that womb that was really a tomb; and then he came out of that womb. He rose from the grave, like a seed falling into the ground and it dies. If it doesn't die, it brings forth nothing. It must die as a seed; so it is the earth which is its womb and becomes for a moment its grave. But to prove the grave is transformed into a womb, something grows. So when it grows and comes out bearing a hundred-fold, then that which was a grave became a womb. And out of the womb...he loosens the womb and something comes out. The very one that hurled himself into it came out. He came out of that loosened womb.

And then, all that was concealed in him which is fatherhood began to appear; for before him appears his son bearing witness to his fatherhood. He didn't know until that moment that he had a son. It was concealed in the very beginning of time, as told us in Ecclesiastes: "God has put eternity into the mind of man, but he's put it so that man cannot find out what God has done from the beginning to the end" (3:11). Then, suddenly, at the end he comes out, that which was concealed in his mind, and he stands before him, and he does call him "my Father." He calls him "Adonay," "my Father, my God and the Rock of my salvation" (Psalm 89:26). Doesn't call him John, doesn't call him Robert, doesn't call him Neville; he calls him Father.

Yet not for one moment did you until *that* moment in eternity ever believe *you* were the *answer* to the riddle. How could you? You can't make one hair of your head; you can't add one hour to the span of your life as you're told. Not an hour can you add to the span of your life, in spite of all the false claims to the contrary. You make your exits and your entrances from the stage on time, and no one adds to or takes from that span of time. As we are told, "Who by taking thought, who by being anxious, can add one cubit to his stature?" (Mat. 6:27). Well, that translation in the *Goodspeed Bible* is "Who by being anxious can add an hour to his span of life?" So, they've changed it completely to conform to the real basic meaning of·the phrase. You do not come in before your time and you don't leave before your time. Even when you seem to take your life, you don't leave before your time, no one does. And no one comes in before his time.

So here, you didn't realize, you who cannot add an hour to your span of life, who can't grow one hair of your head, who can't grow any of these things, and *you* establish all the ends of the earth? And that you have a son and that son is the princely David of biblical fame? Why, it seems nonsense...until it happens. When it happens, then it doesn't matter what the world will tell you. You can share it with others. And the whole gospel of John, for instance, is completely based upon believing or disbelieving in his message...all that matters. These are the stories that he experienced to interpret scripture. And the rabbis rejected him because they had their own speculations; and he wasn't speculating. He was simply giving his own personal experience of scripture. He said, I came to fulfill scripture, nothing else; Scripture must be fulfilled *in me.* So as the book unfolded in him, he was the grand being who was hurled by Jehovah—and Jehovah hurled only himself. There was no one else to send, so he sent himself. He sent himself into this maelstrom, this horror as it were, this place where you and I are subjected to the incarnation of the tragedy and the glory of the message of God. Well, we must not lose our vision of the glory in the tragedy. So while we are passing through all the afflictions, let us keep alive the vision of the glory. It's going to come, and *you* are the answer to the riddle.

So "Who established all the ends of the earth? What is his name and what is his son's name? Canst thou tell?" Well, I know in my own case, I have talked with so many rabbis and ministers and those of different aspects of the faith since it happened. I haven't found one who is teaching it who will listen even with interest. They are so completely sold on the belief that God is something on the *outside*, and that he has one unique son, called Jesus Christ, and that is it. You can't sway them for one moment. They will say after they read your book, "You know, I see and feel in your book a certain sincerity, Neville, but..." and there the book is closed and the mind is closed.

So when he said, "Take my yoke upon you" he's asking you to accept and exchange the yoke you now wear, based upon the false traditions, the speculations of the priesthoods of the world, for *his* yoke, which is his knowledge based upon *experience* of the scriptures of God. He tells you, I am he. Before I came into incarnation, I dictated it through my servants the prophets. They only served me. And throughout the centuries men have searched eagerly all through the scriptures to find that of which they spoke. They couldn't find it by their speculations; it comes only by revelation. When it was revealed to one and he told it, they rejected the revelation and held onto their traditions. So he said, you will circumnavigate the earth to make one proselyte, and you've thrown away the key; so you can't get in, and you stop him from getting in, because you become a slave to your traditions, and your traditions are keeping you out.

So I will share it with you, but I can't compel anyone to take it. I tell you, the name of that father is "Father"...and it's you. But you don't know that your name is Father, who is really the God who established all the ends of the earth, because you emptied yourself of that knowledge when you took upon yourself the limitations of a man, and became obedient unto death, even the death upon the cross of man (Phil. 2:7). So here you are nailed upon this cross of man, having emptied yourself of your primal form, your immortal self; and then you had to dream the dream of life that you had predetermined, for a purpose. And the purpose was to exercise your creative talent, called in scripture "your son"; for, he's called "your son" and he is, in scripture, nothing more than the power and the wisdom of the God that *you* are (1 Cor. 1:24). But you're told it takes the son to set you free; you will continue to dream the dream of life until the son appears (John 8:36). It comes only in the end, and when he appears he sets free his father who dreamed him into being. He was hidden in his father from the very beginning, and it took the entire dream to bring him forward and have him presented as son.

And so, "Where is your father?" The word is asked in the Book of Samuel, "Whose son are you, young man?" and he said, "I am the son of thy servant Jesse the Bethlehemite" (1 Sam. 17:58). That's who I am...I am the son of your servant Jesse. The word Jesse is I AM. So when he appears he calls you Father. And who is he calling Father and who is Father? You say, "Well, I am the father. He called me Father, so *I am* his father." But he doesn't call you Jesse, any more than I call my father Joe Goddard. Others would call him Joe Goddard, but I always called him Father. So he can call anybody else the name Neville...he can't call me that, he has to call me Father. So he calls me Father. You look at him, and you see him, and you are his father, and he is your son.

So I will tell you the answer to that riddle: You, as you are seated here, regardless of the name you bear on earth, *you* are the Father and your son's name is David. Because your son's name is David and you are his father, and *my* son's name is David, *the* David, the same David, and I am his father, then we are one. That's the only way you and I will know of our unity. We never lose our identity in this union. We are still completely individualized. In fact, this journey through death, when the curtain comes down on this fantastic drama, and we all awaken as the father of the one son called David, we will be individualized beyond that which we were when the drama began. When we began this drama, we did it for the purpose of increasing our individualization. We're all individualized, and we tend forever towards ever greater and greater individualization. There is no absorption in this union; there is simply a unity, a oneness. We are *all* that being that was in the very beginning, called in scripture, the Elohim. The God—it's plural—the gods created it all. It was the gods who hurled themselves into their creation. And they agreed to dream in concert, so the whole would be a dream in concert. When the concert is over, they all will return completely, not only without loss of consciousness or loss of individuality but an *increase* of individuality. And all together form the one God and that God is Father.

Then there's the next step. What that step will be that you and I will conceive for the fifth act, I do not know. I can only share with you the ending of the drama as it has ended in my life. Every story as told of Jesus Christ in scripture is true, but man himself has to realize it. As he realizes it he exchanges the yoke of the traditions of his fathers for the yoke of Jesus. And Jesus means Jehovah, that's all it means. The word Jesus means "Jehovah saves." It was Jehovah who threw himself into this maelstrom; it's Jehovah who will rise; it's Jehovah who will loosen the womb and save himself and bring him out; and when he comes out he is Jesus. And so, it was to Jesus that David in the Spirit turned and said, Adonay. So in the end, only one name; and at that name every knee in the world should bend and every tongue will confess that he is Lord to the glory of God the Father. He *is* God the Father. He said, "Why do you ask me to show you the Father? I have been so long with you, and yet you do not know me, Philip? He who has seen me has seen the Father; how then can you say, 'Show us the Father?'" (John 14:9). And then he unfolds who he is as Father by revealing (if they will listen to him) his Son.

But the traditions could not accept it, for time separated the event from the one he claims who called him in the Spirit, Adonay. For a thousand years separated the two events. If I go back 2,000 years, I hear the drama unfolded. I must go back 3,000 years to hear the promise and the question asked of the youth who could actually bring down the tyrant that annoyed Israel, and that youth was called David. His name was Olam and it's translated "the eternal youth" in scripture. He took this youth, this eternal youth, or the personification of all the generations of humanity and all of their experiences and personified it into one single youth. But when the whole is over it's *because* of all the generations of humanity and all of the experiences of man that you could extract from it all that eternal being called David. You pass through the furnaces, pass through all the afflictions, and because you've passed through all the afflictions and experiences—not in some other way but actually experienced it—you could bring him forth. It takes all of the fires to bring out of you that which you buried in the beginning. So he took eternity and placed it in the mind of man so that man could not find out what God had done from the beginning to the end. That which he put in the mind of man was Olam, and Olam means "the lad, the youth, the *stripling*." So I will set your father free if I can only find the name of your father, so "Whose son are you, young man?" For I made a promise: Whosoever's son should destroy the enemy of Israel, I'm going to set the father free.

So the Father is dreaming and dreaming and dreaming the dream of life until he brings forth David. When he brings forth David, David has *conquered* life; he's conquered all the generations of man. He's passed through every experience that man could ever experience, really. Having passed through it, and memory being kind to him—not letting him remember the horrors of the past—he only now knows the glory. He hasn't forgotten the glory in the tragedy through which he had to pass to bring forth David. So he brings out David. And when the king of earth, his name is Saul, and he sees this heavenly youth and that he was the conqueror, he remembers his promise: He is going to now set free the father of that youth. He cannot enslave him any longer in the dream of life. So the king of the earth must set free one of the dreamers who aided in the great concert. He has to go free. So tell me, "Who is your father?" "Jesse." And Jesse is I AM.

And so you will know the answer to the riddle. When you know it, really, you step aside, and you take the yoke off of you. In the gospel of Matthew, "I'll take it from myself." For in that one small little three or four verses (it's all crowded together) he tells you that "No one can know the Son but the Father; and no one can know the Father but the Son, and anyone to whom the Son chooses to reveal him" (11:27). So, I will now choose to reveal my father: Said he to the king, "My father is Jesse." Up to that, he didn't know; but he's looking for the father of that son to set him free, for he has to fulfill his promise. But until then, the fathers are enslaved. We are the fathers, we are the Elohim, we are the gods spoken of in Acts (14:11). "Great indeed is this day!" said the writer—whoever wrote the Book of Acts, the one who wrote the Book of Luke—"For the gods have come down to us in the likeness of men!" They've all come down and worn the forms of men, and they're enslaved while they wear the forms of men; and they will continue to be enslaved until they find the Son. Because no one can set him free but the Son, and the Son will decide when he will choose to reveal his Father. So in that 18th verse of the first John, first chapter of John: "No one has seen the Father; but the Son, who is in the bosom of the Father, he has made him known." You see John, you see Mary, you see Neville, you see all these characters of the world, the masks that the Father wears, but you haven't seen the Father. And not one knows the Father but the Son; and when he comes, he calls him, Adonay, in fulfillment of scripture. For the 89th Psalm...and the 89th Psalm makes the statement: "I have found David. He has cried unto me, 'Thou art my Father, my God, and the Rock of my salvation" (verse 26).

So here, Jeremiah, who threw so much light on it, makes the statement in his 23rd chapter...he is complaining about the false prophets of the world...oh, yes, they have dreams and they tell you the dreams came from God; but he tells you they're not from God, they are the ambitions of men. So they have dreams and dreams and they try to encourage all in a strange optimistic way. Well, they haven't had the dream that came from the depths of the soul. He's asked them a very simple question, Did you stand in the council of the gods? Did you really stand in the assembly of the gods? They could not answer yes unless they lied. He said, then you have not been sent. Were you addressed by him? No? And so, he put these questions to them and the answer is no. If you were not in the assembly of the gods, if you were not *addressed* by him, then you've not been *sent* by him...and so you're false prophets. So that was Jeremiah's message to the world.

When you are brought in, in Spirit, into the council of the gods and asked a question *by* the risen Christ—the being that's now about to embrace you and therefore you *are* he from that moment on—then you are sent on a mission because you are sent by him. And he doesn't leave you, he goes with you. That's the mystery: How could he go with you and still be there in the divine council, embracing one after the other, as he sends them on a mission? Well, that's the great mystery. I fill all, said he, I fill all heaven and all earth; there's no place where I am not. You take the wings of the morning and fly to the ends of the earth, he's there. If you make your bed in hell, he's there (Jer. 23:24). No matter where he sends you, and he'll send you through hell that you may tell them of the *true* yoke, the true understanding of scripture, and have them exchange their yoke, which is a misunderstanding of scripture, for the true understanding based upon experience. He said, "Take my yoke upon you and learn from me. My yoke is easy and my burden is light."

So when he addresses God the Father, you are misled, because he's speaking *of* God the Father. But then, one doesn't search long enough to find he tells you *he is* the Father. It's like communion with self. He is communing with self while he is in search, while he's playing the game, while he's playing the part he predestined himself to play. He was, in the beginning, foreknown by himself. "And those that he foreknew, he also predestined, and those whom he predestined, he also called; and those whom he called, he also justified; and those whom he justified, he also glorified" (Rom. 8:29). The glorification is simply the *complete* gift of himself at the *end* of the drama, when he returns to his prenatal state; when he returns to that primal form of which he was emptied when he assumed the limitations of a garment, and stepped upon the stage, on time, and played all the horrible parts of the world. It took all of these to expand and increase the creative power that he had prior to entering the great drama.

So in the end when the curtain comes down, we'll all gather together and we'll understand clearly what the great wonderful tragedy meant. We'll all rejoice, because, in spite of it all, all tears are washed away, all scars are gone, and nothing but joy remains; with an *expanded* creative power for another drama, which you and I together, in concert, will agree before we hurl ourselves into the garment. Having seen it clearly in the beginning, then we hurl it in forgetfulness and *become* the part. Then, having played it fully, whatever is then the one to be brought forth at the end of the drama we'll bring him forth. We can't fail because God can't fail...and you are he.

So now, let's go into the Silence and take...you can take the answer and the hope that *you* will now be able to tell it from experience rather than from belief in one whom you trust who has had that experience. Now let's go.

* * *

Q: (inaudible)

A: Everything has been played. He said, "No one takes my life, I lay it down myself" (John 10:18). He's speaking for everyone. Don't put him aside on the outside as a being speaking; this is God *in* every man speaking. So he said to the one who said, 'Don't you know I have power to set you free and power to crucify you?' he said, "You would have no power over me were it not given to you from above." So the play is fixed and the play is on, and your entrance and your exit; and you make many entrances and many exits during the play. When you come out you are the Father, and you are the one who established all the ends of the earth. And you have a son, a son which is really your creative power. And you brought him forth at the end, because it was he in you that you use as a creative power, and he comes forth. He doesn't condemn you for putting him through the furnaces; he sets you free. You can't separate a man from his creative power. So it doesn't make sense... because our doctors today are telling us that because of our know-how in chemistry that we are prolonging the life, as though they really knew what the span was in the beginning. So they say if you drink too much you get cirrhosis of the liver. Daddy lived to be eighty-five. Mother never drank in her life, died at sixty-two, never smoked. He led a rugged, full life, with *excessive* drinking...so eighty-five. All the doctors who warned him that they were going to bury him, he went to their funerals, all of them. He knew he couldn't make his exit before that moment in time. And the day he died he said to my brother Collin, "Col, today is the day"...fully conscious, knew exactly what he was doing, dictating policy for business.

Every day they consulted him as to what should be done in the many ventures that we have all through the islands, and Daddy would state his opinion and state it forcibly. The very day he died he said to my brother Collin in the morning, he said, "Col, this is the day." He said, "No, Daddy." He said, "This is the day, boy, today. Get ready." And so it was the day, right on the button. So, read the words carefully, "Who by taking thought can add one cubit to his stature?" That is in the King James Version. The Revised Standard Version has "Who by being anxious can add a cubit to his span of life?" But the Goodspeed translation is "Who by worrying can add one hour to his span of life?" So if we can only get back to the original meanings of the ancient scripture; but men as they interpret it, they're forever trying to give it sense, and theology is man's reasoning about the word of God, as science is man's reasoning about the works of God. But now, to understand God's mystery it must be revealed. He unveils himself and he unveils himself in you and you find that you are the being all along that you've been seeking. You've been in search of self, for that's God.

And so, our exits and our entrances...and if you've ever known any playwrights in this world, they don't want any messing around with their play. When they say "I want this one to enter stage right, that one enter stage left, I want it on time," don't let the actor think he knows better than the director and the one who conceived the play. Well, the gods conceived it and hurled themselves into the play, but they had to forget they were gods to become man. He said, "How could he do it?" Well, he emptied himself of his divinity, and took upon himself the form of man; and being found in the form of man, he became obedient unto death, and even death upon the cross of man (Phil. 2:7). Having been found in that form, then God has highly exalted him, so that now he has been given the name, a name that is above every name, that at the name of Jesus every knee should bow...and every tongue confess that Jesus Christ is Lord, to the glory of God the Father. So that's the name you're going to get in the end, because it's David who calls Jesus, Father. So when he calls *you* Father, aren't you he? He only calls one Father, so all will be he. So in the end, "the Lord is one and his name one, and he's king over all the earth."

Any other questions, please?

Q: Is everything predestined, including suicide?

A: I said exits and entrances are predestined, but within the framework of the play the actor can change parts by a reinterpretation of parts. But he doesn't change his exits and his entrances. Man is born physically by the actions of powers beyond himself; he's also born spiritually by the actions of powers beyond himself. A little child comes into the world and, well, the so-called doctors of the world and the parents of the world will say that it came because of a certain creative act based upon the ___(??), or if it's a eugenic child, well, based upon some scientific experiment. So the child came by the action of powers not its own. That's a physical birth. Well, he's born spiritually by the action of powers beyond himself.

So that we are told, "He who began a good work in you, he will bring it to completion at the *day* of Jesus Christ" (Phil. 1:6). Jesus Christ is the one who discovers fatherhood, and you can't be a father unless there is a child. He discovers he was the father of David, for David in the Spirit called him Father. And he tried to share his knowledge of scripture with the world, and the world rejected his yoke. They wouldn't take his yoke upon them. They think they're going to earn it; they're going to work out their salvation by the sweat of their brow; and they're going to by keeping the outer yoke going by constant attendance in the churches, contributions to charities, and by doing all the things that they think ought to be done in this world they will earn it. And they do not know it's all grace. Your physical birth, certainly, was a gift, and your spiritual birth is a gift.

So he not only hurls himself, but at one moment he rises. "Jehovah will rise"...and then again, "Jehovah will loosen the womb." And he does, he loosens the womb. *You* don't roll away the stone; suddenly the stone is rolled away. You push automatically and at a certain moment the stone rolls and you come out. So he loosens the tomb. He loosens that womb which in the beginning was really a tomb. It was a tomb, but you, by your dream, dreaming in it, turned that which was death into sleep, and the sleep into eternal life. You woke from it all into eternity.

Q: If it's all predestined, how about 'Seek and ye shall find it'? That's in the Bible too.

A: I'm not saying that your attempt to change your mind is predestined. No, you can take God's law, but you can't by God's law receive God's grace. He said, You didn't get it by law, you got it by grace. But there is a law of God, that whatever you desire in this world, believe that you have it, and you will have it. So you *can* change the pattern of your life, no question about it. But that was not the question, originally. The question was, "You mean my exit from this world, even though self-imposed, such as a suicide, that that was predetermined?" Scripture teaches that you can't add one hour to your span of life—and we're told that what is not written in scripture is non-existent—in spite of our scientists today who will tell us that by their knowledge of diets and knowledge of this and knowledge of the other we can extend it and are extending it. But I notice in every morning's obituary there are just as many young doctors dying as there are people in other parts of the world who never heard of the name doctor.

This very brilliant chap, the other day over here in Pasadena, a great physicist, just turned in his fifties, so he had the presence of mind to make his exit not by cutting his throat, he had what they call a heart attack. A young fella walking through the park in New York City, thirty-eight years old, brilliant physicist, they found his body on the ground the next morning. Someone played a part of shooting him. And it goes on through life. You can't understand the horror of the play while you're in it. But as Blake said from the Spirit world to us still in the play): "Do not let yourself be intimidated by the horror of the world. Everything is ordered and correct and must fulfill its destiny in order to attain perfection. You follow this path and you'll receive from your own soul an even greater perception of the *beauties* of creation"; and then not only that but you become ever more free from what now to you seems so horrible, so altogether frightening in the world. You will not see it as frightening as the headlines will tell, like the four plane accidents yesterday, but in a drama. May I tell you, I told it in forty-six in my little book *The Search*—not a thing has happened to me to modify the statement—but I said it in closing that tiny little pamphlet. I said: This world, this universe that we study with such care is a dream, and we are the dreamers of the dream, eternal dreamers dreaming non-eternal dreams. One day like Nebuchadnezzar we will awaken from the dream, from this nightmare in which we fought with demons, to find that we never really left our eternal home; we were really never born and have never died save in our dream. Goodnight.

SIGNS AND WONDERS

5/15/64

Tonight's subject is "Signs and Wonders." As we are told in the 6th and 20th chapters of the Book of Deuteronomy, "The Lord brought his people out of Egypt with signs and wonders." Now, the Bible from beginning to the end is divine history. But this history is not history as you and I understand it. In other words, you could never by historical research either prove or disprove it; and any religion in this world that depends upon historical and scientific confirmation really is not a fixed act.

Let us now take the book, this divine history. It's *your* history, a history that you and every child born of woman *will* experience. Every child is Adam, and Adam is compelled to be disobedient. As we are told in the 11th chapter of the Book of Romans, that "God has consigned every man to disobedience that he may have mercy upon all" (verse 32). So Adam is the garment that God wears. And that disobedience is for one outstanding purpose: He eats of the tree of knowledge of good and evil that *conscience* may be born. And so conscience is born by the seeming disobedience. Then he passes through the furnaces of affliction. But at least he does have conscience and he does know right and he knows wrong. He violates it time after time. And so from Adam to Noah it is sheer hell in scripture, because everything is for self-gain; and so, he simply buries his conscience which tells him it is wrong, and simply, well, for the purpose of self-gain. Then we're told this is all wiped out, and then we start with Noah.

Remember these are all states...every character in the Bible is a state of consciousness. They're simply personifications of the eternal states of the soul through which the individual passes like a pilgrim. So he moves first through Adam to Noah. We find now the character called Noah, for here is Noah the first tiller of the land, the first beginning of civilization (Gen. 11:20).

Then he drinks successfully of the fruit of the vine, and he got drunk, and found himself completely exposed, but *completely* drunk, flattened out and uncovered. Then we are told, his son Ham came in and saw him in his nakedness, and then he told his brothers Shem and Japeth. They brought a sheet and walking backwards, without turning around, they covered the nakedness of their father that they would not see his nudity. When he arose from his drunkenness and once more returned to normalcy and discovered that his son Ham had seen his nudeness, he cursed Canaan...didn't curse Ham. He cursed Canaan and said, "Cursed be Canaan; you shall be a slave of slaves to all your brothers" (verse 24). So that is now a new beginning. Well, who is this Noah and the state of consciousness, when you and I start a certain attempt to create a civilization, to really move forward? Who is this Ham that saw my nudity? For the word Ham in Hebrew means "life." It's Cheth Mem—it is life itself. He curses Canaan and Canaan is the world that is cursed.

You can't understand Canaan until we jump now to the next character where you and I really begin in this world. The next character is Abraham. It's really Abram in the beginning of it all which is faith. So all this is a turmoil. Then Abram is put into a deep sleep and then a dread and frightful darkness descends upon Abram. While he is in sleep, the Lord speaks to him and tells him to leave Haran and migrate into Canaan. There he and his descendants will be enslaved as sojourners in this strange land, and they will be slaves of slaves for 400 years; then he will deliver them with signs and wonders. So every descendant of Abraham will go into this land and be completely enslaved. He must leave Haran. Well, Haran means "sanctuary, it's the haven of rest, a comfort." He must leave this innocence and move into a world of experience; and in the world of experience he goes through all the fires of hell. For every conceivable situation that man could ever think of, man, the individual, must pass through as he goes into Canaan. And there he remains for 400 years.

Well, he doesn't mean 400 years as you and I would measure years by the clock. Four hundred is the numerical value of the last letter of the Hebrew alphabet, which has a symbolical value of a cross—it's Tau. And so, the twenty-second letter is a cross. And so I wear this cross for that interval of time called 400 only for its symbolical meaning, its numerical meaning; but not 400 as you and I would measure 400 years. How long it is, well, some claim 6,000 years, others 8,000 years…but, really, who knows? I don't know, I really do not know. I only know there are signs and wonders that tell me the end of the picture. How long I went through this thing as years, I haven't the slightest concept. But reading the Bible carefully, I know by the signs as they begin to appear within me I am at the end, the very end of the journey only by reason of the signs.

Now the story Jesus, Jesus Christ, from his conception by the Holy Spirit to his ascension into heaven is a sign vouchsafed by God to those who will receive it. It's a *sign*. The words are put into the mouth of the prophet Simeon, "And the child is a sign for the fall and the rise of many in Israel" (Luke 2:34). But it is a sign...and people look upon the child as a fact. The child is a sign, as told us in the 2nd chapter of the Book of Luke, when the angel of the nativity told the shepherds she would give them a sign; and this is the sign of the event just before it, "You shall find a babe wrapped in swaddling clothes." They hastened to Bethlehem to find the child, just as foretold, to fulfill prophecy of Micah. In the 5th chapter of the Book of Micah, there you will read, Bethlehem...and then Bethlehem becomes personified as the woman who conceived by the Holy Spirit; and she was so little among the clans of Judah; and how should Bethlehem have this great honor bestowed upon her? We then are told in this 5th chapter that I will deliver you into all things and forget you until she who is in labor brings forth (verse 3). What she brings forth will be the ruler in Israel, but it will be a sign...these are all signs from beginning to end.

So it is not history that any archeologist in this world, by his search, could ever find to support the claim that these things ever took place on earth. Because not one character of scripture walked this earth as an individual, as you walk it, as I walk it. They are the *eternal* states, which one day everyone will see, see in their Imagination—-as I have seen them all, seen them just where they really belong, in my Imagination. I've seen Abraham; not as the world thinks it, to see Joseph, to see every one of them, all in my Imagination. And to see them at a certain focus, when all together they form one man, and that man is Jesus. When you look at him closely, you're looking at yourself. You know who he is, the Lord of Lords, and when you look at him closely with all in him, it's only one. But when it's fragmented, they become unnumbered characters and all these are the states, the states that are eternal states through which every soul must pass.

So here, these signs and wonders as told from the very beginning to the end is the only thing I can tell you that I know: When they begin to happen in you, you *are* at the end. Because I know of no other way of measuring the time between entering the state...for the real thing begins with Abraham. So if he promises him a child and "Abraham rejoiced that he was to see my day; he saw it and was glad" (John 8:56). Well, how could you possibly know Abraham, he preceded me by a thousand years? "Before Abraham was, I AM." Well, I am, as you are, of the Ancient of Days. We were before the whole thing was brought into being, and this was brought for a purpose: to create and to extend our creative power. The only reason for this play is to develop the creative power of God which power is Jesus Christ. As we are told: "Jesus Christ, the power and the wisdom of God" (1 Cor. 1:24). But man thinks that Jesus Christ is an individual on the outside. Isn't so at all! Always think of Jesus Christ as the little child...*always* think of him as the little child. And everyone must bring forth Jesus Christ, as told us in the 3rd chapter of the Book of Galatians. And everyone beginning with Abraham, which is only a state, but we all enter that state of faith and only by faith are we led and simply move forward, bringing at the very end, we bring forth the child. So he saw me and rejoiced that he was to see my day. Saw what? He saw the child, the laughing infant, called Isaac, which really is the prototype of Jesus Christ (Gen. 17:18).

So these are the signs and they are signs from beginning to end in scripture. So I will tell you of the signs, and when they begin to happen, don't look back to ask how long have you been journeying. You've been journeying 400 years, symbolically. The 400 years may be as we measure time 8,000 years. It may be 6,000 years. I do not know, I haven't the slightest idea this night. If I ever get it I'll tell you before I leave. But until then I can only tell you that the signs are the measure of the end. And the first sign which is God's most majestic act in the world is resurrection. That's his greatest sign and all the other signs are understood within the framework of that...that's resurrection. And then you will know who you are, that you were God before you became man. You have never been less than God, but you did it for one purpose and one purpose only that God the one—-"Hear, O Israel: The Lord our God is one Lord." Hear, O Israel: The I AM our I AMs is one I AM (Deut. 6:4)—but for creative powers and for creative reasons it fragments itself into the Elohim. The Elohim is a plural—-the gods. And so every being in this world is one of the Elohim, and scattered beyond the wildest dream. On a frightful journey, a terrifying journey, where in the very end, when he has prepared the way to redeem all, everyone will be redeemed—-not one will be lost—-and come back into the unity that is I AM. And that I AM, as we told you recently, is called the Father—-that's his wonderful name.

So the *first* sign, the real first sign of the awakening is the resurrection, where you awake to find yourself entombed within your skull. And then things begin to happen. Entombed within your skull...A seed must fall into the ground and die before it is made alive. If it doesn't fall into the ground and die, it remains alone and brings forth nothing. If it falls into the ground and it dies, then it brings forth a hundredfold. So the seed, called the Elohim, it falls into the ground which is your skull and there it dies. And then after a frightening dream of creating in this world of death, it still creates, creates all kinds of things, and then it awakens. As it awakens it resurrects, for it was dead, and then it comes out, proving that what was a skull has been turned into a womb. It was a tomb and the tomb became a womb. Then it comes out of the womb, and as it comes out of the womb, the first sign is that of the child, Emmanuel—"God is with us"—the Christ child wrapped in swaddling clothes. So I tell you, go into Bethlehem and you will find this as a *sign*. And so they went quickly and they found the sign. They could not see the event but they trusted the angel's words that it was a sign, and they found the sign.

Following that, now we know another sign is told us in Deuteronomy and told us first of all in Exodus. This is a nature sign, for it always happens and *only* happens when Israel departs from Egypt; and *you* are the Israel, the pure in heart. So only the Israelite can see God and the Israelite is one who is pure in heart. So here we are told that this sign always occurs with the departure of Israel from Egypt, and the sign is that of the serpent. So here is the *other* sign. And so, suddenly you will find *that* sign, whether you see it in the world as some little thing or whether you actually experience it. But sometimes, as it happened this last week...the lady is not here tonight but she lives in the Palisades and she's right on the beach and sees the ocean all the time. Walking down the beach this past week she saw a little object and said to herself, "No, why stop and pick it up? It may be some stupid little glittery little thing." But she said, "Don't be lazy, pick it up." So she picked it up, it was a little ring, almost the size of a child's ring. It was a serpent swallowing itself, with a little tiny, I presume almost valueless, jewel for a head. But nonetheless, there it was. I saw the thing last week. She walked on a few yards and something else caught her eye—the next symbol was a cross, a little silver cross that at one time hung on someone's necklace because it had a loop for the chain. Then she kept on walking, and then a little wooden chalice...here is the cup of wood. She brought the three that she found on the beach. They are only external symbols of the internal signs that she one day will experience. So everything in this world, this outer world, is a shadow of the inner world.

So I saw them last week, right here in the little room behind...that right on our Pacific beach, one after the other, she encountered the three grand signs. First, the serpent was the tempter who said, "You will not really die. He said, 'You will die, but not really.'" So you were made to disobey and so by disobeying conscience is born. How could you ever start the journey unless conscience is born? What conscience?—good and evil. Man must know the difference between right and wrong, good and evil. But he will suppress it for personal gain until he reaches a certain point where then he reaches the point called Abraham. And Abraham believed the most impossible thing in the world, and to him it was accounted righteousness. So he starts the journey, and he leaves the haven, the sanctuary of Haran, and moves into Canaan that is cursed. Canaan is cursed by one whose secret was exposed; for the father was seen in his nudity and he who saw him saw the secret of creation. Seeing the secret of creation he cursed Canaan as a land and sent every descendant of himself into this world that he would learn how to create and to *expand* his power to create in this world. Before we started the journey he sets up a series of signs they are called in the Book of John. They're called miracles in the synoptics, and they're called, by any other name, portents in the Old Testament. So the child will be a sign and a portent. And the serpent will be a sign and a portent. So when they begin to happen, know the end is at hand.

And so, when will they come? Well, I will come like Jonah. And they're all trying to find out what does it mean to come like Jonah. When I come, it will be just like the sign of Jonah. Matthew adds, Jonah was three days in the whale; therefore, he was three days in the earth before he rose (Mat. 12:39). They are all confused as to it. The word Jonah is the Hebrew word for dove; dove in Hebrew is Jonah. I will only give you one sign and that sign is the sign of Jonah. It comes. Wait for it. He will descend upon you and when the vision comes to an end that descent of the dove will not have departed. He's still on you when the vision comes to an end, smothering you with kisses. While the whole thing begins to come to an end, the dove is still upon you, so Jonah is still upon you. That is the descent of the Holy Spirit and it is forever and forever. So, you'll know. When will the end come, O Lord? The end? This generation seeks the sign. There shall be no sign but the sign of the prophet Jonah. The prophet is telling you this is the end and Jonah, which means dove, is the symbol of the Holy Spirit, and he descends upon you as promised in scripture. I will depart...for we all heard this story before we set forth, we heard everything that could ever happen to us...then he departed. Departed where?—he *entered* us; for we *are* the very being who conceived the play, who is playing the play. So, unless I go away then the Spirit cannot come; but if I go away, there is a Comforter, the Comforter will come (John 16:7). And so, I will depart and you will be sad, but I will come again. These are the signs by which I will awaken, and you will know that I never really left you. I am closer than ever before as we are told. So he departs from the visible world by actually becoming invisible, and never was he nearer than when he was invisible.

So *in* man is God, this Holy Spirit, who is taking us through from the beginning of it, whenever that time was, to the end, and the end we know by observing the signs. So by signs and wonders he brings his people out of Egypt. You read it carefully; only by signs and wonders would you ever know. Don't ask, "How long, O Lord, how long?" Wait for the signs. May I tell you, not one in this world will fail, *no* one will fail. It's all ours! You and

I conceived it; we are playing it; and in the end, when these masks are taken off, you and I will know each other more intimately than you and I have ever known anyone in this world. I've been a father of two children and love my wife, love her dearly. I have never known her in this world, though she bore our daughter, as I will know her, and know you, when these masks are off. There's an intimacy when the masks are off which you can't compare to anything here, not a thing here is like it. Here the most intimate relationship is like living at arm's length…just like arm's length. When these are off, we are the Elohim, and the Elohim is a compound unity. It is a unity, a oneness made up of others: "Hear, O Israel, the Lord our God is one Lord." And that's who we are.

So, one by one by one the mask comes off, and you know when the mask is coming off only by the signs and wonders. And they simply…then you are told, the first shall be the last of these signs and the last shall be first. People think in *this* world where we live in terror and are afraid of each other by the masks that we wear, that it means that someone who is now prominent will be demoted by some tyrannical god. No, it means only the signs. The first sign recorded is the dove, in the earliest scripture and that is Mark. So the first event or sign is the dove and the last one recorded is resurrection. Well, *reverse* them. It's going to happen exactly like that: The resurrection is going to come first and the dove is going to come last. So when the dove appears, which is the very last, although recorded first, it really is the last sign. Then, at any moment in time, but not one second before the appointed hour, you will depart from this world. You may be the healthiest being physically, but you're only wearing a garment. Your departure is already cut and dried; not one can add one hour to his span of life, not one being in this world. You can have all the great doctors in the world, you could have all the finest food in the world, all the medicines in the world, and they think they can put you some place where there isn't a germ it is so completely clean; but at your moment in time you make your departure, and you do not add one hour to your span of life. Our entrances and our exits are all predetermined.

But within the framework of God's play, our play, for we are the being who conceived it, we can change all kinds of things to our amusement, really. You can be rich or you can be poor; you can be strong or you can be weak; you can be known or you can be unknown. You are encouraged to use a certain power, a certain talent, to change anything to make your life more desirable. But you aren't going to extend it. "Who by being anxious can add a cubit to his stature?" "Who by being concerned can add a cubit to his span of life?" And the latest translation, "Who by worry can add an hour to his span of life?" So they've finally come down to the real meaning of the word which is stature, which is cubit. So first they gave it a spatial dimension—twenty-two inches would be the cubit—and then they turned it into time and gave the word translated cubit a time measurement of an hour. Then they took the word stature, which would be spatial and then turned it into a time measure of a span of time, span of life. So today, the perfect translation is what Goodspeed has given us: "Who by worry can add one hour to his span of life?"

So your entrance is perfect, your exit is going to be perfect. But within the framework of the play use your talent. Your talent can be used by a simple process: Whatever you desire, no condition attached to it, *whatever* you desire, believe that you've received it and you will. But bear in mind, we began because God imposed upon us disobedience to bring about the birth of conscience. But when conscience is born, don't bury it! So use it! So you are free to imagine anything in this world, but remain aware of the birth of conscience, and conscience is the knowledge of right and wrong, of good and evil. I need not tell you what *you* know to be right and what is wrong. You can always ask yourself this question if you are in any doubt whatsoever, "Would I like it done unto me?" Ask that simple question, for do unto others as you would have them do unto you. So if you are in doubt when you have a longing, an intense desire, would you like it, were things reversed, to have it done unto you? For that is conscience, the knowledge of good and evil. So you begin there. That's how the whole vast world begins as far as God expanding his talent. So you could bury it, you could bury your conscience, and accept the evil because it seems a temporary gain, a little moment of joy, a little moment of a thrill, where you could *take* from someone else what you know in your heart belongs to them, but you would bury your conscience. Well, do it if you will, but then you are only putting upon yourself the most horrible tomorrows. And so use it.

But the real journey begins with faith, and faith is nothing more than Abraham. Abraham is *not* a member of a certain racial group; Abraham is the eternal state where everyone *really* begins the journey in faith. And so you hear the story, the whole story was told you, and then you reacted. You either believed it or you didn't believe it. If you believed it, you start the journey. So as Paul brings out, only the sons of faith are the sons or descendants of Abraham; that no one can claim that because he is a Levite or that he belongs to the tribe of Benjamin or the tribe of someone else that he is a Jew. The *true* Jew is the one who is the descendant of Abraham in faith. As Bishop Pike brought out so beautifully when he was asked, being an Episcopalian and a bishop concerning the Jew, he said, "I am a Jew *because* I am a Christian. I *could* be a Jew and not be a Christian, but I can't be a Christian and not be a Jew." You dwell upon it. Because that's where you start, you start in the faith of Abraham, and unless you have that faith you are still moving between Noah and Abraham. We all start with Adam where conscience is born and consciousness is there; but conscience becomes the child, the first one. And then we go through the most horrible experiences; and then all the signs are set up when you enter the state called Abraham.

I wish I could take everyone with me this night, all together, and show you what you've *forgotten*, because you have forgotten it. Because things that I see today and see constantly now, they're only memories, things I have known forever as you know them. Every one of them you see. I saw the whole thing before I set forth and have been up until now trying to remember them. Then comes the last and the last is simply the signs and the wonders. As they begin to unfold then night after night the vision comes back, and all that you and I shared together before we started the journey is there, all in you. May I tell you, don't ask how long between now and then: "How long, Lord, how long?" As you are warned, "It is not for you to know the times and the seasons that the Father has fixed by his own authority. But wait for the promise from the Father." What is the promise? As told us in 2nd Corinthians, the 1st chapter, "All of the promises of God find their Yes in him" (verse 20). Then you know who you are. So every promise is being realized *in you* by the signs and every promise of God finds its Yes in him. Of whom are they speaking? God's creative power personified as one called Jesus Christ—-that's you. So *every* promise of God will find its Yes in you.

So when you come...suddenly it happens. At first you are so bewildered your response is nothing more than awe and wonder. You can't talk or think of anything but, when the first thing happens. And then when the second one happens, it adds to your confusion and your bewilderment. And you go back and you read the scriptures for intimations and for foreshadowings of what is taking place in you, and you see it had to take place because it was all foretold. The third one happens and then the fourth one happens. Here when the fourth one happens...for the first I would call a double one like two sides of a coin, resurrection and birth come the same moment, just one moment after the other. And so the minute you are awake, you come out of the womb which is the tomb of your skull. So they're are two events but they're really one, one follows on the other at the same moment or the same night, I ___(??). Then comes the second grand event, the discovery of the fatherhood of God; the discovery of *yourself* as God the Father who conceived it and then fragmented himself into all these things. Then comes the third, your real departure from this realm—the serpent.

And then comes the fourth one and that is the end. As you're told, it all started...and he named the fourth one Judah. He is the one, the gate, the

Daleth, through which all things pass. Now, don't for one moment think that because you aren't the fourth child physically you aren't the fourth. May I tell you, you are. There are numberless ways of arriving at the fourth, at the Daleth. You could be the fourth in your class and not the brightest and yet that's the one chosen. You could be the fourth to come through the door one day. You can be then fourth in a million different ways, but in some peculiar way the mystery is so set up that through the door you go, and the door is the fourth. The fourth letter is Daleth and that is the fourth. In my own case, I am the fourth physically of the children of my mother, but it doesn't mean that I would have to be *physically* the fourth. My daughter is my wife's first child, she happens to be my second, but she could be the fourth in her class or she could be the fourth in marks, she could be the fourth in many ways, as you can be. Don't try to analyze it, it's all been done.

But within the framework of what has already been arranged for us you play it beautifully. You just take God's law, assume that you are now this night the man, the woman that you want to be. Live it fully in your Imagination and sleep in it just as though it were true, and fall asleep in that assumption. And be as faithful to that as the state called Abraham is faithful to the vision when he rejoiced that he was to see my day, he saw it and he was glad; and then started the journey leaving the haven of Haran. He left the sanctuary, the comfort of that wonderful home, and moved into a land where he knew by prophecy he would be a slave of slaves to all his brothers. So he moves right into the cursed land, the land of Canaan. And the land is cursed; he takes upon himself the curse of the world and becomes obedient unto slavery; then hoped for, because the memory remained with him, that he would be redeemed by signs and wonders. Then came that moment in time when the first sign appeared. In his case, it was the child, it was Isaac. So Isaac is not some little thing that is born of generation, it's something that was promised. It's only a *sign*. Some will call it (I will go along with them) it's simply the generation of God...and he brings forth his child. But the child is brought forth that's seen by others; the shepherds saw it, but they didn't see the being who awoke; for that being awoke in an entirely different dimension, and that being could not be seen by the eye that would see the sign. So let us go quickly and see the sign this day.

So Simeon saw the sign and knew the sign was for the fall and rising of many in Israel. He knew it, but he couldn't see that which the sign represented. He was only told, as the prophet, that it represented the birth of God this day in Bethlehem. And so in this city of Bethlehem he was born, and go and see the *sign*. When you see the sign, well, certainly you'll see the sign…that is not an unnatural thing…every child is wrapped in swaddling clothes. But you don't see it in the flesh, you see it in Spirit. And so it is supernatural in the sense that you only encounter the child, this heavenly child in the Spirit, as you encounter all the states. David, you encounter him in the Spirit: "Did not David in the Spirit call me Father?" (Mat. 44:28). Not in the flesh! We are separated by, well, 3,000 years, but in the Spirit we aren't separated...he calls me Father. So everyone will experience these things in Spirit...all these signs are yours. So by signs and wonders he brings us, his people, out of Egypt. And when we are all brought out, once more we form the unity that is ours before, for creative purposes, we fragmented ourselves and became a divided, conflicting, fiery state.

So when you read the scripture in the future, bear in mind it is simply an infinite play. It's *divine* history, not ever to be known by any historical research. There is no archeologist who will ever find anything in this world to either prove or disprove the claims of scripture. It was never intended to be understood as secular history, never! And every character in it from beginning to end is a state of consciousness that's eternal. And these states, one day you will see them, actually see them. You will see them sometimes coalesced into one man; and then you will see them scattered into nations, and places, infinite numbers of people, and one day, all together. And as you look, it is really the Lord of Lords, but he has *your* face, and you know it. You're looking right into your own being when the time comes for your return and your departure from this wheel of recurrence.

Now let us go into the Silence.

* * *

___(??) where you and I are invited to ask to be given a sign of his favor: "O Lord, give me a sign of thy favor" (Ps. 86:17). So we are invited... so tonight do it in this way, for we are told if we ask with his name, we'll receive it. Well, the name in our case of asking is "I am." So just assume that you could tell me that you have a sign. Go to sleep this night just as though you could share with me, and allow me to share with everyone here, your experience of receiving the sign. He said, "O Lord, give me a sign of thy favor." And these are the signs spoken of. So don't think because of what I told you earlier that you must passively wait for it. No, I mean by the "fixed things" your exits and your entrances from the stage of life. But within it, use your talent, your creative talent, through your belief in these signs to ask for it. And let the soul...because really when you get it from yourself the depth of your soul reveals it, for it's all in you.

Q: (inaudible)

A: The Q Source is simply the gospels, really, Matthew, Mark, Luke, and John. No one knows who Q is. Q is simply the only source that the Evangelists had, but they claimed that they had it from mouth to mouth, that's what they claim. But as far as we can go back the only manuscript that they had to really use for their interpretation was the Q Source, and that Matthew, Mark, Luke, and John draw from it, but especially Matthew, Mark and Luke. John seems to have something a bit different, but he does draw a bit on the Q Source.

Q: Well, one night you referred to the back of the head...

A: Oh, the back of the head, that's Qoph. I thought you meant the manuscript itself. There is a Q Source of the manuscript; like in Genesis, we have the J Source and the E Source and the P Source: the Prophets, the Jehovah and the Elohim and they're only initials. But when you said the Q, I thought you meant the letter Q, and so there is, but the Q Source is the only source for the New Testament, Matthew, Mark, Luke, and John. But, Q as a letter—the back of the head, Qoph. And so its value is a hundred in the numerical value of the Hebrew tongue. And so, he was a hundred years old when the child was born. It doesn't mean he was a hundred as a person would be a hundred years old, but it means it is born from the back of the head. You do come out through the base of the skull. So the letter Q or Qoph in Hebrew has the numerical value of a hundred. It is said of him that he was a hundred years old when Isaac was born, and so he's simply telling us, symbolically, in a metaphorical sense, that man will come out of the back of that skull. And then as he comes out, the sign that he did get out of his tomb and therefore is born from above, will be present. The shepherds will be present to witness the sign, and he himself will see it. Because Abraham saw Isaac; he saw it and held it, held his Isaac, and it's simply the Christ child. But the child is only a *sign*. It is *you* who will come out at the back, or the Qoph, the Q, of your head. You'll come right out by rolling it away without effort. So you rise to find yourself entombed; the tomb turns itself into a womb out of which you come... and that's the hundred. So you are then the Abraham fulfilling the promise made to him that when at this time of the year, I will return and you will have a son. And then when the angel returned he was a hundred years old and the hundred is the back of the head.

Q: How do you explain the fact that our lifespan has been increased so much in the past few years?

A: I'm not denying that within the past few years that *seemingly* a man's life has increased, but who knows that before he came in that was his lifespan? That we, judging things against another frame, we think that we are expanding it by our new knowledge of diets and new knowledge of chemicals and new knowledge of sanitation and all these things, we *think* we do. I'll take you into little Barbados where there's, in a certain area, there is no indoor plumbing and no sanitation. ___(??) I'll introduce you to a thousand people who have passed a hundred. They get an occasional piece of meat because they can't afford it, and they eat nothing but starches, sweet potatoes, potatoes, yams, get a little fish, smoke their tobacco.

Q: (inaudible)

A: No, do exactly what you're going to do anyway. I mean, people are so geared they will not believe scripture. Listen to the words of scripture: "Is there a thing of which it is said, 'See, this is new'? It has been already. But there is no remembrance of former things, nor will there be any remembrance of things to come after among those who will come later. There is nothing new under the sun" (Eccles. 1:9). So the arguments we make today, at that point in time as the wheel turns that argument is always made. And if you will take the lives of doctors who have all these things with them, their expectancy is no more than ours, none whatsoever. I know fellows, friends of mine, who abused their bodies so they should have been dead many times over, but they're not; and those who have lived clean, wholesome, wonderful lives and then at a tender age they're gone. And, of course, then the doctor steps in and tells you why after the event. Well, anyone can do that...after the event.

Q: You said the dove is the last. If one had the experience of the dove before the others preceded it, where would it fit into the picture?

A: My dear, I can only give you my experience and scripture. The first recorded incident in the earliest gospel which is Mark and it is the dove. The dove is not only a symbol of tranquility and peace, but of the creative power of God—that is really his symbol, the creative power. The creative power descends upon him and remains on him. For the only purpose of all this drama is to develop and expand the creative power. So the *symbol* of creative power comes at the very end and then you see it; it descends upon you and remains on you. So I can only go along with scripture and my own experiences that parallel scripture. So the symbol of peace yes, because you're told in the 9th chapter of Isaiah when the names are given, the four names of this one, this child will bear, and peace is the end (verse 6). Some translations will break it into five, but I notice that all new translations break it into four. (Tape ends.)

JESUS: GOD'S PLAN OF SALVATION

5/19/64

Tonight's subject is "Jesus: God's Plan of Salvation." God's plan of salvation appears so different in prospect from what it really is in retrospect. If you haven't experienced it and you trust the one who has, do not at any time forget or ignore the out and out supernatural character of this plan of salvation and never try to interpret it in some naturalistic way. That's what the whole vast world tries to do with the plan of salvation. It's supernatural from beginning to end. The whole drama takes place *in* the *inner* man: The inner man is Jesus Christ. Jesus Christ *in you* is the hope of glory, so it hasn't a thing to do with something on the outside. The whole drama is taking place on the *inside*. And so, I have experienced it, and let me share with you what I have experienced.

But first of all, let me thank you for what you've done over the last few months in sharing with me your letters, your experiences in the use of God's law, and in your visions, your wonderful mystical experiences. This morning's mail brought three perfectly wonderful letters, all visions. Let me give you the highlights of two of them. One I will take at some future date, it's too long. But, I've told you in the past that the entire space-time history of the world is laid out and you and I only become aware of increasing portions of it, successively. You and I did not choose it. We were made subject unto futility, not willingly but by the will of him who subjected us in hope; and that hope was that you and I would be set free from this bondage to corruption, and obtain the glorious liberty of the children of God (Rom. 8:20). We find ourselves here, and we must admit we were born of the action of powers not our own, and this is the physical birth. Let us now admit that we are also born spiritually by the actions of powers beyond ourselves. We certainly didn't do it physically; we found ourselves here.

Don't let anyone tell you that by some effort on your part that you're going to be born spiritually into some wonderful world. It's all being done by the one who subjected us to this wheel of futility.

Now this morning's letter brought...this mail brought this letter. She said, "My mother died in '53. She was, I would say, seventy years old—-she might have been seventy-one, two, but she was in her late sixties or early seventies. I met her in my vision and mother was radiantly beautiful. She looked about thirty, and the joy, I can't describe the joy of my mother. She told me that when she left here she moved into the age or the year 3,804 at the age of twenty-one. She found herself twenty-one years old, living in the year 3,804. Then I asked her many questions. There were many interruptions by people and circumstances, but I tried to get as many questions across as I could. She seemed to be quite familiar with your teaching, although in this world where she left eleven years ago she never heard of you in any way whatsoever. But your name was not a strange thing to her in that circle where she now lives. I got the impression that she's married. And I tried to find my father and my brother Art to share with them my experience that I met mother. She told me she is living in a part of Pennsylvania. I asked her if death to her in that world of 3,804 is like death to us in this world, and she said it was the same thing. They feared it as we fear it, and they know it is the inevitable as we know it is the inevitable. Then she said, 'Our moral code, our ethical code is just like your code, same thing.' But she also said, 'We have no choice in that time sequence into which we are placed. I found myself twenty-one years old. At death being seventy, I was twenty-one in a time sequence that is the 3804th year A.D.'"

Now, in the Bible we're taught that there is nothing new under the sun: "Is there a thing of which it is said, 'See, this is new'? I tell you it has been already, in ages past. But there is no remembrance of former things, nor will there be any remembrance of things to come after, among those who will come later; for there is nothing new under the sun" (Eccles. 1:9-11). That's difficult for man to understand. And then he reads the Book of Ezekiel, where there are wheels within wheels within wheels, all turning. Then he reads the Book of Romans where you and I, not willingly, but subjected to the will of God for a *divine* purpose, that we would, being subjected, one day be freed from this futility and obtain, having gone through it, the glorious liberty of the children of God. And that liberty comes; and it is inaugurated by a divine event and we call that event resurrection.

But resurrection seen from a certain angle comes seemingly at the last, and it doesn't. The great mystery: It comes not at the end of history, it comes within history. This very night it could come to all of you, or to one of you. I do not know, no one knows. So when they asked the question, "When, O Lord?" he said, "It is not for you to know the times and the seasons that's fixed by the authority of God" (Acts 1:7), by his own authority. But wait for the promise of the Father, just wait—he has promised to redeem you. Redeeming you is redeeming himself, he's not redeeming another. It is *God* who fell asleep in the great creation called "the wheels and wheels within wheels" for educative and creative purposes. That by putting himself into the state likened unto death—it's not really death but it's so still, so altogether a sound sleep that it seems like death. But the ancient scripture, the Old Testament, does not use the word "resurrection," it implies it. But I would rather go back and use the term that is used in the Old Testament. The New uses the word "resurrection" throughout, and I love it, it's a marvelous term, and I use it here night after night. But in the old scripture, they only speak of "waking from sleep."

The 78th Psalm, which is a maschil, meaning special instruction, it is a recapitulation of the entire history of Israel, which is divine history. We come to almost the end, the 65th and 66th verses, it's a very long chapter, and then suddenly we're told that God or "the Lord God awoke as from sleep" (Psalm 78:65, 66). He awoke as from sleep and then he chose Judah and chose David. Then we come to the end of the glorious *awakening* of the being who was asleep, as the whole story was being told. You start in the beginning of that chapter, the 78th chapter, and he simply tells the traditions of the fathers: "I will open my mouth in a parable, and I will utter dark sayings from of old." And he tells all the stories of Israel, the horrors of the world, and the conquering of Jehovah—how he conquers, and he overcomes and he overcomes and he overcomes. Man still falls back, but God overcomes...and then the Lord God awakes. He awakes as from sleep. When he wakes from sleep, then the whole thing comes to an end.

Now we are all told to please tell it just as it happened. Don't embellish it, don't add to the word of God; don't take from the word of God. Well, the word translated word—in the New Testament the word logos—has as a root meaning "that which is behind the thing." That is, the sense or the meaning of the thing. So when we are told, "In the beginning was the word, and the word was with God, and the word was God" (John 1:1) that word logos, translated "word," means "that something that is the sense or the meaning behind the event, whatever that event is." So when you tell it, tell it clearly. So at the end of Luke we are told, "They related their own experience"; they told what had happened, not embellished, don't add to it. And that's why I don't quarrel with the use of the word resurrection, for it is part of the event. But I would go back to the 78th Psalm and rather use that terminology. For in my own case, when I was taken off the wheel of recurrence but left on it to tell the story, for I must tell it until this garment comes off; and when it comes off now it comes off for the last time. I do not find myself—like my friend Larry's mother who found herself in the year 3,804—I am through with the wheels within wheels within wheels. But I must remain on the present wheel, the year 1964, and tell it until that time when the garment is taken off, and this time for the last time; for I am not going through death any more.

But I must tell you, the night it happened to me, that force, I can't describe it save it was the most *intense* force. We call it an electrical force or charge. But, every morning I wake and I feel myself coming-to into this world and I wake. But *that* day, four years ago, I felt myself coming-to, and I thought it would be like the normal waking here. But it wasn't! The most intense vibration I've ever felt, and I'm waking alright, but I'm waking to find myself in a tomb, and the tomb, the sepulcher is my skull, an entirely different form of awakening. So they say in the 78th Psalm, "And the Lord God awoke as from sleep." I awoke from sleep, but it was a different waking from any waking I've ever had, that I have any memory of. I awoke to find myself entombed. So I can see the use of the word resurrection, for how could you possibly come out of a tomb, therefore resurrected, unless you were dead? But I had no sense of being dead; I felt I was waking from sleep. That's what the Old Testament teaches. So I was waking from sleep and I awoke to find myself in a tomb. So I could only then conclude if I am now in a tomb I *must* have been dead or someone *thought* me dead, because you don't put anyone in a tomb and seal it, as I was sealed in that tomb, unless you were dead. And so, the only sensation of being dead was that I am now in an *actual* sepulcher, a tomb.

And then you come out, and you come out and you are born from above. For this is the area of the tomb; it's your skull. So when you come out of your skull, as you're told in the Book of 1st Peter, "We are born anew by the resurrection of Jesus Christ from the dead" (1:3). Only Jesus Christ is ever awakened, ever resurrected; so everyone who resurrects or who is awakened to find himself entombed, he is Jesus Christ. He is now telling the story to the world, and they can accept it or reject it, it's entirely up to them. But he *must* tell the story, and it is so important that the story of Jesus and the salvation of God be told, and then let man respond to it. He will accept it, sometimes modified. Let him just reject it completely or let him in some way just toy with the idea.

But all the minds who hear the story from the one who has experienced it are like certain soils in the world, and he, the one who tells the story, is the sower who goes forth to plant, and he spreads the seed of truth. It falls sometimes on the highway. It falls on the highway and then the birds devour it (Mat. 13:3). The birds are simply all the great rumors: "After all, that man is just a normal person like yourself, he's been married twice, he has children, he knows what it is to know a person intimately, he is a meat eater, he drinks, he does all these things, so forget it." And so, quickly the idea is gobbled up. Another one hears it with *eagerness*, but the cares of the day are more than his attention can cope with, and so the seed, the idea, is choked. And then you go from one to the other and all different soils of the world. You may find in a gathering…but we're told in scripture you will always find a remnant. The remnant is considered ten percent, told in many ways in the Bible. There is always ten percent of any gathering who would listen to you, who will be the soil on which it can fall. It falls on *that* soil and brings forth a hundredfold, meaning that it will come forth. When it comes forth then he will have the identical experience—while you have been detached from the wheels of recurrence.

Now let me share with you another story that comes into this, this morning. This gentleman writes, he said, "I felt myself sitting on a nest. Of course it might have been prompted, said he, by the story you told of the dove that is now in your tree outside of your window, but I felt myself sitting on a nest as a dove would sit. Then I felt something move under me, like something alive, and I raised myself slightly, and then I looked and observed an egg. As I observed the egg, I felt the egg breaking. Suddenly the egg began to break and it broke, and out came *you*. You were about two inches tall but you were fully proportioned, everything was perfect in proportion. As you came out you said, 'Bill'— that's his name. And then he said to me, 'But Neville you are so little!' and I said to him, 'In God's creation everything begins small and then it expands and expands and expands' and at that, before my eyes you grew to immensity before my eyes. Then, relative to you I was the little one and you were this immense being standing before me. Then you went over to another nest, and there you took from this nest our mutual friend Jan Johnson and you brought her. And with your hand on Jan and your hand on me, you still remained this immensity, and Jan was my size relative to you. We are both the same little ones and you are this immense being, and you took us both, each in a hand, and together we walked up into the sky."

Now you have a vision, don't discard it. Go back into scripture and search diligently for something that would throw light on it. Now, let me give you, if you're in the audience tonight, the passage: it's the 7th chapter of Amos, the 2nd verse. So you go back and you read the ancient scripture for some foreboding, some shadow, some intimation of what you had in the depths. For are we not told, "If there be a prophet among you, I the Lord will make myself known unto him in a vision, and I will speak with him in a dream" (Num. 12:6). And so, you had it. Only God speaks to you in dream. There's only one source of dream in scripture and that source is God. So he's telling you something— go back into his word, his ancient scripture, and search. Well, in the 7th chapter you'll find it and these are the words: "O Lord God, forgive! How can Jacob...how can Jacob stand? He is so small!" (Amos 7:2). How can Jacob stand? He is so small! And then we are told in that same chapter the Lord forgives and said, "It shall not be" and then he allowed Jacob to stand. Now, the word Jacob means, by the concordance, our biblical concordance, "to enlarge, to expand." And there is no limit to the expansion, that's the word Jacob. It's called "the supplanter" on the surface, but in definition, it is "the capacity to enlarge and to expand." So, here is the little one, "How can Jacob stand? He is so small!" and then God repented, changed an attitude towards this that is coming out, and allowed it to expand to the limit. And there is no limit to expansion, there's only a limit to contraction; there's no limit to translucency, there's only a limit to opacity. So if my friend would go back into scripture and read it and search, he would find the secret of his vision, for I came out from that little egg.

Well, a few months ago, last year really, when the voice said to me, "The whole vast world is only for hatching," that's all that it is. The whole vast world is for hatching. And so, worlds within worlds, all turning, and so you slip from this age 1964 into 3804— and the purpose is only for hatching. At some moment in time man thinks now that this world is moving from moment to moment to moment in some linear progression. It isn't, it's a cycle. And so 1964 and 3804 are taking place at one and the same time. Columbus is now discovering this country for the first time on that wheel as it turns. Everything is turning at the same time...and we are inserted.

But she also said this to her son, "We have no choice in that time sequence into which we are placed, none whatsoever." Then you go back and read the scripture. "What is *that* in scripture?" she said that to him. And you go back and read the 8th chapter of the Book of Romans, that "The creature was made subject unto futility, not willingly but by reason of the will of him who subjected him in hope that the creature would be set free from this bondage to corruption and obtain the glorious liberty of the children of God" (verse 20). So *we* are subjected, but who subjected it? God, subjecting himself; it's only God. It is God who awakes from this fantastic creation and when he wakes, he has by this strange subjection increased his capacity to create. For the only purpose of it all is to develop one's creative power. And God is not absolute, as the world would call it, God is forever expanding. If God were absolute, the whole thing would be dead. God is *potentially* absolute and can create and create forever and forever. And God is man.

So to come back to this plan of salvation, the plan is in scripture. It begins...the whole thing is inaugurated with an event we call his resurrection from the dead; the first-fruits of those who slept; the first-born from the dead (Rev. 12:5). But the *first-born,* not the *only* born. So a great judgment is passed upon those who teach that the resurrection is past already. Read it in Paul's letter, the 2nd letter to Timothy, he said: There are those who are teaching that the resurrection is past and over. They are misleading the people, and in misleading them they're turning them from the faith (2:18). And he pronounces on them an uncompromising condemnation, for the resurrection has *started.* It is *taking* place. And moment after moment after moment you and I are being detached from this wonderful wheel where we were born out of it as it were. But being in it...if we were not in it, we could never develop beyond what we were prior to coming into it.

So we are told in scripture, the 20th of Luke: And the Sadducees—-the Sadducees are the wise people, they are the scientists of the day—-and they asked a question: Master, Moses in the law said that if a man marries leaving no offspring and has brothers, the brothers should marry the widow and raise up issue. Well, there were seven brothers; and the first one who's married, he died leaving no offspring; and the second took her to wife and he left no offspring when he died, then the third, and finally all of them married her, and then they all died, and then she died. Whose wife is she in the resurrection (verses 27-36)? They did not believe in the resurrection, for they thought it just couldn't be. They saw people die and that was the end of them, like all scientists of the world, or most of the scientists. And he said to this wise scientist, "You do not know the scripture. The sons of *this* age marry and are given in marriage; but those who are accounted worthy to attain to *that* age, to the resurrection from the dead, they neither marry nor are they given in marriage, for they can die no more; they are now sons of God and sons of the resurrection" (verse 34). Well, by that very statement he implies that they do, in dying, still die. So he tells you they die no more. Well, here he talks to someone who is awake, who must actually go through the experience of death, physical death, but he's telling you he dies no more. But these who seemingly die will continue to die, like my friend Larry's mother. She knows that they fear death as we here fear death; they experience death as we experience death. And she will slip from the year 3804, however long she lives there--it may be 3890 before she makes her exit from that wheel—-to find herself in a wheel that is behind it in so-called time. For all are moving together. So what is up and what is down if the wheel is moving? This is now the apex and this is the nadir; but if the wheel is moving, this that is now the apex becomes the nadir, and this is apex. So what is up and what is down when the wheels are moving within wheels within wheels? And it's all for the bringing out of this turning nest. It's a nest...for the voice said, "The whole vast universe is for hatching, only hatching."

This morning's mail can bring two letters from two entirely different friends of mine. They meet here socially, but only in the last few months they met each other in this room. Prior to that, my friend Larry has been coming here for years, and my friend Bill, who wrote the other letter, only came here last November. So they only met here in the last few months... and they dovetail, one bringing out the hatching story that was told me, and the other bringing out the wheels within wheels. So here, 3804 she told him as he understood it. She knows that she never heard of me here in the year 1964. When she died in '53, she never heard of me, I was completely unknown. But my works are known to her in the year 3804 and my name is not a stranger to her.

So it was *always* so. That's part of the game, that's part of the great play. And we come out of it in the most wonderful manner. But it begins... the whole thing is inaugurated by that event that we call resurrection—his resurrection from the dead. After the resurrection comes the birth, and after the birth comes that end of the book of the 78th chapter of Psalms. For as he awakes as one from sleep and becomes one who shouts as a man filled with wine, and he puts all of his enemies to rout, all adversaries are routed and they are everlastingly put to shame. The whole vast wheel is now put to shame as far as he who has awakened from it. For it subjected him to the most horrible things in the world. Then he awakens from it. Then he calls Judah, and then he calls David, and takes David from the flocks where he was taking care of the ewes, those that were "in lamb." And David is then the third one. You find him, and you discover him, and discovering him you know who you are. In the same chapter of Luke that we quoted earlier, when the Sadducees asked about resurrection, on the heels of his answer he then brings up the question and asks the question concerning David. And then he answers the question and tells you who David is. But no one sees it.

That's why I said at the beginning of this message tonight that this mystery of salvation, it appears in prospect so different from what it really is in retrospect. Who by reading the story would see it in prospect as it really is? It isn't as the world will tell you. Seeing it in prospect, it *took* place two thousand years ago and he is something unique on the outside, and you worship him on the outside. And that isn't so at all. It *takes* place in the *new* man. The new man is in every man being formed. When he's completed, when he's formed, then it unfolds like a flower *in* that new man who is in every man; for every man contains Jesus Christ. Well, "Do you not know that Jesus Christ is within you?" "Test him and see" (2 Cor. 13:5). Long before he unfolds these petals—which is simply the resurrection; and the birth; and the discovery of the fatherhood of God; and the ascent into heaven in the form of a serpent; and the descent of the dove upon him, where he's blessed and smothered with the affection of the Holy Spirit—*long* before that, test him and see if he's not within you. For by him all things were made, and without him was not anything made that is made (John 1:3). So test him and see.

So the Jesus Christ of scripture is the Jesus Christ *in* you, the only Jesus Christ; and he is your own wonderful loving human Imagination. There never was another Jesus Christ. God and God alone became man. In becoming man he's Jesus Christ. He now has to awaken. As he awakens, it's nothing but God. There's *no* intermediary between yourself and God, none whatsoever, as you're told in the 43rd and the 45th chapters of Isaiah: "I am the Lord thy God, the Holy One of Israel, your Savior...and besides me there is no savior" (verses 3, 5). No savior besides me and I am the Lord your God. He became man that man may become God. But in becoming man he and he alone goes through all the furnaces of affliction as he turns the wheels and wheel after wheel.

What determines the jump in time between 1953 when she made her exit and 3804? Strangely enough, she said, I awoke there; I was twenty-one. When he saw her he estimated her age at thirty, within the range of thirty... that would be the growth. So they still grow. They do exactly what you do, what I do, they have all the conflicts, but the year differs and all things differ. They make their exit through a grave to find themselves awake at a certain age in a different time-slot as it were. But this world here is the very *limit* of contraction. I have slipped into these worlds unnumbered times. When I speak of *this* world, not other worlds, ___(??), when I speak of this world, they are scared to death. This world to them is hell. They can't conceive of anyone recovering from this world, they can't.

I stepped into a world and here was Heine, and Heine, the brilliant German poet, essayist, artist, and Heine was instructing them. Heine said to me, "You know, they don't call this world of yours where you just came from, they don't call it Earth, they call it Woodland. They can't conceive that anyone could ever recover from that descent to Woodland." Well, now search the scriptures for it. Is it called Woodland? It is, in the 8th chapter of the Book of Mark (verse 24). You go back into Mark and the eye was opened. When the blind man, born blind, had his eyes opened he was asked, "What do you see?" and he said, "I see men; like trees walking." So they call this...if a man would ever come here, he'd become like a tree, a tree walking. So he would lose all identity, he would lose his humanity, he would lose what he is by coming here. This is the limit of contraction. No one wants to come here. And when I decided to return to this world, and had to go, for my time was come to depart from that world, and I began to say goodbye, they all rushed because they didn't believe my story. They said, "What an imaginative being! What stories he's talking about!" But I was telling them only the things of Earth but they wouldn't believe me. And they came...when I began to descend and a voice said "All down for Woodland" you should have seen the fear, sheer ghastly fear on their faces when I began to descend. Only one came with me and she was the old dowager, one who belonged to a certain group who had usurped my estate in my absence when I came here. These are fantastic stories but they're all true.

So we're living in a world...you think, well now, this is the most real world, and tomorrow we develop the present energy into something else, to something else, and it'll go on forever in one direction. Don't believe it! We're going to turn the wheel, the wheel is turning, but the wheel is so large, we can't see around the corner. Like you can't see...the ship goes off to sea and it disappears; it hasn't dropped off the Earth, it's the curvature of space. Well, time is curved just as space is curved, and so things disappear in time. We see them disappear in space by the curvature of space. Well, they disappear in time but it's only curved, and they're turning. But the wheels are wheels within wheels. So you see a large wheel, when will it be turned? And man has no memory. "So is there a thing of which it is said, 'See this is new'? It has been already, in ages past. But there's no remembrance of former things, nor will there be any remembrance of things to come after among those who come later." For there is nothing new under the sun, and how difficult that is to tell to anyone who knows in his own short little span of time that he's never seen *this* before.

I say, with anyone living in this world today, born when I was born, where we had candle light, and then we had oil lamps, and we had gas lamps, these little gas mantles, and then came the day we had electricity. So I go back in my short space of time of fifty-nine years back to my grandmother's day or your great-grandmother's day. For your great-grandmother can't go back beyond the time that I go back in my fifty-nine years, for I was put into a different space down the wheel. The space on which I was placed on this wheel of the same age, the 20th century, was so limited that my background would take you back, in your more marvelous way, back into the 19th century. I wasn't born then. I was born in 1905. Well, 1905 is the space where I was placed on the wheel, goes back in the comforts of life back into, well, say 1850. Can I not see them now cleaning the chimneys and cleaning all these things and all outdoor plumbing. That was Barbados, where the kitchen was on the floor, I mean the floor, the earth; I don't mean wood. And so, that is the space of the same wheel. So there are wheels within wheels within wheels. And then man is lifted off the wheel.

So when you have the experience, go back into the ancient scripture and seek and seek and seek. A great help is the Concordance, Strong's Concordance, and take Strong's Concordance, take a word and look it up. Don't take anything for granted, just look it up and see what it means. Take the word resurrection, for instance, and you think in terms of resurrection as someone resurrected physically. Hasn't a thing to do with that. The word, as defined in the Bible, in the Concordance, means "to rise up; to stand upright; to awake from sleep." Read it—to awake from sleep. Well, I know in my own case exactly what happened: I awoke from sleep. But the awakening was something entirely different: It was the inauguration of the grand unfolding of God's plan of salvation. For, that was the first event, and on the heels of it came the child, and the men who saw the symbol called the child, and I took the child. And then, after that, came the others, one after the other.

So, resurrection as defined is "to awake from sleep." But I didn't know I was asleep until that moment in time. I always thought I went to bed at night and woke in the morning, so when I woke in the morning I was awake. I didn't know that until that moment in time back in 1959 I had been sound asleep, and sound asleep in a tomb where someone placed me there because to them I must have been dead. For, you're placed in a tomb only because you're dead. So everyone in this world who is walking through the world, who will make their exit from this world, are just as sound asleep; and they are to those who behold this death, dead. So Blake tells us of the great eternal ones who contemplate death and say, "What seems to be to them, *is,* to those to whom it seems to be, and is productive of the most dreadful consequences to those to whom it seems to be, even of despair and eternal death; but divine mercy steps beyond and redeems man in the body of Jesus" (Blake,*Jer.*,Plt.36). Well, there's *only* the body of Jesus, and that body of Jesus is in man.

So he awakens that body, and as it awakens, then these things begin to unfold within him, and the very first act is the resurrection. That inaugurates the entire process: His resurrection from the dead; then comes his birth from above; then comes his discovery of the fatherhood of God through the son called David; then his ascent into heaven in serpentine form; and then the descent of the dove who smothers him with affection, which is he never in eternity will leave him, it smothers him and remains upon him. And everyone goes through the identical experience. So this is God's plan of salvation. Everyone will be saved, for the simple reason everyone is now being occupied by God. God is only redeeming himself. And before he entered into the wheels that turn, he had planned his own pathway of return and his return is simply the development of his own creative power.

Now let us go into the Silence.

* * *

Q: I have two questions. First, on this wheel of recurrence is there any retention of spiritual progress? And, secondly, what authority is behind the Bible Concordance so that one would know that they were reading something...

A: Alright, first of all, take the second. *James Strong's Concordance* which is called the exhaustive concordance, I personally think of the many concordances that I have that it is the greatest, the most exact translation of the original meaning of the words. He spent forty years compiling it, it was not done overnight. And he took these ancient manuscripts and compared them and compared them and compared them, and came up, after forty years, with this fantastic work. And it is truly an *exhaustive* concordance. So, if you...you don't need to know Greek or Hebrew because you simply look up the little number that is next to the word. You look the word up in English, at the extreme end of the column you find a little number; then you turn, if it's a Hebrew word that is in the Old Testament, you look up the number in the Hebrew section; if it is in the New Testament, you look up the number in the Greek section. And it simply defines the word for you as it was *originally* intended, because words change their meaning from year to year. Even in this century we have changed words; in fact, today more than ever we have what is known as newspeak. When the Russians use the word democracy they don't mean what you and I mean, but everything is "democracy" there. You have no choice in the matter... you vote for one man, and you simply put your vote in and affirm what a very small minority will tell you the populace wants. That's "democracy." It's not my concept of it, yet they use the word all day long. And so, all through the world words change their meanings, and so we go back to the original intention of the prophet when he used the word. But I find that *James Strong's Concordance* gives me the best light on these words.

Now to come back to your first question again…

Q: I asked if you're on this wheel of recurrence is there any retention of spiritual progress?

A: My dear, by the vision of this gentleman and his mother, certainly there was infinite joy, beauty beyond measure. He said, "All the pictures of my mother taken of her when she was a young girl and a young lady don't compare to the beauty of my mother today. I wanted so much to share her beauty and her joy with my brother Art and my father, but the interruptions, the people came through; and then circumstances changed and I couldn't pump her with enough questions." Yet she was quite willing to answer these questions. So there's a certain retention, because God is simply not a God of retribution, he's a God of love. God is infinite love. And the only purpose is to go through this play and to come out as the one who is the author of the play and then the actor in the parts. God plays all the parts.

Q: In the 65th and 66th of Psalm 78, the Lord God awakes, and chose Judah and chose David, do we hear of Judah as judgment?

A: Well, Judah means "praise." But Judah—bear in mind, there are so many facets of it—-Judah is the fourth son of Jacob, and Jacob is the little one that she said he regretted and Jacob began to expand. The word means "to expand without limit". No limit to the expansion of the little one who comes out to expand as *God*. He was contracted to the limit, and now as he breaks the shell, as Blake brings out, "At length for hatching ripe he breaks the shell." But now you can't limit him to the little one who broke the shell. Let him expand forever and forever without limit until some future date when he conceives a new play of contraction for the purpose of developing his creative talent, and then break it once more, and then expand forever and forever. But, Judah is the fourth, and as we told you the last time, the fourth doesn't necessarily mean the fourth child of the womb of woman. It could be the fourth in your class, the fourth that came through the door tonight, the fourth in any sense, the fourth into a restaurant. I mean four, four means "the door." It's the fourth letter of the Hebrew alphabet, which is Daleth. He said, "I am the door. Anyone who comes through any other way is a thief and a robber." One must go through simply by having the experience *themselves.* And so, I am…when he called me, he didn't say "Neville is my father," he called me Father. And I didn't say, "So Neville is your father," I said, "I am." It's "I am your Father."

So, I am the door. He was standing against an open door, and there's this open door, and David is looking out upon a pastoral scene. Here was the symbol of the door and he calls me Father, but he doesn't say Neville. I don't speak of so-and-so as his father, *I am* his father. You will say not "Tom is his father," I am his father. Everyone will say "I am his father." So he calls *us* Father and that I am the door. The door is the fourth letter of the Hebrew alphabet, Daleth. He said, I am the door; anyone who comes in towards the sheepfold in any other way is a thief and a robber (John 10:9). And he was looking out on a pastoral scene, and he's called the shepherd. For when they came to get him, they said, he's out with his flocks and he said, "I will not sit down until you bring him in, bring him in. And as he was brought in, the voice of the Lord said, "That is he. Rise and anoint him" (1 Sam. 16:12). The Lord's anointed, his Son, who calls you Father, therefore, you are the Lord. He calls you Father; therefore, everyone must have it themselves. If they don't have it themselves, then they're still on the wheel, and they'll make extravagant claims and all kinds of things because there are false prophets in the world, too. As told us in Ezekiel and Jeremiah: There are those who will not feed my sheep. They'll feed my sheep only to take from my sheep to fatten themselves. And so, they make all the false claims in the world—-that they are sent, that they are this, they are the other—-and they are all thieves and robbers, speaking without experience and not believing one word of scripture. But this is a nice little gimmick as far as they're concerned. But that's part of the play too. Let them go...they'll make their little exit, and all people their exit, and then they move automatically without choice on their part into that wheel necessary for their awakening, whatever it is.

Q: Does the word valley have any significance?

A: Valley?

Q: ___(?) any similar word to valley?

A: Certainly. The Bible is full of the use of the word valley. We go down to the valley of death. The dark convolutions of the brain are called valleys and out of that we come. I would have said of everyone here, don't despair, don't despair because God has planned your redemption, everyone's redemption. I would only plead with you to be honest, rather die than be dishonest about it. If you can't explain it, alright, be quiet. Don't have to explain it. If someone asks of you and you can't explain it, don't make up something, just, alright, be quiet. You have your belief, you believe that this is God's plan of redemption, well, believe it! And if some wiseacre tries to dethrone you through argument, alright, leave him alone, perfectly alright. That's what the Sadducee tried when he said, "Master, (this is the story)...whose wife is she?" and he thought he could dethrone him. So I would say to everyone, don't be concerned; just live in hope that this will quickly awaken within you.

I'm thrilled beyond measure, an audience of this size, when this morning's mail could bring me three letters—-one I didn't touch tonight it's too long—-from three young fellas in this audience. Well, why, what percentage is that of these visions? If they enclosed in this morning's mail a large big check, may I tell you, it couldn't be equal to their letters. If they wrote me a letter where they thanked me for my time here and enclosed a large check, that couldn't compensate. That would be nothing compared to the letter that they wrote in which they told me their vision and shared with me their visions. That's wealth beyond the wildest dream of this world...that vision of three young men in an audience the size of this.

Goodnight.

GOD HAS A PURPOSE

5/22/64

Tonight's subject is "God Has a Purpose," an *infinite* purpose, and no one will thwart it. But within the framework of his purpose, you and I could have *unnumbered* objectives, and no one, really, could thwart it if we really understand his law; the law that was given to us...how we, too, can realize these purposes. A purpose, in a strict sense, is a deliberately conceived plan proposing a certain action, or a plan to be executed within that action.

Now tonight let us take it first in the most simple way. Many months ago I asked a very simple question, "Why, why did you create the universe, just why?" I never doubted that there is a God, for I've stood in the presence of the Ancient of Days...but why? And the voice came from the very depth, "Hatching, just hatching." So the very end of it all is hatching. Hatching what? He's hatching out himself. Who by looking at a little worm, one of these little caterpillars, could ever predict his future as a painted butterfly? Who by looking at an egg, not knowing the contents, could predict the beauty of the peacock or maybe another beautiful, beautiful bird? Who by looking at man could predict Jesus Christ? Who in this world by looking at man could see that man is but the egg and out of man will come Jesus Christ? Not one will fail, for his purpose is that not one will be lost in all my holy mountain.

But within the framework of his purpose, you and I can take the same technique and we cannot fail. Now, it is for *hatching*. Well, we are not nesting correctly if we ever fall asleep in any nest *other* than the feeling of the wish fulfilled. For at night all the birds return to their nests. Through the day they have intervals upon that nest. You go out to make a living in the world of Caesar, and you may forget, and numberless things may happen that cause you to even forget for a moment that there is such a thing as a nest. But you must remember that there is on that nest that you built, as you prepared it or you conceived it, it's a deliberate constructive plan on which you will sit. As we are told in Habakkuk, "I will stand upon my watch and see what the Lord will say unto me, and what I will answer." The next verse, Every seed, really, has its own appointed hour—for he's telling us that all the visions, well, the vision is simply your little seed or your egg—"The vision has its own appointed hour; it ripens, it will flower. If it be long, then wait; for it is sure and it will not be late" (Hab. 2:3).

For, there are different time intervals for all the different eggs of the world. I may have an egg based upon a yearly income, or an egg based upon a weekly income, or a monthly income. If I take it over a long period of time, well, then wait. If the first day, week, month or even the first six months are slow but I am faithful to that egg which is a yearly income, at the end of the year I will look back upon the most fantastic year I've ever had. So in the course of a day I will fly from that nest and do all kinds of things and forget; but at night let me return to that nest and keep that seed warm, keep that egg warm. And then do, as we're told in Habakkuk, "I will stand upon my watch, and I will watch to see what the Lord will say unto me and what I will answer." Well then, the Lord is simply the whole vast world pushed out, for the Lord is *I AM.* So I am sitting on this state and then I look upon my world, my world is myself fragmented, and that is what the Lord is saying unto me. When I think of my friends and see them mentally in my mind's eye, what are they saying? Are they congratulating me? Am I accepting their praise graciously? Well, then I will now sit upon this nest and fall asleep in this assumption, in this state; for I am standing upon my watch and watching to see and to hear what the world (the Lord) will say unto me and what I will answer. What is my response when they say what they must say seeing me as their friend so successfully lifted up in this world?

So if you will do that, night after night, no power in the world can stop me from bringing forth from that egg—which is simply my assumption—all that it is implying...if I will do it. I may leave it and not really sit upon the egg. We have seen that in all the barnyards of the world, for eggs are dropped and no one thinks in terms of ever warming them or incubating the egg. But you and I, if I know what purpose really means—purpose in the strict sense is a *deliberately* conceived *plan* proposed for action or executed in it. I plan a campaign. And that action...but not only the action, something must be executed in it. Why am I planning the campaign, to sell merchandise? I plan a campaign or plan the campaign of war, why?—that I may be victorious in this action. So I will execute this plan in the action that I have now proposed. Well, the action is simply this night I will stand upon my watch and watch to see what and hear what he will say unto me—and how I will answer, knowing in my heart that the vision has its own appointed hour, it ripens, it will flower; and if to me it seems long then let me wait, for it is sure and it will not be late. So I simply stand on my nest and go to sleep in that state. If in the course of a day I can't come back to it too often, it wouldn't addle. If I am faithful night after night, it will not addle.

Just before I came on the platform, not more than one minute before, my very dear friend, who is here this night, she said, about two years ago a friend of hers won what she called—-I have never heard of this award before until tonight—-it's called a Lulu, it's like an Oscar in the fashion world. And so, it is given to some lady in the fashion field, whether you be in department stores, TV, radio, well, any aspect of displaying your fashion. She said when the friend won it, "I'll win one too." She did it just as lightly as that. But she did something about it and tonight she brought it, it's in her purse, this lovely Lulu. It's a little statuette, a first prize for *her* work. Only recently has she joined the May Company, and so for the May Company she's been doing all of their displays, all of their advertising, and she won the Lulu. Just did it naturally. And this is not just for this city, every state west of the Mississippi is within that picture of the Lulu. So I tell you, sit upon your nest and let it hatch out. Everything comes out this way, but if you don't have a definite objective, well, you can't, so that you either succeed or that you fail.

But *God* has a purpose and his purpose is to bring forth from man Jesus Christ, and Jesus Christ is God himself. He's bringing out of us Jesus Christ. *He* will not fail. As we are told, "As I have planned it, so shall it be; as I have purposed, so shall it stand" (Is. 14:24). And, "the anger of the Lord will not turn back until he has executed and accomplished the intents of his mind. In the latter days you will understand it clearly" (Jer. 23:20). In the latter days you will understand why you went through all the things in this world...because out of you is coming, actually coming, Jesus Christ. He could not emerge from man were he not actually present in man. So at this very moment he's buried in every being in the world, and God is bringing him forth. When he brings him forth, he brings forth himself, and it's you. But while he is bringing him forth, he has given us his own talent: The talent of using our Imagination to create everything in this world.

A letter given me this past week from this young lad who is here tonight, he said, "I found myself in the high school, and my teacher—-my teacher was the Latin teacher, her name was Miss Divine—-and as I entered, there was an examination taking place. And so I sat, and on the board were two columns; there were twenty-one problems. On the right side there were from zero to ten, say, eleven problems; on the left side from eleven to twenty. Down in the middle of the column on the right side there were two words that I had to define. They were separated by a word which I couldn't quite discern, but the two words were crucifixion and resurrection. The left hand column, there were from eleven to twenty, and I couldn't discern the words save two, and the words were map and route. And so, I took my paper, I began to define crucifixion; and I defined it by quoting the words of Paul from the 2nd chapter of Galatians: 'I have been crucified with Christ; it is not I who live, but Christ who lives in me'" (verse 20). That's how he put down the definition of crucifixion.

Then he discovered that his paper wasn't big enough for all the answers, so he turned to Miss Divine—-bear in mind the name of this teacher, Divine—-so he turned to Miss Divine and asked her for permission to go and get a piece of paper. She said to him, "Go to my desk and get a piece of paper" so he did. He came back with a larger sheet. On his way back, he realized that in his pockets were all the answers to all these questions on a smaller piece of paper. So he sat down and tried to transfer from the smaller piece of paper to the test paper all of the answers. And then, suddenly, the test was halted, and then all the test papers were collected. Then Miss Divine began to read the answers as she got all these test papers together. And she turned first to the left hand column to the words map and route and she said: "Neville Goddard has the map and the correct route. If anyone wants the map and the correct route, let them go to Neville Goddard." With that it was all dismissed, and then he took his papers and tore them up into shreds, and started towards the exit to throw them into the waste basket. She asked him for the papers. At first he said no, and then she glared at him, and with that he gave her these torn pieces of paper. Then with his books in his hands, towards the exit he walked out saying to himself, "I am expelled."

Then, it was early in the morning, so he woke, wrote the whole thing down in detail as I've just told it to you, and then fell asleep. And this is the epilogue, the epilogue is marvelous. He heard a voice and the voice was the voice of the broadcaster, the announcer of the Angels, the baseball game. Bear in mind, they're the Angels, not the Dodgers, they're the Angels. And this Don Wale(?) said, "This is the fourth game that the Angels have played in the last twenty-four hours, and there are 400 people present." The fourth game in twenty-four hours and there are 400 people present. Well, 400 is the numerical value of the twenty-second letter of the Hebrew alphabet, which is Tau, and it has the symbolical value of a cross. Remember, he defined only one word—he defined crucifixion. The 400 were present. So he defined the crucifixion in his test. And then, there were four games, that's the fourth letter, which is Daleth, which is a door. He said, "I am the door. Anyone who comes through any other way other than through this door (and I am the door) is a thief and a robber" (John 10:9). Twenty-four in the *mystical* Hebrew is a horse, it's ___(??), and that is the mind. The whole thing is coming out of the mind of man. It's the mind that man has to control. That is the horse, the unbridled beast that must be broken in by man and ridden by man himself. And so, he found the horse, told in the form of a number: in twenty-four hours. He found the door—"I am the door"—in the form of a number: four games. You wouldn't play four games in twenty-four hours. And then there were 400 people present. They do get very, very small audiences, I grant you that, but not 400...they haven't fallen that low. But bear in mind, they were Angels, they were not Yankees; not these, Angels. All of this is symbolism.

Well, what strikes me forcefully in the entire picture is not that Miss Divine—there's the name, she's the teacher—said that Neville Goddard has the map and the correct route…I love that in the picture. But what really to me is significant in the entire vision is his quote from Paul in the definition of the crucifixion. For when I stood in the presence of the Ancient of Days and he asked me, "What is the greatest thing in this world?" I, too, quoted Paul. I answered in the words of Paul, "Faith, hope and love, these three abide; but the greatest of these is love" (1 Cor. 13:13). At that, infinite love embraced me, and I fused with him and became one forever with the body of God. And I wonder, after his letter to me, do we all answer in the words of Paul? I'm asking a question. He shared with me his experience. I hope you will share with me your experience when a similar vision takes place with you, for I answered in the words of Paul and he answered in the words of Paul. He answered the one question, the crucifixion, and it came up in the epilogue, there were four hundred people present at the Angel game, and that's the crucifixion.

And so, when you think the greatest figure in Christendom is Paul, really. Who has done for Christianity what Paul has done? You ask yourself a thousand times over, who then is the one who first awoke? Who *is* he that awoke? If we read the gospels, and the Evangelists are Matthew, Mark, Luke and John, anonymous names, unknown, completely unknown; no one knows who they are, and then you ask yourself this question concerning this fantastic creature that is Paul (the little one). Paul means "little," and he is the "little one." Then he tells you that "I am a descendant of Abraham, of the tribe of Benjamin." Benjamin means "son of the right hand." "The Lord said unto my Lord, Sit thee at my right hand until I make of thy enemies a footstool for thee" (Heb. 1:13; Mat. 22:44). You ask...all kinds of things go through the mind concerning who is this one that we call "the little one" that is Paul.

He never denied his faith. In fact, he insisted that his religion was not a *new* religion it was the fulfillment of one as old as the faith of Abraham. He never gave up the Hebrew religion; he only saw the flower, the fulfillment of it. To him the whole thing was the unfolding of all that was prophesied and promised to Abraham. So, Christianity was simply the fulfillment of the *faith* of Abraham. We have in the western world these three great religions, the religion of Islam which is complete kismet, fatality, complete. They call themselves...most of them are named, and there are 400,000,000 of them, Abdullah (slave of Allah, complete slave of Allah). Then comes this great rock, the Hebrew religion, and it begins with faith, Abraham. He believed the promise made by God, God *would* fulfill, and he was able to fulfill it, and the promise was an heir.

All the way through, the promise continues in changing form. "I will raise up after you a son that will come forth from your body. I will be his father and he shall be my son" (2 Sam. 7:12). That's the promise made to us: Raise up out of us a son that will be God's son. God will be his father and that which he pulls out of us will be his son, something so unlike the form that we see here; and unlike the form called man as the butterfly is unlike the caterpillar; as unlike this glorious winged creature to the egg. So we are told in Philippians: "Our country is in heaven, from which we await a Savior, the Lord Jesus Christ, who will reform and change our lowly body to be like his glorious body, by the power by which he is able even to subject all things to himself" (Phil. 3:20). The word translated "change to be like" means, literally, "to be of one form with him." Actually, something is coming out of every being in this world that is Jesus Christ. And the form is that glorious form that is the form of God: "Return unto me the glory that was mine, the glory that I had with thee before that the world was" (John 17:5). So he gives man himself. He brings out of man, his egg, himself. He is hatching it out, and *he* is faithful.

All he's asking of us that we be as faithful or *try* to be as faithful as we can to our modified desires as he is to his grand scheme, which is to bring forth out of man, himself. For, he's bringing out of man, himself. No one's going to fail because we aren't doing it. But while he's bringing it out, he's asking us to take the talent that he gave us, while be are being turned over and over in this world, to take that talent and become what we want to be in this world. Do it for ourselves or do it for others. You can take any being in this world if you are faithful. And the faithful time is when you have the unbroken few hours of the night, just as you are settling down to retire into the deep, and you know the day's over, and you're simply going to relax into some state. Take that moment and then stand upon your watch and view the world to see what the Lord is going to say unto you. The Lord, being the fragmented I AM, everything that you're doing, you're saying, "I am doing it." So, that's the Lord viewing his fragmented self. And see what it is saying to you, is it sympathizing? Get off that nest! Is it now with great *empathy*? Alright, good! Are they rejoicing with you, all of them, because of your good fortune? *Stay* on that nest, and go sound asleep viewing the world from your watchtower, knowing in your heart that what you are sitting on mentally has it's own appointed hour. It is ripening and it will flower; and if to you because of your anxiety it seems long, you know you must wait, for what you're doing is *sure* and it will not be *late*.

So we're told that his promise is faithful and sure. These promises are not some little thing done because of some emergency; they were done of old, and they are faithful and sure we are told. Not something that suddenly, because of some plan in the world of man, that God is now instituting some emergency thinking. No, his plans are of old. Man is allowed all the freedom in the world to make all the mistakes in the world, perfectly alright. He will correct it. He doesn't condemn man, he corrects man. He corrects all kinds of things but allows us within the framework of his purpose to do anything in this world that we desire. He doesn't have the same code that man tries to impose upon man. He allows us quite a wide range of everything in this world.

So I say, God has a purpose and his purpose is to bring forth himself out of his egg called man. But while the egg called man is living in the world of Caesar, he allows it to use a certain talent; the talent is the gift he gave of himself which is man's Imagination. Man can take his Imagination and create anything in this world. You think of this story of the Lulu. For here is a lady who only recently started working for the May Company and how many artists must there be between the Mississippi and the West Coast who simply wanted that? This is a fist prize, this is not something down into the bottom of the barrel, this is the Lulu. I never heard of it until tonight, so she brought it in her purse and picked it up. It's like an Oscar. It is an Oscar to those who are in her profession. And this covers the entire water front; this is not confined to department stores, it isn't confined to TV or to radio or to moving pictures but to every aspect of the art world where ladies are involved in fashion. And she gets it! She's only been there a few months and she gets it, because she wanted it…and she knows the principle; and the others who I think by her own confession will be equally talented, they didn't know the principle. So they didn't sit upon the nest and simply view it as she did. So she sat upon the nest.

So I say to every one of you, don't get off that nest until it hatches out, and then go for a bigger nest and a still bigger nest. If anyone tells you that you shouldn't want things, turn a deaf ear to them; completely turn a deaf ear to them. You're not going to be enslaved by things if you know this principle. You'll get things and be quite willing to drop them on the way. But you'll simply test your talent. You're exercising your talent; and a talent that isn't exercised is like the limb that is not exercised, it atrophies, it does. And so, day after day you must take your dreams, your noble purposes, and simply settle down and nest them and simply bring them to pass in your world. Every one will hatch out, for we are told, "Not one is lost in all my holy mountain." Not one child born of woman will ever fail to bring forth what God has demanded; and God demands only one thing: "I will raise up out of you a son that will come forth from your body. I will be his father and he shall be my son." That son will say of his father, "I and my Father are one," because he is the creative power and wisdom of God (John 10:30). So when he comes forth, personified, he will say of the very power that drew him out of that body, I am the power and wisdom of God (1 Cor. 1:24). I *am* he. You *are* he. And everyone will come out...not one will fail.

So I tell you, try it. Try it over and over and over...and don't ever admit failure, don't for one moment admit it. The most impossible thing in this world, still try it. For here, we will not accept paganism, we will start with Israel, that's where the whole creative world starts, really, and it's based upon faith. Christianity is the fulfillment. If an orthodox Jew will not believe that it happened, alright...he will eventually. At least he has the faith that it is *going* to happen. But I tell you that it *has* happened. But I will go back now to that definition of my friend Tom with the crucifixion, and go to another aspect of it, which you find in the 6th chapter of Romans. He took his from the 2nd chapter of Galatians, but the 6th chapter of Roman: "If we have been united with him in a death like his, we shall *certainly* be united with him in a resurrection like his" (verse 5). So now Paul, the same grand Paul, is now saying to his, what he calls "my son Timothy," and he said: There are those who are teaching that the resurrection is past already. They are misleading the people and turning them from their faith (2 Tim. 2:18). His condemnation of those who said it was past already, once and for all, is, well, you can't quite describe the condemnation, uncompromising. It's *not* past once and for all. It *took* place, it is *taking* place, and will *continue* to take place until everyone gives up that Son of God. It's the Son of God *in man* that is buried that makes man alive. Were it not for the Son of God in man, then there would be no living being in this world.

So if I have been crucified with him, alright, I have enjoyed that death. I'm crucified with him, and in that crucifixion I have union with him. Now, certainly, I will also be united with him in a resurrection like his. Well, I can tell you from experience it has happened to me. So I know the joy of the union in my crucifixion with him, and I now experience the joy in my resurrection with him. It's one. I do not differ from any child that walks the face of this earth, we're all one. I can't share with you that body which he has transformed to be like his glorious body. I tried it once and didn't quite succeed in revealing the glory of the body that is one…but she is not far off from seeing it for herself. But here, it's the most fantastic glory...the joy of this body. Human face yes. I will recognize you?—certainly, forever and forever. But I can't describe the glory of the body; it's something entirely different.

So we are subject to this humiliation of these bodies of blood, bodies of flesh...but not for long. And so, if someone this night...like my friend Tom who has had this experience...and you will say "Well, why should he have it?" No one knows Tom's background. No one knows how long he has been treading this winepress in this world. No one knows it. And so, if in many ways you may think he is young or even limited in expression, don't! Because the minute it happens to one, limitations fall away. These things that seem so wonderful here that we acquired through labor will not be used, because it's all then a creative power in operation. So don't judge anyone. And may I tell you, if perchance you should entertain such a thought, bear in mind the story of Job. Job's story is the story of man. Here is the most cruel experiment ever performed on an innocent being, that which is performed on Job. Job in the very end didn't condemn the Lord. He thought the Lord was justified in everything that he did. And then he turned from himself, for he felt sorry for himself, and he prayed for his friends, and as he prayed for his friends his own captivity was lifted (Job 42:10). So turn from self to a friend and wish them well. Well, that's really what love is, to wish a friend well, and *sincerely* wish him well. May I tell you what will happen to you? You'll simply bloom. Out of the nowhere things that are now hidden from you will come into view and they're all yours by sincerely wishing a friend well. So when Job turned from himself and prayed for his friends his own captivity was lifted. So that is what we're here to do. Turn to someone this night, I don't care who he is, who she is, and see them in your mind's eye in some blessed state. And feel the *thrill* that will be yours as a friend because they *are* what you're now representing them to yourself as being.

Someone once said, and for years I had to agree with them and even to this day I would go along with them, that if someone is hurt, a thousand will rush in sympathy; and if some member of the neighborhood falls heir to a fantastic fortune, you don't find the joy, you find envy. So we have so many words to express sympathy, compassion and all these things, but possibly only one which is not a good, not a good word in a sense because it isn't known. You speak of empathy, how many people even know what the meaning of the word is when you use it? So it isn't used. It's used in cultured society among the educated. They know the meaning of the word but they don't use it, because it's not in use. They will use it in their writing and someone reading their works will rush to the dictionary for definition of the word, because we're not given to rejoicing with those who have good fortune smile upon them.

In fact, one of the disciples whose name is only mentioned among the twelve, he's not mentioned saying that he's one of the twelve, is Thaddeus, and Thaddeus means "praise." It's so little exercised by man that there is no story of Thaddeus in the Bible. He's only called. He is called...he has to be part of the awakened man, for the awakened man must have Thaddeus within him awake; but in the actual story he isn't there. He's only named among them, and he's the tenth disciple, and the word is praise. How many of us can rejoice when we hear of the good fortune of another? We wonder, "Why didn't it happen to me?" That's the reaction. You read in the morning's paper someone won $150,000 with a two dollar bet, some daily double in Florida or someplace or down in Caliente, and instantly you say, "I wish I had it!" No one thinks of the joy in that household, that moment when he goes home to his family with a hundred thousand dollars in cash. We think, "Why didn't I make it?" So really empathy is an empty word until it becomes so alive that we use it as frequently as we use sympathy. We can sympathize with one who lost his home because he had a hot tip and put the house down on the horse that didn't come in. We can sympathize with his wife at home who must now give up the house, but we cannot rejoice with her when he comes home with the fortune. So Job rejoiced in the good fortune of his friends, and as he did so his own captivity was lifted.

So to come back to our theme which is God has a purpose. That end you can accept as Abraham accepted it. He heard the promise, he believed it, and then in spite of the hell of the 400 years in this land where he was a stranger, where he was a slave of slaves, he still remembered the promise. He believed the one who promised was capable of fulfilling that promise. And then, "He rejoiced that he was to see my day; he saw it and was glad" (John 8:56)...and went through hell faithful to the promise made to him by God. And so, you become *that.* I tell you he's coming out of you, one that is completely glorified, and the body he wears is the body of God. Not some little tiny thing...something is coming out of *all* of us that is the most glorified thing in this world. It's an immortal body and the body is the body of God.

But, before it comes out and you wear it and you are one of the immortals, while you are still telling the story and moving through the world of Caesar, use the same talent to play your own part of sitting on your nest. Night after night, take the most glorious idea. If you're in business, augment it, double it, treble it. Let no one tell you that you're too hungry, you're too anxious, forget what they're saying. You double it! You're making x number of thousands a year, double it, you treble it, and test God and see if it doesn't work. And so, when you go to bed this night you sit on your nest of an income and you name it; and then stand upon your watch and see what God is saying to you. And God speaks to you through the faces of every person in this world that you contemplate. So you think of me, and you've just written me the most fantastic letter of your good fortune, and hear me tell it from the platform. So think of me this night telling from the platform *your* good fortune. Think of your mother, if you have one in this world or if not in this world—she's still in this world, you know, for the world is simply sections within sections—so think of her. Don't think because she's not physically present she's not aware of it. Think of her and let her see your good fortune. Let all of your friends see your good fortune. And go to bed sitting on that view of things, which view implies the fulfillment of your desire. And see how it comes to pass. It may take twenty-four hours, some things hatch out in twenty-four hours, some things hatch out in a week, some things in a month, six months, a year. I do not know the time interval of your desire. But your desire, your mere wish is an egg, you laid it. Your wish...you laid an egg…I mean in the true creative sense, not in the theatrical sense. And so, you have an egg and then you simply sit upon your egg and bring it to pass. Let the whole thing come out in this fabulous world of yours.

Now let us go into the Silence

* * *

Q: Neville, you said last week, last Tuesday that we are inserted into different time intervals as these wheels turn. They're not turning together, they're turning and we're inserted. Now, once before you told us that once you ___(?) like this man, your example of a man putting coal down the cellar, he's always doing that. Now I can't reconcile that, would you explain it? I mean, if we're inserted...we leave this sphere and are inserted into another wheel, are we still doing that?

A: No. First of all, the lady is asking a question based upon an experiment that William Ramsey made under a controlled withdrawal from this world. William Ramsey took ether, chloroform, and in his presence were nurses and secretaries, and they gave him these doses of chloroform as he asked for them, and he withdrew from this surface mind. As he went deeper and deeper into himself he recorded audibly for his secretary to put down what he was experiencing. And he said, I saw—-and he was in London and he saw a man delivering coal to a certain home, and said he to his secretary, "At this moment in time, one would think that that man was delivering coal because someone ordered coal; but at this degree of withdrawal, I would say that that man is delivering coal because he is part of the eternal structure of the universe. He is *always* at that moment in *time* delivering coal. So if you went back to, say, he delivered coal on the morning of July the 6th, on July the 6th of that year of that wheel, he is *always* delivering coal." So when Hamlet enters the stage, at a certain moment when he has the argument with his mother and tries to persuade her to assume a virtue if she has it not, he is always at *the* moment of the play. He doesn't bring it in at the first act; he brings it in after the murderous thing that the uncle and his mother contrived. So he does not ask the mother to assume a virtue until he knows the mother is in need of that radical change of attitude. So he couldn't come before. But at that moment of the play, he's always trying to persuade her to change her attitude. That's the whole vast structure. But we are not the garment that we are wearing. We are that being that God is bringing forth. On the surface we are no more than the eggs; but buried in us is God and God is bringing forth himself, his creative power which is personified in scripture as his son.

Q: ___(??) where Jesus rose from the tomb and Mary approached him and he said, "Do not yet touch me, I have not yet ascended to my Father."

A: Did you hear the question? "Do not touch me, I have not yet ascended to my Father." First of all, this is a mystery. We can't see it as a man getting out of any tomb…can't do that. The drama takes place in you, Bill, the whole thing takes place in you. *After* it takes place in you and you're completely ascended, everything that has happened as told in scripture or the gospel is only a revelation of the risen Christ. And so, in the appearance of a man, that great title "Lord" is conferred upon any man to whom Christ has risen. So he's telling the story. The world is now his Mary as it were. And they're trying to...you can't touch it through the flesh, you can't touch it in any way whatsoever. I have ascended but not completely until the body is taken off. And so, ___(??) while one is still in the body, while he still tells the mystery as he experienced it, let no one try to touch him to make something spectacular out of him. This man doesn't need to be worshipped; he said, "Worship *God*. I'm a man just like you." So he's asking the whole vast world not to make an idol of him. He hasn't yet ascended, but when he does he goes no place other than where you will be in the not distant future. So it's a drama within a drama. It's a mystery…if you tell as it has been told of some little place where someone came out of a tomb…and the only tomb out of which Christ ever rose is the skull of man. And he can't show it to another. They either believe it or don't believe it, and most did not believe. So he told them what happened. In fact those five words at the end of Luke are the most provocative words: "They related their own experience." They told what had happened; and then to most people who heard it they seemed like the words of an idle tale, and did not believe it. And so, out of man comes this fantastic glorious being, which you may try to show to another, but the eye is veiled, they can't see it. And even he who wears the garment is not aware of his glory while still in the body. But he knows what has happened to him and the whole thing that has happened in scripture has happened to him.

Of course, one translation of that same statement is this, "Do not hold me back." That is what Moffat has. Instead of "do not touch me," he has that translated "do not hold me back"...that you by your sense of loss will bind me to where you are. For, I'll be always called by you for your sense of loss. Then do not hold me back, let me go. So the sense of ____(??) if someone that you admire as a teacher and hold them high in your mind's eye is now departing from the world, your sense of loss and their feeling for you would hold them close. Do not hold me, do not keep me back; for I can serve better when completely free and then control from above.

Goodnight.

CALL THE NEXT WITNESS

5/26/64

___(??) which is the last for a little while. We'll be returning on the 6th of October. And this has been a perfectly marvelous session. I want to thank you for your case histories. As far as I'm concerned they are tops, not only in the working of the law but in your visions which you have shared with me and allowed me in turn to share with others.

Well, tonight's subject is "Call the Next Witness." Everyone in the world will be called as the *next* witness. We are told in the Book of Isaiah: "And now go, write it upon a tablet and inscribe it in a book that it may be for the time to come as a witness forever" (30:8). So the first witness is the book, that book is our Bible. It is a witness forever. But our Bible, in this instance, is the Old Testament, that's the witness. That is the *external* witness. But, as we are told in the Old Testament, in the Book of Deuteronomy, the 19th chapter, that only on the evidence of two witnesses, or three witnesses, can a charge be sustained (verse 15). So here we have one witness, the external witness of scripture, and there must be a second witness to sustain the charge. This is God's promise to the whole vast world. And then we are told we are called one by one: "I will gather you one by one, O people of Israel" (Is. 27:12). Everyone is called and the one who is called is the witness, the next witness; and he has to parallel by his own experiences this that is the external witness, recorded in scripture.

So when the first one comes into the world who has the witness of scripture, it is said of him he is the first-born of the dead, the *faithful* witness. You read this in the Book of Revelation, the 1st chapter, the 5th verse: "And he is the faithful witness, the first-born of the dead." But no one believed him, or few believed him, because they expected a different kind of a witness. They thought some mighty giant would come from outer space and be their leader, to enslave those who had enslaved them, and raise them to some victorious state in the world. And that's not the picture of scripture. You and I will be, one by one, called as we can parallel that testimony as described in scripture.

So we are told, if two persons who differ, like two witnesses, if they agree in testimony it is conclusive. And so we have the Old Testament and we read it carefully—that is the external witness. Now, I differ from that, for I will say I didn't write it but I was told about it or I read it. Now, can I actually have an experience that parallels that which is recorded in the external witness? So there must be an external witness of scripture and the internal witness of the Spirit. So here comes one who makes the statement: "Scripture must be fulfilled in me. For all that was written about me has its fulfillment, and beginning with Moses in the law and the prophets and the psalms, he interpreted to them in all the scriptures the things concerning himself" (Luke 22:37; 24:44). Every passage in the Old Testament that was in any way related to himself he showed them where this had to be experienced by him. He couldn't share it with them, for the experiences take place in the soul of man. It doesn't take place that the mortal eye could see. And then he began to tell them what had happened to him. Then we are told the one who really believed it in this world, though he fought him in the beginning, that in the end of his days he expounded the matter from morning to night, trying to convince them of the reality of Jesus, using all the scripture as his argument; and some believed while others disbelieved. And that's the entire story.

I can tell you this night, you may believe it or you may disbelieve it, but the story is this: It's not enough to hear the testimony of Jesus, one must hear it with faith. For we are told that those who heard it heard it as we hear it; but it did not profit them who heard it, because it was not received with faith in the hearers (Heb. 4:2). Let us not now fail as they failed by not mingling what we have heard with faith. So I can't take you with me into the depths of my own soul and show you the moment in time and the experience that was my experience when it happened to me, I can only tell you. But we are told when this was made aware, they asked, "When is this going to happen to us?" and he said, "It is not for you to know times or seasons, seasons fixed by the authority of the Father." Wait for the promise of the Father, "For you shall receive power when the Holy Spirit comes upon you" (Acts 1:8). But I can't tell you the time or the season. Everyone here this night would ask me, "When is it going to happen to me?" I can't tell you. I do not know. It's not given to us to know the times or the seasons. They are fixed by the Father by his own authority. I can only ask you to *wait* for the promise of the Father, because I know from experience that you shall receive power when this is given to you when the Holy Spirit descends upon you.

You'll have the power, the most fantastic power in the world. Nothing in this world…you speak of nuclear energy…there's *nothing* comparable to the power that is given you. Here you come into room like this, you could take a bomb and blow everyone up and destroy it. You think you could. You could destroy it, but that moment prior to the moment of destruction remains forever, so you can't really destroy more than the instant that you think you did, and that instant remains in time. But with this power of which I speak, you come into this room, and you could turn off from within yourself that which allows everyone to be aware of being alive. And turning it off, they will believe themselves no...as a lady present knows from being turned off...that they are nothing, but absolutely nothing. That there's nothing, they are nothing. And then you turn it on and then wherever you stopped it, they simply pick it up at that moment in time, and they go on, and they become someone again. So you know the power that you can really exert, you can turn off. You can not only turn it off, may I tell you, I've done it. Not on this level, I have done it. You turn it off and then you rearrange the structure of the intentions of those that you turned off. When you turn it on again they have not the intention they had when you turned it off, and they move in an entirely different direction.

You could take the whole vast world, may I tell you, if you were so given...but you would not be given this power were you not completely immersed in love. For were you not completely immersed in love, you could turn it off and rewrite the script on the minds of men and march them, without effort on their part, into the ocean beyond their height, and fill it with humanity, and therefore drown them. You could; that's the power. There's nothing in this world comparable to the power that is yours when you awake from this dream of life. So you're told, wait for the promise of the Father, for you shall be given power when the Holy Spirit comes upon you. That's the kind of power, for "as the Father has *life* in himself, so he has granted the Son also to have life in himself" (John 5:26).

Now, this is the witness of which I speak this night. The Bible is the first witness, it's the external witness. Now "bring me the second witness," and you one day will be called that second witness, because you will have all the experiences as prophesied in scripture. For scripture is only talking about you, your biography. Everything said in scripture you must experience, and then you'll know beginning with Moses and all through the prophets and in the psalms, that everything said about you must have its fulfillment. You will interpret to those who will listen. They may not listen, but you'll interpret for them.

Now let us begin with the witness, "Bring me the next witness." Now we are told in scripture "God has taken his position in the divine council; in the midst of the gods he holds judgment" (Psalm 82:1). Is that true? I know from experience that it is true. I was taken in Spirit into the divine council, and presented to the Ancient of Days. And God, may I tell you, is man. When you stand in his presence, you stand in the presence of infinite love. *Infinite* love! And he's going to ask you a question and you will answer based upon scripture. I am not going to say tonight that the question asked me will be the same question asked you. A friend of mine, who is present tonight, was asked a different question, but he answered it based upon scripture. He did it just as automatically as I did it. I was asked the question, "What is the greatest thing in the world?" and my answer came from the Book of Corinthians, Paul's letter to the Corinthians, the 13th chapter, "Faith, hope and love, these three, but the greatest of these is love" (verse 13). At that, infinite love in the presence of man, embodied man, embraced me. As he embraced me our bodies fused and we became one body. I have no consciousness of any separation after that embrace. I have never felt such joy in my life when he embraced me and I became one with infinite love. And then I was sent to do what I'm doing, to tell the story, a command that I could not resist: Go and tell the story.

Well, this is the 82nd Psalm. So I'm a witness to the truth of the statement in the 82nd Psalm that God has taken his place in the divine council; in the midst of the gods he holds judgment. The gods are simply you, the whole vast world, awakened. When man awakes he becomes a part of the gods where God holds judgment. He doesn't judge you and then gives you some sentence. He's not a God of retribution; he's a God of love. He's only asking you a question, and then you are divinely prompted to make a confession of faith. So he's not going to condemn you. You, first of all, couldn't possibly make a mistake because you are prompted by God what you *ought* to say. So when you are brought into the divine council, don't be concerned what you are going to say; for you are going to be prompted and you're going to be prompted what you ought to say.

Here's one. I can say now that wonderful chapter of the 42nd Psalm...I can testify to that (verse 4). For I, too, found myself in a moment of a sadness of heart...and who hasn't...when you are sad and you wonder, "Why am I so down within me, why is it?" And then you turn to memory and suddenly this thing happens. I can say with the Psalmist today, these things I remember, when I joined the throng in this grand procession and I led them in procession, and there was joy, a multitude keeping festival—that I recall vividly walking in an enormous crowd. I can't measure the number, but in that crowd I walked with them. The 42nd Psalm tells us, I remember these things, when I joined this crowd and led them in procession to the house of God. Well, we were moving toward some invisible Jerusalem, invisible Mecca, it was the house of God, when a voice rang out and the voice said, "And God walks with them." Then a lady at my side said, "If God walks with us, where is he?" and the voice answered, "At your side." Then she turned to her left and looked into my face, my eyes, and then she became hysterical. She said, "What, is Neville God?" and she was really hysterical with laughter it struck her so funnily. The voice replied, "Yes, in the act of waking."

And then that same voice heard only now by me—not by the multitude, this festive multitude— heard only by me, and it came from the depths of my soul; and the voice said to me, "I laid myself down within you to sleep, and as I slept I dreamed a dream. I dreamed..." and I knew exactly what the finish of the sentence was: He was dreaming that he's me. But at that moment when I heard it, the thrill, the joy! Then I was nailed upon this body as though nailed on a cross, but unlike what the world talks about the crucifixion it was sheer delight. My hands, my feet, my head, my side were vortices, and each vortex was joy beyond the wildest dream of man. And so, he nailed himself upon me (the dead). And so "I have been crucified with Christ; it is not I who live, but Christ who lives in me; and the life I now live in the flesh I live by the faith of God, who loved me and gave himself for me" (Gal. 2:20). So to *that* statement of scripture I bear witness...I have experienced it.

Now we come to the series of events which is God's plan of salvation. God's plan of salvation was made very, very clear from the scripture, once the *key* was given to us by the testimony of Jesus. No one believed it. And you can't really blame anyone for not believing it. Because a man, a normal man as I'm a normal man, you're a normal man, walking the earth not knowing the time is now fulfilled, at this moment in time it is fulfilled, like an egg coming to its ripeness. You don't know the contents of the egg and suddenly this little thing breaks. You look at a caterpillar and it seems to you nothing, and suddenly it breaks and out comes the butterfly. Out comes from the egg this glorious feathered being. Out comes from this concept of God, which is man, the being you cannot describe: It is God coming out.

And so, who could actually believe a man who was born a normal person, one of many brothers, who had sisters, who lived in a normal environment, who had no background whatsoever, and suddenly out of *this*, when the time was fulfilled, that the prophecy is really true? That man who was made an animal, as told us in the 4th chapter of the Book of Daniel: He took himself and put himself in the form of an animal, gave himself the mind and the heart of a beast, and allowed seven times to pass over him until he knew that the Most High rules the kingdom of men, and *gave* it to whom he would, even to the lowliest of men (verse 16). So he takes the lowliest, a man who has no qualifications whatsoever for the claim that he could possibly be the fulfillment of all that was prophesied in scripture; and suddenly it begins to happen in him. It didn't happen in some little physical manger in the Near East, no three shepherds came out of the night to see the event; all of this takes place in the *soul* of man. So he tells what happened to him. He goes back into scripture and searches the scripture and finds where it was prophesied. He tells them this is what it meant. No one believed him. He believed it. And then came a second event, the third event, the fourth event, and event after event, as he found it in scripture, it is taking place in the soul of an individual. He is the first-fruit of those who slept, the first-born from the dead.

And so, he comes into this world, as you came into this world, and maybe you this night will be that witness, I do not know. For no one knows the time: "It is not for you to know the times or seasons fixed by the Father by his own authority. But wait for the promise of the Father, for you shall receive power when the Holy Spirit comes upon you." And no one in this world knows and no one can prophesy for you. Let no one tell you that they can read some horoscope or some chart to tell you when that time will arrive. It could come this very moment to anyone in this room or the world. But, when it comes, *you* are then the witness that is called; so only God sees the second witness. Man judges from the outward appearances, but God judges from the heart.

No one in this world unless he believes me could actually know what I have experienced. My most intimate person, my wife, where I've shared it with her and tell her these experiences, I believe that she believes me one hundred percent, but I can't share with her the experience. Neither can I tell her that she will be the next in line, I cannot. Much as I love my daughter, I can't tell her that she will be the next in line. She may be a way down the line to be called to witness to the word of God. So bring me the next witness. And only God knows when he calls them: "I call them one by one, O ye people of Israel" (Is. 27:12). And so he's calling everyone in his own good order, but I don't know the order that he calls them.

I only know that he called me. He called me and everything said in scripture concerning Jesus Christ I have experienced in the soul of my being, beginning with the first one. All the others were preparatory, like finding myself in the divine council where God was holding court, and being welcomed, embraced and then sent, like an apostle. That preceded... all the other things preceded it. My finding myself in that section of the book of the ___(??), where I'm in this enormous multitude keeping festival, that preceded it. But the *real* beginning of the awakening began with the resurrection, where suddenly a power that I've never felt in my life was applied to my head. And I don't know, I can't tell you how it was applied. I only know it was applied to my head—and I who thought up to that very moment I was always awake found myself waking. I'm waking and I thought this is a normal waking, and it isn't a normal waking; I'm awaking in my skull. My skull is not just a skull if one woke in the skull, but at the moment that I awoke I *knew* it was a tomb. That's the strange part of it, my skull was a tomb. Here was a tomb, and suddenly I'm being born out of the tomb, so the tomb becomes a womb. And this begins the birth of God in man. I come out as one that is being born, and everything said in scripture concerning the birth of Jesus Christ I experienced.

So I came out of it. The three men were present to witness it. And then comes the most unearthly wind that man could ever experience. And so we're told, "All was foretold me, naught could I foresee. But I learned how the wind would sound *after* these things should be." I couldn't envision the wind. I didn't know. I was told it as you were told it, everyone was told the story of God before we set forth; and so, all was foretold me but I couldn't foresee it. But *after* the event I knew what that wind would be. And so, here I heard this fantastic wind. And then the whole thing was over; that was the fulfillment of scripture of the birth of God which he promised: "I will bring forth out of man a son, but that which I bring forth will be *my* son and I will be his father" (2 Sam. 7:12). May I tell you, *you* are the one brought forth. You're not something that you remain here and something else comes out of you, you are pulled out of yourself. This thing here was the dead, this was the sepulcher; this was the tomb into which God immersed himself. He is extracting himself individualized *as* you. So when he brings himself out, you are he.

To prove now that you *are* he, he gives you the next event. For he only extracts himself. God could not emerge from man in whom he was not present. Christ Jesus could not come out of one in whom he's not present. And so, he draws *himself* out of you. When he draws himself out of you, to prove it is himself, the next event is the one that reveals it. And the next event is when he shows you his son, and his son is your son. So you look into the eyes of God's only begotten son (Psalm 2:7) and that only begotten son calls you Father, as told you in the 89th Psalm. "I have come only to fulfill scripture. Scripture must be fulfilled in me" (Luke 22:17). So the 89th Psalm: "I have found David and David has cried unto me, 'Thou art my Father, my God, and he Rock of my salvation" (verse 26). So you find him, and there's no uncertainty in this discovery: He was always your son. So if he is *your* son and he is God's *only* begotten son, well then, God succeeded in his purpose in extracting himself from that tomb into which he had entered.

He enters the tomb of man; man is dead; and then extracts himself multiplied a thousand-fold beyond what he was when he buried himself in the tomb called man. He comes out, and to prove it, comes the third event. The resurrection is first, the birth second, and this one is the third: The discovery of the fatherhood of God where he succeeded in giving himself to you as father because you have a son. Then comes the fourth event where he raises himself into Zion: "And as Moses lifted up the serpent in the wilderness, so must man be lifted up" (John 3:14). So man, *you*, you are lifted up in the same manner that Moses lifted up the serpent—which is only a symbol, all the outside things were simply symbols—but now *inwardly* you must experience what outwardly was only a sign. Inwardly you become alive and you lift yourself up in the most miraculous manner, right up like a serpent into your skull. So that's the next one.

And the *final* one is when he succeeds now in really giving you the power, which you will not exercise save governed by love. There is no temptation in this world that could make you turn a stone into bread, or cast yourself down to prove to anyone that his angels would bear you up, or in any way take any temptation of sleeping humanity. That's why he now gives you...and the last gift is the gift of the Holy Spirit, which descends upon you in bodily form as a dove, and *smothers* you with love, but completely smothers you with affection. And while he is enveloping you in love, the whole thing vanishes, and you awake on the level of Caesar. You're here, endowed with the power that he gave you, but you could not in eternity use it save governed by love.

So when you first encounter love, you first see the one that is infinite might. And then you know, as the years go by, that you will have infinite power in proportion to your capacity to love. For love is the greatest in the world. That no one in this world could ever have infinite might until he's first embraced by love, for what would he do with it if he was not actually embraced by love? He would destroy the universe; he would destroy anything in this world. So he asked this little question: Who told you of things from of old? Ask him and let him tell you of what is yet to be. Did I not tell you the things from of old? And so, the old is that Old Testament, the 44th Book of Isaiah I'm quoting, 44th chapter (verse 8): "Did I not tell you these things from of old?" If there's one who can tell you, let him tell you the things yet to be. I have told you all the things to come, and then he closed the book. But the time has not yet fulfilled. When it is fulfilled, I will come forth, and then it will never end; my salvation shall never have an end. My redemption shall never come to an end. So one by one by one I call them.

So the witness is simply when you suddenly—maybe this night, it's my hope it is this night—that it will break. For, may I tell you, you could have a billion, and you may, you could have all the glamour in the world, and if you were not awake, what does it really matter? You're tied to the wheel of recurrence. And tomorrow...as my friend saw his mother, radiantly beautiful and moving through the year 1953, suddenly finding herself in the year 3804. But no transforming power in that transition, the same lovely lady, this time more beautiful, married, ___(??), with the same fear of death that she had here prior to her own death at the age of seventy but now at the age of thirty and beautiful beyond measure. As happy as any beautiful lady would be here with means, at the age of thirty, but in fear of death. Death follows man forever on these wheels within wheels within wheels. It is only when we are lifted out of the wheel of recurrence that we have conquered death, for we die no more. So what does it matter if you owned the earth and you were not extracted from the wheel of recurrence?

All you have to do is to turn on the radio or the TV and hear the junk that is on today in this election year. Someone will quote a man, doesn't tell you who he's quoting, but he quotes the most marvelous things concerning a person; and he tells you everything about this wonderful man, that he really should be our leader of leaders, as I got it exactly before I came out. And then you heard… I've just quoted you the words of Nelson Rockefeller, what he said two years ago about Goldwater, the most marvelous things... that's two years ago. They're only quoting, they're quoting exactly what he said when he introduced him at this party, but you could never improve upon the joy of that moment. But now this is two years later...now he wants the same job…because the other fellow was less fitted for it…and so now we have Rockefeller today. But all of this is part of the wheels within wheels of a deadly sleep.

And so I tell you, I come here to bear witness, the second witness—"Call me the next witness"— and I'm telling you what happens. You can hear what happened to me, but it will not benefit anyone who hears me unless they accept it with faith. If you think this is all hallucination, if you think, well, this is a strange dream the man had, and you don't believe it is true concerning you as of tomorrow, well then, you heard it but you did not mix it with faith; and the word of God falling upon the mind, which is the soil, did not receive the necessary fertilized and prepared soil, and you're simply tied upon the wheel, the wheel of recurrence. I can only hope that when I talk to you that I will actually receive from you a certain receptivity that it may bury itself in you and grow; for unless it is accepted by you it can't grow.

So how long you remain on the wheel, may I tell you, is irrelevant. It doesn't really matter. It is only when it is accepted—after he sends one as his witness to tell you what has happened to him, and you hear it and accept it—will it grow. How long that interval of time between acceptance and fulfillment? That I do not know. I only know until he is accepted that the wheel...it doesn't really matter. But may I tell you, when you see the wheel and you stop it, and see that the whole power is turned off *within you*...and they are nothing, they're dead, I mean *really* dead. It doesn't matter what you do to the dead, it doesn't really matter, any more than they took off that head of the mermaid in Denmark. It was dead. You desecrate something and they were all annoyed that someone would dare take a lovely piece of art and do it...but it didn't hurt her. So when you see the whole vast world and you turn it off and everything stands still. And you can turn it...I have turned it and changed the pattern, and it moved in an entirely different direction. I've done it with a train. It seems so fantastic to tell you this, but you can not only turn it, you can turn it backwards. You can do anything with this wheel; it's a machine. But out of this machine God is bringing himself, extracting himself from the wheel of recurrence which is the wheel of death.

And the day will come every word I've told you you will know is true. So let me go back to the Book of Acts, You "wait for the promise of the father...for power will come upon you when the Holy Spirit has come upon you; and then you will be my witnesses in Jerusalem, and in all Judea, and Samaria, and to the ends of the earth" (Acts 1:4,8). You, every one in this world, will be a witness to the truth of what I told you this night. I don't care who you are and what you are. Your social position, intellectual position, financial position means nothing in the eyes of God, but *nothing*; for you are destined to inherit the kingdom of God. You are destined to inherit God: "Give them no inheritance. *I am* their inheritance" (Ezek. 44:28). That's what we're told. So man himself inherits not only the kingdom of God, he inherits God. He inherits the *power* that is God, the *wisdom* that is God. And so, out of this fabulous world of ours we're extracting the being that is buried in it.

So believe me, I am a witness to the truth of all that is recorded in scripture, first in the Old Testament and then in the New where the testimony of Jesus is the spirit of prophecy. Listen to it carefully, there is nothing more important for any of us than to hear that testimony and then respond to it. It doesn't matter what you've done. If you've been horrible, brutal, unkind, you may be sorry for it, but, may I tell you, these things in themselves, that's not important. Hear the testimony and accept it, for it grows, it grows within you. You may be kind and generous and wonderful and not believe in the testimony. Until you hear it and respond to it with acceptance, it can't take root and it can't grow. So here, we go back to our premise, only on the evidence of two witnesses can a charge be sustained. The first witness is the external witness of scripture; the second witness is the internal witness of the Spirit. If these two agree in principle, in testimony, it is conclusive. I don't care what the world will say if they agree. So when you have an experience go back and see if the external witness of scripture in any way parallels what you had. If they agree then it's conclusive. Read the scripture and see if it is something that parallels your own experience.

Now before I close tonight I want to tell you, the Promise is a gift, you don't earn it. God's law you operate. I'll be back in October and everyone here could be any being that they want to be, really they could be if they were really faithful to the law. He said, "I have come not to abolish the law and the prophets…I have come to fulfill them," to tell you what the law really means (Mat.5:17). So he reinterprets the law and shows us that the law is *mental*, it's not physical, that causation is imaginal. So when a man imagines himself to be what he wants to be and remains faithful to that imaginal state as though he were, he becomes it. There's no power in the world that can stop him. That, when you know what you desire, "When you pray, believe that you have received it, and you will" (Mark 11:24). If you can really be faithful to the imaginal act, knowing that you are what you want to be, the whole vast world would reshuffle itself to mirror the fulfillment of your imaginal act. Everyone in this room if they are faithful to it could give you not one but dozens of case histories when I return in October as many of you have given me in the past few months. If you are faithful to it! You could this night assume that you are the man, the woman that you want to be, and believe it implicitly, that you *really* are, and view the world mentally as you would physically, and see it mentally as you *would* see it physically were it true. Night after night, sleep in that assumption just as though it were true and it will become true. You'll become the man that you want to be, you'll become the woman that you want to be. That is God's law.

His Promise comes in its own good time, for it's not for us to know the times and the seasons when it comes. So I can tell you, because the Promise has been fulfilled in me I am a witness to the truth of scripture. I only hope that you will believe me and accept it, that in the not distant future you, too, will be a witness to the truth of scripture. For everything said in scripture concerning Jesus Christ, the first witness—-he is called the first-born from the dead, the first-fruits of those who slept—there isn't a thing said in that book concerning him I have not experienced in the deep of myself. So it doesn't really matter now when my physical departure takes place, for that has happened in me. I know it will happen in every child born of woman. But we may delay the planting, for the word falls upon man and man rejects it. I hope that you will not reject it.

So tonight, when we call the next witness, we're simply asking anyone who had the experience...as my friend Tom did today and Larry the other day...all this is scripture, all these visions that they gave me. That's part of the preparation for the grand events that begin to unfold the Promise of God. All things come just before it, and so both of them really are fulfilling scripture. But Christianity is based upon the affirmation that a *certain* series of events happen in which God revealed himself in action for the fulfillment of his promise to man. So what they have brought forth or through, they come prior to the unfolding of that *definite* series of events, beginning with the resurrection and ending with the descent of the Holy Spirit in the form of a dove.

Now let us go into the Silence.

* * *

Q: Will you tell us again why God became man so that man might become God?

A: Why God became man that man may become God? First of all, there's only God, there's nothing but God in the world. And when we say God became man, man as we see man is an eternal part of the structure of the universe. God buries himself in man for, I would say, creative purposes, to develop his creative power. Because when we speak of Jesus Christ in the Bible, bear in mind what Paul said about Jesus Christ: "Jesus Christ is the power and wisdom of God" (1 Cor. 1:24). So he buries his power and his wisdom in his own creation, animates it, puts himself through all the hell of the world, then extracts himself. So that God is not a static state, God is not an absolute, which would be static and therefore dead. God is an ever-increasing illumination, an ever-increasing power of creativity. When a man thinks that God is finished, it couldn't be this infinite power, seemingly infinite potential. And so it limits itself to man: He took upon himself the form of man and became obedient unto death, even the death upon the cross of man (Phil. 2:7). And so here is the limitation of the power, the creative power of God, and then creates it, animates it.

I can't tell you the thrill that is in store for you the night that you are moved in Spirit, and come upon a scene, a very simple scene, undoubtedly it will be, and you will know intuitively that you can shut off, turn off, a power within yourself by arresting it. And you know what's going to happen if you succeed in doing it. You will know that if you do it, the animated world that you perceive will stand still. It doesn't have power in itself; it's only an animated you, that your perception animates the world that you perceive. People don't realize that. But you'll know it one night and when you do it, well, I can't describe the thrill. And then you will turn it on again and the intentions unfulfilled will continue and they'll be fulfilled, like eating what it intended to eat, flying where it intended to go, moving where it intended to go, and all these things. You'll have other experiences of turning it off and turning it on; and then you'll begin to experiment and you will change the pattern of the intention. And you will see what's going to happen. They who intended to do this, when you change the intention, they don't do that, they simply fulfill your changed pattern. And you realize what man is. Then you come back to scripture, "You have no power over me were it not given to you from above" (John 19:11). You are operating then when you have this motion from above.

Well, a lady who is not here this night could tell me that ten days before Kennedy was assassinated that she saw the headline on the same color paper that it was brought out ten days later. And we think this is something altogether initiated by the individual who played the part? They're like puppets, as you're told in the Book of Ecclesiastes. Nothing frightens man more than that Book of Ecclesiastes. The priesthood rejects it, the scientists reject it. Because they say, "Is there a thing of which it is said, 'See, this is new'? It has been already, in ages past. There is nothing new under the sun" (1:10). And man can't believe it... he doesn't want to believe it. He thinks all of his efforts are simply in some strange way changing things. You don't change it this way, you change it only by an inner attitude of mind, and you change patterns by a simple change which is called in scripture, well, I call it reversing, I call it revising. Scripture calls it by some other name, which is not remorse as the world would call it, which is not regret, but the word is repentance. Repentance is not remorse; it's a complete radical inner attitude of mind that is changed. You change radically and then you do see it here on the surface.

But then will come the moment in time when you don't do it this way. You know you can do it and you stop it, stop the whole thing.

Then as you stop it, you'll change it, deliberately, and then turn it on again and watch what they do. Suppose I could take you this very night and stop you and change your intention and send you elsewhere in this world. You could go astray, couldn't you? Well, that's life. It doesn't make sense but it's true.

Q: Neville, in conjunction with that, do you consciously work toward this or does this just happen at an appointed time?

A: The Promise happens at a point in time. But until the Promise is given you which is God's grace we're called upon to use his law. And use it, use it lovingly, but use it. Don't accept a drifting state in this world. In other words, interfere with the stream of life, interfere with it. If you're moving toward a certain end, don't accept that; interfere with it by a radical change of attitude towards life. It doesn't mean because you change it time and time again that you're any nearer the Promise. The Promise is not for anyone to know when God gives it. It's his grace. We're told to put our hope fully on the grace that is coming to us at the revelation of Jesus Christ (1 Peter 1:3). So set your hope fully upon it. But you can't ask when it's going to happen, because no one knows the times or seasons…that's fixed by God's own authority.

But, nevertheless, believe in it. And while you're waiting for the Promise to be fulfilled, use his law. His law is that you can be any man, any woman you want to be in this world by controlling your own inner attitudes of mind: Seeing what you want to see and *only* what you want to see. If you will remain faithful to that inner change of your mind, it will objectify itself, it will come to pass. But it doesn't mean that because you are successful in the use of this that you are in some way closing the gap towards the Promise. The Promise is something that is in God's own hand: I call the children of Israel one by one (Is. 27:12) and no one knows when he'll be called. You may be called tonight! And no one in this world can tell you how near you are to that call. Because they all ask the same question, Lord, when? Will you now this day restore the kingdom to Israel? It's not for you to know the times or the seasons which the Father has fixed by his own authority (Acts 1:7).

But you simply remain faithful and wait for the Promise of the Father. You *shall* (which is a promise), you shall receive power when the Holy Spirit comes upon you. Until it comes upon you, *wait* for the Promise. The Promise comes in a peculiar, strange unfoldment of a series of events: resurrection, birth, the discovery of the fatherhood of God, the ascension into heaven, and the descent of the Holy Spirit in the form of a dove. It comes that way, there is a sameness to the unfolding picture. Until it happens (and it happens suddenly) use your talent that God gave you, that imagining creates reality. So imagine only the best for yourself and don't...because it costs you nothing to imagine good for others, doesn't take it from you, imagine the best for others. Imagine the best for everyone in this world and see it come to pass. It *will* come to pass. No power can stop it.

Q: (inaudible)

A: Lynn, my dear, everything in this world has been shown you before you set forth, everything. We saw the Promised Land before we left *it* and went into exile—this is the exile. We have forgotten it but we were shown it. And while we are in exile, the story is told to man that he may accept it with faith. You did not a thing in this world that was wrong to cause the exile. God himself exiled himself; it's only God playing all the parts. "God has consigned all men to disobedience, that he may have mercy upon all" (Rom. 11:32). No man in this world is responsible for the exile, it's God. God conceived it and God is playing it, playing all the parts. The purpose of the play is to develop his creative talent, his creative power; and when he extracts it, you are he. The day will come you'll actually know this, you'll see it. You'll see yourself in the depths of your soul in deep, deep meditation. And you will say, as Carl Jung said, "So it is he who is meditating me: and you will know that when he awakes from his sleep, you, on the surface, will no longer be, because you are *he*. When he awakes, you on the surface will vanish but you are he.

I saw it so clearly. I saw this when I came upon myself in deep meditation, *profound* meditation, a glowing being like a Buddha in the lotus posture. I looked at it and I was amazed to see myself in this profound state. If I struck it over the head it wouldn't move. It was in such a deep sleep no blow from me, the surface, could ever disturb it. As I looked at it and saw myself, it glowed like the sun. But I didn't use the words that Jung used. But when Jung came upon a similar situation Jung was frightened, and when he came back to the surface he said, "So it is he who is meditating me, and when he awakes from his sleep I will no longer be" (*Memories, Dreams, Reflections*). So God placed himself into a profound state of sleep—this is the dream of God—and when he awakes in you, you the surface will vanish but you will be he who was the dreamer, who is now awake, that is God.

So no one can fail. How could you fail? Nothing can fail! I only ask everyone to recognize it for what it is and dream nobly. So I would say to everyone tonight, regardless of headlines and all the rumors in the reports, if you have a real urge to bring about a certain objective, don't give up because of rumors. Just simply persist in your controlled waking dream.

Until October...thank you.

THY DEAD SHALL LIVE

11/13/64

Tonight's subject is taken from Isaiah, the 26th chapter, just as a title because it's really not on that chapter. The title is "Thy Dead Shall Live." To understand this we have to go all through the Bible and take pieces from here and pieces from there and put them all together. So we turn now to the Book of Romans, the 6th chapter, you'll find it in the 3rd and 4th verses. I am quoting from the *New Age Bible*. I find it far more clear when it comes to this passage, in fact, many, many passages. But in this a question is asked—in the other Bibles they state "Do you not know"—that passage has been interpreted "Have you forgotten?" All the difference in the world! Have you forgotten that when we were baptized into union with Christ Jesus, we were baptized into his death and lay dead? By baptism we were buried with him and lay dead, in order that Christ would rise in the splendor of his Father; then comes a hope, so also we would step into this new life (Rom. 6:3,4).

So you and I through what he called baptism—it doesn't mean the baptism that you and I experience when we couldn't even experience it, for we were just simply days old—hasn't a thing to do with that earthly baptism. He's telling us, before the whole thing was, you and I were incorporated into one body, all of us, and we lay dead. And then like life coming out of the depths, like the seed falling into the earth—"Unless the seed falls into the earth and dies it remains alone; but if it dies, it bears much fruit"—the mystery of life through death. So, all of us have union with Christ. You can't think now, if you believe this, of God as "other," can't be other. So we are told, As a body is one and has many members, so it is in Christ. By one Spirit we were all baptized into Christ, and all were made to drink of one Spirit (Rom. 12:4). Well, that you can see. I say "Who are you?" and as you reply you say "I am John." And before you go any further I can stop you and turn to another and another and all will begin "I am" and then they'll say so-and-so. We all say the same thing. You ask me "Who are you?" I am...I may say Neville, I may say I'm an American by adoption, I may say anything; but before I say anything I first say "I am." So we're all made to drink of one Spirit and that Spirit is God. There's nothing but! So God is not "other." Until that comes into man's consciousness and remains there and he feeds upon it, he will die in despair. So, have you forgotten? he asked. So we've all forgotten. We've drunk deeply of the Spirit and lay dead; and now we're about to be resurrected, raised from the state of death. But how did we simply die?

Now let me tell a story. It's taken from 1st Kings, the 13th chapter. It's a strange story but a fascinating story...the entire chapter, not just a verse. "And the man of God came from Judah by the word of the Lord, and came to Bethel." As he came to Bethel, he pronounced this I wouldn't call it a curse but a prophecy on the altar of Bethel, for it was used for idolatry, and said it would be destroyed and all the ashes would be poured out. The king, Jeroboam— whose name simply means "may the people be multiplied, may they become numerous or unnumbered like the sands of the sea," that's his name, that's what it means—he was at the altar and when this prophecy was made against the altar of Bethel the king stretched forth his hand to injure and the king said, "Take hold of him, this man of God." And as he did so his hand stiffened and withered so he could not bring it back to himself. And he knew he was in the presence of the man of God. Then he said to the man of God, "Entreat the Lord your God to restore my hand" and so the man of God entreated his Lord and the hand was restored to its former healthy state.

Then the king said to him, "Come into my house and refresh yourself and dine and drink with me." He said, "By the word of the Lord I cannot eat in this place or drink in this place, neither can I return by the way that I came." And so, he started by a different way. Then there was an old, old prophet in Bethel, and his son came to him and told him of the man of God and what he had done to the altar of Bethel. The old man said to his son, "What direction did he go?" and the son pointed the direction where the man of God departed. So he said, "Saddle my ass," then the ass was saddled and the old prophet started in search of the man of God. When he came to him he found him under an oak tree—think in terms of Abraham the father of the multitudes found under the oak tree as you read that in the 18th chapter of Genesis. And he said to him "I too am a prophet. An angel of the Lord said to me, come after you and have you dine with me, eat with me and drink with me." But he said, I cannot, because the Lord told me, he said, "I am the prophet and angel of the Lord."

Of course, the angel lied. It was a lying angel. And so he did, believing it was from the voice of God. Having dined, then the old prophet said to him, "Because you disobeyed the voice of the Lord your God, you shall *not be* buried in the tomb of your fathers"—a nice way of saying you shall not reach home, you shall die on the way. Then the prophet saddled the ass and gave it to the man of God. The man of God started on his ride and a lion destroyed him, a lion came out of the nowhere and killed him. Then the people passed by and here was the ass, here was the lion, and here was the man of God lying dead. So when news came to the old prophet, the old prophet set out in search and came upon these three—the man dead (the man of God), and the ass and the lion. The lion killed him but had not eaten him, and the lion had not torn the ass. Then the man of God was taken by the old prophet and buried in his own grave, in the old prophet's grave, and then he said to his son, "When I die, bury me in the grave of the man of God that my bones be with his bones."

Now you read that story and you say, what is it all about? What a glorious story! The man of God disobeyed God. Well, then who made him disobey? Now we turn back to Romans, the 11th chapter from which we quoted earlier. In the 11th chapter it is said that "God has consigned all men to disobedience, that he may have mercy upon all" (verse 32, RSV). So who is playing the part? It's *all* God! There is nothing but God. Now this 11th chapter ends on this note, that God is the source, the guide and the *goal* of all things. The source, the guide and the goal of all things! There's nothing but God. God is not other. He has consigned all to disobedience, that he may have mercy upon all. So, "Unless I die," said God, "thou canst not live, but if I die I shall arise again and thou with me." (Blake, *Jer.*,Plt.96). You couldn't possibly breathe were it not for this death of the man of God and when we die we are buried in the same grave. And so, the weary man enters his grave, his cave, and there he meets his Savior in that grave. So when I die—as the prophet who was fooled by the so-called angel of God—I am buried in the grave *with* God. So the question is asked, Have you forgotten when we were baptized into union with Christ Jesus that we were baptized unto his death? That by baptism we were buried with him and lay dead, in order that as Christ was raised from the dead in the splendor of the Father, so also we would step in this new way of life (Rom. 6:4).

Now I say experience must seal the truth of scripture. Everyone is going to have this experience, but everyone. It must be sealed only by experience. He said, "The word is true, every word of it is true." Well, I could tell you unnumbered stories to show survival, but that's not what the Bible is speaking about. Survival *is*—that I know. As Blake said, "Death awakes to generation." That I know from my own personal experience. "Death awakes to generation. O Lord, arise and rend the veil." I don't want to awake to generation...I have it here. I live in a world of generation, and all death unless resurrected awakes the generation. "Arise, O Lord, and rend the veil": tear it so there is no more generation in my world. For, all the dead are restored to life only to die again, as told us in the 20th chapter of the Book of Luke. When we are asked by the Sadducee...and the Sadducee simply is the man who does not believe in the resurrection. That is the wise man of the world, the scientist of today, the brilliant mind who understands the structure of the physical world. And he can't find the soul no matter how he opens up the brain. He can't find anything that could survive the dissolution of the body. And so they're called in the ancient world the Sadducees who did not believe in the resurrection. And they said to him, "Teacher, Moses in the law said that when a man dies and leaving no children and having a brother, the brother should marry the widow to raise up children for his brother. Well, there were seven brothers. And one died, leaving no offspring, and the second took her. He died leaving no offspring, the third took her, and finally they all married her and left no offspring, and finally she died. Whose wife will she be in the resurrection?" He answers, "The sons of *this* age marry and they are given in marriage; but those who are accounted worthy to attain unto *that* age and to the resurrection from the dead, they neither marry nor are they given in marriage, for they cannot die any more, for they are now sons of God and sons of the resurrection" (Luke 20:28-36). He distinguishes between *this* age which he calls "the age of death" and *that* age which is "the age of life."

So Blake was right, the dead awake to generation. They don't realize that this is the world of death, none of us do. We think *this* is the world of life, and when a man goes to the grave that's the world of death. No, that's simply going through a little veil to be once more awake to generation. You're restored to life, automatically inserted into your wonderful time sequence best suited for the awakening as the being that you really are who is God. This is a self-imposed state of sleep, a sleep so deep that it appears as death. As you are told, "In great Eternity those who contemplate on death said thus, 'What seems to be *is* to those to whom it seems to be, and is productive of the most dreadful consequences to those to whom it seems to be, even of despair and eternal death. But Divine Mercy steps beyond and redeems man in the body of Jesus'" (*Jerusalem*, Plt.36). So while we are here, what seems to be *is* to those to whom it seems to be, and is most productive, whether it be for something lovely or something horrible. But it's only a grand dream. You and I are in the body of Christ and we are here dreaming until he awakens us in his body *as* that body, as that Christ. There aren't two Christs. So when we awaken, his body is our body, and he and I are one. We are all one in the end. So "In that day the Lord shall be one and his name one." All awaken...but in our own good time, that is, in *his* good time. But when we awaken we are he, therefore, it's really in *our* good time.

So do we really survive? I could tell you of unnumbered cases where I know from my own experience and from the experience of my friends who shared with me their experiences in continuity. For you meet someone who died...many years ago, while I was here in this city, the first year I came here, my secretary died. I received a cable saying that Jack was dead. Well, Jack had no one but the speaker. He had a sister living somewhere, where I didn't know. She popped up at the last moment to get some money out of me, I know. But before that, I knew nothing of her and Jack never breathed anything of any relative. He was simply a lone wolf. He simply died on one hot August day when I was out here, my first year. So I went back and took care of the funeral, buried him up in Haverstraw, New York.

My sister-in-law always said to me, "I love you because you take care of my sister, but I don't believe one word that you say. I don't believe in immortality. I believe that we are immortal only through the loins—-our children who are our extension in this world." I said to her, Aren't you a good Christian? She said, "Oh, yes!" Well, she is a pillar of her church, the Episcopalian church. So I said, "How can you say you are a good Christian and say there is no immortality? Why, the foundation stones of Christianity are: the fatherhood of God, the brotherhood of man, and life everlasting. You can't remove one of these stones and not have the whole thing topple. So you say you are a good Christian, but you do not believe in life everlasting. You may have the first two—-fatherhood of God, brotherhood of man, but you can't rub out the third, for this is a God of the living, not a God of the dead." She said, "I still don't believe in your teaching." Alright.

Six months went by after Jack died. One night in question, I'm fully awake but I am not in this world, I am in that world, through this little gossamer...it's sort of...thin little veil between here and there. And so, here is Jack standing in my room and here is my sister-in-law, and she said to me, "I still don't believe what you teach, you know." I said, Well, how can you say that and see Jack? She said to me, "What has Jack to do with it?" I said, Jack died you know. I came back and buried him. At that moment her face becomes now aware of the truth of what I've said. She's fully conscious that Jack died and she's seeing Jack. But Jack now intercedes and Jack said, "Who's dead?" I said, "Jack, you're not dead but you died." He said, "That's stupid! I'm not dead but I died." I said, "Jack, you died. I came back from California and I buried you. You're buried, that little body that you wore is buried right now in Haverstraw, up in New York." With this, he thought the whole thing was stupid. I said, "Come over here." He did. I said to Al, "I'll show you how solid he is." I put my hand this way on his thigh and squeezed it. I said, "You see my hand doesn't go through the thigh, he isn't made of gossamer, he's as solid as I am, as you are. And Jack did this to me as he would have done in this world. He said, "Take you hand off!" just like that and slapped my hand with his hand in a very friendly manner. And suddenly the whole thing after a few more scenes, then the whole thing dissolved.

I could multiply these experiences of the reality of continuity. Jack was not transformed one iota, not one change in Jack, the same Jack that he was here. I say, death here is simply a passage through a door where you can't see them from this side, and they are restored to life to continue. It's a continuous state, but resurrection is discontinuous. It's a different world altogether, things that the eyes have not seen and ears have not heard what God has prepared for those in that day of resurrection. And the resurrection is taking place now at every moment of time, for all of us are one in Christ Jesus. When we awake, we aren't another; we are Christ Jesus, and that body we wear is that glorious body of God. And it isn't another, all one. So I can say when the question is asked, "Have you forgotten?" yes, the whole vast world has forgotten. "Have you forgotten when you were baptized into Christ Jesus, into that union with him, and that that baptism meant death with him?" Well, the old prophet knew it. Whoever wrote that Book of Kings, that 13th chapter, he knew it: "So when I die bury me in the grave with the man of God."

And may I tell you, all of these experiences you are going to have. You, too, will be called the man of God and strange powers will be yours. The first night I was called the man of God I found myself in a strange, strange area standing at the opening of a cave, and in that cave lived the most horrible, monstrous looking thing, the witch of witches, a horrible thing instructing a brood of children in the misuse of Imagination, complete misuse. The witches of *Macbeth* had nothing compared to this thing. She looked up and she screamed at me and she called me "man of God" and she said, "Man of God, what have you to do with me?" Well, she knew as far as she was concerned she was powerless in my presence. But I wouldn't raise, in that moment, I wouldn't raise a finger to stop her misuse of my power. For Christ Jesus in scripture is described as the power and wisdom of God. You read it in the very first chapter of the 1st epistle of Paul to the Corinthians, "Jesus Christ, the power and the wisdom of God" (verse 24); only one power, only one wisdom. And so, the *power* is Christ. You stand in the midst of some misuse of the power that is yours, that you are yourself, and you wouldn't raise a finger to change...it has all to be done.

Then, a second time that I came upon this same strange power, I found myself in a city that I knew so well, but it had changed, the whole thing had changed. I came to a junction and I thought, "Well, this is a radical change of the city since the last time I saw it." And a policeman dressed in black across the way—the voice of authority. Whether it be a king, a soldier, or a policeman, any form of uniform would be one of authority—here is the law. It could be Jeroboam as king or it could be a simple policeman across the way; in this case, a simple policeman. As I looked around wondering of this radical change, he rushed across the square and took me by the arm and started leading me away. I asked him, "What are you doing?" He said, "Your actions look suspicious to me." I said to him, "For the insult to the man of God, your voice is now still and the hand that touched me is just as still as the voice." And they were. He couldn't move the hand and he couldn't speak, and the expression on his face was one of stark fear. Then that scene came to an end.

So I know all of these things of scripture are true and every child born of woman *must* experience it. As he wakes in us, you are the man of God deceived by yourself, by a false, lying prophet. For in the very beginning there was only God who deceived man, the first man. For you're told, the word Yod He Vau He in its base although we interpret it as I AM (good interpretation, it's true), still it's primitive meaning, the primal meaning was "to fall or to cause to fall; to blow or to cause to blow." So who caused the fall was Yod He Vau He, the I AM. So I caused myself to fall for purposes beyond the wildest dream of man on this level. So the whole thing is done *by* God; he's the source, it's now *through* God, and the *goal* is God. So he crystallized and took upon himself the limit of contraction, the limit of opacity which is man; and then he starts bursting through from here, because there's no limit to translucency and none to expansion. It begins to burst beyond the wildest dream. But he took upon himself...like the little story of the seed, the grain of wheat, falls into the earth and dies...if it doesn't, it remains alone. But if it falls and dies it brings forth much. And so, here we are the great grain of seed, all gathered together in one body, one Spirit, and we all drank of that one Spirit, so we can all say "I am." And though we can say "I am" and do marvels in this world by the wise use, or even the misuse of Imagination, it's the same power. One day we suddenly are awakened from it all, and we enter the world called the world of resurrection—not continuity, but discontinuity.

Now here is a story told me this past week. A lady said she bought a franchise—didn't tell me the nature of the franchise—to discover right after she'd paid for it that the president of the concern was a fraud. And so, the investigator downtown asked her to secure a photostatic copy of the check she paid. But, she said, "I couldn't produce it because it was a check given to me by Bache and Co., the brokers. They sold some stock of mine for a little over $3,000, and I took that check and endorsed it over to the person with the company for the franchise, and I couldn't produce the check. That was in the company of Bache. But I applied this principle towards it and kept on working on it, just as you teach. Four months went by and Bache called me up and said that "the check issued to you for over $3,000 has not passed through the bank, therefore, we have put a stop on it, it's too long, and now we will issue you another check." And so, she got every penny back. How that check did not go through, who knows? She said, "I've never heard of it before, but, nevertheless, I have all the money that I gave this so-called fraud."

Well, he might have been a fraud in her eyes and maybe he had intentions that way, but it's God. Maybe this wonderful story of having faith in God's promise, God's law...that whatever you desire in this world, believe you have received it and you will (Mark 11:24). Even though reason denies it and your senses deny it and everything denies it, could you at a moment like that, knowing the man is a fraud, or you believe he is, and you gave him over $3,000, and time goes by, and you can't locate the check because it wasn't your personal check, it was a check that you endorsed that you received from your broker, from Bache and Co., and could you in the face of all that still believe that you'd get it back, and feel the reality of it, and actually believe in the reality of the imaginal act? Well, she did. Now, what caused the displacement of that check she doesn't know and she doesn't care; she got the money back! So Bache called up and said, "It hasn't passed through, so we've stopped it and now we'll issue another check in lieu of that." So I say to everyone here, it doesn't matter what the world will tell you, when you *know* what you want, assume that you have it and then walk just as though it were true.

Even though you haven't yet been raised from the dead, while you are dreaming dream noble dreams. For this death spoken of in scripture is a death of a profound sleep, that's the death; for in the 2nd chapter of Genesis we're told, "And God caused a profound sleep to fall upon man and he slept" (2:21). Not a thing is said of waking that man until Christ awakes. So all through the Bible the command is, or the plea is, "Rouse thyself! Why sleepest thou, O Lord?" (Ps. 44:23). Not another, God is the one that fell into that state. It is God in man who is dreaming. And the Bible recognizes only one source of dreams: All dreams, all visions proceed from God, whether it be a waking dream or the dream of the night (Job 33:14; Num.

12:6). So why not have lovely dreams if everything comes from the same source. Your dream produces an effect in the world. It can either scare you to death (your own dream) or enlighten you. So everyone here can dream the most marvelous dreams in the world, because it comes from God, and *all* things are possible to God.

So in this story of...there is no death, really, although you see them die. I can tell you—and multiply it many times over, when I talked with friends—that continuity of the same state, same pattern in this world. But like Blake, let your prayer be "Arise, O Lord, and rend the veil." You reverse all the currents of life when the veil is torn from top to bottom; and then what goes out in generation turns into regeneration and you rise into a world completely subject to your imaginative power. No waiting for it...you are now God and create by simply imagining.

In this state, you are still God but in a state of dream…and we're having bad dreams, horrible dreams. This past week I bought Wednesday's *New York Times.* To show you there is not anything in this world called fiction… don't believe it…there is no fiction! If you conceive something and you call it fiction because it's not based upon external fact, you may think, "Well now, this is fiction because I have no external fact to support my theory or my Imagination," don't believe it! A month ago, two of my friends, who come with me every week here, and my wife and myself went off to see a picture. Here was this comedy laid in Greece and Turkey, and the story is the plot to steal this fabulous bejeweled sword that was under real strong guard in Turkey. They had this fantastic way of getting this sword. Well, they got it, but they were caught and imprisoned. While they were all in jail, the one who held the idea was a woman, and the men were simply tools of her idea. And so, they were parted by the rails, she's on the one side, and as the curtain is coming down, she said to the men on the other side, all in their prison garb, "I have an idea: the jewels in Russia. I know a secret pass way into that fabulous museum there." And so, as the curtain is coming down, here they are trekking through the snows of Russia towards the fulfillment of her idea.

Well, this current week, this past Wednesday, on the front page of the *New York Times*, Russia for the first time revealed this fantastic robbery that took place of this jeweled sword this past year in Russia. The most unique way they got into that museum and took this bejeweled sword. They finally located it. They did not bring it out in the papers of Russia until they redeemed the sword. It took them about a year before they could find where the thieves had taken it. In the same paper two different articles, one is saying such things couldn't happen in Russia as they could happen in a capitalist country. But it happened in Russia! Just as this so-called fiction just to give a good laugh, because as the curtain is coming down here she is in her prison garb and she has another idea which will put them in jail again. And if it didn't take place in Russia!

I say there is no fiction! You can sit here alone and think, "But no one knows what I'm thinking." Not a thing that you do in the dark is kept in the dark; it's always revealed in the light. And so, you could be this night in a dungeon and you could hate the world and lose yourself in hatred and be the invisible cause of the most fiery conflict. The cause need not spring from the leaders of the world at all. Some woman in a dungeon treading the winepress of hate could produce tomorrow's real, real conflict. So that no one really can stop you, because who can stop you from doing it? You're a dreamer. And while you are in the state of sleep not yet awakened, not yet resurrected, it's entirely up to you to use your talent, which is the talent of dreaming. If you hear someone who knows the story, and believe him, you will stop the bad dream and produce the good dream but still a dream; in the hope that it won't be too long before you are resurrected from this wheel of recurrence and enter into the world of resurrection. We're all destined to enter that world anyway.

I tell you, the whole story as recorded in scripture is true, and it's all about *you*, every word is about you. So you're the one that he made in the very beginning, so you can truly say, "Before that the world was, I am." Because, before the thing is made the creator must exist. So, before the world was, I am. And if in the beginning I was actually by baptism united in the body of Christ Jesus and buried with him, well then, before the world was, I am. I can say, when the world shall cease to be, I am. For I am a world within myself...the whole vast thing is contained within me...and now I'm dreaming. You can't conceive of something in this world that isn't possible to God, you can't conceive of it. Everything possible to be imagined is an image of truth. It could be a horrible state, but it's still truth. So tonight, I appeal to everyone to take the most glorious concept of yourself and your friends and your circle, and though at the moment everything denies it, dare to believe that it's true. Just dare to believe it's true and feel yourself right into that state as though it were true, and then let it unfold in your world. It will. No power in the world can stop it.

So here, when you go home read that 13th chapter of the Book of 1st Kings, and as you read it put yourself into the place of the man called the man of God. He comes from Judah. Now a lion killed him—that's all imagery, beautiful symbols. The words for "scatter" in the Bible—"and he scattered them all over the face of the earth"—they were one people with one language, and the Lord said, Let us go down and scatter them, and give them all the different tongues of earth so they will not understand each other. The word translated "scattered" in scripture is defined in the biblical concordance as "the fall." For here I point it this way, then scatter it; yet it is still bound, one body...many members but one body. And so he breaks it and becomes fragmented. So the "fall" killed him by being scattered. So he was simply a scattered being or a fragmented rock. So you're told in scripture, "You've forgotten the Rock that begot you" (Deut. 32:18). So the Rock is fragmented and we are all the pieces. But when we are gathered together, we form one body, one Spirit, one God, and we are that being.

So you take it tonight and try it...costs you nothing. Doesn't cost you a penny to imagine that things are as you would like them to be, and see how they mold themselves in harmony with your assumption. You remain faithful to your assumption and they all become a dream projected, objectified, in your world; for we are dreaming it until we awaken from the dream.

Now let us go into the Silence.

If there aren't any questions, thank you. Goodnight.

GATHERED ONE BY ONE

11/17/64

Tonight's subject, as usual, is all about the reality we call God. We titled it "You Shall Be Gathered One by One." Tonight I hope to make it a very practical picture.

Do not be ashamed of your own testament to our Lord, for our Lord, as far as I am concerned, is our own wonderful human Imagination. If you've experimented and you've proven it, then don't be ashamed no matter what the world would say to tell it. I have just quoted from the 1st chapter of 2nd Timothy: Do not be ashamed of our testimony to our Lord. If you've proven it in performance so what does it matter if the whole world denies it? You tell it, because what you and I know from experience we know more thoroughly than we know anything else in this world...if we know it from experience. So don't ever hesitate to tell it. In fact, the individual who has actually experienced God's word cannot escape the responsibility of telling its meaning to others. He just can't do it. He *must* tell it to everyone in the world for the simple reason we're only one. There's only one being in this world and that being, when one awakes, they call Jesus the Christ, the only being in the world. So you put yourself to the test—not another, not testing another—testing self. There is no other. And when you test yourself and it proves itself in performance, then because there is no other you share it with every being in the world.

The Old Testament is simply a series, the most marvelous permanent series of states through which you and I pass. The New Testament is its fulfillment. Last Friday night, I asked you who were here to read the 13th chapter of 1st Kings. I hope you did. I hope you read it seriously and contemplated it. If you were not here, and there is someone tonight who is here for the first time, or maybe was not here last Friday, let me give you the highlights. And behold, a man of God came from Judah and he came with a message. The message was the destruction of that which was not faithful to God. It worshipped false gods; it was the altar of Bethel, the house of God. But he was given a certain condition: He must not eat bread and drink water in the area that he came to pronounce this prophecy, and he must not return the way he came...he *must* not. In the story he was deceived by a false spirit; and so he ate of the bread of that area and he drank of the water. Then the prophet who had received the *false* message said to him, "Because you disobeyed the word of the Lord your God you shall not return to the tomb of your fathers." In other words, he would *die* on his way back. And it was fulfilled. He was killed on his way back.

When you read that you wonder, "What is it all about?" Let me share with you what it's all about, for I have experienced this in its positive state. I did not eat or drink in the area where I was sent to give a message, and I returned to the tomb of my Father. If you do *not*, you cannot return to the tomb of your Father. So let me share with you this strange and wonderful mystery. If you haven't had it, you're going to have it, because there is only one being in the world and that being is God...and *you* are God. You're playing all of the parts in the world, and these are placed like an obstacle race and you and I pass through them, coming towards the ultimate end which is *God awakening*, that's all. You begin as God, the way is God, the end is God...there's nothing but God.

Well here, maybe ten years ago, I saw what I should not see if reason prevailed, for I'm seeing the most wonderful interior of a fabulous building. Consciousness followed vision, and I stepped into the vision that I contemplated, and I explored. Then I saw two ladies and I told them, "Ladies, this is a dream, this is a vision." They were afraid. They were frightened because to them that world was no vision, that was real like this it was solidly real. Yet I knew the origin was vision, and because all ends run true to origins, if the origin was a vision, the end is vision. So I told them this whole vast world is a dream and I am the dreamer of the dream. Well, they were afraid, they were frightened, and they got as far as they could from me; and then when they got out of sight practically they ran. I did not eat their bread. To eat of one's bread is to believe one's beliefs. They told me that what I said wasn't true. I was adamant. I believed it implicitly because I saw it. It began as a vision, the end must be vision. So I was not diverted by their behavior, therefore, I did not eat of their bread. I did not drink the water of *their* truth, because they believed that they were living in a solidly real world as this is real.

And I returned not the way I came. How did I return? I stepped into *that* world as I came onto this stage tonight. I walked onto this stage tonight; that's how I walked into that world. But I didn't return walking from that point in space *back* to where I was on my bed. This is how I went back...another vision. Many years before, I found myself in a dream, and I knew it was a dream, but I prolonged the dream 'til I got to a stationery object. It was a huge pillar driven into the sea, a pillar about that ___(??) in diameter and I felt that if I could hold it—it's stationary, it's not a movable object like an animal or something, say man, it was simply stationary—if I could hold it and not let it go, I may prove to myself what inwardly I knew. I felt that if I in a dream could hold an object and not let it go and make myself wake, I would awake in the dream. I found myself in water and there were these pillars driven into the sea. The bridge that it formerly supported was gone, but the pillars remained. And I held it, I wouldn't let it go, and I made myself awake, and I awoke in my dream. I was just as awake as I am now in this room. I am no more awake now in this room than I was then when I held this pillar. And I knew that *feeling* was the secret…if I could but touch it.

And then memory returned…I went back to the 27th chapter of Genesis. These fantastic stories...empires come and go but the truth of the word of God remains forever. Isaac is blind and he said to the voice that he heard, "Come close, my son...you sound like my son Jacob, come close." So Jacob came close. He said, "Who are you?" and Jacob answered, "I am your son Esau." "Come close, for I am blind, I cannot see." So Jacob clothed in skins to resemble his brother Esau came close and the blind father touched him and the blind father said, "Your hands feel like Esau and you have the smell of Esau, but you sound like Jacob." But I will now pronounce the blessing based upon feel. And he pronounced the blessing and he gave reality to what he felt, and Jacob supplanted his brother Esau. Jacob means "the supplanter."

So I felt this thing and I felt it to be solid. When I touched it my hands didn't go across each other and meet this way, they simply were as far apart as the object of my vision, and I held it and I wouldn't let it go. I said, Wake, come on, wake up! and I woke. I woke in my dream and my dream was just like this, just as real as this. Then I waded ashore. As I waded ashore onto this tropical isle—not the Caribbean for I know them well. I do not know the Pacific as of this moment in time, but it seemed to me like the Pacific, homes built on stilts, either to avoid the animals or to avoid floods, but what I don't know. Homes were built on stilts. As I got ashore, I saw a strange looking animal, a horrible looking thing, and it came towards me. Then I returned by a way I did not come. I was frightened out of my wits as it were. So the statement "frightened unto death" isn't really far off, amiss. As it came towards me I was simply frightened, and then I broke the entire thing and found myself back on my bed. But the world *from* which I returned was just as real as the world to which I returned. So I know that it started as a dream, the end must be a dream. It started as vision, the end must be a vision. This is just as much a vision. It started as a vision and the end is a vision, and we are the dreamer of the dream, and that I do know. I know it from my own personal experience.

Now in the 13th chapter that I asked you to read of 1st Kings he was warned not to eat the bread of that place and drink the water of that place. He was deceived by a lying spirit, and he ate the bread and drank the water. Then the old prophet said to him, "Because you've disobeyed the word of the Lord your God you shall not return to the tomb of your fathers" and so he was killed on the way. Had I not obeyed the voice of God the body to which I returned would have been dead. I returned to this body. When I told the ladies the whole thing is a vision and the end is a vision, they did not believe me. Their disbelief would have caused me to actually live in that world of reality. It seemed so real just like this. I would have feasted on their beliefs of that reality and not been faithful to the message that I brought, which was: It began as a vision; the end is a vision, for all ends run true to origins. I remained faithful to my message that I took. So when I came back the body was cataleptic...it was dead. I entered it...I'm a living presence in a dead body...I animated it after how long I do not know. But I animated it and it returned, it was restored to life.

Then I experienced the 11th chapter of the gospel of John. That's the story of John the Baptist. No "other" did it; there is no "other"; you *are* Jesus Christ. So when Jesus Christ restores the body and makes it once more alive, it is from within, it's not from without. "Jesus Christ *in you* is the hope of glory" (Col. 1:27). "Do you not realize that Jesus Christ is in thee?" Not outside animating you (2 Cor. 13:5). So I returned and found the body dead, but I did not disobey the word. I delivered a message. The message is: The whole thing is a dream, it's all a vision, for it started as a vision and the end must be a vision. And then they tried to give me other bread and other water. But their world is real and it was real. This is no more real than that world, may I tell you. This little thing here, this lectern, is no more solidly real than the things I touched in that world. But I did not forget the origin of the whole thing: it was all vision. So I couldn't forget the origin and the end had to be consistent with the origin.

So I did not eat of their beliefs, I did not drink of their truth, and I did not return the way I came, for I walked into that world just as I walked into here tonight. But I returned by a way I discovered years before that—the way of feeling—where I actually felt this huge pillar and woke within a dream. And so I knew if I could now feel a pillow behind my neck and actually feel it, I would return by the way I did not come. So I felt a pillow under my head while standing in this hallway, and then in a little while I could *feel* the pillow, and instead of being vertical I was horizontal. And I am in a dead body: This body here that is now animated was cataleptic and *dead.* I came into it in a dead body. How long I remained trying to animate it I don't know. Could have been a minute, could have been an hour, I don't know. I only know that after awhile the little finger could move, and then the wrist could move, and then the elbow could move, and then the body could move, and finally I, with tremendous effort, I could open the eyelids. The eyes opened upon a familiar scene that told me I was back in my home on El Camino in Beverly Hills. So I returned not by the way I had gone into the other world.

The command was, "a man of God suddenly appeared..." Where? He appeared from Judah. The word Judah is spelled Yod He Vau Daleth He. The name of God is in the name—Yod He Vau He is in the name of Judah. Only one letter is put into it—other than Yod He Vau He—and that letter is Daleth. Daleth is "a door." He said, "I am the door" (John 7:9). You get it? Who sent him? The word Judah is defined as "he himself"; it's defined as "the hand, the *creative* hand of God." If there is one thing in this world that separates man from the whole vast world of creation it's the hand. A monkey thinks it has a hand...or you think it has a hand...no, it's used only to convey food to its mouth and to swing from branch to branch. A man's hand fashions. You could be the most brilliant being in this world, without a hand you could only be a smart monkey. It takes a hand to create in this world, and the hand separates the whole vast world of creation from man. Man is God! He has a hand, he can fashion, he can create. No matter how brilliant the mind is, if you didn't have a hand you could not express yourself.

So the word Judah—Yod He Vau Daleth He—is defined as "a hand, dominion, power, that creative power that is God." So when you are told, Behold, a man of God came from Judah, came from what? *He himself* came. But in these stories of the Old Testament they are told negatively, and so you do not return the way you came. You *fail* to be faithful to the vision. You entered a world that was real, so real you're carried away with the reality of it. And so, when you told your story, and they showed you how *real* it was and you could actually test the reality of it, you forgot the origin, you forgot God. For, the origin of it was the dreamer, and the dreamer is God. It started in *you* as a dream. That dreamer which is yourself is God. You didn't forget it (after awhile) that it started as a vision and therefore it still is a vision. So you did not go into a false god. So when the man of God came, in the Book of Kings he came to destroy the altar that worshipped false gods. They were carried way. And he ate of the bread of the world into which he came. It seemed so real he partook of it. He drank the water of that world, the truth of that world he partook of it, and forgot the origin of it all. So on his way back he did not return by another way. He came back and he was killed on the way.

In the New Testament, the positive aspect of it is: He did not return the way he came; he remembered. He remembered the cause of it and, therefore, the end of it must be equal to the cause. In the Book of Zechariah, which is almost at the very end, the 38th book of the Old Testament, "On that day the Lord will be one and his name one." The word Zechariah means "Jehovah has remembered." He remembered. He didn't forget the origin of the phenomena of life, he remembered. His name is one. We're all one. And that one, when we awake, we will call Jesus the Christ, and you and I are he. As we actually awake we are he. So I told you a week ago that the one whom he loved is the one that he restored to life. It didn't fail, memory returned. So he came into a dead body. And the story is told as though someone on the outside awoke him; no, not someone on the outside—from within *himself*. He was faithful to the vision and he returned and came out, for *he* is Jesus Christ. He had not yet realized the grand turning point which is resurrection—that comes after—but he restored his body to life.

A friend of mine in San Francisco last September, a surgeon, and he told me that ten percent of all autopsies reveal no cause of death. Now you will see who they are who were not faithful to the vision. So they fell asleep one night and suddenly vision took place, and they went into the world that they contemplated, and it seemed so real. And it is, may I tell you, there's nothing in this world more real than these worlds into which you step. And the world is so real they are carried away with the reality of it and they eat of the bread and drink of the water of that world and they never get back. They never return to the tomb of their father, for the tomb of the father is this body. We are buried in it. We are the fathers and we're buried in these bodies. You never return to the tomb of the fathers as told you in the 13th chapter of 1st Kings. But if you do *not* eat of that world and accept the solid reality of it, as we do here, you will return by a way you did not come. May I suggest, if this night you have not had the experience or you can't bring it back and you find yourself moving into such a world, the way back is *feeling*. You feel anything in this world—which is the world of your father, for this body is the tomb of the father—so anything that is familiar here and you touch it and you don't let it go and make yourself wake within, you awake here in this tomb. If it takes you a minute or an hour or longer, you *will* activate it, you will animate it. You will restore it to life in this world, and they won't take your body to the morgue and cut it up to find no cause of death.

And I am told this is a universal picture, that all over the world those who operate on dead bodies as they do day after day to find the cause of death—especially in a world where everyone is insured they must for insurance reasons find out some cause—and ten percent reveal no physical cause of death. They are the ones who did not obey the command of the Lord, not to eat and drink in the place where you are sent...just give the order. In my case, I was sent to tell them the world is a vision; that I know it because it just happened to me. It started as a vision, therefore it still is a vision and the end is a vision. And they didn't believe me. But in spite of their disbelief they did not persuade me to modify my conviction. I was persuaded and remained convinced that it is a vision, and I returned convinced, and animated my body. Therefore, that was the story of Lazarus (John 11, 12). He was the one that Jesus loved you're told, and Jesus is the reality of every being in the world. Jesus is the true identity of every child born of woman. It's called the soul of man and the soul is the animating principle of a being. It animates anything and makes it alive. That's Jesus Christ.

So here in this fabulous world...he goes on in the very end of the story, in the Book of John we're told, it is he, the one he loved who now tells the story. He tells us all these words are written by the one who testified to the truth of these things. Only a very small section of the tradition of Jesus Christ is recorded. He tells us in the very last verse, if everything that he did were recorded, the world itself would not be big enough to hold the books (21:25). These are the experiences that you pass through. So I say everything in scripture is true. The Old Testament is simply, these are states, eternal states through which you and I pass. I can share it with you. I would be amiss if I did not this night tell you of my personal experiences. For the individual who has experienced the Word of God, I can't see how he can avoid or escape responsibility of telling the meaning of that experience to others. So you read it as something that took place a thousand years or 2,000 or 3,000 years ago to find you experience it, and it's contemporary, it's taking place now. It's not something that happened 3,000 years ago, it's happening now as we become more and more radiant as it were, and begin to awake.

So we are told in the *last* book of the Old Testament, "A son honors his father. If then I am a father, where is my honor?" (Mal. 1:6). A son honors his father. If then I be a father, where is my honor…where is my son? And you turn over the page, you come into the New Testament and you find the son. So the last book, the thirty-ninth book, Malachi, which means "the messenger or the angel of God" and the angel of God was strictly called Jehovah Elohim: God himself. But here was the grand forgetfulness, the dream. He knew the story in the depth of his soul but he hadn't found the son. And then comes the fulfillment of it, as you turn the page over, and here you come into Matthew. Matthew shows you who the son is that honors the father, and I and my father are one. Then comes the unfoldment of the picture.

So tonight, may I tell every one of you, if you have an experience don't conceal it. Any experience that you have of the word of God, scream it from the housetops, no matter who believes it. Because tomorrow—-maybe in twenty-four hours or twenty-four years, when I do not know—-you, too, will find yourself opening, and the eye within you will open, and as they open you are seeing a world just as real as this. Consciousness will follow vision and you will step into that world, and you will be tempted to feast on the reality of that world, for it's not less real than this. And if you do, you will not return...not to the tomb of your fathers. They will find your body and they will call it dead. If you do *not* feast and remain faithful to the vision—-the origin is a vision, therefore the end is a vision; and you tell them whether they believe it or not—you will come back knowing that in this world that seems not more real than that, it too is a vision. And this whole thing here is a vision. For the origin of it was as much a vision as the origin of that world. That is as real as this was vision.

Then one day you will awake for the *last* time and you will say with Paul: "The time for my departure has come. I have fought the good fight, I have finished the race, I have kept the faith. Henceforth there is laid up for me a crown of righteousness" (2 Tim. 4:6). And so when you close your eyes here, after your faithfulness to deliver your message, and your return to re-animate and restore this garment—like a Lazarus coming out of the tomb—you will have, before you make your exit here, you will have the experience of the true resurrection, which is not described in any page of scripture. It's only mentioned but not described. I have described it to you to the best of my ability in my latest book. I am now bringing out a little tiny pamphlet, not bigger than the size of *The Search*, where the whole thing is confined to the four acts of the unveiling of God's image. When my friend Jack will bring it out, I do not know...it's entirely up to him. But I gave him the script confined completely to these four scenes. It is not described in scripture. I have made every effort to the best of my ability to describe it in detail just how I experienced it.

For I know that everyone in this world...now he who wrote that story and the four evangelists did not describe the event. They named it but they didn't describe it. And I feel no compunction to be, I would say, modest about it. Whether the world believes it or not, I have told it in detail just as it happened to me and given the scriptural support for the event, knowing that there is only one of us in the world: Everyone in the world is Jesus Christ. If you have the works of Blake, the 38th plate of *Jerusalem* : "We live as One Man; contracting our infinite senses we behold multitudes, or expanding, we behold One Man"—only one man if the centers begin to expand—"and that One Man we call Jesus the Christ; and he in us and we in him live in perfect harmony in Eden, the land of life, giving, receiving and forgiving each others' trespasses" (line 17). Only one man when the senses begin to expand. The whole vast world is one man.

I saw it one night with Blake. Blake tells you he dined with Isaiah and Ezekiel. May I tell you, I didn't dine with him, but I certainly spent the night with him...yet he died a hundred-odd years before I was born, seemingly. But I wasn't born in 1905. As you're told in scripture, "Before the world was I am." So we are all in one before that this world began. And Blake showed me so clearly how to fall and to look. So I took his advice and I fell backwards like some meteor falling through space. I came to a moment of stillness, and looked as he told me how to look. I saw one man; the man's heart glowed like some living ruby, and he glowed. I contracted my senses and there were multitudes of nations within one man. I expanded it, I saw *one* man, and that one man was myself containing the whole vast world of humanity. All races, all nations, every one was contained within the one man. And one day, you're going to see yourself containing the whole: Only one man and that one man is Jesus Christ. So if anyone should ever tell you, "Look, there he is!" or "Here he is!" don't believe it (Mark 13:21). Why? Because, "Although it does not now appear what we shall be, we know that when he appears, we shall be like him" (1 John 3:2). When you see him it's just like you, and it contains the whole vast world of humanity.

So tonight I've shared with you two great secrets. One in the negative state, the 13th of 1st Kings—that if you are not faithful to the message you take into that world when you step into it, you will not return to the body of your father, to the tomb, which is this. If you are, you'll return (that's the 11th chapter of the Book of John), you'll return and although it seems dead you will animate it, you'll make it once more alive and restore it to life. *You* will do it, for *you* are Jesus Christ. But you'll go through to the very end and then you'll write the story, because you will have the experience of the *true* resurrection. That's restoration [Lazarus]; that's not resurrection. You will have the true resurrection not recorded in any book in scripture, and you, too, will tell it just as it happened to you. And so you're told, "If it is my will that he remain until I come, what is that to you? Follow me" (John 21:22).

And this is the disciple whom Jesus loved, who testifies to all these things and who has written all these words. And we know that his testimony is true.

So you, too, will tell it. You write the entire story and leave it behind you, because you're departing from this world for the last time. But because you are every being in the world you can't be detached from it. You become one of those Blake spoke of "Those who in Eternity contemplate on death," knowing that "what seems to be *is* to those to whom it seems to be" (Blake, *Jer.*,Plt. 36). You contemplate on it, because they actually become what they contemplate and believe; what seems to be *is* to those to whom it seems to be. You become one with the immortals, the eternal beings who contemplate on death, knowing and waiting eagerly to step beyond and redeem one in the body of Jesus; for there is no other body into which anyone can be redeemed. All eventually become one being, one body and that body is Jesus Christ.

Now let us go into the Silence.

* * *

First of all, before we take questions, my friend Jack has a small book at a ridiculous price, one dollar and fifty cents. It's only the Bible. Who arranged it no one knows, so I'm told, so there's no royalty on the book. It's arranged in 365 days for a daily reading. The first page you may completely discount, it's just a little thought by Billy Graham, but he didn't write the book. It's all Bible, no one word in the book is other than the Bible. A week ago they gave me this sample copy that someone sent them. I must tell you it's perfectly marvelous. Pick it up at random and read any page...only the Bible...and the way they've arranged it, Old and New Testament all in the book. Not one word is changed and no comments, no commentary, no analysis, just a simple lovely arrangement in a peculiar manner. So the first page by Billy Graham, you can tear it up if you want to (unless you like him), but the book itself, this simple little thing, for only a dollar and a half. So, it isn't one nickel in my pocket, but I so liked it that I would like to share it with you. It's called *Daily Light.* He doesn't have more than a dozen. Why he doesn't have more I don't know, but it's a little wonderful book of 365 days ___(??), morning and evening. You have a morning reading and an evening reading.

Now, are there any questions?

Q: Neville, in referring to what you said about this autopsy thing, ten percent, does that imply that ninety percent of the people then know what you're talking about?

A: No, I wouldn't say that. No, Bill, I wouldn't say that. I just said, my friend the doctor who is a surgeon when I told him of my experience in answer to a question from the audience, after the meeting he said to me, "You know, we as doctors…I'm a surgeon, I'm in surgery every day of my life…I am called upon to perform numberless autopsies. And I share my experience with you as I share it with all the doctors when we get together at our conventions, and this is a universal statement, whether you be in China, Africa, America, Europe, no matter where you are, ten percent of all autopsies reveal no cause of death." So someone can't get back. In other words, they feasted on the bread and the water of the world into which they stepped. And may I tell you, that world is just as real and as solid as this. But if you forget your message—it began as vision therefore the end is vision—and you're trying to awaken everyone in the world. So you tell them, "Ladies, this is a vision." Well, they're scared to death. They don't believe you. So you tell them it is a vision, it started as a vision, and therefore the end must be a vision; for all ends run true to origins: "See yonder fields, the sesamum was sesamum, the corn was corn; the silence and the darkness knew, and so is a man's fate born" (Arnold, *Light of Asia*).

So it *began* that way, the *end* is that way, all ends run true to origins (Gen. 1:11,12). So you scream it. They don't believe you. But you don't feast on their disbelief and now forget the origin. And you come back not the way you entered that world. You walked right into it, as I walked in here, but you don't, you *feel* your way back into this. As I told you earlier, when I held the post that was driven into the sea and wouldn't let it go, I made myself awake holding a stationary object. I awoke in the dream to prove the origin is a dream and the end—though solidly real and I'm waking in a world and it's just like this—it still must be a dream. And so, you can take anything here and hold on to it, and don't let it go until you awake in it! Whether it be money that you want in this world, fame that you want, anything that you want in this world, hold on to it, and give it reality in your imaginary hand; for Imagination is sensation, really...you can *feel* the thing, you can actually feel it. Well then, don't let it go. Though you can't see it, feel it anyway. "Come close, my son," said Isaac, "come close, that I may *feel* you," for he's blind, he can't see. And so this one comes clothed like his brother Esau, and he puts upon himself skins with hair on it. He comes forward and Isaac said, "Come close.

You sound like Jacob, but come closer that I may feel you." He uses the word *feel* with emphasis. He said, "You feel like my son Esau and you smell like him (he brought two senses to play), although the voice sounds like my son Jacob." But he pronounced the blessing upon what he *felt* because he couldn't see.

So you can't see right now your success, but what would it feel like? What would you feel in this world were it true? Hold onto it. That is a solid reality. I've proved it, for I found myself in water and I knew it was a dream, and I prolonged the dream until I came to a pillar. I felt, now I'm going to hold this pillar solidly, I'm not going to let it go, and make myself wake within it. And I held it and I wouldn't let it go. Then I awoke within my being and I'm standing in water, just as wet as any water in this world. And I waded ashore in a world just like this, having held (like Esau) he made something he felt and touched real. That's the story. So I'm sharing with you. So to repeat myself, the individual who has experienced God's Word cannot escape the responsibility of telling its meaning to others.

Goodnight.

WHAT DOES THE LORD REQUIRE?

11/20/64

Tonight's subject, that is, the title of the subject is taken from the Book of Micah, the 6th chapter, the 8th verse. In this verse he asks a very simple question. First, he makes the statement, "He has shown you, O man, what is good; and what does the Lord require of you but to be just and kind and live in quiet fellowship with your God." Nothing else is required of man after man has been told what is good, these three fundamentals. Outside of these the outer ceremonial is an affront to God. It's an attempt to bargain him into accepting from man *less* than he wants of man. So, all the rituals, all the ceremonials, everything on the outside is really an affront to God. All he asks of us is to be just, to be kind and to live in quiet fellowship with our God. Well, how would we go about living in quiet fellowship with our God?

I think tonight you are going to find this a very, very practical approach to living in this quiet fellowship with your God. To understand it, let me go back now into the Book of Psalms, the 4th chapter, the 4th verse: "Be angry, but do not sin; commune with your own hearts upon your own beds, and be silent." How would I do it? Would that really be living in quiet fellowship with God? Yes. Well, how do I know? I'll tell you this night how I do know. There are supposed to be a billion Christians in the world. And I wonder what percentage...it would be so small it would be ridiculous. If I would ask a very simple question of the whole billion, "Do you not know that Jesus Christ is in you?"—I'm quoting from Paul's second letter to the Corinthians, the 13th chapter, the 5th verse; he's asking the Corinthians, "Do you not know that Jesus Christ is in you?"—if we were honest, the billion of us who claimed that we are Christians, our answer would be, no, we do not know that Jesus Christ is in us. All you have to do is go to any home, especially the homes of those who put up pictures and little icons, and look and see what they have on the wall to represent Jesus Christ. It doesn't faintly resemble any member of the family, far less the one who occupies the home as owner. It doesn't resemble in the most remote manner any member of the family. And most of them are painted or done by very poor artists… they're monstrosities. But there they are, all over the walls, all over the places in all these homes that call themselves Christians. They do not know that Jesus Christ is *in them.*

Tonight, you do this in a simple way, for I'm speaking from experience. You are told to be angry, and the word translated "angry" is "perturbed, enraged." So something disturbs you, burns you up, but do it in the seclusion of your bed. Do it in the silence of the night, the darkness of the night. Let it off your chest. You're required to help someone; and that someone has been helped, then they go back and go back a hundred times, and you are made aware of their falling back. How often Lord…seventy times seven (Mat. 18:22). But get it off your chest, tell them exactly what you think, and then, do not sin. These are the words, "Be angry, but sin not" (Eph. 4:26). Sin is missing the mark; sin is having a target and failing to hit it. You have a goal in life, either for yourself or for another, and if that goal isn't reached, well, then you've sinned. So be angry, but sin not.

Then comes the technique: "Commune with your own hearts upon your own beds, and be silent." So after you've gotten it off your chest, you bring them into your focus once more and see him as he *ought* to be seen, hitting the mark. You bring about your inner conversations either with this individual or with others, implying he, she or they have realized the goal regardless of what that goal is. If you now put into your picture that you are kind, would you like it done to you? Yes! Well, then that's right. That's one of the fundamentals. Is this now just? That's just, you can forgive sin and you must be kind, and now live in quiet fellowship with your God. Well, am I communicating with God? I am. Well now, do I know that what I am doing now is really seen by God? How do I know that God is actually seeing this...because with God all things are possible. Well, I'll tell you exactly how you can know, if you'll trust me. I now turn to the 42nd Psalm, and in this Psalm (you're all familiar with it), "As the hart panteth after the water brooks, so panteth my soul after thee, O God." That's how this wonderful Psalm begins. He wonders when he will come and behold the face of God, for all day long men say to him, "Where is your God?" As he pours out his soul, they are always asking, "Where is your God?" Then he calls upon a memory and he said, "These things I remember, as I pour out my soul: when I went with the throng and led them in procession to the house of God, in joyful songs of thanksgiving, a multitude keeping festival" (verses 1,3,4). He remembers that.

Well, now let me share with you an experience that parallels this—how I *know* that Jesus Christ is in us. I'm not unique, Jesus Christ is in every child born of woman, but people do not know it. So when they ask "Do you not know that Jesus Christ is in you?" they can't honestly say, "Yes, I know." They might have heard of it through someone else, they might have read it, as you read it in the scripture, but they don't *know* it. They haven't experienced it and they have not that inner conviction that it really is true. Now, what I'll tell you now I did not hear from a man, I was not taught it, it came to me by revelation of Jesus Christ. Many years ago I found myself in vision leading a throng in a gay procession towards some invisible house of God. The crowd was thick, and as far as vision could go, an enormous crowd, all in gay Near East costumes. As we walked toward this invisible crowd, a voice rang out from out of space, and the voice said, "And God walks with them." To my right, this woman (she appeared to be Arab) and she asked the voice, "If God walks with us, where is he?" and the voice replied, "At your side." She took it literally and turned to her side. I happened to be on her left side as we were leading this procession. Then she became hysterical. I mean, it struck her so funnily that she simply had hysterics. She said to the voice, "You mean Neville is God?" and the voice replied, "Yes, in the act of waking." The same voice, now heard only by me, not by the crowd...for everyone heard that voice, in her voice and the voice, the announcement that God walks with them; the question "Where is he?"; "At your side"; "You mean Neville is God?"; "Yes, in the act of waking"—all that was heard by the whole throng as we moved in procession to the house of God.

But now the voice speaks in the depths of my being, heard only by me, and the voice said, "And God laid himself down within *you* to sleep, and as he slept he dreamed a dream, he dreamed..." and I knew exactly the finish of the sentence: "He is dreaming that he's me," I knew it. And at that moment, sheer ecstasy, for I was actually sucked into this body by whirling vortices. This hand is a vortex, this hand a vortex, my soles of both feet a vortex, and my head a vortex, and the right side of my body a vortex. Far from pain it was sheer ecstasy as I was nailed upon this body. Well, *who* was nailed upon the body? For I was not the body...this thing took place in vision and I, a living reality, a soul that animates bodies, actually was riveted on this body; and with a joy, an ecstasy that you can't describe in words. It's something entirely different. And I knew what it meant to be asked, "Do you not know that Jesus Christ is in you?" I knew then, at that very moment, from experience that the dreamer in me is Jesus Christ, for he laid himself down within me to sleep—there was a purpose—and as he slept he dreamed a dream. Well, who is dreaming a dream but the dreamer, and he's dreaming that he's me. Don't I feel I am the being that I am? Am I not the dreamer dreaming this that I am? So commune with your *own* power upon your bed and be silent.

So tonight when you are in your bed and you think of someone and you set up a pattern that you want to hear for them—whether it be health, wealth, good fortune, success, I don't care what it is—and just simply bring it into your mind's eye, believing that the being who has done that is Jesus Christ. If he annoys you prior to that or something disturbs you, you are told in the 4th Psalm, Be angry, be perturbed, be enraged, but do not sin. In other words, get it off your chest, but sin not. The next stage is now to set up the pattern once more. You took a picture and you either over-exposed it or maybe destroyed it after it was realized...can't find it now. You brought success into his world or you brought him into some other state of joy, a state where he's gainfully employed. Then he's fired at the end of a day, week, month or maybe some time later, and you hear of his distress again. You hear that, well, he got into the people's hair as it were and they simply couldn't keep him any longer. And he's lost job after job after job and he turns to you once more. Seventy times seven! And being very human you are invited in the 4th Psalm to be angry, to be enraged, to be perturbed, but now do not sin. Right after it gets off your chest then go ___(??).

Who is doing it? Jesus Christ is doing it. Christ actually laid himself down with man, humanity, for a purpose: to sleep. What is the call in scripture? "Wake, sleeper, arise from the dead," as you're told in the Book of Ephesians (5:14). As we're told in the 44th Psalm, "Rouse thyself! Why sleepest thou, O Lord?" (verse 23). Well, who is the sleeper? He is calling upon *God* to awaken. Well, where will he awaken if he entered me to sleep? This seems to be his sleeping place. He sleeps in man and the sleep is so profound it is to the world death. So he's called upon to awaken from this state called death. While he's in it, he's dreaming and he's dreaming the dream of life.

Now, you can modify that dream by communing with your heart on your bed at night, just as simple as that. You read it when you go home, the 4th chapter, the 4th verse of the Book of Psalms. After you get it right off and you explode and just tell them off as it were; but do it at night in your bedroom, in the seclusion of your bed, in the stillness of the night, when you are quiet. That's when you're told to do it. All you need do is to see does it fit now these three fundamentals. Does it fit justice? Am I asked now to do to someone else what I wouldn't want someone else doing to me? If someone came here this night and said, "You know so-and-so is in my way and I want him fired." Well, is that justice? No, it doesn't fit my code; it isn't my code, so I couldn't accept that request from anyone. Someone said to me, "You now, he's in my way, I want him to die. Get him out of my hair altogether, I want him to actually die." Would I want someone to ask that for me? No I wouldn't. So do unto others as you'd have them do unto you. It isn't just...that's not one of the fundamentals.

Now the next one is kind, be kind. Alright, would it be kind if I saw the man promoted? Oh, yes, that would be kind. Would I want to be promoted? Yes, well, now that's alright. It comes within, it fits the frame. And the last one—there are only three he gave us—what does the Lord require of you? The third one is so very simple: to live in quiet fellowship with your God. Well, I found who he is: he is the dreamer in me. I must be in quiet fellowship with that dreamer. I don't want any bad dreams, that's not being in quiet fellowship with the dreamer. I have found Jesus Christ to be the dreamer in man, in every man in this world. And by man, I mean generic man—male, female. Every child born of woman…the dreamer in that child is Jesus Christ. So when you go to bed tonight, do not let the sun go down upon the anger. Be angry if you want to, to clear the whole atmosphere like lightning clears the atmosphere. And after the whole thing is cleared, then come and set it up again, and set up that scene that you really want to take. For the being that is setting it up is Jesus Christ. He actually *became* man that *man* may become Christ.

So I am not quoting only Mr. Blake; I *know* this from experience. Long before I read Blake I had this experience. I was not the poet to put it into words like Blake. So when Blake said that God became man that man may become God, I read the words of Blake long after I had the experience. But I was not given to writing. I do not consider myself at this very moment, though I have brought out twelve books, I am not in my own mind's eye a writer. Blake was a writer, he was the grand poet. He was a painter, the artist in every sense of the word. So he could take an experience like mine and put it into such beautiful, beautiful English. And he said, "All that you behold, though it appears without, it is within, in your Imagination of which this world of mortality is but a shadow." How beautifully he stated it.

Well, if Jesus Christ is the core of my being, the dreamer, and he fills all, he's all in all, what could I encounter that is really in a true sense without? He is dreaming it into being. Well, I can modify the dream, for it isn't going to alter the pattern that I gave him. I give him a pattern and he'll perpetuate that pattern indefinitely unless I modify the pattern. So how often must I do it?—until it's done. If it comes within the code of these three fundamentals...that's all he asks of me. What does the Lord require of you? And then he answers it, But to be just and to be kind and to live in quiet fellowship with your God. Well, having found God as my own wonderful Imagination, for my Imagination is the dreamer in me, I can't think of anything without Imagination. I couldn't dream anything whether it be a daydream or a night dream without the use of Imagination. So isn't my Imagination Jesus Christ?

When Blake said that "The eternal body of man is the Imagination, and that is God himself" he had the experience (*Berk.*,Pg.775). He must, to have remembered walking with the throng and leading them in procession to the house of God. I know I did. And I heard the voice at my right, I heard the voice in space, and I heard the voice in the depths of my soul—-when it said to me, God laid himself down within *you* for a purpose, to sleep, and as he slept he dreamed a dream, he dreamed...and I knew exactly what he was dreaming: He laid himself down within you to dream and he's dreaming that he's you. And that dreamer can take any dream and externalize it, because with God all things are possible. So you start with the dream; and no power in this world can stop it from externalizing itself and becoming objective in your world. They can't stop it. You don't need them! As you are told, "Go within, shut the door and your Father who sees in secret he'll reward you openly" (Mat. 6:6). In the Psalm you're told, "Commune with your *own* heart upon your own bed, and then be silent." That's all you do, commune with your own heart and then be silent. You don't raise one finger to make it so. You simply believe in the reality of this imaginal act, that's all that you do. You must give reality to what you've done.

So I know from experience that revelation is the principle source of religious insight. Revelation has made me the speaker feel so secure in what I tell you. Before it, I might have speculated, I might have trusted wise men, and because they could speak in so many ways and they were so brilliant in the eyes of men, I might have repeated what *they* said. I don't any more... it doesn't matter what *they* said. My only source now outside of vision is the Bible. So I go back and I read the Bible *after* the vision, and I search it thoroughly for confirmation of the vision, because if it's not recorded in scripture it's non-existent. This is an eternal word, and everything else comes and goes and vanishes, but the word remains forever. And so, I went back and here came the 42nd Psalm. I do remember this, I remember when it happened to me, exactly the night it happened, and how this crowd appeared and suddenly I am leading them in this gay procession, where?—-to the house of God. I had no doubts in my mind where we were going. I knew we were on our way to this invisible Mecca, the house of God, and all these lovely gay clothes around me, a *festive* crowd. I knew the search that was mine prior to this, for the Psalm begins, "As the hart panteth after the water brooks, so panteth my soul after thee. My soul thirsts for God, for the living God." Well, that was my search from the time I was a child, that constant search. It was a thirst that not a thing in this world could satisfy but an experience of God. Then comes this fabulous night of the crowd and the voice telling me exactly who I am: A sleeping garment as it were of God. That when he entered this death's door with me he did it for one purpose: To share with me my visions of eternity and dream with me until together we awake; and we aren't two then, we are only one (Eph. 2:14,15).

So he came into this garment and it's dead. He emptied himself of his primal form, took upon himself the limitations of this form to dream with me my dreams of the world of death, really. (Phil. 2:7). For things come, they wax, they wane, they vanish; and all things come and vanish in this world, all things begin and end. The world of death...he took upon himself the world of death as he entered this garment which I now call myself. But I know it isn't my being, because I was actually nailed upon *it*. No, I know what I am. So I can say to the world that that act of the crucifixion where six points were pierced (not five)—my two hands, my two feet, my head and my side; there were six like the Mogen David, the six-pointed star—and they were whirling vortices and they produced in me a joy that you can't describe. So this was the *remembrance* of the *initial* crucifixion. For we are told, "If we have been united with him in a death like his, we shall certainly be united with him in a resurrection like his" (Rom. 6:5). So everyone is united in this death, just like that; and it's God in you or you couldn't even breathe, you couldn't move, you couldn't be here this night. You couldn't in any way be a conscious entity were it not that God is in you as the dreamer.

Now tonight when you go to bed, don't think of some little being that must rise before morning and rush off to the job; it is *God* sleeping that night and *all* things are possible to God. Regardless of what happened to you today on the job—you might have been threatened with being discharged, maybe your creditors are pressing you—alright, everything is possible to God. So when you put your head on the pillow commune with self and that communion is actually in this quiet fellowship with your God. This is the God of whom the Bible speaks—when you say "I am" that's he. Now, what are you doing? You say, "Well, I'm thinking of John, and John needs, well, he needs a good job. He has a wife, he has children, he has to support them, and it's not enough." Raise him up in your mind's eye. Well, how would you raise him up? Well now, do you know a friend, a third party who would tell you of John's good fortune after the event? Alright, bring that third party into the picture and just hear the conversation between you and the third party discussing John's good fortune. That's all that you do. Now *believe* in the reality of *that* imaginal act. That's all that you do. Just trust it and know, *really* know that the being that is doing it is Jesus Christ.

So that's why I said earlier, go into the homes and say, "Where is a picture of your Lord?" and they point to the wall. And then you say, "Bring your children, your uncles, your aunts, your grandparents, bring me all the pictures," and it doesn't faintly resemble the picture on that wall. And yet he became you so thoroughly that he *is* you. Not like another, just like *you*. He took that mold and is raising you to be just as he is, without loss of identity. So when you see him he's going to be just like you. That is Jesus Christ.

So you're told in the same Psalm, "When will I come and behold the face of God?" In the 27th Psalm, "Thou hast said, 'Show me thy face. My heart longs to see thy face" (verse 8). And I tell you, you are going to see that face. The day you see it, you'll be startled beyond measure—you're going to look right at your own face, not another. It's you raised to the nth degree of beauty, of majesty, of dignity, of a strength of character, of...you can't conceive of your beauty when you see the being who is meditating you. You'll actually have an experience where you come upon a being; as you look at him he's glowing and it's yourself. That's Jesus Christ who so *became you* that he doesn't resemble anyone but you. And so you're told: "If any one should say, 'Look, there he is!' or 'Look, here he is!' believe him not" (Mark 13:21). Why should I not believe him?—because, "When he does appear we shall be like him" (1 John 3:2).

So don't be ashamed to know that the being in you is actually Jesus Christ. "Do you not know that Jesus Christ is in thee?" Well, the honest answer to that question from the one billion Christians actually is, "No, I don't know that at all." But I tell you from experience this is all revelation and revelation makes us sure. So you can argue the point, do all kinds of things. What does this same 5th verse of the 13th chapter of 2nd Corinthians tell us? He tells us to test it and see. He said, "Examine yourselves, to see whether you are holding to your faith. Test yourself and see. Do you not realize that Jesus Christ is in you?" So we are invited to examine ourselves to see if we are holding to the faith. So tonight after you do what I hope you'll do, tomorrow examine yourself to see if you really believe in that creative act. That was a creative act; see if you really believe in it. Now you put yourself to the test: In the not distant future, what you did tonight should externalize tomorrow or in the not distant future. See if you are holding to your faith. Well, that's your faith. Your faith may be...but no one here, I doubt that anyone here, would have faith in some little icon or in some little service at the altar. I tell you, it is an affront to God, all this palaver that goes on all the time, as though some being on the outside is watching it and is chalking up to our little credit what our little attendance inserts. Hasn't a thing to do with true Christianity. Christ walks wherever you are in this world. If this very night you stand at a bar, or you leave here and you go into a coffee break, wherever you are seated that's where God is seated.

But he's dreaming; he hasn't yet awakened in man. He awakes in the individual, one after the other. He *will* awake in every being in the world. Until he awakes in all it isn't over. It can't come to an end until all awake. But do believe the words of one who has had the experience of waking; and the being who awoke, may I tell you, was the being who became me. We aren't two anymore, we're only one. In the story as told in the scriptures, you and I are born again through the resurrection of Jesus Christ from the dead (1 Pet. 1:3). I speak of a universal Christ, not *a* little Christ, a universal Christ. He actually became every being in the world and so you are born again through the resurrection of Jesus Christ from the dead. Well, when he resurrects, it's you—-because you have no change of identity and you have no feeling that another one rose with you, it's all you. That's how unique it is. *You* rose from the dead. And yet scripture tells you, only Jesus Christ rises from the dead. So if only Jesus Christ *rises* from the dead and you have the experience of *having risen* from the dead, well, then you know who you are.

And you aren't ashamed of it. You make no excuses to those who think this is blasphemy. You go back to ancient scripture and that's what they said 2,000 years ago, and that's what they'll say every moment of time to anyone who makes a similar claim. Have you ever wondered why in all that is written of Jesus Christ in the scriptures that there is no personal description of him? There isn't one word to describe him in any of his person or in his habits. Others are described, but not one word to describe Jesus Christ—-whether he was tall, whether he was short, whether he was fat, whether he was thin. Why do you think that there is no description of him? Because there was nothing unusual about the outer man. He is the *supernatural* being. You can't see him. He's just like you when you see yourself supernaturally; therefore, why describe the outer garment, which is his sleeping garment? So it isn't described at all. More words are written about Jesus Christ than about any man that ever walked the face of the earth. I don't care who may have these biographies. There is nothing said about our great Lincoln...or go back beyond Lincoln, go back to the early characters...nothing is said of any character that faintly comes to what is said of Jesus Christ—and yet no description of him.

You write some story of our late President...or you go back, say, to Mr. Roosevelt. You couldn't write a biography of him without saying the man was paralyzed; he couldn't stand on his own feet unassisted; that he always had a cigarette in his face with a long holder, and you'd paint such word pictures of a man and you can see him vividly in your mind's eye. But not a thing is said about Jesus Christ. The 11th chapter of Matthew makes one little statement, comparing him to John. They said John had a demon because he came neither eating nor drinking; and when Jesus Christ came, he came eating and drinking and they called him a glutton and a drunkard and a friend of sinners and tax collectors. But that doesn't describe the man. I could be a drunkard and be very, very thin or very, very fat, or I could be a glutton and still be very, very thin or very, very fat. I could be a small little fella as a glutton and a drunkard or a very big fella. But that doesn't describe to say that I'm a drunkard, I'm a glutton and I love sinners. He didn't come to save the righteous—they are already in their own mind's eye so complacent, he left them alone—only those who were missing the mark in life. So he was a friend of sinners.

So who is this being who is *not* described in scripture? His personality is not at all described. He sits right here this night in everyone who is here. And when you just think of your home right now, that act of thinking that was Jesus Christ. You think of a home that you wanted to have, instead of what you have, that's Jesus Christ. Is everything possible to Jesus Christ? Well, then trust that imaginal act and see how he externalizes that act in your world. He will! He doesn't need the help of any being in the world to do it. But when you tonight do it, do it quietly. Get it off your chest first if you are going to think of someone else who has annoyed you—it could be a husband, a wife, a child, a friend, and you would like to tell them off and tell them something. So you're told to do it: Be angry, but sin not. Don't carry it with you into the depth. Don't fall asleep in the act of telling someone off. Tell him off and clear the atmosphere, just like lightning clears the atmosphere. And then, in the silence of that room, in communion with your own heart, bring it into your mind's eye, if it's now seventy times seven, and just take another picture. And hear the voice of either the individual or a friend of that individual or some mutual friend telling you that the one is all of the things that you wanted for him. And then drop off, in confidence that that is a perfect picture and it's done!

You don't need anyone else. Paul came saying you need no intermediary between yourself and God. Rub out all intermediaries between yourself and God. When God revealed himself to him, he said, "To whom would I turn?" Then in that 6th chapter when they all left him and he turned to Peter, he said, "Would you go also?" He said, "To whom would I go? Have you not the words of eternal life?" (John 6:66). This drama is taking place *in man*. Peter finds him; because when Peter found him and named him, he said to Peter, Well, where do you get it? These are the words, "What do you think of the Son of man?" Instead of saying Son of man now, which is the title he always used, he said, "Thou art the Christ, the Son of the living God." He said, "Flesh and blood has not told you this but my Father who is in heaven has revealed it unto you" (Mat. 16:13-16). So he found him, and having found him to whom now would he turn? Because he made the most fantastic statement in that 6th of John: "Drink my blood, eat my flesh or you have no life in you" (verse 53). "My blood and my flesh are the words that I speak and they are living words"—feast upon them, assimilate them—"because no man can come unto my Father save through me." They said, "That's a hard saying; who can accept it?" and they all left him, never to walk with him again. So he turns to Peter, "Would you go also?" He said, "To whom, to whom would we go? Have you not the words of eternal life?" (verse 68).

These are things that you didn't compose yourself; they are revealed from the depths of your soul. Just like that journey was revealed. I certainly didn't sit down after having read the 42nd Psalm...I didn't read the 42nd Psalm prior to it. I went back and searched the scripture for the experience. Because it happened to me in New York City on a night I didn't really expect at all. In fact, you go to bed quite quietly and simply and these things happen. Then you go back to God's word, the external witness, and see if you have any external witness to support the internal witness of the Spirit. Because you must have two witnesses, for only on the evidence of *two* witnesses shall a charge be sustained. So you have one witness, the witness of the Bible, that's one external witness. But you can't bring one, you must have two, and the second witness is the witness of the Spirit, where you have the identical experience, and then they agree in testimony. If two different ones agree in testimony, then that testimony is conclusive, it's done. You can't change that if two different ones agree. Well, the Bible is one and your experience is another, and they come together and they parallel. So you go back and you read the scripture. So when my eyes fell upon the 42nd Psalm, after the experience, I knew I had my two witnesses. I couldn't deny my own experience and here is something written 3,000 years ago. So, I've come, as everyone has come, really, to bear witness to the scripture. I've come to experience scripture...but nothing else.

So I can do anything here in my outer dream if I know who I am; in the hope that night after night I will have the experiences of scripture until I completely fulfill them. For all that is written about me has its fulfillment and must be fulfilled *in* me. So then you go tomorrow into the world of Caesar once more. While you're in the world of Caesar, why not be comfortable? Why not have a good income? Why not have all the lovely things in the world of Caesar? You don't have to be saturated with it, but you can do it if you want to. The day will come you will not really *want* things. They'll be there for the dream if you want a dream; but you won't find security or think you want security in things, you won't really.

But while you're in the world of Caesar dream the things. You have to pay taxes, pay rent and do all the things that you're told in scripture. They asked him, "Do you believe in taxes?" He said, "Give me a coin. Well, whose inscription is that?" He said, "Caesar's." Alright, render unto Caesar the things that are Caesar's. Does he want taxes? Bring me the gold from that fishes mouth (Mark 12:15-17). He doesn't say, I will not pay the tax—he knew he could simply dream anything. And so that same being spoken of in scripture is the being seated here tonight—when you say "I am," that's he.

So tonight you go back...just the few verses I quoted, read that 8th verse of 6th of Micah, and the 4th verse of the 4th chapter of Psalms, and then the 42nd Psalm (it's a very short one). These are the only ones I pulled on tonight to illustrate this point that you can't answer in the affirmative when the question is asked of you, "Do you not know that Jesus Christ is in you?" So when it is asked of you in the future you can tell. You take the whole verse, the 5th verse of the 13th of 2nd Corinthians, so just the one verse, "Examine yourselves to see whether you are holding to the faith. Now test yourselves and see. Do you not know that Jesus Christ is in you?" Well, if tonight you do what I ask you to do you're putting it to the test. If tomorrow the results appear on your tree, then you've found him.

Now don't forget him after you've found him. And keep on dreaming noble dreams day after day after day, not only for yourself but for everyone. See that it comes within the framework of these three fundamentals as named as the thing that God requires of every man: To be just, to be kind, and to live in quiet fellowship with your God. Not a thing you do on the outside. If you want to give to charity, give. It doesn't mean a thing as far as the scripture goes. You have to live in quiet, wonderful, simple fellowship with your God. So whatever you do mentally see that it fits the framework of justice and kindness, that's all. So if it is just then it's right. Is it kind? Alright, if you are in doubt, ask yourself a simple question, "Would I want it done to me?" Well, no. Well, then that's not for you; it doesn't fit the frame. And then after it fits the frame, very simply commune with your own heart upon your own bed and be silent.

Now let us go into the Silence.

* * *

Q: ___(??) can you combine imaginal acts?

A: Certainly. For instance, if you have a desire for yourself and one for friends, would you celebrate if all came true—say a little party, a dinner party, a tea party, a cocktail party? I mean, if you had a party...say six or eight came together and they discussed their own good fortune and all are telling lovely things about what has happened to them...couldn't you conceive of just such a little gathering where all are expressing their joy because of their good fortune? You simply listen to a voice, a familiar voice of one, go to the other one, go to the other one, just as though it were a party. Always do that which implies the fulfillment of the dream. But if you can't bring them together take them separately. You can have a group picture, or you can have just simply a single picture of one party. But try it! You're invited just to try it. You may stumble upon something that you can tell me that I can share with others, because it is infinite, as he unfolds his great secret. He is really your wonderful, wonderful Imagination. That's why the great old man Fawcett, whom I quoted in my latest book, he said, "The greatest of all secrets is this great secret of imagining." If one could only unravel that secret!

Q: In John 11, Thomas said, "Let us also go that we may die with him." It came to me that the "him" could be Lazarus, rather than Jesus as in the preceding verse.

A: The story in that whole chapter is Lazarus and so you are right. They want to have the identical experience. It was *not* resurrection. That was restoration, where something that was dead was restored to life—because afterwards, the same one is writing the story of resurrection; because resurrection happens not at the end of one's history, within it. And so, he went beyond the experience that he could tell the experience. And so, the 24th verse, he tells you that these are my words; he tells you these are the experiences of which I bear witness. He is witnessing all that he is recording in that book. It tells you that they are *his* words, and then he tells you at the very end, if everything that was done by him really were recorded, the world couldn't hold the books. So he's telling you of the unnumbered experiences because he's speaking of the universal Christ. But man has seen *a little* Christ, not the universal Christ that is actually in all.

So there's the descent; the ascent (which is the rising again); and then another descent that it may fill all things. So nothing can ascend unless it first descended, and the *second* descent is the *dove*, that you may fill all things. So the first is death: God became man that man may become God; that's the descent of *God*, where you are nailed, actually nailed here, in ecstasy. Then you rise during the state when you awaken from the dream, but you do not break the dream as yet. Then you have all these experiences of restoring the body, as you're told in the 11th of John; and then you go on with experience after experience until the very end. And then comes the descent, the second one, that you may fill all things, because you must fill all things when you break this wheel of recurrence, the very wheel of death. And so, John is really the cue...uh... Lazarus is the cue in the Book of John.

Q: Do you create these imaginal activities each night? Do you do it for a certain amount of time? ___(??) Sabbath?

A: Well, to me the Sabbath is simply satisfaction—he saw his work and it was very good, and he rested. A complete satisfaction with what I've done so I'm not anxious, I'm not concerned. It's like becoming aware through symptoms of pregnancy...not a thing you can do after the symptoms of pregnancy are upon you. All you can do is simply wait for the appointed hour to be delivered of what you're carrying. Any interference with it is going to produce, either mentally or physically, a miscarriage. And so, there will be no anxiety after you can reach the state of Sabbath. So, after he saw his work and pronounced it very good he rested and called it the Sabbath. So the Sabbath is a moment in time that follows satisfaction with what you've done.

Q: ___(??) Zechariah 13: "Two parts therein shall be cut off and die; but the third shall be left therein."

A: Give me an evening on that. Every time I speak, there's always...if I speak to one or I speak to ten or I speak to a thousand, I have been promised in scripture: Elijah ran away and said, "There is no one" and he said, "Get on back, for there's always my remnant." So he ran, thinking when he left that city that was doomed there would be no one to hear him and hear the word of God, and he sent Elijah back, because he said, There is always my remnant. Wherever I send you there will always be a remnant to receive the word of God. The field must be prepared. And so, he may be the most brilliant man in the world, but the field is not prepared to receive the word of God. So he tells us in the 13th chapter of Matthew the four different soils in which the seed fell. These soils are only *humanity*, for he tells you by analysis the seed is the word of God, and man is that field on which the word of God is planted. Some reject it instantly—that falls on the highway. Then some eagerly accept it, but it's not yet prepared for it, so it springs up quickly but has no roots; not deep enough for the roots, because the soil has not been prepared properly enough. Then comes a third, and finally a fourth. It brings forth, and brings forth sixty and one hundred-fold, the properly prepared soil.

But you could be the most brilliant man in the world and be, relative to the Bible, the highway, where you have no soil whatsoever to accept the word of God. You could be a simple person, ignored by the world, and you can be seeded. This past year in Barbados I passed one of the most touching scenes. These two women on the street, they were without shoes, clothes clean but possibly their only dress, and one was holding the Bible this way. The other, mouth to mouth or mouth to ear, this one was telling her...she would quote the passage and this one would continue it. She had committed to memory the Bible just from sheer hearing it. She knew her Bible from one word, from the beginning to the end. So, when she makes her exit from here, to be instantly restored in another time sequence, in the depths of her soul she has the word of God. She may be put into another sequence where the Bible is not part of her world, not on the surface mind, but in the depth of her soul it's been planted and so it will rise and she will have these experiences. So the word must be heard by man.

I saw these two in a very small little alley. There they were, undoubtedly, they might not even have been working, I don't know. It was the time of day that if they were really on a job they'd be on the job, but there they were, almost in the gutter. One had the Bible open and the other was repeating it, word for word. She would say something—it struck me so, like I can't tell you the thrill that was mine to see them—and she knew her Bible, from beginning to end. Chances are she could not read the normal paper...just from sheer hearing of the word of God. Well, when she makes her exit from this world, she, like all of us, will be restored and inserted into a time sequence best fitted for our unfoldment.

Until Tuesday...thank you.

GO DOWN TO THE POTTER'S HOUSE

11/24/64

Tonight is like every night, really, the same story told over and over and over. The title is taken from the 18th chapter of the Book of Jeremiah. "And the word of the Lord came to Jeremiah: 'Arise, and go down to the potter's house, and there I will let you hear my words.' So I went down to the potter's house, and there he was working at his wheel. The vessel that he was making of clay was spoiled in the potter's hand, and so he reworked it into another vessel, as it seemed good to the potter to do" (verse 1). Now the word potter by definition is your own wonderful human Imagination... that's the potter. So, if I go down to the potter's house, I simply turn my interest within and wonder what am I imagining? So I hold myself or I hold you or some situation in my mind's eye and it's not as I would like it to be, so I am making something that seemingly at the moment is spoiled. But I don't discard it. I reshape it into another state, as it seemed good to me to do. So I am called upon to practice this wonderful art of reshaping images that are not as they ought to be based upon my desire for them. So I hear something of a friend and it's not good, alright, I'm holding it if I heard it in my mind's eye. I am told not to accept it because reason dictates it, my senses allow it, but to reshape it into another vessel as it seems good to me to do.

Now the entire chapter, the 18th chapter of the Book of Jeremiah is devoted to *repentance*. If I say that I will give evil to this nation and they repent, then I will repent of the evil that I intended. If, on the other hand, I say I will do good and they turn from their way into the evil way, I will repent of the good that I said I would do for them (verse 10). So the whole thing is based upon change of mind and the whole thing is based upon God. There is only *God* in this world, and God is your own wonderful human Imagination. So, I go down to the potter's house and the potter is Imagination. It shapes, it fashions. One of the definitions is "To determine, to make a resolution." So you resolve to do this, that or the other. So at the moment when you resolve to do it, to be successful in this world or to be something in this world other than what you are—-at the moment of your resolution reason denies it, your senses deny it, but you resolve to do it— you are told to remain faithful to that resolution. If you remain faithful to it, trusting in your imaginal act as though it were *fact*, then it will externalize itself within your world...*if* you remain faithful to the imaginal act. That's what the story is telling us.

Now, let us turn to the 8th chapter of the Book of Ezekiel. It shows you what man does in this world. And so we are told, the voice came to Ezekiel—-the word means "God strengthens"—and here he calls him "Son of man," the one title used of Jesus Christ. He always referred to himself only by the name "Son of man." So in the Book of Ezekiel, Ezekiel is called "the Son of man." "Son of man" and he takes him in Spirit, for he never left physically. Ezekiel, if you read the story carefully, he never left Telabib, which means "the top of the mount of the flood." He never left that area physically, but he's always transported in Spirit, and transported in Spirit into these areas that the Lord would show him. So he brought him to the court. As he brought him to the court, he said, 'Son of man, look' and there as I looked I saw a hole in the wall. Then said he to him, 'Son of man, dig'; and so he dug, and as he dug he saw a door; then said he to him, 'Son of man, go in and see the vile abominations that they are doing here.' As he went in, on all the walls all around he saw all the creeping (or portrayed upon the walls) all the creeping things of the world, these violent abominations all around. And then he said to him, 'Son of man, do you see what frightful abominations the elders of Israel are doing in the dark, every one in his own room of pictures? And they say to themselves, 'The Lord does not see us, the Lord has forsaken the land'" (verses 5-14). Around on the walls...well, where is this wall? He saw a hole and the hole he dug, and the hole became a door that he could enter and see the elders of the house of Israel performing these abominations out of the things engraved upon the wall. They were all creeping things and horrible monstrous things, all brute force.

What does it mean to us? Well, it means this much: If there is one thing that man worships in this world it is power, it is force. We speak of brute as force, and force as brute force. Any man who falls victim to it falls below the level of man; he enters the brute world—-whether you be a politician, a religious leader, a social leader, anyone who thinks of power, sheer brute force. It can be financial power, social power, political power...and they all are in their room. Well, what is this room? It's all here, right in your own wonderful skull. "Everything that you behold, though it appears without, it is within, in your own wonderful human Imagination of which this world of mortality is but a shadow" (Blake, *Jer.,* Plt.71). So, from this combination of these brutes, these creeping strange things engraved upon the mind, man makes patterns and externalizes these things in his world.

Then what is this little hole spoken of? If I read a simple little statement in scripture, "'Son of man, look!' and behold I looked and I saw a hole in the wall." Now you would think a hole in the wall it would be like I take a little hole through that wall there. But don't take anything in scripture for granted. Look it up in your Concordance, because you and I are living in a different age. Go back 2,000 years to find out what the inspired prophet meant when he wrote a word which is now translated as hole, h-o-l-e. Well, to us a hole could be a hole in the sock, it could be a hole in the piano, but does it really mean *that*? So go back and take a sentence and look it up, and what does the word "hole" mean in the Concordance? "The crevice of a serpent; the cell of a prison," that's what it means. It means the crevice of a serpent, just imagine, the crevice of a serpent, and the cell of a prison, that's what it means.

Now the 42nd chapter of Isaiah: "And they were all trapped in holes and hidden in prisons" (verse 22). The 14th chapter of the 1st Book of Samuel: "Behold, Hebrews are coming out of holes in which they have hid themselves" (verse 11). And you ask all these strange questions, what is this thing, Hebrews are coming out of holes in which they hid themselves and all of us have been trapped in holes and hidden in cells? Well, I know from my own personal experience what this fantastic mystery is all about, and I share it with you: Here in man's own wonderful skull the whole drama is taking place. This is the rock out of which something was taken. And then God himself, this is the sepulcher in which God was buried, the rock-hewn stone in which he was buried, and with him all things are there.

Now why is it the crevice of a serpent? Why, you mean, out of here? This is a hole somewhere and he digs it, and he can enter it, and he's called Son of man, and it's called a door? Well, who made the statement, "I am the door"? He said, "I am the door. Anyone who attempts to come in by any other way is a thief and a robber. I am the door" (John 10:7). So he is the Son of man who could enter and see what is taking place in this fabulous world within man. You and I not knowing, because we say "The Lord does not see us, he has forsaken the land," so I think that if I stand here and I don't talk, I'm just thinking, that no one knows what's going on because it's all alone, I haven't articulated it, I haven't expressed it. So I sit in the Silence and I think no one sees it—-certainly God doesn't see it—-because I do not know who God is. So I think I'm all alone and I can take from this imagery these vile horrible things and I can take all the creeping things and these abominable beasts, and from these horrible concepts I hold of man I can fashion what I want, and delight myself, and no one sees it, so I think. So he said, "Son of man, do you see what the elders of the house of Israel are doing in the dark?" Well, who are the elders of the house of Israel? We are! We are the fathers, all of us, we are the fathers who fell asleep, fell asleep in this tomb, this sepulcher called the skull of man. And in this we are creating the most horrible monstrous things that we externalize in the world of shadows, and we think the reality is there. And the origin of it all is here, all within us, what we are doing.

Now you can test it. I ask you to test it. Take someone you think is out there...a friend who lives 3,000 miles away. Maybe he's in New York City and you've heard from him and things are not going well, and you will think he is 3,000 miles away. Alright, I ask you now to test the actual origin of all phenomena. In your mind's eye you bring him and hear him tell you the most fantastic story about his good fortune, his success—and believe in the reality of that imaginal act. Trust God...for God is doing it. Begin to prove who you really are, and wait for confirmation seemingly coming from there. The origin is here, all within your own wonderful human Imagination. That's where God is. And so you take your friend seemingly out there, you bring him into your mind's eye, represent him to yourself as the man that you would like him to be, hear him tell you all the lovely things that you want to hear, and believe in the reality of what you imagined, that you have heard, and wait for confirmation seemingly coming from without the garment. Because, a seed falls into the ground and it has an interval of time between being sown in the earth and reaping in this world. So every little thing has its own appointed hour. As we are told: "The vision"—-your vision now—-"has its own appointed hour; it ripens, it will flower. If it be long, then wait: for it is *sure* and it will not be late." That's from the 2nd chapter of Habakkuk (verse 3). Every vision in this world, if you don't disturb it, it has its own appointed hour. So, that's your vision of one who seemingly can't make the grade in this world—-he's unemployed, he can't make any money, he can't get beyond the eight-ball as it were—-and you simply represent him to yourself as you want to see him. See him clearly in your mind's eye.

And then one day this fabulous mystery will unfold within you: "And I looked and behold, the Hebrews were coming out of the holes, where they had hidden themselves." Oh, what a fantastic story that is! All of a sudden one day, unexpectedly—and a surprise beyond your wildest dreams—you are torn in two. Suddenly you find yourself looking at molten gold, and you know it is yourself, and you fuse with it, and like a serpent you go up right into that hole. The Son of man must be lifted up: "As Moses lifted up the serpent in the wilderness, so must the Son of man be lifted up" (John 3:14). And you find yourself just like a serpent moving through that hole right into heaven, a redeemed being, completely redeemed. The word is "redeem or deliver." In scripture when I read the word "deliver"—look it up in your Concordance—-what does it mean? A flux of blood. A flux of blood: "Saved by the blood of God." You are severed in two from the top of your head to the base of your spine, and there you stop and stare at the parted body, like a cleft tree. At the base of the spine is molten gold; it's the blood of God, but you know it is yourself. Knowing it's yourself, you fuse with it. The word "flux of blood" also has the definition "fusing." Look it up in your Concordance. So you fuse with it as your very being, and then like this slippery being up you go, right through that hole. And that hole is nothing more than you are told in your Concordance, "a cleft, the cleft of the serpent." Can you imagine that, the cleft of the serpent, the cell of a prison? Man is imprisoned in his skull. Everyone in this world is imprisoned in this rock. And the word rock in scripture, if you look it up in your Concordance, is "to encase, to confine." So man is completely confined within himself in his skull. And the moment will come when suddenly these things will happen to you and you will simply find yourself as this wonderful being, glimmering being, moving up into an entirely different new world.

Then you go back and you ask, well, who is this serpent of the 3rd chapter of Genesis, who was he? What is this serpent who said to me I would not die? You were told that you would die, yes, but really in the end you would not really die. And you ask, what is this serpent? Then you read it, "to cause to fall"...and the word Yod He Vau He its primitive meaning was "to cause to fall, or to cause to blow, or to cause the wind to blow." So who made us fall? Then you go into the Book of Romans, "And God consigned all men to disobedience that he may have mercy upon all" (11:32). Well, if the serpent caused me to disobey and *God* caused all men to disobey that he may have mercy upon all, who is the serpent? And therefore who is that serpent that now goes up through the hole, for the hole is the crevice of a serpent. And you go up just like a serpent in a fiery manner right through that hole into your skull. So you think about it and you dwell upon it.

Until it happens to you, may I tell you, come let us go down to the potter's house. So I will go down to the potter's house and there I see him working at his wheel. "And the vessel that he was making of clay was spoiled in the potter's hand, but he reworked it into another vessel, as it seemed good to the potter to do." So before this thing happens to you, as it has happened to me, then let us go to the potter's house and prove this law. Is this really true? Alright, I will take someone now in my world and imagine that he is exactly as I want him to be. So if he is not as he should be *now*, then it's spoiled in my mind's eye. I'm not going to throw him away, I will not discard him as a friend—no one ought to be discarded—bring him back into my mind's eye and then simply reshape him and see him as I would like him to be; and then believe in the reality of what I've seen for I have imagined. And wait, for all things have their own appointed hour, wait for it and see it externalize within my world.

Now we are told in the Book of Numbers that "If there be a prophet among you, I the Lord will make myself known unto him in a vision and I will speak with him in a dream" (2:6). Well, this morning's mail brought a letter Special Delivery from a lady who is here tonight. These are revelations...and you listen to them carefully. She gave two. She said, "I found myself in a very small room, very sparsely furnished. I was greatly disappointed for I was looking for a man and he wasn't there. Suddenly the room began to fill with pearls—the vase, the table, all things began to fill with pearls, luscious, lovely, shimmering pearls. Then a voice said to me, 'You formerly had false pearls, and then you had cultured pearls, man-made pearls, and now you have the *real* pearl. *He* will find *you*.'" You don't have to search anymore. You've been looking for him and you had your false pearls and cultured pearls. Now he will find you, because you have found the *real* pearl, the true pearl.

On the heels of this comes a second vision. The second is this, she found herself in another world, an enormous crowd that she's addressing, and she's telling them that imagining creates reality. No one believes it. It's a luscious crowd—the costumes and the gowns of the ladies and their jewels, and the attitude of mind of the men simply bespeak opulence. They're all successful. And, of course, they laughed and ridiculed the thought that imagining creates reality...when they have all these things, and these are not at all the cause or the result of imagining, these are something entirely different. And so they asked her to give up this stupid concept of hers, this nonsense they called it. She said, "I will not part with my knowledge that imagining creates reality for one million dollars." At that moment a cart is wheeled towards her and on the cart stacked in neat piles, beautifully piled, is one million dollars which they offered to her. She said, "Not [for] ten times this amount would I part with this thought, this knowledge that I know: imagining creates reality." So they whispered among themselves before this cart came in.

Then, she said, when the cart came in to her, she rejected it, she simply waved her hand and whisked it away. Then her oldest daughter appeared and the oldest daughter said to her, "Well, mother, why didn't you take it if you didn't want it and give it to me?" Now said the lady in her after-thought—-that was the end of the vision—-"Every time this daughter, which is very seldom she does, but every time she appears in my dream she represents reason." She said, "Neville, she's a very nice, devoted, sincere, ardent Catholic. Her church teaches, and she has accepted it one hundred percent, that Catholicism appeals to the *reasonable* man, and so that would be reasonable (she represents reason) to take it." Alright, she ought to take it...that's the reasonable man...in other words, play the game, the world of politics. That's what she really believed that is what it represents.

She said, "She never speaks of you by name, would never call the word 'Neville,' she always refers to you as 'him.' So when I come home from your lectures on Tuesdays and Fridays and I go and get my Bible and my Concordance and Blake, and look up the references that you've used, she knows, well, if it does *this* to you, that you go to the Bible, she said, well, what can you do with a mother who quotes the Bible? But as far as *you* are concerned, you are the anti-Christ." So these were the visions and these comments are all after the visions. The vision was, she was offered a million dollars to deny the reality that imagining creates reality, deny the truth, which she rejected. Then comes her daughter who personifies to her reason. Reason would have told anyone, well, take it anyway, what does it matter? Take the million dollars. You don't have to really give it up, take it. But she rejected the million dollars. And then came the after-thoughts analyzing these things for the speaker.

So I say to you, let us all go down to the potter's house tonight. The potter's house is not out there—it's just where we're seated, where I'm standing, where you're seated—and see what he's doing in this chamber of imagery. For within the chamber of imagery are engraved all kinds of creeping things and abominable beasts. When you think of someone, you think he's no good and you represent him as simply a glutton, a pig, a lion, a tiger, and you represent him in our own words, you represent him by reason of these things that are engraved upon the mind. It could be the most horrible thing in the world that you're thinking of him. You're called upon to recognize the fact that you're not really alone. You say that no one sees us, the Lord does not see us, and the Lord has forgotten the land. I tell you, he hasn't forgotten the land, for the simple reason he entered death's door when you entered it. When man entered death's door, God entered it with him. And he entered it—-and it seems crazy to tell you—-in the form of a serpent. He caused you to disobey, and came down, and entered with you. And so, the hole through which you entered is the crevice of a serpent, also the cell of a prison. So you are imprisoned in that. In fact, you're dead. You are so still and so profound in your sleep you are, to all appearances, as though you are dead. But you are not dead! You are dreaming...and dreaming these horrible dreams all over the world.

Now *knowing* this you can start to change it and prove you can change and modify the most horrible dream in the world, and bring it into a lovely dream; and externalize the lovely part, as we have done through the ages the unlovely dreams. Everyone can do it. Here, tonight, just before I came on the platform, a lady who imagined herself in the picture with Elvis Presley... well, the first one didn't come to pass, alright, she still didn't give up because it didn't work. She just completed the last picture with him finished only a few weeks ago. Not one thought in the world would have allowed her to believe she could have made it with him. She did. She simply didn't take no for an answer and simply imagined it. Now what you think of Presley has no point, hasn't a thing to do with the outside values. It's what you can make come to pass in this world that's important! Can you imagine something and in spite of all things to the contrary produce it and make it come to pass? That's all that matters.

I tell you that God became you, just as you are, assuming all the limitations; and he's buried in a sepulcher; and the sepulcher is that rock-hewn state I call your skull. That's where he's buried and there he dreams. And he dreams, he dreams all kinds of things, the most horrible dreams, until one day he awakes. When he awakes he comes out. That whole thing is split right down the middle. And then you will understand all these strange words of scripture: "Behold the Hebrews are coming out of the holes where they have been hidden," the 14th chapter of the Book of 1st Samuel. Then go back and read the 42nd chapter of the Book of Isaiah, and there they were all hidden in these holes, in these prisons. So we were imprisoned and hidden behind these holes. Then comes the splitting of the entire temple of God, and here you see your "deliverer" and the word deliver in scripture is defined as "flux of blood." You look at it and it is golden, radiant energy, it's liquid, molten gold. You look at it and you know it is yourself. As you *know* it, you *fuse* with it. Another definition of the word deliverance is fusion. And you fuse with it. Up like a serpent you go through that hole. That's how the New Jerusalem is being established, every one redeemed—"not one will be lost, not one in all my holy mountain." No one can be discarded, for it would be God discarding himself. That's unthinkable.

So no matter what a man has done, no matter what a man is doing, it's only a nightmare if it isn't along the lines of love. Alright, he'll come back to it. But you, knowing this, believe. Like the lady who remembered, even in vision she remembered the statement from the platform "Imagining creates reality." To remember that while in vision, and deny one million dollars and say "Take it away"; then to have the personification of reason come into her world, her own child, and say, "If you didn't want it yourself, why didn't you take it and give it to me?" She recognized what the child represented. The child only represented reason; for she believes that her own Catholicism is the reasonable man's philosophy of life. It modifies and changes itself from day to day based upon the tacking of the wind. Just as the wind goes it goes. Today if it is not, well, productive or financially beneficial to go along a certain archaic line, so they will patch it.

I saw in today's *Time* magazine this present council has now signed into law, at the moment, that Protestants...at first they said, "Protestants have found him in scripture"...no they mustn't...took out the word, not "*found* him", "they *seek* him in the scriptures." Well, ___(??) you could put that ___(??). You can't find him there; scripture only confirms what you find in yourself. So, in a way, you can almost say they're right. You first find him in yourself. All the symbolism unfolds in *yourself*; *then* you go back in scripture and you read from the Holy Word of God confirmation of what has happened in you. That's perfectly alright. So you read about the hole in the wall. And then you know what happened to you, how you went up, just like a slippery serpent in a fiery manner, just as you're told in scripture. Well then, you go back into scripture and you have confirmation of what happened to you.

Then you are told that only the Son can reveal the Father (John 1:18; Mat. 11:27). It happens to you and then you realize that these so-called ancient stories aren't ancient at all; they are all contemporary. That these are symbolic persons, and that Abraham, Isaac, Jacob, David, Moses, all of them are eternally true, and you know them more intimately than you know anyone in this world. For everyone in this world is wearing a mask. Well, you don't know him, he's wearing a mask. Everyone in the world is hidden; you don't know them really. I think I know my wife, I know my children, my father and mother, my friends, and they're all hidden by a mask. But these characters, eternal characters of scripture are not. You know them more intimately...no one has to introduce you to David when you meet David. You've always known that relationship of yourself to David, and he always has been your Son. No one has to introduce you to Moses when you meet Moses. When you meet any character in scripture you've known them forever. Before the world was, all these were. We knew them all. They're parts of the great play, the great drama. And so when you encounter these characters in the depths of your soul in vision, no one tells you who they are, you know it more surely than you know anything here on earth. And then the whole thing unfolds within you and the whole tree begins to blossom. This is the great story of our scripture.

So here tonight, you and I can go down to the potter's house and take any person—-I don't care what it is, no matter how far gone he seemingly is in the world of, well, our social world—-and bring him back as you would have him. Be a good potter and mold him and fashion him into your own image of what he ought to be, and believe in the reality of that. Listen to the words carefully: "I went down to the potter's house, and there he was working at his wheel. And the vessel that he was making of clay was spoiled in the potter's hand, but he reworked it into another vessel, as it seemed good to him to do." Didn't discard it! "How often Lord? Seventy times seven." So you have a child or you have a daughter-in-law, a son-in-law, a father-in-law, someone who is not as you think he or she ought to be, don't discard them. Just bring them back seventy times seven into that image and be the *good* potter, be the good artist, and fashion him as you would like him to be. And then *know* that this thing is going to harden, and then externalize itself upon the screen of space, and you will see it in your world. Everyone could do it. So I challenge you to try it. You can be the man you want to be. I don't care what you are now; you *can* be what you want to be.

What you're ultimately going to be that is in God's hands, and no one is going to thwart it: "He who began the good work in you will bring it to completion by the day of Jesus Christ" (Phil. 1:6). Jesus Christ is the image of the invisible God, so when the image is complete, based upon his determined effort, well, then he unveils it. No one is going to stop that image because it's his image; he's doing it. But within the framework of his purpose you and I are invited to be imitators of God as dear children. He's the great potter and he's molding me. So today's pain, don't condemn yourself because of it; tomorrow's hurt, don't condemn yourself. It takes all these things to produce that image. But while we're being put through the works as it were we can be what we want to be within the framework of man. He has his own purpose and no one's going to stop it: "As I have planned it, so shall it be. As I have purposed it, so shall it stand" (Is. 55:11). And no one's going to thwart it. Every child born of woman is destined to bear the image of Jesus Christ, because Jesus Christ is the image of the invisible God. So he who started the good work in you brings it to completion by the day of Jesus Christ. So everyone is destined to actually be shaped as Jesus Christ. Then comes the unveiling, and you are unveiled in four mighty acts; and when the four mighty acts are completed, you are the image of the invisible God, with life in yourself. Not now worked upon but a being who has life in himself. But while that is being done on you and in you, you are invited to imitate him, and bring others into our world's eye and simply mold them in lovely patterns, and see them become these lovely ladies and lovely gentlemen in our world. We can do it, everyone can do it. So we're invited to do it.

Now let us go into the Silence...and go down to the potter's house.

* * *

Q: I don't know what part of scripture it's from, Neville, but I'd like an explanation of, "Since we are all men most miserable, if I'm dreaming let me dream on."

A: That's not scripture. It's familiar, but it's not scripture. We are dreaming. As you're told throughout scripture, "Rouse thyself! Why sleepest thou, O Lord?" That's the 44th Psalm (verse 23). Then we're told in the 5th chapter of Ephesians, "Wake, sleepers. Rise from the dead" (verse 14). And so, throughout there's a call to God buried in man to rouse himself and awake from the dream and bring with him not only himself the dreamer, but what he was dreaming —he's dreaming that he's you— bring you with him into full maturity. But what you quoted, that isn't scripture. But, Bill, we'll look anyway...not scripture.

Q: I didn't get it out of any Bible, it was just on a note that said, "Bible quote." I couldn't find it in the Concordance.

A: No, it's not scripture. It's so unlike scripture, as you quoted, so unlike scripture. When you become familiar with scripture, you can tell if it's Genesis...you can almost name the sixty-six books from which it must have been taken, because they all differ. You can hear and you can feel the very rhythm of the words. So it's not scripture.

Q: Does the potter represent my true being?

A: Yes, my dear, you are the potter.

Q: And we're to fashion things?

A: You are the potter. You're told (I think it's the 64th chapter of Isaiah) "O Father, thou art our potter; we are the clay; we are the work of thy hand" (verse 8). So he's conceding that whatever is taking place now—-for purposes beyond his knowledge at the moment—-is in the hand of the one he calls his Father who he designates as the potter. "O Lord, thou art our Father, thou art our potter, and we are the clay." So that here man is in the hands of God, and can the clay say to the potter, what are you making? "Woe be unto the man who will say, 'What are you begetting?' or to the woman, 'With what are you in travail?'" (Is.

45:10). And so he had *one* purpose. His purpose is "Let us make man in our image" (Gen. 1:26). That's the primal wish. Nothing can divert it. That's the primal wish. So if I am in pain, let no one tell you because I suffer today that I did something that was wrong. I am the clay in his hands and he's forming an image; and as Paul tells us, the glory that is to be, you can't compare any of the sufferings of man to that glory that is the fulfillment of the work (Rom. 8:18). So when people go and tell you that you did so and so, serves you right, forget it, just forget it! You are being fashioned into the image of God and you'll be beautiful beyond the wildest dream of man. No man could conceive himself so beautiful, so majestic, so perfect. Because you are Jesus Christ...when you come out it's the image of the invisible God; and yet no loss of identity, none whatsoever, no loss of identity and a perfection beyond the wildest dream of man.

But in the meanwhile, while that is being done on us in us we are given freedom to imitate him as dear children. "Be ye imitators of God as dear children" you're told. So he's fashioned me this way as the potter...I'll become a potter. I can fashion myself, I'll fashion you, fashion my child, fashion my friend, and see that they are better and better than they thought themselves to be. Within the world of Caesar they become this, that and the other, all lovely things. I stopped using the *brute* force. So, engraved upon the imagery of man's mind are all the creeping things and abominable beasts. I won't use them. I won't liken him to a fox, the sly fox who's trying to get the better of me with his soft words. I wouldn't liken him to something else, I would not use this. I would simply become a good potter and fashion him according to my own concept of what I would like done to me. Always do unto others as you would have them do unto you. If that's your code you can't go wrong. And so, would I like to be better than I am? I would; alright, then let someone hold me in their mind's eye as that, and let me do unto others as I would have them do unto me.

Any other questions?

Q: (inaudible)

A: You try it my dear. May I tell you, in the end we are all one. There's only one. His name is one and we are one. Because I know from experience the day when I look in my mental state and see my David, this radiant being that supposedly lived 3,000 years ago, and I know the relationship of my son to myself his father. And he called Jesus Christ in scripture, "my lord." "My lord" is the expression used by a son of his father. Every son spoke of his father as "my lord," so he's saying "my father." And you know the relationship regardless of the words and you see him. Memory returns and as a man begins to awake, the whole thing returns. We suffer from amnesia, total amnesia. Then comes the Son and he calls you Father, and you know who he is. But you also know that every child born of woman is going to have that identical experience; therefore, if you are the father of my son then you and I are one, are we not?

Goodnight.

ADVENT

11/27/64

Tonight's subject is "Advent." Advent begins on Sunday. It's the first Sunday nearest to the 30th day of November, which is called Andrew's Day. And then for four Sundays men are watching—this is all traditional—and they're watching for the coming of a great event, the second coming of the Christ at the end of *this* age. So that's what man watches for, for the second coming which will end this age. But they look to find someone coming from without, and he never comes from without, he comes from within. For the first has taken place: God limits himself in the incarnation. God became us that we may become God—that's already accomplished. But while he is in us, then he awakens in us at the end of this age as far as we're concerned. God limits himself. Actually to achieve his purposes in this world he imposes upon himself this self-limitation by a certain specialization, a certain selection, a certain contraction, in order to expand. For the only purpose of it all is for *God* to expand.

Now Andrew is the one who is called upon to start the watch. He is the first one of the apostles who found him, and having found him he went and called his brother Peter. So Andrew is the first to discover the one of whom the prophets wrote, the one of whom Moses in the law wrote; and having found him he called his brother Peter to tell he had found him, found the Messiah. Andrew was among the four who always accompanied him. We speak of Peter, Andrew, James and John. And so, in the 13th chapter of the Book of Mark, he takes the four up into the mount, the Mount of Olives. ___(??) It isn't said who asked him the question or who made the statement, but one made the statement, Look at the buildings, these glorious buildings; and he replied, "Not one stone will be left standing upon another. It will all be cast down. And they wondered, when, when will it happen? Not one stone will be left upon another" (Mark 13:1). What is he talking about, buildings in our city here? No. Not one *concept* that man would have of life based upon his own reasoning will stand the test of time, not one—his theory of evolution, his theory of man, every concept that man holds so dear. And there are libraries the world over about all that man knows—not one stone will be left standing, all will be cast down. It's so completely *unlike* what man believes it to be, for the wisdom of man is foolishness in the eyes of God (1 Cor. 1:25).

Now, in the 40th chapter of the Book of Isaiah, we read the words: "Have you not known? Have you not heard? Have you not been told from the beginning and have you not understood from the foundations of the earth? It is *he* who sits above the circle of the earth...calling them by name...his mighty power...and by his great power not one is missing," not one (verses 21-26). He calls everyone by name and not one is missing by his mighty power. He is the one who sits *above* the circle of the earth. And when you sit above the circle of the earth and see it, it's so completely unlike what man believes it to be. It's dead; the whole vast world seen from above is dead. Then God by self-limitation to achieve his purposes comes down by selection and assumes your body, my body, all these bodies, and every body is related. The minute you enter it you animate it and then everything starts.

But everything in this world is completely finished, everything is finished. You can't conceive of a situation in the world that isn't already worked out. Blake saw it so clearly and told it in his 13th Plate of *Jerusalem*, where everything in the most minute detail is worked out, all the relationships of men, everything. And any man who dares to come down—I said man, I mean God comes down—and assumes a state. The minute he animates *that* state the whole vast world related to *it* comes into animation and the whole thing starts to move. It's so completely unlike what the wise man of the world believes it to be. So Blake made the statement in his dictated poem called *Jerusalem* and he gave us the theme of: "The Sleep of Ulro and of the passage through eternal death and of the awakening to eternal life." Then, said he at the very beginning, "Awake! awake O sleeper of the land of shadows, wake! *expand*! I am in you and you in me, mutual in love divine."

Now who is this that actually came down? We're now waiting, beginning on Sunday in the traditional concept, waiting for the Second Coming. Tonight I'll tell you he's come. It's the second coming they're waiting for. How did he come? Well, he's spoken of in scripture as Christ Jesus, defined in scripture as the power of God and the wisdom of God (1 Cor. 1:24). The power of God and the wisdom of God is buried in man.

That power and wisdom is called Christ Jesus. It's *personified* as a being called Christ Jesus. He's spoken of as the Son of God, but he makes the claim, "I and my Father are one." So God himself comes into man, buries himself in man, and is the reality of man. And that God *in* man, which is Christ Jesus, has to come the second time; this time not from without, he comes from within.

He awakens *in* man...something that may not be easy to grasp. But may I tell you, if you reject it…I will quote the 12th chapter of John, for when you reject a man's words you reject him. "He who rejects me has a judge; the word that I have spoken will be his judge on the last day" (John 12:48). He won't be heard because the same being...but on the last day when it happens to *you*, you will know how true the word was. So "He who rejects me has a judge; the word that I have spoken will be his judge on the last day." That last day could come tonight. For when it comes it comes suddenly, comes like a thief in the night. You don't really expect it, it suddenly happens to you; suddenly *you* awake and you realize that the being you thought to be Jesus Christ and looked because of the misunderstanding of Jesus Christ, you thought him to be another. And you look eagerly for a second coming, some being who would come out of space and save you and your nation and your race and all these things, and it doesn't come that way at all. It's all specialization: God actually achieves his purpose by self-limitation by selection. He selected you in this fabulous state and limits himself to *you*, and took upon himself that contraction that is you that he may expand. For the whole thing is based upon his contraction. As he contracts himself and takes on *this* limitation, then something happens in you. He breaks it, like a seed becoming alive, and it begins to grow. So he takes upon himself the limitation called Neville. I think I was born of my mother, I think I have a certain background, of a certain family background, and all this thing man taught me. I was told that I evolved from some strange thing out of the mud, and all of a sudden here came man and then another man and another man, and finally I find myself *this* man. Don't believe it. Every stone that man has simply piled up on this glorious building of his, called the wisdom of man, the whole structure is going to fall, and not one stone is going to be left standing upon the other.

The day will come you will actually have the experience of the 40th chapter of the Book of Isaiah: "Have you not known? Have you not heard? Has it not been told you from the beginning? Have you not understood from the very foundations of the earth it is *he* who sits *above* the circle of the earth...calling them by name? Every one called by name." We are afraid of billions? Multiply billions by billions, more than the sands of the sea, and every one is named. He calls every one—he specializes—all by name. And as he calls them by his mighty power, not one is missing. "Not one can be lost in all my holy mountain."

The day will come you will have the vision of the mystics, the vision of Blake. I have seen it. One night he showed me how to look and I saw it. I'm not alone in this, others have had the experience of actually being above the circle of the earth and seeing everything here as dead, and how they could not animate it from there. They had to come down. They must leave that high, exalted level and come down and assume the state. So Blake tells us, when you enter into the state, everything else seems shadowy and unreal, but the state seems to be the only substance. Before you enter the state you see it as something dead. But if you dare to enter the state and take upon yourself the restrictions, the contraction of that state, and move it, animate it, everything related to that state becomes alive and everything else is shadowy and unreal. So, said Blake, "If one could only enter into these states in his Imagination, approaching them on the fiery chariot of his contemplative thought...if he could make a friend and a companion of one of these states in his Imagination...then he would rise from the grave...then he would meet the Lord in the air and then he would be happy" (*Vision of Last Judg.*, Pps.82-84).

Well, that's what God did. God sent himself called Jesus Christ—Jesus Christ being the power and the wisdom of God—for that's what God desires to expand. He took upon himself the limit of contraction that is man, the limit of opacity that is the darkness, called in scripture the devil or called Satan. He took *that* upon himself. And then, wearing it for awhile—Blake calls it 6,000 years—the seed breaks and suddenly it's the *second* coming. The first coming was the contraction and assuming the limitation of that contracted state; and the second coming is when he, as *you*, rises in your skull, and *you* awake in your skull…not another. Then you realize who Jesus Christ really is. So when you read the word "he's the power and the wisdom of God"...and this is how he actually came the second time: He was born from above. For, we are told in the Book of Peter, 1st Peter, the 3rd verse, "We are born anew through the resurrection of Jesus Christ from the dead." Man is born anew through the resurrection of Jesus Christ from the dead, and all of a sudden *you* are born anew. But no other being came into your world. Then you realize who Jesus Christ really is—*you* are resurrected from the dead. You awoke within yourself, and having awakened *within* yourself you come out and now are born anew.

Then you realize the story as told in scripture as they record it. They're not recorded according to the position that they occupy in chronological sequence, but they are recorded according to their content. And events that coincide in content are simultaneous. So the resurrection that should come, say, fifty years later or 6,000 years later—for if the journey is 6,000 years, and we have been crucified with him in a death like his and we shall be resurrected with him in a resurrection like his, well, this is a 6,000-year span—they should be *so* recorded. But they're *not* so recorded. Because events that have mingling in content are really, though separated in time, they are really simultaneous, they are together. I can tell you from experience these two *really* are together.

Now there are signs that precede it, no question about it. One of the signs is the sign I'm speaking of this very night. You will have the experience of being seated above the circle of the earth looking down on a world that is dead, I mean dead, just dead. You have the experience of coming down from that circle and entering what you see as your own body. You will animate it once more. As you animate it, your world becomes alive. If you didn't come down and re-animate it, the world remains dead as far as you are concerned. For, none of these here really are what they appear to be. Every stone is going to topple. Not one stone will stand above the other when he comes. And when he comes he precedes his coming by these experiences. You have the experience of sitting on the circle above the earth and watching it all as something that is inanimate. You'll have the experience of returning and animating a body that seemingly was dead. You have the experience of stopping and starting the machine and realize that they aren't there at all. The whole thing is taking place within you, for the purpose of it all is to have life in ourselves: "As the Father has life in himself, so he has granted the Son also to have life in himself" (John 5:26). And you realize what life *really* is.

You won't find it in any laboratory in the world. I am told today that fortunes are being spent, something, a very hush-hush process, to find out the secret of life. I'm told that great foundations are giving fortunes right here in our land. They think they're on the very verge of it. And I have news for them you will never find it in a test-tube. You will never find it in anything that man thinks that is the origin of life: it's all in you. Life is an activity of your own wonderful human Imagination. One day you will so control it you will stop it and start it at will, and the whole vast world will stop and start at will. But, before you have *that* control, you will sit on the circle above the earth and watch it as something that is completely dead, and make your selection, make your specialization, and come down and take that contracted form, and bury yourself in it, and assume the complete limitation of that contraction for one purpose: for expansion. But to do it means you must dream the dream of life and you will dream the dream of life. At the very end of the dream something will break within you. As it breaks, you awake, and you awake to find yourself in your own wonderful skull, the sepulcher wherein you were placed when you made your decision. It is all God.

And then you realize the words of the 11th chapter of Romans, all things were made by him, and through him, and for him. Then the 15th chapter of 1st Corinthians, and ultimately it will be revealed that he himself is everything. There is nothing but God and *you* are he. Nothing in this world but God and you are God. It's God who actually took upon himself this restriction for the purpose of expansion. And this restriction is called by Blake, the great dream, the great sleep, where he passes through death. When you read these words—and he claims they were dictated by the spirit of love—well, how could you actually have a passage through death? He said, "The sleep of Ulro and the passage through eternal death and the awakening to eternal life." Well, how could you have a passage through eternal death? When you see it, you realize that's the death, and you go right down and actually take possession. You select it.

Then, at the very end, you come out, called by name, and yet you are Jesus Christ. In the end there's only one name, really, it's Jesus Christ. But you are called by the name—it's not Jesus Christ—by your own wonderful name. He calls them by name and not one is missing, we're told. You read it carefully in the 40th chapter of the Book of Isaiah. Start from the 20th through the 26th verses...just that short six verses. And he asks us as though, why have we forgotten? "Have you not known? Have you not heard? Has it not been told you from the beginning? Have you not been told this from the very foundations of the earth?" Then he tells us what we were told but we forgot. And may I tell you, when you come here you have to drink the drink of forgetfulness. God completely empties himself and completely *forgets* that he's God when he becomes man, completely forgets. So you do not know anything but the relationships of birth; and you're proud of your background, of your race, of your nation, of all these things; and none of these things are you, in the true sense of the word. You brought them all into being and there they are part of the eternal structure of the universe. But you took upon yourself this structure—which was the *limit* of contraction— for the purpose of expansion. For there is no limit to expansion, only to contraction; there is no limit to translucency, only to opacity. So you took upon yourself the most opaque state in the world and felt yourself completely shut out, and all dark. Then you move from darkness to light, from this contraction to expansion.

Now, while we are in *this* world of ours, having completely contracted ourselves, we can still test this principle on this level. While a man called John Brown—and John Brown may be poor, or he may be unemployed, or he may be this, that or the other, and he desires to be other than what he is at the moment—he could dare to assume that he *is* the man that at the moment of his assumption reason denies and his senses deny. And if he dares to assume that he is, he's doing the same thing that he did from a higher level when he came down and assumed the fact he was John Brown. So he came down and took upon himself the restriction of John Brown. As John Brown, he need not go on forever in that one place. He could change from state to state to state. And when he enters a state, all the other states seem so unreal; but the state he enters seems to be the *only* reality, the only substance, as he enters that state.

So you could this night assume that you are this very night the lady or the gentleman that you want to be and although everything denies it, just *dare* to assume that you are it. Then remain loyal to that assumption, as you in the beginning swore to yourself you'll remain loyal to being man until you woke in man as an individualized being, completely individualized. That was your pledge—not to another, for there was no other—it was your pledge to yourself. Now, as *that* pledge is being kept while you are here and completely shut out and everything is forgotten, you could now assume that you are and you name what you want to be, and see it actually unfold before your eyes, the whole thing has become a fact. If you know what you want to be or if you know what you would like someone you love to be, then dare to assume that they are it or you are it or others are it. And then, try to remain as faithful as you can to that assumption as you are now remaining, and you will remain, to this present and most unique assumption when you specialized in becoming man. For, you're not going to break it. If you die this very moment, you don't really die. You restore yourself to life, really, and insert yourself in the same circle that is here, where you were above it before you came down. No loss of identity, but none whatsoever. With the same identity you're re-inserted into a time sequence best suited for your awakening.

And so, the moment will come in time, at the very end, when you will awaken; and you will understand this great mystery being celebrated this coming Sunday by the Christian churches of the world, the Day of Andrew. Behold the man...they are waiting for him. But the whole vast world is waiting for him to come from without. Many of them sell their possessions and go off to some mount waiting for him to come. And you're told he does not come by watching; he comes suddenly when you least expect it…and that I know from experience. No expectation, no even looking for him, suddenly, a very normal day, a normal night, and suddenly you begin to awake. You think, at the beginning of the awakening, that this is a normal waking, but it doesn't feel like it, it's more intense. Your head becomes so intense and then you awake to find yourself in a sepulcher, and the sepulcher is your skull. Then you know, and you push a certain hole at the base of the skull, and out you come and you are born from above.

Here, these two events that should be separated in time between birth and resurrection, and if you are, say, sixty-years old, birth should be separated from resurrection at least by sixty years, but it isn't...the same night. Because the contents of the two events coincide, and so in their mystical language they coexist, they're simultaneous. And then the other event follows quite closely on it, a few months later, and altogether all part of the same complex, all within a matter of three-and-a-half years. And what should really be a long spell of time, but in the last days they rush upon you, and all are culminated in three-and-a-half years, after the end of a long dream. A horrible dream in many respects, yet not altogether horrible; many parts of it were lovely. But as Blake said, "Joy and woe are woven fine, a garment for the soul divine." It's not *all* woe and it's not all joy, but they are woven fine, a garment for the soul divine. And then you weave your garment through 6,000 years of this dream, and then when you come out, you're clothed as he is clothed, clothed with the Spirit. And you had the experience of the dream of life while wearing the restrictions of the garment called man.

So, this is Advent. Advent, the coming of a great event: The second coming of Christ at the end of the age, this age. For when it comes at the end of *this* age, you have broken the thing called death. You can die no more, as told you in the 20th chapter of the Book of Luke (verse 35). You are now a son of the resurrection, a son of God, returned, enhancing the glory of God. For when a son comes back he brings back by his breaking through death, he brings back an increase of power, an increase of wisdom to God. For bear in mind the son is defined in the 1st chapter of Paul's 1st letter to the Corinthians as "the power of God and the wisdom of God" (verse 24). So when that son returns, having gone into death and destroyed death—for that's the last enemy to be destroyed; he destroys death as far as he is concerned—and returns with an increased power and an increased wisdom. And that's the only purpose for this creation. Hasn't a thing to do with the natural order at all; simply to extract his sons *from* the natural order. And the whole vast creation *groans* waiting for the revealing or the unveiling of the sons of God. And they are unnumbered, more than the stars of the heavens, more than the sands of the sea, and yet everyone is unique, everyone is known by name, and not one is missing. Not *one* can be missing when they return, and altogether to unite into a single man who is God...a single man and that one man is God. The fragmented being taking upon himself—having seen exactly what it's going to be—but that was for a purpose and God achieves his purposes by self-limitation, by specialization, by selection, by contraction in order to expand.

And so, you were chosen and no one in the world could have entered that expansion of God for you, no one. God's only begotten Son actually became that one particular thing that you call you; and it's in-woven in you, and sleeps in you dreaming the dream of life. And then he wakes and you are he. And that's the glory of it all! Then that whole wonderful story as you've been told it for centuries now begins to return, memory returns. It was never another that he sent; he sent himself. He who sends me came with me, and, therefore, he who sees me sees him who sent me. If you will not receive my word, then you reject me; if you reject me, you have a judge. I will not judge you and no one else will judge you, but you have a judge; the word that I have spoken will be your judge on the last day. For on that last day you will experience it and having experienced it you are self-judged; and you will know the truth of the word you heard and you rejected.

So everyone, *everyone* will be saved, but no one is lost. No one is unredeemed at the end of the dream, for God is calling everyone by name. And he actually sits above the circle of the earth, that's his home, but he comes down and assumes the restrictions and the limitations of man. And when you see it from above, believe me, it's dead. It seems so alive here—three and a half billion animated bodies moving all over—but when you see it from above they're dead, everything is dead. And then you'll see even wearing a garment that you yourself wear and you will come down and animate it. Only as it is animated does the world related to it become animated. And then it becomes animated because you animated the body that you specialized, that you actually selected, and wove yourself into that limited state...and then this becomes animated.

Then one day you'll have other experiences of turning it off and turning it on. All these precede...he said, what are the signs of the destruction of the temple? He doesn't analyze any of the signs, but he implies, he intimates some of the signs. You read it in the 13th chapter of the Book of Mark. He doesn't actually spell it out but these are the signs that I'm telling you from experience. These signs you shall have, the signs of moving into a world within a world, returning to this world to find a dead body that you left behind. And then you restore it to life; then you know the mystery of Lazarus. It was not another: it was Jesus Christ in you, who is your very being, who restored that body, because Jesus Christ restored that one, and "Jesus Christ *in you* is the hope of glory" (Col. 1:27). As we are told, "Do you not know that Jesus Christ is in you?—unless, of course, you fail to meet the test" (2 Cor. 13:5). Well, the test is to animate the body; for only Jesus Christ can animate it; for he is the resurrection and the life. For if you come into a body that is dead, cataleptic, and it won't move, and then suddenly after, well, how long I do not know, maybe a minute, maybe minutes, maybe longer, then the thing becomes once more animated, reactivated, then you know who Jesus Christ is.

And then, ___(??) comes that final state at the *end* of the play, before you depart from this world, because your time has come at the end when you're going to depart from the world. "For the time for my departure has come," said he. "I have fought the good fight, I have finished the race, I have kept the faith." What faith? That faith in the beginning when I came down and limited myself for the purpose of expansion—I've kept the faith and "Henceforth there's laid up for me a crown of righteousness" (2 Tim. 4:6). So here, everyone goes through the same thing; so in the end, everyone is that one being, without loss of identity. That's the amazing part, no loss of identity, and yet all the Son of God. And the Son of God is one with God the Father: "He who sees me sees the Father. How can you say, Show me the Father? If you see me you see the Father" (John 14:8). For he who sent me hasn't left me, he's one with me; so whoever sees me sees him who sent me. And so it was a self-decision when man as God comes down and takes on the limitation of man.

Now to put it to the test...tonight, you put it to the test…you take some noble dream for yourself. Make it a *noble* dream and dare to assume now that you are the man, the woman that you would like to be, and then look mentally into your world for confirmation. They're all dead; just look at them, and then animate them, let them see you as you are seeing yourself. Let every one of them see you as they would have to see you were it true. Then see them become alive in your mind's eye and hear their conversations implying that they see in you what you want the whole vast world to see, just let them see it. Now that's another state you've animated while still waiting for the end, for the second coming or the awakening of Christ within you. Before he awakes within you, you can put him to the test, because he is dreaming. He's dreaming this whole vast world and you can modify the dream and change it to suit your heart's desire.

So tonight, you take yourself, take a friend, take anyone, and just simply try it. May I tell you, if you try it, it won't fail you. You don't need any intermediary between yourself and God because you are he. God became you that you may awaken to find yourself God. So you don't need anyone between yourself and God. So try it. Do you know of someone in need? Well, alright, represent him to yourself as the man, or the woman that you would like him to be, or like her to be, and just believe in the reality of that imaginal act, just believe in it. And be as faithful to that as you are now faithful—and may I tell you, you will remain faithful—to your initial decision to restrict yourself for the purpose of expansion.

When you see it in this light and you go back and you read Blake, the whole thing becomes awake, for he sees it so clearly. That first line of his, after he gives us the theme, he said: "This theme calls me in sleep night after night and wakes me every morn"—and he tells us of this wonderful being called the Spirit of Love—"spreads his beams of love over me and dictates the words of this mild song." But the first dictated words are "Awake! awake O sleeper of the land of shadows, wake! *Expand*! I am in you and you in me, mutual in love divine"...the first dictated words of this glorious poem, which he claims God himself dictated and did this night after night. As he was waking he could feel the words and hear the words coming through twelve, twenty lines at a time.

So, the whole thing is simply to awake after having imposed this profound sleep upon self. So we're the ones spoken of in the 2nd chapter of Genesis, where he caused a profound sleep to fall upon man and he slept (Gen.2:21). Now, the waking is the second coming of Christ. And all through scripture the words are "Awake! Rouse thyself! Why sleepest thou, O Lord?" (Ps. 44:23). It's always a call to awake. But may I tell you, you *will* awake at the end—that end which is called Andrew's Day, the second coming of Christ, you'll awake. And the words that I've told you from this platform and I've told you in my latest book, *The Law and The Promise*, that last chapter, are true. There are some who will reject it because of their traditional concept of the second coming. They expect him to come from without and not to awaken from within, and so they will reject it. But I will repeat, from the 12th chapter of John, "He who rejects me has a judge; the word that I have spoken will be his judge on the last day." Not going to condemn him; he will see how true it was when he heard it a year, a century, or centuries ago. It will all come back to him that he heard it and he rejected the word of God; and now he fulfills the word of God. And so now *he* tells it to find himself rejected...and so the old, old story. So now he goes out and tells it expecting acceptance from him, when he rejected it when he first heard it. That's the old, eternal story.

Now let us go into the Silence.

* * *

Q: Neville, would you explain this from 1st Corinthians, the 10th chapter, 9th verse "Neither let us tempt Christ as some of them also tempted and were destroyed of serpents."

A: Let us not tempt Christ as others tempted him and were destroyed of serpents? Well, that goes back to the Book of Exodus where those who would look at him *risen* when lifted up were instantly cured of any disease that they had. Those who would not look were destroyed by the disease, whatever disease they had. And so, they were told to look at the serpent that was lifted up on the rod that budded, and everyone who would look to this lifted-up-serpent were cured. Well, the lifted-up-serpent was simply the Son of Man raised from the dead. Hear the story and believe it. You're looking at it, you're seeing it, you're accepting it. If you know it—"to know" and "see" are one in Greek—and so if I know it because I have accepted it, I'm seeing it. So I'm looking at the risen serpent and no one was destroyed who looked at the risen serpent. Those who were bitten by serpents, who would not look at the *risen* serpent, were destroyed. For we speak of the serpent wisdom, well, the wisdom of man is serpent wisdom, and they're so wise in their own conceit; they know it all.

There are some who are going to live forever in the garments of flesh. Why, I would never know. We come to the very end, as Shakespeare describes it, sans teeth, sans everything, yet they still want to vegetate, without any reason for living, not a thing that is left. Making us all ___(??), the one thing they valued. And all the other things go with it, but they want to live forever. In fact, I saw a sign here "How to live forever" right on the street at Hollywood and Vine, a huge, big sign advertising some lecture. This man is going to show them how to live forever. Because he goes on the theory, as others have, the way to make his exit from this world tonight, why should he care? As long as he's still here he can get away with it and fool everyone until he makes his exit, which is inevitable, and the day he makes his exit he isn't going to be concerned about the millions he fooled. And so, let the millions come and pay him for living forever. He's not alone; it's been going on forever—so the serpent and the wisdom, human wisdom, up against the serpent that is God.

Blake speaks of this wonderful serpent, he calls it Orc. When the child was born it was named Orc and it came from the serpent that was coiled in the south, and to Blake the south is the eye. And so, here he sees this thing coiled, in vision, and then when it brought forth a child the world screamed, and they called the child Orc.

Any other questions, please?

Q: What determines the individual awakening? You keep saying that none will be lost, but what determines the individual awakening?

A: Well, my dear, I can only give you my own experience. No one in this world of the three billion and a half who walk the face of the earth (and I am one of them) no one ever told it to me, I never suspected it, it just happened. And when it happened, it came so suddenly, so unexpectedly, no one was more startled. I was born and raised in a Christian home, raised in the Christian tradition, and I wasn't taught it this way. With all of my teaching across this country I wasn't taught it this way. I was taught that Jesus Christ was another, some other being, and didn't realize it's the universal, the cosmic Christ which is the power and the wisdom of God. I read it in scripture, but because of my background and training I didn't see what was there to be seen. It's so difficult for man to change his opinion of events once they've become fixed traditionally in his mind's eye. When as a Christian I was raised to believe Christ in a certain way, I didn't realize that the sepulcher in which he was buried was my own skull. I didn't know it. The birth of Jesus Christ I thought *took* place; I didn't realize it is ever taking place, on the heels of the resurrection. So you go back and you read scripture and in that 1st chapter, the 3rd verse of 1st Peter, "Man is born anew"—that is that second birth—"by the resurrection of Jesus Christ from the dead." Well, it comes right on the heels of your resurrection…and you realize how it is conditioned on the resurrection. You wouldn't think a birth is conditioned on resurrection, would you? It doesn't make sense. And yet there are the words in scripture: "Man is born anew through the resurrection of Jesus Christ from the dead."

But when man is taught to believe he did it 2,000 years ago, then our second birth would follow because he did it as a resurrection...isn't so at all. He is resurrected in *you,* and on the heels of his resurrection in you, *as you,* you are born from above. That's how it happens. And it happens without anyone taking thought. You came to the end of your journey. We are on a very long journey, a pilgrimage where man is enslaved; God is enslaved. He took upon himself the form of a slave and was born in the likeness of man...you (Phil. 2:7)...that's the one he took upon himself. And one night when you least expect it...it could be a very simple day, as it was in my case, certainly not expecting it, because I never heard it. No man taught it to me. I never read it in a book where I understood it. Yet it is in scripture, but scripture isn't taught that way by those who teach scripture. They have a complete misunderstanding of this great mystery. And so, when he wakes in you, at that very moment you are born...you come right out. You wake in a skull to find it a sepulcher, and you know it's a sepulcher. You push the base and out you come. All the symbolism as given us in the Book of Matthew and Luke appear before you, the men, the child, the wind, everything. The whole thing comes and you don't invite any of it, it just happens.

And then you come back to this so-called normal world and you stand bewildered, just bewildered. What is this secret of God's selective love? For you don't feel worthy of what has happened to you. You're the same man that you were the night before you went to bed. And yet you know what has happened, that everything said of Jesus Christ has happened to you, right now. And yet you know your background, memory hasn't failed you, and so you know the mistakes you've made, the things of which you are ashamed. Things that you would not do over, you hope, if given the same opportunity—you'd be more of a man—and yet you can't deny you did them. And you realize what God's grace *really* is. So what is his selective love? What is the secret of his selective love? It remains his secret.

So I say to everyone, just as you're told tonight, not one will be missing. Because of his mighty power he calls us by name, and not one will be missing. So you can tell that to the whole vast world. "Though your sins be as scarlet, they shall be as white as snow." That's a promise made in the very early part of Isaiah, either the first or second chapter of Isaiah, "Though you're sins be as scarlet, they shall be white as snow" (1:18). And who hasn't made these mistakes in his life? Show me the man who will claim that he hasn't and I'll show you a liar. So my memory hasn't faded, I recall the mistakes I've made. I'm still aware of what I have done in my sixty years...and yet it happened to me. So it is said of him, he comes into the world eating and drinking, a glutton and a winebibber, so how could *he* embody the Messiah that is the expected one in this world? So he comes a normal man from a normal family doing the normal things, a friend of sinners, a friend of tax collectors, everything that they would not expect the coming one to represent. So he comes in that garb...that was his selectivity...and while he selected that constricted state within him he wakes. He took upon himself *that* limitation and then he woke within himself. Everything said of him happens in you.

Any other questions, please?

Q: A strange question perhaps but how have organized churches gotten so far off the path through the centuries?

A: How can organized churches get so far from the truth, from the path? All I can say is they are men without vision. And let us not, because a person calls himself an ordained minister think for one moment that he was *sent* by God. He was appointed politically by those around him. He was best fitted for the job, as they saw it. He knew how to raise large sums of money, how to meet the right people, how to give them the best seats in church, and how to smile at the one who is richer than the other, and all these things they know. And they know what is known as church law, not God's law. If you dare…I've tried to begin to discuss this just at a little gathering, a dinner party, with any member of the cloth, they go blanch. They don't want to discuss it. They are above it all, and you are a layman, so who are you to discuss God's word? So, that's been true since the beginning of time. Go back and read scripture, he was not from the tribe of the Levites. They were the traditional priests of the world and came from the tribe of Judah, not from the tribe of Laban. And Laban was the tribe of the priests of the world. So how can you tell the Sanhedrin anything? He confounded them with his arguments, but they still could point to the fact he was not from the tribe of Laban. They will ask you, "What is your college?" and you say none, well, right away they close the door. "What are your degrees?" None...well, that closes it all the more. And so, they have these little codes that they set up.

So, I am speaking from experience, not from theory. I can stand here without batting an eye and say to you in biblical terms, take my yoke upon you and learn from me. For "the yoke of the law" is the common rabbinical expression for the study of the scriptures. But, my study of the scriptures is based upon experience and not upon theory, I'm not speculating. When I offer you my yoke in exchange for yours, I'm offering my *experience* for anything you may have that's not based upon experience.

Goodnight.

YOU ARE MY WITNESSES

12/1/64

___(??) in which he asked the question, "Have I not told you from the beginning and declared it? Is there a God besides me? There is no God, I know not any" (Is. 44:8). Now the word translated God in the first is the Elohim; the second is singular, and it's translated in the Revised Standard Version as Rock. So when we read it in the Revised Standard Version "Is there a God besides me? There is no Rock, I know not any," we search the scriptures to find out what is it all about, what is this Rock of which he speaks?

Well, tonight, you and I are called upon to be witnesses, to witness to the truth of God's word. For we are told, "Every word of God is true. Do not add to it lest he rebuke you, and find that you are a liar" (Prov. 30:6). So do not add to the words, just leave them just as they are until you actually have the experience of the words of God. Now what is this Rock of which he speaks here? In the 20th chapter of the Book of Luke a question is asked and the words are put into the mouth of Christ Jesus, and the words are, What does this text of scripture mean—and then he mentions the stone—"the stone that the builders rejected that becomes the chief cornerstone?" (verses 1-7). Then Paul in his 9th chapter of his letter to the Romans, "Behold, I am laying in Zion a stone." He tells us it will be a stumbling stone to some and it will fall upon others. But the stone suddenly turns into a person: "He who believes in *him* will not be put to shame" (verse 33). I am laying in Zion a stone, and he who believes in him will not be put to shame.

Now, you and I are called to testify, to witness to all these things. Now, first of all, let us see what is a witness. A witness is one who has firsthand knowledge of a fact or an event. We are told in Deuteronomy, the 19th chapter, that unless there are two witnesses or three witnesses then a charge cannot be sustained (verse 15). There must be at least two, but, alright, have three or more, but not less than two witnesses to sustain a charge. Well, if two different persons agree in testimony then it is conclusive. We are told, "Write it, inscribe it in a book that it may be for the time to come as a *witness* forever." We have that witness today in the form of our Bible. You who are not familiar with it possibly or you want to check it, the 30th chapter of the Book of Isaiah: "Inscribe it in a book, because it will be for the time to come as a witness forever" (verse 8). So we have an external witness called the Bible. You and I must now be the second witness; you and I must *experience* scripture. As we experience scripture, we form the second witness. And we stand self-judged. If our witness, our experience coincides with that of scripture, then we know how true God's word is.

Now, can I really stand here tonight and testify to the truth of this strange statement concerning a Rock? "You were unmindful of the *Rock* that begot you and forgot the *God* who gave you birth" (Deut. 32:18). I begotten of a Rock? "You were unmindful of the Rock that begot you and forgot the God who gave you birth." And they are associated, the Rock and God. Can I stand before you tonight and swear I have had that experience and tell you that it is true beyond the wildest dream of man? I can. So I'm called upon to testify to the truth of scripture. Here, what is this Rock? We are told in the 20th chapter of the Book of Luke: If this stone falls upon you it will crush you. If *you* should fall upon *it*, it will break you into pieces (verse 18). The word fall is "to alight; to come upon it suddenly, unexpectedly." Well, one day, sitting in the Silence, thinking of nothing in particular, turning my attention inwards, as always happens with me, all the dark caverns of the brain began to grow luminous. As they grew luminous, suddenly before my eyes came the rock, a quartz. I never thought anything of it, just looked at it, and suddenly it shattered, it fragmented into numberless pieces. Then it was gathered together by some invisible force or hands, and as it was gathered together it formed itself into a lovely seated, meditating form. As I looked at this meditating being, I discovered I'm looking at myself: I am the Rock that was fragmented.

I came upon it. As I'm told in the 20th chapter of the Book of Luke, If you come upon it—and it's called "if you fall upon it"—and the word fall is "to alight, to alight upon; to simply come upon, simply come upon it unexpectedly." You come upon it and suddenly it fragments. But you are told in scripture *you* are broken. Well, if *it* that is broken into numberless pieces now are gathered together, all these pieces are gathered together and forming itself into one being, and I am the being that I'm looking at, then can I deny that *I* was broken? I'm looking at my own being and the being is the most majestic being that one could ever conceive—a strength of character, a beauty beyond the wildest dream of man, majesty, you couldn't conceive of such majesty, all in this wonderful being that is meditating me. And I realized then that he is my very being. It glowed like the sun.

So here is this wonderful Rock spoken of in scripture, and everyone will have this experience. You are called upon to simply not touch the word of scripture, leave it just as it is. Do not add to it, do not take from it, leave it. What is it trying to tell me? Here are the words, "Is there a God besides me? There is no Rock besides me, I know no other." You mean I must have such faith in myself, such complete *confidence* in my own wonderful imaginal acts that these are creative? I must! There is no other. I must actually believe in this Rock. And I saw the Rock...and the Rock fragmented, reformed; and when it reformed itself, it formed itself into a form, and I am that form. Here is a being looking at me and I'm looking at him...he's not looking at me…I'm looking at it. Because it's in profound meditation, deep, deep meditation: It's dreaming me. And when it comes to the end and the whole journey is over, I am he. The journey begins with the call of Abraham, this wonderful state of faith. As we are told, "I told you from the beginning," said he, "Have I not told you from of old?" Everything was foretold man, and the state called Abraham is the one that could say, I believe the most incredible thing in the world, I believe it; and then I enter the state called Abraham, and I move through the most horrible dream. This is all a dream. It comes to a climax and fulfillment in the little inn in Bethlehem, that's the climax. It comes from Abraham who believes the most impossible thing to the climax of the little inn in Bethlehem. Everyone is going to have this experience.

Now, before we testify to other things tonight, let me tell you one simple little story concerning this fragmentation. How you and I...right now you must hear it and respond. You may not believe it. That is also stressed in scripture, that man is free to reject it completely or to accept it. If you accept it, go all out and let no one disturb it, no one. If you really believe that this Rock is your own being and there is no other God—when you say I am, that's God, and there is no other God— believe it implicitly. I have experienced it. I saw the Rock fragment itself, gather together, form itself into the form of a meditating being, and I am looking at myself, and he is the one meditating me. I can suggest a change in pattern; I cannot change the ultimate dream. For you and I in the beginning, as we entered into that state called Abraham, we agreed to dream in concert, and we will not violate that covenant. All of us agreed to dream in concert. But within the dream I can change and modify certain states. But I am called upon to tell every person in this world that they can change anything within the framework of this little field in which we now operate.

Now let me be very, very personal. I told you the story of my daughter who when everyone tried to help her failed. They loved her dearly and tried to get her into certain jobs. All the doors were open, but there was no job, and on her own she answered a little ad, just a little box number to the *L.A. Times*. They responded and she got the job with Prudential Life, and they started her at a hundred and ten a week, her first little job, she's never worked before. But on one of these many doors that opened prior to this, one lady said to her in a very insolent way, "What makes you think you can come in here and get a job in the script department before you have *any* experience?" When she came home that night, she was really burned up because of the attitude of this one who interviewed her. "What makes you think you can come in here and do these things?" And she said to us, "What must someone do to get a job? Here I've graduated from college, I've majored in English, I want to write, and this is what she told me, 'Go and get something published before you can dare come in here.'"

Alright, there's a lady present tonight...whether she knows this story or not I do not know, a very *dear* friend of ours…and she took my daughter into her confidence and told her a story of a horse, a blind horse that she owned, the family owned, that was brought into the High Sierras, and this other horse that was not blind would bring it down when the snows began to fall; and bring it down through all these crevices and all these rocks, all the way down to safety. My daughter went home and banged that story out, just in synopsis form, *moved* beyond measure, and then said to me, "Daddy, post this for me to Disney." Alright, I think I'll register it for you, so I did. And today, this very day, came a letter from Disney accepting the story, asking her to name her price and saying, "You must remember that it will take a lot of professional work to bring it to maturity," but they liked the story and they want it, and asking her to name her price. So if she only got one dollar, at least she has a check from Disney for the story, and they will undoubtedly give her credit because it's the idea that she presented. She can go back to the same woman and say, "Alright, you want some professional recognition, here it is."

To whom did she turn? She didn't turn to me; I never saw the script. Didn't turn to her mother; her mother never saw the script. Didn't turn to anyone. To whom did she turn?—that Rock that begot us. "You were unmindful of the Rock that begot you and forgot the God who gave you birth." The Rock is God. I saw it. I saw the Rock inside, I fell upon it, and then the Rock fragmented. It gathered itself together in to a form, the human form, and here it was in deep, profound meditation. As I looked at it, I'm looking at myself, *I am* the Rock. There is no other God. That being is meditating me. *That* being—-looking just like you, raised to the nth degree of beauty and perfection—-is meditating you. You and I are the Elohim. We are the gods who agreed in the beginning to dream this dream in concert, and then we forgot the being that we are.

Well, that's alright. May I tell you, the crowning infamy is not that you and I *forgot* God, but to apologize to anyone for the faith we have in God. All of the wise people of the world, they're always apologizing for their faith in God. The wiser they get in the eyes of the world the more remote they become from this faith in God; there is no God to them. Half the world, two thirds of the world deny the existence of a God, and a very large section of the remaining third have little icons that they make and call that God. That's not God. There is no God but your own wonderful human Imagination; that's the *only* God. And when you see it, and you come upon it and you stumble upon this—-as the word fall means "to light upon"—-unexpectedly you light upon it, and here it is a rock, this huge quartz, and before your eyes it fragments. And before your eyes it gathers itself together forms itself in to a form. You look at it and you stand amazed that you're looking at yourself, only glorified beyond the wildest dream of man. It's yourself and *he* is meditating you.

You can modify his dream by wishing for wealth at the moment you may be impoverished, wishing for recognition when at the moment you're unknown, wishing for an open door to get in and write a script when they all are closed against you. So don't take it out on anyone. She drove my Vicki to go home and bat that thing out, and send it off in this amateurish way to have it accepted. So here is acceptance of a script. And the lady who gave her the idea happens to be here this night. Whether she's heard it before this meeting, I do not know. It only happened today. And what she's batting out now, I don't know...maybe another Shakespeare ___(??). But I mean, this is the concept of this Rock that we are. There is *nothing* but God. But don't think of a "him"—I'm speaking of *you*. Listen to the words, the Rock becomes a person: "I am laying in Zion a stone, and he who believes in *him* will not be put to shame." I'm laying a stone...and suddenly a stone becomes a person...and the "him" becomes the being who is reading it. The whole vast Bible is about you. There is nothing in that book but you, and may I tell you, there's nothing in the world that is not in that book. If it's not in the book, it's non-existent. That's the story of scripture.

Now, let us now testify this night to other aspects of the great story, the 82nd chapter of the Book of Psalms. And here in this 82nd chapter we read that "God has taken his place in the divine council, in the midst of the gods he holds judgment" (verse 1). Is that true? May I tell you, I know from experience that is true; for I was taken in Spirit into that divine council and stood in the presence of the Ancient of Days, infinite love. Infinite love asked me a very simple question, "What is the greatest thing in the world?" and I answered, "Faith, hope and love, these three abide, but the greatest of these is love." At that, he embraced me and we fused and became one body, one with infinite love who is God. So I can say to you standing here, I know that God is man. I don't care what the whole vast world will tell me, I know God is man and that man is infinite love. You can't conceive until you are embraced by him what such love is. And from that union you are never divorced. You are sent off to tell the story supported by that memory, but you are never separated from that love. So I know the truth of that statement of the 82nd Psalm that "God takes his place in the divine council, in the *midst* of the gods he holds judgment." You are the gods. We are the Elohim and we are called, one by one, into that divine council and asked a very simple question. So that 13th chapter of 1st Corinthians is true; for when it comes to the summary and names all these things, it summarizes all the talents and all the powers of the world, and then it comes down to love is the greatest of them all. So he asked me a very simple question, "What is the greatest thing in the world?" and I answered correctly. Having answered correctly I was embraced by him. So I know that that is true.

Now, return ___(??) to the Book of Luke where he's speaking now of bringing man forward towards a new concept of life altogether. First of all, the Pharisees asked a question, and then come the Sadducees; and the Sadducees are asking questions that they do not believe. They ask the question concerning resurrection. They said, "Moses in the law said that if a man marries and dies leaving no children, well then, if he has a brother, the brother should marry the widow to raise up offspring. Well, there were seven brothers; the first married and he died leaving no offspring; and the second took the widow and he died; then the third took her, and finally seven took her, and they all died leaving no offspring, and eventually she died. Whose wife is she in the resurrection?" Then he said, "The sons of this age, they marry and they are given in marriage, but those who are accounted worthy to attain to *that* age, to the resurrection from the dead, they neither marry, nor are they given in marriage, for they cannot die anymore. They are sons of God and sons of the resurrection" (Luke 20:27-36).

Now, I know from experience...I have had *that* experience, actually resurrected from the dead. It's not at all as churches teach it. Hasn't a thing to do with what the world tells you. I am only speaking from this platform of *you*. And know who you are?—you are Jesus Christ. There is only Jesus Christ in the world. Jesus Christ became us that we may become as he is. Jesus Christ is the power and the wisdom of God" (1 Cor. 1:24). And the power and the wisdom of God actually sunk itself or emptied itself or limited itself to take upon itself the limitations called man. In this limitation it travels for these unnumbered years—Blake calls it 6,000 years. The journey regardless of the years, the journey starts in Abraham and climaxes in the inn in Bethlehem. So I know from experience the climax. And the resurrection precedes that little picture of the inn only by moments. You awaken in a tomb and the tomb is your skull. You come out of your skull and find yourself in an inn. The inn, a very simple, very modest inn, and in this, here is the Christ child wrapped, just as you're told, in swaddling clothes. It's put into your hands and like Simeon you rejoice because you know now, "Let your servant depart in peace" (Luke 2:29). You've served him faithfully, served yourself faithfully, and now let your servant depart in peace. For I have held in my hands the infant Christ which is a symbol of my own redemption, my own, I would say, release from this world of recurrence. So that, I can testify to that as I stand before you.

I can testify to the fatherhood of God, for no one in this world will ever know truth, God the Father, unless it's revealed to him by the Son. And the Son of God in biblical language is David: "Thou art my son, today I have begotten thee" (Ps. 2:7). And so, David comes into your world and David calls you Father. And there is no shadow of a doubt of this relationship. You know him more intimately as your son than you know anyone in this world. I who love my daughter Vicki dearly, and I trust my wife implicitly that I did sire that form called Vicki—but the relationship between Vicki and myself, dear as it is, is not as intimate as the relationship between David and myself. I know David so *intimately*...it was *always* so...before the beginning of the world this relationship was established. And then came this forgetfulness; I forgot the Rock that begot me. Then comes that very end of the journey, and when you come to the end of the journey, David comes back into your world, and here is your only begotten son. You know him so intimately and you love him beyond the wildest dream—all your whole spring of love rushes towards him, and it's returned from David. So I know the truth of that statement in the 2nd Psalm, the 7th verse: "Thou art my son, today I have begotten thee."

So I can testify to this—the outside word called the Bible, that's one, and my inner experience parallels it. So I brought the two witnesses and if two different persons agree in testimony, it is conclusive. And so, I have the testimony to match that of scripture. So I know today beyond all doubt of the reality of the fatherhood of God, that I am truly that Father. So I can say with the 14th chapter of John: "When you see me, you have seen the Father. You ask me to show you the Father? Have I been so long with you and you do not know me? He who sees me sees the Father; how then can you say,

'Show me the Father'" (verse 9). Everyone is going to have this experience, therefore, in the end *everyone* having had that experience will be the same Father and we will be this compound unity that makes *one* God. And we'll understand that *greatest* of all commandments, "Hear, O Israel: the Lord our God is one Lord" (Deut. 6:4). The I AM, our I AMs, is one I AM. This is a compound unity; all of us together form *the* I AM. But each must have the experience of being father; for *the* I AM is the father of David, and everyone must have the experience of being *that* father. And you can't know it unless David calls you Father.

And now the story of the ascension, I can testify to that. I can witness to the fact that the Son of man must ascend as the serpent ascended when man departed from Egypt. The Son of man must ascend just as the serpent did; and when he does ascend he ascends in the manner of the serpent (John 3:13). And that, I can attest to that, I've experienced it. I can attest to the fact that the temple of God which is man...as you're told, "Ye are the temple of the living God" (1Cor. 3:16), and "the curtain of the temple must be split in two, from top to bottom." (Mat. 27:51). And that I have experienced...the top to the bottom, from the top of my skull to the base of my spine. I know this day what it is to be saved by the *blood* of God; for when you are split in two you behold at the base of your spine this pool of golden light. It's liquid, moving, living gold, unalloyed. And you know it's yourself. You fuse with it; and as you fuse with it, you move up in the serpentine form right into your skull. And that I can attest to that.

I also can attest to the fact what he does when he completes his work and unveils it and is satisfied with what he has done, he descends upon that work in bodily form as a dove. So he comes down in the form of a dove, and he descends upon you and smothers you with affection, kissing you all over your face, the top of your head, your neck, all over from your neck up, and completely smothers you. There is a voice who does say to you—not what you read in scripture, it wasn't my experience—but there is a voice and the voice does say to you, "He loves you." Scripture records it "This is my beloved Son, in whom I am well pleased" (Mat. 3:16). But there are many modifications of that phrase in scripture; none of them agree, and none can really be superimposed one upon the other. I will give you my own experience: There is a voice and a very objective voice, because she stands at your left, and she does speak and she makes a statement "He loves you." Then you reply... it's obvious that he loves me because you couldn't deny the smothering of this affection of the dove that moves all over your face. Then she tells you what is *not* recorded in scripture, and so far I have not found it in recorded scripture. It may be in Apocryphal scripture, I do not know. But she said to me, "They avoid man because man gives off the most offensive odor, and to avoid the odor they avoid man. But he so loved *you* he penetrated the ring of offense, and came down to demonstrate his love for you." Now, that I have not found in scripture. I only know the dove *does* come down and rests upon you and smothers you with love.

What I am trying to get over to you this night is that *you* are the Rock spoken of in scripture. I have experienced it. And that Rock when you light upon it fragments itself, as told. You're told in scripture *you* are broken, well, you *are* broken. If the Rock breaks, and then you see the Rock reassemble itself into human form, and *you* are the form into which it is reassembled, was it not you that broke? So you're told, "If anyone lights upon it"—-the word is called falls; the word "falls" means "to alight or alight upon, to come upon suddenly." So if you do come upon it suddenly, then you are broken in pieces. But who is broken in pieces? The Rock was broken in pieces. But am I the Rock? Yes. Because I saw the Rock before my eyes... then reassemble all of these broken pieces into this wonderful human form, the most glorious vision; and I am looking at myself. So *I* was broken into pieces when I lit upon the Rock. How true scripture is! And then you look at this glorious being, majesty beyond the wildest dream. And then you return to the world of Caesar to tell it to anyone who will hear it. Alright, some will hear it and believe it; others will hear it and deny it. It's entirely up to them. But the story of Jesus Christ must be told to everyone in the world. Everyone should hear it and respond to it.

So the little story I told earlier concerning Vicky, take it to heart. She didn't turn to the left or the right, and here she simply trusted only herself, only herself, and the courage to send it off this way. And then in two weeks to get a response that it is accepted. She only trusted that one Rock...and the Rock is herself. "Of the Rock that begot you, you are unmindful, and you've forgotten the God (which is that Rock) who gave you birth." For this is the emanation of this meditating being. I am meditating this for purposes not quite made clear in this world. For all of us, together, agreed to dream in concert and meditate all these forms, through all the horrors of the world, and then to awake. And awakening from it all, we have expanded beyond what we were when we agreed to this play. So all of us together—not one greater than the other, not one—all of us are one, for his name is one and God is one. So let no one tell you that one, because he actually encountered one of these words of God within himself and experienced it, that he is, because he preceded you in it, is better than you are. Let no one tell you that. Jesus Christ is called the faithful witness, the first *fruits* of those who slept, the first *risen* from the dead. But don't let anyone tell you because it's the first that Jesus Christ mentioned in scripture is other than the Jesus Christ in you. When you awake, *you* are that Jesus Christ. So in the end, all, only Jesus Christ awakes in everyone, and *everyone* is God.

Now tonight, you try it, you just try this simple thing of believing in this Rock that you are. For I'm testifying to the truth of scripture: the Rock is literally true. I think I mentioned it in my latest book that the truth is literal, the words used are figurative. But, nevertheless, on a higher level it is literal. So when you read the words that you are a Rock and God is a Rock and that Rock begat you, don't let anyone tell you although it is figurative on this level it isn't literally true on a higher level. For I speak from experience, it is literally true on a higher level. And so you see the Rock, so you can't rub it out. So you're told in the 30th chapter of the Book of Proverbs that every word of God proves true—do not add to his words lest he rebukes you and calls you a liar. So the wiser you become in this world the more you tend to change the word of God to give it sense, to give it meaning on this level. It doesn't belong on this level, because on this level you will find experiences related to the world of Caesar. But, may I tell you from my experience, *every word* of God is literally true on a higher level. "As Moses lifted up the serpent in the wilderness, so must the Son of man be lifted up." On this level, it doesn't make sense, and yet I tell you from experience that is true. Just as a serpent was lifted up on that rod that budded, so must the Son of man, which is the title of Christ, be lifted up. And you *are* lifted up in the same serpentine manner just as the serpent was lifted up.

So I ask everyone to come with me and believe me implicitly. As I stand before you, I'm only testifying to what I know from experience of the word of God. And it's far more important than all the things in the world. What would it really matter if tonight you had a billion and you didn't have any experience of the word of God? You would like the rich man of scripture be called this night and to leave it all behind, to be restored to life and inserted into another aspect or time sequence of this long 6,000 years. You leave here the billionaire to find yourself, still without loss of consciousness, inserted into a time sequence best suited for your awakening. Why not believe now and start to awaken? Now there is a passage in scripture that is very comforting. It's the 5th chapter of John that "He who hears my word and believes him who sent me, will inherit eternal life…and pass from death to life" (verse 24). To hear it and to completely accept it seems to, in some strange way, bring it all together and one passes from death to life. Read that in the 5th chapter of the Book of John. I'm glad I've had the experiences, but if I standing here being very human could relieve the whole vast world (because it's all myself anyway) of having experiences as witnesses, I would this night grant it. And the 5th chapter of John grants it, based only on the acceptance of his word. He who hears my word and believes in him who sent me will inherit eternal life and pass now from death to life.

Let us go into the Silence.

* * *

Now are there any questions, please?

Q: Would you please explain the Son of man and the Son of God.

A: Well, you're told in scripture in the 7th chapter of 2nd Samuel, and the prophet is speaking to David, and the prophet said to David, "When your days are fulfilled and you lie down with your fathers"—which means when you die and you're buried— "I will raise up your son after you, who will come forth from your body. I will be his father, and he shall be my son" (verse 12). So if it comes forth from man it is man's son, is it not? But if now that which is brought forth from man is now adopted by God as God's son, then it's the Son of God. So he brings forth from man that which he adopts as his own son. But you can't deny man the right of giving birth to him; were it not for man he couldn't bring him forth. So, "I will raise up from you your son, who shall come forth from your body. I will be his father, he shall be my son." So the third act of the unveiling of the story is Son of man. The last act when this dove descends upon man—and God sees his image and it's perfect as he intended that it should be, and he smothers it with affection, and shows his appreciation for what is done, and his satisfaction—then *that* is Son of God. So there are four unveilings. The first is a double act, which is the resurrection and birth; they come together, resurrection preceded by a matter of moments. The second act is a single act which is the discovery of the fatherhood of God when David reveals you as his father, and David is God's only begotten son. The third act is a double act. That is the splitting of the temple from top to bottom, and the ascension of the Son of man into a new creation. And then the fourth act is the satisfaction shown by God of his image—it's good, it is very good, and smothers it with affection.

Q: Neville, we're told that Jesus said to Peter, "Thou art Peter, a rock, and upon this rock I will build my church." I don't know Hebrew...exactly where the word Peter comes from. In French, literally, Pierre, which is the same word, same name, is rock or stone. Is this also true in Hebrew?

A: Yes, the word is Petros, which is rock. The first, he was introduced by his brother Andrew as Simon, which means "to hear." And so, Andrew found Jesus Christ...and so "I found him of whom Moses and the law and the prophets spoke." And so he brought his brother Simon, and he said to him, "So you are Simon...from now on your name is Peter." And Peter means stone; it's Petros, the petrified, the rock, the most condensed, the most congealed; but on *this* I will build...and the church is *not* any church on the outside in the world, for "Ye are the temple of the living God" (2 Cor. 6:16). And from this congealed state I will shatter it and show you the being that is really meditating the whole vast world. And that being happens to be you.

Well, until...now don't forget we're not here on the 18th but we are here until the 15th. Thank you. Goodnight.

THE PRIMAL STATE

12/4/64

Tonight's subject is "The Primal State." We read in the works of Shakespeare, "It has been taught us from the primal state that he which is was wished until he were." For the primal state with us is "Let us make man in our image." That's the very first wish recorded in scripture. And we are told that he who began this work in us will bring it to completion at the day of Jesus Christ (Phil. 1:6); that no power in the world will stop it. That was his wish and he will complete it.

Now, in the Book of Ephesians, the first chapter of Ephesians, we read the words, "In Christ, he chose us before the foundation of the world"... that you and I were chosen in Christ before the foundation of the world. Christ is the power and the wisdom of God, so by his wisdom and by his power we were chosen. Now he tells us why: To be full of love. These are the words, the 1st chapter, the 4th and 5th verses: To be full of love; God being love, to be full of God. He is filling us with himself until we overflow with God. Then we are told "He destined us" and then it's explained why he destined us. For this, we're told, such was his will and his pleasure that we may be accepted as his sons. For the whole purpose, the whole vast world was brought forth as a theater wherein God and God alone might develop beings fit for his sons. So let no one scare you about not being saved, because you choose yourself. Let no one tell you that you are not being brought out just as God, for it is all *God* doing it. He began the good work in us and God will bring it to completion at the day of Jesus Christ. And no one can be lost, but no one. Our sonship is not earned, it is all grace; and our fitness is the consequence not the condition of his choice. And so, everyone in the world because they can't earn it, everyone is given it, but everyone.

Now, let me share with you a letter that came to me last Tuesday. This lady writes that she was dreaming and she knew she was dreaming, and in the dream she remembered this teaching and said to herself, "Neville tells us that if I know that I am dreaming and decide to awake in it I could; and awake right in the dream and prove to my own satisfaction that a dream is not what the world thinks it is. If I awake in it, it takes on objectivity and becomes just as real to me, the dreamer, as the world is to those who think they are awake. So I will awake in it. Well, I know it was a dream and I did what you told us to do. So I sat at a desk, and I discovered that the desk was joined to the chair, one piece of furniture. I realized that this enormous hall was the hall in some institution of higher learning. When I made my decision, I awoke in my dream. The professor was giving a lecture. There weren't very many people present, but he was talking to the few who were present in this very large hall. I noticed to my right a stairway led from the upper floor. At the base of the stairway there was a group of young men, all talking. So I sat at the desk, and two of them detached themselves from the little group and came over to where my desk was and got on both sides of me and locked me in. Well, here the desk was attached to the chair, and the only exit for me would be to the sides, and they stood at my sides.

"Then one shouted to the crowd, that is, the group gathered at the stairway, 'Here is another one of them' said this youth to the others over there. 'Here is another one of them.' Seven left the little gathering and came over and got in front of me, implying that I was a visitor, and I was not the first visitor from a very strange land…that they were seeing something, and I was one of them. I realized from their attitude towards me that I should get out of there. Again, I remembered your teaching, that if I could feel a bed under me and a pillow under my head I would depart from this area. Quickly as I imagined I was on a bed and a pillow under my head, I felt myself dissolve from this chair and felt myself on my bed, leaving an empty chair for the nine of them to observe. So they all thought they saw someone who was a visitor from some other world or some other planet, as far as they're concerned, and they shouted to the crowd, 'Here is another one of them.'"

Now, that same technique you use to put yourself into anything you want in this world. You don't have to use it only to return to this world from another place; you use it here to put yourself from one state into another state in this world. You take the state of poverty...now what, instead of a bed and a pillow, on what would you rest if now you were *not* poor? On what would you rest if now you were gainfully employed? On what would you now rest...and you use the same technique to move from one state here into another state here. You don't have to use it only to get back to this world from another section of this world. Because, really, she was really in this world, but "this world" runs thousands of years. She was in another time sequence, and if at this very moment she went back in time and you saw people dressed differently, if you slipped back in time a thousand years and you saw people dressed a thousand years ago, you would think you were in another world. You'd be forgetful of the fact that that same world in which you now slip was once called "this world," and we now reflect upon it as the past history of this world. But to you, relative to this it's another world. It's only *this* world, and you slip into all these different time sections of *this* world. If you don't know it, anyone functioning there now will look upon you as a visitor from another planet, from another world. It's another *section* of this world.

But while we are in this section of *this* world, we can use this same technique to move from our present state into another state. To understand this principle, you must always bear in mind the great distinction between infinite states and the occupant of the state. When I speak to you I'm not speaking to states, I am speaking to the occupant. And tonight, no two are in the same state in this room, we are in different states. But I am speaking to the occupant of the state, and that occupant is God. Actually, I'm speaking to God. I can't speak to anyone else; there is no one else. And so, God became that state, entered that state, regardless of the nature of that state. Whether it be restricted or free, it's a state. Man, not knowing it's a state, he thinks he *is* the state and he doesn't know how to get out of the state.

Well, you take this lady's experience. For I can tell you from my own experience unnumbered times of finding myself deliberately making a choice to wake in a state. And so, I could wake in a dream to find that I could explore that dream, and the world was just as real as this, solidly real. The people are real; I talked with them, they talked to me. And then I could dissolve from that world and find myself back here in this section of time, pick up the threads where I left them the night before when I fell off to sleep. This seems mad, but as Blake said, "There are states of consciousness in which the visionary is declared a madman." Yes, there are numberless states where you would be considered, if you told it to another group other than you, I would be declared an insane person. But I can trust you. You know I am sane (I think I am) and yet I can share with you all these strange experiences, because I am not confined to the evidence of my senses here. Falling asleep and deciding—not every dream of mine I want to awake in it—some dreams are not pleasant. I wouldn't want to awaken in that section of time. Other dreams are most pleasant, and so you could awake in that. Consciousness follows vision, you awake in the dream, and the dream takes on all the properties of this external world. While you're in it you explore.

But the technique by which you awoke and the technique by which you return is the same technique to move from one state to the other in this world. If I use it to move from one section of time here to another section of time of the same world, yet the time stretches, say, 6,000 years...but I don't want 6,000 years...I want to take it back now in another state right here. So there are infinite states and you are the pilgrim moving through states. You're moving toward the ultimate state, which is the inn. The inn wherein the symbol of your awakening takes place: It is called the birth of Christ. The birth of Christ is simply a departure from the entire wheel of recurrence into a new creation altogether. But you don't depart that night. You reach the end of your road and you remain long enough to tell it to encourage every being (who happens to be God) that the word of God is a true story. Everything is true about it. And so you remain, but when you do depart it's your last experience on the wheel of recurrence. You can say with Paul, "The time for my departure has come. I have fought the good fight, I have finished the race, I have kept the faith. Henceforth there is laid up for me a crown of righteousness" (2 Tim. 4:7). But that may come tonight, it may come next month, may come next year, or, maybe, ten years from now. It doesn't matter, because you reach the end of the road when you reach the inn. That lovely little poem of Christina Rossetti, she calls it *Uphill.*: "Does the road wind uphill all the way? Yes, to the very end. Will the day's journey take the whole long day? From morn to night, my friend. But is there for the night a resting place, a room, for the slow dark hours begin. May not the darkness hide it from my face? You cannot miss *that* inn."

Don't be concerned, you *cannot* miss that inn. You come to it and you don't even realize you're on it; and suddenly you're in the inn, and the child is coming forth, bearing witness to the event that was in the beginning predetermined. You didn't determine it. "Let us make...let us make man in our image" (Gen. 1:26). We didn't say, "Let us make God in our image." God said, "Let us make *man* in *our* image"; that's the primal wish. It is his responsibility and no one in the world can stop him from bringing to fulfillment that which was in the beginning that primal wish. And it ends... it comes to fulfillment in the inn, when suddenly all that was foretold concerning Jesus Christ...for he is the image of the invisible God. Jesus Christ, the image of the invisible God. So when he completes the image he has completed Christ, because as he completes his image you are Jesus Christ. And Jesus Christ is the power and the wisdom; but the power and the wisdom of God is personified and it's you.

So let no one in any way divert you by telling you of some other concept of salvation. He prepared the way of his return before the world was made. Listen to these words, and how can you interpret these five terms and reach any other conclusion other than that we are *predestined* to be conformed to the image of his son. "Those whom he *foreknew* he also *predestined* to be conformed to the image of his son. And those whom he predestined he also called; and those whom he called he also justified; and those whom he justified he also glorified" (Rom. 8:29). But I don't see how anyone could take these five terms—foreknew, predestined, called, justified, glorified—and arrive at any conclusion other than that we are predestined to be God. For to be glorified...listen to the words, "And now, Father, glorify thou me with thyself with the glory that I had with thee before that the world was" (John 17:5). He asks for the return of a glory that is his, that was one with God the Father, therefore, he *is* God the Father. It's God's purpose to give *himself* to us, as though there were no others in the world, just God and us. But the *us* is a compound unity, it's a oneness, because all of us form one. He's bringing that one being out of the *seeming* many and yet we do not lose our individual identities.

But here, you take this simple, simple picture of withdrawal from one state into another and you work it out. She said, A bed and a pillow, and so I'll return because it didn't look...but I thought it might be...in the beginning it seemed a bit threatening when these seven came and stood before me. I said, get out of here quickly…and I remembered the teaching. Having remembered, I put it into practice and I felt myself dissolve from that chair, leaving it empty for them to contemplate the empty chair, while I felt myself securely placed upon my bed. Well, you can take anything and do it using the same principle. I have taken ladies who want to be married. Well, alright, what dissolved from one state, what state? Where I can't feel a ring here; and then all of a sudden I *feel* a ring, a ring that would imply the fulfillment of my desire to be married. Well now, put another quality to it, to be *happily* married. Not just to be married but to be happily married, to be proud of the name I bear and to be proud when you say, "I want you to meet my husband"; or if it happens to be a man, he may not wear a ring, but there's something else he could actually feel, as the lady would feel the ring, and then be proud to say, "I want you to meet my wife."

So whatever you would do, do it in the same way, so you would move from one state to the other state. They're all states, infinite states, but you, the occupant, you are not a state. Imagination is not a state. Imagination is the man himself, and that man is God. For, "Man is all Imagination and God is man, and exists in us and we in him. The eternal body of man is the Imagination; that is, God himself" (Blake, *Ann. to Berkeley/Laocoon*). So here, when we speak of the real you, I'm speaking to your Imagination, and that is God. Well, what did she use to move back? She used her Imagination. She imagined a pillow under her head, she imagined a bed under her body, and felt herself detach itself from that chair, and she found herself safely back in her own room. A mother of five small children, she certainly didn't want to leave five small children in this world. They're all just simply tots. The fifth one happens to be named after me and Blake, his name is Neville Blake. And so I'm a godfather, I'm the godfather of all five of them. So she didn't want to leave five children in this world. But she did remember the teaching she got from this platform, which to me is a marvelous thing, because the waking person remembers. If you don't remember, you're sound asleep. While in it she remembered the teaching and decided this is the one dream in which I want to awake. Her husband is a teacher. She is qualified to teach and it interested her that here is a hall of higher learning and here is a professor giving a lecture—-not many listening to him, but, nevertheless, he's giving a lecture. And so, she awoke in the dream to discover that what I'm saying from this platform is true. And then while in it, she also remembered when it became threatening and someone said "Here's another one, someone from outer space or from some other world, here she is." And so she felt a little bit uneasy with this threatening attitude of the nine of them, and decided to return. But how to return? And she remembered. She remembered that I told her what happened to me.

Now may I tell you, as I've told you, not recently but a long time ago, one day you're going to see it: This whole vast world is dead and you are the life of it. The whole vast world is dead and you really are the life of it; for what God is giving to his sons that he formed is himself. And God is the God of the living, God is life; so "As the Father has life in himself, so he's granted the son also to have life in himself" (John 5:26). And how do I know it? I knew it from many experiences as I've shared them with you in the past. Well, here is one. I said earlier, the whole vast universe was brought in to being as a theater for God to manifest his power and his love in the development of beings fit to be called his son. And his son is life, for the son has life in himself. Well, one night from this platform I couldn't answer a question that was asked by a lady. She said, "Neville, I'm terribly concerned about the future development of the animal world. Could you throw any light upon the evolution of the animal?" Well, I couldn't. I had never had an experience, and any answer that I might have given to this lady would have been based upon speculation not upon anything that I knew from experience. So I told her, I can't answer you intelligently now. I could tell you what I've read. I could tell you what the evolutionists claim is the future of an animal, the survival of the fittest, and so on. We can project some picture, but that may not be a true picture. So I can't really honestly answer your question, but if I ever have a vision where the answer is given in vision, I'll tell it to you.

Well, I was blessed with the answer a few days later. A few days later, I found myself at the top of a very tall ladder and down below were all the beasts of the jungle, the tigers, the lions, every wild animal down below... and they were angry, really angry. And I was afraid. I was alone at the top of a very tall ladder and all these were living, moving, angry, beings. And then I remembered that the whole vast world was myself made visible, so the animal would have to be myself made visible. I saw it one night with people, and a bird, and leaves, and all these things, where they were alive because I made them alive; and when I stopped that activity in me they all stood still. Well, the same thing should be true here now. So at first, when I lost my fear, these enormous big cats became docile like domesticated cats. The tiger wasn't angry, the lion wasn't angry, and they were simply lovely, lovely living things, but not angry. And I was completely unafraid. When I lost my fear I went beyond it now and I stilled in me the activity that allowed them to move. As I did that, they all froze; then I went down that stair. When I came back down, they were all dead, just as though they were made of clay. Every one was just as still as this, as though they were made of clay. So I looked at them, and then once more I began to release them from that ___(??) from within me. They became once more alive, but not angry... and I dissolved back into *this* section of time.

So I know there are levels in man where he will discover that this whole vast world is simply fixed states forever and forever. It's fixed. It was brought into being after God made his decision to bring forth sons. You and I preceded, as told that story in the 1st chapter of Ephesians, you and I were part of this plan of God before he brought forth the world. This is not an after-thought, this is not some emergency thinking on the part of God. The whole thing was planned in detail before he even brought forth the universe. The universe was brought forth for a purpose, and the only purpose is to beget sons, sons like himself, companions forever. Infinite sons and yet altogether form one being...and that one being is God.

So here, take this simple technique, and while we're still living in the world of Caesar use it. I can't take you in detail and show you what I would do were I you to change a state. But you have intelligence, you can do it. The one with the lady with the ring, I've see that many, many times working beautifully; the one with the change of position, change of this or the other. What would you feel if now you were the person that you want to be? What would you feel? Well then, feel it...as she felt the pillow to prove she was back from that world into this world. Then what would you feel? For, really, feeling truly is the secret. Blake tells us that the door of feeling is closed in man. Yes, it is closed, but I'm trying with you to open it. Because feeling is the Western gate, he tells us, and the Western gate in man is closed: It's the sense of touch. He calls it "the tongue." Well, the tongue is touch, and so, the sense of touch or taste, and these are one in scripture. They only speak of four rivers in scripture and four senses: sight, sound, scent, taste and touch. Sight, sound, and scent are three separate ones in the fallen state; and taste and touch form one, for both depend upon contact, and he tells us that is the one that is closed in man. So what depends upon contact? Well, touch. You can feel the pillow, you can feel the bed. And that gateway in man is closed; man doesn't know it. But he speaks of Imagination as spiritual sensation. Just extend your feeling and just feel what is not here to be felt, if you're going to use only your eyes to see it or your other senses. But now, what is here that if you could touch it would imply that you have or you are what you want to be? Whatever you can *touch*, for that's the closed door in man. So extend your senses and feel it. You'll feel it; then you'll find yourself actually moving from one state into another state, the state that you are dreaming.

So this is the story of this primal wish. "It has been taught us from the primal state that he which is was wished until he were." And so, you wish it. Do the same thing. We're called upon to imitate God as dear children. Well, if this is the way God does it, well then, I'm told to imitate him, and "he calls a thing that is not seen as though it were seen, and the unseen becomes seen." If that's how he calls it into being then I must do the same thing. That verse is taken from the 4th chapter, the 17th verse of Romans: "He calls a thing that is not seen as though it were seen and the unseen becomes seen." So I will call the bed that isn't seen. I'm sitting in a chair at a desk and there are seven men in front of me and two at my side, and so there's no bed here and there is no pillow. But if I could only *feel* the presence of a bed under my body and a pillow under my head, then I would detach myself from this strange behavior of these nine men, and so I would actually find myself where I want to be. Well, we do the same thing in moving from any one state into another state.

Just...well, I don't know what you really want this night. It could be money...and may I tell you, not a thing is wrong with wanting money. I don't care what the world will tell you. They'll tell you, you shouldn't want it. If money, said Blake, is something we should not pray for, there's practically nothing left to pray for. So when they told him that he shouldn't want money, he said, well, if you don't want money and that's one thing you shouldn't pray for, well, there's nothing one should pray for. He was the most down-to-earth practical being in the world. Didn't care for it, yet he had to have it. Went to his grave not having any to leave behind him, but he lived seventy wonderful, marvelous years, and left behind him a wealth you cannot estimate in dollars and cents. There's no money enough that you could bring out to buy one of his ___(??). How could you buy one of his six copies of *Jerusalem*? He has one that is now the only one that is in color at Yale University. Well, you couldn't offer Yale two million dollars for it and have them accept your offer. And so, he left behind him what today runs in to...you can't measure in wealth...plus what he's done to the minds of those who really found him.

So imagining is spiritual sensation and use that spiritual sensation to touch the object of your desire. For, he who is was wished until he were. Well, now the thing that we want to be, touch it, and wish it to be real until it becomes fact. Just as someone one night in my Bible class in New York City, I asked if she knew what she wanted. She named it down to the penny. She said, "My withholding tax is so much, and I don't want less than so much in my envelope." I asked if she could feel it? She said, "I could." Could you now count the contents? Yes. Can you smell money? Yes. She brought all of her senses to play upon the contents of that envelope. She could shake the contents; then feel paper plus change, and then she counted off right down to the penny what she would receive were it true. Within one week she had *that* job, earning *that* amount of money.

It can't fail you. But it doesn't operate itself. We are the operant power because we are God, and there's nothing but God in this world. So God actually came down to the limitation here, and then he's moving up to where he was before, taking with him, us, taking all of us...but one by one. So I am inviting everyone to try it. And do share with me your results, because I want stories to tell to everyone to encourage all to try it. Because unless I can take these stories and bring new stories all the time, people get tired even of the thousand and one stories that I could tell you. They don't want to hear the same thing, they want another story. So don't be silent about it, tell me your stories, that from this platform—with your permission, naturally—I can encourage others how you can move from one state into another state and externalize the contents of that other state. For, they're only states, infinite states. When you open the Bible and you read of these characters like Abraham, and you read Isaac and Jacob and David, they are states. The persons represented are not really meant there; they only simply represent the state, the significance of that state, but not the individual. Every one there is a state, and we pass through all these states. Our journey starts when we enter the state called Abraham...that's the state of faith. We can hear the most incredible story and believe it because we believe him who said it. And we believe that all things are possible to God, and we heard it from God from the depths of our soul. And so, we enter that state and then the journey starts, and we remain faithful across the journey until we come to the inn when it comes into fulfillment. For,

"Abraham rejoiced that he was to see my day; he saw it and was glad" (John 8:56).

You come into the state of Moses. The word Moses means (from its Egyptian verb) "to be born." Yet it's a play on the word "to draw out"; for the word Mosheh is "to draw out." For she said, "I found him and drew him out of the water." And so, not the mother, she claimed she adopted him, who was the daughter of Pharaoh. So the word Mosheh, Mem, Shin, He, does really mean "to draw out." You turn it around, it's Heshem, and the word Heshem is "name." You take the middle letter out and put it first, it's Shema, and that is "heaven." So, heaven is within you. So you're really drawing out, out of the depths of your own being by the power which is symbolized here as Moses. But the word actually means by its ancient word, it's really an Egyptian word, "to be born." It's a prototype of what is really to be born... because Moses could not enter the Promised Land. He came to the end and then he turned all the power over to Joshua. Joshua is simply the Hebraic form of the Anglicized word Jesus; Jesus and Joshua are the same word. And so, Joshua is spelled...I think it is spelled Jehovah—Yod He Vau Shin Ayin. Yod He Vau He would be Jehovah. You put a Shin and you put an Ayin in the name, but the base of the word, which is Yod He Vau begins Joshua, and it is the same word for Jesus, and therefore the same. Jehovah is the same. So it is Joshua who moves into the Promised Land. So this is another state.

Now the whole vast world has been trying to find over the centuries a real live living history of Jesus. You aren't going to find it, because you are he...*this* is his history and he wakes in you. The whole story is told so beautifully, but people are looking for him on the outside, and trying to find confirmation in fact in the pages of history when the whole drama unfolds within us. The whole wonderful story of Jesus Christ is taking place in us. It starts with the call of Abraham and comes to its culmination in the inn at Bethlehem...and that's you.

So tonight you try this, just as the lady did. I don't know what you're going to use to touch, to imply that you have what you want. I have seen people take with the piano...when you couldn't buy a piano during the war years...and this lady took an area of her apartment in New York City, cleaned off everything in the area where the piano would go had she the piano, and would actually feel the piano in that presence—when someone called her and said to her, "I'm moving to the coast, and I have a wonderful piano, and I don't really want to sell it, could you use the piano? I don't want to sell it to you. I will give it to you if you will take it. I don't want to take it to the coast." And she fell heir to the piano, a wonderful concert grand piano. I know the family well, I know the piano well. And she simply cleaned the area where the piano would go when it arrived, and she got the piano. This happened in this last...the 2nd World War. So as you're told in the Book of Kings, "You say you want rain, dig ditches"—prepare for the reception of what you say you want. So you won't dig the ditches and you say you want rain...and there isn't a cloud, not the size of a man's hand... but I say, in spite of the absence of the sign of rain, prepare for the reception of rain. So prepare for the reception of the good that you seek by actually feeling its reality *now*, and then it comes into your world. Well, if you do so, you enter the state and then all these things belonging to that state externalize themselves in your world.

So the primal state began with a wish, and he which is was wished until he were. So you begin and imitate God like a dear child. And so you want something, begin with the wish, and then wish it until it is. You wish a thing by assuming that it is. For this grand being within you which is your Imagination will do nothing that you wish until you have imagined the wish fulfilled. You must imagine the wish fulfilled before you can get it into action. If you don't imagine the wish fulfilled, it remains quiet. So not until the wish is *imagined* fulfilled do you move the being from one state into another state.

And may I tell you, as Blake said in his wonderful *Vision of the Last Judgment*: "I do not consider either the just or the wicked to be in a supreme state, but to be every one of them states of sleep which the soul may fall into in its deadly dreams of good and evil." So all these states *are*; every conceivable state is already part of the eternal structure of the universe, and you the pilgrim, you move from state to state. And it's entirely up to you. As we are told in Deuteronomy, "I place before you this day life and death, good and evil; choose life, choose blessings" (30:19). But it is entirely up to you. He said, "I made the good; I also made the evil. I fashioned the light and form the darkness…and there is no one to deliver out of my hands" (Is. 45:7; Deut.32:40). Who else could make darkness? Who else could make evil?—none but the only creator. So he made every conceivable state. When you read the Bible carefully, there isn't one thing possible for man to experience, good, bad or indifferent that is not openly discussed in the Bible. Every conceivable vice, every violation of the so-called moral code, *everything* is in the Bible. And so, it's entirely up to man to choose what he wants. You can choose this, that or the other; and as you choose you move into it, and you will experience the results of your choice. If you don't like it, you get out of it, just like the lady. It was her decision to awaken in this particular dream. It had something about it that interested her. Her husband is a teacher, she is qualified to teach, and this was simply an institution of higher learning. So she awoke in it to find it was not quite as desirable as she thought in the beginning. But instead of regretting it, she detached herself from it and returned to her home and her family. And so, I invite everyone here to single out the dream, the initial wish now, this night, and then wish it until it is.

* * *

Q: (inaudible)

A: Meek? What does the word meek mean? It really means "to be disciplined," as a wild animal is disciplined and falls into the state of being domesticated. "Blessed are the meek, for they shall inherit the earth." That's the self-disciplined mind. For you take an animal... it's really used in the same way that you take an animal that is a wild animal and train it. You can break an animal, a horse, for instance, so that you can ride that horse. Normally, you couldn't take an animal out of the wilds and ride it, but you could take that same wild beast and train it and eventually ride it.

Well, the mind is as wild as the wild horse. You set it a task, and it's almost impossible with even the disciplined mind to move logically from A to D, far less from A to Z. Take a sequence and see how quickly the mind jumps and bolts and goes in some other direction. But if you take, say, a sequence like the lady took..."I'll take a pillow, I'll take a bed, very simple...I can feel my pillow and I can feel the bed"; then she dissolved, leaving an empty chair to be observed by these people. So she took a short little sequence, but try taking even four...by the time you hit the third the mind has jumped to Z ___(??) You take any little sequence...bring before your mind's eye a friend, congratulating you on your good fortune, and you start to say how wonderful it is, and in no time flat you're justifying the previous failure or some other thing. Try to hold it and keep it right as you would hold the reins of a horse along a certain path. So the meek is really the self-disciplined mind. It's tamed in the way that you tame the wild animal. That's what the word means.

Q: Neville, would you interpret this word "buy, b-u-y, in the Revelation 3:18, "I counsel thee to buy of me gold refined by fire that thou mayest become rich."

A: Yes, the coin you use is patience and diligence. You don't use the coin of Caesar. This is the book of the Spirit, and the values, the monies you bring in Spirit would be simply diligence, I would say a self-disciplined mind. That's the coin you use, patience, courage, all these are the coins of heaven. And so, if you brought this coin, then you'd buy it with that.

Yes, Tom?

Q: Would you mind, if it's possible in just a few moments to indicate the significance of the advent on Peter, Andrew, James and John?

A: Well, to me Andrew is simply watching. Andrew is like the first of the Old Testament—his name would be Rueben, "the corresponding one", and Rueben is the oldest son. He was the first son and Andrew was the first one called. Andrew by definition is called "memory" but that doesn't convey anything. But to me, Andrew is simply "to watch carefully"—know exactly what you want to see and don't be diverted. Just see it as clearly as you possibly can...that would be Andrew. Peter is faith. He's called "the rock." "I call you no longer Simon, I call you Peter." James is "righteous judgment." A righteous judgment always would involve repentance. That is, if you see anything in this world and it doesn't please you, rearrange it so that it pleases you. That's right judgment, because, anyone who masters the art of repentance need never despair; because he can always repent, and repentance is a change of state. And John, well, to me John is love. And so, I always say to everyone whenever you use your Imagination use it lovingly. Whenever you use your Imagination lovingly on behalf of another, you are mediating God to that other, for God is love. So the choice is man's. But use it lovingly, no matter what you do, always use it lovingly. And let this be your code, "Do unto others as you would have them do unto you."

Q: Why do we find, Neville...the other night I noticed this, the 18th Psalm, the words are almost identical with 2nd Samuel, chapter 22.

A: They are, almost to the word.

Q: Why is that?

A: I couldn't tell you, Bill. You find many verses that are duplicated. After all, Samuel deals completely with David. And you'll notice in that 18th Psalm the very long, I would say, introduction to that Psalm trying to emphasize the fact the whole thing is by and of David.

So you find at least what would be three verses, all put into one paragraph prior to the 18th Psalm trying to stress that point that this is all by and for and to David. And so, the Book of Samuel is all about David. He is his choice in Samuel—that God sees the heart, not the outer appearances, so he chose David, rather than the first brother or the second brother or the third brother. He wanted David because he saw the heart: I want a man after my own heart (Acts 13:22). Then it was David who brought down the enemy of Israel. It was David then who set his father free, because whoever brought down the enemy of Israel, his father would be set free (1 Sam. 17:25). We are the fathers when our David appears; and by his appearance he sets us free, because you can't be free until the Son sets you free (John 8:36).

Goodnight.

FOR HATCHING

12/8/64

Well, tonight's subject is "For Hatching." There is a voice in man that if you listen to it and expect it, you will at rare intervals hear it. It's the voice of authority and it never lies. Over the years I have heard this voice. It has never led me astray and everything that it prophesied has come to pass, but everything. So, in the Silence...and you are not concerned but you ask a question—it may come or it may not come that night—but you ask the question "What is the purpose of it all?" You do not question for one moment that God *is*, for you met God, you know God; you were embraced. But this was a moment of not I said concern, just in not even an idle moment, you ask the question "What is the purpose of it all?" and the voice answers in the depth of your soul, "For hatching." For hatching what? For hatching everything in the world, like a huge big egg, but specifically for hatching God—God in man, brought to the surface *as* that man in whom he is buried. Like the old hymn of Isaac Watts: "Wrapped in the silence of the tomb the Great Redeemer lay, 'til the revolving skies bring the third, the appointed day."

Now let me share with you an experience given me this week by a friend of mine, where he was brought to the third, the appointed day. For the purpose of life is to find God and God, when you find him, is God the Father, that's God. "In many and various ways," we're told, "God spoke to our fathers through the prophets; but in these last days he has spoken to us through a Son" (Heb.1:1). If he spoke to us through a Son, then he's Father. As we are told in the last book of the Old Testament, the Book of Malachi, "A son honors his father. If then I be a father, where is my honor?" says the Lord of hosts. Where is my son if I am a father? I have no way of knowing that I am a father unless there is a son to bear witness to the fact that I am his father. So, if a son honors his father and I be a father, where is my honor, where is my son? So here, "Wrapped in the silence of the tomb the Great Redeemer lay, and then the revolving skies bring forth the third, the appointed day."

So this friend will allow me to tell you the story. And to give you just a little background, just a few words, he said, "My father died when I was eight, and my world was shattered. I felt an outsider. Every family in the neighborhood seemed to be a complete unit, but I felt an outsider, and I took this feeling with me into school. I was never once a part of the student body, always an outsider. When I left school I took the same feeling with me into business; and though I worked for very large companies and I served them well, and they were good to me, still I was never part of the company, I was always an outsider. This feeling of being an outsider drove me to the point of suicide, and this feeling also caused me to hurt those I loved dearly. Those I love most in this world I seemed to have hurt by the feeling of being an outsider.

Well," he said, "three months ago, the most authoritative voice, this thunderous voice, spoke from within me and the voice said, 'I took away your father that you might find out who the Father is.' Several weeks later, the voice repeated that sentence, 'I took away your father that you might find out who the Father is.' And then a few weeks later with even a greater authority and a still louder voice it spoke the same thing but it changed the pronoun." This is the change, and listen to it carefully, "I took away *my* father that *I* might find out who the Father is." Everything is a plan. He said, "When I awoke, I reflected on my life, and I saw it, the entire life, in a beautiful light, as I've never seen my life before. Prior to that it was one of sadness, one of loneliness, one of chaos, one of confusion; and now I saw everything perfectly ordered, everything precisely ordered, everything done as it ought to be done, because I, for purposes known at the moment of my decision, I decided to impose upon myself that state. And so, *I* took away my father that I might find out who the Father is. For the outside father is but a *symbol* of authority, a *symbol* of power, and I had to find that power, that authority within myself. I knew I couldn't find it on the outside, so I took away the outside symbol. I didn't know it when it happened, I was but eight, and here, everything was ordered, everything was a plan that I may find in me the power and the authority represented by a father."

You're told in scripture in the 23rd chapter of the Book of Matthew, "Do not call anyone on earth father, for you have *one* Father, and he is in heaven" (verse 9). In spite of this, we have organizations the world over who will simply promote people as teachers, as priests of the world, and first thing they want to be called is "father." And they all accept it, from the top down they're all called "father." And yet we are told in this Book of Matthew, "Do not call anyone on earth father, for you have *one* Father, and he is in heaven." In the same gospel we are told, "And heaven is within you." From *within* you this Father will come, and when he comes you are he.

Now, what is this whole plan? We are told, "As I have planned it, so shall it be, and as I have purposed it, so shall it stand" (Is. 14:24). Purpose, in the strict sense, is "the deliberately conceived plan proposed for action, or to be realized in it." A plan proposed for action, or else to be executed in it. And so, no one can stop the plan of God from coming to pass. Well, what is his plan? Listen to it carefully: "They shall have no inheritance; *I am* their inheritance: and you shall give them no possession in Israel; *I am* their possession", the 44th chapter, the 28th verse of the Book of Ezekiel. That *I* inherit *God*, that God is my possession...that is the plan.

Now, he speaks of an anger—my friend used the words "chaos, loneliness," all the things that you would associate with an angry God. It was not an angry God as he knows today. But the Bible speaks of anger: "And the anger of the Lord will not turn back until he has executed and accomplished the intents of his mind. In the latter days you will understand it clearly," here from the Book of Jeremiah, the 23rd chapter (verse 20). And so, in the latter days you will understand it clearly. It cannot turn back until it executes and accomplishes the intents of its mind, and the intent is that you and I inherit God. Well, God is father. It was revealed clearly in the New Testament. It is mentioned in the Old but not revealed. In the New it is completely revealed. But man will not see it, or, at the moment, he feels himself unable to grasp it.

Now, let us go to the first book of the New Testament. "This is the book of the genealogy of Jesus Christ, the son of David, the son of Abraham" (Mat. 1:1). That's how the book begins. When you read it you wonder "What is it all about?" For if you read it, he's supposed to be the son of Joseph, and David is supposed to be the son of Jesse, and Abraham the son of Terah. And here we find this opening wonderful dramatic statement: "The book of the genealogy of Jesus Christ, the son of David, the son of Abraham." Well, every rabbi would admit that if in the genealogy of Messiah you mention Abraham and David, these would be the high-water marks, no question about it. For all would concede that it was to Abraham and his seed that the promises of God were made, no doubt about it as you go back and read the promises. So here, on that they will agree—but Jesus Christ the son of David? It isn't mentioned in scripture. Then what is it all about? As I stand before you tonight, I am not theorizing, I speak from experience and I *know* this is true. But when man begins to awake, he first becomes his own father; and then he becomes his father's father. To become my own father, David being my father, because I'm David, to become my father's father, and if Abraham be his father, then I am Abraham, the father of the multitudes.

Now, is this true? I tell you it *is* true. This genealogy is not physical; it's all spiritual, the entire Bible is spiritual. Man not knowing that he tries to trace it in a physical line and it's not a physical line. The whole thing is spiritual. Man had no idea that this was altogether true, that man would eventually *inherit* God. He would actually awake to find himself the being that he formerly worshipped as something on the outside, to discover it is himself. And there was no way in eternity that he could ever reveal it to himself save through a son. That no one knows, "No one has ever seen God; but the only begotten son in the bosom of the Father, he has made him known" (John 1:18). And you are taught to believe it was, and the Bible will tell you, that is, the priests will tell you that it was Jesus Christ. It isn't so. They'll tell you, yes, Jesus was his son. Every priest in the world, every minister I've ever met, if I ever have an argument with them it is because of this point. All I can say, "You haven't had the experience." When I quote scripture to them they stand confounded, but tradition is a powerful force and they can't quite overcome their training. So you say to them, listen to the words carefully, "You want to see the Father?" "For no one has ever seen the Father," they'll tell you. "Well, he who has seen me has seen the Father. How then can you say, 'Show us the Father? I have been so long with you, Philip, and yet you want me to show you the Father? He who has seen me has seen the Father. How then can you say, 'Show us the Father'?" You quote that from the 14th chapter of the Book of John and they stand amazed (verse 8). They can't deny scripture, but reason cannot allow them to accept it. Here is the 14th chapter of the Book of John, now we go forward into the 16th chapter, "I have spoken to you in figures; the hour is coming I will no longer speak to you in figures but tell you plainly of the Father" (verse 25). I have talked about the Father but from now on I will tell you *plainly*, said he, of the Father.

Well, who is he? Listen to the words again, "I took away my father that I might find out who the Father is." When you come to the third, as the hymn brought forth, as the skies in their revolutions brought forth the third, the appointed day...what did they bring forth? Wrapped in the silence of the tomb was the Great Redeemer—and the tomb is the skull of man—completely wrapped in swaddling clothes, *in* the skull of man. When I first heard it years and years ago from my old friend Abdullah, he said, "Neville, never think of Christ save you think of him as a child"—people paint pictures of a matured man—"Always think of Christ as the Christ child, always." I couldn't quite grasp it, didn't quite understand it. These words have been told me by a Negro Jew, born in Ethiopia, of the Jewish faith. He knew more of Christianity than all the priests of the world. Just like Paul he was born a Jew, born of the tribe of Benjamin. "I'm a son of Abraham after the faith, but if you took it even physically" said he "I would still be after the flesh, but now I know the spirit." And he said to me, The Christ child is always the child. Now we turn to the 8th chapter of the Book of Proverbs and here is a child speaking: "I am the first of his works of old. Before he brought forth the heavens, I was beside him as a little child. I was daily his delight, and rejoiced in the works of men" (verses 22,30). The little child, scholars say personify that, or rather, that is the personification of the wisdom and power of God. With that I do agree. It *is* the personification in the form of a little child of the power and wisdom of God. "I was daily his delight"...God delights in his creative power, personified as a little child, wrapped in swaddling clothes in the silence of the tomb; and the tomb is the skull of man.

Comes that day in the life of a man, individual man, when suddenly he realizes *I* took away my father, my outside father that I might find out who the Father *really* is. The day comes he finds the Father. Well, if I am a father, then where is my honor, where is my son? And then the son comes and looks you right in the face and calls you Father. He calls you "my lord." Well, "my lord" is an expression that every ancient boy used of his father. He always referred to his father as "my lord", Adonay, always. And so David calls him "my Father." So he asks the question, "What think ye of the Christ? Whose son is he?" And they answered, "The son of David"... for that's traditional. He said, "Why then did David, in the Spirit, call him Lord? If David thus calls him Lord, how could he be David's son? And no one asked him any other question" (Mat. 22:42). Here is the most glorious experience, and every child born of woman is moving toward this experience, for the end is to awaken as God. The end is to inherit God.

Now the promises were made to all of us, but the promise made to us differs from *obtaining* the promise. You and I who received the promise, we are regarded as heirs because we received the promise; but it differs from obtaining the promise. When we receive the promise, then we have received what was promised. And that which was promised is God himself. In between receiving the promise and receiving that which was promised is the pilgrimage of man. He moves on this earth as a pilgrim for unnumbered years until he comes to the point where he *receives* the promise in its fullness...that which was promised. And what was promised?—God. "They should have no inheritance; I am their inheritance: give them no possession in Israel; I am their possession." You possess God in his fullness: you become God, you inherit God. God is father, so you will never know you have really inherited God unless God's only begotten son stands before you and calls you "my lord." And you know it beyond all doubt as he stands before you and calls you "my lord." No doubt whatsoever when David stands there; and then you fulfill that portion of scripture, "Thou art my son, today I have begotten thee" (Psalm 2:7).

So the journey is on, and this whole vast world of ours has but one purpose: for hatching. "At length, for hatching ripe he breaks the shell" (Blake). And when he breaks the shell, then out comes that which calls you Father. So I know from the depths of my soul that this voice has never lied to me, never. And so, "Why did you make it?" and then it replied, "For hatching, just for hatching"...for hatching out everything in this world. You can hatch out success, same world, hatch out failure. He allows you to hatch out anything in the world. But you will not thwart his purpose, which was to hatch out God. For God entered death's door and laid down in the grave of man to share with man all of his visions of eternity; and then he comes out, and when he comes out you are he. You have no way of knowing that you are he were it not that *his* son calls you Father. So if *his* son calls me Father, then I am he. So I can say with the central figure, "I and my Father are one" (John 10:30).

This whole drama is a peculiar mystery. The mystery of Christ—you and I confront morning, noon and night as we read the Bible or hear it discussed—is no less a mystery today than it was in the day of the scribes. They couldn't understand it either, as they were inspired to put it down. And so, the mystery that confronts us, the person of Jesus, is no less a mystery than it was then. If you and I come at it with our, I would say, prefabricated misconceptions we are no wit better off than they. They, too, have the same misconception: They are looking for a savior on the outside—as someone had a father which is a representative of power and authority on the outside. And "Call no man on earth father, for you have but *one* Father, and he is in heaven...and heaven is within you." It isn't that you deny fatherhood as a physical state. You love him dearly, more so than ever. You see the part he plays. You see him in a new light, as a brother. Well, brotherhood without fatherhood is impossible. But you see everyone, including your own earthly physical father, as brother. You see your own children as brother, you see everyone in the world as brother. But there could be no brotherhood without a fatherhood, couldn't be. Any more than there could be a resurrection without death. How could you conceive of resurrection without death? So, "Wrapped in the silence of the tomb the Great Redeemer lay, 'til the revolving skies bring forth the third, the appointed day."

So in his case, it was the third. Here, the first one, and the first one stated it in simple terms as though another spoke, "I took away *your* father that you might find out who the Father is." That is, affirmed it, to fulfill the 41st of Genesis, where the dream or the voice repeats itself. If it doubles it, then it means that shortly it shall be brought to pass, the significance of it; and so, the second one was a repetition, word of word, of the first. But the third, the pronoun's changed, "I" becomes now a different "I" altogether. The first, the "I" was another one speaking, but now, listen to the words, "I took away *my* father"...can't be another one speaking now... "I took away *my* father that I might find out who the Father is." Not that *you* might find out or *he* might find out, but that *I* might find out who the Father is.

Then you see the whole thing in an entirely different light. To use his words, "I saw my entire life in a beautiful new light, that everything was ordered, everything was perfect. There was no confusion any more. That when my father made his exit from this sphere at my age of eight my world then was shattered. I know now that was my purpose in the beginning: to find my *true* Father. So that disappearance was all in order from my world. It drove me to the point of suicide and caused me to hurt those I loved best, and now on reflection, the whole thing was ordered." So, "As I planned it, so shall it be, as I have purposed, so shall it stand" (Is. 14:24). And the purpose, as we defined it earlier, is a deliberately conceived plan. You conceived it for its ultimate end, which is God the Father. That's the plan of God to you and everyone in the world would inherit him. If I inherit God and God is one, and you inherit God and God is one, and *we* inherit God and God is one, then are we not one? So in the end, there is only *one*; therefore, there's only one Son and that one Son is David. If I am his father, and you are his father, and we are his father, are we not the Father?

So it's a brotherhood and a fatherhood; *one* brotherhood, *one* fatherhood. This is the great mystery. So Paul in his letter to Timothy, he said, "Great indeed, we confess, is the mystery of our religion" (1Tim. 3:16). He uses the word mystery no less than eighteen times. He knows it's a mystery; and the world thinks that it's a little secular history, and it isn't. It's the *great* mystery: Contained within us is this one who is wrapped in the silence of the tomb, the tomb being our skull, and he's wrapped in the swaddling clothes...and here is Christ, who is God the Father. And so, when you come and you awake, you are Christ, and, therefore, God the Father. How will you know that you are? Well, you'll ask the question "What do you think of Christ?" "Oh, he's the son of David." "Then why did David in Spirit call him Father, call him 'my lord'? If David thus calls him 'my lord,' how could he be David's son?" And you have the experience.

You look into the mirror the next morning and the beard is still there to be shaved, you still have to wash this garment, you still have to feed it. And all that you were taught about Christ Jesus falls away. You see the garment that hides him now, for you had the experience. You know it's not the outer garment of flesh, for flesh and blood cannot inherit the kingdom of God. But you had the experience of Spirit and you know who you are. So you shave it and you feed it, and you go through the day, the normal day, knowing that you're going to fulfill scripture. And they will say to you, "Well, if this happened to you, go and show yourself, certainly you want to display it." Then you will say, after the words recorded in the 7th chapter of the Book of John, "For even his brothers did not believe in him"...his brothers did not believe in him. So they want him to become a magician and go out into the world and be magical, do fantastic things. And he knew in the depths of his soul if he did everything in the world that man could never do, they still would not believe. You can't believe until it happens.

You may take it on credit as it were, take it on approval. When I was a little boy we charged everything and sent it home on approval. And so, mother put the little shoes...and so if they didn't fit you sent them back… but you took them on approval; you didn't have to pay for them. So you put all your clothes on "on approval," and at the end of the week, after you tried them all on, and either they didn't look right or they didn't feel right, mother would simply call the place where she had them sent "on approval," and they sent and picked them up. How they survived, I don't know. But that's how we conducted business when I was a boy. So what I tell you now, you may take home on approval and then send it back to me, reject it. For his brothers did not believe in him. And so, if he did a thousand things he knew that would not be convincing. They would ask for the thousand and one. So no matter what you did, neither the number nor the character of the signs that he performed convinced them to the point where they believed, where they accepted it, and became sons of the faith of Abraham. So I tell you from experience this is going to happen to you.

This morning, between 5:30 and quarter of six (and the gentleman is here tonight) as I was coming back from the depths of my soul I heard the voice, and the voice is speaking to this gentleman who is here tonight. The voice asked a question and his answer was, "I'm a student of Neville." The voice said to him (I am like an eavesdropper), "If you are a student of Neville, you are far, far along the path of salvation," and then I woke. It was quite dark, but the mornings are dark now, so I would say between 5:30 and quarter of six. So I can say to him what I heard the voice say. What voice? I heard it, but it was the voice in the depths of my own being. For in the end, there is only one voice that speaks with authority, only one voice.

If you know in the depths of your own soul all that you've had is recorded in scripture, and it goes back thousands of years, and you're only fulfilling scripture—"Scripture must be fulfilled in me"—and if everything recorded there you have experienced, then that is *your* voice.

The day will come you will know it isn't another, though you may have heard it from another. In this case, it came to him as another speaking with an authority. And so he knows that what I'm telling you is the truth. I'm not manufacturing it; this is not the product of emergency thinking. I'm not trying to in some way contrive it to tell you something. All this is simply what I have experienced. And so, I know that all these characters of scripture are contained in us, every one. But the important ones...as stated in the very first verse, "This is the book of the genealogy of Jesus Christ, the son of David, the son of Abraham." So man matures when he becomes his father's father. The whole thing begins with Abraham. Are we not told that all the nations of the earth will bless themselves *because* you believed. Read it in the 22nd chapter of the Book of Genesis: Every one in the world will bless himself because Abraham believed (verse 18).

So he goes back to that state. And who was that "believing one" but God. The word Abraham means "the father of multitudes," that's what it *really* means. And so, you go right back. The father of Jesus Christ, David? Well, David calls him "my Father." And then, David the son of Abraham? That is not analyzed in scripture, because you go right back to be the father of your father, and then you know who he is. It is God who willed himself to go into this fabulous world of death and bring back an experience that would expand him beyond what he was when he started the journey. Now you know who he is, that God actually imposed upon himself this limitation and started this journey, a predetermined journey, that not a thing in the world could in any way divert it or stop it. And at the very end he comes out, but he comes out expanded beyond what he was when he started the journey. So you and I are coming out, inheriting God, expanded beyond the wildest dream as we can conceive it here.

So this experience of my friend is a *fantastic* experience, really. "I took away your father"—that's the first—"that you might find out who the Father is." And after that was repeated and affirmed comes the change in pronoun, "I took away *my* father that *I* might find out who the Father is." "Call no man on earth father"—so I took him away—"when you have but one Father and he is in heaven." So if he's in heaven and heaven is within me, I must find him. If I *find* him though I have no child on earth and I find Father, then show me the child. "For a son honors his father. If then I am a father, where is my honor?" So if I have found him, bring me that child; he's got to call me Father, and I must know without any uncertainty that he really is my son. And may I tell you, you do not know anything in this world with the same assurance. You do not know any relationship... we trust our wives and we trust that our wives trust us...I mean, that is all taken on trust. So when we say, well, they have a little child, my father. in a humorous mood when he toasted a friend of his would always say, "Well, here's to the man who rocks his child and rocks his child alone, for there's many a man that rocks another man's child and thinks he's rocking his own." But in *this* case you have no uncertainty when you see David. It is *your* son and there is no other father; and may I tell you, no mother, just you and your son. And you know it more surely than you know any relationship in this world. And so, everyone is destined to have *that* relationship, *that* experience. So he who has it fuses with me, for we are one. Everyone who has it fuses with me, without loss of identity. Therefore, in the end "the Lord is one and his name is one" (Zech. 14:9).

So here, the voice said to me, and it has never lied, "It is for hatching" and the hatching is to bring forth God. Where, outside? No, can't be brought forth on the outside; brought forth in you *as* you, that's the hatching. Well, if he's brought forth within me *as* me, this must be just like a big egg; and when the egg is broken I come out and I am he. So the whole world is for hatching. But while we're playing our parts in the world of Caesar, we can hatch out success, hatch out health, hatch out better relationships, hatch out anything. But first of all, you must *want* to. It starts with a desire, it starts with the urge. God's imaginal dynamic is called "anger" in the Bible: "And the *anger* of the Lord will not turn back" (Jer. 23:20). That's the imaginal dynamic. You must *lust* for it, for God *lusts* to give himself to everyone, as though there were no other in the world, just God and you; and finally, only God, because you are God. That was the dynamic that could not turn back "until it had executed and accomplished the intents of his mind; in the latter days you will understand it clearly."

So the same *urge*...if you want to succeed in this world, you must have that same drive, that same desire in this world. A friend of mine gave me the paper yesterday the *Observer*, comes to us on Monday, and today she called to ask if I had seen, on the thirteenth page, a letter among the letters where Goldwater didn't have the *lust* for power, and that no person ever sat in our White House who didn't have that lust for power. You must have *lust* for power to sit in the body that represents the greatest power in the world, you must. If you have other things in your world, you don't have that same lust. So I'm not saying that you should have it, but if you wanted something in this world other than what you now enjoy, you must *really* want it. Don't ask how, just really want it! And then if you *really* want it, this world is for hatching...it'll hatch it out. You may not want it after you get it, but that's alright. You can simply bring it to pass and then want something other than what you bring to pass. But you must want it. You start with a desire, with a lust. In fact, one of the words used to define the word "prayer" is lust, longing. It's a longing and then a yielding to that after which you long. That's how it's defined.

But regardless of what you bring to pass in this world, I assure you, from my own experience, God cannot fail in his purpose for you, and that purpose is that you inherit God. So, if you have to impose upon yourself at moments a sad experience or some other thing in this world, bear in mind that when it comes to you on that third day, the appointed day, when you hear who the Father really is, you'll reflect upon your life and see it in a more beautiful light, and see it all is ordered, all is perfect, just as it ought to be, because of your *predetermined* goal.

Now let us go into the Silence.

First of all, we're closing a week from tonight, closing on the 15th instead of the 18th. The club needs this area for the annual party, which will be held on the 18th, so we're closing a week from tonight, and reopening on the 5th day of January. So that will be also a Tuesday. I think it is, yes, a Tuesday. I will not be sending out notices to remind you, so bear it in mind. I will have a little ad in the *L.A. Times*, but I'm not sending out notices between now and then. So I will be open on the 5th day of January, the usual schedule, every Tuesday and Friday in this place. We're closing a week from tonight, so we have but two lectures left, Friday and next Tuesday. My friend Jack, who is bringing out my little pamphlet called *He Breaks the Shell* has promised it for next Friday. So, it's just a little pamphlet the size of *The Search*, and so anyone who is coming may pick it up, it's *He Breaks the Shell.* I have related my own personal experiences in these four mighty acts of God as he unveils his finished portrait. For "Let us make man in our image" was the primal wish, and not a thing will stop him from fulfilling that wish. When he's fulfilled it, he unveils his image in four mighty acts, and so I have recorded the four mighty acts as I, personally, have experienced them. And, it's a little pamphlet, just about the size of *The Search,* and he tells me he will have it next Friday. We really only have two days more, Friday, and then we close on Tuesday.

But I know, in New York City I went through Hallmark's new building on 5th Ave. and 56th St. It's a beautiful building and marvelous cards. I saw many a card there for $2.50 and $3.00 and more...just a card. Well, this is truly the story of God's final work. It may not be told...in fact, I will confess it has not been told as a Shakespeare would tell it or a Blake would tell it. I am not equipped to tell it in that manner, but I have told it as clearly as I possibly can, without embellishment, and I haven't added one thing to it or taken one thing from it. I've just told it just as it happened and tried to relate it to all of the passages of scripture. So I put a little subtitle to it *A Lesson in Scripture.* For all the things that happened to me I pointed to scripture where it ___(??) told me. So it will be here next Friday. I, personally, do not send Christmas cards, and I doubt that I would send cards a dollar fifty apiece; but, nevertheless, I can say I have seen cards in New York City, $2.50 and three dollars and more per card, and it's not a message, just a beautiful, lovely arrangement as a card. That's a hint to send it as a card, you see.

* * *

Are there any questions?

Q: Would you please explain again God the Elohim and God Jehovah.

A: The word Jehovah is defined for us as I AM; it's singular, I AM. The word Elohim is plural. He said, when asked the question, "What is the greatest commandment?" he didn't mention any of the ten as recorded in scripture. But he did mention this, from the 6th chapter of the Book of Deuteronomy, "Hear, O Israel: The Lord our God is one Lord" (verse 4). If I would now put it into our language, "Hear, O Israel"—Israel is simply everyone who has the faith of Abraham. Israel is one of the pure in heart, a man without guile. They said, "Behold an Israelite, indeed, in whom there is no guile" when he spoke of Nathaniel…so anyone who fits that pattern, one who would be incapable of hurting another for personal gain. You could hurt others unwittingly, that's not it, but to hurt them deliberately for personal gain would not be an Israelite. So an Israelite in Spirit, not an Israelite after the flesh, for he addresses now those who are coming towards the fulfillment of his purpose. So, "Hear, O Israel: The I AM, *our* I AMs, is one I AM." It's a compound unity, one made up of others.

So you will not lose your identity in that day when you see David and David calls you "my lord"; and, therefore, on that day you and I will be one in the true sense of the word, without loss of identity. So we are the Elohim, and all of us will one day experience the fatherhood of God. There's only one Father, so on that day he'll be king over all the earth, and he will be one, and his name one, just one, without loss of identity. And we all return from that predetermined play where we, in the beginning, agreed to dream in concert towards *the end,* which was agreed upon before we started. When all of us, the Great Redeemer which is I AM, just simply wrapped in the silence of the tomb, started the dream.

Q: Neville, ___(??) riding the white horse?

A: Christ riding the white horse? Well, the white horse in Revelation is the mind completely under the control of the rider of that mind. And so, the white horse...a friend of mine sent me a dream where he was on a boat and there was a white horse who got aboard the boat, and it knocked someone down, even injuring others, and there was confusion. It was a battleship, it was a British man-of-war, and he was among the Britishers (although he is an American). They were shooting up some air ___(??), and the horse jumped overboard. When the horse jumped overboard, this battleship ran aground and there was confusion. One threw a spear at the captain and it went right through the captain. Then he pulled the spear from himself and threw it at someone else and almost severed the head of another. Well, there was complete confusion when the white horse jumped overboard. There was no control; there was no mind in control. So, I would say to him (he's here tonight) a dream is a private parable and the earthly form that it takes is always secondary to its meaning. Don't try to give meaning to all the little parts of the frame. It has one jet of truth. In this dream of his, the horse is the jet of truth. The horse should be ridden by Christ: "Let this mind be in you that was also in Christ Jesus" as we're told. If that mind is not in you, well, then you can't ride the white horse...he falls overboard. You're not in control of your mind. And then comes confusion and the captain was speared, and others were speared, the boat that should be afloat ran aground, because the mind is not in control.

Q: [inaudible]

A: I said that man matures when he becomes his own father. He completely awakes when he becomes his father's father. So, it begins "This is the book of the genealogy of Jesus Christ, the son of David, the son of Abraham." If he is the son of David...and he contradicts that by asking a question, "What think ye of the Christ? Whose son is he?" and they answered, "The son of David." He said them, "Why then did David, in the Spirit, call him 'my Lord'?" and quoted the 110th Psalm: "And the Lord said to my lord: 'Sit at my right hand, till I make your enemies your footstool.'" That's the 110th Psalm. So he calls him "my lord," therefore, he can't be his son, for "my lord" is an expression that a son uses of his father. So, really, David is calling him "my father." Now we go back, if now he calls him "my father" then he must be Abraham. For the book is, "This is the book of the genealogy of Jesus Christ, son of David, son of Abraham." Abraham, who then is he? Who is this being called Abraham that is the father of the multitudes? Ab is father; Resh is life, ___(??) life. Here, the spirit of life. Well, you're told the Father has life in himself: "As the Father has life in himself, so he has granted also the Son to have life in himself" (John 5:26]).

So here, no rabbi would deny that these two characters...at least not Jesus Christ...but David and Abraham are the high-water marks in any genealogy of the Messiah. Well, the word Christ means "Messiah," and so you could use the word Messiah instead of Jesus Christ; that this is "the genealogy of Messiah, who was the son of David, the son of Abraham." So when one awakes, he sees the whole thing is Spirit. He stands in the presence of one called David. Well, David is one who called Jesus Christ "my father." Well, if the Bible tells you Abraham is his father in Spirit, then who is Jesus Christ?

Goodnight.

ETERNITY IN MAN'S MIND

12/11/64

Tonight's title, I should say, is "God has put Eternity into the Mind of Man." It's taken from the 11th verse of the 3rd chapter of the Book of Ecclesiastes. It's considered the most disputed verse in the book. It begins: "God has made everything perfect in its time; and he has put eternity into the mind of man, yet so that man cannot find out what God has done from the beginning to the end." That each event in life comes in a setting in which it fits. That God had, by the limitation of man's power, made it impossible for man to comprehend the whole of his purpose. So man cannot quite see the purpose behind it all.

Now the entire world rejects this almost in its entirety...that everything is predetermined. Well, that's what the book teaches. There are a few inserted verses, which if you're serious as a student you can find them. They were inserted by some zealous religious leader, who tried to make God some great judge where he's a God of retribution. That's not what this one is talking about. He said the rich and the poor they go to the same end, that the wise and the foolish they go to the same end. He invites us all to simply enjoy life, eat and drink, and simply rejoice in what you do; for the end of all as far as he's concerned it's the same. He said, "That which has been is that which will be. That which has been done is that which will be done; and there's nothing new under the sun. Is there a thing of which it is said, 'See, this is new'? It has been already, in ages past. But there is no remembrance of former things, nor will there be any remembrance of things to come later among those who will come after" (Eccles. 1:9). But man rejects that completely; he can't believe that for one moment.

But, we'll come into this present generation of ours, and here are the words of one of the truly great physicists of the day, Professor Feynman at Cal Tech. Professor Feynman made the statement—-and it isn't new, he only confirms but he doesn't know he's confirming Ecclesiastes—that having observed the strange behavior of the positron, where this little particle produced by atomic disintegration, starts from where it hasn't been and it speeds to where it was an instant ago; arriving there it's bumped so hard its time sense is reversed, and then it returns to where it hasn't been. That's Professor Feynman. This is *this* generation. He said, "Now, having observed the strange behavior of this little particle, we have to change our entire concept of the world. No longer can we believe that the future is unfolding gradually out of the past. We must now see the entire space-time history of the world laid out, and we only become aware of increasing portions of it, successively." The whole vast thing is a world of recurrence.

Well, that's what the writer of Ecclesiastes saw. He calls himself Koheleth. No one knows what the word means, because it only appears in this book, so they've guessed at it. But these are the words, "These are the words of Koheleth, the son of David king in Jerusalem." That's all that it says. So they have concluded that it means either an assembly, or the speaker before the assembly, a preacher, a teacher—one who has gathered together all the wisdom of the world and tries to convey it to an assembly. That's what they believe the word means. But the words are this, "These are the words of Koheleth, the son of David." That's how the New Testament begins, "The book of the genealogy of Jesus Christ, the son of David." Is this Koheleth? Now we go to the end of the Bible, the Book of Revelation, in the very last chapter: And "I Jesus" say to my angel, "I am the *root* and the *offspring* of David, the bright morning star" (22:16). I am the root, therefore, I am father, I am the origin; I am also the offspring. I am the origin of the flower, of David. I conceived him, I am his father, and yet I am the flower. Here is the great mystery. "I will bring forth from you" said the voice to David "a son from your body. I will be his father and he shall be my son" (2 Sam. 7:12).

Now we go back to the statement of the 3rd chapter, the 11th verse, and listen to it carefully, for you can't quite grasp it unless you understand the meaning of the word which is translated "eternity." "God has put eternity into the mind of man, yet so that man cannot find out what God has done from the beginning to the end." Now the word translated eternity is the Hebrew word Olam—-Ayin, Lamed, Mem—-and we sound it Olam. You turn to your Concordance and you look up the word and find its many definitions, its many meanings. Here are a few: "something hidden, something kept out of sight; hide oneself; eternity, the world; something veiled from sight; a young man, a youth, a *stripling*, a lad." All of these are the meanings of the word Olam.

Now, what *did* God put into the mind of man and did it in such a manner that man cannot find out from the beginning to the end what God did? Only in the end can he find out, at the very end. Well, what did he put into the mind of man? Well, I'll tell you that in the beginning, before we unfolded, he put himself, he hid *himself,* in the mind of man. Well, when he hid himself in the mind of man he was already a father, and because he hid the whole of himself, he had to hide his son. So he hid his son and he hid himself in the mind of man. God himself entered death's door which is the human skull, and laid down in the grave of man to share with man his visions of eternity. At the end of the great vision, when the whole thing is over and this son conquers everything, then the son awakens the father who is the dreamer. And then in that awakening of the dreamer, he awakes from the dream of life.

Now let me try to explain it to you. This is a mystery. A mystery is not a matter to be kept secret, but it is a truth that is mysterious in character. How can God enter the grave called man? How can he condense himself to this thing? Well, in Hebrew thought history consists of all the generations of men and their experiences fused into a great whole, and this concentrated time into which all the generations of men are fused and from which they all spring is called Olam. Olam, then, is history...a compact whole, that's what Olam is. So when we speak of Olam as eternity, all the generations, the play is finished. That's what Koheleth is saying, the whole play is finished, and it repeats and repeats itself forever and forever. While he awakens within the play and escapes from it all, he warns us not to be amazed, not to be surprised, when we see day after day or year after year all the great...well, what would I say to describe it? Every morning's paper brings it and you and I remain shocked when we see all the stealing going on in the world among officials. And he warns us not to be surprised because all officials are encouraged by the example of those above them to make what gain they can from their vocations. So we read in a morning's paper that some trusted official suddenly embezzles so much the firm goes broke. Or someone that you and I voted for and thought he was the one to lead us to some greatness, and he entered politics as a poor man, married a poor girl, served only us, supposedly, and at the end of his faithful service (really to himself) he comes out with, say, twenty million dollars. And so, he warns us in the 5th chapter *not* to be surprised, not to be amazed when we see such things taking place among officials. This is a play. You can't blame anyone when you see it. They don't know they are sound asleep, as though they were really in a state of amnesia. But they don't know it, and you and I don't know that they don't know it. We think that they are completely awake. So he warns us of all these things in the story. And man refuses to accept it, because he can't believe that this thing is a play. But the book itself, from beginning to end, warns it, with few exceptions, which all scholars agree are insertions by these zealots, religious zealots, trying to give some kind of reason behind it all...and you can't do it. God himself did it.

Now let us turn to the word Olam, for that gives us the cue. What does it mean? What did he put into my mind, into your mind, into our mind, and put it in such a way that you and I can't detect it until the very end? And I tell you, the word means "a stripling," it means "a youth," it also means "to hide oneself." Alright, I say in the beginning he put himself into the mind of man; and if the word is translated eternity: "Eternity exists and all things in eternity, independent of creation, which is an act of mercy" (Blake). So he put the whole thing in my mind. Therefore, I agree with Blake: "All that I behold, tho' it appears without, it is within, in my Imagination, of which this world of mortality is but a shadow." If he put eternity in my mind, I can't see anything, really, outside of myself. There isn't one thing outside of my self. But he will not allow me to discover just what it is and the process until the very end: It's really himself. I make this statement: The whole is contained within man, but the important thing in man is God the Father and his Son. His Son is his creative power and his wisdom (1 Cor. 1:24). It's *personified* in scripture as David. David is called "the adventurer"; David is called "the one who goes forward against all opposition and conquers." He is the conqueror. He never fails, he goes forward, and when he conquers completely he sets his father free as told us in the Book of Samuel (1 Sam. 17:25).

Now we come to a certain passage in the Book of Samuel. Listen to it carefully. This whole story takes place in Spirit, not on earth. Here in Samuel…and David is brought into the picture, a youth, he's just a youth, and the king said to his lieutenant Abner, "Abner, whose son is that youth?" and he replies, "As your soul liveth, O king, I cannot tell." Well, the word translated "youth" is Olam. He's inquiring about Olam, "Whose son is that youth?" He asked another question, he said, "Inquire whose son the *stripling* is." The word "stripling" is Olam. Nobody knows, so the youth steps forward, and he holds the head of the giant in his hand, the Philistine, the one who was the opponent of Israel. And he turns to the youth now, he said, "Tell me, whose son are you, young man?" The word "young man" is Olam (1 Sam. 17:56). So, "Whose *son* are you, young man?" I'm trying to find out the father of this lad, I'm not asking about the lad at all. I'm not saying, "Who are *you*?" I'm saying, "Whose *son* are you, young man?" Whose son are you—and "young man" is Olam—so tell me. Well, he replies "I am the son of your servant Jesse the Bethlehemite." Jesse means "I AM"... that's all that it means. Jesse is the same word translated Jehovah. Jesse is the same word translated Jesus. This is who I am: I am the son of Jesse the Bethlehemite. Now, the promise is made that if I can find the one who destroyed the enemy of Israel, I would set his father free. I must now set the father of this one free. Well, who is the father of that being? I am. So, when you see him he sets you free.

So the mystery contained in the mind of man is God and his creative power, personified as a youth called David. God being man, his attributes are men. So his son which is the personification of his creative power is David. And when I put myself into death, the last thing to be conquered is death. So I enter death's door, and play my part, sending my son into battle, my creative power, and my creative power conquers and conquers and conquers. As it conquers, as we are told, I will give to him who overcomes… the morning star (Rev. 2:26,28). In the end, we are told, "I am the root and the offspring of David, the great morning star" (22:16). So he gives himself. His own creative power is now redeemed. He brings it back enhanced beyond the wildest dream of anyone on earth, having gone through death and overcome death. He dies: He becomes man. This is death. This whole vast world, believe it or not, is dead.

I've seen it. I have seen the whole thing stand still. You can turn it back...so then you read the words, And he took the world and turned it back from its shadow ten degrees (2 Kings 20:9). How could you take the sun and the shadow that it cast upon the earth and turn the shadow back and tell me that the world is what the scientists believe that it is? If I can turn it back ten degrees, I can reverse its course, if I can turn anything back. How can I make it stand still? Well, I've made it stand still. I've made those I saw in the focus of my being, I've made them stand still, and they all stood still; and then I allowed them to move on in their course. So they moved on in the wheel of recurrence, but I had the satisfaction of tasting of the power of the age to be. Didn't change them…I made them stand still, and then the birds stood still, the leaves stood still, everything stood still. Then, when I released within me—not in them—the activity which I arrested, they all continued to perform their intention. Their intention is predetermined; it's a wheel within a wheel within a wheel.

And man will not believe it, he can't seem to believe it. And so this is the most disputed book in the Bible, and the verse we chose for tonight's subject is the most disputed verse in the book, the 3rd chapter, 11th verse (Eccles.). He has made everything perfect, everything—that every event in this world comes into a setting in which it fits—but by the limitation of man's power, man is not able to see the full purpose of God's plan. And man will not believe it.

Now he makes this statement...all through the book he uses the words "I saw" or "I have seen." He reminds us of the Book of Acts when John and Peter are told, if they are not silent they are going to be imprisoned and persecuted and beyond that. They said to the Sanhedrin, "If it is right in the eyes of God...no, whether if it is right in the eyes of God to listen to you rather than God, you must judge. But we cannot speak of anything other than that which we have seen and heard." So, whoever Koheleth is, is saying: These things I know, I have seen them, I've experienced them. Whether I understand them or not, I'm telling you what I have seen. And now he tells you—this is the 4th chapter, the 15th verse—he said, "I saw all the living that move about under the sun as well as the second youth, who is to stand in his place. There was no end to all the people. He was over them all. Yet those who will come later will not rejoice in him." He saw all the people moving about under the sun, but he also saw the *second* youth, who is to stand in his place. And here, this one is over everyone—as we're told in Ezekiel, the 37th chapter, And David is my prince over all, but no one will rejoice in him. So I tell you this story. And if tonight you are hungry for money, your concept of that so far transcends any thought I could ever tell you about David that you couldn't even compare them. You have no ears to hear the story of the one who is coming to stand over all—the conqueror of your own being, your creative power, personified as the second youth. All through scripture it's the second one that takes the place. So Cain slew Abel, and Cain I hated and Abel I loved; Jacob took the place of Esau; Ephraim took the place of Manasseh; and all through the entire Bible the second takes the place—this peculiar mystery that is taking place.

Now listen to these words, the word "Olam" also means, it's the same word translated in the book of Isaiah as "the virgin" in the 7th chapter, the 14th verse: "And a virgin shall have a son and call his name Immanuel." That word "virgin" is Olam. Here in the 9th chapter: "Unto us a *child* is born, to us a *son* is given...and his name shall be Wonderful Counselor, Mighty God, Everlasting Father, Prince of Peace" (verse 8). Everlasting Father, if I would spell it in Hebrew would be Ab Olam. That's his name, Everlasting Father. Now these two, the child and the son given are entirely different. "Unto us a child is born," that's one. It's not the same as "the son is given." A child is born; the son is given. That son that is given is David, and "God so loved the world he gave his *only* begotten son" (John 3:16). What is his only begotten son? "Thou art my son, today I have begotten thee," the 2nd Psalm the 7th verse addressed to David.

So to this David a son is given. And one of his names—he has four names—is Everlasting Father. So right into the mind of man is placed the Everlasting Father. For if he's a father and he's all, you can't take from him fatherhood, therefore, where is his son? His son is his own creative power and his wisdom. He buries his creative power in this world of death; and sends him through death to conquer death, and he comes out, and the last enemy to be conquered is death. When he has conquered all, he comes out and extracts from the world of death his son that was the warrior, who performed all the actions as the Father dreamed it. When the Son has completed all the actions the Son returns, and as he looks into the eyes of his Son, that heavenly face and knows it to be his Son returned, he awakes. He awakes from the dream and he's conquered death.

Now you understand the story of the prodigal son. He sends the *second* son into the world. The prodigal son was the second, not the first. He sends the second son into the world, and he goes into the pigsty and lives off of husks. He does *everything*, and then he remembers; he comes to his senses. And the Greek word translated "and when he came to his senses" literally means "and when he came to his senses after fainting." Have you ever fainted, completely fainted, and then all of a sudden you'll be on the floor, and then you come to your senses after fainting and the whole world returns? Well, this was like a faint and he comes to his senses *after* fainting and returns. In that interval he remembers, the Father remembers, and now his creative power is once more placed upon the throne as it were. The robe is put upon him, the ring, and shoes upon his feet, for only slaves went without shoes. He's no longer the servant, he's no longer the slave; he is now a free being. He brings back his creative power; and is risen from the world of death because he conquered death.

Now, does this give us any opportunity while we are in the world of death to modify it and change it? The book does not show it but the New Testament does. One who has returned from death can tell you a story. Until one *returns* from death, he doesn't know of the story of repentance, he knows nothing of it. Prior to that, it's simply a world of recurrence, and it's over and over and over, and you wonder if ever in eternity one will ever come out. So he said, "What has man who amasses enormous fortunes, at the end he must leave it at death to those who did not toil. How does he differ from the poor man? And the *wise* man, how does he differ from the fool?" He only saw recurrence in this world. Well, when one rises from the dead…when that second one...he saw it only in shadow, that's all that he saw it (Eccles. 4:15). He saw the second one, but he didn't see it vividly. Read it carefully. There's no description of the second one, he only knows it's Olam; he only knows it's the second, it's not the first. He doesn't in any way describe that second son, that second youth. But when that second one returns from his venture in the world of death and conquers everything, he awakens his father and sets his father free; and the father extracts his creative power from the world of death. He overcame it.

So here, not until someone rises from the dead can he tell the story of repentance. Repentance is simply, while one is still venturing in this turning wheel, where things recur and recur and recur: "Go and tell them that the time is fulfilled and the kingdom of heaven is at hand. Repent and believe the gospel." This Book of Ecclesiastes shows us that humanity's most urgent need is for the gospel that waited for the fullness of time, the most *urgent* need. Because, man seeing only the wheel...like Professor Feynman, the whole vast time-history of the world is laid out and we only become aware of increasing portions of that which already is. But when one rises from the dead and extracts his creative power, he can tell everyone—if they'll believe him, who have not yet *risen* from the dead, for they haven't found the son that was lost—"This is my son, he was dead, and he's alive again; he was lost, and now he's found" (Luke 15:24). So the prodigal has returned; my creative power in the world has returned. I lost it, I was sound asleep; to me it was dead. I am sound, sound asleep. And now, he conquered everything, he conquered death. Having conquered all he is returning, and he's waking me, his Father, and he and I are one. I can't separate myself from my creative power.

And so, when I now resurrect and completely return but enhanced beyond the wildest dream of what I was prior to my venture into death, I can now say: I can send my angel into the world and tell them that repentance works. That you don't have to consider this wheel forever, you *can* interfere with the otherwise mechanical structure of the brain. You don't have to actually observe this and that as it unfolds before your eyes. You can see what you *want* to see—though the wheel of recurrence would deny it—and change the pattern. And while you are in the wheel of recurrence, change the pattern and not be a slave of it. This exercise is the exercise that David needs, and then he will overcome and overcome all the things presented for his observation. And overcoming it, finally he overcomes death; and he returns to awaken his Father.

So God placed into the mind of men, Olam; and Olam really is himself and his son. He placed the history of humanity, that's what he did. The whole compact history of the whole vast world he placed in the mind of man. So man cannot observe anything outside of himself. But he can interfere with this mechanical structure of the brain by repentance. Repentance is simply a radical change of attitude towards life. And so, I really need *not*, I need not go on forever just observing the wheel of recurrence with no hope of redemption—for there's no hope in the Book of Ecclesiastes, none whatsoever. Enjoy yourself whether you're poor or rich, he tells you, for your end is the same whether you're wise or foolish, whether you're known or unknown. Whatever you are, simply enjoy yourself. Said he, I have amassed fortunes, I have raised buildings, I have known the love of women, all the things. He refused nothing; he could indulge himself; and he saw the whole thing as a wheel turning and no escape.

But he did have the vision, a faint vision of a second son; but he didn't know what the second son represented. He knew he was *above* all, and he knew that everyone he saw moving under the sun would be *under* this second son. But he also knew that those who would come later would not rejoice in him at all. So you could talk about him and tell about him and no one would care anything about David. Oh, he lived a long time since. Don't tell me of David, tell me of today's story, what is the president doing? What is the leader of Russia doing? What is the head of society doing? So you can say, well, today...and then you tell the story that those who were prominent only a few days ago are gone. But it doesn't register. Khrushchev is gone from this sphere, but it doesn't register at all. "Who's the one who can take his place? Let me know him. If I could only know him I could better myself"...and they don't understand the wheel is turning.

So the whole vast story is the same; they will not listen about David. So listen to the words, "Those who will come later will not rejoice in him." I tell you there is no escape from the world until David returns from his conquering venture, and brings back the head which is the vital part of man, and brings back the head of the enemy of man. He brings it back and the king said, "Whose son are you, young man?" He answered, "I am the son of Jesse." Son of Jesse? Yes, I am the son of I AM. So he looks you right in the face and calls you Father. Well, who is he calling Father? He's calling you, and if you answered you'd say, "Well, I am his Father...called me Father...I am his Father." He is the son of Jesse. At that moment you are redeemed; you've conquered death; you die no more. Until then, all death... you are restored at death only to die again. But when this thing happens in your life you die no more, you're completely redeemed. But you put yourself into death to *conquer* death. You can conquer everything, but the last enemy to be conquered is death, and death is conquered when David appears, having returned from the slaughter of the enemy of Israel. And so, this is the story.

So I ask you to dwell upon it. When you go home, it's only a very few chapters, there are only twelve chapters, and he tells you that "Take these words of the shepherd, for they are like nails that are properly driven in" (Eccles. 12:11). A good translation of that phrase would be that you take the idea of one who's had the experience and you drive it in, the idea of one man driven into the minds of many so they become fixed. I am telling you of my own experience. So let me become the one who will drive the nail in, and let it become fixed in your mind, for these are the stories. And when they are well driven in, he said, the words are like nails firmly fixed, and all these words that are gathered together under one heading, by one shepherd, so let them be firmly fixed. One shepherd (meaning one man who has had the experience) let him take this experience and drive it into the minds of many so they become fixed in the minds of many, that you may be supported by it. Because the day is coming, you'll have the experience.

In the meanwhile, you are not doomed to eternal recurrence as the book implies. You *can* repent, and no man is lost who dares to repent. To repent is to change your attitude towards life, and to change your attitude towards life is to change the phenomena of life. You will not see the same thing you would see had you not repented. Indulge yourself and enjoy it while you're waiting for your creative power, personified as David, to return from the slaughter, to bring back the victory. Then you look into the face of your victorious son...for it was your son that you sent. He gave his only begotten son, his creative power, that's his son. Not some little being on the outside, your own being. Your own creative power is always personified as a son, and that son is David. And therefore eternity, in the true sense of the word, is not the old man that the Greeks used but eternal youth. That's your son. He was beside you in the very beginning, your eternal delight, your creative power, as told in the 8th of Proverbs: "He created me in the very beginning of his way, the *first* of his acts of old. I was daily his delight and he joyed in the affairs of men, a little child. I stood beside him as a little child" (verse 22).

So here, this son is only the personification of your own creative power. Exercise it tonight by changing your attitude towards life, anything in this world, an individual. And you gradually catch on to how it's done. It's a simple process when you catch on to it. You don't burst a blood vessel. You reach a certain moment of actually *feeling* something that reason denies. At that moment, you feel a thrill as though some electrical current went right through you. Then you do nothing. Watch how you conquered it. Who did it? Your creative power, just watch it. You just bring into your mind's eye a friend and see him as you would like to see him, and then at a certain moment, I can't quite describe it other than to tell you it's like some electrical current. It goes right through you; every atom of your being seems to explode. At that moment it's done. You overcame whatever he faced as a problem, you overcame it for him. Doing that you overcame it, because you're overcoming everything. In the very end, having overcome all, you return, having conquered all; and you conquer death and you return to awaken your Father who sent you, his son.

So the Father and the Son are one. Where is the sacrifice? asked the prototype of the Son. Isaac asked his father, "Where is the lamb for a burnt offering?" and the father answered, "The Lord will provide *himself* a lamb" (Gen. 22:7). *He* is the lamb for a burnt offering. So I and my creative power I can't divorce them. How can I divorce myself from my thinking, from my imagining? I can't do it. I can't put them apart. And so here I seem to send my imaginal act into the world; it returns bringing back exactly what I imagined. And so I overcome and overcome and overcome, and finally this personified power stands before me and calls me Father. At that moment I awaken from it all, and leave behind me a record of how I overcame; and tell the world, you're not completely enslaved by the wheel of recurrence, you can repent. If you repent, you can change and change and change while you wait for the final consummation, which is the return of the prodigal, the second son. And when he returns, you put shoes on him because he's free now, and you put a robe on him, and the ring of authority on his hand, and a banquet beyond the wildest dreams.

And those who did not go into the power will sit back and criticize. They wouldn't go...the first son wouldn't go. There are those who do not venture. Not everyone will venture into the world of death. For when you see it—-and I've seen it from on high—-I've had those who have not ventured tell me that no one could return. When I returned to them and told them one night that I came from the world that I called Earth, and they called it Woodland, they couldn't believe that anyone could ever return from Woodland. So there are those who will not venture, and those who will not venture are called the first son. And those who *dare* to venture into the world of death and experience the whole, when they return they are enhanced beyond the wildest dream.

Now let us go into the Silence.

* * *

Now before we take the questions, I call your attention to my little pamphlet that came off the press this week, called *He Breaks the Shell.* It's very simply told, but because it is something different from what man believes, it will be difficult to grasp. But may I turn to Blake...Blake was criticized by the Reverend Doctor Trussler and Trussler told him his works were too obscure and he needed someone to elucidate his ideas. He said to the great Rev. Dr. Trussler that "that which could be made clear to the idiot isn't worth my care…and that the ancients considered what was not too explicit fittest for instruction, because it rouses the faculties to act." And so, I'm going to ask you...it's very simply told, not a word in it would send you to a dictionary, but it may be in conflict with your prefabricated concepts of religion or scripture. So read it and read it and read it. It's all based upon my own personal experience. I haven't told one thing in that little pamphlet that I heard from another. I've only related my own experience. It's the unveiling of the image of God, when he sends his power into the world on a predetermined plan to conquer death, and brings it back enhanced beyond the wildest dream. It comes back as his image, and he unveils it, and there are four mighty acts in which he unveils the returned son on a higher level. For it's a new creation when you return from death; it's not the same creation. You're ready now for a new venture. And so that's what the story's all about. It's a very simple little thing. You can read it in, say, two, three minutes. But don't say because I read it, well, I'll put it aside. May I suggest that you read it and read it and read it. It's not something that ninety-nine point ninety-nine percent of the Christians of the world, and the Jews of the world, will accept. But I tell you it is true. Hasn't a thing to do with orthodoxy. It is true based upon my own personal experience.

Now are there any questions, please?

Q: (inaudible)

A: As far as I am concerned, God is all Imagination. But people have such a strange concept of Imagination. You can take a very simple little story, you will say of someone, oh, that's just his Imagination. Haven't you heard that said "Just his Imagination"? And then someone does the most marvelous job, and he increases the returns of a business that ___(??) and all of a sudden he had Imagination and saw what could be done as against what was being done. There, he's a man of Imagination! Same word Imagination. And so, we speak of all kinds of ways of using the word, and it's right, it's everything, all inclusive. But I use it in a way that to me God is all Imagination and so is man, because God and man are one.

Q: (inaudible)

A: Eternity? Eternity...the word Olam is "something hidden." Well, certainly Imagination is hidden from the world, because they don't believe what they are imagining is creative. Isn't that hidden? And so, it is something hidden, something kept out of sight in time, both past and future. They can't see the past, they can't see the future, so they deny the past still exists, then deny the future exists now. So it's out of sight. They don't know David, so they can't see that Olam, which is eternity, is "the youth, the stripling, the lad, the young man." So when you mention to those who have not experienced him, they do not rejoice in him. I have gone on programs on TV and radio with ministers, rabbis, priests, and they stand appalled. I had one say to me, "Well, tell me...first of all I don't believe you" said he "and secondly what do you propose to do to spread it if you really believe what you're talking about?" I said to him, well, as far as I'm concerned, I am reaching you, at the moment, and right now on TV I'm doubling the exposure to, maybe, a half-million people. An nth part, always a little remnant will know, for I've planted it in their minds, driving it right in. I will leave behind me in printed form quite a few thousand books.

Well, if I go back in time to what you believe, where it started, there was no book, no book. If I go back to what you call the beginning of, say, one A.D., there's no book. We had no record of the story until fifty or sixty years after someone had the experience and told it. So you now think you represent a section of one billion Christians, but they all grew in the interval when there was no book, and no TV as you say. But TV and radio came before...it was always part of the picture, but no one knows it. If Feynman, who worked on the atomic bomb and worked on our nuclear bomb, and he's still a very young man today, and considered one of the top theoretical physicists in the world, not just in our land but in the world, and he said: "The entire space-time history of the world is laid out, and we just become aware of increasing portions of that which already is, successively" then said he in an after thought, "it doesn't matter what direction of time you take." And he's right, would it matter? And this is today's man in this century. Well, if it is true today, it was always true, that the entire space-time history of the world is laid out. That's what Blake meant in his wonderful *Vision of the Last Judgment* that "Eternity exists and all things in eternity, independent of Creation, which was an act of mercy." He need not bury himself in the dead to overcome death. But I saw it, it was all dead, everything was dead; and see it from a higher level, past, and the present, and the future coexist in the world of death. And you enter it, and then set yourself in motion, and overcome death.

Well, it's nine...and so, may I remind you we're closing next Tuesday. I intended to close on the 18th, but the club needs the place for their yearly Christmas party. So next Tuesday will be our last for the year, and we're reopening on the 5th of January. I'm not going to send out notices to remind you. I will put an ad in the paper, the *L.A. Times*, the week before I open. But outside of that simple ad I will not be notifying you that I'm reopening on the 5th. So try to remember I'm reopening right here in the same place on Tuesday, January the 5th.

Until next Tuesday. Goodnight.

THE TRUE STORY OF CHRISTMAS

12/15/64

Well, this is our closing night for a little while. We close tonight and reopen on January the 5th, which is really three weeks from tonight. I will not be sending notices. I will take an ad in the *Times* just about a week or a few days before we reopen, so do not expect a notice and titles. It will be appropriate, the title and the subject, when we reopen.

Because I am not speaking beyond tonight and this is the Christmas season, I would like to tell you the story of Christmas, the true story, not as hundreds of millions of people really believe it. For ten days from today hundreds of millions will celebrate Christmas, and they will think in terms of some being who was born 2,000 years ago in some strange and unique manner. And that is true...but not as the story is told. Any attempt by theologians to equate faith with historical information or scientific facts or philosophic, I would say, speculation, is bankrupt. That is not the story of the birth of Christ. When Christ is formed *in us*, he is born. We are the cocoon as it were; we are the egg in which Christ is being formed. And when he's formed, at that very moment when he's formed, and the time is fulfilled, then it is alive, it is awakened—it's our very self—and we come out and we are born. This is the story. I wouldn't care if the whole vast world rose in opposition. I am only telling you what I *know* from experience. This is not theory, I'm not speculating. And so any attempt to put it into any other form is folly. It isn't so at all. Everyone in this world is simply being formed into Christ Jesus and Christ Jesus is the image of the invisible God. It takes all the pains and the sufferings of the world to produce it, and when it's completely formed in us, at that moment then it comes out.

Now, let the churches this coming fortnight be bursting to overflowing. It makes no difference, it's good. Let them hear it even though it's distorted.

Let all the priesthoods of the world tell their story in a distorted manner, it's perfectly alright. But I'll tell you, the few that are here, how it *really* takes place. And may I tell you, no one knows until that moment when the hatching is about to take place, but no one knows. I will tell you this night and tell you in detail in the hope that you'll remember it. But when it happens it is so startling, so bewildering, you will forget, but not really. Something in the depths of your soul will know what is taking place, and then you will simply return to the outer scripture and read it for confirmation of the experiences that you've just had.

It will come in the most wonderful manner. You're told in scripture that it came so suddenly and unexpectedly in an unobserved inn. The inn was completely unobserved. No one knew that something great would take place in this inn, and no one knew that the occupant of the inn was selected that moment in time. And here, you make a journey from wherever you are living. So you were living—wherever you are that's home, that's base—and for reasons that you need not explain you make a journey. The scripture tells you that they went off because it was decreed they should all pay taxes. And at that moment came this moment of delivery. Well, paying taxes...we all pay taxes, it's been going on forever. So if you go from here on a journey, it's a vacation. If you go to visit a friend, if you go on a business jaunt, whatever you do, it's removed from where you are, and you invariably stop at an inn. You may call it a hotel, call it a motel today, call it a friend's home, I don't care what you call it; it is that you are removed from where you were. And so, you make your journey physically. And you retire quite normally in a simple inn, not knowing that this is the moment for you to be delivered of that which has been formed in you, your very being. And while you retire quite simply, suddenly the most *intense* electrical power seems to be applied to your brain. You've never felt anything in this world like it. Here, you begin to awaken and awaken and awaken, and then you are completely awake as you've never in your life been awake before. I think I'm awake now. I see you, I see you vividly. Everyone in this room I can spot and those that I know by name I could call by name, in this area. But this is like a dull, dull state compared to *this* awakening. There's a clarity, there's a translucency you've never known before, and you awaken, and you find yourself in your own skull.

And then one moment not of panic but of *deep concern* that you are in a skull. You don't think of it only as a skull, you think of it, strangely enough, as a sepulcher. You know that you are in a sepulcher, and *if* you are in a sepulcher then someone must have thought you to be dead to have placed you here. For here I awake...I awake in a tomb. Why am I in a tomb and the tomb is my own skull? So if I'm awake in this tomb, someone placed me here...or did I voluntarily go into it and fall asleep? I don't know. I simply found that I am in a tomb, and for a moment I think it's sealed, completely sealed. Then one moment later I feel that if I could but push the base of the skull, something would give and I would come out. And so I push the base of the skull and I come out just as I thought I would, head down. When I start moving out, pushing myself out, then I pull the remaining portion of me out, and there I am, I am out.

That's the beginning. I awoke from a state of death. I didn't realize I was dead. Someone thought me dead because I was placed in a tomb. I come out of it, I find myself now completely out of the tomb. I open my eyes to the world and I look back, and strangely enough although I am out of the tomb, the thing out of which I came is still present. That's the strange part. For I came out of the tomb and the tomb was my skull; and yet here is the thing, the body, out of which I came. That doesn't make sense but it's true. There it is, I look at it, it's ghastly pale, pale as snow. And then a wind, the most unearthly wind is disturbing me, and I cannot tell where it comes from or where it is going. I look around and then I think it's over there. I turn my attention for a moment over there. As I look over there wondering is this thing so strong it's going to blow the whole area down—I'm not diverted more than moments—when I look back and the body is gone.

In its place sits—and I'll tell you because you are few tonight; I didn't tell it in my little circle, in my little booklet; I told it impersonally, but I will repeat it—my three brothers were there. I say this to you tonight for a purpose, my three brothers were present. The oldest, called Cecil, was at the head; the second, called Victor, was at the right foot; and the third, called Lawrence, was at the left foot. They heard the same wind that I heard; but they didn't see me, they couldn't see me. I could see every thought that they entertained. My vision was so clear that they couldn't think unless it became objective to me. Everything they thought I saw. That's what I was at that moment. They couldn't see me for one moment. Lawrence, my third brother, was the most disturbed and he went off to see where the wind was coming from. He hadn't gone more than one or two paces when something attracted his attention, and looking down he said to my two brothers who were sitting on the bed, "Why it's Neville's baby!" and they in turn said, "How can Neville have a baby?" in the most strange, unbelieving manner. He didn't argue the point. He lifted up the evidence and placed it on the bed. Then I took the babe wrapped in swaddling clothes and into its little heavenly face I looked and I asked, "How is my sweetheart?" It just simply broke into a smile. And then the whole thing dissolved.

Now, I tell you tonight from experience, everything written about Jesus Christ in the Bible is a *sign*, but everything, from beginning to end. The manner of his birth is a sign to those who know who he is. But everything, I don't care what it is it's all a sign if you know who Jesus Christ is. I tell you this for a reason. It's all true, every *word* is true. It happens to us when Christ is formed in us. And you have no way to reveal it to another on this plane, if they are anchored on this plane, to satisfy them. A few days ago, last Saturday, the religious editor of the *Los Angeles Times* received a letter. In the letter he was offered five thousand dollars if anyone in this world could produce evidence that Jesus Christ lived. One condition imposed upon it, he would give $5,000 to anyone who could prove that Jesus actually lived, but you cannot produce any book, any writing in evidence. He wanted scientific facts. He wanted historical truth, as he considers historical truth, not even philosophic speculation, just scientific facts, archeological facts.

Well, he will hold that check forever. He will never be able to part with it, because this is not based upon this world at all. You are told a story and you either believe it or you don't believe it. When you *believe* it, it takes root. You may be here for unnumbered centuries. You don't begin because you come into the world; you are already in the world. "Eternity exists and all things in eternity, *independent* of creation, which is an act of mercy." So the whole vast world is here, and you don't move from where you are to the formation of Christ *in* you by the mere passage of time. You move only when the idea of God's plan of salvation is heard and believed. When you hear it and believe, then you start a journey...still in the same world. And the journey, may I tell you, is a journey of horror, a journey of dismay, of real affliction. But the affliction is for a purpose: It fashions you into the image of God. When it is completed you are awakened and brought forth, and you are one with God.

So you could be here and reject it completely. And the mere passage of time in this world— as the tyrant of tyrants, as the wisest of the wise, as the richest of the rich—will mean nothing until heard and *accepted*. Not just heard, but you hear it and you accept it on faith. You can't have...you can have no proof in this world based upon scientific facts. So I stand before you to plant the seed. I tell you it is true. Every thing that happened in my world is recorded in scripture. This is a sign you are told. A sign, what sign? That something has happened—that a savior was born. What savior? Well, the only savior mentioned in scripture is God. He has moved to a higher level of his own being. His creative power came into the world of death personified as a man, and the whole vast world takes the personification and worships it. And that's not it at all. Hasn't a thing to do with the personification. It's his creative power buried *in us* in the world of death. Then he tells a story and we hear it and we believe it. Those who believe it have accepted the seed which is the seed of God, and then we come out. For this remains, the whole vast world of death remains. Everything here is part forever of the eternal structure of the world. And he simply plants his seed upon man and lets it grow...if it is accepted.

I hope you will accept it. I tell you every word I have told you is true. The child in my hand is a fact, I can feel it now, I can see its face now. I can see the entire picture from beginning to end, as this power took place in my brain and awoke me from a long, long sleep. Then I found myself in the sepulcher. I came out. As I came out I looked back and that out of which I emerged was ghastly pale, as told in scripture. And here was the evidence of my birth in the form of a child, and those who witnessed the *sign* couldn't see the twice-born man.

Now, how could I prove to anyone save in faith that I've experienced it? Well, let me tell you a story. You and I speak of death; it's obvious things die every moment of time. You and I have gone to funerals and we've said goodbye to friends that we hope we will see...but we hope. We speak of the cold hand of death, we speak of the jaws of death, we speak of the king of terrors, and people speak, "Oh well, alright, that's just some poetical expression." Is that really true? Is there such a thing as a hand of death? Well, let me share with you an experience. It took place six years ago. We were living then on El Camino, it's a little street just at the end of the Strip, north of the Strip. One morning my wife said to me when we met for brunch, "I had the strangest experience this morning." She said, "I awoke and I sat up in bed, and then you came into the room and you sat on the bed. And then as you sat on the bed, a hand came out of nowhere and a hand grasped my hand. I didn't see the face of the hand, I didn't see what possessed the hand, it was just a hand and it held me in a firm grip. Then *you* looked up seemingly at the body where the hand was attached, and you said, 'Oh, my friend Death.' And then I said to you, 'But I don't want to die.' I said, 'Are you afraid to die?' and she said, 'No, I'm not *afraid* to die, but I don't want to die *now*.' Then I said, 'Alright, if you don't want to die now, alright' and the two hands disengaged, and she returned to her normal state here."

May I tell you, at that time in her life six years ago, she felt quite low in spirits, quite low physically, and really entertained the thought that she would make in the not distant future her exit from this world. So the hand of death is *not,* as the world thinks, some wonderful poetical figure of speech. God is *man* and everything in this world is personified as man, yes, even death, but everything in this world. And I knew him well. And that was before I had the experience of being born from above. I would have to have known him well to reach the point where I could be born from above, for every man goes through death after death after death in this world having accepted the idea that he would come out as God. And so I saw what I called my friend, I knew him so well.

So here, I tell you everything in scripture is true. This story of Christmas is a true story, but not as hundreds of millions will be told it ten days from today. They will be told that some unique experience took place 2,000 years ago, and they'll be told that it was something that happened in a natural thing, like a man not knowing a woman and the woman having a child through her womb. Christ is not born that way. Christ is formed in the *skull* of man. You and I are born naturally in this world from the womb of woman. But Christ *in us* is being formed by our life in this world, fashioned and shaped into the image of the invisible God. And when it's perfect, but really perfect, then it is awakened; and it's you and you are Christ. And we're all gathered together into one body and that body is Jesus Christ. You *are* Jesus Christ, the being formed into the likeness of Jesus Christ; and when you are completely perfect you are extracted from the skull and brought into the body of Jesus Christ.

So if I say I stood in his presence, what presence?—the presence of the risen Christ. Jesus appeared, this universal humanity, and I saw his form, and it is man. He embraced me when I knew who he was, for he asked me a simple question, "What is the greatest thing in this world?" I answered, after stating faith and hope, I said, "Love, the greatest of all is love." And then love embraced me. Now, may I tell you, when John wrote these words in the epistles of John he wasn't speculating (whoever John was). I believe the character, which is not really Lazarus; it's called Lazarus, the one who'd experience the ___(??), restoration from death, that was Lazarus—but whoever wrote the epistle when he said "God is love," I tell you he didn't speculate. This was not his conclusion after he thought in some philosophical manner. This was revelation, when God *revealed* himself. I didn't know that God...I heard it...but I didn't know that God was *actually* love, *infinite* love, until he unveiled himself before me. So when I was brought into his presence and stood in his presence, I couldn't think of anything but love, infinite love. Here, when he asked me the question and I answered as he intended that I should, and he embraced me, I became one with the body of love. And may I tell you, from that day to this, I am never divorced from it. I am *in* the Father and the Father in me, even though he sent me to do what I'm doing. As Paul made his statement to the Philippians, he said, Whether I should depart from this world and be one with Christ or remain...he didn't know. But he had no choice; he said there was a work to be done—this is the first chapter of Philippians (verse 23)—and there's a job to be done while he was in the body. He thought he had to remain in the body to complete the work and tell the world, but his longing was to depart from this world and to be one with Christ. For having felt the ecstasy, who on earth could find anything comparable to it? There's nothing here that compares to it, and you long to be one with that which you felt. You're still with it, but you're insulated because you're still wearing this body. And he uses the word "while in the body." And so, I am in the body, said he, and I long to depart from this world and be one with Christ, but there is a job to be done while still in the body.

So anyone who has had the experience, they cannot for one moment find anything in this world that holds them, that interests them to the point where they want to succeed in it...they really don't. I'm speaking from experience. I can't conceive of anything in this world that I have as an objective, really, save for individuals. But I don't have an objective for myself beyond that. I can't conceive of another objective, I just can't. And so I will take anyone's request and hear it and I'm quite confident it will work. I am *confident* that every request if I hear it and accept it it'll come to pass. Of that I am sure! Because I will hear nothing that I would not myself want as man. If you ask me to hear that someone is hurt, I couldn't hear it. If you ask me to hear that someone is unwell, I couldn't hear it. It's not part of my world. If you ask that you should have money, I could hear that; that you have a better job, and all these things, I could hear these things, and they'll all come to pass. I know it! But for myself I have no desire for these things at all. I feel like Paul. I can't wait for that moment of departure and yet I know there are things to be done while I wear the body. I must, too, wear the body. That's what he said in his first chapter to the Philippians. You read it carefully. If you take the new translation, called the *New English Bible*, it will give you a little different slant on the original Greek, but they're all good anyway. But the archaic language of the old Bible doesn't quite reveal what he intended to tell the world.

So I tell you the story of Jesus Christ is true...*not* as the world understands it. Jesus Christ is being formed in man. He's formed in the skull of man, and the very moment that he is formed he is awakened, and that is called resurrection. God's *mightiest* act is resurrection. Then comes the birth on the heels of the resurrection, and then comes the unfoldment of the entire picture. He knows who he is now. Because the purpose of it all is to give himself to his image, that's God's purpose. Not just to make an image but to endow it with the same power that he possesses which is life in himself. Well, if he gives himself to his image that he has formed and he was prior to that attempt a father, then the image at the moment that he succeeds in his transference of himself must be a father. And that's the second act. And so, he actually transfers himself, he *gives* himself to his image; and the image awakes; and the image becomes the Father; the very

Father that is God. For God is the Father of this heavenly Son. He sees his Son and the Son calls him Father.

And after that comes the next sign—-they're all signs—the splitting of the temple from top to bottom; and he sees the sacrifice that was God. For now God is himself, and he sees the blood of himself which is called in scripture the blood of Jesus Christ, and he fuses with his own blood. Then he moves up into heaven. And then comes the final picture, where God sees the whole thing and it's good and *very* good, and smothers him with affection, in bodily form of a dove. And he sees the whole thing unfolding within himself.

So I tell you the story that will be told ten days from today, where they have a little child on the outside, and animals all around, and wise men. I said earlier the wise men come...tradition has it that the wise men were brothers and they were kings, Melchior, Gaspar and Balthazar, that's what tradition has it. Scripture does not record it. But as far back as we can go, the early fathers, someone had the experience; and now tradition has it that there were three brothers, one the king of India, one the king of Arabia, one the king of Persia. These were three kings and they were brothers, and they came to witness the event. So I record this to this small audience that you may know the thing is true. Whether it is always so that you have three brothers, I do not know. On the other hand, when David appeared in my world and I was David's father…and not one moment prior to that event did I ever entertain such a thought. Well, three could come into your world and strangely enough they could be your brothers. You can have the same feeling, the same certainty about this relationship that you'll have to David. For I *know* these three brothers in my world, Cecil, Victor and Lawrence, I know them. They are still in my world. It was Lawrence (who was a doctor) who got off the bed in search of the wind to find the babe. And the Book of Luke tells you that he was a doctor (Col. 4:14).

Well, this thing is so fantastic, for it happens in the mind of man. So, all...I consider every one...just as David came into my world—and not for one moment prior to that entrance into my world did I entertain the thought that we were related—to discover he is my *son* and always has been my son. Then, these brothers that I know now...if you do not have brothers, it could happen tonight and the three who would come into your world would have the same sense of relationship that my three earthly brothers have to me. I'm only suggesting that; I do not know *that* from experience. But I do know that when David came, I had no sense of uncertainty about the relationship. And so, when these three men come into your world, whether you have brothers here in this world or not, they will to you be like three brothers. For somewhere along the centuries back they felt that the three wise men were brothers, and they called them Gaspar, and they called them Melchior and Balthazar, and said they were three kings who were brothers. So I leave it with you to do what you will from this.

But the story of Christmas is a true story, eternally true. And when you've had the experience and you make your departure from this world, you leave it just as it is, having told your story. I can't conceive...as Paul said in his letter to the Philippians, he wanted so much to make his exit on the heels of the experience but he could not. He had to wait, wearing a body, tied to this earth, to tell the story to all who would hear it and would accept it, but eagerly waiting for his departure. For as far as he was concerned the race was over, the fight was over, he kept the faith (2 Tim. 4:7). He heard it somewhere along the way. So don't think for one moment that this story *took* place once and forever 2.000 years ago; it is ever taking place every moment of time the world over.

May I tell you that the story of the Bible this is *sacred* history, it's not secular history. You begin with Abraham and come all the way through the entire line. Read the eleventh chapter of the Book of Hebrews and these are the characters that are eternal *in you.* And whether someone believes it or not, until you accept *this* story it doesn't matter what you do or accomplish in this world. There's no record of any Buddha, or Confucius, or a Plato, or an Aristotle, or a Socrates, or a Karl Marx, or a Hitler. These are not mentioned in this sacred history. None of these characters are mentioned, only from Abraham through to the end of the prophets. And Jesus Christ is the fulfillment of the entire picture. The Old Testament ends upon the note of expectancy, and the New Testament begins on the note of fulfillment; and the two are one; you can't separate them. The Old and the New are one; you can't interpret one without the other. The New only interprets the Old and the Old expects the New. And here is *your* story.

So everyone in this world has it, but it's not fertilized. Inwoven into man is the story. He hears it and the hearing would fertilize it *if* accepted. If he doesn't accept it, it bounces off. He remains in the world and moves from state to state to state, and makes every effort to anchor himself here forever. And they do today, trying to live physically for an extra hundred years...and vegetate. When I think of these lovely fellows that have lived so beautifully in this world I think of Winston Churchill. Here is a perfectly marvelous wonderful fellow. He's done such a marvelous job in the world, but at ninety the body shows its age, and here, well, he's not the Churchill that you and I knew. None of them are and yet someone today wants to put it on for 200 years and maybe a thousand years. If you lived a billion years and Christ was not formed within you, it wouldn't really matter.

Christ has to be formed *in man*, and Christ is the image of the invisible God. When formed, he awakens his image and gives to his image himself, and calls his image his son. He is declared son, why?—through his resurrection from the dead. You can't quite grasp…you can grasp it in a way, but when you find yourself waking in your skull and know what it is, it's not just a skull, it's a sepulcher. So that lovely thought: "Were you there when they crucified my Lord?" May I tell you, you can answer, "Yes, I was there." "Were you there when they placed him in the tomb?" Yes, you were there. Do you know where the tomb is? Maybe, that you don't know. May I tell you, the Bible tells you. Well, some call it Golgotha and others call it Calvary and still others call it "the place of the skull." Well, then I must go and awaken my Lord, for they took my Lord and they crucified him, crucified him on the place of the skull. So the father goes...this is the story told in scripture...that they were servants, the prophets, who went into the field and asked for some return of the vineyard, and they beat them and chased them away. Then he sent other prophets and they beat those and threw them out. Then he sent his son (his creative power) and they said, "Now, he is the heir, let us kill him, for the whole thing will be ours if we kill him" (Mat. 21:33). So they killed the son. And then the father went and the purpose of the visit of the father was to awaken his son: "This my son was dead and he's alive again; he was lost and he's found" (Luke 15:24). So here is the story of every one of us sent into this world of death, and then told the most *heavenly* story of recovery. Some believe it and some don't. So I ask you to believe it tonight, for *if* you believe it I can't tell you when the thing will be finished in you, but only after belief does the work begin.

Now let us go into the Silence.

* * *

We're closing tonight and opening three weeks from tonight, on the 5th of January. So may I call your attention to the book table. My little booklet is out, called *He Breaks the Shell*. It's the story of the unveiling of the image of God. And so you may take a look at it. There are other books there that I think you would like. Are there any questions, please?

Q: In your reference to the skull, where and of what is it?

A: Pardon me?

Q: Of what and where is it?

A: The 24th chapter of the Book of Luke, you'll find...read the 22nd chapter...and they name it Calvary, the Latin form; Golgotha is the

Jewish form. But Luke calls it by its name you and I understand: And when they came to "the place of the skull"…there they crucified him (John 19:17). So he calls it by the name that you and I understand. Well, Calvary means "skull" and so does Golgotha mean "skull." We're told in the Book of Romans, the 6th chapter, "If we have been united with him in a death like his, we shall certainly be united with him in a resurrection like his" (verse 5). And think in terms of the first one that simply awoke. But we're all together in that state. But for some strange reason it seems that only as the word is heard with *acceptance* does it start to grow, which is told us in the story of the sower who plants the seed, which is called the word of God; and it falls on four different types of soil and only on one type of soil does it grow (Mat. 13:18).

And people completely reject it. Those who completely reject it, alright, they reject it. It doesn't mean they cease to be. No, no one ceases to be. They simply go from state to state to state in this fabulous world of God, hearing the story at another moment in time, and maybe by then they will be more receptive to the story. But when someone can offer $5,000 to anyone who could produce evidence that Jesus lived—you can't produce a book in evidence or any paper—-he wants scientific facts. Well, Jesus Christ is a supernatural being. The birth is supernatural. Everything about him is supernatural. You can't produce any evidence, any more than my wife tonight could produce the arm that held her arm. And when I looked up and saw the face and knew him so well and said, "Oh, my friend Death," how could I present to anyone save in words the existence of a personification of a fact which is death? Death is a fact. People die; you can't deny that all things die. Well, how can I take that personification of death which was a hand... all the poets have written about the cold hand of death…but I saw it, she saw it. And I knew him so well, because I have passed through these stages of death, and how often he has taken me by the hand until I overcame him. For you overcome death when you are raised *from* the dead. For the last enemy to be overcome is death.

But in the meanwhile he's been your friend. He took you from one state to the other state to the other state. You leave this state to be inserted into another time slot for a purpose that is beyond one's knowing at the moment. But after having gone through so many, you certainly would know him as a friend. But how could I prove to this man who offers $5,000? As the editor said, "He has a firm grip on his $5,000." He wants the proof here in this world. Well, you can go to the Near East forever and ever, and excavate all of the Near East trying to find the sepulcher where he is buried. And may I tell you, some pope in the past or some emperor in the past named it, and that is now called the Church of the Sepulcher. That isn't the sepulcher at all; it's your own skull. That's where he's buried. But the story isn't told.

So this coming Christmas it will be told in the same old form again. After 2,000 years they finally conceded that the Jews did not kill Jesus Christ. After 2,000 years! What else will they concede tomorrow? I hope that someone present is a good orthodox Catholic and Protestant who will go and tell the story that tomorrow in some other council they will concede that it is not what they so far believed. Hasn't a thing to do with the garments that you wear outwardly. God does not judge from outward appearances, as you're told, he sees the heart...that deep belief in man.

Well, what I told you this night is true. Every word is true, because I'm speaking from experience. I am not theorizing.

This being my last night until the new year, may I wish you all a true Christmas in the sense that may it happen to you! Thank you.

GLOSSARY

Affliction - Experienced for the purpose of fashioning man into the image of God which when completed the individual is inwardly awakened and shown to be God (one's own I-am-ness).

Awakening - The soul of man awakens from a profound sleep of "6,000" years to his true divine identity (the return of long memory). Man experiences a series of six visions: resurrection/birth from above; David and the father- hood of God; splitting of the temple of the body/ascension into Zion; the descent of the dove, over a period of three and a half years—all are signs of your transformation from limited man back into God.

Bible - All parable. Not secular history but salvation history. Man's spiritual autobiography. The Old Testament is adumbration and prophecy, while the New Testament is fulfillment of the prophecies: the events depicted in the story of Jesus Christ which man experiences.

Bible Characters - Personifications of eternal states of consciousness (not historical beings). Two lines of personifications run through scripture: the inner man and outer man; e.g. Eve (inner) culminating in Jesus; Adam (outer) culminating in John the Baptist.

David - The symbol of humanity—all of its generations, experiences, and the concentrated time in which they spring, fused into a grand whole, and personified as a glorious youth who (in vision) calls you "Father." God's only son (Ps.2:7); the anointed, the first born from the dead, the Christ. Also, eternity, a lad, a stripling; personification of the resultant state; symbol of man's creative power that overcomes all challenges. Only David reveals the Father.

Egypt - This age of illusion; the state of ignorance that I AM is he, as opposed to "that" age, the awakened state.

Enemy of Israel - All false gods and beliefs in causation other than the only God which is I AM (your I-am-ness or awareness of being).

Faith - Response to revelation rather than discovery of new knowledge. An assumption persisted in; an experiment that ends in experience. Loyalty to unseen reality. Opposite of faith is worry. To determine a thing.

Glory - God's gift of himself to each individual soul, ultimately. Achieved by an internal transformation of man into God by God (man's inner being) (2 Cor. 3:18). The state of awareness man enjoyed prior to the descent into man (John 17:5). Man's true identity returned, greatly expanded having experienced and overcome death.

Imagination - The eternal body of man; God himself. Man's awareness of being; the inner five senses; God's/man's creative power; the I AM (called God, Lord, Jehovah, Jesse, Jesus, the Dreamer, the Father). Man's creative power keyed low is human Imagination, the son—but the same in essence.

Imagining - Picturing a scene that implies the wish fulfilled, feeling the present reality of it, drenching self with that feeling, believing it is done, and remaining faithful to the imaginal act until it manifests.

Israel - "He who shall rule as God" (all of humanity at the end of his/her journey as man); a man in whom there is no guile.

Jesse - Any form of the verb "to be" (hence I AM; God the father of David, Ps.2:7).

Jesus - The I AM (Exod.3:14); the Father. Also called Jehovah, Lord, Jesse. Means "Jehovah is salvation." Anglicized Hebrew word Joshua. God individualized is when you say "I am." Universal humanity.

Christ - (See David above) The power and wisdom of God personified (1Cor.1:24)

Jesus Christ - Personification of awakened Imagination and man's creative power. God awake in man (two having been transformed into one, Ehp.2:14). Personification of man's soul; the animating principle of a being. Bifurcated term: "Jesus and his Christ" (Rev.11:15; 12:10). Father/Son.

Man - God (Imagination) is man, the son, the creative power keyed low. Destined to be awakened as God. Man's power is greatly expanded by overcoming this world of the senses, of extreme limitation, opacity and contraction.

Old Testament - Series of permanent states of consciousness through which man must pass, personified as characters; New Testament is Old Testament's fulfillment.

Parable - A story told as if it were true, leaving the hearer to discover its fictitious surface character and learn its hidden meaning. (See Mat.13:3 and 13:18 for instruction on how to solve the riddle of parable.)

Paul - To find the I AM; to desist in seeking (as opposed to Saul, one who seeks; also humanity still suffering from amnesia). Paul is the symbol of anyone who awakens; one in whom the six visions has occurred.

Potter - The Imagination personified (Jeremiah 18:1). Also teaches revision of facts in order to get new results. Lord (Imagination) and Potter linked (Is. 64:8).

Power - One's ability to create by use of Imagination. The inner five senses used to to assume the wish fulfilled, which contains the way to bring it into being.

Pray/Prayer - To imagine. Defined as: motion toward, accession to, in the vicinity of, nearness at. A mental-emotional movement into a new state of consciousness by assuming the feeling of the wish already fulfilled, along with gratitude therefore. Not supplication.

Primal Form - A being of fire in a body of air.—not flesh and blood.

Purpose of Life - To learn to create imaginatively and to exercise the power of love to overcome this limitation called man. Eventually, to regain the exalted state of God, without loss of identity…a gift to man (Luke 12:32).

Repentance - A deliberate radical change of attitude towards life, called revision by Neville (called repentance in scripture). Not contrition or remorse.

Time - Two times exist simultaneously: Eternity or big time; and sidereal time or man's view of a past, present and future (temporary and part of this dream's illusion).

Transformation - The inner process conducted entirely by the Inner Being (God) on the individual to change man into himself. Man cannot earn it, nor do anything to shortcut the process or the time required to accomplish it. A loving result of the journey of the soul through fires of experience as man.

Vision - Revelation. Contains three elements: the supernatural, parallels stories in scripture and quite vivid. Issues from the only source, God (Num.12:6; Job33:14).

Visions of The End (Six) - Signs to man that the internal transformation into God (by God, your "I am") has been completed and the promises to man have been fulfilled. (For a list see above "Awakening")

World - A dream dreamed in concert for the purpose of sentient experience and expanding our creative power. The world is dead if not animated by Imagination (as is man). Also, the individual (aka, nations, cities, rivers, mountains, etc., all man).

A few sources of the quotes used by Neville:

James *Strong's Exhaustive Concordance of the Bible* (with Hebrew and Greek dictionaries, containing the original meanings of words); Bayley's *Lost Language of Symbolism; The Complete Writings of William Blake*; *The Bible— Revised Standard Version* (most used).

PRODUCTION NOTES

1. The word Imagination is capitalized because it is synonymous with Lord, God, I AM, Jehovah.

2. The set of figures ___(??) is used to indicate a missing word, words, even a phrase, inaudible on the tape from which it is typed.

3. Parentheses are used at the end of a sentence to indicate book, chapter orverse of a biblical quote or other source used in the lecture but not identified by the speaker.

4. Italicizing of a word usually indicates voice emphasis made by Neville. Also used to indicate a book, magazine, newspaper and sometimes reference to a chapter within them.